Published by Bloomsbury USA, New York
175 Fifth Avenue, New York, NY 10010, USA

www.benschott.com

First US Edition 2008 · 1 2 3 4 5 6 7 8 9 10

ISBN-10 1-59691-542-0 · ISBN-13 978-1-59691-542-8

Library of Congress Cataloging-in-Publication Data have been applied for.

papers used by Bloomsbury USA are natural, recyclable products made from
od grown in well-managed forests. The manufacturing processes conform to
the environmental regulations of the country of origin.

Designed and typeset by BEN SCHOTT
Printed in the USA by QUEBECOR WORLD FAIRFIELD

* * * *

Also by BEN SCHOTT

Schott's Original Miscellany
Schott's Food & Drink Miscellany
Schott's Sporting, Gaming, & Idling Miscellany
Schott's Miscellany Diary (with Smythson of Bond St, London)
Schott's Almanac Page-A-Day® Calendar (Workman Publishing Co.)
British and German editions of *Schott's Miscellany* are also available.

Sch

Misce

2 0 (

LIBER PRAETERITORUM ET PO

An Alma

Everyone spoke of informatic

but what there was, in fact, was a non-i

— RICHARD SAUL WURMAN, *What*

C

Po

The

th

The

Schott's Miscellany

2009

An Almanac

LIBER PRAETERITORUM ET POSTERITATIS CARMEN

· *The book of things past and the song of the future* ·

Conceived, edited, and designed by

BEN SCHOTT

US Editor · Bess Lovejoy

UK & Series Editor · Claire Cock-Starkey
Assistant Editor · Victoria Kingston
German Editor · Alexander Weber
Researcher · Iona Macdonald

BLOOMSBURY

Preface

A calendar, a calendar! look in the almanack;
find out moonshine, find out moonshine.
— A Midsummer Night's Dream, III, i

Completely revised and updated, *Schott's Miscellany* 2009 picks up from where the 2008 *Miscellany* left off, to create a seamless biography of the year. ❦ The celebrated wit James Thurber (1894–1961) once observed, 'So much has already been written about everything that you can't find out anything about it'. If this is true, and it seems increasingly so, then mechanisms for filtering news and opinion become ever more valuable. *Schott's Miscellany* aspires to be one such filter – stepping back from the torrent of rolling news to offer an informative, selective, and entertaining analysis of the year. ❦ The C21st almanac is necessarily different from its distinguished predecessors, which were published in times when the year was defined by matters astronomical, ecclesiastical, or aristocratic. By exploring high art and pop culture, geopolitics and gossip, scientific discovery and sporting achievement, *Schott's Miscellany* endeavors to describe the year as it is lived, in all its complexity.

— *Schott's Miscellany* is an almanac written to be read.

THE MISCELLANY'S YEAR

In order to be as inclusive as possible, the *Schott's Miscellany* year runs until late August.

Data cited in *Schott's Miscellany* are taken from the latest sources available at the time of writing.

CHERISH TRUTH, PARDON ERROR

Every effort has been made to ensure that the information contained within *Schott's Miscellany* is both accurate and up-to-date, and grateful acknowledgment is given to the various sources used. However, as Goethe once said: 'Error is to truth as sleep is to waking'. Consequently, the author would be pleased to be informed of any errors, inaccuracies, or omissions that might help improve future editions.

Please send all comments or suggestions to the author, care of:

Bloomsbury USA, 175 Fifth Avenue, New York, NY 10010, USA
or email *editor@schottsalmanac.com*

In keeping with most newspapers and journals, *Schott's Miscellany* will publish any significant corrections and clarifications each year in its Errata section [see p.368].

Contents

EARLY ALMANACS OF NOTE

Solomon Jarchi	*c.*1150	Zainer (at Ulm)	1478
Peter de Dacia	*c.*1300	Francis Moore's Almanack	1698–1713
John Somers (Oxford)	1380	Poor Richard's Almanack	1732
Nicholas de Lynna	1386	Almanach de Gotha	1764
Purbach	1150–1461	The Old Farmer's Almanac	1792
After the invention of printing		Whitaker's Almanack	1868
Gutenberg (at Mainz)	1457	The World Almanac	1868
Regiomontanus (at Nuremberg)	1474	Information Please Almanac	1947

'MISCELLANY' & 'ALMANAC' vs 'ALMANACK'

The *Oxford English Dictionary* (*OED*) defines 'miscellany' as 'a mixture, medley, or assortment; (a collection of) miscellaneous objects or items' – noting the word is now commonly used to describe 'separate articles, treatises, or other studies on a subject collected into one volume; literary compositions of various kinds brought together to form a book'. [The word derives from the Latin 'miscellanea'.] The *OED* credits Ben Jonson with an early use of the term in *The Fountaine of Selfe-Love* (1601), in which he wrote, 'As a miscellany madame [I would] inuent new tyres, and goe visite courtiers'. The American pronunciation of 'miscellany' – stressing the first syllable [*mis*–el–any] – may be the most authentic. According to the *OED*, the modern British pronunciation, which stresses the second syllable [mi–*sel*–any], might reflect a later trend in the pronunciation of four-syllable words like 'accompany', 'epiphany', and 'mahogany'. ❦ The spelling and etymology of 'almanac' are disputed. The *OED* cites an early use of 'almanac' by Roger Bacon in 1267, though Chaucer used 'almenak' in *c.*1391; and Shakespeare, 'almanack' in 1590. Variations include almanach(e), amminick, almanacke, &c. A number of etymologies for *almanac* have been suggested: that it comes from the Arabic *al* [the] *mana(h)* [reckoning or diary]; that it comes from the Anglo-Saxon *al-moan-heed* ['to wit, the regard or observations of all the moons'], or from the Anglo-Saxon *al-monath* [all the months]; or that it is linked to the Latin *manachus* [sundial]. In 1838, *Murphy's Almanac* made the prediction that January 20, 1838, would be 'Fair, prob. lowest deg. of winter temp'. When, on the day, this actually turned out to be true, *Murphy's Almanac* became a bestseller.

SYMBOLS & ABBREVIATIONS

>	greater than	≈	approximately equal to
≥	greater than or equal to	km	kilometer
<	less than	m	meter
≤	less than or equal to	mi.	mile
♂	male/men	'/"	feet (ft)/inches (in)
♀	female/women	C	century (e.g., C20th)
c.	*circa*, meaning around or roughly	m/bn	million/billion

Throughout the *Miscellany*, figures may not add to totals because of rounding.

Chronicle

Time has too much credit ... It is not a great healer. It is an indifferent and perfunctory one. Sometimes it does not heal at all. And sometimes when it seems to, no healing has been necessary. — IVY COMPTON-BURNETT (1884–1969)

─────────────── SOME AWARDS OF NOTE ───────────────

Time magazine Person of the Year [2007] · VLADIMIR PUTIN
'At significant cost to the principles and ideas that free nations prize, he has performed an extraordinary feat of leadership in imposing stability on a nation that has rarely known it and brought Russia back to the table of world power'

Scripps National Spelling Bee . . . . Sameer Mishra (13 years old), IN
Pantone Color of the Year . . . . Blue Iris
Webby Awards Person of the Year . . . . Stephen Colbert
United States Barista Champion . . . . Kyle Glanville, CA
World's Ugliest Dog . . . . Gus (Chinese crested), FL
Best Dressed Real Man [*Esquire*, 2007] . . . . Frank Kelly, FL
Game of the Year [Spike Video Game Awards, 2007] . . . . BioShock
Entertainer of the Year [*Entertainment Weekly*, 2007] . . . . J.K. Rowling
American Cheese Society Best in Show . . Snow White Goat Cheese [Carr Valley, WI]
World Car of the Year Mazda2
Consumer Electronics Show Best in Show [CNET] . . . . Philips Eco Flat TV
Sexiest Vegetarian Celebrities [PETA] . . . . Leona Lewis & Anthony Kiedis
Cigar of the Year [*Cigar Aficionado*] . . . . Padrón Serie 1926 No. 9
National Teacher of the Year . . . . Michael Geisen, OR
Bookseller of the Year [*Publishers Weekly*] . . . . Vroman's Bookstore, CA
Best Young Entrepreneur [The Stevie Awards] . . . . Lauren Berger, Intern Queen Inc.
Wallpaper Design Awards Best City . . . . Los Angeles
Will Eisner Comics Industry Awards Best Writer/Artist . . . . Chris Ware
Miss Universe . . . . Dayana Mendoza, Venezuela
Airline of the Year [Skytrax] . . . . Singapore Airlines

─────────────── DOUBLESPEAK AWARD ───────────────

Each year the National Council of Teachers of English 'honors' an American public figure with its Doublespeak Award, for 'language that is grossly deceptive, evasive, euphemistic, confusing, or self-centered'. The 2007 'winner' was former Attorney General Alberto Gonzales, who treated Senators to the following phrase during his testimony on the US attorney firings scandal: *I have in my mind a recollection as to knowing as to some of these United States attorneys. There are two that I do not recall knowing in my mind what I understood to be the reasons for the removal.*

───── MISC. LISTS OF 2008 ─────   ─2009 WORDS─

TOP PUBLIC INTELLECTUALS

As ranked by 20,000 people, from a list by Prospect *and* Foreign Policy *magazines:*

1 . . . . . .Noam Chomsky
2 . . . . .Umberto Eco
3 . . . . .Richard Dawkins
4 . . . . .Václav Havel
5 .Christopher Hitchens
6 . . . . .Paul Krugman
7 . . . . .Jürgen Habermas
8 . . . . .Amartya Sen
9 . . . . . . .Jared Diamond
10 . . . . . . Salman Rushdie

GREATEST TV ICONS

Compiled by TV Land & Entertainment Weekly:

1 . . . . Johnny Carson
2 . . . . Lucille Ball
3 . . . . .Oprah Winfrey
4 . . . . Bill Cosby
5 . . . . . . .Walter Cronkite
6 . . . . Carol Burnett
7 . . . . .Mary Tyler Moore
8 . . . . .Jerry Seinfeld
9 . . . . . .Homer Simpson
10 . . . . Dick Clark

BANNED NAMES

Below are some of the names given to children that have been banned by various authorities, according to the BBC:

Yeah Detroit; Stallion; Twisty Poi; Sex Fruit; Keenan Got Lucy; Fat Boy; Cinderella Beauty Blossom; Fish and Chips (twins)

BEST HOSPITALS

The 'honor roll' on US News & World Report's *annual list:*

1 . . . . Johns Hopkins
2 . . . . Mayo Clinic
3 . . . . .Ronald Reagan
    UCLA Medical Cntr
4 . . . . . . Cleveland Clinic
5 . . . Massachusetts Gen.
6 . . . . . . New York Presb.
7 . . . UCSF Medical Cntr
8 . .Brigham & Women's
8 . . . Duke Medical Cntr
10 . . U of Penn Hospital
10 .U of WA Med. Cntr
[8th and 10th place were tied]

WORDS TO BANISH

Lake Superior State University's list of words and phrases to be stricken from the language:

Perfect storm · Webinar
Waterboarding (back to the beach where it belongs)
Organic · Wordsmith/ Wordsmithing · Author/ Authored (why not 'paint- ered?') · Post-9/11
Surge · Give back
___ is the new ___
or X is the new Y
Black Friday (contradicts 'Black Tuesday')
Back in the day
Random (overused by teenagers) · Sweet (as a synonym for 'good')
Emotional (overused by reporters) · Pop (overused as a verb on design shows)
It is what it is
Under the bus

─2009 WORDS─

The following words celebrate anniversaries in 2009, based upon the earliest cited use traced by the venerable *Oxford English Dictionary*:

{1509} *elocution* (oratorical or literary style) · *refulgent* (resplendent with light) · {1609} *baritone* (male voice, from lower A in the bass clef to lower F in the treble) · *pipe office* (humorous term for the mouth) · *queen bee* (the reproductive female in a colony of social bees) · *stateswoman* (a female statesman) · {1709} *blood-relation* (one related by birth or consanguinity) · *story-teller* (one who...) · {1809} *ambulance* (a movable [army] hospital) · *ginger beer* · *jollification* (the act of making merry) · {1909} *air conditioning* · *caravanner* · *cinema* (abbreviation of 'cinematograph') · *gaffe* (inadvertent error) · *oo-er* (expression of surprise or innuendo) · {1919} *ad lib* (speaking extempore) · {1929} *balls-up* (an inch away from a cock-up) · {1939} *dognapping* (stealing dogs for a reward) · *jitterbug* (the dance) · {1949} *Big Brother* (Orwell's leviathan) · *tweenager* (almost or just a teenager) · {1959} *binge eating* · {1969} *moonwalk* (not the dance)

SOME SURVEY RESULTS OF 2007–08

%	*(of American adults, unless otherwise stated)*	*source & month*
88	use at least one electronic device in the bathroom	[American Standard; Aug]
87	believe the US should have its own missile defense system	[ORC/CNN; Aug]
86	of employees said that they liked their managers	[BPI/BVA; Feb]
80	of college students have been injured by their textbooks	[Zogby; Jan]
80	rated their listening skills as good or excellent	[Hyatt Place; Aug]
78	of workers reported feeling 'burned out' at work	[CareerBuilder.com; Jul]
72	of drivers have stains on their car interiors	[Milliken & Co.; Mar]
71	of marketing execs think office April Fools' jokes unsuitable	[Creative Group; Mar]
70	said that speculators were profiteering by driving up the price of oil	[ATA; Jul]
70	of likely voters said the IOC was wrong to give the Olympics to China	[Zogby; Apr]
68	of those aged ≥65 got a flu shot in 2007	[CDC; Jan]
61	planned to celebrate Valentine's Day	[BIGresearch; Feb]
60	of those aged 18–64 have never been tested for HIV	[CDC; Aug]
58	expressed a distrust of credit card companies	[CreditCards.com; Aug]
57	were less likely to buy a product if it had been made in China	[*Fortune*; Jan]
57	planned to watch Super Bowl XLII as much for the ads as the game	[Harris; Feb]
57	believe God can save a dying family member	[Univ. of Connecticut; Aug]
56	never read blogs that discuss politics	[Harris; Mar]
55	always recycle cans, bottles, and newspapers	[BBMG; Nov '07]
54	thought that homeschooled children often lack social skills	[LifeWay; Aug]
53	have regular, weekly sex [see p.100]	[Durex; Mar]
52	would rather die than live with a severe disability	[Disaboom; Jul]
51	of American Jews are over the age of 50	[Pew; Feb]
49	of business travelers always specify a liquor brand for cocktails	[idrinkwell.com; Aug]
47	of internet users have looked for themselves on a search engine	[Pew; Feb]
41	believe the 2nd Amend. protects an individual's right to bear arms	[Harris; May]
41	consider themselves to be an 'environmentalist'	[Planet Green/ABC; Jul]
39	nominated Simon Cowell as their favorite reality TV villain	[AOL; Jul]
39	of women hide clutter in unseen places (under beds, inside closets)	[SC Johnson; Jul]
38	think the air inside their homes is cleaner than that outside	[Johns Manville; Aug]
38	of teens avoided school because they were embarrassed by acne	[Galderma; Jul]
36	of men (46% of women) defined 'passion' as a loving, longing embrace	[Ipsos; Jul]
35	were less likely to buy a product if it had been made in India	[*Fortune*; Jan]
34	said they believed in ghosts	[AP/Ipsos; Oct '07]
29	said they use a meat thermometer	[Int. Food Info. Council; Jan]
26	consider the debt they are carrying to be unmanageable	[Harvard Bis School; Feb]
23	of high school students said they didn't know how to write a check	[Huntington; Jul]
22	of gays and lesbians have no health insurance (12% of heterosexuals)	[Harris; May]
16	of teens reported they had been a victim of cyber-bullying	[Horatio Alger Assoc.; Aug]
15	weigh themselves every day	[Synovate; Jan]
13	of those of 57–85 report verbal, financial, or physical mistreatment	[U Chicago; Aug]
10	of parents consider their children excellent listeners	[Mom Central; Aug]
10	consider themselves 'spontaneous' travelers	[Hotwire.com; Aug]
8	were aware that there are no early warning signs of glaucoma	[US Nat Eye Inst.; Mar]
6	of men wear a necktie to work every day	[Gallup; Oct '07]

SIGNIFICA · 2008

Some (in)significa(nt) footnotes to the year. ❦ The US Navy was forced to spend $682,000 to alter a base in California that resembled a swastika when viewed from the air. Although building officials had been aware of the structure's shape, it did not become problematic until the invention of Google Earth. ❦ A disgruntled Belgian citizen put his entire country up for sale on eBay; bidding reached $14m before the auction was canceled. ❦ Roads were closed, buildings sealed, and an anti-

terrorist chemical response team was dispatched to the Soho area of London after residents complained of a noxious smell. The cause turned out to be 9 pounds of chilis left roasting by a Thai cook. ❦ The US government reported that the average price of cocaine nationwide had hit a 5-year high, and now costs $118·70 per gram. This higher price was attributed to scarcity, itself a sign of success in the 'war on drugs'. ❦ After the brutal 2007 Myanmarese crackdown on monk-led demon-strations, residents resorted to one of the few forms of protest open to them: switching off their lights and television sets during the evening news (i.e., propaganda) broadcasts. ❦ According to the European Tissue Symposium, the average Briton uses 110 rolls of toilet paper a year; this compares with 98 rolls per year for Americans, and a restrained 73 rolls for Germans. ❦ A Tanzanian man requiring brain surgery was mistakenly given a knee operation after hospital staff confused him with another patient who shared the same first name. He later died, and the knee-surgery patient, who was given a brain operation, was left paralyzed. ❦ The tree that comforted Anne Frank as she hid from the Nazis in Amsterdam was saved from felling after a Dutch judge ruled that authorities should find a way to preserve it, despite a severe fungal infection. ❦ In the middle of a severe drought, the governor of Georgia held a multidenominational service during which he asked the crowd to 'pray up a storm', and said the drought was God's way of bringing to our attention the need for resource conservation. ❦ An Italian retailers' asso-ciation reported that 20% of Italian shops regularly pay money to the Mafia in order to carry on their business unhindered. The association also claimed that the Mafia rakes in $120bn a year – 7% of Italy's GDP. ❦ Researchers at the University of Copenhagen alleged that the furniture giant IKEA names its cheaper products (doormats, draft guards, &c.) after Danish towns and its more expensive lines (chairs, beds, &c.) after Finnish, Norwegian, and Swedish towns. IKEA rejected the claim as 'nonsense'. ❦ As property prices collapsed in parts of America, some houses became less valuable than the copper pipes and wiring within them. As a result, there were reports of a crime wave of break-ins at foreclosed houses, where metal was stripped out to be sold on the black market. ❦ Mexico City opened a free outdoor ice-skating rink in the city's central square in December 2007; at 34,000 sq ft, it was said to be the world's largest. ❦ Sales of Neapolitan mozzarella fell by 30% in March 2008, amid fears that 15 years of trash dumping and burning in the city had contaminated local water buffalo milk with dioxin, a potent carcinogen. ❦ Market research data on the food preferences of US voters found that support-ers of John McCain enjoy Chips Ahoy cookies, while Barack Obama fans seem to have an intense dislike of vanilla wafers. ❦ In July, a New Zealand judge made a 9-year-old girl a ward of court so that the name she had been given by her parents

—————————SIGNIFICA · 2008 cont.—————————

could be changed: the girl had been called 'Talula Does the Hula from Hawaii'. ❦ Press reports revealed that a common nickname for the Thai Prime Minister, Samak Sundaravej, was 'Mr Rose Apple Nose', since his schnozzle is said to have a striking resemblance to the 'pear-shaped Asian fruit'. ❦ Officials in the English village of Lunt debated changing the name of their conurbation to thwart vandals who repeatedly defaced local signs by adding a single stroke of a pen. ❦ The French parliament introduced a bill to combat eating disorders that would punish (with fines and even prison sentences) websites, blogs, and other media that encourage 'excessive thinness'. ❦ Congolese police arrested 13 men accused of using black magic to steal or shrink other men's penises, in what was said to be an attempt to extort cash. ❦ Global Language Monitor predicted that the English language will celebrate its millionth word on April 29, 2009. There are currently 995,844 official words in English. ❦ The mayor of a remote Australian mining town faced calls for his resignation after telling a local paper, 'May I suggest if there are five blokes to every girl, we should find out where there are beauty-disadvantaged women and ask them to proceed to Mount Isa'. ❦ The Vatican was forced to deny reports that Pope Benedict XVI wore Prada shoes. The pontiff's footwear is apparently made by Adriano Stefanelli from Novara, and repaired in the Borgo by Antonio Arellano. ❦ Jim Bob & Michelle Duggar, from Springdale, AR, have given all of their 17 children names that begin with the letter *J*: Joshua, Jana & John-David (twins), Jill, Jessa, Jinger, Joseph, Josiah, Joy-Anna, Jedidiah & Jeremiah (twins), Jason, James, Justin, Jackson, Johannah, Jennifer. In July, it was reported that Michelle was expecting another child in January 2009; the couple were said to be canvassing suitable names. ❦ A Finnish MP proposed that the country's employees be granted paid weeklong 'love vacations' in order to connect 'both at an erotic and emotional level'. It was hoped such holidays would reduce the country's high divorce rate. ❦ A Swedish engineering firm plotted the most efficient Christmas Eve route for Father Christmas, and found that Kyrgyzstan was Santa's ideal delivery hub. Delighted, Kyrgi officials announced plans to make Kyrgyzstan 'the land of Santa Clauses', and to rename a local peak Mount Santa. ❦ A May 2008 survey by *Consumer Reports* revealed that Americans frequently exhibit 'risky mowing behavior' while tending their lawns: 77,000 ER visits a year are caused by mowing accidents, and 12% of Americans admit to drinking beer while using a mower. ❦ A female voice-over artist who recorded safety announcements for the London Underground was fired after recording spoof messages for her website, including one that advised American tourists they were 'almost certainly' speaking too loudly· ❦ A teenager from Reykjavik prank-called the White House and  was put through to George W. Bush's secretary after claiming to be the president of Iceland. He later faced questioning by the CIA. ❦ A *New York Times* report on dental problems in Kentucky noted that 1 in 10 residents of the state are missing all of their teeth. ❦ Officials in Hanover, Germany, were criticized for including a real-life serial killer in a cartoon advent calendar designed for children. Fritz 'the Butcher of Hanover' Haarman – responsible for at least 24 brutal murders between 1919–24 – was depicted lurking behind a tree and brandishing an enormous ax. ❦

———————— WORDS OF THE YEAR ————————

CLIENT 9 · NY Governor Eliot Spitzer's alleged alias with the 'Emperors Club VIP' prostitution ring. The *NY Post* ran the headline HO NO!; the *Daily News* ran PAY FOR LUV GOV; and many dubbed Spitzer ELIOT MESS [see p.27].

TERRORIST FIST JAB · DAP · see p.15.

CARLA EFFECT · the rise in French President Nicolas Sarkozy's popularity after he divorced his wife Cécilia and married pop star Carla Bruni.

DUMBLEGATE · brouhaha following J.K. Rowling's October 2007 revelation that her *Harry Potter* character Albus Dumbledore was homosexual.

NIGHTTIME SPINACH · euphemism for illegal bushmeat traded and cooked (at night) by refugees in E Africa.

SILVER TSUNAMI · the wave of baby boomers applying for social security.

CHÁVISM · the political philosophy of Venezuelan leader Hugo Chávez. *Also* 21ST-CENTURY SOCIALISM.

FATHER OF THE NATION · the deliberately vague description of Vladimir Putin's place in Russian politics.

DEBAUCHERISM · debauched tourism, with drinking, gaming, &c. [see p.212].

SANCTUARY CITIES · US cities accused of 'don't ask, don't tell' policies towards illegal immigrants (SF, NY, LA, &c.).

YAWNS · Young & Wealthy but Normal · billionaires who eschew ostentation.

TIME HORIZON · new euphemism for the 'timetable' of withdrawal from Iraq.

ANGEL FLIGHTS · military term for flights repatriating dead soldiers.

THRISIS · a thirtysomething crisis.

MOMPRENEURS · mothers who combine child care with a home business.

ECONOMIC HIV · the severity and impact of Zimbabwe's unstoppable hyperinflation [see p.27]. *Also* MOLLAR · Zimbabwean slang for Z$1m. *Also* ZIMBABTHEM · sad allusion to the arrogance of Zimbabwe's rulers [i.e., not Zimbab-we]. *Also* MUGABE'S TSUNAMI · the mass of refugees fleeing Zimbabwe.

SECULAR SABBATH · one day a week (more or less) when all electronic inputs (email, phone, &c.) are turned off.

SHLUMPADINKA · Oprah Winfrey's onomatopoeic word for a woman who dresses like she has completely given up.

GUYLINER · makeup for men.

PEAKNIKS · those who predict the end of oil, and with it the fall of capitalism.

WALL STREET GOT DRUNK · Bush's 'off the record' analysis of the economy.

RECESSIONISTA · one who predicts, talks up, or invests in expectation of a recession. *Also*, one who manages to maintain their lifestyle in a downturn.

SCRIMP & SPLURGE · the recessionary trend of saving on some items, while still being prepared to pay for luxury.

UNDERWATER · description of houses worth less than the mortgage secured upon them. *Also* MORTGAGE FAMINE · the dearth of affordable mortgages.

—————— WORDS OF THE YEAR cont. ——————

BLUE-SKY DAYS · low pollution target set for Beijing's air quality during the Olympics. [100µg/m³: twice the WHO level]

SOCIAL NOTWORKING · the avoidance of work through social networking.

IPOD GENERATION · Insecure, Pressurized, Overtaxed, Debt-ridden.

GREAT HAUL OF CHINA · description of UK's Olympic medal tally [see p.23].

DISTAVORE · one who (deliberately) sources food from far-flung places.

STOP LIST · the Kremlin's list of those banned from appearing on the media.

PROTESTIVALS · festivals with political agendas.

GREEN GOLD · valuable material that was previously given away for recycling.

PIIGS · Portugal, Italy, Ireland, Greece, & Spain · The European countries most at risk from an economic downturn.

HYPERMILING · using a variety of driving techniques (e.g., preemptive braking) to increase fuel efficiency.

BOREOUT · burnout by boredom.

ALLERGY BULLYING · exploiting food (or other) allergies to torment others.

AGFLATION · agricultural inflation. *Also* SILENT TSUNAMI · The UN's term for rising world food prices [see pp.16–17].

EIGHTH BLUNDER · the less-than-idyllic reality of Dubai's Palm Jumeirah.

TANOREXIA · addiction to (fake) tans.

NEAR ABROAD · Russian term for former Soviet areas [see p.31].

FAT, MUSCLE, BONE · supposedly the three stages of corporate redundancies, as the least talented are fired first.

CLEAN TEAMS · investigators untainted by any involvement in torture, selected to prosecute Guantánamo detainees.

FLAME OF SHAME · demonstrators' term for the Olympic torch [see p.231].

BEIJINGOISM · China's Olympic pride.

BEAR MOUNTAIN COMPACT · Vegasesque agreement among some NY state lawmakers where 'illicit' activities north of the State Park are kept quiet. *A.k.a.* THE TAPPAN ZEE BRIDGE RULE.

TAXODUS · the relocation of firms or individuals to lower-taxed jurisdictions.

QUEASICAM · filmmaking that aspires to verisimilitude by mimicking raw, amateur footage from cell phones &c. *Also* MUMBLECORE · emerging indie movie genre characterized by an awkward twentysomething slacker sensibility, low-key plots, and realistic, casual, and often improvised dialogue.

DWP · Driving While Primping.

LKBC · those who combine a powerful influence with a low profile: the Least Known, Best Connected.

A SOLDIER OF IDEAS · Fidel Castro's self-defined role after resigning [see p.68].

DRUNKOREXICS · those who starve or purge in order to mitigate the calories they later consume in alcohol.

———————————— WORDS OF THE YEAR ————————————

BAITING · tactic of the US Army in Iraq of leaving items useful to the insurgency (explosives, ammo) and targeting with snipers those who collect them.

JUNK FEES · exploitative charges levied by mortgage lenders and others.

RANK-LINK IMBALANCES · where people are 'good at vertical relationships with mentors and bosses, but bad at horizontal relationships with friends and lovers' – coined by David Brooks.

UNFITNEY · a Britney Spears moniker.

AUTO OWNER GIVE-UPs · insurance industry jargon for fraudulent car fires and staged car thefts [*LA Times*].

DESKWICH · sandwich eaten '*al desko*'.

CHILD PROTECTION SPACES · areas set up to provide security for children orphaned after major disasters.

PRECAUTIONARY BUYING · political euphemism for panic buying.

3Gs · households that, out of necessity, contain 3 generations of the same family.

FALSE TERRIBLES · Rob Lowe's term for the allegations reportedly made about his family by a former employee.

QUAKE LAKE · see p.29.

BOOMTOWN BRATS · the daughters of Bob Geldof: Peaches and Pixie.

HERMIT STATE · North Korea [see p.30].

WIDOW SIX SEVEN · Prince Harry's army call-sign during his short-lived (10-week) tour of duty in Afghanistan.

SEE-HEAR-BUY · near-instantaneous purchase and delivery of goods (e.g., music heard at Starbucks and downloaded there and then via iTunes &c.).

ANTHROPOCENE · see p.188.

PLAIN VANILLA · traders' term for the simplest forms of financial investment.

BEERBOARDING · extracting information by getting someone drunk.

SHOPDROPPING · placing items *onto* store shelves for the purpose of political activism, artistic expression, or self-promotion. *Also* DROPLIFTING.

DEFICTIONIZE · actually manufacturing a hitherto fictional product, such as the real-life confectionary based upon sweets in the *Harry Potter* series.

LEANOVER · a mild hangover.

SPORNO · the heady convergence of sporting and sexual imagery; such as David Beckham's underwear ads for Armani, and the Italian football team's ads for Dolce & Gabbana.

STAYCATION · see pp.19, 212.

NUKING THE FRIDGE · new version of 'jumping the shark', based on a scene in *Indiana Jones & the Kingdom of the Crystal Skull*, where Indy survives a nuclear blast by hiding in a refrigerator.

KAROSHI · Japanese term for 'sudden death from overwork'.

TOXIC TITLES · houses that have been abandoned by owners and banks.

PHELPS PHEVER · see pp.22, 230.

———— OBJECT OF THE YEAR · THE HAND ————

One of the year's most iconic images was of the ink-stained fingers of voters in Zimbabwe. Indelible ink has prevented voter fraud in undeveloped areas since at least the 1920s, and George W. Bush boasted of the ink-stain of freedom in Iraq's 2005 elections. But under Robert Mugabe's vicious regime, those who could not show ink-stained proof of voting risked assault by Zanu-PF thugs, since the only candidate in the presidential runoff was Mugabe himself [see p.27]. ❦ Superficially, few things could be less modern than the hand or its component fingers. In 1888, the anthropologist Frank Baker wrote, 'The hand is so intimately connected with the brain as the executor of its behests that the savage mind naturally ascribes to it a separate and distinct force independent of the rest of the body – makes it, in fact, a fetish'. The ancient Greeks, for example, 'cut from the body of a suicide the hand which had committed the deed and buried it in a separate place'. ❦ Yet, in 2008, hands and fingers linked the most fragile societies and the most modern technologies. As Zimbabweans struggled with democracy, so millions were getting to grips with Apple's iPhone which, for the first time, put multi-touch technology into the hands of the masses. Apple, Microsoft, and many others are now pioneering (and attempting to patent) a vocabulary of touch-screen 'tactile events' (*tap*, *swipe*, *drag*, *flick*, *pinch*), in the most significant innovation in gestural communication since the invention of sign language in 1775. ❦ Palmistry has long held that hands can foretell the future, and fingers have tracked the past since the clay fingerprint seals of the Han Dynasty (206 BC–AD 220). Now security systems are bridging this divide by using biometric finger and palm scans, as well as techniques of gesture recognition and authentication by 'typing pattern'. ❦ In an increasingly mediated society, where computers 'handshake' across networks and Facebookers 'poke' one another, human touch remains resolutely significant. In 2008, the 'Harare handshake' between Mugabe and Morgan Tsvangirai proved almost as newsworthy as the 'fist bump' between Barack and Michelle Obama – sneered at by Fox News as a 'terrorist fist jab'. In Paris, Nicolas Sarkozy engineered a curious three-way handshake with Israel's Ehud Olmert and Palestine's Mahmoud Abbas, while in N Ireland, Gordon Brown was baffled by Bush's 'homeboy' handshake. Brown also drew a clumsy distinction between *receiving* the Olympic torch and refusing to *touch* it, and before the Games, the Chinese were told it was rude to shake hands for longer than 3 seconds. (The buttock-obscured hand signals of bikini-clad Olympic beach volleyballers proved irresistible to the media.) The hand also lingers as a culprit in the communication of disease, evinced by the link between hand washing and MRSA [see p.111]. And, as ever, individual fingers hold their own significance: a photograph of Madonna's ringless fourth finger catalyzed a wave of speculation about her marriage, while Conrad Black was snapped presenting a different digit to reporters outside his trial. ❦ But we could be forgiven for letting much of this pass us by. As the anatomist Charles Bell wrote in his 1833 monograph on the hand, 'Is it not the very perfection of the instrument which makes us insensible to its use?'

WORLD FOOD CRISIS

After many years of relative food price stability, the cost of basic foodstuffs escalated alarmingly during 2007–08, resulting in severe food shortages, social unrest, and fears of hunger and starvation in many of the world's poorest regions. As of August 2008, riots and protests over food prices had erupted in *c*.30 countries – reflecting the fact that the UN's index of world food prices had more than doubled since 2000, as the chart [right] illustrates.

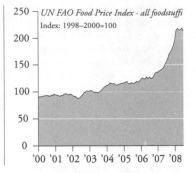

The causes of this agflation (agricultural inflation) were numerous and interrelated. Inevitably, the soaring price of oil touched almost every aspect of food production, processing, and transportation [see p.308]. And disasters like Cyclone Nargis skewed food's supply and demand. But much of the crisis was driven by the price of grain, which rose due to a confluence of events, including: six years of drought in Australia (a major wheat-producing nation); lower agricultural yields due to global warming; the expansion of the Indian and Chinese middle class, hungry for (grain-fed) meat; and a wave of panicked protectionism that cut food exports. The impact of biofuels was much debated. Diverting land from food to fuel crops necessarily cuts the supply of food, yet while America claimed its biofuel subsidies were responsible for only 2–3% of global agflation, the World Bank reckoned the impact at *c*.75%. ❦ Whatever the causes, the consequences were dramatic, and the World Bank estimated that 100m people were at risk of being driven into poverty. In June, the UN's World Food Program announced $1·2bn in food aid for 60 struggling nations, and in August it announced a $214m plan for 16 'hunger hot spots' (including Somalia, Ethiopia, Haiti, Liberia, the Palestinian territories, and Mozambique). However, many argued that aid could only be a temporary measure and, as the world's population continues to grow, agricultural research is needed to find ways of producing more food on less land. ❦ Charted below is the rise in the price of various foods since 2006:

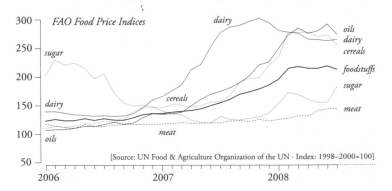

[Source: UN Food & Agriculture Organization of the UN · Index: 1998–2000=100]

WORLD FOOD CRISIS cont.

Below are some revealing reports on the food crisis from around the world:

In March, Egyptian President Hosni Mubarak ordered his country's army to bake bread, after shortages of subsidized loaves led to riots in which at least a dozen 'bread martyrs' died. ❦ Frustrated by the slow pace of international relief, nations forged individual deals to help one another: Ukraine agreed to allow Libya to grow wheat on 247,000 acres, in exchange for access to construction and gas deals; Uganda agreed to sell more coffee, milk, and bananas to India; and China signed a free-trade deal with New Zealand (a major food exporter) – China's first such deal with a developed country. ❦ In April, a week of food riots in Haiti killed >5 and forced out PM Jacques-Édouard Alexis. ❦ Also in April, US chains Sam's Club and Costco limited the quantity of rice their customers could purchase – despite official assurances that there was no US rice shortage. ❦ In May, the newly created Philippines Anti-Rice Hoarding Task Force accused 33 people of hoarding rice, diverting subsidized rice, and other illegal rice-related activities. ❦ In June, the US Dept of Agriculture reported that agflation during 2007 had increased the number of the world's hungry by 14%: an additional 122m people – roughly the population of Japan. ❦

Although most American consumers are insulated from the worst of global agflation, the charts on the right show the rise in some US food prices over the past year. Yet it seems unlikely Americans will be facing a food shortage anytime soon. According to the Stockholm Water Institute, 30% of all US food is thrown away each year.

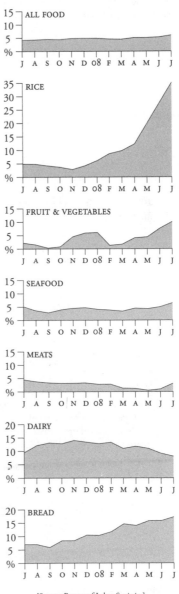

US food inflation, 12-month change (%)

[Source: Bureau of Labor Statistics]

──────────────── US CONSUMER CONFIDENCE ────────────────

The highly uncertain state of the US economy was evident in a range of indicators, including a steep decline in consumer confidence since mid-2007, as illustrated by the Consumer Confidence Survey, conducted for the Conference Board by TNS:

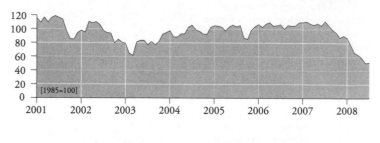

──────────────── US HOUSE PRICES & DELINQUENCY ────────────────

July 2008 figures from the US Office of Federal Housing Enterprise Oversight illustrate the dramatic rise and fall in house prices across America since 1992:

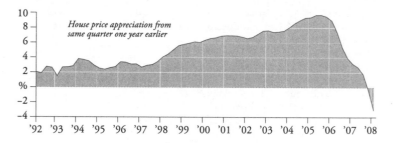

Data from the Mortgage Bankers Association indicate that the US mortgage loan delinquency rate was 6·35% at the end of the 1st quarter of 2008. This rate includes loans that are at least one payment past due, but not loans in the process of foreclosure (which, in that quarter, was 2·47%). Foreclosure actions were started on 0.99% of all loans during Q1 2008. Below, these two indicators are tracked since 2001:

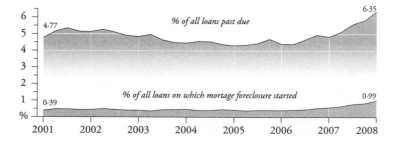

---------------- US CONSUMER CREDIT ----------------

US consumer credit continued to rise in the summer of 2008, as individuals used credit cards and loans to bridge the gap between higher prices and static wages. In June 2008, consumer credit rose $14·33bn (a 6·7% rise on June 2007) to $2·586 trillion. (Some noted that this higher-than-expected rise may have been catalyzed by the expectation of 112·4m stimulus payments worth $91bn.) Illustrated below, from Federal Reserve data, is the staggering escalation of consumer credit since 1943:

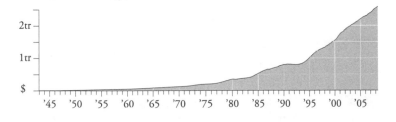

---------------- US INFLATION & GAS PRICES ----------------

The credit crunch was exacerbated in 2008 by rising inflation across a range of expenditures. Below are some unadjusted price changes from July 2007–July 2008:

All items............................5·6%	Transportation ....13·4
Food [see p.17] ....6·0	· gasoline (all types)................37·9
· food at home ....7·6	· public transport....................14·5
· food away from home..............4·6	Medical care..........................3·5
· alcoholic beverages ....3·3	Recreation............................1·7
Housing.............................3·9	Education ....5·7
· shelter.............................2·5	Communication ....1·5
· household energy..................18·2	· telephone services..................2·8
· fuel oil & other fuels ....61·1	· personal computers &c.........−11·8
· natural gas & electricity..........14·8	Tobacco & smoking products......7·9
· water, sewer, & trash collection...5·5	
Apparel..............................0·8	All urban consumers (CPI-U) [Source: BLS]

Charted below is the rise in retail gas prices, which hit $4/gallon for the first time:

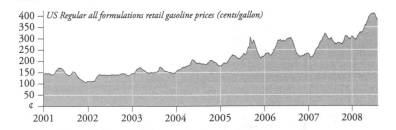

US Regular all formulations retail gasoline prices (cents/gallon)

——— AFGHANISTAN CONFLICT ———

516 US troops have died in Afghanistan (at 7/31/08); below is a breakdown (2001–):

Year	US fatalities
2001	12
2002	49
2003	48
2004	52
2005	99
2006	98
2007	117
2008 *to date*	86

In addition, the following troops from other coalition countries have been killed:

Australia.......6	Finland.........1	Lithuania.......1	Romania........7
Canada.......90	France........12	Netherlands..16	S Korea.........1
Czech Rep.....3	Germany.....25	Norway.........3	Spain.........23
Denmark.....15	Hungary........2	Poland..........5	Sweden.........2
Estonia.........3	Italy...........12	Portugal.......2	UK..........115

Despite the presence of *c*.65,000 troops in Afghanistan – including *c*.34,000 from America and *c*.8,000 from Britain – the UN Office on Drugs and Crime reported in 2008 that 'the area under opium poppy cultivation in Afghanistan increased 17% in 2007, with cultivation expanding to a record high of 193,000 hectares in 2007. Global opium poppy cultivation, as a result, rose 17% in 2007 to almost 234,000 hectares. Afghanistan's share of global cultivation remained 82%'. The chart below illustrates how Afghanistan's opium production has grown since 1990.

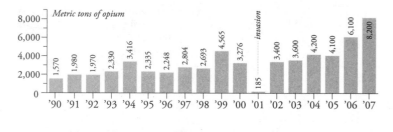

——— COMBAT EXPERIENCE IN IRAQ · 2007 ———

A US Army report into the mental health of soldiers in Iraq surveyed the 'combat experience' of troops (rank E1–E4, see p.267) during 9 months in theater in 2007:

	% experiencing
Receiving incoming artillery, rocket, or mortar fire	78·4
Knowing someone seriously injured or killed	72·1
Seeing destroyed homes and villages	61·1
Seeing dead bodies or human remains	60·2
Working in areas that were mined or had improvised explosive devices	59·8
Receiving small arms fire	57·7
Having a member of your unit become a casualty	55·6
Being attacked or ambushed	51·7
Seeing dead or seriously injured Americans	48·7

IRAQ CONFLICT

4,142 US troops had died in Iraq (as of 8/14/08); below is a breakdown since 2003:

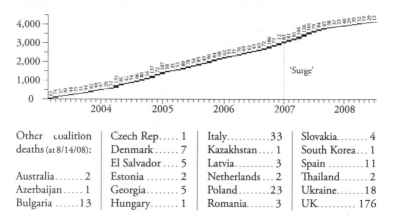

Other coalition deaths (at 8/14/08):	Czech Rep..... 1	Italy............33	Slovakia........ 4
	Denmark...... 7	Kazakhstan.... 1	South Korea... 1
	El Salvador 5	Latvia.......... 3	Spain 11
Australia....... 2	Estonia 2	Netherlands ... 2	Thailand....... 2
Azerbaijan..... 1	Georgia........ 5	Poland........23	Ukraine.......18
Bulgaria 13	Hungary....... 1	Romania....... 3	UK.......... 176

As of August 2008, there were *c*.149,233 coalition troops in Iraq, of which *c*.140,000 were American; the remaining *c*.9,233 were from 4 countries. Below are the number of US and other troops since 05/03, and a breakdown of current coalition support:

Country	approx. troops
UK..................	4,000
Poland	900
South Korea...........	650
Romania	600

On 8/10/08, *c*.2,000 Georgian troops were airlifted from Iraq to fight against Russia [see p.31]

The calculation of civilian deaths in Iraq is problematic and controversial, and opinion differs as to which estimates are most accurate. As of 8/14/2008, the Iraqi Body Count (IBC) estimated that the documented civilian death toll from violence in Iraq was 86,609–94,490. Below is the IBC's estimate of fatalities since 3/2003:

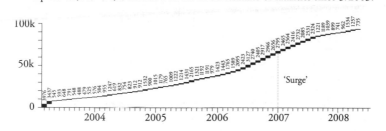

[Sources for the page: The Brooking Institution, *Iraq Index*; iCasualties.org; Iraq Body Count]

—————————— OLYMPIC GAMES · BEIJING 2008 ——————————

At 8·08pm on 08/08/08 the XXIX Olympics opened in Beijing. An unforgettable 4-hour ceremony of synchronized music and acrobatics set the scene for 16 days of sporting achievement. The creation of 38 world records and 85 Olympic records – in a series of stunning venues – would significantly, but not entirely, obscure China's problematic record on human rights, political oppression [see p.231], and pollution.

The undisputed star of the Games was the 23-year-old swimmer Michael Phelps, who shrugged off the frenzy of 'Phelps Phever' to break 7 world records while amassing 8 Olympic golds. In so doing, he beat both Mark Spitz's 1972 haul of 7, and all but 8 of the national squads. As headline writers ran short of superlatives, the 'People's Republic of Michael Phelps' vowed to add to his career tally of 14 Olympic golds at London 2012. ❦ Phelps's only rival for column inches was the Jamaican sprinter Usain Bolt. On 8/16, 'Lightning' Bolt stunned spectators by running the 100m in a world record time of 9·69s. That he achieved this feat after slowing down mid-race to celebrate (and with a loose shoelace) only added to his appeal. On 8/18, Bolt ran the 200m in 19·30s – shaving ·02s off Michael Johnson's 'unbreakable' best. Bolt's third gold and world record came in the 4×100m relay. ❦ Inevitably the Games were not without incident or accident. As the opening ceremony drew nearer, concern grew that Beijing's notoriously polluted air would not meet even the lowest standard of quality. To ensure 'blue sky days', authorities limited the use of private cars and temporarily shut down factories and building sites. And, in an attempt to improve standards of civility, campaigns were launched to encourage queuing and clapping and discourage swearing and spitting.

More disturbingly, groups such as Amnesty reported that draconian security measures were used to sweep criminals, vagrants, and drug addicts, as well as dissidents and protesters, out of the media's sight. This desire for presentational perfection was also behind the use of a 'cute' 7-year-old girl to mime the singing of a child deemed less photogenic during the opening ceremony, and the broadcasting of computerized fireworks rather than the actual display. ❦ Rigorous testing ensured the Games were relatively free from doping scandals, although 5 athletes were expelled for drugs, including Ukrainian heptathlete Liudmyla Blonska, who was stripped of her silver after testing positive for an anabolic steroid. (Bizarrely, 4 horses were ejected from the show-jumping after testing positive for capsaicin – a chili that is rubbed onto a horse's legs to encourage it over the jumps.) Many attributed the breaking of 25 swimming world records to the popularity of the Speedo LZR Racer swimsuit – which employs NASA technology for improved aerodynamics. Although these suits are perfectly legal, some called the use of such high-tech equipment 'technological doping'.

The Chinese authorities had every right to be pleased with the Games, which were spectacular in scale and effect, and free from boycotts, podium protests, or serious diplomatic censure. It remains to be seen what the much vaunted 'Olympic legacy' or the slogan 'One World One Dream' will mean for the ordinary Chinese citizen.

—— OLYMPIC GAMES · BEIJING 2008 · MEDALS TABLE ——

#	Country	Gd	Sv	Bz	All	#	Country	Gd	Sv	Bz	All
1	China	51	21	28	100	52	Bahrain	1	·	·	1
2	United States	36	38	36	110		Cameroon	1	·	·	1
3	Russian Fed.	23	21	28	72		Panama	1	·	·	1
4	Great Britain	19	13	15	47		Tunisia	1	·	·	1
5	Germany	16	10	15	41	56	Sweden	·	4	1	5
6	Australia	14	15	17	46	57	Croatia	·	2	3	5
7	Korea	13	10	8	31		Lithuania	·	2	3	5
8	Japan	9	6	10	25	59	Greece	·	2	2	4
9	Italy	8	10	10	28	60	Trinidad/Tobago	·	2	·	2
10	France	7	16	17	40	61	Nigeria	·	1	3	4
11	Ukraine	7	5	15	27	62	Austria	·	1	2	3
12	Netherlands	7	5	4	16		Ireland	·	1	2	3
13	Jamaica	6	3	2	11		Serbia	·	1	2	3
14	Spain	5	10	3	18	65	Algeria	·	1	1	2
15	Kenya	5	5	4	14		Bahamas	·	1	1	2
16	Belarus	4	5	10	19		Colombia	·	1	1	2
17	Romania	4	1	3	8		Kyrgyzstan	·	1	1	2
18	Ethiopia	4	1	2	7		Morocco	·	1	1	2
19	Canada	3	9	6	18		Tajikistan	·	1	1	2
20	Poland	3	6	1	10	71	Chile	·	1	·	1
21	Hungary	3	5	2	10		Ecuador	·	1	·	1
	Norway	3	5	2	10		Iceland	·	1	·	1
23	Brazil	3	4	8	15		Malaysia	·	1	·	1
24	Czech Rep.	3	3	·	6		South Africa	·	1	·	1
25	Slovakia	3	2	1	6		Singapore	·	1	·	1
26	New Zealand	3	1	5	9		Sudan	·	1	·	1
27	Georgia	3	·	3	6		Vietnam	·	1	·	1
28	Cuba	2	11	11	24	79	Armenia	·	·	6	6
29	Kazakhstan	2	4	7	13	80	Chinese Taipei	·	·	4	4
30	Denmark	2	2	3	7	81	Afghanistan	·	·	1	1
31	Mongolia	2	2	·	4		Egypt	·	·	1	1
	Thailand	2	2	·	4		Israel	·	·	1	1
33	DPR Korea	2	1	3	6		Rep. of Moldova	·	·	1	1
34	Argentina	2	·	4	6		Mauritius	·	·	1	1
	Switzerland	2	·	4	6		Togo	·	·	1	1
36	Mexico	2	·	1	3		Venezuela	·	·	1	1
37	Turkey	1	4	3	8						
38	Zimbabwe	1	3	·	4		Individuals	Gd	Sv	Bz	All
39	Azerbaijan	1	2	4	7	USA	Michael Phelps	8	·	·	8
40	Uzbekistan	1	2	3	6	JAM	Usain Bolt	3	·	·	3
41	Slovenia	1	2	2	5	GBR	Chris Hoy	3	·	·	3
42	Bulgaria	1	1	3	5	AUS	Stephanie Rice	3	·	·	3
	Indonesia	1	1	3	5	CHN	Kai Zou	3	·	·	3
44	Finland	1	1	2	4	AUS	Lisbeth Trickett	2	1	1	4
45	Latvia	1	1	1	3	AUS	Leisel Jones	2	1	·	3
46	Belgium	1	1	·	2	USA	Matt Grevers	2	1	·	3
	Dominican Rep.	1	1	·	2	CHN	Wei Yang	2	1	·	3
	Estonia	1	1	·	2	USA	Aaron Peirsol	2	1	·	3
	Portugal	1	1	·	2	USA	Ryan Lochte	2	·	2	4
50	India	1	·	2	3	USA	Jason Lezak	2	·	1	3
51	Iran	1	·	1	2	JAP	Kosuke Kitajima	2	·	1	3

———————— 2008 PRIMARIES · VOCABULARY OF NOTE ————————

Phrases, quotes, and bon mots from the interminable 2008 presidential primaries:
PINGATE · Fall 2007 non-scandal prompted by Obama's initial refusal to wear a flag pin on his lapel. (In September, he said: 'I'm less concerned about what you're wearing on your lapel than what's in your heart.') ❦ HILLRAISERS · Those who collected ≥$100,000 for Hillary's campaign, including Norman Hsu. ❦ FAIRY TALE · Bill Clinton's January description of Obama's opposition to the Iraq war; in December, Bill said that an Obama presidency would be 'A ROLL OF THE DICE'. ❦ SUPER-DUPER TUESDAY · 24 states voted on 2/5/08, the largest 'Super Tuesday' ever – *also* TSUNAMI TUESDAY *and* THE TUESDAY OF DESTINY. ❦ CELESTIAL CHOIR · Hillary's snarky allusion to Obama's rhetoric, in February: 'Let's just get everybody together, let's get unified, the sky will open, the light will come down, celestial choirs will be singing, and everyone will know we should do the right thing, and the world will be perfect.' ❦ SNIPER FIRE · In March, Clinton said that during a 1996 trip to Bosnia, 'I remember landing under sniper fire ... we just ran with our heads down to get into the vehicles to get to our base.' (Later, after pictures revealed her to have walked calmly across the tarmac, she said she MISSPOKE). ❦ UNITY TICKET · Hillary and Obama in some combination of POTUS and VP. ❦ 3 AM · A Clinton TV ad in February portrayed her as the candidate best able to handle a crisis. The (racially charged) ad began: 'It's 3 am, and your children are safe and asleep. But there's a phone in the White House, and it's ringing.' ❦ LUCKY · In March, Geraldine Ferraro resigned from Clinton's finance committee after arguing that Obama had benefited from being a black man: 'He happens to be very lucky to be who he is.' ❦ MONSTER · In March, Obama foreign policy adviser Samantha Power resigned after saying, to the *Scotsman*, of Clinton: 'She is a monster, too – that is off the record – she is stooping to anything.' ❦ BITTER & BITTERGATE· At a San Francisco fund-raiser in April, Obama said, 'it's not surprising' voters struggling financially 'get bitter ... they CLING to guns or religion or antipathy to people who aren't like them...' ❦ A NATION OF WHINERS · In July, McCain's (now former) economic adviser Phil Gramm told the *Washington Times*: 'You've heard of mental depression; this is a MENTAL RECESSION ... We have sort of become a nation of whiners'. ❦ NUTS · The part of Obama's anatomy that Jesse Jackson said, in July, that he'd like to cut off. ❦ YES WE CAN! · Obama's relentless campaign slogan; in Spanish: SI SE PUEDE! (After Ben & Jerry's endorsed Obama, some suggested the flavor YES, PECAN!). ❦ FIRST LAD · what Bill would have become had Hillary won. ❦ PUMAs · Hillary supporters who refused to back Obama, stating Party Unity My Ass. ❦ CONE OF SILENCE · During an August 'civil forum', Pastor Rick Warren told his audience before Obama began answering questions, 'We have safely placed Senator McCain in a cone of silence'. It was later revealed McCain had actually been in his car en route, leading some to allege an unfair advantage. ❦ ENCYCLOPEDIA BARACKTANNICA · *Slate.com's* splendid compilation of >800 Obama-inspired neologisms – ranging from the sublime (Nirbama) to the ridiculous (Dalai Lobama). ❦ OBAMANIAC, McCAINIAC · Passionate supporters of each. ❦ NOBAMA · Anti-Obama monicker. *Similarly*, McLAME; McSAME; McSHAME. ❦ D-AMTRAK · reference to Obama's running mate, Joe 'RARE MIX' Biden, who invariably mentions that he takes the train home each night. ❦ HOCKEY MOM · one of the few things known about McCain's running mate Sarah Palin – whose basketball nickname was SARAH BARRACUDA.

—— ENDORSEMENTS ——

Notable celebrity endorsements:

BARACK OMABA

Kareem Abdul-Jabbar; Ben Affleck; Halle Berry; Jessica Biel; George Clooney; Matt Damon; Robert De Niro; Tom Hanks; Hulk Hogan; Scarlett Johansson; Eddie Murphy; Chris Rock; Will Smith; Sharon Stone; Gene Wilder; will.i.am

HILLARY CLINTON

50 Cent; Cher; Ted Danson; Danny DeVito; Elton John; Magic Johnson; Quincy Jones; Madonna; Rob Reiner; Carly Simon; Jerry Springer; Martha Stewart; Barbra Streisand; Donald and Ivanka Trump; Renée Zellweger

JOHN McCAIN

Wilford Brimley; Arnold Schwarzenegger; Curt Schilling; Tom Selleck; Sylvester Stallone; Rip Torn

MIKE HUCKABEE

Ric Flair; Chuck Norris; Ted Nugent

JOHN EDWARDS

Kevin Bacon; Harry Belafonte; Danny Glover; Bonnie Raitt; Tim Robbins; Susan Sarandon

DENNIS KUCINICH: Melissa Etheridge; Larry Flynt; Woody Harrelson. ❦ RUDY GIULIANI: Robert Duvall; John O'Hurley; Ben Stein; Ron Silver; Jon Voight. ❦ FRED THOMPSON: Pat Sajak ❦ RON PAUL: Arlo Guthrie ❦ MITT ROMNEY: Pat Boone; Donny and Marie Osmond.

Key to table right: figures are % votes for each major candidate, from the *New York Times*. Am[erican] Sa[moa]; Pu[erto] Ri[co]; Vi[rgin] Is[lands]; Dem[ocrats] Ab[road].

—— STATE RESULTS ——

Paul	Romney	Huckabee	McCain		Obama	Clinton	Edwards
				%			
3	18	41	37	AL	56	42	1
17	44	22	16	AK	75	25	.
4	35	9	47	AZ	42	50	5
5	14	60	20	AR	27	70	2
4	35	12	42	CA	43	51	4
8	60	13	18	CO	67	32	.
4	33	7	52	CT	51	47	1
4	33	15	45	DE	53	42	1
8	6	16	68	DC	75	24	.
3	31	13	36	FL	33	50	14
3	30	34	32	GA	66	31	2
.	.	.	.	HI	76	24	.
24	.	.	70	ID	80	17	1
5	29	16	47	IL	65	33	2
8	5	10	78	IN	49	51	.
10	25	34	13	IA	38	29	30
11	3	60	24	KS	74	26	.
7	5	8	72	KY	30	65	2
5	6	43	42	LA	57	36	3
18	52	6	21	ME	59	40	.
6	7	29	55	MD	61	36	1
3	51	4	41	MA	41	56	2
6	39	16	30	MI	.	55	.
16	41	20	22	MN	66	32	.
4	2	13	79	MS	61	37	1
4	29	32	33	MO	49	48	2
25	38	15	22	MT	56	41	.
13	.	.	87	NE	68	32	.
14	51	8	13	NV	45	51	4
8	32	11	37	NH	36	39	17
5	28	8	55	NJ	44	54	1
14	.	.	86	NM	48	49	1
6	28	11	52	NY	40	57	1
8	.	12	74	NC	56	42	.
21	36	20	23	ND	61	37	1
5	3	31	60	OH	44	54	2
3	25	33	37	OK	31	55	10
15	.	.	85	OR	59	41	.
16	.	11	73	PA	45	55	.
7	4	22	65	RI	40	58	1
4	15	30	33	SC	55	27	18
17	3	7	70	SD	45	55	.
6	24	34	32	TN	40	54	4
5	2	38	51	TX	47	51	1
3	89	1	5	UT	57	39	3
7	5	14	72	VT	59	39	1
4	4	41	50	VA	64	35	1
22	15	24	26	WA	68	31	.
5	4	10	76	WV	26	67	7
5	2	37	55	WI	58	41	1
.	67	.	.	WY	61	38	.
.	.	.	100	Am Sa	42	57	.
.	.	.	100	Guam	50	50	.
4	.	5	91	Pu Ri	32	68	.
3	19	.	31	Vi Is	90	8	.
.	.	.	.	Dem Ab	67	33	.

———————— MYANMAR & CYCLONE NARGIS ————————

On May 2–3, 2008, Cyclone Nargis, which had developed in the Bay of Bengal, made landfall in Myanmar. By the time it hit coastal communities, Nargis had been upgraded from Category 1 to 3–4, and the >120mph winds wrought devastation across *c*.5,000km² of the low-lying Irrawaddy delta. To the south and west of the capital Yangon [née Rangoon], coastal villages that stood just 5' above sea level were deluged by a 12' flood surge, which also threatened *c*.65% of Myanmar's rice production by contaminating the filigree of paddy fields with seawater and corpses.

As the death toll rose from hundreds to tens of thousands, the impact of Nargis was compared to the 2004 SE Asian tsunami. Yet if 2004's aid 'air bridge' was a model of cooperation, efforts post-Nargis were obstructed by the mistrust, superstition, xenophobia, and bureaucracy of Myanmar's idiosyncratic and secretive junta. After some days, aid trickled in from trusted neighbors, but charities complained that their staff were denied entry visas, and repeated offers of assistance, notably from US troops on exercise nearby, were rebuffed. Only on 5/8 were the first UN aid flights permitted to land but, within hours, these flights were suspended when the junta declared that it would accept aid to distribute itself, but would ban 'rescue and information teams from foreign countries'. As the military confiscated enough high-energy biscuits to feed 95,000, and refused to waive import duties on aid, charities warned of a 'second catastrophe' of 'apocalyptic proportions' as hunger, exposure, and disease threatened >1·5m. ❦ In a series of surreal photo-ops, Myanmar's generals were shown handing out TV sets and single bags of rice; press reports claimed that these leaders also affixed their names to foreign aid for pro-army propaganda. In the midst of the crisis, on 5/10, the junta forced a referendum on a constitution designed to secure its power and ban opposition leader Aung

San Suu Kyi from ever holding office. Although polling was delayed in the worst-hit areas, anger was voiced that a (plainly rigged) vote took precedence over the feeding of a people (opposing the constitution carried a 3-year prison sentence).

On 5/12, a single unarmed C-130 transport plane carrying US aid was permitted to land in Yangon. On the same day, the UN Sec-General expressed 'immense frustration' at the delay, disclosing that he had been unable to contact Myanmar's military leaders. ❦ Frustration gave way to outrage after it was reported that Myanmar was *exporting* rice, and that the junta was *selling* foreign aid to its own people. Yet a French suggestion that the UN exercise its 'responsibility to protect' by air-dropping aid was blocked by China and Russia. ❦ Those who hoped that Nargis might force change on the junta were disappointed. On 5/27, Suu Kyi's house arrest was extended for another year, and in June the regime accused the media of fabricating stories about the disaster. In July, the UN stated that the cost of Nargis to Myanmar's assets was $4bn, and calculated that $1bn was required over 3 years to assist the survivors. In total, *c*.600,000 hectares of farmland were destroyed or damaged, along with *c*.800,000 houses; >800,000 people were displaced, and it was estimated that 84,537 people had died and a further 53,836 were presumed dead.

———————OTHER MAJOR STORIES IN BRIEF———————

Economic stimulus package

On 2/13/08, George W. Bush signed the Economic Stimulus Act of 2008, to prod America's flagging and subprime-weakened economy. The Act provided for $100bn in tax rebates to individuals, $52bn in tax cuts for business, and a temporary increase in the size of mortgages that the Federal Housing Admin, Fannie Mae, and Freddie Mac were allowed to insure. As a result of the Act, most who filed 2007 taxes received up to $600 as a rebate ($1,200 for married couples filing jointly). Yet while Congress moved with unusual speed and bipartisanship to approve the Act (progressing from discussion to signing in under a month), economists were divided on the wisdom of the package, noting that worried consumers might save their rebates rather than spend them, and that funds for the rebates would increase the deficit. At the time of writing, the Act's effects on the economy remained unclear, though few cash-strapped Americans objected to some extra income.

Eliot Spitzer

On 3/12/08, Eliot Spitzer resigned as the 54th governor of New York after it was alleged that he had links with the 'Emperor's Club VIP', which was said to be a 'high-end' prostitution ring. Faced with the accusation that he was the 'Client 9' referred to in a federal wiretap operation, Spitzer said, 'I have acted in a way that violates my obligation to my family and violates my or any sense of right or wrong'. Days later, Spitzer, a lawyer and politician feared for his combative defense of the moral high-ground, told a press conference, 'Over the course of my public life, I have insisted – I believe correctly – that people regardless of their position or power take responsibility for their conduct.

I can and will ask no less of myself'. Many of those against whom Spitzer had directed his ethical zeal failed to suppress a shiver of schadenfreude that the man known as 'the Steamroller' and 'the Sheriff of Wall Street' appeared to have been hoisted by his own petard. ❧ At the time of writing, it was unclear what, if any, action might be taken against Spitzer. Legal proceedings were under way against some of those alleged to be involved in the 'prostitution ring'. ❧ Spitzer was succeeded as governor by David Paterson – the first black governor of New York and the second legally blind governor in US history. Soon after his swearing in, in what was described as a 'preemptive' strike against future scandal, Paterson and his wife both admitted to having had extra-marital affairs. He later admitted to using cocaine and marijuana in his 20s.

Zimbabwe's elections and economy

On 3/29/08, in an environment of relative calm, Zimbabweans voted in parliamentary and presidential elections. After days of delay and allegations of corruption, it became clear that Morgan Tsvangirai's Movement for Democratic Change (MDC) had toppled Robert Mugabe's Zanu-PF parliamentary majority for the first time since independence in 1980. The official result of the presidential elections was even more delayed. On 5/2, Zimbabwe's Electoral Cmsn declared that Tsvangirai had won 47·9% of the vote: more than Mugabe's 43·2%, but short of the absolute majority required. On 5/10, despite the violent harassment of MDC supporters, Tsvangirai announced that he would stand in a runoff election, later set for 6/27. However, as the weeks passed, Zanu-PF's systematic campaign of intimidation, starvation,

—————— OTHER MAJOR STORIES IN BRIEF cont. ——————

arrest, abduction, arson, torture, rape, and murder intensified. Mugabe even boasted, 'We are not going to give up our country for a mere X on a ballot. How can a ballpoint pen fight with a gun?'. On 6/22, Tsvangirai withdrew his candidacy, refusing to participate in a 'violent, illegitimate sham', yet this halted neither the election nor Mugabe's campaign of terror. By election day, the MDC told its supporters to vote for Mugabe (the sole candidate) if only to stay alive. On 6/28, Mugabe was sworn in for his 6th presidential term, claiming to have won >85% of the vote. ❦ The backdrop to these events was the rapid collapse of Zimbabwe's economy and civil society. In May, the central bank issued Z$5bn, Z$25bn, and Z$50bn notes in rapid succession; and in June, the official inflation rate was 2·2m%, though 10m% was more realistic. On 8/1, days after issuing a Z$100bn note, Zimbabwe lopped 10 zeros off its currency, making Z$1bn=Z$1. This did nothing to curb inflation or unemployment (*c*.80%), or the acute shortages of water, power, fuel, medicine, and food. The flood of refugees into neighboring countries only intensified. ❦ In July, soon after Mugabe's 'victory', encouraged by international pressure and the 'quiet diplomacy' of S Africa's president Thabo Mbeki, Mugabe and Tsvangirai met (and shook hands [see p.15]) in Harare to discuss power-sharing. ❦ Even with Mugabe being offered an 'honorable' exit as ceremonial head of state, at the time of writing the prospects of a swift and peaceful end to Zanu-PF's rule looked bleak. But not as bleak as the future of the country and its people. The UN warned that in 2009, >5·1m would face hunger in what was once considered to be the 'breadbasket of Africa'.

Polygamous sect raid

On 4/3/08, Texas law enforcement raided the Yearning for Zion (YFZ) ranch outside Eldorado, TX. Over several days, officials seized *c*.460 children, claiming they were at imminent risk of physical and sexual abuse. Yearning for Zion is owned by the Fundamentalist Church of Jesus Christ of Latter Day Saints (FLDS), a breakaway Mormon sect known for practicing polygamy, founded by 'prophet' Warren Jeffs. For years, reports had circulated that young girls were pressured into marriages at the ranch, often with much older men who were already married to several other women. Authorities were moved to act against the ranch after a call to an abuse hotline in which a caller who claimed to be 16 said she was abused at the ranch by her 49-year-old husband. (The caller was never identified, and the call itself was later thought to be a prank.) The children of YFZ were transferred to holding facilities and then foster care, where they became the subject of an anguished national debate over the limits of religious tolerance and state authority. Amidst poignant cries from mothers, and growing media curiosity, the Third Court of Appeals in Austin ruled on 5/22 that the state had failed to establish an immediate danger to the children, and that their seizure had been illegal. On 5/29, the TX Supreme Court upheld the ruling. The YFZ children were soon reunited with their families, and church leaders said they would from then on forbid underage marriages. At the time of writing, both criminal and child welfare investigations were ongoing. And while many families have now chosen to live away from the ranch, it seems likely the sect has not seen the last of the spotlight from both the press and police.

――――――― OTHER MAJOR STORIES IN BRIEF cont. ―――――――

The Sichuan earthquake

On 5/12/08, at 2:28pm local time, a 7·9 Richter earthquake hit the mountainous region near Chengdu, in the Sichuan province of W China. The quake was felt >1,000 miles away in Beijing and Shanghai. Within days, the death toll was *c*.20,000, and *c*.4m homes were said to have been destroyed. In some areas, 80% of all buildings were in ruins. ❦ Mindful surely of the upcoming Olympics (and the outrage at Myanmar's response to Nargis [see p.26]), the government reacted with uncharacteristic speed and transparency. *c*.130,000 soldiers, medics, engineers, &c., were ordered to the region; assistance was solicited from (selected) neighbors; and both the President and PM were filmed visiting the area. ❦ However, the inaccessibility of the region, the destruction of vital infrastructure, bad weather, and the scale of the devastation combined to hinder rescue efforts. As the death toll hit *c*.50,000, it was reported that >3m tents were urgently needed. Miraculous reports of people rescued against all odds did little to ameliorate the tragedy. Soon, pride in China's resilience gave way to anger that many of the rural region's buildings, not least schools, appeared cheaply and corruptly built. The death of >10,000 children led local authorities to suspend China's one-child policy for parents who had lost their only child (though this was of no comfort to those who were too old to conceive or who had been sterilized). ❦ A series of aftershocks terrorized the area after the quake, and within days millions were placed in further jeopardy by *c*.34 'quake lakes' – vast, unstable, and fast-rising reservoirs formed after rivers had been dammed by landslides. Notably, >250,000 were forced to evacuate from the 'Tangjiashan Lake', whose waters threatened >1·3m people before they were partially drained in June. ❦ At the time of writing, *c*.88,000 were reported dead or missing, *c*.5m were homeless, and many thousands had been left childless. Clearly, the psychological, political, and socio-economic consequences of the quake will emerge only in time. But, although not perfect, China's response to the tragedy marked a shift in the regime's relationship with the international community, the media, and its own people [see p.32].

California & gay marriage

On 5/15/08, the California Supreme Court ruled 4–3 that denying same-sex couples the right to marry violated California's constitution. Striking down a 1977 law and a 2000 proposition that defined marriage as a union between a man and woman, the ruling made California the second state to permit gay marriages, following Massachusetts in 2004. While noting that California's 'domestic partnership' provisions give same-sex couples the same legal privileges as marriage, the court ruled that calling homosexual unions by a different name deprived same-sex families of the equality afforded them by the constitution. Chief Justice Ronald George said that 'an individual's sexual orientation, like a person's race or gender, does not constitute a legitimate basis upon which to deny or withhold legal rights'. (Scholars noted this was the first time a state Supreme Court has ruled sexual orientation is a protected class.) Yet as jubilant couples (and retailers) celebrated, other advocates cast a worried eye towards November, when a referendum to ban gay marriage would appear on the state ballot, and gay newlyweds seemed likely to become a lightning rod in the presidential elections.

──────── OTHER MAJOR STORIES IN BRIEF cont. ────────

Midwest flooding

In early June 2008, unusually heavy rains in the upper Midwest caused the Mississippi River and its tributaries to overflow, leading to the region's worst flooding in about 15 years. Throughout the month of June and into early July, the flooding displaced >40,000, killed *c*.24, injured 148, and wrought *c*.$6bn in damage. Iowa suffered the worst destruction: 83 of the state's 99 counties were declared disaster areas, and Cedar Rapids alone suffered $1bn in damage. The floods also damaged crops in the nation's breadbasket, putting further pressure on corn and soybean prices already inflated by biofuel production [see p.183]. At the time of writing, the federal government had provided $2·6bn in assistance for victims of the flood and was considering a $3·96bn tax relief package. Yet for many residents, it will take a long time to rebuild and recover from what some Midwesterners called 'our Katrina'.

North Korea's nuclear ambitions

In February 2007, N Korea agreed to end its nuclear program in return for a thaw in diplomatic relations and much-needed economic aid. And, on 6/26/08, six months behind schedule, N Korea submitted a 60-page declaration of its nuclear program to the Chinese, who, along with Japan, Russia, S Korea, and the US, are engaged in the '6-party process' to denuclearize the Korean peninsula. In return for this declaration, the US agreed to remove N Korea from its list of state sponsors of terrorism, lift some sanctions (including those imposed by the Trading with the Enemy Act), and open the way for loans, aid, and increased trade. A day later, N Korea demolished the cooling tower at its nuclear reactor in Yongbyon

which had produced the plutonium for Pyongyang's first nuclear test in 2006. ❦ Some were critical that N Korea had neither fully disclosed its nuclear arsenal nor addressed the issues of proliferation or what nuclear assistance it had given Syria. Others saw the declaration and the tentative resumption of talks as a sign that progress, albeit slow, was being made to disarm one of the world's most secretive and paranoid countries.

Supreme Court & guns

On 6/26/08, the Supreme Court struck down a Washington, DC, ban on handguns, ruling 5–4 that the 2nd Amendment protects the right of an individual to keep a gun for personal use. At issue was the court's interpretation of the amendment, which reads: '*A well regulated militia, being necessary to the security of a free state, the right of the people to keep and bear arms, shall not be infringed*'. Writing for the majority, Justice Antonin Scalia concluded that the prefatory statement ('*a well regulated militia*') should not be taken to limit the right set forth in the operative clause ('*the right of the people to keep and bear arms*'). Gun-control advocates had long argued that the right to bear arms should be understood in the context of service to a militia, and did not create a right to a gun for personal use. A 1939 opinion by the court was widely understood to have rejected the individual's right to a gun; Justice Scalia wrote that such an interpretation of the 1939 decision was mistaken. While the decision was viewed as historic, it seemed likely to have little impact on most of the nation's gun restrictions – Scalia noted that the court's decision applied only to the right of 'law-abiding, responsible citizens to use arms in defense of hearth and home', and should not be

———————— OTHER MAJOR STORIES IN BRIEF cont. ————————

seen to contradict rules prohibiting the ownership of guns by felons, 'dangerous and unusual weapons', or other restrictions. Yet within days of the decision, the libertarian organization that organized and financed the DC challenge followed with a suit in a federal district court challenging Chicago's gun laws, which are among the nation's most restrictive. Across the country, activists on both sides began preparing for a series of challenges to test the limits of the Supreme Court's decision.

Georgia vs Russia

On 8/7/08, as the eyes of the world were on Beijing, Georgia launched a surprise attack on South Ossetia – a bordering province supported by Russia which for years had been agitating for independence. ❦ Tensions in the region, palpable since the Soviet Union's collapse, had worsened in 2008, as the newly reelected (and not uncontroversial) Georgian President Mikhail Saakashvili sought closer ties with the US, and NATO promised Georgia membership sometime in the future. Both of these moves dismayed Russia – already angered by Western interference in its 'sphere of influence' and by America's 'defense shield'. ❦ On 8/8, Moscow reacted to the incursion by sending an overwhelming force of troops, tanks, and air power deep into Georgia. The ensuing fighting killed c.1,500, forced tens of thousands to flee, and spread into Georgia's northwestern breakaway province, Abkhazia. On 8/10, reeling from Russia's attack, Georgia declared a cease-fire and said its troops had withdrawn from S Ossetia. Moscow brushed aside these claims – and US condemnation – and continued its assault. Over the next few days, with France acting as EU mediator, Russia

spun out the peace negotiations while maintaining its strong military presence in Georgia. America attempted to exert pressure on Russia by flying c.2,000 Georgian soldiers home from Iraq and sending in humanitarian aid. Yet for all their words of support, it was evident that neither the US nor NATO was willing to engage the Russian military. ❦ At the time of writing, diplomacy was still under way, as the phrase 'new cold war' gained momentum. Despite NATO warnings, Russia was in no hurry to withdraw all its troops from Georgia. Indeed, Poland's agreement on 8/20 to site the US missile shield on its soil only intensified Moscow's desire to exert control over her 'near abroad'.

Pervez Musharraf's resignation

Pakistan's president Pervez Musharraf resigned on 8/18/08 – days before he was due to face impeachment charges of corruption and violating the constitution laid by the coalition government elected in February. ❦ Musharraf seized power in a bloodless coup in 1999 and for c.9 years ruled Pakistan as a military dictator (only in 11/07 did he resign as army chief to govern as a civilian). After 9/11, he allied Pakistan with America and became a pivotal player in the 'war on terror', exchanging tough action against Islamic extremism for >$10bn in military aid. However, this stance was unpopular domestically, and was blamed for fueling the Taliban insurgency and terrorist attacks across the country. ❦ Musharraf's peaceful exit, though welcomed by many, left a power vacuum in Pakistan just when the country faced economic turmoil, judicial instability, violent terrorist attacks, growing sympathy for Islamic extremism, and further threats of militancy in the North West Frontier Province.

———————— PERSON OF THE YEAR · HU JINTAO ————————

Before his elevation in 2003, profiles of China's new president were often prefaced, 'Not much is known about Hu Jintao'. Five years on, we know only a little more about the man who leads the most populous nation on Earth. ❦ Two events intensified the world's gaze on China in 2008: the tragedy of the Sichuan earthquake and the triumph of the Beijing Olympics. Yet neither of these was clear-cut. For while the quake catalyzed an unusually open (though not perfect) state response, it also exposed China's structural corruption and rural poverty. And while the Games were spectacular, their scale and security were premised on a firmly authoritarian grip. These tensions characterize both modern China and Hu himself. ❦ Hu Jintao was born in 1942 to a family of tea merchants. He grew up in Taizhou, Jiangsu, and in 1959 entered Beijing's Qinghua University, where he excelled in hydroelectric engineering. It was here he met his wife, with whom he has a son and daughter. In 1964, Hu joined the Communist Party and worked as a political instructor, before the Cultural Revolution banished him to the countryside for 'reeducation'. In 1968, he was sent to the desolate Gansu province, where he labored for a year before he was promoted to technician. Hu worked assiduously, traveled extensively in the region, and formed powerful Party allies. In 1982, he was transferred to Beijing, and in 1984 he headed the Communist Youth League. A year later, political intrigue forced him back to the provinces as Party Secretary in Guizhou. Yet he shone in this role too, and in 1988 became the first civilian Party Secretary in Tibet. Interpretations differ as to Hu's role in the bloody suppression of the 1989 Tibetan unrest, but he proved himself no squeamish moderate, and after Tiananmen Square he did not hesitate to voice his support for the Party. ❦ In 1990, Hu returned to Beijing, where he was propelled by Deng Xiaoping, the author of China's reform era, to the top ranks of the political hierarchy. After a decade's tutelage, Hu succeeded Jiang Zemin as China's top party, government, and military leader between 2002 and 2005. ❦ Some were warily optimistic of Hu as China's paramount leader, considering him technocratic, pragmatic, and even reforming. His response to the 2003 SARS outbreak was initially secretive, but he responded to international criticism with greater transparency. Similarly, he reacted to protests in Hong Kong by shelving an anti-subversion law. Hu's ideological innovation is 'scientific development', whereby economic growth is tempered by social and ecological considerations for a 'harmonious society'. Yet while this 'people first' approach has ameliorated corruption, pollution, inequality, and incivility, Hu is unwavering over Tibet and Taiwan, and severe in his treatment of political dissidents, religious activists, and media critics. Hu is working to focus China's awesome potential so that the environment and the poor are not crushed in the stampede. But he is far from ushering in Western capitalist democracy. As he said in 2007, 'only socialism can save China and only reform and opening up can develop China, socialism, and Marxism'. ❦ Hu is expected to retire in 2012, the year London's Olympics will be compared to Beijing's. Expect profiles to begin: 'Not much is known about Hu's successor...'

—— SCHEMATIC · WORLD EVENTS OF NOTE · 2007–08 ——

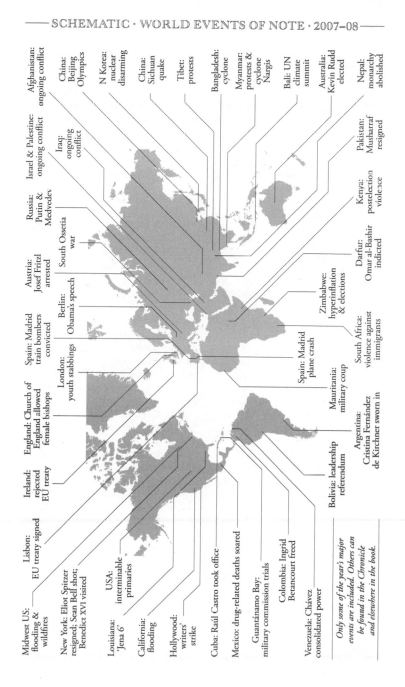

Afghanistan: ongoing conflict

China: Beijing Olympics

N Korea: nuclear disarming

China: Sichuan quake

Tibet: protests

Bangladesh: cyclone

Myanmar: protests & cyclone Nargis

Bali: UN climate summit

Australia: Kevin Rudd elected

Nepal: monarchy abolished

Israel & Palestine: ongoing conflict

Iraq: ongoing conflict

Pakistan: Musharraf resigned

Russia: Putin & Medvedev

Kenya: postelection violence

South Ossetia war

Austria: Josef Fritzl arrested

Darfur: Omar al-Bashir indicted

Zimbabwe: hyperinflation & elections

Berlin: Obama's speech

South Africa: violence against immigrants

Spain: Madrid train bombers convicted

Spain: Madrid plane crash

London: youth stabbings

Mauritania: military coup

England: Church of England allowed female bishops

Argentina: Cristina Fernández de Kirchner sworn in

Ireland: rejected EU treaty

Bolivia: leadership referendum

Lisbon: EU treaty signed

Midwest US: flooding & wildfires

New York: Eliot Spitzer resigned; Sean Bell shot; Benedict XVI visited

USA: interminable primaries

Louisiana: 'Jena 6'

California: flooding

Hollywood: writers' strike

Cuba: Raúl Castro took office

Mexico: drug-related deaths soared

Guantánamo Bay: military commission trials

Colombia: Ingrid Betancourt freed

Venezuela: Chávez consolidated power

Only some of the year's major events are included. Others can be found in the Chronicle and elsewhere in the book.

——————— IN BRIEF · AUGUST – SEPTEMBER 2007 ———————

The daily chronicle below picks up from the 2008 edition of Schott's Miscellany.

{AUGUST 16} US citizen José Padilla was convicted of terrorism conspiracy charges after a 5-year detention. ❦ A seismic jolt killed 3 rescue workers trying to save 6 miners trapped in UT. ❦ The US signed a deal to give Israel $30bn in military aid. {17} The Fed cut its discount rate and urged banks to borrow from it directly, citing risks of a recession. {19} Hurricane Dean killed *c.*13 in Jamaica. {20} RIP @ 87, hotelier Leona Helmsley. {21} The CIA declassified a report from its inspector general citing pre-9/11 failures. ❦ Space shuttle *Endeavour* landed safely. {22} 14 US soldiers died in a N Iraq helicopter crash. {23} A National Intelligence Estimate was released raising doubts about the Iraqi government. ❦ Hurricane Dean killed *c.*10 in Mexico. ❦ Midwest US floods abated after killing *c.*26. {24} Forest fires began in Greece, killing 64 over several days and threatening antiquities. ❦ Officials said US 'friendly fire' had killed 3 UK soldiers in Afghanistan. {25} Twin bombings killed >40 in Hyderabad, India. {26} Iraqi PM Nouri al-Maliki criticized US Senators who had called for his exit after the intelligence estimate. {27} Attorney Gen. Alberto Gonzales announced his resignation. ❦ Sen. Larry Craig [ID-R] admitted pleading guilty to disorderly conduct after being arrested in a Minneapolis airport bathroom in June; he denied wrongdoing. ❦ NFL star Michael Vick pled guilty to dogfighting charges. {28}

Nouri al-Maliki

I am not gay. I never have been gay.
– SEN. LARRY CRAIG

Craig said his guilty plea had been a 'mistake'. ❦ Abdullah Gul was sworn in as President of Turkey. ❦ A battle between rival Shiite groups killed *c.*50 in Karbala, Iraq. {29} Hillary Clinton's campaign said it would give to charity $23,000 raised by donor Norman Hsu, after reports of Hsu's questionable fund-raising practices and an unrelated outstanding arrest warrant. ❦ A VA state panel released its report on the VA Tech massacre, criticizing officials for failing to warn students earlier. ❦ The Taliban freed 12 S Korean hostages held since 7/19. {30} The Taliban freed 7 remaining S Korean hostages. {31} Sen. John Warner [VA-R] said he would retire at the end of his term. ❦ The Justice Dept said it was investigating possible campaign finance violations by Hsu; he surrendered to CA officials on his arrest warrant. ❦ White House Press Sec. Tony Snow announced he was resigning.

SEPTEMBER · {1} Sen. Craig said he would resign effective 9/30. ❦ UT rescue efforts ended after officials said there was no hope of finding the miners alive. {4} A GAO report said Iraq had failed to meet 11 of 18 progress benchmarks. ❦ Mattel recalled 775,000 Chinese-made toys over lead paint concerns. ❦ Millionaire adventurer Steve Fossett disappeared during a flight in NV. ❦ Danish police arrested 8 for al-Qaeda links, and on suspicion of plotting bomb attacks. {5} German police arrested 3 Islamic militants suspected of planning imminent major attacks. ❦ Rep. Fred Thompson announced his presidential candidacy. ❦

——————— IN BRIEF · SEPTEMBER 2007 ———————

Hsu disappeared after failing to appear in a CA court; another arrest warrant was issued. ❦ Craig said he would try to reverse his guilty plea and, if successful, might not resign. ❦ The Pentagon said a B-52 had been mistakenly armed with nuclear warheads and flown across several states. ❦ RIP @ 71, tenor Luciano Pavarotti. ❦ Hurricane Felix killed *c*.100 in Nicaragua. {6} Israeli troops killed 10 in S Gaza. ❦ Syria accused Israel of an air attack. {7} The parents of 4-year-old British girl Madeleine McCann, who disappeared 5/07 in Portugal, were named suspects by Portuguese police. ❦ The FBI arrested Hsu in CO. ❦ Congress passed legislation increasing aid for college students. ❦ Bin Laden released his first videotape in 3 years. {9} Roger Federer won his 4th consecutive US Open [see p.245]. {10} Gen. David H. Petraeus and the US ambassador to Iraq, Ryan C. Crocker, testified before Congress on the war in Iraq; Petraeus said he would begin reducing troops to pre-'surge' levels but warned against a hasty withdrawal. ❦ Former Pakistani PM Nawaz Sharif returned to Pakistan, but was deported within hours of his arrival. ❦ Sen. Craig filed court papers to withdraw his guilty plea. ❦ RIP @ 90, actress Jane Wyman. ❦ RIP @ 64, Body Shop founder Anita Roddick. {11} Palestinian rocket fire wounded 40 Israeli soldiers near Gaza. ❦ Americans commemorated the 6th anniversary of 9/11. {12} Japanese PM Shinzo Abe announced his resignation. ❦ Russian PM Mikhail Fradkov resigned; President Vladimir Putin appointed Viktor Zubkov as

Benazir Bhutto

*We are Americans ...
protecting Americans.*
– ERIK PRINCE, Blackwater CEO

his replacement. ❦ 3 earthquakes hit Indonesia over 2 days, killing *c*.24 and raising tsunami fears. {13} In a national address, Bush said he would withdraw 5,700 US soldiers from Iraq by Christmas 2007, and reduce the total number of combat brigades from 20 to 15 by 7/08. ❦ The NFL fined the New England Patriots coach $500,000 and denied the team the 1st-round draft pick after a staff member allegedly videotaped another team's signals. {14} Exiled former Pakistani PM Benazir Bhutto said she would return home. {16} A plane crash in Phuket, Thailand, killed >88. ❦ O.J. Simpson was arrested and charged in Las Vegas for an alleged armed robbery involving sports memorabilia; he denied wrongdoing. ❦ A Baghdad shoot-out involving US security firm Blackwater killed 17 Iraqis. {17} Bush nominated retired federal judge Michael Mukasey as Attorney General. ❦ Hillary Clinton unveiled a health insurance overhaul. ❦ Blackwater defended its actions during the shoot-out; the State Dept promised an investigation; Iraqi officials said they would suspend the company's license. {18} The Fed cut its benchmark interest rate by half a point, in an attempt to contain the subprime crisis. ❦ Obama unveiled a major tax cut plan. {19} Israel declared Gaza 'hostile territory'. {20} A bill to withdraw combat troops from Iraq by 6/08 failed in the Senate. ❦ An Iraqi government report said the Blackwater shoot-out had been unprovoked, and called for all foreign security forces to be replaced with Iraqi forces. ❦ Floyd Landis was stripped of his 2006

—————— IN BRIEF · SEPTEMBER – OCTOBER 2007 ——————

Tour de France title after an arbitration panel upheld doping charges. ❧ Thousands protested in Jena, LA, over the treatment of 6 black teenagers accused of beating a white schoolmate [see p.302]. {21} 2 students were shot and wounded at Delaware State University, prompting a campus lockdown. ❧ Britney Spears was charged with a hit-and-run and driving without a valid license in CA. {22} RIP @ 84, Marcel Marceau [see p.57]. {23} Japan's ruling party voted in Yasuo Fukada as PM. ❧ *c.*35,000 marched in Myanmar during several days of protests against the country's military junta. {24} Iranian Pres. Mahmoud Ahmadinejad spoke at Columbia University in NY, drawing protests. ❧ United Auto Workers went on strike against GM. {25} Bush announced sanctions against Myanmar. ❧ In a UN Gen. Assembly speech, Ahmadinejad said, 'the nuclear issue of Iran is now closed', and vowed to ignore sanctions. ❧ The House approved an expansion of the State Children's Health Insurance Program (SCHIP). ❧ Mormon sect leader Warren Jeffs was convicted of being an accomplice to rape. ❧ Vick was indicted on state dogfighting charges. {26} Myanmar security forces attacked protesters, arresting *c.*3,000 and killing 31 over several days; the US, EU, and UN condemned the violence. ❧ Israel killed 12 Palestinians in Gaza. ❧ The GM strike ended. ❧ Sen. Craig said he would remain in the Senate until a judge ruled whether he could reverse his guilty plea. ❧ The trial of music producer Phil Spector, charged with the 2003 death of Lana

M. Ahmadinejad

Race is not a major local issue.
– MURPHY MCMILLIN
Mayor of Jena, Louisiana

Clarkson, was declared a mistrial. {27} The US issued sanctions against Myanmar as protests there continued. ❧ Musharraf formalized his reelection bid, amid controversy over his position as both president and army chief. ❧ The Senate gave final approval for a SCHIP expansion despite a threatened Bush veto. {28} At a DC climate-change summit, Bush called for long-term emission targets but rejected mandatory limits. {30} Darfur rebels staged a major raid against African Union peacekeepers, killing >10.

OCTOBER · {1} The FBI announced a probe of the Blackwater incident. ❧ Israel released 86 Palestinian prisoners. {2} Blackwater's chief appeared before a House panel to defend his company. ❧ Britain said it would withdraw 500 troops from S Iraq. ❧ The leaders of N and S Korea held a 3-day summit. ❧ A coroner's inquest into Princess Diana's death opened in London. {3} N Korea agreed to dismantle all of its nuclear facilities by the end of 2007. ❧ Bush vetoed the SCHIP expansion. ❧ The *New York Times* reported on secret 2005 Justice Dept memos authorizing harsh interrogation techniques. ❧ An accident trapped 3,200 miners in S Africa; all were freed. {4} The House passed a bill to make government contractors in combat zones subject to US criminal law. ❧ Sen. Craig said he wouldn't resign, after a judge rejected his request to rescind his guilty plea. ❧ Dems demanded to see the secret 2005 Justice Dept memos; the White House said it had never permitted torture. {5} Track star Marion Jones publicly admitted steroid use, pled guilty to lying to federal investigators in the BALCO case, and announced her retirement. {6} Pakistanis voted in a presidential election; the country's high court said results would not be official until it ruled on whether Musharraf was eligible to run. {7} An Iraqi government investigation concluded that Blackwater contractors had committed 'deliberate murder' in the 9/16 shoot-out. ❦ A runner died and hundreds fell ill at the Chicago marathon [see p.241]. ❦ A 20-year-old deputy sheriff killed 6 in Crandon, WI, then died in a police shoot-out. {8} UK PM Gordon Brown said he would halve the British troop presence in Iraq by spring 2008. ❦ Jones returned 5 medals won at the 2000 Olympics. ❦ Rescue workers found the bodies of 7 whose plane had crashed in the Cascades a day prior; 3 remained missing. {9} Private guards killed 2 women in Baghdad, adding to the debate over contractors in Iraq. ❦ The Supreme Court rejected an appeal by a German who claimed he was abducted and tortured in a CIA 'rendition'. ❦ The bodies of the remaining 3 plane passengers were found in the Cascades. {10} A House committee voted to recognize WWI killings of Armenians in Turkey as genocide; Turkey condemned the move. ❦ A Cleveland, OH, high school student went on a shooting rampage, injuring 5 before killing himself. {11} Doris Lessing won the Nobel Prize in Literature [see p.161]. ❦ A US attack on insurgents N of Baghdad killed 15 civilians.

Marion Jones

Simply, it was no longer possible.
– CÉCILIA SARKOZY

❦ Turkey recalled its ambassador to the US and threatened to withdraw support for the Iraq war. {12} Al Gore and the IPCC won the Nobel Peace Prize [see p.66]. ❦ Myanmar's junta rejected a UN statement calling for negotiations with the opposition. {14} A 31-vehicle crash killed 3 on I-5 in CA, leaving parts of the highway closed for days. {15} Israel and Hezbollah held a prisoner exchange. ❦ SoS Rice said, 'It is time for the establishment of a Palestinian state'. {16} Putin visited Iran. ❦ Bush met with the Dalai Lama. {17} The Turkish parliament approved an offensive against Kurdish rebels in N Iraq. {18} Bombs killed >100 near a convoy carrying Bhutto as she returned from exile. ❦ The House upheld Bush's SCHIP veto; Dems vowed to send the bill to Bush again in a month. ❦ Mukasey earned criticism during his confirmation hearings for refusing to say whether waterboarding was torture. ❦ French president Nicolas Sarkozy and wife Cécilia announced their divorce. {19} The US military said 2 marines would be court-martialed over the 2005 killings in Haditha, Iraq. ❦ Bush imposed further sanctions against Myanmar. ❦ Sen. Brownback abandoned his presidential bid. ❦ J.K. Rowling said she'd always thought of *Harry Potter* character Albus Dumbledore as gay. {20} LA elected the US's first Indian American governor, Bobby Jindal. ❦ Iran's chief nuclear negotiator, Ali Larijani, resigned. {21} Kurdish rebels killed *c.*12 Turkish soldiers near the Iraqi border. {22} Bush asked Congress for $196bn for the wars in Iraq and Afghanistan. ❦ 250,000 were

————— IN BRIEF · OCTOBER – NOVEMBER 2007 —————

told to evacuate wildfires in S CA. {24} Bush declared the CA wildfires a 'major disaster'. ❧ Turkish planes attacked Kurdish rebels near the Iraq border. {25} The US announced new sanctions against Iran's Revolutionary Guard Corps, its Quds division, and 4 state-owned banks. ❧ Prominent biologist James D. Watson resigned from the Cold Spring Harbor Laboratory after controversial remarks about the intelligence of people of African descent; he later apologized 'unreservedly.' ❧ A revised SCHIP bill passed the House, but lacked the votes to override another Bush veto. {26} As CA evacuees returned, reports showed the wildfires had burned *c.*2,000 buildings and killed 7. ❧ FEMA admitted officials had posed as journalists during a 'fake' news conference on the CA wildfires. {27} Darfur peace talks opened in Libya, with some rebel groups boycotting; Sudan declared a unilateral cease-fire. {28} A fire in Ocean Beach, NC, killed 7 college students. ❧ Cristina Fernández de Kirchner was elected to succeed her husband as president of Argentina. ❧ The Red Sox swept the World Series [see p.234]. {29} Russia's 'Chessboard Killer' was sentenced to life for murdering 48. ❧ A suicide bomber killed *c.*29 in Baquba, Iraq. ❧ Israeli PM Olmert said he had prostate cancer. {30} The State and Defense Depts agreed that the military would supervise all State Dept security contractors in Iraq. ❧ Joe Girardi was named to succeed Joe Torre as Yankees manager. {31} A Spanish court sentenced 21 in connection with the 2004 Madrid train bombings.

Nicolas Sarkozy

No money, no funny.
– WGA strike chant [see p.150]

NOVEMBER · {1} The SCHIP expansion passed the Senate. ❧ The UN said 103 children a French aid group tried to fly out of Chad on 10/25 were not orphans, as the group had claimed. ❧ Stephen Colbert's satirical presidential bid ended after the SC Dem. Party refused to list his name on the ballot. ❧ Japan recalled its navy from Afghanistan. ❧ Hurricane Noel killed *c.*107 in the Caribbean. ❧ Joe Torre was hired by the Dodgers. {3} Musharraf declared emergency rule in Pakistan, citing a rise in extremism and problems with the judiciary [see p.31]. ❧ Astronauts repaired a solar panel on the International Space Station during a 7-hour space-walk. {4} Pakistani security forces seized *c.*500 opposition members; officials said elections could be delayed by a year; the US said it would review aid. {5} The Writers Guild of America (WGA) went on strike [see p.150]. ❧ Thousands of lawyers in Pakistan mounted several days of protests against Musharraf; *c.*600 were arrested. ❧ Google announced new ventures into mobile phone technology. {6} Protests continued across Pakistan, police arrested *c.*100. ❧ A bomb attack targeting lawmakers in N Afghanistan killed *c.*50. ❧ The Senate Judiciary Cmte voted 11–8 to approve Mukasey as Att. General. {7} Bush telephoned Musharraf, urging him to hold elections and step down as military ruler. ❧ Georgia's president declared a state of emergency after protests against his leadership. ❧ A container ship collided with the SF-Oakland Bay Bridge, spilling 58,000 gallons of oil. {8} Musharraf said he would hold elections by Feb. 15. ❧ The Senate confirmed Mukasey. ❧ The Senate voted 79–14 to override Bush's veto of a water projects measure; the first veto override of Bush's presidency. ❧ Georgia's president called for a special presidential election Jan. 5. ❧ Brazil announced a major oil field off its SE coast. {9} Former NY police commissioner Bernard Kerik pleaded not guilty to charges of corruption and making false statements. {10} RIP @ 84, author Norman Mailer [see p.57]. {11} Musharraf pledged to hold parliamentary

Pervez Musharraf

elections by Jan. 9, but said his emergency rule would last until then. ❧ A Black Sea storm sank 11 ships, spilling 1,300 tons of oil and raising concerns of environmental damage. {12} Bhutto was placed under house arrest for 7 days in an attempt to block a major march of her supporters. ❧ The former Khmer Rouge foreign minister and his wife were arrested by Cambodian police to face charges of crimes against humanity at a UN-backed Cambodian genocide tribunal. {13} Bush vetoed a $606bn health and education bill. ❧ A congressional report said the wars in Iraq and Afghanistan would cost $1·6 trillion through 2008. ❧ Preliminary FBI findings said 14 of the 17

I am quite sure it will work in humans. – scientist S. MITALIPOV, after cloning a monkey embryo

Blackwater shootings on 9/16 had been without cause. ❧ RIP @ 78, author Ira Levin. {14} Oregon researchers said they had successfully cloned a monkey embryo. {15} Bhutto's house arrest was lifted; Musharraf named an interim PM to oversee elections. ❧ The IAEA said Iran was providing more information on its nuclear program, but still

enriching uranium in defiance of the Security Council. ❧ Barry Bonds was indicted on perjury and obstruction of justice charges; he denied any wrongdoing. ❧ Cyclone Sidr hit Bangladesh, killing *c*.3,000. {16} The Senate rejected a war funding bill calling for troop withdrawal; Defense Sec. Gates warned funding was needed by February. {17} The IPCC released its final 2007 report, saying climate change was 'unequivocal' and could lead to 'irreversible' changes. {18} A mine explosion in Donetsk, Ukraine, killed *c*.63. {20} Scientists announced a method of creating embryonic stem cells from skin cells, bypassing the need to create or destroy embryos. ❧ The Supreme Court agreed to decide whether the 2nd Amendment allows individuals to keep guns for private use. ❧ Warren Jeffs was sentenced to 10 years in prison. ❧ RIP @ 88, former Rhodesian PM Ian Smith. {21} Pakistani officials said they'd released 3,416 detainees (the figure was disputed). {22} Pakistan's top court dismissed the final legal challenge to Musharraf's reelection. {23} Lebanese President Emile Lahoud resigned; a vote to elect his successor failed amidst political infighting. ❧ Bombs in Baghdad and Mosul, Iraq, killed *c*.28. {24} Dozens were arrested over several days of opposition rallies in Moscow, including former chess champion Garry Kasparov. ❧ Kevin Rudd was elected Australian PM. {25} Sharif again returned to Pakistan, this time successfully. ❧ Riots in the Paris suburb of Villiers-le-Bel erupted after 2 youths were killed in a crash with a

——— IN BRIEF · NOVEMBER – DECEMBER 2007 ———

police car; >100 police officers were wounded over 2 days. {26} Senate minority whip Trent Lott [MS-R] announced his resignation. {27} The Red Cross fired its president over his relationship with a subordinate. ❦ RIP @ 24, Washington Redskins safety Sean Taylor, after an armed attack at his home. {28} Musharraf resigned as Pakistan's army chief. ❦ Bush and Mideast leaders concluded peace talks in Annapolis, pledging to work towards a deal by the end of 2008; SoS Rice named Gen. James Jones special envoy for Mideast security. ❦ A 19-day strike by the Broadway stagehands' union in NYC ended after an agreement was reached with theater owners and producers. {29} Musharraf was sworn in as a civilian President; he promised to lift emergency rule by 12/16. ❦ Sudan convicted a British teacher for inciting hatred and insulting Islam after she allowed pupils to name a teddy bear 'Muhammad'. ❦ In an audiotape aired on al-Jazeera, bin Laden called on Europeans to stop aiding the US in Afghanistan. {30} A man demanding to speak to Hillary Clinton took several hostages at her NH campaign office; the 5-hour ordeal ended without injuries. ❦ A plane crash in Turkey killed 57. ❦ RIP @ 69, daredevil Evel Knievel [see p.57].

Hugo Chávez

I believe in my Mormon faith and I endeavor to live by it.
— MITT ROMNEY

elections. ❦ Venezuelan voters defeated a constitutional referendum that would have made Chávez president for life. {3} A National Intelligence Estimate said Iran halted its nuclear weapons program in 2003, contradicting earlier intelligence. ❦ Sudan freed the jailed British teacher. ❦ Israel freed 429 Palestinian prisoners. {4} Bush said Iran remained a threat despite the new intelligence findings, and vowed to continue pressing for sanctions. ❦ Hsu was indicted for fraud and violating federal election law. {5} A gunman killed 8, then himself, at a mall in Omaha, NE. {6} The CIA admitted destroying 2 videotaped interrogations of terror suspects in 2005; there was concern the destruction could qualify as withholding evidence. ❦ In a letter to Kim Jong-il, Bush offered normalized relations if N Korea fully disclosed its nuclear programs. ❦ A gas explosion in Linfen, N China, killed 105 miners. ❦ Bush unveiled a plan to help homeowners hit by the subprime crisis. ❦ Presidential candidate Mitt Romney gave a speech defending his Mormon faith. {7} The Senate Intelligence Cmte promised an investigation into the destroyed CIA tapes. ❦ An oil tanker hit by a barge spilled 2·7m gallons of oil off S Korea's W coast. {8} Oprah Winfrey and Barack Obama held a major rally together in Des Moines, IA. ❦ The Justice Dept and the CIA's internal watchdog launched an investigation into the destroyed tapes. {9} A gunman killed 4, then himself, in shootings at 2 CO churches. ❦ Robert Pickton was convicted of 2nd-degree murder in the deaths of 6 women near

DECEMBER · {1} John Darwin, a Briton declared dead in 2003, walked into a London police station claiming amnesia; he was later charged with fraud. {2} Putin's United Russia party won a landslide victory in Russian parliamentary

IN BRIEF · DECEMBER 2007

Vancouver, BC. ❧ An ice storm hit the Midwest; *c.*24 died over several days. {10} Putin endorsed Gazprom chairman Dmitri A. Medvedev as the next Russian president. ❧ Vick was sentenced to 23 months in prison for dogfighting. ❧ Newspaper magnate Conrad Black was sentenced to 6·5 years in prison for fraud and obstruction of justice. ❧ Libby dropped his appeal in the CIA leak case. ❧ A UN deadline for negotiating the status of Kosovo passed without a deal for the province. {11} Medvedev endorsed Putin as PM. ❧ 2 suicide bombs in Algiers killed *c.*60, including *c.*11 UN workers. {12} 3 car bombs in Amara, Iraq, killed *c.*41. ❧ Bush vetoed another SCHIP expansion bill. ❧ 5 central banks, including the Fed, announced plans to inject *c.*$90bn into the global credit system. ❧ RIP @ 76, Ike Turner. {13} Former senator George Mitchell released his inquiry into steroid abuse among MLB players; he alleged 89 had used performance-enhancing substances. {14} The Justice Dept refused to give Congress details on the CIA tapes inquiry. ❧ Hillary Clinton apologized for a staff member's comments on Obama's youthful drug use. ❧ Tropical storm Olga killed 38 in the Caribbean. {15} A UN climate change conference in Bali ended with a 'roadmap' for negotiating a post-Kyoto treaty, after a last-minute U-turn by the US. ❧ Musharraf lifted Pakistan's state of emergency. {16} Turkey bombed Kurdish rebels in N Iraq. ❧ Britain transferred control of Iraq's Basra province to the Iraqi government. ❧ RIP @ 56, singer-songwriter Dan Fogelberg. {17} Russia said

Dmitri Medvedev

Everyone involved in baseball shares responsibility.
— GEORGE MITCHELL

it had delivered nuclear fuel to Iran's Bushehr plant, in defiance of the US; Iran announced plans to build a 2nd plant. ❧ Saudi Arabian King Abdullah pardoned a rape victim whose sentence of 200 lashes had provoked a global outcry. ❧ World leaders pledged $7·4bn in aid to Palestinians. {18} News broke that Jamie Lynn Spears, Britney Spears's sister, was pregnant. ❧ Congress passed the Energy Independence & Security Act, mandating new fuel standards and increased biofuel use [see p.183]. ❧ The FCC passed 2 corporate ownership rules, tightening restrictions on cable ownership but allowing newspaper owners to buy radio and TV stations. {19} Congress passed a bill delaying an expansion of the alternative minimum tax. ❧ The CIA agreed to give documents on the tape destructions to the House Intelligence Cmte. ❧ Congress passed a $555bn spending measure, including $70bn in war funding, without the troop-withdrawal constraints earlier sought by Dems. ❧ The EPA ruled that CA couldn't set its own auto emissions standards. {21} NASA delayed a Mars mission to 2013 after discovering a possible conflict of interest with a project finalist. ❧ A suicide bomber killed *c.*50 in NW Pakistan. ❧ Japan agreed to delay a humpback whale hunt. {22} Declassified documents showed that J. Edgar Hoover planned to imprison 12,000 citizens and suspend habeas corpus during the Korean War. {23} RIP @ 82, jazz pianist Oscar Peterson. {25} A tiger escaped in the SF Zoo, attacking 3 and killing 1. ❧ The Queen made her Christmas

———— IN BRIEF · DECEMBER 2007 – JANUARY 2008 ————

Day broadcast. {26} Landslides in W Indonesia killed *c*.78. ❧ A gas pipeline exploded in Lagos, Nigeria, killing *c*.34. ❧ A Chadian court sentenced 6 French aid workers to 8 years hard labor over kidnapping charges; the group denied wrongdoing. {27} RIP @ 54, Benazir Bhutto, assassinated leaving a rally in Rawalpindi, Pakistan; days of riots followed, killing *c*.60 [see p.57]. {28} Pakistan named an al-Qaeda-linked militant the chief suspect in Bhutto's death. ❧ Nepal's parliament voted to end its monarchy and become a republic. {29} The Patriots beat the Giants 38–35, giving them pro football's first perfect regular season in 35 years. {30} Mwai Kibaki was declared president of Kenya; the opposition disputed the results, and resulting riots killed *c*.500.

Jamie Lynn Spears

JANUARY 2008 · {1} *c*.50 died in a W Kenya church set afire amid post-election violence. ❧ A suicide bomber killed *c*.32 in Baghdad. ❧ A smoking ban took effect in French cafés and restaurants. {2} The Justice Dept announced a formal criminal inquiry into the destruction of the CIA tapes. ❧ Pakistan postponed parliamentary elections in the wake of Bhutto's death. ❧ CA sued the EPA over the right to regulate emission standards. ❧ Oil hit $100 a barrel for the first time [see p.310]. {3} Obama won IA's Dem. caucuses; Mike Huckabee won among Reps. Both wins were seen as major victories and threats to party establishments. Dems Chris Dodd and Joe Biden withdrew from the race after poor showings. ❧ Israelis

My mother always said democracy was the best revenge.
– BILAWAL BHUTTO

killed 9 Palestinians in Gaza after a long-range rocket landed in Ashkelon, Israel. ❧ Musharraf denied involvement in Bhutto's murder. ❧ Britney Spears was hospitalized for evaluation after a reported child custody dispute and police standoff. {4} Hsu was sentenced to 3 years' prison for fraud. {5} Spears was released from the hospital. {6} Mikhail Saakashvili won reelection as President of Georgia; the opposition claimed fraud. ❧ NY Yankees pitcher Roger Clemens appeared on *60 Minutes* to defend himself after being named in the Mitchell Report. {7} The Pentagon said Iranian ships had threatened 3 US Navy ships in the Persian Gulf a day prior; Iran called the encounter 'an ordinary occurrence'. ❧ Hillary Clinton choked up at a campaign event in NH. ❧ The war crimes trial of former Liberian President Charles Taylor resumed at The Hague. ❧ The Golden Globes gala was scrapped in favor of a news conference due to the WGA strike [see p.150]. ❧ A warehouse fire in Incheon, S Korea, killed *c*.40. {8} John McCain won the NH Rep. primary and Clinton the Dem. primary, amid record turnouts; both wins were interpreted as comebacks for troubled campaigns. ❧ The Pentagon released video of the Persian Gulf encounter; Bush called the confrontation 'a provocative act'. ❧ Bush signed a bill preventing the severely mentally ill from buying guns. {9} Iran said the ship footage was fake. {10} Iran released its own footage of the naval incident. ❧ Bush paid his first presidential visit to Israel. ❧ A

---------- IN BRIEF · JANUARY 2008 ----------

suicide bombing in Lahore, Pakistan, killed *c*.25. ❧ Colombian rebels freed 2 hostages held for >5 years, after negotiations engineered by Chávez. ❧ RIP @ 88, Sir Edmund Hillary [see p.57]. ❧ Bill Richardson dropped out of the presidential race. {11} Marion Jones was sentenced to 6 months in prison. {12} Iraq's parliament approved a law allowing some Baathists back into the government. {13} Bush called on Arab states to confront Iran 'before it is too late'. ❧ The Obama and Clinton campaigns sparred over Clinton's remarks on Martin Luther King. ❧ S African police chief Jackie Selebi, head of Interpol, resigned amid a corruption investigation. {14} Militants stormed a luxury hotel in Kabul, Afghanistan, killing *c*.7. ❧ The US said it would send 3,200 Marines to Afghanistan. {15} Romney won MI. ❧ *c*.18 Palestinians and 1 Israeli were killed during an Israeli raid in Gaza. ❧ The FDA ruled meat and milk from cloned cattle, pigs, and goats were safe to eat. ❧ Citigroup, the largest US bank, reported a 4th-quarter loss of $10bn. {17} Gaza rockets hit Sderot, Israel; an Israeli airstrike in Gaza killed *c*.5. ❧ RIP @ 64, Bobby Fischer [see p.57]. {18} Bush unveiled a *c*.$145bn economic stimulus package. ❧ Israel sealed its border with Gaza. {19} Romney won NV among Reps, Clinton among Dems; McCain won SC. {20} The Patriots beat the Chargers for the AFC championship; the Giants beat the Packers for the NFC title [see p.236]. ❧ Gaza officials cut power to the area after running out of fuel. ❧ 2 small planes collided near LA, killing 5. {21}

John McCain

I had such great hope for him.
– MEL GIBSON, on Heath Ledger

Worldwide stock markets plunged dramatically amid fears of a US recession. {22} In a surprise move, the Fed cut its main interest rate by ¾ of a percentage point, the largest rate cut in *c*.2 decades. ❧ Thompson quit the presidential race. ❧ RIP @ 28, actor Heath Ledger [see p.57]. ❧ Padilla was sentenced to 17 years prison. {23} The Congolese government signed a peace deal with rebel groups to end fighting in the country's east. ❧ Gazans flooded into Egypt in search of supplies, after Hamas destroyed part of the Gaza-Egypt border. ❧ A Mosul, Iraq, bombing killed 34. {24} Bush and House leaders agreed on a stimulus plan. ❧ Italian PM Romano Prodi resigned after losing a Senate confidence vote. ❧ French Bank Société Générale said a rogue trader had cost the company $7·2bn. {25} Dem. Dennis Kucinich quit the presidential race. {26} Obama won SC. ❧ Hamas opened new sections of the Gaza-Egypt border. ❧ The US offered to send troops to Pakistan to fight insurgents, but was rebuffed by Musharraf. ❧ A US aid worker was kidnapped in Kandahar, Afghanistan. {27} Died @ 86, former Indonesian dictator Suharto [see p.58]. ❧ 19 died in Kenya amid ongoing post-election violence. ❧ The SAG Awards were held in LA, drawing more attention than usual as the season's major film awards gala. ❧ RIP @ 97, Mormon leader Gordon B. Hinckley. {28} Sen. Edward Kennedy endorsed Barack Obama's presidential bid. ❧ Bush delivered his final State of the Union address [see p.292]. ❧ 5 US soldiers were killed by a roadside bomb

──────── IN BRIEF · JANUARY – FEBRUARY 2008 ────────

in Mosul, Iraq. ❦ Jérôme Kerviel was charged with breach of trust, falsifying documents, and breaching computer security in the Société Générale case. {29} McCain won FL, earning 57 delegates and front-runner status. ❦ The House approved the stimulus package. ❦ Iraqi officials said they'd approved the execution of 'Chemical Ali' for his role in the 1988 Anfal campaign. {30} John Edwards and Rudolph Giuliani quit the presidential race; Giuliani endorsed McCain. ❦ The Fed lowered short-term interest rates half a percentage point.

Jérôme Kerviel

❦ A former Israeli inquiry found 'grave failings' among its leaders in the 2006 war with Lebanon. {31} Obama and Clinton appeared in their first one-on-one debate.

F EBRUARY · {1} 2 suicide bombers, reportedly mentally disabled women, killed *c.*72 at a Baghdad pet market. ❦ Microsoft made a $44·6bn takeover bid for Yahoo. {2} Rebels seized N'djamena, Chad. ❦ Sarkozy married Carla Bruni in Paris. ❦ 5 were killed in a Tinley Park, IL, mall shooting. {3} The Giants beat the Patriots at the Super Bowl, dashing the Patriots' hope of a historic perfect season [see p.236]. ❦ Egypt resealed its border with Gaza. ❦ 2 earthquakes killed *c.*40 in Rwanda and Congo. {4} Bush presented a $3·1tr budget proposal to Congress. ❦ A suicide bombing in Israel, the first in a year, killed 1 in Dimona. {5} 24 states voted in 'Super Tuesday' primaries: neither Dem. candidate took a decisive lead, while Romney was damaged by a

Our economy is undergoing a period of uncertainty. – GEORGE W. BUSH

surprise showing from Mike Huckabee. ❦ National Intelligence Director Mike McConnell said 3 al-Qaeda operatives had been waterboarded in 2002 and 2003; the first details on the use of the interrogation technique. ❦ The death toll in Kenya violence reportedly hit 1,000. ❦ *c.*55 were killed as tornadoes hit 4 S US states. {6} Senate Reps blocked a Dem. plan to expand the stimulus package. ❦ The US military released an al-Qaeda training video showing (apparent) child soldiers. {7} Romney withdrew from the presidential race, citing the need for GOP unity. ❦ The Senate passed the stimulus plan. ❦ Scotland Yard said Bhutto died from head trauma during the attack on her car. ❦ A gunman killed 5 at a Kirkwood, MO, city council meeting. ❦ An explosion at a sugar plant near Savannah, GA, killed 7. {8} A female student shot and killed 2 at Louisiana Technical College, and then committed suicide. {9} Obama won LA, WA, and NE; Huckabee won KS and LA; McCain took the WA caucus. ❦ A suicide bomb killed *c.*25 in NW Pakistan. {10} Obama won ME. ❦ Clinton replaced her campaign manager, Patti Solis Doyle. ❦ East Timor President José Ramos-Horta was shot and critically wounded near Dili. ❦ The 50th Grammys were held [see p.144]. ❦ Yahoo rejected Microsoft's bid. ❦ A car bomb N of Baghdad killed 23. ❦ WGA leaders approved a tentative contract with Hollywood studios [see p.150]. ❦ A fire destroyed the 600-year-old Namdaemun Gate in S Korea. {11} Thieves stole 4 C19th masterpieces worth *c.*$163m

IN BRIEF · FEBRUARY 2008

from a Zurich museum. ❧ The US charged 6 Guantánamo detainees with murder and war crimes related to 9/11. ❧ RIP @ 80, former CA Congressman Tom Lantos. {12} Obama and McCain won MD, DC, and VA. ❧ The Senate approved a Foreign Intelligence Surveillance Act (FISA) overhaul, granting immunity to phone companies involved in the domestic wiretapping program. ❧ Director Steven Spielberg withdrew as artistic adviser to the Beijing Olympics, citing China's stance on Darfur. ❧ Australia's PM apologized for past mistreatment of Aborigines. ❧ WGA members voted to accept a new contract and end their strike [see p.150]. {13} The Senate approved a bill banning CIA waterboarding and other 'enhanced' interrogation techniques. ❧ Hezbollah commander Imad Mugniyah, long sought by the US, was killed by a car bomb in Syria. ❧ Bush signed the stimulus package. ❧ Clemens told a House panel he had never used human growth hormone. {14} Romney endorsed McCain. ❧ The Pentagon said it would try to shoot down a failed US spy satellite carrying toxic fuel. ❧ A gunman killed 5, then himself, at Northern Illinois University. ❧ The FISA overhaul stalled in the House. ❧ The House voted to hold 2 former Bush staffers in contempt for failing to cooperate in the US attorney firing investigation. {16} 8 were killed at a street-racing event in MD after a car was driven into the crowd. {17} Kosovo declared independence from Serbia. ❧ A suicide bomber in S Afghanistan killed c.100. ❧ A CA company recalled 143m pounds of beef

Amy Winehouse

From today onwards, Kosovo is proud, independent and free.
— Kosovo PM HASHIM THACI

after an undercover Humane Society investigation. ❧ Ryan Newman won the 50th Daytona 500 [see p.248]. {18} The US formally recognized Kosovo as a nation, as did 17 EU countries; Russia and China were opposed. ❧ A suicide bomber in S Afghanistan killed 38. ❧ George H.W. Bush endorsed McCain. ❧ 2 of the paintings stolen in Zurich were recovered. {19} Fidel Castro resigned as President of Cuba [see p.68]. ❧ Obama and McCain won WI; McCain won the WA Rep. primary; Obama won HI. ❧ Serbs set fire to UN border checkpoints in N Kosovo to protest against independence. {20} The Teamsters endorsed Obama. ❧ Shuttle *Atlantis* returned to Earth. ❧ The military shot down the failed spy satellite. {21} Serbian protesters attacked the US Embassy in Belgrade. ❧ Clinton and Obama debated in TX; Clinton accused Obama of supporting 'change you can Xerox' [see p.24]. ❧ McCain defended himself after a *New York Times* article discussed close ties to a female lobbyist in 2000. {22} Turkish forces entered N Iraq in raids against Kurdish rebels. ❧ Rep. Rick Renzi [AZ-R] was indicted on corruption charges. {24} Raúl Castro, Fidel's brother, became President of Cuba. ❧ Ralph Nader announced an independent presidential bid. ❧ A suicide bomber killed c.40 Shiite pilgrims S of Baghdad. ❧ The 80th Academy Awards were held in LA [see p.154]. {25} A suicide bomb in Rawalpindi, Pakistani, killed the country's surgeon general. ❧ The Drudge Report published a photo of Obama in the dress of a Somali elder during a 2006 visit to Kenya, stirring controversy. ❦ The Pentagon said 8,000 troops would remain in Iraq at the end of the 'surge'. {26} The New York Philharmonic played a concert in N Korea [see p.146]. ❦ Clinton and Obama met for their final debate. {27} Dodd endorsed Obama. ❦ NYC Mayor Mike Bloomberg said he wouldn't run for President. ❦ Gaza rockets killed 1 in Sderot, Israel; Israeli air strikes killed 8 in Gaza. ❦ FARC rebels released 4 Colombian hostages held for 6 years. ❦ RIP @ 82, William F. Buckley [see p.58]. {28} Kenyan leaders signed a power-sharing deal. ❦ Israeli missiles killed 20 in Gaza. ❦ The FBI said it was investigating whether Clemens lied to Congress. ❦ International press reports revealed Prince Harry had been covertly serving in Afghanistan since December, breaking a news embargo. {29} Prince Harry was withdrawn from Afghanistan. ❦ Authorities said a vial of ricin had been found in a Las Vegas hotel room.

Eliot Spitzer

M ARCH · {1} Turkey withdrew its forces from N Iraq. ❦ A suicide bomber killed 35 at a funeral in NW Pakistan. {2} Medvedev won Russia's presidential elections. ❦ Palestinian leader Abbas suspended contact with Israel after assaults on Gaza killed *c.*100 over several days. ❦ A suicide bomb in NW Pakistan killed *c.*40. {3} Israel withdrew from Gaza. ❦ The UNSC approved a 3rd round of sanctions against Iran. {4} McCain won enough delegates to secure the Rep. nomination; Huckabee conceded.

His conduct on operations in Afghanistan has been exemplary. – GEN. SIR RICHARD DANNATT, on Prince Harry

Clinton took TX, OH, and RI, ending Obama's winning streak; Obama took VT, and maintained his overall delegate lead. ❦ Green Bay Packers' quarterback Brett Favre announced his retirement. {5} Bush endorsed McCain. ❦ Abbas agreed to resume peace talks with Israel. ❦ The House passed a bill requiring equal insurance coverage for mental and physical ailments. {6} A gunman killed 8, and was then killed, at a Jerusalem seminary. ❦ 2 bombs killed *c.*50 in Baghdad. ❦ Thai police arrested a Russian businessman in Bangkok, suspected of being one of the world's leading arms dealers. ❦ The FAA fined Southwest Airlines a record $10·2m for safety violations. {7} An Obama adviser resigned after calling Clinton a 'monster'. {8} Obama won WY. ❦ Bush vetoed a bill preventing the CIA from using 'enhanced' interrogation techniques. {9} Pakistani leaders signed a power-sharing agreement, threatening President Musharraf. {10} NY Governor Eliot Spitzer apologized after allegedly being linked as a client to a prostitute ring [see p.27]. ❦ A suicide bomber killed *c.*8 US soldiers in Baghdad. {11} Obama won MS. ❦ Adm. William J. Fallon resigned as CENTCOM commander. {12} Spitzer resigned, saying he needed to atone for 'private failings'. ❦ Geraldine A. Ferraro, the 1984 VP nominee, resigned from the Clinton campaign after saying Obama had benefited from his position as a black man. {13} The White House unveiled a plan to tighten regulations on mortgage brokers. ❦ Monks led several days of protests in Lhasa,

———— IN BRIEF · MARCH – APRIL 2008 ————

Tibet, against Chinese rule; *c.*80 were killed and hundreds reported arrested. {14} Obama's pastor, Rev. Jeremiah A. Wright, resigned as a campaign adviser after a series of controversial speeches. {15} A crane collapse in NYC killed 7. {16} The Tibetan protests spread through W China; the Dalai Lama called for an inquiry into their suppression and accused China of 'cultural genocide'. ❦ With Fed. Reserve financing, JP Morgan Chase bought Bear Stearns, a victim of the subprime mortgage crisis. {17} A female suicide bomber killed 43 at a shrine in Karbala, Iraq. ❦ China blamed the Dalai Lama for the violence in Tibet. ❦ The FL Dem. Party said there was no chance of redoing its disqualified primary. ❦ David A. Paterson was sworn in as NY Governor; in his first week, he admitted to several extramarital affairs [see p.27]. {18} Obama delivered a groundbreaking and controversial speech on the state of race in America. ❦ The Supreme Court began considering the DC handgun ban case [see p.30]. ❦ The Fed cut interest rates for the 6th time in 6 months. ❦ RIP @ 90, author Arthur C. Clarke [see p.58]. ❦ RIP @ 54, director Anthony Minghella. {19} Bush marked the Iraq war's 5th anniversary with a speech urging against withdrawal; protests took place across US cities. ❦ Bin Laden released an audio message threatening the EU over the republication of the Danish cartoons of Muhammad. {20} Plans to redo MI's disqualified Dem. primary collapsed. ❦ 'March Madness' began [see p.239]. {21} Richardson endorsed Obama. {23} The US death toll for the

The Dalai Lama

He has never been my political adviser – he's been my pastor.
– BARACK OBAMA, on Rev. Wright

Iraq war hit 4,000, according to the AP. {24} Detroit Mayor Kwame M. Kilpatrick was charged with perjury and obstruction of justice for concealing an affair with a staff member; he said he would not resign. ❦ Bush marked the 4,000th US death in Iraq by saying the outcome of the war would 'merit the sacrifice'. ❦ The remains of 2 US contractors kidnapped in 1/07 were found in Iraq. ❦ Yousaf Raza Gilani became PM of Pakistan; he freed dozens of judges detained by Musharraf. ❦ The Olympic torch was lit in Athens, beginning a 21-country relay. {25} A 160-sq-mile chunk of ice collapsed at the edge of the Wilkins ice shelf in Antarctica. ❦ Iraqi security forces began a major operation against Shiite militias in Basra. {28} N Korea test-fired missiles into the Yellow Sea. ❦ The Treasury announced plans to overhaul the US financial system's regulatory agencies. {29} Zimbabwe voted in a general election, seen as a major test for President Mugabe. {30} Shiite cleric Moktada al-Sadr called a truce in Basra, ending fighting that killed *c.*370. ❦ Israel said it would remove 50 roadblocks from the West Bank. ❦ N Korea threatened to reduce S Korea to 'ashes'. {31} The Olympic torch was welcomed in China at a ceremony in Tiananmen Square. ❦ Housing and Urban Development Sec. Alphonso Jackson resigned following allegations of favoritism; he denied any wrongdoing.

APRIL · {1} The Justice Dept declassified a 2003 memo that allowed military interrogators

———— IN BRIEF · APRIL 2008 ————

to use 'enhanced' techniques. {2} Official Zimbabwe election results showed Mugabe's party had lost control of parliament; no presidential election results were released [see p.27]. ❦ Irish PM Bertie Ahern said he would resign. ❦ A UT man was charged in connection with the ricin case. {3} NATO endorsed Bush's plan for a European missile defense system. ❦ The UN war crimes court acquitted Kosovo's former PM of persecuting Serbs in 1998. ❦ Police raided a polygamous sect's ranch in Eldorado, TX, after a teenager reported sexual abuse; 416 children were taken into state custody over several days [see p.28]. {4} Somali pirates attacked a French yacht off the African coast; 30 crew members were held hostage [see p.73]. ❦ The Labor Dept said the US had lost 80,000 jobs in March, the biggest such loss in 5 years. {5} RIP @ 84, Charlton Heston [see p.58]. {6} Hillary Clinton's chief strategist, Mark Penn, resigned amid allegations he sought approval as a lobbyist for a trade pact Clinton opposed. ❦ A suicide attack before a marathon in Sri Lanka killed 14. ❦ The Olympic torch relay was disrupted in London by pro-Tibet demonstrators. {7} Protesters disrupted the Olympic torch relay in Paris; organizers canceled the last leg of the relay. ❦ The coroner's inquest concluded that Princess Diana had been unlawfully killed by reckless driving on the part of her chauffeur and the paparazzi; outlandish allegations of a royal plot to kill Diana were rejected. ❦ Bush asked Congress to pass a controversial trade pact with Colombia. {8} Gen.

Robert Mugabe

David Petraeus told 2 Senate panels that security gains in Iraq were 'fragile and reversible' and that no further troops should be withdrawn after the last of the 'surge' troops left Iraq in July. ❦ The father of Dodi al-Fayed, killed alongside Princess Diana, said he accepted the inquest's verdict and would not continue to press claims the couple had been murdered by a British royal plot. {9} American Airlines grounded >1,000 planes, stranding tens of thousands, after the FAA ordered safety inspections. ❦ The Olympic torch visited SF; protests forced organizers to reroute the relay. {10} Bush endorsed Petraeus's plan to halt troop withdrawals after the summer. ❦ The House blocked action on the trade deal with Colombia. ❦ Chinese officials said they had uncovered a terror plot targeting the Olympics, and arrested 35. {11} France said the yacht held by Somalian pirates had been released and 6 pirates arrested. ❦ Obama was criticized for saying people in small towns were 'bitter' due to economic woes, and clung to 'guns and religion' as a result; he later said his remarks had been misconstrued. ❦ Zimbabwe banned political rallies amid a crisis over the country's unresolved election. {12} Haiti's PM was fired by opposition senators after days of rioting over food prices [see p.16]. ❦ An explosion at a mosque in Shiraz, Iran, killed 12. {13} Iraq fired 1,300 security personnel who had deserted or refused to fight in Basra. {14} Delta and Northwest announced a merger deal that, if approved, would create the world's largest airline. ❦

The champagne bottle's been pushed to the back of the refrigerator.
— GEN. DAVID PETRAEUS, on Iraq

— IN BRIEF · APRIL 2008 —

Berlusconi's coalition won general elections in Italy, making him PM. {15} Pope Benedict XVI arrived on his first official visit to the US [see p.338]. ❧ A plane crash in Goma, DR Congo, killed *c*.40. ❧ A federal jury convicted 'DC Madam' Deborah J. Palfrey of running a prostitution ring for elite Washington clients. {16} The Supreme Court ruled that KY's method of lethal injection was humane and thus constitutional, allowing the resumption of executions across the US [see p.117]. ❧ Bush called for the US to halt the growth of greenhouse gas emissions by 2025. ❧ *c*.20 Palestinians died in clashes with the Israeli military in Gaza. {17} A suicide bombing killed *c*.50 at a funeral in Diyala province, Iraq. ❧ Kenya's opposition leader was sworn in as PM, in part of a power-sharing deal designed to end the country's political crisis. {18} The Pope addressed the UN [see p.338]. ❧ Former president Carter met with the exiled Hamas leader Khaled Meshal in Syria, drawing some criticism. ❧ A TX judge ruled children from the polygamous ranch would stay in state custody until June, and ordered maternity and paternity testing. {19} 3 Gazan suicide bombers attacked an Israeli border crossing, killing themselves and wounding 13. {20} The Pope held mass at Yankee Stadium, and blessed the site of the 9/11 attacks [see p.338]. ❧ Street fighting between Ethiopian troops and Islamist fighters in Mogadishu, Somalia, killed *c*.80. ❧ Israeli forces killed *c*.9 in Gaza. ❧ Carter said Hamas would accept Israel if Palestinians ratified a peace deal. {22}

Pope Benedict XVI

Quite frankly, I'm not sure what we're going to do. — JUDGE BARBARA WALTHER, on the Texas sect children

Clinton won PA. ❧ Hamas proposed a 6-month ceasefire in Gaza. {23} The military said Petraeus would be nominated to lead CENTCOM [see p.264]. ❧ A battle between Tamil rebels and government troops in N Sri Lanka killed *c*.90. ❧ Clinton's campaign said it had raised $10m in the hours after her PA victory. {24} The US accused N Korea of helping Syria build a nuclear reactor bombed by Israel 9/07. ❧ Wesley Snipes was sentenced to 3 years in prison for tax evasion. {25} A Queens judge acquitted 3 detectives charged with killing Sean Bell [see p.302]. ❧ China agreed to meet with Dalai Lama envoys. ❧ Clinton admitted she'd made a 'mistake' saying she'd dodged sniper fire while traveling to Bosnia in 1996. {27} 3 were killed in Kabul during an assassination attempt on Afghan President Hamid Karzai. ❧ Austrian police arrested Josef Fritzl, a 73-year-old they said kept his daughter imprisoned for 24 years while fathering her 7 children. {28} The Supreme Court upheld an IN law requiring voters to show photo ID. ❧ Rev. Wright gave a series of speeches defending his earlier sermons. ❧ 2 trains collided in Zibo, China, killing *c*.70. ❧ 3 tornadoes struck VA, injuring *c*.200. {29} Obama denounced Wright's remarks, calling them divisive and offensive. ❧ RIP @ 102, inventor of LSD Albert Hofmann [see p.58]. ❧ *Grand Theft Auto IV* was released [see p.199]. {30} The Fed cut interests rates for the 7th time in 8 months. ❧ The military said 49 soldiers died in Iraq in April, the highest toll in 7 months.

—————— IN BRIEF · MAY 2008 ——————

MAY · {1} Bush proposed $770m in food aid to address rising food costs in poor countries. ❦ 2 suicide bombs in Diyala province, Iraq, killed *c*.35. ❦ Congress passed a bill banning genetic discrimination by insurers and employers [see p.90]. ❦ 'DC Madam' Deborah J. Palfrey was found hanged. {2} Conservative Boris Johnson was elected Mayor of London, replacing 'Red' Ken Livingstone. ❦ Zimbabwe's Electoral Cmsn officially announced the results of the 4/29 election, saying opposition candidate Morgan Tsvangirai had more votes than Mugabe, but not enough to avoid a runoff [see p.27]. ❦ A plane crash in Sudan killed 21, including the country's defense minister. ❦ *c*.10 tornadoes hit Arkansas, killing 7. {3} Obama won the Guam Dem. caucuses. ❦ Cyclone Nargis hit W Myanmar [see p.26]. ❦ Big Brown won the Kentucky Derby; 2nd-place Eight Belles broke both ankles and was euthanized at the track. {4} Microsoft dropped its bid for Yahoo, after negotiations had failed to agree on a new sale price. ❦ Chinese officials and the Dalai Lama's envoys held talks. {5} Chinese authorities said an outbreak of hand-foot-mouth disease had struck 11,905 and killed 26; a significantly higher toll than previous counts. ❦ Iran called off Iraq security talks with the US until the US ended a crackdown on Shiite militias in Iraq. {6} Clinton won IN; Obama won NC. ❦ The death toll from Cyclone Nargis was estimated at *c*.22,500. ❦ GA carried out the country's first execution since the 2007

Jeremiah Wright

I want to register my deep concern – and immense frustration.
– BAN KI-MOON, on Myanmar

moratorium [see p.117]. {7} Medvedev was sworn in as president of Russia; as expected, he appointed Putin as PM. {8} The Olympic flame was lit on Mt Everest. ❦ Battles erupted in Beirut between Hezbollah supporters and Sunni government loyalists. ❦ Mexico's acting chief of federal police was assassinated, apparently by a drug cartel. ❦ Israel celebrated its 60th anniversary. {9} Myanmar's military seized UN aid shipments and said foreign aid workers were not welcome [see p.26]. ❦ Obama gained 9 superdelegate endorsements, tying with Clinton by some counts. {10} Tornadoes in MO, OK, and GA killed >20. ❦ Hezbollah gunmen began withdrawing from Beirut and Tripoli, Lebanon, after 4 days of gun battles that killed *c*.80. {12} A 7·9 earthquake hit SW China; initial reports were of 10,000 dead [see p.29]. ❦ Myanmar allowed in the first plane with US relief supplies. ❦ Former GA Rep. Bob Barr launched a presidential bid as a libertarian candidate. ❦ RIP @ 82, artist Robert Rauschenberg [see p.58]. {13} The death toll in the Chinese earthquake rose to >13,000. ❦ Clinton won WV. ❦ 7 bombs in Jaipur, India, killed *c*.60. {14} Edwards endorsed Obama. ❦ The House passed a $289bn Farm Bill, despite a Bush veto threat. ❦ The Interior Dept declared the polar bear a threatened species. ❦ Francis Bacon's *Triptych* sold for $86·3m, the most expensive work of contemporary art ever sold at auction; a day earlier, Lucian Freud's *Benefits Supervisor Sleeping* sold for $33·64m, a new record for a living artist. ❦ NY Gov. Paterson ordered state agencies to recognize gay marriages performed elsewhere. {15} The CA Supreme Court overturned a ban on gay marriage. ❦ The House rejected $163bn in funding for wars in Iraq and Afghanistan. ❦ McCain said that he would bring most troops home from Iraq by 2013 if elected. ❦ In a speech before the Israeli Knesset, Bush said negotiating with terrorists was 'the false comfort of appeasement'. {16} The death toll in Myanmar reportedly rose to 78,000. ❦ RIP @ 94, CA winemaker Robert Mondavi. ❦ A pipeline explosion in Ijegun, Nigeria, killed *c*.100. {17} The US commander in Baghdad apologized to Iraqis after a soldier admitted using the Koran for target practice. ❦ Sen. Kennedy was hospitalized after a seizure. {18} China declared 3 days of national mourning for quake victims [see p.29]. {19} WV Sen. Robert Byrd endorsed Obama. ❦ Anti-immigrant riots in S Africa killed 22. {20} Obama won OR, Clinton won KY; Obama claimed the lead in pledged delegates. ❦ Sen. Kennedy was diagnosed with a malignant brain tumor. {21} Bush vetoed the Farm Bill; the House overrode him, despite a procedural snafu. ❦ Bush signed into law the bill banning genetic discrimination [see p.90]. ❦ Rival factions in Lebanon reached a deal ending the country's political stalemate and giving Hezbollah additional powers. {22} The Senate passed a $165bn war-funding bill. ❦ UN Sec. Gen. Ban Ki-moon met with Myanmar's PM. ❦ A TX appeals court ruled that the state had seized children from the polygamist ranch

Ban Ki-moon

illegally. {23} Myanmar officials said foreign aid workers would be allowed into the country. ❦ Clinton apologized after appearing to link Robert Kennedy's 1968 assassination with Obama's presidential run. {24} The Lebanese parliament elected former army commander Michel Suleiman as president. {25} Colombia's defense minister said the leader of the FARC rebels had died. {26} An IAEA report said Iran was continuing to withhold information about its nuclear program. ❦ Canada's foreign minister Maxime Bernier resigned after he admitted leaving government documents at an ex-girlfriend's house. ❦ RIP @ 73, director Sydney Pollack [see p.58]. {27} The Supreme Court ruled that civil rights also protect those who complain about discrimination against others. {28} White House officials expressed dismay over a controversial book by former press secretary Scott McClellan – *What Happened*. ❦ Israel's defense minister called for PM Olmert to resign amid a corruption scandal. {29} The TX Supreme Court upheld the ruling on the polygamous ranch. ❦ Myanmar said a constitutional referendum held immediately after Cyclone Nargis had passed [see p.26]. ❦ The World Bank announced a $1·2bn fund to help poor countries cope with high food costs. {30} Obama resigned from his church. ❦ A crane collapse in NYC killed 2; it was the second such accident in 3 months. {31} The Democratic National Cmte decided to seat delegates from Michigan and Florida at the party convention, but with half a vote each.

This is not the Scott we knew.
– White House spokeswoman
DANA PERINO, on Scott McClellan

——————— IN BRIEF · JUNE 2008 ———————

JUNE · {1} Clinton won PR. ❦ RIP @ 71, fashion designer Yves Saint Laurent [see p.59]. ❦ A fire at LA's Universal Studios damaged sets and classic film prints. {2} A TX judge ordered that children taken from the polygamous ranch be returned to their parents. ❦ RIP @ 79, Bo Diddley [see p.59]. {3} On the last day of the primaries, Obama won MT, while Clinton won SD. After a surge of superdelegate endorsements, Obama claimed victory as the Dem. nominee, becoming the first African American  can to head a major party's

Barack Obama

presidential ticket. {4} Obama named a vice presidential search committee, amid speculation as to whether Hillary Clinton would be offered the job. ❦ Obama fund-raiser Antoin Rezko was convicted of fraud, money laundering, and bribery. ❦ The Detroit Red Wings won the Stanley Cup [see p.240]. {5} Defense Sec. Gates dismissed the 2 top Air Force leaders, after an inquiry found serious and systemic problems in the force. ❦ Zimbabwe ordered all aid groups to cease operations in the country; a group of US and UK diplomats were briefly detained. ❦ Alleged 9/11 mastermind Khalid Sheikh Mohammed and 2 conspirators appeared at a military tribunal at Guantánamo Bay; they said they welcomed execution. {6} Tamil Tiger rebels blew up 2 buses in Sri Lanka, killing 23. ❦ Crude oil saw its largest price jump ever, rising by $11 to $138. ❦ A Fox News anchor referred to a fist bump shared by the Obamas on 6/3 as a 'terrorist fist jab' [see p.15]. {7} Clinton conceded and endorsed Obama, noting her campaign's historic

milestones and urging Democrat unity. ❦ Big Brown lost the Belmont Stakes, dashing Triple Crown hopes [see p.241]. {8} A man drove a truck into a central Tokyo crowd and went on a 'stabbing spree', killing 7. ❦ The FDA warned the public to avoid certain types of tomatoes, linked to a salmonella outbreak. {9} Apple unveiled a 3G iPhone. ❦ Defense Sec. Gates recommended Gen. Norton Schwartz as Air Force chief. ❦ Ken Griffey Jr hit his 600th home run, only the 6th player so to do. {10} A plane exploded on landing at Khartoum airport in Sudan, killing *c.*28. ❦ Tens of thousands in Seoul, S Korea, demonstrated against renewing imports of US beef. ❦ Chinese soldiers drained a Sichuan Province lake formed by the earthquake, after evacuating >250,000 [see p.29]. {11} The head of Obama's VP search team resigned amid concern over his business activities. ❦ 4 died when a tornado struck a scout camp in Iowa. {12} Irish voters rejected the Lisbon Treaty on reforming the EU. ❦ The Supreme Court ruled 5–4 that foreign prisoners held at Guantánamo can challenge their detention in US courts. {13} RIP @ 58, journalist Tim Russert [see p.59]. ❦ R&B star R. Kelly was acquitted on 14 counts of child pornography. {14} Bush said Iran had rejected a new round of incentives to halt uranium enrichment. {15} 83 IA counties were declared disaster areas amid major flooding. ❦ China said 55 had died in flooding after torrential rain. {16} Al Gore endorsed Obama. ❦ Despite a knee injury, Tiger Woods won the US Open, his 14th major championship,

The path will be a little easier next time.
— HILLARY CLINTON

——————— IN BRIEF · JUNE – JULY 2008 ———————

in a sudden-death playoff. {17} A Baghdad car bomb killed *c*.51. ❦ The Boston Celtics won the NBA Finals [see p.238]. {18} Israel and Hamas agreed on a Gaza cease-fire. ❦ Officials said the IA floods had killed *c*.24 and caused $1·5bn in damage. ❦ The CDC said 383 had been sickened by eating salmonella-contaminated tomatoes. ❦ Bush called for the repeal of an offshore oil-drilling ban. {19} Obama became the first presidential candidate to reject public financing for his campaign, reversing an earlier comittment. ❦ House and Senate

Hillary Clinton

leaders agreed on a compromise FISA overhaul. {20} The House passed the FISA overhaul. {21} A ferry capsized in the Philippines after being struck by a typhoon; >150 were killed. {22} Zimbabwean opposition leader Tsvangirai said he would pull out of the run-off election with Mugabe, citing violence against his supporters. {23} The UNSC issued a statement condemning violence in Zimbabwe and saying a 'free and fair' election would be impossible [see p.27]. ❦ The EU approved a new round of sanctions against Iran. ❦ RIP @ 71, comedian George Carlin [see p.176]. {24} An Israeli policeman shot and killed himself during a farewell ceremony for Sarkozy. ❦ Myanmar raised the Nargis death toll to 84,500. {25} The Supreme Court ruled that the death penalty was unconstitutional as a punishment for child rape, and for crimes other than murder or those against the state. ❦ A number of African leaders, including Nelson Mandela, issued statements chastising Mugabe. ❦ The Supreme Court reduced Exxon's

Only God who appointed me will remove me. – ROBERT MUGABE

punitive damages for their 1989 oil spill from an original $5bn to $500m. {26} The Supreme Court overturned a DC handgun ban, ruling that the 2nd Amendment protects an individual's right to own guns for personal use [see p.30]. ❦ The Senate passed a bill funding the wars in Iraq and Afghanistan into 2009. ❦ N Korea delivered an accounting of its nuclear weapons program, as promised in 2007 talks; in return, the US lifted some sanctions and said it would delist the country as a sponsor of terrorism. ❦ A suicide attack near Baghdad killed 23. {27} Amidst reports of violence and intimidation, Zimbabwe held its run-off presidential election; Mugabe 'won' >85% of the votes. ❦ N Korea demolished the cooling tower at its nuclear reactor in Yongbyon. {29} 2 medical helicopters collided in AZ, killing 7. ❦ Obama supporter and retired Army Gen. Wesley Clark caused comment by saying of McCain, 'I don't think getting in a fighter plane and getting shot down is a qualification to become president'. {30} The Pentagon announced war crimes charges against Abd al-Rahim al-Nashiri, alleged mastermind of the 2000 attack on the USS *Cole*. ❦ Obama gave a speech defending his patriotism, amid concern over Clark's comments.

JULY · {1} The AU, meeting in Egypt, called for a unity government in Zimbabwe. ❦ A coal mine collapse in NW China killed 18. {2} The Colombian army freed from FARC rebels 15 hostages, including 3 US contractors and former Colombian

──────────── IN BRIEF · JULY 2008 ────────────

presidential candidate Ingrid Betancourt. ❦ A Palestinian attacked a bus in Jerusalem with a bulldozer, killing 3. ❦ Residents of Big Sur, CA, were ordered to evacuate amid a major wildfire, one of 1,100 burning in the state. {3} Critics accused Obama of flip-flopping after the candidate said he might 'refine' Iraq withdrawal plans after meeting with military commanders. {4} RIP @ 86, Jesse Helms [see p.59]. ❦ Iran responded to an incentives package aimed at ending its nuclear program, saying it was open to dialogue. {5} The CDC said tomatoes may not have been to blame for the salmonella outbreak after all. {6} Bush said he would attend the Olympics opening ceremony. ❦ A suicide bomber killed *c*.15 in Islamabad, Pakistan. ❦ Rafael Nadal beat Roger Federer at Wimbledon, Federer's first such loss in 5 years [see p.245]. ❦ Jesse Jackson was caught on a microphone saying that Obama 'was talking down to black people', adding 'I want to cut his nuts off'. {7} A suicide bombing in Kabul, Afghanistan, killed 41 and wounded *c*.140. {8} The Czech Rep. agreed to host part of the US anti-missile shield, despite Russian opposition. ❦ The G8 endorsed a plan to halve greenhouse-gas emissions by 2050. ❦ Gunmen killed >7 UN peacekeepers in Darfur. {9} Jackson apologized for his 'crude and hurtful remarks', saying he hadn't realized his microphone was live. ❦ Iran said it test-fired 9 missiles, drawing US criticism. ❦ The Senate passed the FISA overhaul. ❦ Gunmen attacked the US consulate in Istanbul, leaving 6 dead. {10} Iran tested a second round of

Ingrid Betancourt

missiles, drawing a warning from SoS Rice. ❦ Rove refused to testify before the House Judiciary Cmte in the US attorney firings investigation, citing executive privilege. ❦ The Senate confirmed Petraeus as head of CENTCOM. ❦ Bush signed the FISA overhaul. {11} CA's IndyMac bank failed and was taken over by the FDIC. ❦ A N Korean soldier shot and killed a S Korean tourist N of the demilitarized zone. {12} A deal to verify N Korea's nuclear disarmament was reached during six-nation talks. ❦ RIP @ 53, former Press Secretary Tony Snow [see p.59]. ❦ Angelina Jolie gave birth to twins [see p.120]. {13} 9 US soldiers were killed in NE Afghanistan. ❦ The Treasury and Fed announced a plan to resuscitate mortgage lenders Fannie Mae and Freddie Mac. {14} Bush lifted an executive ban on offshore drilling; a Congressional ban remained in effect. ❦ The ICC charged Sudanese president Omar Hassan al-Bashir with genocide. {15} Bush authorized the State Dept's No. 3 official to meet with Iran's nuclear negotiator, the countries' highest-level contact since 1979. ❦ Suicide bombers killed >28 in Iraq's Diyala province. ❦ The MA Senate voted to repeal a law that barred the state from marrying gay couples whose union would be invalid elsewhere. {16} Israel exchanged 5 Lebanese militants for the remains of 2 Israeli soldiers. ❦ A train crash in N Egypt killed 40. {17} The FDA said tomatoes were safe to eat, and began focusing on hot peppers as the potential cause of the salmonella outbreak. {18} Bush and al-Maliki agreed to set a 'time horizon' for withdrawing US troops from

I am so very happy.
– RAFAEL NADAL, after Wimbledon

─────── IN BRIEF · JULY – AUGUST 2008 ───────

Iraq. ❧ McCain's top economic adviser resigned, after comments on 7/9 calling Americans 'a nation of whiners'. {19} Obama arrived in Afghanistan on the first stop of a foreign tour; he called for transferring more troops to the country. {21} Iraqi officials said the end of 2010 was an 'appropriate time' for withdrawal; the comment was seen as a victory for Obama, who advocated withdrawal within 16 months of taking office. ❧ Former Bosnian Serb leader and war crimes suspect Radovan Karadžić was arrested near Belgrade; he was disguised and working as an alternative medic. ❧ The FDA confirmed jalapeño peppers as the likely source of the salmonella outbreak, blamed for sickening 1,200 since 4/10. ❧ The war crimes trial of Osama bin Laden's former driver, Salim Hamdan, began; it was the first military commission trial at Guantánamo. ❧ Mugabe and Tsvangirai agreed to hold power-sharing talks in Harare, Zimbabwe. ❧ Portugal shelved its highly controversial inquiry into the disappearance of Madeleine McCann, citing a lack of evidence. ❧ A federal appeals court threw out the FCC's fine against CBS for the 2004 Super Bowl 'wardrobe malfunction'. {22} A TX grand jury indicted Jeffs on charges of abusing children. {23} A housing and mortgage rescue package passed the House; Bush dropped a veto threat. ❧ Hurricane Dolly hit SW TX, causing damage estimated at *c.*$750bn. {24} Obama gave a speech before 200,000 in Berlin, emphasizing a renewed partnership with Europe. {25} McCain met the

Radovan Karadžić

I will step aside properly in an honorable and responsible way.
— Israeli PM EHUD OLMERT

Dalai Lama in CO. ❧ Obama met with Sarkozy in Paris. ❧ CA banned transfats, effective 2010. ❧ Bush expanded sanctions against Zimbabwe. ❧ A plane bound for Australia was forced to land in the Philippines after developing a gaping hole in its fuselage. ❧ RIP @ 47, 'Last Lecture' professor Randy Pausch. {26} The Senate passed the housing rescue package. ❧ *c.*16 bombs exploded in Ahmadabad, India, killed *c.*45. {27} Carlos Sastre won the Tour de France [see p.242]. ❧ 2 bombs killed 16 in Istanbul, Turkey. ❧ A gunman killed 2 at a church in Knoxville, TN. {28} Suicide bombings in Baghdad and a bomb in Kirkuk, Iraq, killed *c.*50. ❧ An internal Justice Dept investigation found political bias in hiring under Gonzales. ❧ The White House said the deficit would hit $482bn by 2009. {29} A 5·4 earthquake struck S CA; there were no reports of major damage. {30} Bush signed the housing rescue package. ❧ Amid a corruption scandal, Israeli PM Olmert said he would resign in the fall. ❧ Bush issued an executive order reorganizing intelligence agency powers. {31} Karadžić was charged with genocide and war crimes at The Hague. ❧ Stevens pleaded not guilty. ❧ Army scientist Bruce Ivins, a suspect in the 2001 anthrax attacks, committed suicide.

AUGUST · {1} Barack Obama proposed an 'emergency economic plan' that included an energy rebate. {2} Iran ignored a deadline to reply to a further incentives deal. {3} *c.*145 were killed during a stampede at a temple in N India. ❧

──────── IN BRIEF · AUGUST 2008 ────────

11 climbers died in an avalanche on K2 in Pakistan. ❦ RIP @ 89, author Alexander Solzhenitsyn [see p.59]. ❦ Moktada al-Sadr's Mahdi army in Iraq said it would disarm and focus instead on social services. {4} Attackers killed 16 police in NW China. {5} The US charged 11 with stealing 40m credit card numbers. ❦ John 'Junior' Gotti was arrested and charged with links to cocaine trafficking and 3 murders; he denied wrongdoing. {6} The FBI released evidence it said proved Ivins was solely responsible for the 2001 anthrax letters. ❦ A Guantánamo military commission convicted Hamdan of providing material support for terrorism. ❦ The Olympic torch arrived in Beijing. ❦ 9 were feared dead after a firefighters' helicopter crashed in N CA. {7} Hamdan was sentenced to 5 months in prison, counting time served. ❦ Army officers staged a coup in Mauritania. ❦ Bush gave a speech in Thailand criticizing China's human rights record; China rebuffed the remarks. ❦ Detroit mayor Kilpatrick was jailed for violating his bail terms. ❦ Georgia attacked the capital of S Ossetia [see p.31]. {8} The opening ceremonies of the Beijing Olympics were held. ❦ John Edwards admitted to an extramarital affair. ❦ Russia sent troops to S Ossetia and launched bombing raids across Georgia. ❦ The EU tightened trade sanctions against Iran. ❦ A bus crash in TX killed 14. {9} Russia and Georgia began fighting in Abkhazia, a breakaway Georgian region to the northwest of the country. ❦ A stabbing attack in Beijing killed the father-in-law of a US Olympic coach.

Vladimir Putin

I started to believe that I was special.
– JOHN EDWARDS, admitting his affair

❦ Michael Phelps won his first Beijing gold medal. ❦ RIP @ 50, comedian Bernie Mac. {10} Georgia called for a cease-fire; Russia bombed Georgia's capital, Tbilisi. ❦ Violence by Muslim separatists in NW China killed 11. ❦ RIP @ 65, singer Isaac Hayes [see p.59]. {11} Russian troops pushed deeper into Georgia, capturing Gori; Bush called Russia's actions 'unacceptable in the 21st century'. ❦ Bush proposed changes to the Endangered Species Act. {12} Russia agreed to a provisional cease-fire in Georgia, though fierce fighting continued; tensions within the international community grew. ❦ Phelps won his 10th and 11th career gold medals, making him the most successful Olympian of all time [see p.230]. {13} Bush sent troops to deliver humanitarian aid to Georgia. ❦ The chairman of the AR Dem. Party was shot and killed in his office. ❦ A roadside bomb killed c.18 in N Lebanon. {14} The US and Poland agreed to the siting of a missile defense system in Poland, angering Russia. {16} Phelps tied with Mark Spitz for the most gold medals in one Olympics, after winning the 100-meter butterfly by ¹/₁₀₀th of a second. ❦ Russia signed a revised cease-fire deal. {17} Russia said it would withdraw troops into S Ossetia and a surrounding 'security zones'. ❦ To world acclaim, Phelps won his 8th Olympic gold medal, breaking Spitz's 1972 record [see p.230].

──────────────

The daily chronicle will continue in the 2010 edition of Schott's Miscellany

——————SOME GREAT LIVES IN BRIEF——————

MARCEL MARCEAU
3·22·1923–9·22·2007 (84)

Undoubtedly the most famous mime artist in the world (few can name another), Marceau enchanted all ages and nationalities with a gift that transcended maturity and language. He will best be remembered for his creation 'Bip' (the shambolic white-faced clown with a flower in his hat) and for a host of routines, including 'Youth, Maturity, Old Age, Death', in which the ages of man are lived in just a few moving minutes.

NORMAN MAILER
1·31·1923–11·10·2007 (84)

One of the giants of US letters, Mailer was celebrated as much for his Pulitzer-winning prose as his pugnacious personality and uncompromising private life (he had 9 children with 6 wives). Yet, like Hemingway, with whom he was often compared, while the legends of his life will live long, works such as *The Naked and the Dead* and *The Executioner's Song* are likely to live longer.

EVEL KNIEVEL
10·17·1938–11·30·2007 (69)

Undoubtedly the most famous daredevil motorcyclist in the world (few can name another), Knievel trod that well-worn path from insurance salesman to stuntman. In a series of ever more extreme stunts, Knievel broke most of the bones in his body, earning him fame, fortune, and female companionship. As he said: 'Bones heal, pain is temporary, chicks dig scars, but glory is forever'.

BENAZIR BHUTTO
6·21·1953–12·27·2007 (54)

The glamorous and populist daughter of a political dynasty, Bhutto became Pakistan's first female leader – and one of the first in the Muslim world. Yet she proved to be a divisive figure, and was dismissed on corruption charges from each of her 2 terms as PM. After a period of exile, she staged a triumphant return to Pakistan in 2007, only to be assassinated shortly thereafter.

EDMUND HILLARY
7·20·1919–1·11·2008 (88)

At 11:30 on 5/29/1953, Hillary became the first man to ascend Mount Everest, the planet's highest point. (Hillary later admitted that Sherpa Tenzing Norgay was 10' behind him.) The news of this Commonwealth triumph (Hillary was born in New Zealand) was broadcast on the morning of Elizabeth II's coronation, as was his famous boast – 'Well … we've knocked the bastard off'.

ROBERT 'BOBBY' FISCHER
3·9·1943–1·17·2008 (64)

The archetypal chess genius – eccentric, mercurial, arrogant, paranoid – Fischer made cold war history when he took the world title from Boris Spassky in 1972. After this, Fischer became ever more idiosyncratic: he forfeited his title, refusing to defend it; rejected his country, claiming persecution; and later praised the 9/11 attacks. Yet he will be remembered as one of the greatest-ever players (and popularizers) of chess.

HEATH LEDGER
4·4·1979–1·22·2008 (28)

Ledger's premature death from an accidental (it is assumed) overdose shocked a legion of fans – many of whom had been captivated by his Oscar-nominated role in *Brokeback Mountain*. His legendary status will be sealed by a bravura performance as the Joker in Christopher Nolan's Batman movie *The Dark Night*, released after Ledger's death to critical acclaim and box-office fortune.

———————— SOME GREAT LIVES IN BRIEF cont. ————————

SUHARTO
6·8·1921–1·27·2008 (86)

From a peasant background, Suharto rose through the ranks of the army, mysteriously surviving a botched coup in 1965 to become Indonesia's president in 1968. For three decades Suharto (like many Indonesians he used one name) ruled his country repressively and corruptly, though he did transform its fortunes before the S Asian economy collapsed in 1997, and with it his regime.

WILLIAM F. BUCKLEY
11·24·1925–2·27·2008 (82)

A writer and editor of erudition and conviction, WFB played a leading role in vivifying US conservatism, not least by founding the *National Review* (1955), presenting *Firing Line* (1966–99), and directing against the left the forceful exuberance of his wit: 'Liberals claim to want to give a hearing to other views, but then are shocked and offended to discover that there are other views'.

ARTHUR C. CLARKE
12·16·1917–3·18·2008 (90)

One of the most popular and influential sci-fi writers of the genre, Clarke entertained a global audience without losing the respect of scientific experts. He will best be remembered for collaborating with Stanley Kubrick on *2001: A Space Odyssey* (1968), though since his DNA was blasted up into space in 2001, clones of Clarke may yet one day return.

CHARLTON HESTON
10·4·1923–4·5·2008 (84)

Heston used his imposing presence and rugged good looks to dominate Hollywood's most monumental roles, including Ben Hur, Michelangelo, and Moses. At 75, he became president of the National Rifle Association – a position he held for >5 years until the symptoms of Alzheimer's took their toll. Famously, at the NRA's 2000 convention, he held a musket aloft and vowed it would only be taken 'From my cold, dead hands'.

ALBERT HOFMANN
1·11·1906–4·29·2008 (102)

Hofmann was a Swiss chemist who in 1938 accidentally discovered lysergic acid diethylamide (LSD). In 1943, he deliberately ingested '0·5cc of ½ promil aqueous solution of diethylamide tartrate', and was so unnerved by its effects that he cycled home as his surroundings 'transformed themselves in more terrifying ways'. The anniversary of this first 'acid trip' is still celebrated by amp heads every April 19, aka 'Bicycle Day'.

ROBERT RAUSCHENBERG
10·22·1925–5·12·2008 (82)

Rauschenberg eschewed high seriousness in favor of a relentless experimentation that helped American art's transition from Abstract Expressionism to Pop Art. After a series of spare, conceptually driven works (most famously *Erased De Kooning* in 1953), he began creating 'combines' using paintings, sculpture, and found materials to infuse everyday objects with meaning, surprise, and beauty.

SYDNEY POLLACK
7·1·1934–5·26·2008 (73)

Pollack may have called directing 'like hitting yourself in the forehead with a hammer', but he still clearly enjoyed it. Notably he directed *They Shoot Horses, Don't They?* (1969), and *Tootsie* (1982), and won two Oscars for *Out of Africa* (1985). Pollack will be remembered for directing and producing liberal-hued mainstream hits, and for an on-screen presence that seldom disappointed.

————— SOME GREAT LIVES IN BRIEF cont. —————

YVES SAINT LAURENT
8·1·1936–6·1·2008 (71)

YSL first made his mark on fashion when, aged just 21, he became chief designer of the House of Dior. From then, though his professional and personal life veered between triumph and despair, he dressed some of the world's most elegant women and changed the way the rest aspired to dress. Fashionista Diana Vreeland called YSL a 'genius', dubbing him 'the Pied Piper of fashion'.

BO DIDDLEY
12·30·1928–6·2·2008 (79)

Inspired by John Lee Hooker, Diddley himself inspired countless musicians with his trademark (and much copied) 'shave and a haircut' rhythm and grinding guitar. 'The Originator' had a series of hits, including *Who Do You Love?*, *Road Runner*, *Mona*, and *Say Man*, but justifiably complained that the flattery of recognition and imitation 'didn't put no figures in my checkbook'.

TIM RUSSERT
5·7·1950–6·13·2008 (58)

Russert was steeped in politics, first as a counselor to Daniel Patrick Moynihan and Mario M. Cuomo and later as a journalist, most famously as moderator of *Meet the Press* for *c*.17 years. Russert combined a plainspoken and homespun manner with detailed research and inquisitorial questioning – a formula that opened up the political process to millions outside the Beltway.

JESSE HELMS
10·18·1921–7·4·2008 (86)

During >50 years as an icon of Southern conservatism and five terms as a North Carolina senator, Helms defined himself by what he was against: communism, abortion, gay rights, welfare, AIDS research, modern art, Fidel Castro, and 'the ultraliberal establishment'. Known for blocking ratification of the Comprehensive Test Ban Treaty and the Kyoto Protocol, among other measures, his refusal to compromise earned him the nickname 'Senator No'.

TONY SNOW
6·1·1955–7·12·2008 (53)

Poacher turned gamekeeper, Snow was a respected political journalist and pundit before becoming George W. Bush's press secretary – a job he called 'the most exciting [and] intellectually aerobic', and one he undertook for 17 months with wit and opinionated vigor. His tenure at the White House was interrupted by a recurrence of the colon cancer that would finally claim his life.

ALEXANDER SOLZHENITSYN
12·11·1918–8·3·2008 (89)

Solzhenitsyn exposed the horror of Stalin's labor camps (in which he spent eight years) in a series of brutally honest books – one of which, *The Gulag Archipelago*, led to his exile from Russia in 1974. His legacy was encapsulated in 1970 by his Nobel Prize citation, which praised 'the ethical force with which he has pursued the indispensable traditions of Russian literature'.

ISAAC HAYES
8·20·1942–8·10·2008 (65)

Hayes's 1969 album *Hot Buttered Soul* and his soundtrack for the 1971 blaxploitation classic *Shaft* secured his reputation, in Aretha Franklin's words, as 'a shining example of soul at its best'. He acquired an unlikely new fan base in his 50s, voicing Chef on the cartoon *South Park* – before he quit the show after it mocked the Church of Scientology, which Hayes had joined in the 1990s.

The World

The world is a severe schoolmaster, for its frowns are less dangerous than its smiles and flatteries, and it is a difficult task to keep in the path of wisdom.
— PHYLLIS WHEATLEY, 1774

———— CLOCK OF THE WORLD · 2008 ————

Every 2 seconds, someone in America requires a blood donation. [American Red Cross] ❦ Every 5 seconds, a child dies from hunger. [UN FAO] ❦ Every 6 seconds, someone dies from tobacco use. [World Health Organization] ❦ Every 6 seconds, an Australian buys an item of clothing on eBay. [*The Age*] ❦ Every 6 seconds, someone is killed or injured on a road somewhere in the world. [Make Roads Safe] ❦ Every 7 seconds, the Irish Samaritans receive a phone call. [*Irish Times*] ❦ Every 25 seconds, someone in the US is burned or scalded in their home. [*Health News Digest*] ❦ Every 26 seconds, a student drops out of an American public high school. [America's Promise Alliance] ❦ Every 30 seconds, someone in the world commits suicide. [World Health Organization] ❦ Every 30 seconds, a child with birth defects is born in China. [*China Daily*] ❦ Every 30 seconds, someone in the world loses a limb as a consequence of diabetes. [*US News & World Report*] ❦ Every 35 seconds, a child in the US is reported neglected or abused. [*KansasCity.com*] ❦ Every 45 seconds, a plane takes off or lands at Heathrow Airport in London. [*The Economist*] ❦ Every minute, 1,000 people around the world sign up for a cell phone. [*TheStar.com*] ❦ Every minute, 253 children are born. [US Census Bureau] ❦ Every 4·8 minutes, violent, profane, or sexual content appears during prime-time 'family hour' television programming. [Parents Television Council] ❦ Every 8 minutes, a woman in a developing country dies of complications from an abortion. [World Health Organization] ❦ Every 15 minutes, someone in Scotland has a heart attack. [British Heart Foundation] ❦ Every 38 minutes, Louisiana loses a football-field-sized portion of its wetlands. [*Science Daily*] ❦ Every hour & 44 minutes, there is a case of 'dowry death' in India. [*The Guardian*] ❦ Every 2 hours, someone in New Zealand fractures a hip. [Osteoporosis New Zealand] ❦ Every 10 hours, a driver with a suspended license crashes in Maine. [*The Morning Sentinel*] ❦ Every day, 1·6m blog posts appear online. [Technorati] ❦ Every day, 6,800 people are infected with HIV. [United Nations] ❦ Every day, *c.*100 veterans are buried in an American veterans cemetery. ❦ Every 2 weeks, a language falls out of use. [*New York Times*; see p.74] ❦ Every month, 300 specialist nurses leave S Africa. [World Health Organization] ❦ Every month, the US government adds *c.*20,000 names to its terrorist watch lists. [ACLU] ❦ Every month, *c.*130m people ride the New York City subway. [Metropolitan Transportation Authority] ❦ Every year, the average American eats nearly 200 pounds of meat, poultry, and fish. [*New York Times*]

─────────────── YEAR IN DISASTERS · 2007 ───────────────

Although somewhat overshadowed by the events of 2008, 399 natural disasters hit worldwide in 2007, killing *c.*16,517 and costing *c.*$62·5bn, according to the UN International Strategy for Disaster Reduction. Below are 2007's worst disasters:

Disaster	*deaths*
Cyclone Sidr (Nov, Bangladesh)	4,234
Flood (July–August, Bangladesh)	1,110
Flood (July–September, India)	1,103
Flood (August, North Korea)	610
Flood (June–July, China)	535
Earthquake (August, Peru)	519

Heat wave (July, Hungary)	500
Cyclone Yemyin (June, Pakistan)	242
Flood and landslides (June, Pakistan)	230
Flood (July, India)	225

8 of the worst disasters were in Asia – a pattern the UN says is consistent with climate change.

Below is a breakdown of 2007 disasters by disaster type, with the number killed:

Disaster type	*no. in 2007*	*deaths*
Flood	206	8,382
Wind storm	103	5,970
Extreme temperature	24	1,011
Earthquake	19	654

Slides	10	264
Wildfires	18	161
Wave/surge (incl. tsunamis)	3	64
Volcano	6	11
Drought	10	N/A

According to Columbia University's Center for Hazard and Risk Research, Taiwan is the country most exposed to natural hazards – 73% of its land area is exposed to some type of potential disaster.

─────────────── AIDS & HIV ───────────────

In 2007, 33·2m people around the world (0·8% of the world's population) were living with HIV, according to the UN. This figure represents a significant drop from the 39·5m estimated in 2006, a difference due almost entirely to improved research methodology that better extrapolates the total number of infections from sample populations. A breakdown of the global HIV population in 2007 is given below:

Region	*No. infected with HIV*	*adult prevalence %*	*AIDS deaths*
Sub-Saharan Africa	22·5m	5·0	1·6m
Middle East & North Africa	380,000	0·3	25,000
South & Southeast Asia	4m	0·3	270,000
East Asia	800,000	0·1	32,000
Oceania	75,000	0·4	1,200
Latin America	1·6m	0·5	58,000
Caribbean	230,000	1·0	11,000
Eastern Europe & Central Asia	1·6m	0·9	55,000
Western and Central Europe	760,000	0·3	12,000
North America	1·3m	0·6	21,000

The UN estimates that new HIV infections peaked in the late 1990s, at >3m new infections per year; *c*2·5m people were infected in 2007. [For HIV rates by country, see the Gazetteer section, pp.84–85.]

—NUCLEAR POWER WORLDWIDE—

439 nuclear reactors were in operation worldwide as of November 2007, down from a record high of 444 in 2002, according a report from European parliamentary group, the Greens. The World Nuclear Industry Status Report 2007 surveyed the state of reactors across the globe and concluded that predictions of a nuclear 'renaissance' (driven by increasing global energy needs and climate change concerns) were greatly exaggerated. According to the report, 338 new reactors would need to be built before 2030 to maintain the same number of plants as those operating in 2007, yet as of November 2007, only 32 reactors were listed as 'under construction' by the International Atomic Energy Agency. Tabulated on the right is the report's snapshot of nuclear power in some countries of note.

† The life span of a reactor is *c*.40 years, though the mean age of the 117 reactors closed thus far is 22 years. ‡ Share of electricity data is 2006.

	number of reactors	average reactor age†	under construction	new reactors planned	% share of electricity‡
Argentina	2	29	1	1	7
Brazil	2	16	0	1	3
Canada	18	23	0	4	1
China	11	7	5	30	2
Czech Rep	6	16	0	0	32
France	59	23	0	1	78
Germany	17	25	0	0	32
India	17	16	6	10	3
Iran	0	0	1	2	0
Japan	55	22	1	12	30
Mexico	2	16	0	0	5
Pakistan	2	22	1	2	3
Russia	31	25	7	8	16
S Africa	2	23	0	1	4
S Korea	20	14	2	6	39
Sweden	10	28	0	0	48
UK	19	26	0	0	18
Ukraine	15	19	2	2	48
USA	104	28	1	7	19
TOTAL	439	23	32	91	16

Although nowadays the 'peace sign' ⊕ is usually considered synonymous with 1960s hippies, the symbol was actually created in 1958 as a logo for British antinuclear groups. According to *Peace: The Biography of a Symbol*, released in 2008 to celebrate the sign's 50th anniversary, the symbol was created by designer Gerald Holtom by combining the semaphore for 'N'(uclear) and 'D'(isarmament) [right] over a circle symbolizing Earth. Since its debut at a 1958 antinuclear march in England, the sign has been used by civil rights, environmental, and countercultural movements, although it has also been dismissed as a 'chicken footprint' and reviled as a Satanic sign.

'D'

'N'

—LANDMINE CASUALTIES—

According to the most recent information from the International Campaign to Ban Landmines, casualties from landmines are declining: 1,367 people were killed and 4,296 injured in 2006, a 16% decrease from 2005. The 2006 casualties by region:

Asia-Pacific.............*casualties* 2,510
Sub-Saharan Africa..............1,205
Americas.........................1,127
Middle East & North Africa 539

Commonwealth of Ind. States†.... 205
Europe.............................165

† Former Soviet states

——— IBRAHIM INDEX OF AFRICAN GOVERNANCE ———

The Ibrahim Index of African Governance was developed as a tool to assess governance in the 48 countries of sub-Saharan Africa. Released by the Mo Ibrahim Foundation, the index is designed to quantify the delivery of 'political goods' through measurable outcomes. For example, a country's safety is judged on the number of battle deaths, the level of violent crime, the number of refugees, and other quantifiable measures. Each country is scored in the following five categories: safety and security; rule of law, transparency, and corruption; participation and human rights; sustainable economic development; and human development. These category scores are then averaged to create an overall score. In 2007, the following countries were judged to have the best and worst all-round governance:

Best governance	*Worst governance*
1 ....Mauritius	48..............................Somalia
2 ....Seychelles	47.........Democratic Rep. of Congo
3 ....Botswana	46.............................. Chad
4 ....Cape Verde	45..............................Sudan
5 ....South Africa	44.......................Guinea-Bissau

In November 2007, former Mozambican president Joaquim Chissano won the inaugural Mo Ibrahim Prize, which was created to encourage African leaders who promote development while improving the lives of their people. After taking office in 1986, as Mozambique was grappling with civil war and national disasters, Chissano brokered peace talks, launched a new constitution, and instituted an economic recovery program. Reportedly the world's richest award, the Mo Ibrahim Prize includes $5m over 10 years, ≤$200,000 for the winner's causes, and $200,000 annually for life thereafter.

——————— CHILD SOLDIERS ———————

According to a 2008 report from the Coalition to Stop the Use of Child Soldiers, 2004–07 saw a decrease in the number of conflicts involving child soldiers following peace agreements in Afghanistan, the Democratic Republic of Congo, Liberia, and elsewhere. Yet *c*.200,000–300,000 children, some as young as 8, are still used as soldiers by government forces or armed rebel groups around the world. According to various human rights groups, child soldiers† are currently used in:

Africa	Burundi, Chad, Côte d'Ivoire, Democratic Republic of Congo, Rwanda, Somalia, Sudan, Uganda
Asia	Myanmar (Burma [see p.75]), Afghanistan, India, Indonesia, Laos, Philippines, Sri Lanka
Middle East	Iran, Iraq, Israel, Palestinian Territories, Yemen
Americas	Colombia
Europe	Chechen Republic of the Russian Federation

† In some reports, 'child' is defined as any person <18; some entries are disputed. ₩ In 2000, the UN adopted an Optional Protocol to the Convention on the Rights of the Child, prohibiting the forced recruitment of those <18, and their use in hostilities. [Sources: Human Rights Watch; CSUCS]

────── ASYLUM LEVELS & TRENDS · 2007 ──────

Asylum applications rose 10% between 2006 and 2007, the first increase recorded by the UN High Commissioner for Refugees (UNHCR) in 5 years. This upsurge was largely due to applications from Iraqis, which nearly doubled in comparison to 2006. Below are the top countries of origin for asylum seekers (defined by the UN as those seeking international protection and formal refugee status) during 2007:

Origin	applications	'06–'07 ±%			
Iraq	45,247	+98	Somalia	11,487	+43
Russian Fed.	18,781	+19	Mexico	9,545	+41
China	17,141	–7	Afghanistan	9,309	+8
Serbia	15,366	–2	Iran	8,627	–19
Pakistan	14,262	+87	Sri Lanka	7,548	+31
			TOTAL	306,857	+10

The US was the top destination for asylum seekers in 2007, with 15% of applications, followed by Sweden (11%), France (9%), and Canada and the UK (both 8%).

────── WORLD'S TEN WORST DICTATORS ──────

The weekly magazine *Parade* annually publishes a list of the world's worst dictators, based on their record of human rights abuse. The 2008 top ten ('07 rank in brackets):

No.	dictator	age	country	years' reign	facial hair?
1 (2)	Kim Jong-il	66	North Korea	14	none
2 (1)	Omar al-Bashir	64	Sudan	19	goatee
3 (6)	Than Shwe	75	Myanmar	16	none
4 (5)	King Abdullah	84	Saudi Arabia	13	cavalier beard
5 (4)	Hu Jintao	65	China	6	none
6 (7)	Robert Mugabe	83	Zimbabwe	28	Hitler-esque
7 (3)	Sayyid Ali Khamenei	68	Iran	19	bushy beard
8 (15)	Pervez Musharraf	64	Pakistan	9	mustache
9 (8)	Islam Karimov	70	Uzbekistan	19	none
10 (13)	Isayas Afewerki	62	Eritrea	17	full mustache

────── EXECUTIONS ──────

1,252 people were executed in 2007, and at least 3,347 were sentenced to death, according to Amnesty International. China executed more people than any other country, although Saudi Arabia had the highest number of executions per capita. The countries in which the most people were executed during 2007 are listed below:

China........470	USA............42	Afghanistan ... 15	[Source: Amnesty
Iran...........317	Iraq.............33	Libya 9	Intl, 2008. Totals are
Saudi Arabia..143	Vietnam.......25	Japan 9	minimums, given
Pakistan 135	Yemen.........15	Syria.............7	frequent state secrecy.]

STABLE & UNSTABLE COUNTRIES

The violent power struggles, crime, and paucity of border controls in the Palestinian Territories make them the most unstable place on the planet, according to an assessment by the intelligence firm Jane's Information Group released in March 2008. Jane's ranking was based on a yearlong investigation into the politics, society, economics, military, and threats facing 235 countries or territories around the world. The top 10 most stable and most unstable countries or territories were:

Most stable		Most unstable	
1 ....Vatican	6 ....San Marino	1 ...Palestin. Ter.	6 ....Haiti
2 ....Sweden	7 ..Liechtenstein	2 ......Somalia	7 .....Zimbabwe
3 ..Luxembourg	8 ....UK	3 ....Sudan	8 ....Chad
4 ....Monaco	9 ...Netherlands	4 ...Afghanistan	9 ....Congo
5 ......Gibraltar	10 ....Ireland	5 ..Côte d'Ivoire	10. Cnt. Af. Rep.

INTERNATIONAL DEVELOPMENT & AID

The Organization for Economic Cooperation & Development (OECD) stated that in 2007 development aid from the Development Assistance Committee (a group of the world's major donors) was $103·7bn: an 8·4% fall from 2006. The US was the largest donor in 2007, and, as before, only 5 of the 22 major donors gave in Overseas Development Aid the UN target of 0·7% of their Gross National Income:

Country	ODA $m	% GNI			
Australia	2,471	0·30	Luxembourg	365	0·90
Canada	3,922	0·28	Netherlands	6,215	0·81
Denmark	2,563	0·81	Norway	3,727	0·95
France	9,940	0·39	Spain	5,744	0·41
Germany	12,267	0·37	Sweden	4,334	0·93
Ireland	1,190	0·54	UK	9,921	0·36
Japan	7,691	0·17	US	21,753	0·16

[Provisional figures, 2007]

The top 10 beneficiaries of US aid, according to latest figures from the OECD:

Iraq	$4,781m	Colombia	$721m
Afghanistan	$1,403m	Pakistan	$490m
DR Congo	$818m	Egypt	$407m
Nigeria	$787m	Zambia	$380m
Sudan	$739m	Ethiopia	$316m

[Source: OECD, 2006. In 2006, the US's total budget for aid to developing countries was $22,005m.]

Between 1990 and 2005, armed conflicts in Africa cost their countries' economies roughly the same amount as they received in development aid, according to a 2007 report by Oxfam, the International Action Network on Small Arms, and Saferworld. The report found that, during this period, the GDPs of African countries that had experienced armed conflict shrunk by 15% when compared with the GDPs of economically similar countries that did not experience conflict. These losses amounted to $284bn, about the same sum of aid given by OECD countries during these 15 years.

—————— NOBEL PEACE PRIZE ——————

The 2007 Nobel Peace Prize was awarded in equal parts to ALBERT GORE (1948–)
and the INTERGOVERNMENTAL PANEL ON CLIMATE CHANGE

*for their efforts to build up and disseminate greater knowledge
about man-made climate change, and to lay the foundations for
the measures that are needed to counteract such change*

Albert (Al) Arnold Gore Jr was born in 1948 in Washington, DC, the son of a prominent Tennessee congressman. After a childhood in Washington and Tennessee, he graduated from Harvard in 1969, after which he served in the army and fought in Vietnam. Gore was elected to the House in 1976, and the Senate in 1984. While in Congress, he cosponsored hearings on toxic waste and the first congressional hearings on global warming. After being elected Vice President in 1992, he led the Clinton administration's environmental efforts, spearheading work on the Kyoto Protocol. Yet it was only after his controversial defeat in the 2000 presidential election that Gore became a full-time 'climate crusader', traveling the world to lecture on the dangers of climate change. In 2006, he released an eco-documentary based on his lectures; *An Inconvenient Truth* became one of the highest-grossing documentaries of all time, earning two Academy Awards in February 2007 and establishing Gore's place at the vanguard of the green movement. For some, Gore's Nobel Prize even raised hopes of another presidential run in 2008. Yet, the 'Goracle' has not been without critics – including those who argue his film is alarmist and exaggerated, those who criticize his personal energy consumption, and those who question whether awarding the prize to a 'celebrity' detracts from the credibility

Al Gore

of the Peace Prize. ❦ The award to the Intergovernmental Panel on Climate Change (IPCC) was less controversial. Founded in 1988 by the UN Environmental Program and the World Meteorological Organization, the IPCC comprises *c*.2,000 scientists who assess the latest climate change data and produce summaries for policy-makers. IPCC reports are generally deemed the most authoritative word on climate change – though they are approved line by line by 113 governments. According to the Nobel committee, 'over the past two decades, the IPCC has created an ever-broader informed consensus about the connection between human activities and global warming'. Indeed, many saw 2007 as a turning point in the global opinion on climate change, thanks to IPCC reports. ❦ Inevitably, some questioned the link between climate change and peace. Yet as the Nobel committee noted, global warming 'may induce large-scale migration and lead to greater competition for the earth's resources', in turn leading to conflict and war. In June 2007, UN Secretary General Ban Ki-moon discussed the connections between drought caused by global warming and the atrocities in Darfur. It seems that climate change may present a uniquely global threat to world peace, one the Nobel committee felt needed to be addressed both by a popular leader and by rigorous science.

HIGHLY VIOLENT CONFLICTS

According to Germany's Heidelberg Institute for International Conflict Research, there were 328 conflicts around the globe in 2007, of which 31 were considered 'highly violent'. Of these, 6 were categorized as wars, and 25 as 'severe crises'. Listed below are these 31 highly violent conflicts:

Conflict issues

Country	parties	resources	secession	national power	ideology	autonomy	regional predominance
WARS							
Pakistan	*Waziristan militants, government*	·	·	·	·	·	×
Sri Lanka	*Tamil Tiger rebels, government*	·	×	·	·	·	·
Somalia	*Islamic Courts Union, transitional gov.*	·	·	×	×	·	·
Sudan	*rebel groups, Sudanese gov. in Darfur*	×	·	·	·	·	×
Afghanistan	*Taliban, government*	·	·	×	×	·	·
Iraq	*insurgents, government*	·	·	×	×	·	·
SEVERE CRISES							
Central African Rep.	*rebels, government*	·	·	×	·	·	·
Chad	*rebel groups*	·	·	×	·	·	·
Chad	*Arab and African ethnic groups*	·	·	·	·	·	×
DR Congo	*rebels, militias, government*	·	·	×	·	·	·
Ethiopia	*separatist rebel group, government*	·	×	·	·	·	·
Kenya	*ethnic groups, government*	×	·	·	·	·	·
Nigeria	*ethnic groups, government*	×	·	·	·	·	×
Colombia	*FARC, ELN revolutionaries*	×	·	·	×	·	×
Colombia	*FARC revolutionaries*	×	·	·	×	·	×
Mexico	*drug cartels*	·	·	·	·	·	×
India	*Kashmiri, Pakistani separatists, govt*	·	×	·	·	·	·
India	*Naxalites, government*	·	·	·	×	·	·
Myanmar	*rebels, military groups, government*	·	×	·	·	·	·
Myanmar	*political opposition, government*	·	·	×	×	·	·
Pakistan	*Islamists, government*	·	·	·	×	·	·
Pakistan	*militant Sunnies, militant Shiites, govt*	·	·	·	×	·	×
Thailand	*Muslim separatists, government*	·	×	·	·	·	·
Algeria	*Islamist groups, government*	·	·	×	×	·	·
Iran	*Kurdish nationalist groups, government*	·	·	·	·	×	·
Iraq	*Moqtada al-Sadr militia, government*	·	·	×	×	·	·
Iraq	*Abu Musab al-Zarqawi militia, government*	·	·	×	×	·	·
Israel	*Fatah, Hamas*	·	·	·	×	·	×
Israel	*Fatah, Hamas, Pal. Auth., Israeli govt*	×	×	·	×	·	·
Lebanon	*Hezbollah, Fatah, government*	·	·	×	×	·	·
Turkey	*Kurdish militants, government*	·	·	·	·	×	·

According to the Institute, a SEVERE CRISIS is a conflict 'in which violent force is used repeatedly in an organized way'. The Institute defines a WAR, in part, as a conflict in which violent force is used 'in an organized and systematic way … [and the] extent of destruction is massive and of long duration'.

LONGEST-REIGNING LEADERS

When Fidel Alejandro Castro Ruz resigned as President of Cuba on Feb 19, 2008, he also stepped down from his post as the world's longest-reigning leader. Below are the longest-serving leaders (aside from kings and queens†) as of Feb 2008:

Leader	country	in power since
Omar Bongo	Gabon	1967
Muammar Gadhafi	Libya	1969
Maumoon Abdul Gayoom	Maldives	1978
Teodoro Obiang Nguema Mbasogo	Equatorial Guinea	1979
Jose Eduardo dos Santos	Angola	1979
Robert Mugabe	Zimbabwe	1980
Hosni Mubarak	Egypt	1981

[Source: Associated Press] † Thai King Bhumibol Adulyadej is the world's longest-reigning living monarch. Crowned in 1946, he is revered in his country as semi-divine. On December 5, 2007, tens of thousands of Thais thronged the streets of Bangkok to celebrate his 80th birthday. Queen Elizabeth II is the world's second-longest-reigning living monarch, having served since 1952. On December 20, 2007, she also became Britain's oldest ever monarch, passing the record set by Queen Victoria.

GLOBAL FREEDOM

The US pressure group Freedom House annually compiles a *Freedom in the World Survey*, classifying countries by the political rights and civil liberties their citizens enjoy. Countries are judged to be: FREE, PARTLY FREE, or NOT FREE. In 2008, 47% of the world countries were deemed FREE; 31% PARTLY FREE; and 22% NOT FREE. The following countries were classified by *freedomhouse.org* as being NOT FREE:

Algeria · Angola · Azerbaijan · Belarus · Bhutan · Brunei · Burma [see p.75]
Cambodia · Cameroon · Chad · China · Congo (Brazzaville) · Congo (Kinshasa)
Côte d'Ivoire · Cuba · Egypt · Equatorial Guinea · Eritrea · Guinea · Iran · Iraq
Kazakhstan · Laos · Libya · Maldives · North Korea · Oman · Pakistan · Qatar
Russia · Rwanda · Saudi Arabia · Somalia · Sudan · Swaziland · Syria · Tajikistan
Tunisia · Turkmenistan · UAE · Uzbekistan · Vietnam · Zimbabwe [see p.27]

SAKHAROV PRIZE

Presented by the European Union since 1988, the Sakharov Prize for Freedom of Thought rewards individuals who challenge oppression and fight for human rights. The prize is named after Soviet physicist Andrei Sakharov (1921–89), who helped develop the hydrogen bomb but later won the Nobel Peace Prize for his work campaigning against nuclear weapons. In 2007, the €50,000 prize was awarded to human rights lawyer and Sudanese parliament member Salih Mahmoud Osman, who for over two decades has worked alongside the Sudan Organization Against Torture to provide free legal representation for victims of human rights abuses.

CONTESTED LAND

During 2008, a number of countries were preparing to submit claims for valuable underwater territory to the UN Commission on the Limits of the Continental Shelf. Under the UN Convention on the Law of the Sea, countries may submit claims for 'extended underwater territory rights' up to 350 miles from their shores within 10 years of ratifying the Convention. As global warming reshapes topography and technology improves access to oil and gas reserves, some of these regions have become even more valuable, and several major countries, including the UK, face a May 2009 deadline to submit their claims. Below are some of the contested areas:

Area	claimed by	significance
ANTARCTICA	*Argentina, UK, Norway,*	iron, copper, gold, & other
	France, Chile, Australia, New Zealand	minerals; hydrocarbons
ARCTIC CIRCLE	*Russia, Canada, US,*	potential *c.*10bn tons oil & gas;
	Denmark, Norway	fishing & shipping routes
ROCKALL BASIN	*Iceland, Ireland, Denmark, UK*	potential oil and natural gas
FALKLAND ISLANDS	*UK, Argentina*	possibly 60bn barrels of oil

Some worry that these claims could add to the world's list of long-simmering land disputes. Below is a sampling of such current conflicts between sovereign nations:

Area	claimed by	significance
ARUNACHAL PRADESH	*China, India*	historical border dispute
ATACAMA CORRIDOR	*Bolivia, Chile*	oil & gas, maritime access
AVES ISLAND	*Venezuela, Colombia*	territorial rights to large
		portion of E Caribbean
CHAGOS ARCHIPELAGO	*Mauritius, Seychelles,*	uncertain status of inhabitants
	British Indian Ocean Territory	evicted for military base
CYPRUS	*Republic of Cyprus, Turkey, Greece*	Greek Cypriot Rep. of Cyprus
		claims island – Turks disagree
EAST CHINA SEA	*China, Japan*	vast reserves of natural gas
ERITREA-ETHIOPIA BORDER	*Eritrea, Ethiopia*	demarcation never resolved
		after Eritrean independence
GIBRALTAR	*Spain, UK*	gateway to Mediterranean
GREATER & LESSER TUNBS;	*Iran, United*	strategic placement
ABU MASA	*Arab Emirates*	in Persian Gulf
GULF OF GUINEA	*9 West African nations*	potentially *c.*24bn barrels oil
KASHMIR	*China, India, Pakistan*	Hindu-Muslim strife &c.
NAGORNO-KARABAKH	*Armenia, Azerbaijan*	ethnic dispute
SPRATLY ISLANDS	*China, Malaysia, Philippines,*	potentially 17·7bn tons oil;
	Taiwan, Vietnam, Brunei	shipping route; fishing rights
TIMOR SEA	*East Timor, Australia*	oil & gas reserves†
WESTERN SAHARA	*Morocco, Algeria*	phosphates, possible oil;
		rebels seek self-determination

† Australia and East Timor have signed a revenue-sharing agreement for Timor Sea oil and gas reserves but have deferred a decision on maritime boundaries. [Sources: *Foreign Policy*; CIA World Factbook]

MOST POLLUTING POWER SECTORS

A November 2007 survey of carbon dioxide (CO_2) emissions produced by the world's power plants concluded that the Australian power sector releases the most CO_2 per capita (11 tons per year), although American power plants weren't far behind (9 tons per year). The survey, released by the Carbon Monitoring for Action project, compiled data on CO_2 emissions from 50,000 power plants and 4,000 power companies to create a global inventory of carbon emissions produced by the power sector. Below are the countries whose power sectors annually produce the most CO_2:

annual power sector CO_2 emissions		
United States	2·79bn *tons*	Japan 400m
China	.2·68bn	Germany 356m
Russia	661m	Australia 226m
India	583m	South Africa 222m
		United Kingdom 212m

EXPERT TIPS TO SAVE THE WORLD

In November 2007, the UK's Environment Agency asked 25 scientists, authors, and environmental experts to each recommend up to 5 ways of saving the planet. Their top 10 tips, ranked by the number of times each was recommended, are below:

1	*use less electricity: make products more efficient, say good-bye to stand-by* [see p.195]
2	*prioritize the environment as an issue for faith groups*
3	*employ solar energy on a much larger scale*
4	*ratify a tough and binding successor to the Kyoto Protocol*
5	*use micro-scale, decentralized methods of energy production*
6	*use 'green taxes' to make eco-goods cheaper and harmful goods more costly*
7	*discourage flying and halt airport expansion*
8	*kick the addiction to fossil fuels*
9	*discourage consumption and encourage responsible trade*
10	*transform transport by encouraging green alternatives*

MORE PLANETS NEEDED

The UN estimates that the world currently produces 29 gigatons of CO_2 per year, twice the target the UN considers a sustainable level of emission (14·5 gigatons). Thus, mankind effectively requires 'another Earth' if CO_2 production is to remain at current levels. If the entire world were to produce emissions at the same rate as the US, 9 Earths would be necessary. Below are the number of Earths that would be needed if the entire world produced CO_2 at the same rate as other OECD countries:

Earths needed	Germany	4	Spain	3
Australia 7	Italy	3	United Kingdom	4
Canada 9	Japan	4	United States	9
France 3	Netherlands	4	(World	2)

——PRIMATES IN PERIL——

29% of all primate species are in danger of becoming extinct, according to a 2007 report released by Conservation International, the Species Survival Commission, and the International Primatological Society. Below are some of the 25 species said to be most at risk:

Peruvian yellow-tailed woolly monkey (Peru) · *Horton Plains slender loris* (Sri Lanka) · *Miss Waldron's red colobus* (Ivory Coast, Ghana) · *Sahamalaza Peninsula sportive lemur* (Madagascar) *Gray-shanked douc* (Vietnam) · *Silky sifaka* (Madagascar) · *Brown-headed spider monkey* (Colombia, Ecuador) *Rondo dwarf galago* (Tanzania) *Kipunji* (Tanzania) · *Western Hoolock gibbon* (Bangladesh, India, Myanmar)

——AMPHIBIANS AT RISK——

London Zoo produced a list of the 100 most biologically valuable amphibians threatened with extinction, for the launch of the Evolutionarily Distinct and Globally Endangered (Edge) project in January 2008. Below are the top 10 amphibians most at risk:

Amphibian	*location*
Chinese giant salamander	China
Sagalla caecilian	Kenya
Purple frog	India
Ghost frog	South Africa
Olm salamander	S Europe
Lungless salamander	Mexico
Malagasy rainbow frog	Madagascar
Darwin's frog	Chile
Betic midwife toad	Spain
Gardiner's frog	Seychelles

——————————THE RED LIST · 2007——————————

The World Conservation Union (IUCN) publishes an annual 'Red List' of species that are under threat – classifying them from those considered to be at a minor risk of extinction ('Least Concern') to those that have already been rendered extinct:

Least Concern (LC) → *Near Threatened (NT)* → *Vulnerable (VU)* → *Endangered (EN)* → *Critically Endangered (CR)* → *Extinct in the Wild (EW)* → *Extinct (EX)*

41,415 species were included on the 2007 Red List, of which 16,306 were considered threatened (a rise from the 16,118 in 2006). The status of 76 species declined, the status of 74 improved, and one species was declared extinct[†]. Below are some of the species whose status declined, and the reasons these species are threatened:

Species	*status change*	*threatened by*
Speke's gazelle	VU→EN	hunting, drought, overgrazing
Yangtze River dolphin	CR→CR (PE)[‡]	pollution, development, fishing practices
Gharial crocodile	EN→CR	loss of habitat, fishing practices
Egyptian vulture	LC→EN	poisoning by veterinary drug Diclofenac
Western gorilla	EN→CR	commercial bushmeat trade, Ebola
Red-breasted goose	VU→EN	causes largely unknown

† The woolly-stalked begonia, a herb known only from C19th collections made in Malaysia, was declared extinct in 2007 after searches of nearby forests failed to find new specimens. ‡ Critically Endangered – Possibly Extinct. An August 2007 sighting was being investigated at the time of writing.

———————————————————SLUM DWELLERS———————————————————

Large-scale evictions and forced displacements caused by development, infrastructure projects, and 'mega' events such as the Olympics have led to an increase in the number of slum dwellers worldwide, according to a 2007 report by the UN Human Settlements Program (UN-HABITAT). Although reliable data are difficult to come by, the UN estimates that *c.*31% of the world's urban population lives in slums – defined as areas in which tenants lack reliable, durable housing, clean water, and other basic necessities. Tabulated below are the slum populations around the world:

Total slum population (m)	1990	2001	2005 (est.)	2010 (est.)	2020 (est.)
World	715	913	998	1,246	1,392
Developed regions	42	45	47	48	52
Transitional countries	19	19	19	19	18
Developing regions	654	849	933	1,051	1,331

———————————————THE WORLD'S CHEAPEST CAR———————————————

In January 2008, the Indian firm Tata Motors launched what it claimed would be the world's cheapest car. The Nano will cost just 100,000 rupees ($2,500; £1,277) – about half the annual pay of the average Indian accountant. The Nano will have 4 doors, 5 seats, and a top speed of 65mph, though no air-con or central locking (except in the 'deluxe' version). Tata hopes to sell 1m Nanos in a region where car sales are predicted to more than quadruple by 2016. Inevitably, environmentalists have expressed concern at the ecological impact of cheap cars, though others have questioned why the developing world should not enjoy the fruits of prosperity.

———————————————MOST POLLUTED PLACES———————————————

Six of the ten most polluted places on Earth are located in the developing economies of China, India, and Russia, according to a list released in September 2007 by the Blacksmith Institute, a US-based environmental watchdog, and Green Cross Switzerland. The ten most polluted sites in the world were assessed on the scale of their toxicity and the estimated number of people placed at risk – they are:

Location	pollutants & causes	est. number of people affected
Sumgayit, Azerbaijan	*petrochemical & industrial waste*	275,000
Linfen, China	*smog from industry & traffic*	3,000,000
Tianying, China	*heavy metals in air & soil from industry*	140,000
Sukinda, India	*waste from chromite mines*	2,600,000
Vapi, India	*chemical waste & other industrial effluents*	71,000
La Oroya, Peru	*lead contamination from mining*	35,000
Dzerzhinsk, Russia	*by-products from Cold War chemical weapons*	300,000
Norilsk, Russia	*smog and heavy metals from mining*	134,000
Chernobyl, Ukraine	*radioactive remains from 1986 explosion*	5,500,000
Kabwe, Zambia	*lead from mining and smelting*	255,000

WORLD PIRACY

Reports of pirate attacks rose by 20% during the first 3 months of 2008, following a rise of 10% for the whole of 2007, according to the International Maritime Bureau's Piracy Reporting Center. Much of this rise was attributed to an increase in incidents reported in waters off Somalia and Nigeria. Somalia is one of the world's most unstable states, and pirates along its coastline are launching increasingly frequent and violent attacks on merchant vessels traveling between the Red Sea, the Mediterranean, and the Indian Ocean. In Nigeria, piracy has been encouraged by the political instability of the oil-rich Niger Delta region. ❦ Far from the buckle-swashing ruffians of *Pirates of the Caribbean* or *Treasure Island*, modern pirates tend to be poor dockworkers or fishermen who enlist in criminal syndicates equipped with global positioning systems and modern weaponry such as rocket-propelled grenades. Some have even broadcast distress signals to lure ships to their aid, before raiding them. ❦ As of March 31, 2008, 49 actual and attempted pirate attacks had been reported, compared with 263 such attacks in all of 2007. However, it seems that many shipping companies decline to report piracy to prevent their insurance premiums from escalating, or to avoid ships being impounded for investigations. Below are the attacks in the worst-hit areas in 2008 (as of 3/31/08) and 2007:

Country/region	1/'08–3/'08	2007
Indonesia	4	43
Nigeria	10	42
Somalia	1	31
Bangladesh	2	15
Gulf of Aden/Red Sea	5	13
India	5	11
Tanzania	4	11
Malaysia	1	9
Malacca Straits†	0	7
Philippines	2	6
Peru	2	6

† Between Malaysia & Indonesia, and used by 1/3 of the world's shipping fleets. Piracy has declined after efforts by regional governments.

One of the more dramatic piracy attacks of 2008 began on April 4, when Somali pirates attacked the French luxury yacht *Le Ponant* in the Gulf of Aden, and held the yacht's 30-strong crew captive for a week. Elite French commandos negotiated for the crew's release on April 12, then chased the pirates through the Somali desert, capturing 6 and recovering part of the reported $2m ransom. In response to the attack, and others off Somalia's coast, the UN Security Council adopted in June 2008 a 6-month resolution allowing ships to use 'all means necessary' to repress attacks in Somalia's waters.

WORLD HUMAN RIGHTS

The 2008 Amnesty International *State of the World's Human Rights* report surveyed human rights issues in 150 countries around the world. Released to coincide with the 60th anniversary of the UN Universal Declaration of Human Rights, the report found persistent discrimination and repression across the globe in 2007, including:

Countries where ...	
People are tortured or ill-treated	81
People are denied free speech	77
Unfair trials are held	54
Prisoners of conscience are held	45
Laws discriminate against *women*	23
– against *migrants*	15
– against *minorities*	14

——— GLOBAL ENVIRONMENTAL CITIZEN AWARD ———

Kofi Annan and Alice Waters shared the 2007 Global Environmental Citizen Award, presented since 2001 by Harvard Medical School's Center for Health and the Global Environment. Former UN Secretary General Annan was praised for his commitment to the environment during his term, and for his environmental advocacy since leaving the post in 2006. Restaurateur Alice Waters was honored for her work founding the restaurant Chez Panisse in Berkeley, California, where she has been a vocal and passionate advocate for locally sourced and sustainable foods.

——————— ENDANGERED LANGUAGES ———————

Hundreds of languages across the globe are close to extinction, according to a September 2007 report in the *New York Times*, which estimated that a language dies each fortnight. Some languages vanish instantly when a sole surviving speaker dies, while others are replaced gradually by more dominant tongues like English, Spanish, or Portuguese. The *Enduring Voices* project, backed by the US National Geographic Society, has identified 5 'hotspots' where languages are vanishing most rapidly[†]:

Northern & Central Australia
nearly all 153 Aboriginal tongues in this area are endangered; in the rest of Australia most are extinct

Central South America
high language diversity, little documentation of those languages

US/Canadian Pacific Northwest
dominance of English is causing many to abandon the 54 native languages of the region

Eastern & Central Siberia
government policies are forcing speakers of minority languages to speak regional/national ones

Southwestern US
only 40 Native American languages still spoken in Oklahoma, Texas, and New Mexico

† Hotspots were identified by the diversity of languages spoken, the level of endangerment, and the scientific documentation available.

In January 2008, the BBC reported that three speakers of the Kusunda language of Nepal, previously thought extinct, had been found in two separate locations. The three were brought together, enabling one of them to converse in the language for the first time since she was 10 years old – in 1940.

——————————— MISS WORLD ———————————

Three years after China lifted a ban on beauty pageants, the country hosted Miss World and celebrated its first ever victory. Zhang Zilin, a 23-year-old secretary from Shijiazhaung in the northern Hebei province, beat 106 contestants to be crowned Miss World 2007. The ceremony was held at the Beauty Crown Theatre in the resort of Sanya, Hainan province. Zilin's hobbies include travel, reading, swimming, classical and folk dancing, and her favorite foods are fruit, chocolate, and ice cream. Zilin's inspiring personal motto is: 'Where there's a will, there's a way'.

————————BURMA vs MYANMAR————————

The monk-led protests in September 2007 and devastating Cyclone Nargis in April 2008 [see p.26] led to some confusion over the (politically) correct name of the country known as Burma and Myanmar. Below is a short attempt at clarification:

Historically, 'Burma' was used during informal conversation by Burmese people as a colloquial name for their country. The name 'Myanmar' was the high, formal, and literary title used during official ceremonies and matters of state. While both titles were and are still used inside the country, in English the country was called 'Burma' until 1989, when the ruling military junta changed the country's official title to Myanmar. According to the ruling junta, 'Mynamar' is more inclusive of the region's ethnic minorities, and its

use was an attempt to break with the country's colonial past. However, because the decision was made unilaterally, and by a regime widely considered oppressive, many countries have chosen to continue using the name Burma. Both the US and UK governments call the country by that name, although the UN has chosen to recognize the name Myanmar.

According to linguists, though 'Burma' and 'Myanmar' sound quite distinct in English, in Burmese the two terms sound similar.

Thailand was called Siam until 1939, and again between 1945–49. Côte d'Ivoire is often called the Ivory Coast, but the country's government prefers the French. On the subject of cunning linguistics, in 2008, 3 natives of the island of Lesbos submitted a legal challenge to a Greek homosexual group prohibiting the use of the word 'lesbian' to mean those who share Sappho's sexual preference.

————————SPAIN'S SHORT-LIVED ANTHEM————————

Spain's Euro 2008 triumph [see p.247] was the country's first major soccer title since 1964. One theory blamed this long dry spell on the Spanish national anthem, which has no lyrics. While players from other nations can rely on an adrenaline-pumping sing-along, the Spanish are forced to stand in a somber silence that can do little to energize them. For perhaps this reason (or possibly because merely humming along to an anthem became tiresome), in 2007 the Spanish Olympic Committee was inspired to invite members of the public to submit lyrics for the existing tune. In January 2008, the committee announced that the contest had been won by 52-year-old Paulino Cubero, who bested 7,000 budding lyricists with a hymn to Spain's 'green valleys' and 'vast sea'. However, some Spaniards were offended by the anthem's opening line – *Viva España!* – the rallying cry of Franco. After five days the lyrics were withdrawn, and Spain rejoined the ranks of countries with wordless anthems, including Bosnia and Herzegovina and the minuscule San Marino.

In January 2008, the Iraqi parliament voted to change the country's flag, removing the 3 stars that represented the Baath Party in power under Saddam Hussein. The flag has been changed before: in 2004, a line of script allegedly in Hussein's handwriting was changed to Kufic script, an ancient calligraphy used to transcribe the Koran. Apropos of nothing, the flag of Mozambique currently sports an AK-47 machine gun, despite a 2005 attempt by some opposition members to have it removed.

──────── THE MAFIA'S TEN COMMANDMENTS ────────

In November 2007, Sicilian police announced that a Mafia 'code of behavior' had been discovered in a raid at the home of a top Mafia boss. According to investigators, the document was unearthed among a cache of coded notes on mob administration. The following commandments were listed, under the title 'Rights and Duty':

[1] No one can present himself directly to another of our friends. There must be a third person to do it. [2] Never look at the wives of friends. [3] Never be seen with cops. [4] Don't go to pubs and clubs. [5] Always being available for Cosa Nostra is a duty – even if your wife's about to give birth. [6] Appointments must absolutely be respected. [7] Wives must be treated with respect.

[8] When asked for any information, the answer must be the truth. [9] Money cannot be appropriated if it belongs to others or to other families. [10] People who can't be part of Cosa Nostra – anyone who has a close relative in the police, anyone with a two-timing relative in the family, anyone who behaves badly and doesn't hold to moral values.   [Source: BBC]

──────────── THE FBI'S MOST WANTED ────────────

Fugitive [as at 8/26/2008]	allegation	reward
Osama bin Laden	terrorism	$25,000,000
James J. Bulger	murder; racketeering	$1,000,000
Victor Manuel Gerena	armed robbery	$1,000,000
Emigdio Preciado Jr	attempted murder; assault	$150,000
Jorge Alberto Lopez-Orozco	murder	$100,000
Jason Derek Brown	murder; robbery	$100,000
Robert William Fisher	murder	$100,000
Alexis Flores	kidnapping; murder	$100,000
Glen Stewart Godwin	murder; prison escape	$100,000
Michael Jason Registe	murder	$100,000

─────────── BRIBERY ───────────

A 2007 survey released by Transparency International found that bribery was most rampant in poor countries. The following nations reported the highest percent of respondents who said they'd paid a bribe in the past 12 months:

Cameroon . 79%		Pakistan	44
Cambodia	72	Nigeria	40
Albania	71	Senegal	38
Kosovo	67	Romania	33
Macedonia	44	Philippines	32

─────────── ARMS SALES ───────────

The US sells significantly more arms than any other country, according to a 2007 report from the Congressional Research Service. The top arms sellers in 2006, the latest year of data available:

US	$16·9bn†	Sweden	1·1bn
Russia	8·7bn	Italy	900m
UK	3·1bn	China	800m
Germany	1·9bn		
Israel	1·7bn	† Value of arms	
Austria	1·5bn	transfer agreements	

THE PLANETS

Symbol	Name	Diameter	No. of moons	Surface gravity	Rings?	Distance from Sun	Mean temp	Day length
		km		m/s²		×10⁶ km	°C	hours
☿	Mercury	4,879	0	3·7	N	57·9	167	4,222·6
♀	Venus	12,104	0	8·9	N	108·2	457	2,802·0
⊕	Earth	12,756	1	9·8	N	149·6	15	24·0
♂	Mars	6,794	2	3·7	N	227·9	−63	24·6
♃	Jupiter	142,984	63	23·1	Y	778·4	−110	9·9
♄	Saturn	120,536	60	9·0	Y	1,426·7	−140	10·7
♅	Uranus	51,118	27	8·7	Y	2,871·0	−195	17·2
♆	Neptune	49,532	13	11·0	Y	4,498·3	−200	16·1

In June 2008, the International Astronomical Union announced a new class of heavenly bodies, Plutoids, for all near-spherical dwarf planets orbiting past Neptune. So far, only Pluto and Eris qualify.

PLANETARY MNEMONIC

Many **V**ery **E**ducated **M**en **J**ustify **S**tealing **U**nique **N**inth
ercury *enus* *arth* *ars* *upiter* *aturn* *ranus* *eptune*

THE CONTINENTS

Continent	area km²	est. population	population density
Asia	44,579,000	3,959m	88·8
Africa	30,065,000	910m	30·3
North America	24,256,000	331m	13·6
South America	17,819,000	561m	31·5
Antarctica	13,209,000	(a scientist or two)	—
Europe	9,938,000	729m	73·4
Australia	7,687,000	33m	4·3

THE OCEANS

Oceans make up *c.*70% of the globe's surface. The five oceans are detailed below:

Ocean	area km²	greatest known depth at	depth
Pacific	155,557,000	Mariana Trench	11,033m
Atlantic	76,762,000	Puerto Rico Trench	8,605m
Indian	68,556,000	Java Trench	7,258m
Southern	20,327,000	South Sandwich Trench	7,235m
Arctic	14,056,000	Fram Basin	4,665m

———————— A WORLD OF SUPERLATIVES ————————

Highest city .... La Paz, Bolivia 11,926ft
Highest mountain .... Everest, Nepal/Tibet 29,028ft
Highest volcano .... Ojos del Salado, Chile 22,595ft
Highest dam .... Rogun, Tajikistan 1,099ft
Highest waterfall .... Angel Falls, Venezuela 3,212ft
Biggest waterfall (volume) ..... Inga, Dem. Rep. of Congo .... 1,500,000ft^3/s
Lowest point .... Dead Sea, Israel/Jordan .... −1,300ft
Deepest point .... Challenger Deep, Mariana Trench .... −36,220ft
Deepest ocean .... Pacific .... average depth −14,040ft
Deepest freshwater lake .... Baikal, Russia 5,371ft
Largest lake .... Caspian Sea .... 143,200mi^2
Largest desert .... Sahara .... 3,500,000mi^2
Largest island .... Greenland .... 836,109mi^2
Largest country .... Russia .... 6,592,800mi^2
Largest population .... China .... 1·3bn
Largest monolith .... Uluru, Australia .... 1,114ft high; 5·8mi base
Largest landmass .... Eurasia .... 21,137,357mi^2
Largest river (volume) .... Amazon .... 28bn gal/min
Largest peninsula .... Arabian .... 900,000mi^2
Largest rain forest .... Amazon, South America .... 1·2bn acres
Largest forest .... Northern Russia .... 2·7bn acres
Largest atoll .... Kwajalein, Marshall Islands .... 6·5mi^2
Largest glacier .... Vatnajökull, Iceland .... 3,127mi^2
Largest concrete artichoke ..... Castroville, USA .... 20ft×12ft
Largest archipelago .... Indonesia .... 17,508 islands
Largest lake in a lake .... Manitou, on an island in Lake Huron .... 60mi^2
Largest city by area .... Mount Isa, Australia .... 15,821mi^2
Smallest country .... Vatican City .... 0·17mi^2
Smallest population .... Vatican City .... 821 people
Smallest republic .... Republic of Nauru .... 8mi^2
Longest coastline .... Canada 125,567mi
Longest mountain range .... Andes 5,500mi
Longest suspension bridge ...... Akashi-Kaikyo, Japan 6,529ft
Longest rail tunnel .... Seikan, Japan 33mi
Longest road tunnel .... Lærdal, Norway .... 15·2mi
Longest river .... Nile 4,185mi
Tallest inhabited building ...... Dubai Tower, UAE [but see p.178] 1,680ft
Tallest structure .... KVLY-TV Mast, USA 2,063ft
Most land borders .... China & Russia .... 14 countries
Most populated urban area .... Tokyo, Japan .... 35·2m
Most remote settlement .... Tristan da Cunha .... 1,450mi from neighbors
Least populous capital city ..... San Marino, San Marino .... pop. 4,482
Warmest sea .... Red Sea .... Average temp. *c.*77°F
Longest bay .... Bay of Bengal 1,150mi
Largest banknote .... Brobdingnagian bills, Philippines .... 14"×8½"

Unsurprisingly, a degree of uncertainty and debate surrounds some of these entries and their specifications.

POPULATION BY CONTINENT

Year	World	Africa	N America	S America	Asia	Europe	Oceania
Millions							
1980	4,447	472	371	242	2,645	694	23
1990	5,274	626	424	296	3,181	721	27
2000	6,073	801	486	348	3,678	730	31
2010	6,838	998	540	393	4,148	726	35
2020	7,608	1,220	594	431	4,610	715	38
2030	8,296	1,461	645	461	4,991	696	41
2040	8,897	1,719	692	481	5,291	671	43
2050	9,404	1,990	734	490	5,505	640	45
Percentage distribution							
1980	100%	10·6	8·4	5·4	59·5	15·6	0·5
2000	100%	13·2	8·0	5·7	60·6	12·0	0·5
2050	100%	21·2	7·8	5·2	58·5	6·8	0·5

WORLD BIRTH & DEATH RATES

Births	time unit	deaths	change
133,353,798	*per* YEAR	55,532,963	+77,820,835
11,112,817	*per* MONTH	4,627,747	+6,475,931
364,355	*per* DAY	151,729	+212,625
15,181	*per* HOUR	6,322	+ 8,859
253	*per* MINUTE	105	+148
4·2	*per* SECOND	1·8	+2·5

[Source: US Census Bureau, 2008 · Figures may not add up to totals because of rounding]

URBAN POPULATION

Tabulated below are the percentages of the urban population in various regions:

Region % of population in urban areas ·	1975	2005	2030 (est.)
Africa	25·3	38·3	50·7
Asia	24·0	39·8	54·1
Europe	66·0	72·2	78·3
Latin America & Caribbean	61·2	77·4	84·3
North America	73·8	80·7	86·7
Oceania	71·7	70·8	73·8
World	37·3	48·7	59·9

[Source: United Nations Department of Economic and Social Affairs, 2005]

—————————————— CHILD MORTALITY ——————————————

9·7m children <5 years old died around the world in 2006, the first time the global child death toll fell below 10m per year, according to UNICEF data. Officials attribute this fall to campaigns against measles and mumps, as well as economic improvements and efforts to encourage breast-feeding. Below are the 2006 rates of child mortality around the world, as well as the primary causes of child death:

Children <5 deaths per 1,000 live births		*Cause*	*% of global <5 deaths*
W and Central Africa	186	Pneumonia	29
Sub-Saharan Africa	160	Neonatal causes†	27
E and S Africa	131	Diarrhea	17
S Asia	83	Malaria	8
Middle East and N Africa	46	Measles	4
E Asia and Pacific	29	AIDS	3
Latin America & Carib.	27	Other	13
Central & E Europe & CIS	27	† Including infections, premature birth,
Industrialized countries	6	asphyxia, and tetanus [Source: UNICEF]

—————————————— GLOBAL GENDER GAP ——————————————

The 2007 Gender Gap Index, produced by the World Economic Forum, assessed 128 countries in 4 categories: economic participation and opportunity; educational attainment; political empowerment; and health and survival. Each country was given a score between 0 (inequality) and 1 (equality). Below are the top-ranked nations:

Rank	*country*	*overall score*			
1	Sweden	0·8146	6	Philippines	0·7629
2	Norway	0·8059	7	Germany	0·7618
3	Finland	0·8044	8	Denmark	0·7519
4	Iceland	0·7836	9	Ireland	0·7457
5	New Zealand	0·7649	10	Spain	0·7444
			(31	US	0·7002)

The United States dropped from 23rd place in 2006 to 31st in 2007, a decline attributed to a decrease in the number of female legislators, officials, and managers, as well as lower levels of pay equality.

————————— WAIST MEASUREMENTS WORLDWIDE —————————

Results from the International Day for the Evaluation of Abdominal Obesity (IDEA):

Mean waist circumference (cm)	♂	♀						
NW Europe	97·8	88·3	S Africa	93·6	89·8	Latin Am.	96·4	89·7
S Europe	99·4	91·3	Mideast	98·2	93·4	OVERALL	95·8	88·7
E Europe	96·9	89·7	E Asia	86·4	80·2			
N Africa	93·6	93·1	S Asia	89·3	84·1	[Based on measurements		
			Australia	99·1	89·0	of 168,000 people in 63		
			Canada	101·4	92·2	countries in May 2005]		

— DEVELOPMENT INDEX —

The UN Human Development Index annually ranks 177 countries by health, life expectancy, income, education, and environment. The 2007 ranking was:

Most developed	*Least developed*
1 .... Iceland	177 .... Sierra Leone
2 ....Norway	176 ... Burkina Faso
3 .... Australia	175 .. Guinea-Bissau
4 .... Canada	174 .... Niger
5 ....Ireland	173 ....Mali
6 .... Sweden	172 ... Mozambique
7 ......Switzerland	171 .. C African Rep
8 ....Japan	170 .... Chad
9 ..... Netherlands	169 ...... Ethiopia
10 .... France	168 ....Congo

— PEACE INDEX —

The Global Peace Index, produced by the Economist Intelligence Unit, ranks 140 countries on 24 qualitative and quantitative indicators, including military spending, homicide rates, jail populations, and international relations. According to the Index, the most and least peaceful countries in 2008 were:

Most peaceful	*Least peaceful*
1 .... Iceland	140 .... Iraq
2 .... Denmark	139 ....Somalia
3 ....Norway	138 .... Sudan
4 .....New Zealand	137 .... Afghanistan
5 ....Japan	136 .... Israel
6 ....Ireland	135 .... Chad

— NOTES TO THE GAZETTEER —

Traveling is almost like talking with men of other centuries. — RENÉ DESCARTES

The gazetteer on the following pages is designed to allow comparisons to be made between countries around the world. As might be expected, some of the data are tentative and open to debate. A range of sources has been consulted, including the CIA's *World Factbook*, Amnesty International, HM Revenue and Customs, &c.

Size km²	*sum of all land and water areas delimited by international boundaries and coastlines*
Population	*July 2008 estimate*
GMT	*based on capital city; varies across some countries; varies with daylight saving*
Life expectancy at birth	*in years; 2008 estimate*
Infant mortality	*deaths of infants <1, per 1,000 live births, per year; 2008 estimate*
Median age	*in years; 2008 estimate*
Birth & death rates	*average per 1,000 persons in the population at midyear; 2008 estimate*
Fertility rate	*average theoretical number of children per woman; 2008 estimate*
HIV rate	*percentage of adults (15–49) living with HIV/AIDS; mainly 2003 estimate*
Literacy rate	*%; definition (especially of target age) varies; mainly 2003 estimate*
Exchange rate	*spot rate at 6·30·08 (fms.treas.gov)*
GDP per capita	*($) GDP on purchasing power parity basis/population; from 2007*
Inflation	*annual % change in consumer prices; years vary, generally from 2007*
Unemployment	*% of labor force without jobs; years vary, generally from 2007*
Voting age	*voting age; (U)niversal; (C)ompulsory for at least one election; *=entitlement varies*
Military service	*age, length of service, sex and/or religion required to serve vary*
Death penalty	*(N) no death penalty; (N*) death penalty not used in practice;*
	(Y) death penalty for common crimes; (Y) death penalty for exceptional crimes only*
National Day	*some countries have more than one; not all are universally recognized*

Country	Size (km²)	Population (m)	Capital city	± GMT	Inhabitants
UNITED STATES	9,826,630	303·8	Washington, DC	−5	Americans
Algeria	2,381,740	33·8	Algiers	+1	Algerians
Argentina	2,766,890	40·7	Buenos Aires	−3	Argentines
Australia	7,686,850	20·6	Canberra	+10	Australians
Austria	83,870	8·2	Vienna	+1	Austrians
Belarus	207,600	9·7	Minsk	+2	Belarusians
Belgium	30,528	10·4	Brussels	+1	Belgians
Bolivia	1,098,580	9·2	La Paz	−4	Bolivians
Brazil	8,511,965	191·9	Brasilia	−3	Brazilians
Bulgaria	110,910	7·3	Sofia	+2	Bulgarians
Burma/Myanmar	678,500	47·8	Yangon/Rangoon	+6½	Burmese
Cambodia	181,040	14·2	Phnom Penh	+7	Cambodians
Canada	9,984,670	33·2	Ottawa	−5	Canadians
Chile	756,950	16·5	Santiago	−4	Chileans
China	9,596,960	1·3bn	Beijing	+8	Chinese
Colombia	1,138,910	45·0	Bogotá	−5	Colombians
Cuba	110,860	11·4	Havana	−5	Cubans
Czech Republic	78,866	10·2	Prague	+1	Czechs
Denmark	43,094	5·5	Copenhagen	+1	Danes
Egypt	1,001,450	81·7	Cairo	+2	Egyptians
Estonia	45,226	1·3	Tallinn	+2	Estonians
Finland	338,145	5·2	Helsinki	+2	Finns
France	547,030	60·9	Paris	+1	French
Germany	357,021	82·4	Berlin	+1	Germans
Greece	131,940	10·7	Athens	+2	Greeks
Haiti	27,750	8·9	Port–au–Prince	−5	Haitians
Hong Kong	1,092	7·0	—	+8	Hong Kongers
Hungary	93,030	9·9	Budapest	+1	Hungarians
India	3,287,590	1·1bn	New Delhi	+5½	Indians
Indonesia	1,919,440	237·5	Jakarta	+7	Indonesians
Iran	1,648,000	65·9	Tehran	+3½	Iranians
Iraq	437,072	28·2	Baghdad	+3	Iraqis
Ireland	70,280	4·2	Dublin	0	Irish
Israel	20,770	7·1	Jerusalem/Tel Aviv	+2	Israelis
Italy	301,230	58·1	Rome	+1	Italians
Japan	377,835	127·3	Tokyo	+9	Japanese
Jordan	92,300	6·2	Amman	+2	Jordanians
Kazakhstan	2,717,300	15·3	Astana	+6	Kazakhstanis
Kenya	582,650	37·9	Nairobi	+3	Kenyans
Korea, North	120,540	23·5	Pyongyang	+9	Koreans
Korea, South	98,480	49·2	Seoul	+9	Koreans

———— GAZETTEER · KUWAIT – ZIMBABWE · [1/4] ————

Country	Size (km²)	Population (m)	Capital city	± GMT	Inhabitants
UNITED STATES	9,826,630	303·8	Washington, DC	−5	Americans
Kuwait	17,820	2·6	Kuwait City	+3	Kuwaitis
Latvia	64,589	2·2	Riga	+2	Latvians
Lebanon	10,400	4·0	Beirut	+2	Lebanese
Liberia	111,370	3·3	Monrovia	0	Liberians
Lithuania	65,300	3·6	Vilnius	+2	Lithuanians
Malaysia	329,750	25·3	Kuala Lumpur	+8	Malaysians
Mexico	1,972,550	110·0	Mexico City	−6	Mexicans
Monaco	1·95	32·8k	Monaco	+1	Monegasques
Morocco	446,550	34·3	Rabat	0	Moroccans
Netherlands	41,526	16·6	Amsterdam	+1	Dutch
New Zealand	268,680	4·2	Wellington	+12	New Zealanders
Nigeria	923,768	138·3	Abuja	+1	Nigerians
Norway	323,802	4·6	Oslo	+1	Norwegians
Pakistan	803,940	167·8	Islamabad	+5	Pakistanis
Peru	1,285,220	29·2	Lima	−5	Peruvians
Philippines	300,000	92·7	Manila	+8	Filipinos
Poland	312,679	38·5	Warsaw	+1	Poles
Portugal	92,391	10·7	Lisbon	0	Portuguese
Romania	237,500	22·2	Bucharest	+2	Romanians
Russia	17,075,200	140·7	Moscow	+3	Russians
Rwanda	26,338	10·2	Kigali	+2	Rwandans
Saudi Arabia	2,149,690	28·2	Riyadh	+3	Saudis
Singapore	692·7	4·6	Singapore	+8	Singaporeans
Slovakia	48,845	5·5	Bratislava	+1	Slovaks
Slovenia	20,273	2·0	Ljubljana	+1	Slovenes
Somalia	637,657	9·6	Mogadishu	+3	Somalis
South Africa	1,219,912	43·8	Pretoria/Tshwane	+2	South Africans
Spain	504,782	40·5	Madrid	+1	Spaniards
Sudan	2,505,810	40·2	Khartoum	+3	Sudanese
Sweden	449,964	9·0	Stockholm	+1	Swedes
Switzerland	41,290	7·6	Bern	+1	Swiss
Syria	185,180	19·7	Damascus	+2	Syrians
Taiwan	35,980	22·9	Taipei	+8	Taiwanese
Thailand	514,000	65·5	Bangkok	+7	Thai
Turkey	780,580	71·9	Ankara	+2	Turks
Ukraine	603,700	46·0	Kiev/Kyiv	+2	Ukrainians
United Kingdom	244,820	60·9	London	n/a	British
Venezuela	912,050	26·4	Caracas	−4½	Venezuelans
Vietnam	329,560	86·1	Hanoi	+7	Vietnamese
Zimbabwe	390,580	12·4	Harare	+2	Zimbabweans

—— GAZETTEER · ALGERIA – SOUTH KOREA · [2/4] ——

Country	Male life expectancy	Female life expectancy	difference	Infant mortality	Median age	Birth rate	Death rate	Fertility rate	Adult HIV rate	Literacy
UNITED STATES	75·3	81·1	−5·8	6·3	36·7	14·2	8·3	2·1	0·6	99
Algeria	72·1	75·5	−3·4	28·8	26·0	17·0	4·6	1·8	0·1	70
Argentina	72·8	80·4	−7·6	13·9	30·3	16·3	7·5	2·1	0·7	97
Australia	77·9	83·8	−5·9	4·5	37·4	11·9	7·6	1·8	0·1	99
Austria	76·5	82·4	−5·9	4·5	41·7	8·7	9·9	1·4	0·3	98
Belarus	64·6	76·4	−11·8	6·5	38·4	9·6	13·9	1·2	0·3	100
Belgium	75·9	82·4	−6·5	4·5	41·4	10·2	10·4	1·7	0·2	99
Bolivia	63·9	69·3	−5·4	49·1	22·6	22·3	7·4	2·7	0·1	87
Brazil	68·6	76·6	−8·0	26·7	29·0	16·0	6·2	1·9	0·7	89
Bulgaria	69·2	76·7	−7·5	18·5	41·4	9·6	14·3	1·4	0·1	98
Burma/Myanmar	60·7	65·3	−4·6	49·1	27·8	17·2	9·2	1·9	1·2	90
Cambodia	59·7	63·8	−4·1	56·6	21·7	25·7	8·2	3·1	2·6	74
Canada	78·7	83·8	−5·1	5·1	40·1	10·3	7·6	1·6	0·3	99
Chile	73·9	80·6	−6·7	7·9	31·1	14·8	5·8	2·0	0·3	96
China	71·4	75·2	−3·8	21·2	33·6	13·7	7·0	1·8	0·1	91
Colombia	68·7	76·5	−7·8	19·5	26·8	19·9	5·5	2·5	0·7	93
Cuba	75·0	79·6	−4·6	5·9	36·8	11·3	7·2	1·6	0·1	100
Czech Republic	73·3	80·1	−6·8	3·8	39·8	8·9	10·7	1·2	0·1	99
Denmark	75·8	80·6	−4·8	4·4	40·3	10·7	10·3	1·7	0·2	99
Egypt	69·3	74·5	−5·2	28·4	24·5	22·1	5·1	2·7	0·1	71
Estonia	67·2	78·3	−11·1	7·5	39·6	10·3	13·4	1·4	1·1	100
Finland	75·3	82·5	−7·2	3·5	41·8	10·4	10·0	1·7	0·1	100
France	77·7	84·2	−6·5	3·4	39·2	12·7	8·5	2·0	0·4	99
Germany	76·1	82·3	−6·2	4·0	43·4	8·2	10·8	1·4	0·1	99
Greece	77·0	82·2	−5·2	5·3	41·5	9·5	10·4	1·4	0·2	96
Haiti	55·8	59·4	−3·6	62·3	18·5	35·7	10·2	4·8	5·6	53
Hong Kong	79·1	84·7	−5·6	2·9	41·7	7·4	6·6	1·0	0·1	94
Hungary	69·0	77·6	−8·6	8·0	39·1	9·6	13·0	1·3	0·1	99
India	66·9	71·9	−5·0	32·3	25·1	22·2	6·4	2·8	0·9	61
Indonesia	68·0	73·1	−5·1	31·0	27·2	19·2	6·2	2·3	0·1	90
Iran	69·4	72·4	−3·0	36·9	26·4	16·9	5·7	1·7	0·2	77
Iraq	68·3	71·0	−2·7	45·4	20·2	30·8	5·1	4·0	0·1	74
Ireland	75·4	80·9	−5·5	5·1	34·6	14·3	7·8	1·9	0·1	99
Israel	78·5	82·8	−4·3	4·3	28·9	20·0	5·4	2·8	0·1	97
Italy	77·1	83·2	−6·1	5·6	42·9	8·4	10·6	1·3	0·5	98
Japan	78·7	85·6	−6·9	2·8	43·8	7·9	9·3	1·2	0·1	99
Jordan	76·2	81·4	−5·2	15·6	23·9	20·1	2·7	2·5	0·1	90
Kazakhstan	62·2	73·2	−11·0	26·6	29·3	16·4	9·4	1·9	0·2	100
Kenya	56·4	56·9	−0·5	56·0	18·6	37·9	10·3	4·7	6·7	85
Korea, North	69·5	75·1	−5·6	21·9	32·7	14·6	7·3	2·0	—	99
Korea, South	74·0	81·1	−7·1	5·9	36·4	9·8	6·1	1·3	0·1	98

GAZETTEER · KUWAIT – ZIMBABWE · [2/4]

Country	Male life expectancy	Female life expectancy	difference	Infant mortality	Median age	Birth rate	Death rate	Fertility rate	Adult HIV rate	Literacy
UNITED STATES	75·3	81·1	−5·8	6·3	36·7	14·2	8·3	2·1	0·6	99
Kuwait	76·4	78·7	−2·3	9·2	26·1	21·9	2·4	2·8	0·1	93
Latvia	66·7	77·4	−10·7	9·0	39·9	9·6	13·6	1·3	0·6	100
Lebanon	70·9	76·0	−5·1	22·6	28·8	17·6	6·1	1·9	0·1	87
Liberia	39·9	42·5	−2·6	143·9	18·0	42·9	21·5	5·9	5·9	58
Lithuania	69·7	79·9	−10·2	6·6	39·0	9·0	11·1	1·2	0·1	100
Malaysia	70·3	75·9	−5·6	16·4	24·6	22·4	5·0	3·0	0·4	89
Mexico	73·1	78·8	−5·7	19·0	26·0	20·0	4·8	2·4	0·3	91
Monaco	76·1	84·0	−7·9	5·2	45·5	9·1	13·0	1·8	—	99
Morocco	69·2	74·0	−4·8	38·2	24·7	21·3	5·5	2·6	0·1	52
Netherlands	76·7	82·0	−5·3	4·8	40·0	10·5	8·7	1·7	0·2	99
New Zealand	78·3	82·3	−4·0	5·0	36·3	14·1	7·0	2·1	0·1	99
Nigeria	47·2	48·5	−1·3	93·9	18·7	40·0	16·4	5·4	5·4	68
Norway	77·2	82·6	−5·4	3·6	39·0	11·1	9·3	1·8	0·1	100
Pakistan	63·1	65·2	−2·1	67·0	21·2	26·9	7·8	3·6	0·1	50
Peru	68·6	72·4	−3·8	29·5	25·8	19·8	6·2	2·4	0·5	88
Philippines	67·9	73·9	−6·0	21·5	23·0	24·1	5·3	3·0	0·1	93
Poland	71·4	79·7	−8·3	6·9	37·6	10·0	10·0	1·3	0·1	100
Portugal	74·8	81·5	−6·7	4·9	39·1	10·5	10·6	1·5	0·4	93
Romania	68·7	75·9	−7·2	23·7	37·3	10·6	11·8	1·4	0·1	97
Russia	59·2	73·1	−13·9	10·8	38·3	11·0	16·1	1·4	1·1	99
Rwanda	48·6	51·0	−2·4	83·4	18·7	40·0	14·5	5·3	5·1	70
Saudi Arabia	74·0	78·3	−4·3	12·0	21·5	28·8	2·5	3·9	0·01	79
Singapore	79·3	84·7	−5·4	2·3	38·4	9·0	4·5	1·1	0·2	93
Slovakia	71·2	79·3	−8·1	7·0	36·5	10·6	9·5	1·3	0·1	100
Slovenia	73·0	80·7	−7·7	4·3	41·4	9·0	10·5	1·3	0·1	100
Somalia	47·4	51·1	−3·7	111·0	17·5	44·1	15·9	6·6	1·0	38
South Africa	43·3	41·4	1·9	58·3	24·5	17·7	22·7	2·1	21·5	86
Spain	76·6	83·5	−6·9	4·3	40·7	9·9	9·9	1·3	0·7	98
Sudan	49·4	51·2	−1·8	87·0	18·9	34·3	13·6	4·6	2·3	61
Sweden	78·5	83·1	−4·6	2·8	41·3	10·2	10·2	1·7	0·1	99
Switzerland	77·9	83·7	−5·8	4·2	40·7	9·6	8·5	1·4	0·4	99
Syria	69·5	72·4	−2·9	26·8	21·4	26·6	4·7	3·2	0·1	80
Taiwan	74·9	80·9	−6·0	5·5	36·0	9·0	6·7	1·1	—	96
Thailand	70·5	75·3	−4·8	18·2	32·8	13·6	7·2	1·6	1·5	93
Turkey	70·7	75·7	−5·0	37·0	29·0	16·2	6·0	1·9	0·1	87
Ukraine	62·2	74·2	−12·0	9·2	39·4	9·6	15·9	1·3	1·4	99
United Kingdom	76·4	81·5	−5·1	4·9	39·9	10·7	10·1	1·7	0·2	99
Venezuela	70·4	76·7	−6·3	22·0	25·2	20·9	5·1	2·5	0·7	93
Vietnam	68·5	74·3	−5·8	23·6	26·9	16·5	6·2	1·9	0·4	90
Zimbabwe	40·9	38·6	2·3	50·6	20·3	27·4	21·7	3·0	24·6	91

—— GAZETTEER · ALGERIA – SOUTH KOREA · [3/4] ——

Country	Currency	Currency code	$1 =	GDP per capita $	Inflation %	Unemployment %	Fiscal year end
UNITED STATES	Dollar=100 Cents	USD	—	45,800	2·9	4·6	Sep 30
Algeria	Dinar=100 Centimes	DZD	65·9	6,500	3·7	13·0	Dec 31
Argentina	Peso=100 Centavos	ARS	3·1	13,300	8·8	14·1	Dec 31
Australia	Dollar=100 Cents	AUD	1·0	36,300	2·3	4·4	Jun 30
Austria	euro=100 cent	EUR	0·6	38,400	2·2	4·4	Dec 31
Belarus	Ruble=100 Kopecks	BYR	2,135·0	10,900	8·4	1·6	Dec 31
Belgium	euro=100 cent	EUR	0·6	35,300	1·8	7·5	Dec 31
Bolivia	Boliviano=100 Centavos	BOB	7·2	4,000	8·7	7·5	Dec 31
Brazil	Real=100 Centavos	BRL	1·6	9,700	3·6	9·3	Dec 31
Bulgaria	Lev=100 Stotinki	BGN	1·3	11,300	7·6	7·7	Dec 31
Burma/Myanmar	Kyat=100 Pyas	MMK	450·0	1,900	34·4	10·2	Mar 31
Cambodia	Riel=100 Sen	KHR	4,000·0	1,800	5·9	2·5	Dec 31
Canada	Dollar=100 Cents	CAD	1·0	38,400	2·1	6·0	Mar 31
Chile	Peso=100 Centavos	CLP	480·0	13,900	4·4	7·0	Dec 31
China	Renminbi Yuan=100 Fen	CNY	6·9	5,300	4·8	4·0	Dec 31
Colombia	Peso=100 Centavos	COP	1,741·0	6,700	5·5	11·2	Dec 31
Cuba	Peso=100 Centavos	CUP/C	0·9	4,500	3·1	1·8	Dec 31
Czech Republic	Koruna=100 Haléru	CZK	15·8	24,200	2·8	6·6	Dec 31
Denmark	Krone=100 Øre	DKK	4·8	37,400	1·7	2·8	Dec 31
Egypt	Pound=100 Piastres	EGP	5·3	5,500	11·0	9·1	Jun 30
Estonia	Kroon=100 Sents	EEK	10·1	21,100	6·6	4·7	Dec 31
Finland	euro=100 cent	EUR	0·6	35,300	1·6	6·8	Dec 31
France	euro=100 cent	EUR	0·6	33,200	1·6	8·3	Dec 31
Germany	euro=100 cent	EUR	0·6	34,200	2·3	8·4	Dec 31
Greece	euro=100 cent	EUR	0·6	29,200	3·0	8·3	Dec 31
Haiti	Gourde=100 Centimes	HTG	38·3	1,300	9·0	c.65	Sep 30
Hong Kong	HK Dollar=100 Cents	HKD	7·8	42,000	2·0	4·1	Mar 31
Hungary	Forint=100 Fillér	HUF	155·2	19,000	7·9	7·3	Dec 31
India	Rupee=100 Paise	INR	42·4	2,700	6·4	7·2	Mar 31
Indonesia	Rupiah=100 Sen	IDR	9,280·0	3,700	6·4	9·6	Dec 31
Iran	Rial	IRR	8,229·0	10,600	17·5	12·0	Mar 20
Iraq	New Iraqi Dinar	NID	1,272·0	3,600	4·7	—	Dec 31
Ireland	euro=100 cent	EUR	0·6	43,100	3·0	4·6	Dec 31
Israel	Shekel=100 Agora	ILS	3·2	25,800	0·5	7·3	Dec 31
Italy	euro=100 cent	EUR	0·6	30,400	2·0	6·0	Dec 31
Japan	Yen=100 Sen	JPY	105·5	33,600	0·0	3·9	Mar 31
Jordan	Dinar=1,000 Fils	JOD	0·7	4,900	5·4	13·5	Dec 31
Kazakhstan	Tenge=100 Tiyn	KZT	120·5	11,100	10·8	7·3	Dec 31
Kenya	Shilling=100 Cents	KES	62·0	1,700	9·8	40·0	Jun 30
Korea, North	NK Won=100 Chon	KPW	—	1,900	—	—	Dec 31
Korea, South	SK Won=100 Chon	KRW	1,028·5	24,800	2·5	3·3	Dec 31

Country	Currency	Currency code	$1 =	GDP per capita $	Inflation %	Unemployment %	Fiscal year end
UNITED STATES	Dollar=100 Cents	USD	—	45,800	2·9	4·6	Sep 30
Kuwait	Dinar=1,000 Fils	KWD	0·3	39,300	5·0	2·2	Mar 31
Latvia	Lats=100 Santims	LVL	0·5	17,400	10·1	5·7	Dec 31
Lebanon	Pound=100 Piastres	LBP	1,501·0	11,300	4·1	20·0	Dec 31
Liberia	Dollar=100 Cents	LRD	49·0	400	11·2	85·0	Dec 31
Lithuania	Litas=100 Centas	LTL	2·2	17,700	5·8	3·5	Dec 31
Malaysia	Ringgit=100 Sen	MYR	3·2	13,300	2·1	3·2	Dec 31
Mexico	Peso=100 Centavos	MXN	10·3	12,800	4·0	3·7	Dec 31
Monaco	euro=100 cent	EUR	0·6	30,000	1·9	0·0	Dec 31
Morocco	Dirham=100 centimes	MAD	7·4	4,100	2·0	10·2	Dec 31
Netherlands	euro=100 cent	EUR	0·6	38,500	1·6	3·2	Dec 31
New Zealand	Dollar=100 Cents	NZD	1·3	26,400	2·4	3·6	Mar 31
Nigeria	Naira=100 Kobo	NGN	117·8	2,000	5·5	4·9	Dec 31
Norway	Krone=100 Øre	NOK	5·1	53,000	0·8	2·5	Dec 31
Pakistan	Rupee=100 Paisa	PKR	66·5	2,600	7·8	7·5	Jun 30
Peru	New Sol=100 Centimos	PEN	2·8	7,800	1·8	6·9	Dec 31
Philippines	Peso=100 Centavos	PHP	43·7	3,400	2·8	7·3	Dec 31
Poland	Zloty=100 Groszy	PLN	2·2	16,300	2·5	12·8	Dec 31
Portugal	euro=100 cent	EUR	0·6	21,700	2·4	7·7	Dec 31
Romania	New Leu=100 New Bani	RON	2·3	11,400	4·8	4·1	Dec 31
Russia	Ruble=100 Kopecks	RUB	23·7	14,700	11·9	6·2	Dec 31
Rwanda	Franc=100 Centimes	RWF	543·9	900	9·4	—	Dec 31
Saudi Arabia	Riyal=100 Halala	SAR	3·8	23,200	4·1	c.25	Dec 31
Singapore	Dollar=100 Cents	SGD	1·4	49,700	2·1	2·1	Mar 31
Slovakia	Koruna=100 Halierov	SKK	19·5	20,300	2·8	8·4	Dec 31
Slovenia	euro=100 cent	EUR	0·6	27,200	3·6	4·8	Dec 31
Somalia	Shilling=100 Cents	SOS	—	600	—	—	—
South Africa	Rand=100 Cents	ZAR	7·6	9,800	7·1	24·3	Mar 31
Spain	euro=100 cent	EUR	0·6	30,100	2·8	8·3	Dec 31
Sudan	Pound=100 Piastres	SDG	2·0	2,200	8·0	18·7	Dec 31
Sweden	Krona=100 Øre	SEK	6·0	36,500	1·7	6·1	Dec 31
Switzerland	Franc=100 Centimes	CHF	1·0	41,100	0·9	2·5	Dec 31
Syria	Pound=100 Piastres	SYP	45·7	4,500	7·0	9·0	Dec 31
Taiwan	Dollar=100 Cents	TWD	30·4	30,100	1·8	3·9	Dec 31
Thailand	Baht=100 Satang	THB	32·5	7,900	2·2	1·4	Sep 30
Turkey	New Lira=100 New Kurus	TRY	1·2	12,900	8·8	9·9	Dec 31
Ukraine	Hryvena=100 Kopiykas	UAH	4·8	6,900	12·8	c.7·0	Dec 31
United Kingdom	Pound=100 Pence	GBP	0·5	35,100	2·3	5·4	Apr 5
Venezuela	Bolivar=100 Centimos	VEB	2·2	12,200	18·7	8·5	Dec 31
Vietnam	Dong=100 Xu	VND	16,245·0	2,600	8·3	5·3	Dec 31
Zimbabwe	Dollar=100 Cents	ZWD	—	200	p.27	80·0	Dec 31

—— GAZETTEER · ALGERIA – SOUTH KOREA · [4/4] ——

Country	Voting age	Driving side	UN vehicle code	Internet country code	Military service	Death penalty	National Day
UNITED STATES	18 U	R	USA	.us	N	Y	Jul 4
Algeria	18 U	R	DZ	.dz	Y	N*	Nov 1
Argentina	18 UC	R	RA	.ar	N	Y*	May 25
Australia	18 UC	L	AUS	.au	N	N	Jan 26
Austria	16 U	R	A	.at	Y	N	Oct 26
Belarus	18 U	R	BY	.by	Y	Y	Jul 3
Belgium	18 UC	R	B	.be	N	N	Jul 21
Bolivia	18 UC*	R	BOL	.bo	Y	Y*	Aug 6
Brazil	16 U*	R	BR	.br	Y	Y*	Sep 7
Bulgaria	18 U	R	BG	.bg	N	N	Mar 3
Burma/Myanmar	18 U	R	BUR	.mm	N	N*	Jan 4
Cambodia	18 U	R	K	.kh	Y	N	Nov 9
Canada	18 U	R	CDN	.ca	N	N	Jul 1
Chile	18 UC	R	RCH	.cl	N/Y	Y*	Sep 18
China	18 U	R	RC	.cn	Y	Y	Oct 1
Colombia	18 U	R	CO	.co	Y	N	Jul 20
Cuba	16 U	R	CU	.cu	Y	Y	Jan 1
Czech Republic	18 U	R	CZ	.cz	N	N	Oct 28
Denmark	18 U	R	DK	.dk	Y	N	Jun 5
Egypt	18 UC	R	ET	.eg	Y	Y	Jul 23
Estonia	18 U	R	EST	.ee	Y	N	Feb 24
Finland	18 U	R	FIN	.fi	Y	N	Dec 6
France	18 U	R	F	.fr	N	N	Jul 14
Germany	18 U	R	D	.de	Y	N	Oct 3
Greece	18 UC	R	GR	.gr	Y	N	Mar 25
Haiti	18 U	R	RH	.ht	—	N	Jan 1
Hong Kong	18 U*	L	—	.hk	N	N	Oct 1
Hungary	18 U	R	H	.hu	N	N	Aug 20
India	18 U	L	IND	.in	N	Y	Jan 26
Indonesia	17 U*	L	RI	.id	Y	Y	Aug 17
Iran	16 U	R	IR	.ir	Y	Y	Apr 1
Iraq	18 U	R	IRQ	.iq	N	Y	Jul 17
Ireland	18 U	L	IRL	.ie	N	N	Mar 17
Israel	18 U	R	IL	.il	Y	Y*	May 14
Italy	18 U*	R	I	.it	N	N	Jun 2
Japan	20 U	L	J	.jp	N	Y	Dec 23
Jordan	18 U	R	HKJ	.jo	N	Y	May 25
Kazakhstan	18 U	R	KZ	.kz	Y	Y*	Dec 16
Kenya	18 U	L	EAK	.ke	N	N*	Dec 12
Korea, North	17 U	R	—	.kp	Y?	Y	Sep 9
Korea, South	19 U	R	ROK	.kr	Y	N*	Aug 15

GAZETTEER · KUWAIT – ZIMBABWE · [4/4]

Country	Voting age	Driving side	UN vehicle code	Internet country code	Military service	Death penalty	National Day
UNITED STATES	18 U	R	USA	.us	N	Y	Jul 4
Kuwait	?21 U*	R	KWT	.kw	Y	Y	Feb 25
Latvia	18 U	R	LV	.lv	N	Y*	Nov 18
Lebanon	21 C*	R	RL	.lb	N	Y	Nov 22
Liberia	18 U	R	LB	.lr	N	N*	Jul 26
Lithuania	18 U	R	LT	.lt	Y	N	Feb 16
Malaysia	21 U	L	MAL	.my	N	Y	Aug 31
Mexico	18 UC	R	MEX	.mx	Y	N	Sep 16
Monaco	18 U	R	MC	.mc	—	N	Nov 19
Morocco	18 U	R	MA	.ma	Y	N*	Jul 30
Netherlands	18 U	R	NL	.nl	N	N	Apr 30
New Zealand	18 U	L	NZ	.nz	N	N	Feb 6
Nigeria	18 U	R	WAN	.ng	N	Y	Oct 1
Norway	18 U	R	N	.no	Y	N	May 17
Pakistan	18 U	L	PK	.pk	N	Y	Mar 23
Peru	18 UC*	R	PE	.pe	N	Y*	Jul 28
Philippines	18 U	R	RP	.ph	Y	N	Jun 12
Poland	18 U	R	PL	.pl	Y	N	May 3
Portugal	18 U	R	P	.pt	N	N	Jun 10
Romania	18 U	R	RO	.ro	N	N	Dec 1
Russia	18 U	R	RUS	.ru	Y	N*	Jun 12
Rwanda	18 U	R	RWA	.rw	N	N	Jul 1
Saudi Arabia	21	R	SA	.sa	N	Y	Sep 23
Singapore	21 UC	L	SGP	.sg	Y	Y	Aug 9
Slovakia	18 U	R	SK	.sk	N	N	Sep 1
Slovenia	18 U*	R	SLO	.si	N	N	Jun 25
Somalia	18 U	R	SO	.so	—	Y	Jul 1
South Africa	18 U	L	ZA	.za	N	N	Apr 27
Spain	18 U	R	E	.es	N	N	Oct 12
Sudan	17 U	R	SUD	.sd	Y	Y	Jan 1
Sweden	18 U	R	S	.se	Y	N	Jun 6
Switzerland	18 U	R	CH	.ch	Y	N	Aug 1
Syria	18 U	R	SYR	.sy	Y	Y	Apr 17
Taiwan	20 U	R	—	.tw	Y	Y	Oct 10
Thailand	18 UC	L	T	.th	Y	Y	Dec 5
Turkey	18 U	R	TR	.tr	Y	N	Oct 29
Ukraine	18 U	R	UA	.ua	Y	N	Aug 24
United Kingdom	18 U	L	GB	.uk	N	N	—
Venezuela	18 U	R	YV	.ve	Y	N	Jul 5
Vietnam	18 U	R	VN	.vn	Y	Y	Sep 2
Zimbabwe	18 U	L	ZW	.zw	Y	Y	Apr 18

Society & Health

Man seeketh in society comfort, use, and protection.
— FRANCIS BACON (1561–1626)

——————— PERSONALIZED GENETICS &c. ———————

In early 2008, a new breed of biotechnology start-up garnered press attention. Direct-to-consumer genetic testing companies, such as California-based *Navigenics* (launched in 2008), the Google-backed *23AndMe*, and Iceland's *DeCODEme* (both launched in 2007), offer to scan an individual's genome and provide, for as little as $1,000, a portfolio of information on everything from ancestry to the risks of disease, and inherited traits such as caffeine resistance. While à la carte tests for rarer ailments (such as Hodgkin's disease) have been available for some years, these new services represent a significant development in scope and sophistication. Consequently, such companies have attracted investment from Silicon Valley backers, as well as concern from regulators who question the utility and advisability of speculative gene testing. In June 2008, California sent 'cease and desist' letters to 13 test companies, prohibiting them from soliciting state customers without a license; the action followed similar moves in NY, and an FTC investigation into questions of false advertising. These concerns arose amidst heightened public interest in genes, as research probes the genetic roots of everything from heart attacks to autism, and as gene-based therapies begin to fulfill their promise. (Herceptin, a breast cancer treatment given only to those with a specific mutation of the HER2 gene, reportedly earned $1·3bn in 2007.) Lawmakers have also taken steps to address the potential downside of gene testing. In June, George W. Bush signed the *Genetic Information Nondiscrimination Act* (GINA), which prohibits genetic discrimination by health insurers or employers. For instance, GINA bans insurers from denying coverage based on a genetic marker for a disease and prohibits employers from requesting genetic information. The law (which has been called 'the first major civil rights act of the C21st') follows a decade of debate, and seeks to prevent episodes like those of the 1970s, when insurers denied coverage to blacks carrying the gene for sickle-cell anemia. A 2007 poll by the Genetics and Public Policy Center revealed the percent of Americans who support genetic testing for various purposes:

Those who support the use of genetic testing by ...	%
Researchers diagnosing, preventing, or treating disease	93
Doctors identifying a person's disease risk, when no treatment exists	79
Employers making hiring/promotion decisions	19
Health insurers deciding whom to insure or how much to charge	15

———————————— GENERATIONS ————————————

Some of the American generations since WWI, and their supposed characteristics:

Lost Generation............................ came of age during WWI; 'disillusioned'
Greatest Generation.......... born in the 1920s; fought in WWII; built postwar US
Beat Generation.... came of age post-WWII; rejected traditional mores (Kerouac &c.)
Baby Boomers.......born after WWII; came of age during '60s–'70s counterculture
Me Generation................came of age in the 1980s; self-centered, 'materialistic'
Generation X.................................born in the 1960s and 1970s; 'aimless'
Generation Y....born *c*.1979–*c*.1994 (a.k.a. the Millennials, Echo Boomers, iGen)
Generation Z or *Generation 9/11*..... born after the attacks on September 11, 2001

Some dates are debated. ❋ 'The Lost Generation' also refers to a clan of 1920s expatriate writers; the term is attributed to Gertrude Stein. The 'Greatest Generation' was defined by Tom Brokaw in his 1998 book of the same name. The 'Me Generation' stems from the writer Tom Wolfe, who called the 1970s the 'Me Decade'. The term 'Generation X' was coined by Douglas Coupland.

——————— US RESIDENTIAL POPULATION ———————

303,182,698 people lived in the US in January 2008, according to the Census Bureau. Below are some Bureau estimates of the US population for various years:

1900........76,094,000	1960.......180,671,158	2020.....335,805,000†
1910........92,407,000	1970.......205,052,174	2030.....363,584,000†
1920.......106,461,000	1980.......227,224,681	2040.....391,946,000†
1930.......123,076,741	1990.......249,464,396	2050.....419,854,000†
1940.......132,122,446	2000.......282,194,308	† Projections. 1900–40
1950.......152,271,417	2010.....308,936,000†	data exclude AK and HI.

As of January 2008, the nation was growing at approximately the following rate:

1 birth every..................... 8 secs	1 net foreign migrant every.....30 secs
1 death every...................11 secs	Net gain of 1 person every......13 secs

——————— REGIONAL POPULATION CHANGES ———————

Since 2000, the US West and South have gained significantly more residents than the Northeast and Midwest, according to Census Bureau figures released in 2007:

pop. change 2000–07	*births*	*deaths*	*foreign mig.*	*internal mig.*
Northeast +1,085,844	4,919,082	3,472,720	+1,717,074	−2,218,054
Midwest +1,993,595	6,470,373	4,156,045	+1,057,420	−1,400,179
South +10,218,933	11,047,213	6,601,202	+2,551,575	+3,227,337
West +6,898,183	7,372,804	3,367,221	+2,658,202	+390,896
US +20,196,555	29,809,472	17,597,188	+7,984,271	−

——————— US POPULATION BY RACE & ETHNICITY ———————

The racial and ethnic breakdown of the US, according to the latest (2000) Census:

	%	
TOTAL POPULATION	%	281,421,906
ONE RACE	97·6	274,595,678
· White	75·1	211,460,626
· Black or African American	12·3	34,658,190
· American Indian and Alaska Native	0·9	2,475,956
· Asian	3·6	10,242,998
Asian Indian	0·6	1,678,765
Chinese	0·9	2,432,585
Filipino	0·7	1,850,314
Japanese	0·3	796,700
Korean	0·4	1,076,872
Vietnamese	0·4	1,122,528
Other Asian	0·5	1,285,234
· Native Hawaiian & other	0·1	398,835
Native Hawaiian	<0·1	140,652
Guamanian/Chamorro	<0·1	58,240
Samoan	<0·1	91,029
Other Pacific Islander	<0·1	108,914
· Some other race	5·5	15,359,073
TWO OR MORE RACES	2·4	6,826,228

Race alone or with >1 other race

	%	
Total population	%	281,421,906
White	77·1	216,930,975
Black or African American	12·9	36,419,434
American Indian and Alaska Native	1·5	4,119,301
Asian	4·2	11,898,828
Native Hawaiian & other	0·3	874,414
Some other race	6·6	18,521,486

Hispanic or Latino & Race

	%	
Total population	%	281,421,906
Hispanic or Latino (of any race)	12·5	35,305,818
Mexican	7·3	20,640,711
Puerto Rican	1·2	3,406,178
Cuban	0·4	1,241,685
Other Hispanic or Latino	3·6	10,017,244
Not Hispanic or Latino	87·5	246,116,088
White alone	69·1	194,552,774

According to the 2006 US Census Special Report into American Indians and Alaska Natives, 4,315,865 people (1·53% of the entire US population) reported that they were American Indian or Alaska Native, of whom 2,447,989 (0·87% of the population) reported only American Indian or Alaska Native as their race.

MINORITIES & THE AMERICAN DREAM

African Americans, Asian Americans, and Hispanics hold markedly different views about equality of opportunity in the United States, according to a 2007 poll by New American Media, an ethnic press organization. Below are some of the differences:

'Strongly agree' that if you work hard, you will succeed in the US:	%
African Americans	44
Asians	64
Hispanics	74

'Strongly agree' the criminal justice system favors the rich & powerful:	%
Af. Americans	71
Asians	27
Hispanics	45

'Strongly agree' each American has equal opportunity to succeed:	%
African Americans	30
Asians	43
Hispanics	59

Agree 'there is a lot of discrimination against my community' in the US:	%
Af. Americans	92
Asians	57
Hispanics	85

44% of Hispanics and 47% of Asian Americans said they were 'generally afraid of African Americans because they are responsible for most of the crime'. 46% of Hispanics and 52% of African Americans said they believed that 'most Asian business owners do not treat them with respect'. 51% of African Americans agreed that 'Latin American immigrants are taking away jobs, housing, and political power from the Black community'. 61% of Hispanics, 54% of Asian Americans, and 47% of African Americans said they would rather do business with whites than with members of the other 2 groups.

IMMIGRATION

The US's (legal and illegal) immigrant population hit a record 37·9m in 2007 – 12·6% of the population – according to the Center for Immigration Studies (CIS). The CIS concluded that, 'immigrants make significant progress over time. But even those who have been here for 20 years are more likely to be in poverty, lack insurance, or use welfare than are natives'. Below are immigrant numbers and profiles:

Immigrants in the US		
Millions		% of pop
10·3	1900	13·6
13·5	1910	14·7
13·9	1920	13·2
14·2	1930	11·6
11·6	1940	8·8
10·3	1950	6·9
9·7	1960	5·4
9·6	1970	4·7
14·1	1980	6·2
19·8	1990	7·9
31·1	2000	11·1
37·9	2007	12·6

Selected characteristics	natives	immigrants
Less than high school	7·5%	29·0%
High school only	30·9%	24·8%
Some college	30·7%	17·7%
Bachelor's	20·8%	17·4%
Graduate or professional	10·1%	11·0%
Median annual earnings	$40,344	$31,074
Median household income	$49,201	$43,933
Average household size	2·43	3·11
Average age	35·9	40·5

[For notes, see CIS, *A Profile of America's Foreign-Born Population.*]

————AVERAGE US HOUSEHOLD & FAMILY SIZE————

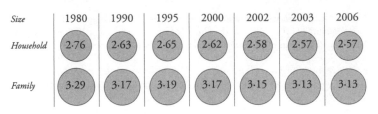

Size	1980	1990	1995	2000	2002	2003	2006
Household	2·76	2·63	2·65	2·62	2·58	2·57	2·57
Family	3·29	3·17	3·19	3·17	3·15	3·13	3·13

————————HOUSEHOLD TYPE————————

Family households..... 77,402,000 *total*
· Married couple 58,179,000
· Male householder† 5,130,000
· Female householder† 14,093,000
· With own children 36,466,000
· Without own children ...40,936,000

Nonfamily h/holds .... 36,982,000 *total*
· Male householder† 16,753,000
· Female householder† 20,230,000

† No spouse present. The 'householder' is the person who rents/owns the house. [2006 data]

————CHILDREN'S LIVING ARRANGEMENTS————

The living arrangements of US children, according to the most recent data [2004]:

70% *live with 2 parents*	26% *live with 1 parent*	4% *live with no parents*

Children who live with ...	%
Biological mother & father	60·8
Biological mother only	22·6
Biological mother & stepfather	5·7
Biological father only	3·1
Grandparents only	2·2
Biological father & stepmother	1·5
Adoptive mother & father	0·9

Other relatives only	0·9
Nonrelatives only	0·8
Bio. mother & adoptive father	0·6
Other mother only (adoptive &c.)	0·6
Bio. father & adoptive mother	0·1
Other father only (adoptive &c.)	0·1
Other arrangement†	0·1

† 2 stepparents or 1 adoptive parent & 1 step

The percent of children who live with siblings, whether full, half, step, or adopted:

21·2%	38·7%	24·8%	10·2%	5%
0 siblings	*1 sibling*	*2 siblings*	*3 siblings*	*≥4 siblings*

Children who live with ...	%
≥1 sibling	78·8
Only full siblings	70·7

≥1 stepsibling	1·7
≥1 adopted sibling	1·5
≥1 half sibling	11·7

85% of fathers and 94% of mothers live with their biological children only; 4% of fathers and 1% of mothers live with stepchildren only; 2% of fathers and 1% of mothers live with adopted children only, and the rest live with other combinations of children. [Source for the page: US Census Bureau]

———————— IMMUNIZATION SCHEDULE ————————

The following is a basic immunization schedule for children from birth to age 6:

Vaccine	standard dose(s)	age of child
Hepatitis B	3	birth · 1–2 months · 6–18 months
Rotavirus	3	2 months · 4 months · 6 months
DTaP	5	2 months · 4 months · 6 months · 15–18 months · 4–6 years
Hib	4	2 months · 4 months · (6 months) · 12–15 months
Pneumococcal	4	2 months · 4 months · 6 months · 12–15 months
Polio	4	2 months · 4 months · 6–18 months · 4–6 years
Influenza	6	yearly from 6–59 months
MMR	2	12–15 months · 4–6 years
Varicella	2	12–15 months · 4–6 years
Hepatitis A	2	2 doses >6 months apart, both between 12–23 months

This chart is based on the Dept of Health & Human Services 2008 schedule. Parents should *always* check with the CDC or their pediatrician, especially for children >6 and for advice on high-risk groups.

———————— FIRST NAMES OF THE YEAR ————————

The Social Security Administration annually lists the most popular names given to babies, based on applications for Social Security cards. The top 2007 names were:

Jacob	*from Hebrew Yaakov*	1	*from the Latin Aemilia*	Emily
Michael	*who is like God*	2	*Spanish form of Elizabeth*	Isabella
Ethan	*Hebrew for 'solid' or 'enduring'*	3	*from Germanic ermen, 'universal'*	Emma
Joshua	*Jehovah saves*	4	*possible variant of Eve*	Ava
Daniel	*God is my judge*	5	*son of Maud*	Madison
Christopher	*bearer of Christ*	6	*wisdom*	Sophia
Anthony	*from the Latin Antonius*	7	*feminine form of Oliver*	Olivia
William	*protector*	8	*my father is joy*	Abigail
Matthew	*God's gift*	9	*from Hebrew for 'grace'*	Hannah
Andrew	*from Greek for 'warrior' or 'man'*	10	*God's vow*	Elizabeth

The most popular names in other decades, based on Social Security applications:

1890s	*1940s*	*1990s*
John & Mary	James & Mary	Michael & Jessica
William & Anna	Robert & Linda	Christopher & Ashley
James & Margaret	John & Barbara	Matthew & Emily

In November 2007 the US Census Bureau released a list of the most common surnames in America, based on the 2000 census. The top 10 most common were:

[1] Smith · [2] Johnson · [3] Williams · [4] Brown · [5] Jones
[6] Miller · [7] Davis · [8] Garcia · [9] Rodriguez · [10] Wilson

———————— AMERICA'S CHILDREN ————————

From: *America's Children in Brief:*
Key National Indicators of Well-Being, 2008

[Forum on Child & Family Statistics]

	previous value	most recent value	significant change
Number of children (0–17) in the US population	73·7m ['06]	73·9m ['07]	↑
Children (0–17) as % of the US population	24·6% ['06]	24·5% ['07]	↓
Children (5–17) in non-English-speaking households	19·9% ['05]	20·3% ['06]	↑
Children (0–17) living with 2 married parents	67·4% ['06]	67·8% ['07]	–
Children (0–17) living in poverty	17·6% ['05]	17·4% ['06]	–
Children (0–17) living in 'food insecure' households	16·9% ['05]	17·2% ['06]	–
Children (0–17) covered by health insurance	89·1% ['05]	88·3% ['06]	↓
Children (0–17) with no usual source of health care	5% ['05]	6% ['06]	–
Children (19–35 months) properly vaccinated [see p.95]	80·8% ['05]	80·5% ['06]	–
Children (3–5) read to every day by a family member	58% ['01]	60% ['05]	–
Children (2–17) who visited a dentist in past year	76·2% ['05]	75·7% ['06]	–
Children (6–17) who are overweight	18% ['03–04]	17% ['05–'06]	–
Children (0–17) with asthma	8·9% ['05]	9·3% ['06]	–
Students who drank heavily[†] – 8th-grade	11% ['06]	10% ['07]	–
– 10th-grade	21·9% ['06]	21·9% ['07]	–
– 12th-grade	25% ['06]	26% ['07]	–
Students who smoked regularly[‡] – 8th-grade	4% ['06]	3% ['07]	↓
– 10th-grade	8% ['06]	7% ['07]	–
– 12th-grade	12·2% ['06]	12·3% ['07]	–
Students who recently used illicit drugs[§] – 8th-grade	8% ['06]	7% ['07]	–
– 10th-grade	16·8% ['06]	16·9% ['07]	–
– 12th-grade	21·5% ['06]	21·9% ['07]	–
High school students who have ever had sex	46·7% ['03]	46·8% ['05]	–
Youths (12–17) involved in serious violent crime	14/1,000 ['04]	17/1,000 ['05]	↑
Youths (16–19) neither in school nor working	7·6% ['06]	7·8% ['07]	–
Young adults (18–24) who completed high school	87·6% ['05]	87·8% ['06]	–

† ≥5 alcoholic drinks in a row in previous fortnight; ‡ daily over past 30 days; § over the past 30 days

———————— CHILDREN'S GLOBAL AWARENESS ————————

American children have comparatively poor international awareness, according to a 2007 survey conducted by Ipsos Mori. Children in 10 countries were asked: [a] if they would go out of their way to understand what was going on in the world; [b] whether they saw themselves as global citizens; and [c] if they felt it was important to learn a foreign language. The countries were scored from 0 (worst) to 7 (best):

Country	*rank*				
Nigeria	5·15	Saudi Arabia	3·74	Czech Rep	2·51
India	4·86	Spain	3·29	USA	2·22
Brazil	4·53	Germany	3·24	UK	2·19
		China	2·97		

——TOP US COLLEGES——	—TOP WORLD COLLEGES—
US News & World Report · 2007	*Times Educational Supplement* · 2007
1 ....Princeton University · NJ	1 ....Harvard University · US
2 ....Harvard University · MA	2 ....Cambridge University · UK
3 ....Yale University · CT	3 ....Oxford University · UK
4 ....Stanford University · CA	4 ....Yale University · US
5 ....University of Pennsylvania	5 ......Imperial College London · UK
5 ...California Institute of Technology	6 ....Princeton University · US
7 ...Massachusetts Inst. of Technology	7 ....California Inst. of Tech. · US
8 ....Duke University · NC	8 ....University of Chicago · US
9 ....Columbia University · NY	9 .....University College London · UK
9 ....University of Chicago	10... Massachusetts Inst. of Tech. · US

Many top US schools reported record-low acceptance rates in 2008. Harvard accepted 7·1% of the high school seniors who applied, Yale accepted 8·3%, Brown 13%, Dartmouth 13%, and Georgetown 18% (each a record for the school). According to the *New York Times*, a spike in the number of high school graduates was in part to blame, along with an increase in college financial aid.

——INTERNATIONAL STUDENTS & STUDY ABROAD——

582,984 foreign students enrolled in US colleges and universities during the 2006–07 school year, the first significant rise (3·2% over 2005–06) since the 9/11 attacks. Below are the top countries of origin and the most popular fields of study:

Place of origin	*% of foreign students*	*Field of study*	*% of foreign students*
India	14·4	Business and management	17·8
China	11·6	Engineering	15·3
South Korea	10·7	Physical & life sciences	8·9
Japan	6·1	Social sciences	8·4
Taiwan	5·0	Math & computer science	7·9

The number of American post-secondary students studying abroad for credit increased by 8·5% during 2005–06, the most recent year of available data, to a total of 223,534 students. Below are their top destinations and areas of academic study:

Destination	*% of US students abroad*	*Field of study*	*% of US students abroad*
United Kingdom	14·4	Social sciences	21·7
Italy	11·7	Business and management	17·7
Spain	9·8	Humanities	14·2
France	7·0	Foreign languages	7·8
Australia	4·9	Fine or applied arts	7·5

The University of Southern California hosted the largest number of international students in 2006–07, followed by Columbia University and New York University. NYU sent the most students abroad in 2005–06, followed by Michigan State University and the University of Texas at Austin. The number of Americans studying abroad has risen 150% in the last decade. [Source: Institute of Intl Education]

————MARITAL STATUS OF THE US POPULATION————

Marital status 2006	% all	% ♂	% ♀
Married	53·4	55·9	51·0
Widowed	6·0	2·4	9·4
Divorced	10·2	8·9	11·5
Separated	2·2	1·8	2·46
Never married	28·1	31·0	25·5

[Source: US Census. Marital status of people ≥15.]

————MARRIAGE & DIVORCE————

Below are the US Census rates (per 1,000) of US marriage and divorce (1970–2005):

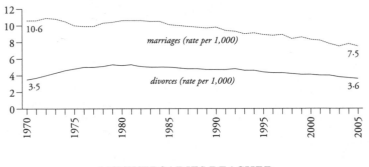

————ANNIVERSARIES REACHED————

For the first time since WWII, couples who first married 25 years ago are facing a less-than-even chance of reaching their silver (25th) anniversary together. Only 49·5% of men and 46·4% of women who married between 1975–79 reached that milestone, according to 2007 data released by the Census Bureau. Below are the % of men and women married in various years who reached some key anniversaries:

Anniversary →	5th		10th		15th		25th		30th	
Married in ↓	♂	♀	♂	♀	♂	♀	♂	♀	♂	♀
1955–59	96	94	88	87	80	79	70	67	67	64
1960–64	95	93	85	82	75	73	65	60	62	56
1965–69	91	90	77	75	67	66	59	55	56	51
1970–74	89	87	75	72	65	61	54	51	46	42
1975–79	88	85	73	70	65	61	50†	46	–	–
1980–84	89	87	74	71	65	63	–	–	–	–
1985–89	89	86	77	73	61	57	–	–	–	–
1990–94	89	87	70	69	–	–	–	–	–	–

† Figures have been rounded; before rounding, the percentage of men reaching this mark is 49·5.

———————WHAT MAKES A MARRIAGE WORK?———————

A 2007 study by the Pew Research Center asked American adults whether they considered 9 characteristics commonly attributed to successful marriages 'very important', 'rather important', or 'not very important'. When the survey was administered in 1990, far more adults said children were key components of a successful marriage, while significantly fewer adults seemed to care about household chores:

Americans who say the following is 'very important' to a successful marriage		*change*
1990 %	**2007 %**	**±%**
95 faithfulness 93		−2
67 happy sexual relations 70		+3
47 sharing chores 62		+15
46 adequate income 53		+7
42 good housing 51		+9
45 shared religious beliefs 49		+4
44 shared tastes & interests 46		+2
65 children 41		−24
11 agreement on politics 12		+1

———————AGE AT FIRST MARRIAGE———————

Americans are marrying at increasingly older ages, according to the US Census Department's data. Listed below are the ages of first marriage during the C20th:

Year · age ♂ ♀	1940......24·3.....21·5	1980......24·7.....22·0
1910......25·1.....21·6	1950......22·8.....20·3	1990......26·1.....23·9
1920......24·6.....21·2	1960......22·8.....20·3	2000......26·8.....25·1
1930......24·3.....21·3	1970......23·2.....20·8	2006......27·5.....25·5

UN statistics gathered between 1990–2002 reveal the following mean age at first marriage for women: Australia [29 *years*] · Bangladesh [19] · Brazil [23] · Canada [27] · China [23] · Egypt [22] · France [30] · India [20] · Ireland [31] · Iran [22] · Iraq [22] · Italy [28] · Japan [29] · Mexico [23] · New Zealand [25] · Poland [25] · S Africa [28] · Netherlands [30] · S Korea [26] · Sweden [32] · UK [26]

———————LEGAL MARRIAGE AGE———————

The legal age for marriage, with parental consent, in various countries of the world:

♂ *age* ♀	China........22.....20	Japan ....18.....16
Egypt.........18.....16	France ....16.....14	Turkey........14.....14
Brazil ....14.....12	GB............16.....16	Venezuela.....21.....18

[Sources: UN; Human Rights Watch] In April 2008, Arkansas repealed a law that mistakenly allowed children of any age to marry if they had parental consent. The law was intended to allow pregnant women <18 to marry, but an extraneous 'not' before 'pregnant' broadened the law considerably.

NUMBER OF SEX PARTNERS

The median number of female sex partners for men in the US is 7, while the number of male partners for women is 4, according to data released in 2007 by the National Center for Health Statistics. Below are the number of partners for various groups:

Median no. sex partners	♂	♀
20–29 *years old*	5·4	3·7
30–39	7·6	4·6
40–49	6·9	3·5
50–59	6·9	2·7
Mexican American	4·7	1·7
Non-Hispanic white	6·2	3·7
Non-Hispanic black	12·5	5·0
Less than high school	8·1	3·5
High school/GED	7·3	3·8
More than high school	6·0	3·7
Below poverty level	6·3	4·3
100%–<200% pov. level	7·4	3·8
≥200% poverty level	6·7	3·5
Married	5·1	2·6
Widowed, divorced, separated	11·5	5·8
Never married	7·4	5·1
Cohabiting	9·7	4·7
ALL (*aged* 20–59)	6·8	3·7

AGE AT LOSS OF VIRGINITY

Below is a statistical breakdown of the age at which Americans first had sex, based on 1999–2002 data released in 2007 by the National Center for Health Statistics:

Age at loss of virginity	% all	% ♂	% ♀
≤15	15·6	19·0	12·3
15–17	41·3	41·2	41·4
18–20	28·4	26·7	29·9
≥21	14·7	13·1	16·3

TIME TAKEN FOR SEX

The length of time spent on foreplay and sex varies significantly around the globe, according to the 2007–08 'Global Sexual Well-Being' survey funded by Durex. Below is the amount of time taken, in minutes, in various countries of the world:

Country	*foreplay*	*'the act'*	*total*
Mexico	22·8	22·1	45
Switzerland	23·3	18·9	42
Italy	20·4	20·4	41
Canada	18·8	18·4	37
Austria	20·2	19·6	37
Germany	18·5	17·6	36
USA	17·0	17·7	35
Japan	17·7	16·0	34
France	17·9	14·6	33
Singapore	13·9	15·2	29
Hong Kong	11·8	15·3	27

The survey also revealed the items most often† found by bedside tables worldwide:

Condoms	59%	Lubricants	33%	Other gels	11%
Pornography	47%	Vibrators	21%	Aphrodisiacs	10%
Massage oil	35%	Sex toys (other)	15%	† 'Sometimes' or 'often'

—————————————— BIRTHS ——————————————

The US fertility rate rose to 68·5 live births per 1,000 women in 2006, its highest level since 1991. Notably, the birth rate for women 15–19 rose 3% from 2005, the first increase since 1991. The birth and fertility rates for various US groups in 2006:

Mothers who are ...	births	rate†		births	rate
White, non-Hisp.	2,309,833	59·5	18–19	296,507	73·0
Black, non-Hisp.	617,220	70·6	20–24	1,080,507	105·9
Am. Ind. or Al. Native	47,494	62·8	25–29	1,182,187	116·8
Asian or Pac. Isl.	239,829	67·2	30–34	950,472	97·7
Hispanic	1,039,051	101·5	35–39	498,566	47·3
10–14 *years old*	6,405	0·6	40–44	105,476	9·4
15–17	138,920	22·0	45–54	6,956	0·6
			TOTAL US‡	4,265,996	68·5

Births to unmarried mothers also rose in 2006, to a record 38·5% of all births: 27% of births to white, non-Hispanic women; 71% to black, non-Hispanic women; 65% to American Indian or Alaskan Native women; and 50% to Hispanic women.

† Fertility rates are the number of live births per 1,000 women in the specified group. Fertility rates by race and ethnicity only include births to women aged 15–44. ‡ Includes all births by mothers <15.

—————————————— ABORTION ——————————————

1·2m abortions were performed in the US in 2005 – according to the latest data from the Guttmacher Institute – a 25% decline from the 1·6m abortions in 1990. Interestingly, the 19·4 abortions per 1,000 women aged 15–44 in 2005 was the lowest abortion rate since 1974 – the year after abortion became legal. Below are the abortion rates since 1992 in various part of the US, according to Guttmacher data:

Region	abortion rate 1992	1996	2000	2005	± 2000–05
Northeast	31·8	29·1	28·0	27·2	–3%
Midwest	18·8	16·9	15·9	14·9	–12%
South	21·8	19·8	19·0	17·3	–9%
West	33·9	26·6	24·9	21·8	–12%
TOTAL US	25·7	22·4	21·3	19·4	–9%

For the purpose of comparison, below are the abortion rates per 1,000 women aged 15–44 around the world, according to the Guttmacher Institute and the *Lancet*:

Area	abortion rate				
Eastern Africa	39	Southcentral Asia	27	Caribbean	35
Middle Africa	26	Southeastern Asia	39	Central America	25
Northern Africa	22	Western Asia	24	South America	33
Southern Africa	24	Eastern Europe	44	Northern America	21
Western Africa	27	Northern Europe	17	Oceania	17
Eastern Asia	28	Southern Europe	18	World	29
		Western Europe	12		

———— US OCCUPATIONAL EMPLOYMENT & WAGES————

The number of employees and their mean hourly wages, by occupational group:

Number employed	major occupational group	mean wage/hour
6,003,930	Management	$46·22
998,590	Legal	$42·53
3,191,360	Computer and mathematical science	$34·71
2,486,020	Architecture and engineering	$33·11
6,877,680	Health care practitioner and technical	$31·26
6,015,500	Business and financial operations	$30·01
1,255,670	Life, physical, and social science	$29·82
1,761,270	Arts, design, entertainment, sports, and media	$23·27
8,316,360	Education, training, and library	$22·41
6,708,200	Construction and extraction	$19·53
1,793,040	Community and social services	$19·49
5,390,090	Installation, maintenance, and repair	$19·20
3,087,650	Protective service	$18·63
14,332,020	Sales and related	$16·94
10,146,560	Production	$15·05
23,270,810	Office and administrative support	$15·00
9,629,030	Transportation and material moving	$14·75
3,625,240	Health care support	$12·31
3,339,510	Personal care and service	$11·53
4,403,900	Building and grounds cleaning and maintenance	$11·33
448,000	Farming, fishing, and forestry	$10·89
11,273,850	Food preparation and serving related	$9·35

[Source: Bureau of Labor Statistics · Table data as of May 2008]

————————OVERRATED CAREERS————————

In December 2007 *US News & World Report* released a list of the 'Most Overrated Careers' – those occupations 'with a mystique that exceeds reality'. While somewhat subjective, the list was based in part on job counseling sessions with 2,600 people, as well as a review of career books, articles, websites, and blogs. Each 'overrated' career was listed alongside a potentially more rewarding alternative occupation, viz:

Overrated career	downsides include …	alternative career
Ad executive	*demanding clients, empty successes*	social marketing
Architect	*housing decline, offshoring, tedium*	interior designer
Attorney	*'contentiousness and chicanery', burnout*	mediation
Chef	*late nights, alienation, too much chopping*	personal chef
Chiropractor	*federal limitations, costly schooling*	physician assistant

Other 'overrated' positions according to the survey: clinical psychologists, medical scientists, non-profit managers, physicians, police officers, real estate agents, small-business owners, and teachers.

——DEPRESSED STATES——

Utah ranks as the most psychologically depressed state in the Union, according to a survey released in November 2007 by Mental Health America. The survey compiled a variety of statistics assessing the level of the depression in each state's population to create an overall 'Depression Index'. Below are the 5 most depressed states in the US:

State	Depression Index[†]
Utah	6·11
West Virginia	6·09
Kentucky	5·90
Rhode Island	4·47
Nevada	4·16

† Based on the percent of the population experiencing depressive episodes in the past year; the percent that experienced 'serious psychological distress'; and average number of days when the population said their mental health was poor.

——MISERABLE CITIES——

Detroit is the most miserable city in America, according to *Forbes*, which in January 2008 released the results of its first '*Forbes* Misery Measure'. The measure builds upon two classic economic indices, the Misery Index (unemployment + inflation) and the Misery Score (based on taxes), by considering also commute times, weather, crime rates, and contaminated toxic waste sites. Based on these criteria, the most miserable cities in the US were:

State	Misery Measure
Detroit, MI	696
Stockton, CA	689
Flint, MI	675
New York, NY[†]	668
Philadelphia, PA	648

† NYC's high tax rates and lengthy commute times were responsible for its high score.

——————UNEMPLOYMENT AROUND THE WORLD——————

189·9m people worldwide were unemployed in 2007, according to the International Labor Organization. Below are the unemployment rates in various world regions:

Region	% unemployed 2007[†]
Developed economies & EU	6·4
Central/SE Europe & CIS[‡]	8·5
East Asia	3·3
Southeast Asia & the Pacific	6·2
South Asia	5·1
Latin America & Caribbean	8·5
Middle East	11·8
North Africa	10·9
Sub-Saharan Africa	8·2

† Prelim. data. ‡ Former Soviet states. [Source: ILO Global Employment Trends, 2008]

——————UNION MEMBERSHIP——————

2007 union membership	%
Men	13·0
Women	11·1
Blacks & African Americans	14·3
Whites	11·8
Asians	10·9
Hispanics & Latinos	9·8
Full-time workers	13·2
Part-time workers	6·5
Age 16–24	4·8
Age ≥25	13·3
TOTAL	12·1% *of employed*

[Source: Bureau of Labor Statistics, 2008]

———————————FOOD & HUNGER———————————

In 2006, 12% of Americans lived in households that couldn't provide enough food for all members for at least part of the year, and were thus deemed 'food insecure' by the US Dept of Agriculture (USDA). In its annual 'household food security report', the USDA assesses food access among US households in the following terms:

Food security definitions Food Secure *consistent access to enough* *food for an active, healthy life* *for all members*	Low Food Security *difficulty obtaining enough* *food for all members, but* *substantial disruption to* *eating patterns avoided* *using food stamps &c.*	Very Low Food Security *food intake of some household* *members reduced and* *normal eating patterns* *disrupted due to* *food insecurity*

Below is a breakdown of the Americans in each food security category during 2006:

Individuals	*total*	*children*	*% of Americans*
In *food secure* households	258·5m	61m	87·9
In *food insecure* households	35·5m	12·6m	12·1
– *low food security*	24·4m	–	8·3
– *very low food security*	11·1m	430,000†	3·8

The following American households were food insecure for at least part of 2006:

Household type	*% food insecure*		
With children <18	15·6	Men living alone	11·4
With children <6	16·7	Elderly living alone	5·9
Married couples with children	10·1	White, non-Hispanic	7·8
Single mothers with children	30·4	Black, non-Hispanic	21·8
Single fathers with children	17·0	Hispanic	19·5
Other households with children	17·5	Below poverty level	36·3
No children <18	8·5	Northeast	9·2
More than 1 adult, no children	6·5	Midwest	10·7
Women living alone	11·3	South	12·3
		West	10·5

The average US household spent $41·67 weekly on food in 2006, whether in restaurants or on groceries. Below are the amounts spent by households of various types:

Household avg. food spending per week		
Food secure	$45	Women living alone	$50
Low food security	$32	Men living alone	$60
Very low food security	$31·50	Elderly living alone	$45
With children <18	$33·33	White, non-Hispanic	$45
With no children <18	$50	Black, non-Hispanic	$35
		Hispanic	$35

† 430,000 children lived in households with 'very low food security among children', meaning the eating patterns of children were disrupted; 12·6m lived in households where there was food insecurity among either children or adults. ❦ 3·8m households (3·3%) used a food bank at least once in 2006.

READING

In November 2007, the National Endowment for the Arts presented a report synthesizing several years of research on American literacy, titled *To Read or Not to Read*. Unsurprisingly, the overall trends were somewhat depressing. In 2006, the average American ≥15 years old spent only 20 minutes a day reading for pleasure:

Average time spent reading for pleasure				
Age	*weekday*	*weekend/hols*	45–54 .... 0:17 .... 0:24	
15–24 .... 0:07 .... 0:10			55–64 .... 0:30 .... 0:39	
25–34 .... 0:09 .... 0:11			≥65 .... 0:50 .... 1:07	
35–44 .... 0:12 .... 0:16			*Average* ...... 0:20 .... 0:26	

The report also showed that teenagers and adults have become less likely to read for fun, though leisure reading rates for elementary school children have improved:

% reading for fun almost every day		*% reading a book for fun in past year*	
	1984 — *2004*		*1992* — *2002*
9-year-olds 53 54		18–24 .... 59 52	
13-year-olds 35 30		25–34 .... 64 59	
17-year-olds 31 22		35–44 .... 66 59	

Not by chance, teenage literacy levels have declined at the same time as the decline in reading for pleasure, while the reading levels in younger groups have improved:

Reading level	*below basic*		*basic or above*		*proficient or above*	
	1992	*2005*	*1992*	*2005*	*1992*	*2005*
% of 4th graders .... 38 ...... 36 .... 62 ...... 64 .... 29 31						
% of 8th graders .... 31 ...... 27 .... 69 ...... 73 .... 29 31						
% of 12th graders .... 20 ...... 27 .... 80 ...... 73 .... 40 35						

While not in significant decline, adult literacy levels have stagnated, according to the report. In 2003, only 13% of Americans ≥16 years old were judged to be 'proficient' readers, meaning they could understand 'lengthy, complex, and abstract texts':

Reading level	*below basic*	*basic*	*intermediate*	*proficient*
Americans ≥16 .... 14% .... 29% .... 44% 13%				

7m Americans (3%) were said to be 'nonliterate' (a figure that did not include those with language barriers that prevented them from taking the survey). The report also demonstrated correlations between adult reading level, employment, and pay:

Reading level	*% employed*	*Reading level*	*% earning ≥$850/week*
Below basic 45		Below basic 13	
Basic 56		Basic 23	
Proficient 78		Proficient 58	

[Employment was for full- or part-time work; earnings included only full-time workers]

——————————HEALTH (CARE) OF THE NATION——————————

The US spends more on health care than any other country. In 2005, the latest year for which data are available, the country spent $1·9 trillion: $6,700 per person, or 16% of US GDP. Below are some CDC figures on the nation's health and health care:

❦ Americans made 1,169,333,000 visits to doctors, outpatient departments, and emergency rooms in 2005 – 4 visits per person, or 4·5 per woman and 3·5 per man. 762,438 medical doctors were active in the US, or 23·8 per 10,000 people. 144,427,000 civilians worked at health service sites – 9·9% of the nation's entire civilian workforce.

❦ In 2005, life expectancy was 77·9 years – 80·4 for women and 75·2 for men, according to preliminary data. Since 1990, life expectancy has risen by 3·4 years for men, and 1·6 years for women. The gap between the life expectancy for the nation's white and black populations has also narrowed: on average, whites lived 5·1 years longer than blacks in 2005, compared with 7 years longer in 1990.

❦ There were 5,756 hospitals in the US in 2005, offering 946,997 beds, with an average occupancy rate of 69·3%. The average hospital stay was 6·5 days.

❦ 9·2% of all Americans rated their health as 'fair' or 'poor' in 2005. 11·7% reported a limitation in their activities due to chronic physical, mental, or emotional problems. The most frequent cause of activity limitation was arthritis and other musculoskeletal conditions.

In 2005, 20% of Americans <65 lacked health insurance for at least part of the year. The percentage of Americans in various groups who lacked health insurance was:

Group	uninsured %	Group	uninsured %
<18 *years old*	13	Black only	22
18–24	35	Asian only	20
25–34	31	White, non-Hispanic	16
35–44	22	Hispanic or Latino	37
45–54	17	Single	34
55–64	13	Married	17
<100% *poverty level*	36	Separated or divorced	31
100–<150%	36	Widowed	25
150–<200%	33	Employed	22
		TOTAL <65	20

Additionally, 19% of Americans ≥18 years (40m people) reported in 2005 that they did not use a needed medical service because they could not afford it, including:

15·4m	*needing* medical care	25·4m	dental care
18·7m	prescription medicine	14·8m	eyeglasses
5·5m	mental health care		[at any time during the past 12 months]

When asked why they had no health coverage, 53% cited its cost, 24% a change in employment, 10% the cessation of Medicaid benefits, and 8% a change in their eligibility for family health coverage.

[Source for the page: *Health, US, 2007*, Centers for Disease Control & Prevention]

—————————————— LEADING CAUSES OF DEATH ——————————————

Below are some of the leading causes of death in the US (2004), broken down by sex:

Cause of death	deaths ♀	♂ deaths	Cause of death
Diseases of heart.	330,513	321,973	*diseases of heart*
Malignant neoplasms (i.e., cancer)	267,058	286,830	*malignant neoplasms (i.e., cancer)*
Cerebrovascular diseases	91,274	72,050	*unintentional injuries*
Chronic lower respiratory diseases	63,341	58,800	*cerebrovascular diseases*
Alzheimer's disease	46,991	58,646	*chronic lower respiratory diseases*
Unintentional injuries	39,962	35,267	*diabetes mellitus*
Diabetes mellitus.	37,871	26,861	*influenza and pneumonia*
Influenza and pneumonia	32,803	25,556	*suicide*
Nephritis, nephrosis, &c.	22,110	20,370	*nephritis, nephrosis, &c.*
Septicemia	18,362	18,974	*Alzheimer's disease*

[Source: *Health, US, 2007*, Centers for Disease Control & Prevention]

—————————————————— CANCER ——————————————————

Cancer killed an estimated 565,650 Americans in 2008, according to the American Cancer Society (ACS). Below is the ACS breakdown of estimated 2008 cancer deaths and new cases by general type, based on a projection of incidence rates in 1995–2004:

NEW CASES		TYPE	DEATHS	
♂	♀		♂	♀
25,310	10,000	Oral & pharynx	5,210	2,380
148,560	122,730	Digestive system	74,850	60,280
127,880	104,390	Respiratory system	94,210	72,070
1,270	1,110	Bones & joints	820	650
5,720	4,670	Soft tissue (incl. heart)	1,880	1,800
38,150	29,570	Skin	7,360	3,840
1,990	182,460	Breast	450	40,480
195,660	78,490	Genital system	29,330	28,490
85,870	39,620	Urinary system	18,430	9,380
1,340	1,050	Eye & orbit	130	110
11,780	10,030	Brain/other nervous	7,420	5,650
10,030	29,480	Endocrine system	1,110	1,320
39,850	34,490	Lymphoma	10,490	10,020
11,190	8,730	Myeloma†	5,640	5,050
25,180	19,090	Leukemia	12,460	9,250
15,400	16,090	Other & unspecified‡	24,330	20,760

Despite these depressing figures, a 2007 analysis by several federal health agencies showed that cancer deaths declined by an average of 2% per year from 2002–04, thanks to advances in prevention, early detection, and treatment. ❦ † An incurable cancer of the plasma cells. ‡ According to the ACS, the number of deaths is higher than the number of cases due to a lack of specificity on death certificates.

———————SOME HEALTH STORIES OF NOTE———————

{SEPT 2007} · After analyzing the drinking habits of 70,033 women, US researchers found that all types of alcohol (wine, beer, and liquor) equally raised breast cancer risk. Women who consumed >3 drinks a day were found to be 30% more likely to develop cancer. ❦ A British study of >10,000 civil servants found that those who reduced the time they slept to <5 hours during the 8-year study period were twice as likely to die from a heart attack. ❦ A British study published in the *Lancet* found that children given drinks with artificial colors and the common preservative sodium benzoate were significantly more hyperactive than those given a placebo. {OCT} · A government study found that, in 2005, US infections from meticillin-resistant *Staphylococcus aureus* (MRSA) caused more deaths than AIDS [see p.111]. ❦ A 5-year University of Pennsylvania study of head and neck cancer patients found that their emotional well-being had no impact on their survival. ❦ Management researchers at the University of East Anglia found that swearing at the office can be a boon for the workplace, since cursing was found to relieve stress and build solidarity. ❦ A study of 740 Taiwanese men published in the *Archives of Dermatology* found that those who smoked >20 cigarettes a day were more than twice as likely to have moderate or severe male pattern baldness. ❦ Microbiology researchers in New York demonstrated that the flu is more common in winter because the virus particles are more stable in cold, dry air: viruses like it no warmer than 41°F, with no more than 20% humidity. {NOV} · After analyzing thousands of studies on the links

Cell phone

between diet, lifestyle, and cancer, scientists at the American Institute for Cancer Research and the World Cancer Research Fund recommended being 'as lean as possible', limiting red meat, and reducing alcohol intake to avoid cancer. ❦ Researchers at the CDC and National Cancer Institute discovered that overweight people have a lower death rate compared to those who are of normal weight, underweight, or obese, largely because they are less likely to die of Alzheimer's, Parkinson's, infections, or lung disease. ❦ A report in *Newsday* said US doctors have begun noticing an alarming rise in cases of rickets, the soft-bone disease that afflicted starving children in the C19th. According to bone specialists, this rise is likely due to a lack of sunshine, milk, and exercise among today's children. In response, scientists at Cincinnati Children's Hospital began a national study to track the bone growth of 1,500 children, to help develop a set of guidelines for healthy bone density. {DEC} · Health Canada found that directly inhaled cannabis smoke contains 20× the ammonia and 5× the nitrogen oxide of regular (tobacco) cigarettes. {JAN 2008} · A study sponsored by a Swiss bank found that concentrated samples of the flu virus, such as those mixed with mucus, can survive on banknotes for as long as 2·5 weeks. ❦ Research funded by the Mobile Manufacturers Forum found that a group exposed to cell phone radiation before bed took longer to enter certain stages of sleep, and spent less time in the deepest sleep stages, compared to those under control conditions. ❦ A study of 1,063 pregnant women published in the *Journal*

—————— SOME HEALTH STORIES OF NOTE cont. ——————

of Obstetrics and Gynecology reported that those who consumed >200mg of caffeine a day (*c.*10oz of coffee and 25oz of tea) had twice the miscarriage rate of those who consumed no caffeine. ❦ A British analysis of 45 studies, published in the *Lancet*, found that women who took the birth control pill greatly reduced their risk of developing ovarian cancer. According to the researchers, a woman reduces her risk by *c.*20% for every 5 years on the pill. ❦ The *New York Times* commissioned a study on the levels of mercury in tuna sushi at NYC restaurants; it found that eating 6 pieces a week would likely exceed the mercury limits deemed safe by the EPA. The study also found that 5 of the restaurants sold tuna with mercury levels high enough for the FDA to take action. ❦ A study in the *New England Journal of Medicine* found that German men were 2·66 times more likely than normal to have heart attacks on the days Germany played in the 2006 soccer World Cup. {FEB} · Baxter International recalled all doses of Heparin Sodium, used as a blood thinner, after a contaminant was found in a Chinese-made active ingredient. At the time of the recall, the contaminated drugs were linked to severe allergic reactions and *c.*20 deaths. {MAR} · The CDC said about 26% of US teenage girls are infected with at least one STD. ❦ A University of California researcher said the 'Gulf War syndrome' reported by some veterans may have been caused by exposure to acetylcholinesterase inhibitors, found in pesticides and in pills given to soldiers to protect them from nerve gas. {APR} · A study that tracked the food consumed by

700 pregnant women, published in the *Proceedings of the Royal Society*, found that those who consumed higher amounts of calories and potassium were more likely to give birth to boys. {MAY} · Research from Harvard Medical School found that a period of starvation can help travelers adjust their circadian rhythms; those wishing to avoid jet lag were advised to fast for *c.*16 hours before their arrival. ❦ A study sponsored by the Pan American Health Org. predicted that deaths from cervical cancer could double in Latin America and the Caribbean by 2030; 20–30% of women in the region were found to have the virus that causes the disease. {JUN} · Univ. of Wisconsin researchers found that middle-aged mice given low doses of resveratrol (a plant polyphenol found in grapes, pomegranates, and red wine) showed anti-aging benefits similar to mice who were put on restricted-calorie diets. ❦ The Intl Diabetes Fed. (IDF) reported that *c.*40% of those with sleep apnea also have diabetes, while *c.*23% of diabetics have apnea. The link was so strong the IDF urged doctors to test all patients with one condition for the other. ❦ An AP/AOL poll of adults who reported high levels of stress associated with debt found that 27% also reported ulcers or digestive tract problems, 44% migraines or headaches, and 23% severe depression. {JUL} · The director of the Univ. of Pittsburgh Cancer Institute sent a cautionary memo to faculty and staff regarding cell phones. Citing early, unpublished data on cancer risk, he warned that children should only use cell phones for emergencies, and that adults should use headsets or speakerphone.

Red Wine

———————————————— STRESS ————————————————

32% of Americans report regularly experiencing 'extreme stress' – according to an October 2007 survey by the American Psychological Association. 48% said their stress level had increased in the past 5 years. Below are the most commonly cited sources of significant stress, and the most commonly reported physical symptoms:

Source of stress	*% reporting*	*Symptom†*	*% reporting in past month*
Work	74	Fatigue	51
Money	73	Headaches	44
Workload	66	Upset stomach &c.	34
Children	64	Muscle tension	30
Family	60	Appetite change	23
Own health	55	Teeth grinding	17
Partner/child health	55	Sex drive change	15
Other family health	53	Dizziness/feeling faint	13
Housing costs	51	No physical symptoms	16
Intimate relationships	47	† Symptoms experienced as a result of stress	

When asked how stress had affected them within the past month, 54% of Americans said it caused them to fight with someone close to them; 48% said they had lain awake at night; and 43% said they ate too much. Only 28% of Americans said they were managing their stress 'extremely well'.

———————————————— ADHD ————————————————

4·5m US children aged 3–17 had Attention Deficit Hyperactivity Disorder (ADHD†) in 2006, according to the latest information from the CDC. Listed below are the percentages of children ever diagnosed with ADHD, by demographic characteristic:

3–17s ever diagnosed with ADHD	*%*		*%*
♂	10·7	Hispanic or Latino	5·1
♀	4·0	*Lived with* mother & father	5·9
3–4 years old‡	0·6	– mother, no father	11·1
5–11 years old	7·4	– father, no mother	8·6
12–17 years old	9·7	– neither mother nor father	10·7
White	7·6	*Family income* <$20,000	9·7
Black or African American	7·4	– $20,000–34,999	8·1
Asian‡	1·5	– $35,000–54,999	7·1
Black or Af. Amer. & White	20·7	– $55,000–74,999	8·8
A. Ind. or Al. Native & White‡	10·8	– ≥$75,000	6·8
		TOTAL US	7·4

† According to the *Diagnostic & Statistical Manual of Mental Disorders* (DSM-IV-TR), 'the essential feature of Attention-Deficit/Hyperactivity Disorder is a persistent pattern of inattention and/or hyperactivity-impulsivity' at levels higher than expected for a person's developmental stage. Symptoms must have been present before age 7, must display themselves in at least 2 settings (i.e., home and school), must clearly interfere with 'social, academic, or occupational functioning', and must not occur exclusively as part of another mental disorder. ‡ Results may be unreliable due to a small sample size.

──────── MRSA & HAND WASHING ────────

2007 saw an alarming spike in reports of meticillin-resistant *Staphylococcus aureus* (MRSA). According to the CDC, there were *c*.94,000 serious MRSA infections in 2007 – *c*.86% were health-care-associated and 14% were community-associated. In total, *c*.19,000 deaths were linked to MRSA. ❦ *Staphylococcus aureus* is a bacterium that *c*.33% of people carry on their skin with no ill effects, though it can cause serious infections if it enters the body, particularly if an individual is undergoing surgery or has a compromised immune system. Meticillin-resistant *Staphylococcus aureus* are strains that have developed resistance to the most common antibiotics. First isolated in the 1960s (when the antibiotic meticillin was introduced), MRSA has become more prevalent since the 1990s. Because MRSA (and similar infections) are spread by cross infection, recent attempts to minimize their impact have focused on hospital cleanliness and hand-hygiene. Doctors, nurses, patients, and visitors are encouraged to ensure that their hands are rigorously washed (sometimes with an alcohol rub) before and after each patient contact. Below is a guide to the most effective method of hand washing, issued by the British Royal College of Nursing:

1. Palm to palm.

2. Right palm over left dorsum and left palm over right dorsum.

3. Palm to palm, fingers interlaced.

4. Backs of fingers to opposing palms with fingers interlocked.

5. Rotational rubbing of right thumb clapsed in left hand, and vice versa.

6. Rotational rubbing, backwards and forwards with clasped fingers of right hand in left palm, and vice versa.

Although 92% of American adults *say* they always wash their hands after using a public washroom, only 77% actually do – according to a 2007 investigation by the American Society for Microbiology and the Soap and Detergent Association†. Furthermore, only 86% say they always wash their hands after using the bathroom when at home; 25% after handling money; and 34% after coughing or sneezing.

† Observers monitored 6,076 adults at Turner Field in Atlanta, the Museum of Science & Industry and Shedd Aquarium in Chicago, Penn Station and Grand Central Station in New York, and the Ferry Building Marketplace in San Francisco. In total, 88% of women and 66% of men washed their hands. Both genders washed more frequently 2 years ago: 75% of men, and 90% of women in 2005.

———————————————— DRINKING ————————————————

Below are the latest (2006) DOH figures for the alcohol consumption of those ≥18:

Characteristic	All %	♂ %	♀ %
DRINKERS	60·8	67·4	54·9
regular	48·0	57·6	39·2
infrequent	12·4	9·2	15·5
light	67·5	58·7	77·5
moderate	24·2	33·1	14·0
heavy	8·3	8·1	8·4
NON-DRINKERS	39·1	32·7	45·0
lifetime abstainers	25·0	17·8	31·5
former drinkers	14·1	14·9	13·5

———————————— SMOKING WORLDWIDE ————————————

There are more than 1 billion smokers in the world, according to a February 2008 report on tobacco usage released by the World Health Organization (WHO). The WHO found 80% of the world's smokers currently reside in low- or middle-income countries, and that ⅔rds of the world's smokers live in one of these 10 countries:

	% adults who smoke†				
	♂	♀	US	28	19
			Japan	43	12
China	57	3	Brazil	20	13
India	33	1	Bangladesh	41	2
Indonesia	63	5	Germany	33	22
Russian Federation†	60	16	Turkey	52	17

The report also noted the price of cigarettes in each of the countries listed above:

China	$1·92	Japan	$2·46	[Cost for a pack of 20 of the
India	$7·04	Brazil	$1·29	most popular brand, in inter-
Indonesia	$2·32	Bangladesh	$1·38	national dollars – which have
Russ. Fed.	$1·53	Germany	$5·01	the same purchasing power as
US	$3·89	Turkey	$4·31	a US dollar has domestically.]

The most affordable cigarettes are apparently to be found in Laos, where a pack of 20 costs just 22¢.
† Percent who smoke daily; other information unavailable. All figures drawn from 2001–06 surveys.

According to the most recent CDC data, in 2007, 20% of US adults were smokers (defined as those who had consumed >100 cigarettes in their life and now smoked 'every day or some days'). The percentage of smokers in various groups is below:

TOTAL US	20%	18–44 years old	23%	Hispanic/Latino	13%
♂	23%	45–64	21%	White	22%
♀	17%	≥65	8%	Black	19%

DRUG SCHEDULES & PENALTIES

The US government organizes drugs into 5 schedules according to: the potential for abuse, its accepted medical use, its safety, and how addictive it is. The schedules, as defined by the Controlled Substances Act of 1970, are summarized below:

I	*high abuse potential; no accepted medical use in the US; lack of safety for use under medical supervision*
II	*high abuse potential; accepted medical use in the US; may lead to severe psychological or physical dependence*
III	*less potential for abuse than I or II; accepted medical use in the US; abuse may lead to moderate or low physical or high psychological dependence*
IV	*low potential for abuse relative to III; accepted medical use in the US; may lead to limited physical or psychological dependence relative to III*
V	*low abuse potential relative to IV; accepted medical use in the US; abuse may lead to limited physical or psychological dependence relative to IV*

Below are selected figures and federal trafficking penalties for some drugs of note:

	Schedule	% use[†]	seizures (kg)	arrests	trafficking penalties (first offense)[‡]
Cocaine	II	2·5	150,739	7,608	*5–40 years prison, ≤$2m fine for 500–4,999g; 10 years–life in prison, ≤$4m fine for ≥5kg*
Heroin	I	0·2	1,774	2,109	*5–40 years prison, ≤$2m fine for 100–999g; 10 years–life in prison, ≤$4m fine for ≥1kg*
Marijuana	I	10·3	1,144,968	5,039	*≤5 years prison, ≤$250,000 fine for >50kg or 1–49 plants; ≤20 years prison or ≤$1m for 50–99kg or 50–99 plants; 5–40 years prison, ≤$2m fine for 100–999kg or100–999 plants; 10 years–life in prison, ≤$4m fine for ≥1,000kg or ≥1,000 plants*
Meth	II	0·8	4,590	2,597	*5–40 years prison, ≤$2m fine for 5–49g (pure) or 50–499g mix; 10 years–life in prison, ≤$4m fine for ≥50g pure or ≥500g mix*
LSD	I	0·3	N/A	25	*5–40 years prison, ≤$2m fine for 1–9g; 10 years–life in prison, ≤$4m fine for ≥10g*

Arrest & seizure data are 2006, the most recent available. † By those ≥12 years old, use within the past year, 2006 data. ‡ First offense by an individual, not involving death or serious injury. [Source: DEA]

CELEBRITY DRUG ABUSE

In a detailed 120-page analysis of the 2007 global drug trade, the UN's International Narcotics Control Board (INCB) included an unexpected comment on celebrity drug abuse. Noting that 'celebrity drug offenders can profoundly influence public attitudes, values, and behavior towards drug abuse', the INCB recommended that criminal justice authorities 'should ensure that public celebrities who violate drug laws are made accountable for their offenses,' arguing that 'cases involving drug-abusing celebrities who are treated more leniently than others breed public cynicism and may lead to youth adopting a more permissive attitude towards illicit drugs'.

──────────── GARBAGE ────────────

Americans produced 251m tons of trash in 2006, of which they recycled 32·5%, according to the latest data from the Environmental Protection Agency. Below are the amounts of trash produced, and percent recycled, by type of material in 2006:

Garbage (millions of tons)	*% recycled*		
85·3......paper/paperboard......	51·6	13·2..............glass............. 21·8
32·4.......yard trimmings.......	62·0	11·8.............textiles .... 15·3
31·3......food/other organic.......	2·2	6·54...... rubber and leather..... 13·3
29·5............ plastics	6·9	4·55......other (in products)..... 24·8
14·2..............steel.............	35·7	3·72.....misc. inorganic waste........–
13·9............ wood	9·4	3·26..........aluminum.......... 21·2
		1·65.........other metals........ 71·5

The amount of trash sent to United States landfills decreased by 4m tons between 1990–2006, thanks to recycling and other efforts. Below are the amounts of trash produced, recycled, incinerated, and sent to landfills over the decades since 1960:

Garbage ... (millions of tons)	1960	1970	1980	1990	2000	2006
Produced	88	121	152	205	238	251
Recycled	6	8	15	29	53	61
Composted[†]	–	–	–	4	17	21
Incinerated[‡]	–	0·4	3	30	34	31
Sent to landfill/other disposal	83	113	134	142	135	138

† Total does not include backyard composting. ‡ Includes only garbage burned to create steam or electricity; garbage incinerated without producing any usable energy is included in 'other disposal'.

──────────── RECYCLING ────────────

77% of Americans recycle at least one type of household item, according to a 2007 report by the Food Marketing Institute. The report found that recycling activity rises with age, education, and income, although no correlation was found between recycling and gender. Below are the percent of Americans who recycle various items:

Aluminum/metal cans .....67% *recycle*	Cardboard............................3
Paper 59	Batteries, fuel oil, hazardous waste ...2
Plastic................................57	Organic materials (food &c.).........2
Glass.................................51	Other...................................3

15% of all respondents said that recycling wasn't available where they live (20% of respondents said so in the South). Some other top reasons given for not recycling:

Too much effort.... 12% *of respondents*	It's too difficult........................5
Costs more...........................12	No recycling center nearby...........5
I don't believe it makes an impact...11	No pickup in our area 4
I'm too busy...........................6	Apt. doesn't provide separate bins....3

——VIOLENT CRIME——

*c.*1,417,745 violent crimes occurred in the US in 2006, a 1·9% increase over 2005. Below are the number of violent and other crimes committed, by type†:

Property crime 9,983,568
Larceny/theft 6,607,013
Burglary 2,183,746
Motor vehicle theft 1,192,809
Aggravated assault 860,853
Robbery 447,403
Forcible rape 92,455
Murder & manslaughter 17,034

† Table data reflects a police reporting practice in which only the most serious offense in a multiple-offense criminal incident is counted.

[Source: *Crime in the US*, 2006]

——————MURDER——————

An estimated 17,034 people were murdered in the United States in 2006, a rise of 1·8% over 2005. Below are the number of people murdered in 2006, listed by selected circumstances:

Arguments, other 3,607
Robbery 1,041
Juvenile gang killings 865
Narcotic drug felony 796
Argument over money/property... 198
Brawl due to alcohol 107
Romantic triangle 103
Brawl due to narcotics 51
Rape 32
Arson 27
Child killed by babysitter 27
Institutional killings 22
Prostitution/commercialized vice.....8
Gambling 4
Sniper attack 2

[Source: *Crime in the US, 2006*]

——— LAW ENFORCERS———

Total law enforcement [2006]	987,125
– ♂	72·9%
– ♀	27·1%
– *civilians*	(30·8%) 303,729
– *sworn officers*	(69·2%) 683,396

Sworn officers are those *'who ordinarily carry a firearm and a badge, have full arrest powers, and are paid from governmental funds set aside specifically for sworn law enforcement representatives'*. [Source: *Crime in the US*, 2006]

———MIRANDA RIGHTS———

In *Miranda* vs *Arizona* (1966) the Supreme Court ruled that before police questioning, suspects must be informed of their right to remain silent, their right to an attorney, and that anything they say may be used against them in court. The warning was named for 23-year-old laborer Ernesto Miranda, who in 1963 confessed to rape and kidnapping without being informed of these rights, and was convicted with his confession as the sole evidence. Contrary to popular (TV- and film-exacerbated) belief, suspects need not be read these rights ('Mirandized') during every arrest, but only before being interrogated.

—BEST-DRESSED POLICE—

Some 2007 'Best-Dressed' awards from the National Association of Uniform Manufacturers & Distributors:

State Agency: WA State Patrol (peaked dark blue hat, bow tie, powder blue pants) · *County Dept*: New Hanover, NC (tan pants & shirt, brown tie) · *University Police*: Vincennes, IN (navy blue shirt & pants) · *City* ≥*200 Officers*: Independence, MO (blue shirt and black tie, optional turtleneck)

---------------------- US PRISON POPULATION ----------------------

America tipped over a significant penal threshold on January 1, 2008, when, for the first time, more than 1 in 100 of all US adults were confined in an American jail or prison. This disturbing statistic was reported in February 2008 by the Pew Public Safety Performance Project, which concluded that such levels of incarceration were 'saddling cash-strapped states with soaring costs they can ill afford and failing to have a clear impact either on recidivism or overall crime'. Pew's calculation was thus:

(Prison population + Jail population) / Adult population = Incarceration Rate
          1,596,127   723,131   229,786,080   99·1

Below is Pew's breakdown of 2006 Justice Dept data, which illustrates the startling disparity in incarceration rates by gender, age, and ethnicity – e.g., the incarceration rate for black men 20–24 was 1 in 9; for white men the same age it was 1 in 60.

Rate incarcerated (1 in x)	ALL				MEN				WOMEN			
	All	White	Black	Hispanic	All	White	Black	Hispanic	All	White	Black	Hispanic
All ages	133	245	41	96	72	136	21	54	746	1,064	279	658
All 18+	102	194	29	64	54	106	15	36	580	859	203	436
18–19	101	191	36	85	57	107	19	47	833	1,235	382	571
20–24	53	103	17	41	30	60	9	24	345	453	157	289
25–29	53	104	17	43	30	59	9	26	333	443	140	328
30–34	54	92	17	47	30	53	9	27	270	343	108	300
35–39	63	104	19	55	36	61	10	32	265	355	100	297
40–44	76	124	24	66	43	71	13	38	352	500	125	358
45–54	153	266	45	101	83	148	23	55	893	1,333	307	709
55+	837	1,249	264	383	391	588	115	184	8,333	11,111	3,571	3,846

The Pew report also offered a range of insights into the financial costs of incarceration, noting that total state spending on corrections was $12bn in 1987, $49bn in 2007, and is estimated to be $74bn by 2011. In 2007, 13 states spent >$1bn of their general funds on correctional systems; California topped the list, spending $8·8bn. In an interesting comparison of spending in different spheres, Pew reported that 4 states spent more on correctional systems than they did on higher education; for every $1 Vermont spent on higher education, it spent $1·37 on corrections. The latest (2005) data indicate that it costs an average of $23,876 to keep a prisoner locked up for a year, though this figure varies widely by state – from Rhode Island which spends $44,860 per inmate per year, to Louisana which spends just $13,009. For comparison, below are the incarceration rates of selected countries worldwide:

Rate per 100,000 population		
USA 762	UK (England & Wales) .. 144	Switzerland 76
Russian Fed......... 635	Australia 130	Japan 63
Israel................ 319	Canada 108	Iceland................ 36
Iran 222	Germany 91	India.................. 32
Mexico 196	France 91	[Source: International Center
	Italy................... 83	for Prison Studies; years vary]

─────── CAPITAL PUNISHMENT ───────

Executions in the US were halted on 9/25/2007, when the Supreme Court agreed to hear *Baze* vs *Rees*, case no. 07-5439. At issue was the constitutionality of Kentucky's method of lethal injection. Two of the state's death row inmates asked the court to rule whether Kentucky's method of lethal injection constituted 'cruel and unusual punishment', prohibited by the 8th Amendment. Like most states that sanction lethal injection, Kentucky uses a cocktail of 3 chemicals (Sodium Pentathol, pancuronium bromide, and potassium chloride); among other issues, critics have noted that the paralysis produced by pancuronium bromide prevents the condemned from expressing pain if improperly anesthetized. On 4/16/08, the court upheld Kentucky's method, 7–2. In the main opinion, Chief Justice Roberts noted all methods of execution pose some pain risk, and that in order to prove a method unconstitutional, a petitioner has to show other 'feasible' and 'readily implemented' methods that would clearly reduce the risk of severe pain. Yet 6 of the 7 justices in the majority wrote separate opinions, suggesting less-than-universal support for lethal injection. Thus, it seems likely this issue will be revisited.

At right is a snapshot of the death penalty in the US. It shows: the methods allowed by state statute; state minimum age; the death row population at 1/1/2008; the numbers executed since 1976, and in 2007; and the 2006 murder rate per 100,000. † NE ruled electrocution illegal 2/08, but has not replaced it with another method. ‡ NJ abolished the death penalty 12/2007.

Key to table – Lethal [I]njection · [G]assing [E]lectrocution · [H]anging · [F]iring squad
ns=not stated · *na*=not applicable
[Sources: DoJ; FBI; Death Penalty Info. Cntr]

	legal methods	minimum age	on death row	executed post '76	executed in '07	murder rate '06
AL	I·E	16	203	38	3	8·3
AK	·	·	·	·	·	5·4
AZ	I·G	ns	126	23	1	7·5
AR	I·E	14	40	27	0	7·3
CA	I·G	18	667	13	0	6·8
CO	I	18	2	1	0	3·3
CT	I	18	9	1	0	3·1
DC	·	·	·	·	·	29·1
DE	I·H	16	19	14	0	4·9
FL	I·E	17	397	65	0	6·2
GA	I	17	107	42	1	6·4
HI	·	·	·	·	·	1·6
ID	I·F	ns	19	1	0	2·5
IL	I	18	13	12	0	6·1
IN	I	18	19	19	2	5·8
IA	·	·	·	·	·	1·8
KS	I	18	9	0	0	4·6
KY	I·E	16	39	2	0	4·0
LA	I	ns	88	27	0	12·4
ME	·	·	·	·	·	1·7
MD	I·G	18	6	5	0	9·7
MA	·	·	·	·	·	2·9
MI	·	·	·	·	·	7·1
MN	·	·	·	·	·	2·4
MS	I	16	64	10	0	7·7
MO	I·G	16	48	66	0	6·3
MT	I	ns	2	3	0	1·8
NE	E†	18	10	3	0	2·8
NV	I	18	77	12	0	9·0
NH	I·H	17	0	0	0	1·0
NJ‡	I	18	0	0	0	4·9
NM	I	18	2	1	0	6·8
NY	I	18	0	0	0	4·8
NC	I	17	173	43	0	6·1
ND	·	·	·	·	·	1·3
OH	I	18	188	26	2	4·7
OK	I·E·F	13	84	87	3	5·8
OR	I	18	35	2	0	2·3
PA	I	ns	228	3	0	5·9
RI	·	·	·	·	·	2·6
SC	I·E	ns	63	39	1	8·3
SD	I	18	3	1	1	1·2
TN	I·E	18	102	4	2	6·8
TX	I	17	373	410	26	5·9
UT	I·F	14	9	6	0	1·8
VT	·	·	·	·	·	1·9
VA	I·E	14	21	102	0	5·2
WA	I·H	18	9	4	0	3·3
WV	·	·	·	·	·	4·1
WI	·	·	·	·	·	3·0
WY	I·G	18	2	1	0	1·7
Fed.	I	18	51	3	0	na
USA	na	na	3,309	1,116	42	5·7

──────── MILITARY FUNERALS ────────

The Dept of Defense states that 'rendering military funeral honors reflects the high regard and respect accorded to military service and demonstrates military professionalism to the nation and the world'. Thus, 'commanders at all levels must support paying a final tribute on behalf of a grateful nation to comrades in arms, and must respond expeditiously and sensitively to requests for military funeral support'. The US Code specifies that the Secretary of Defense 'shall ensure that, upon request, a funeral honors detail is provided for the funeral of any [eligible†] veteran'. This detail must consist of at least two members of the armed forces, at least one of whom must be a member of the deceased's force. ('Each member of the armed forces in the detail shall wear the uniform of the member's armed force while serving in the detail.') At its most basic, a US military funeral ceremony must have the following two components:

Folding & presenting the flag

The Dept of Veterans Affairs issues, on request, one flag per eligible veteran – usually to the next of kin, by order of precedence: surviving spouse; children (by age); parents (including adoptive, step-, and foster parents); brothers or sisters (including half brothers or sisters); uncles or aunts; nephews or nieces; and others (e.g., cousins or grandparents). When placed on or in a casket, the folded flag should be positioned above the deceased's left shoulder; during the commitment ceremony, the flag is held waist high over the grave, and is folded immediately after *Taps*. The flag should not be lowered into the grave nor allowed to touch the ground.

Playing of *Taps*

Taps is a 24-note bugle call now played at all military funerals‡. Its origins are somewhat disputed, but the Dept of Veterans Affairs dates its introduction as a curfew signal to the Civil War, crediting its composition to Union General Daniel Adams Butterfield. In 1862, Butterfield adapted the French curfew call *Tattoo* to replace the existing (and similarly French) curfew call, *L'Extinction des feux*. It seems that *Taps* was first used as a funeral call soon after this, and, in 1891, it was ordered that *Taps* be played at all military funerals. Because of a dearth of bugle players, military regulations now permit *Taps* to be 'performed' at funerals by tape.

The flag is folded lengthways twice (ensuring the stars are visible), before a sequence of triangular folds is made from the right, until the flag's shape is that of a tricorn hat.

In 1963, Army bugler Sergeant Keith Clark became famous for his imperfect rendering of *Taps* at the funeral of John F. Kennedy. Under the pressure of the moment, Clark hit the 6th note off-key – an accident that many commentators thought epitomized the emotion of the event, like a voice cracking with grief. † Military members on active duty or in the selected reserve; former military members who served on active duty and departed under conditions other than dishonorable; former military members who completed at least one term of enlistment or period of initial obligated service in the selected reserve and departed under conditions other than dishonorable; former military members discharged from the selected reserve due to a disability incurred or aggravated in the line of duty. ‡ *Taps* is also played 'to accompany the lowering of the flag and to signal the "lights out" command at day's end'.

Media & Celebrity

One of the drawbacks of fame is that one can never escape from it.
— NELLIE MELBA (1861–1931)

———————— 'PEOPLE' & 'US WEEKLY' COVER STARS ————————

Date	People	Us Weekly
1·07·08	No issue published	Britney & Jamie Lynn Spears
1·14·08	People who lost 'half their size'	Lauren Conrad & LeAnn Rimes
1·21·08	Britney Spears	Britney Spears
1·28·08	Matthew McConaughey	Trista Sutter
2·04·08	Heath Ledger	Miley Cyrus
2·11·08	Michelle Williams & Heath Ledger	Heath Ledger
2·18·08	Britney Spears	Britney Spears
2·25·08	Christina Aguilera & Max Liron	Michelle Williams
3·03·08	Tori Spelling & Liam	Sean & Jayden Federline
3·10·08	Nicole Richie & Harlow	Jennifer Aniston
3·17·08	Drew Barrymore & Justin Long	Heidi Montag
3·24·08	Patrick Swayze	Ashlee Simpson
3·31·08	Jennifer Lopez, Max & Emme Muñiz	Lauren Conrad
4·07·08	Mariah Carey	Reese Witherspoon
4·14·08	Heath Ledger	Britney Spears
4·21·08	Beyoncé Knowles	Beyoncé Knowles
4·28·08	Texas polygamy sect	Mariah Carey
5·05·08	Miley Cyrus	Shiloh Jolie-Pitt
5·12·08	Kate Hudson	Jennifer Aniston & John Mayer
5·19·08	Mariah Carey & Nick Cannon	Heidi Montag & Lauren Conrad
5·26·08	Jenna Bush [see p.328]	Jessica Simpson
6·02·08	Ashlee Simpson & Pete Wentz	Christina Aguilera
6·09·08	Shania Twain	Heidi Montag
6·16·08	Jodie Sweetin	Jessica Simpson & Tony Romo
6·23·08	Elizabeth Smart	Andrew Firestone & Ivana Bozilovic
6·30·08	Tim Russert	Michelle & Barack Obama
7·07·08	Heather Locklear	Reese Witherspoon
7·14·08	Anne Hathaway	Madonna & Guy Ritchie
7·21·08	Nicole Kidman & Keith Urban	Madonna & Alex Rodriguez
7·28·08	Brad Pitt & Angelina Jolie	Reese Witherspoon & Jake Gyllenhaal
8·04·08	Obama family	Angelina Jolie & Brad Pitt
8·11·08	Caylee Anthony	Halle Berry
8·18·08	Angelina Jolie, Brad Pitt, & twins	Christina Applegate
8·25·08	Elizabeth Edwards	Jennifer Love Hewitt

[Heath Ledger was featured on more *People* covers than any other celebrity in the months above.]

—SOME HATCHED, MATCHED, & DISPATCHED · 2007–08—

HATCHED

Harlow Winter Kate	*born to* Nicole Richie & Joel Madden
Max Liron	Christina Aguilera & Jordan Bratman
Usher Raymond V	Tameka Foster & Usher
Thomas Boone & Zoe Grace	Kimberly & Dennis Quaid
Olive	Isla Fisher & Sacha Baron Cohen
Valentina Paloma	Salma Hayek & François-Henri Pinault
Maximilian David & Emme Maribel	Jennifer Lopez & Marc Anthony
Honor Marie	Jessica Alba & Cash Warren
Stella Doreen	Tori Spelling & Dean McDermott
Knox Leon & Vivienne Marcheline	Angelina Jolie & Brad Pitt
Sunday Rose	Nicole Kidman & Keith Urban
Ignatius Martin	Cate Blanchett & Andrew Upton
Levi Alves	Matthew McConaughey & Camila Alves
Clementine Jane	Ethan Hawke & Ryan Shawhughes

MATCHED

Pamela Anderson & Rick Salomon	Las Vegas
Eli Manning & Abby McGrew	Cabo San Lucas, Mexico
Beyoncé Knowles & Shawn 'Jay-Z' Carter	New York City
Jessica Alba & Cash Warren	Beverly Hills
Ashlee Simpson & Pete Wentz	Los Angeles
Mariah Carey & Nick Cannon	Bahamas
Katherine Heigl & Josh Kelley	Park City, Utah

(On New Year's Day 2008, Eddie Murphy and Tracey Edmonds held a 'spiritual' wedding ceremony on a private French Polynesian island, but split 2 weeks later. The marriage was never legally binding.)

DISPATCHED

Liv Tyler & Royston Langdon (*married for* 5 years)	separated
Shania Twain & Robert Lange (14 years)	separated
Cynthia & Alex Rodriguez (5 years)	filed for divorce
Bill Murray & Jennifer Butler (11 years)	divorced
Robin & Marcia Williams (19 years)	filed for divorce
Star Jones & Al Reynolds (3 years)	filed for divorce

——————— PORTMANTEAU CELEBRITY NAMES ———————

The recent craze for combining celebrity couples' names probably started *c.*2002 with the Lopez/Affleck conglomerate 'Bennifer'. It shows little sign of abating, to wit:

Bennifer	*Ben Affleck & Jennifer Lopez*	Spederline	*Britney Spears &*
Billary	*Bill & Hillary Clinton*		*Kevin Federline*
Brangelina	*Brad Pitt & Angelina Jolie*	Speidi	*Spencer Pratt & Heidi Montag*
Garfleck	*Jennifer Garner & Ben Affleck*	TomKat	*Tom Cruise & Katie Holmes*
KatPee	*Kate Moss & Pete Doherty*	Vinnifer	*Vince Vaughn & J. Aniston*

————————— CELEBRITY CHARITY —————————

Raising money for and awareness of various causes has long been an obligatory component of Hollywood celebrity, and the trend showed no sign of slowing in 2008. Below are some celebrities of note and a selection of the causes they support:

Angelina Jolie ...... Goodwill Ambassador for UNHCR; Education Partnership for Children of Conflict; Global Action for Children; Daniel Pearl Foundation
Brad Pitt................Make It Right [rebuilding the Lower Ninth Ward in New Orleans]
Madonna...................................Raising Malawi Orphan Care Initiative
George Clooney...............................UN Messenger of Peace for Darfur
Bono........(RED)†; ONE Campaign [AIDS, poverty]; DATA [Debt, AIDS, Trade, Africa]
Tyra Banks .... TZONE Foundation [female self-empowerment]
Denis Leary ....Leary Firefighters Foundation [funding for equipment, &c.]
Fergie...........................Safer sex/lip-gloss campaign for M·A·C AIDS Fund
Jon Bon Jovi.......Philadelphia Soul Charitable Foundation [poverty & homelessness]
Nicole Kidman........US Committee for the UN Development Fund for Women
Jessica Simpson .... Operation Smile [corrective facial surgery]
Kanye West...............Kanye West Foundation [encouraging high school graduation]
Salma Hayek.................... One Pack = One Vaccine [inoculations against tetanus]

† Since January 2006, (RED)-branded products from Gap, Armani, Apple, Motorola, Converse, Hallmark, American Express, and Dell have appeared on store shelves, in TV ads, and splashed on billboards in major cities. The initiative, cofounded by Bono, funnels a portion of the profits from these red-hued products towards the Global Fund to Fight AIDS, Tuberculosis, and Malaria. However, some have expressed concern as to whether the extensive advertising for (RED) products may, in the final analysis, cost more than the project can raise. [Sources: Sixdegrees.org; LooktotheStars.org]

————————— CELEBRITY BUSINESSES —————————

In April 2008, rapper Kanye West launched a company called Kanye Travel Ventures, to provide airline, hotel, and car reservations for 'Kanye's world-wide fan base'. Below are some other celebrity business ventures, successful and otherwise:

Bo Derek...........................Bless the Beasts [shampoo, fragrance, &c., for dogs]
David Lynch ....David Lynch Signature Cup [coffee]
Francis Ford Coppola.......*Zoetrope: All-Story* [lit magazine]; Rubicon Estate winery
Jay-Z................................The 40/40 Club [sports bars]; Rocawear [clothing]
Jimmy Buffett..........Margaritaville Cafes, drink mixes, salsa, lager, T-shirts, &c.
Lenny Kravitz.................................... Kravitz Design Inc. [interior design]

While not a celebrity business per se, Ben & Jerry's is known for producing ice-cream flavors in collaboration with various celebrities and other figures. Comedian Stephen Colbert has been honored with the vanilla-and-fudge 'AmeriCone Dream'; rock band Phish inspired the chocolate-marshmallow-caramel 'Phish Food'; the Grateful Dead were honored with the creation of 'Cherry Garcia', and the film *Napoleon Dynamite* inspired the cherry & chocolate 'Neapolitan Dynamite'. In July 2008, the company also honored Elton John with a limited-edition batch of 'Goodbye Yellow Brickle Road'.

CELEBRITY RANKINGS & LISTS

FORBES CELEBRITY POWER RANKING
The most powerful media figures in 2008:

1 . . . . Oprah Winfrey
2 . . . . Tiger Woods
3 . . . . Angelina Jolie
4 . . . . . Beyoncé Knowles
5 . . . . David Beckham
6 . . . . Johnny Depp
7 . . . . Jay-Z
8 . . . . The Police
9 . . . . J.K. Rowling
10 . . . . Brad Pitt

PEOPLE's 100 MOST BEAUTIFUL
Kate Hudson was *People* magazine's most beautiful celebrity in 2008. The issue also featured a list of celebs who have appeared most often in *People* over the years:

Halle Berry . . . . . 12 *times*
Nicole Kidman 9
George Clooney 8
Jennifer Lopez 8
Brad Pitt 8
Angelina Jolie 6
M. McConaughey 5
Johnny Depp 5
Alicia Keys 5
Beyoncé Knowles 5
Jessica Simpson 5

MAXIM's HOT 100
1 . . . . Marisa Miller
2 . . . . . Scarlett Johansson
3 . . . . Jessica Biel
4 . . Eva Longoria Parker
5 . Sarah Michelle Gellar
6 . . . . . . Elisha Cuthbert
7 . . . . Eva Mendes

8 . . . . . Christina Aguilera
9 . . . . Lindsay Lohan
10 . . . . Ashley Tisdale

FHM's SEXIEST ♀
1 . . . . Megan Fox
2 . . . . Jessica Biel
3 . . . . Jessica Alba
4 . . . . . . Elisha Cuthbert
5 . . . . Scarlett Johansson
6 . Emmanuelle Chriqui
7 . . . . Hilary Duff
8 . . . . Tricia Helfer
9 . . . . Blake Lively
10 . . . . . . Kate Beckinsale

PEOPLE's SEXIEST ♂
1 . . . . Matt Damon
2 . . . . . . Patrick Dempsey
3 . . . . Ryan Reynolds
4 . . . . Brad Pitt
5 . . . . James McAvoy
6 . . . . Johnny Depp
7 . . . . Dave Annable
8 . . . . Will Smith
9 . . . . Javier Bardem
10 . . . . . . Shemar Moore

COSMOPOLITAN'S FUN FEARLESS MALES
John Mayer · Chris Brown · Dave Annable Dane Cook · James McAvoy · Tony Romo John Krasinski · Dave Salmoni · Common Peter Krause · Tom Anderson · Zac Efron

MODEL.COM'S SEXIEST MODELS
1 . . . . Heidi Klum
2 . . . . . . Gisele Bündchen
3 . . . . Adriana Lima
4 . . . . Tyra Banks
5 . . . . Karolina Kurkova

AOL'S UNSEXIEST ♂
1 . . . . Pete Doherty
2 . . . . Brandon Davis
3 . . . Wilmer Valderrama
4 . . . . Simon Cowell
5 . . . . Howard Stern
6 . . . . . . Kevin Connolly
7 . . . . James Blunt
8 . . . . Pete Wentz
9 . . . . . Josh Hartnett [tie]
9 . . . . Ryan Phillippe
10 . . . . Eric Dane

SMARTEST PEOPLE IN HOLLYWOOD
According to *Entertainment Weekly*:

1 . . . . Judd Apatow
2 . . . . . . Steven Spielberg
3 . . . . . . James Cameron
4 . . . . Ari Emanuel
5 . . . . Will Smith

[The *NY Daily News* named Lindsay Lohan and Kim Kardashian the 'dumbest' in Hollywood in response.]

FILM THREAT'S FRIGID 50
The top 5 coldest people in Hollywood in 2007:

1 . . . . George W. Bush
2 . . . . Angelina Jolie
3 . . . . Jim Carrey
4 . . Comedies not associated with Judd Apatow
5 . . . . Owen Wilson

PARADE'S MOST ANNOYING CELEBS
1 . . . . . . Rosie O'Donnell
2 . . . . Paris Hilton
3 . . . . Ann Coulter
4 . . . . Heather Mills
5 . . . . Perez Hilton

VANITY FAIR'S HOLLYWOOD · 2008

The stars featured on the cover of the 2008 *Vanity Fair* 'Hollywood issue' were:

The 2007 cover stars were: Ben Stiller, Owen Wilson, Chris Rock, Jack Black, and some penguins.

HOLLYWOOD'S WORST-DRESSED WOMEN

Former designer Richard Blackwell has compiled his annual 'Worst-Dressed Celebrity List' every year since 1960. In 2007, Victoria Beckham topped the list for wearing 'one skinny-mini monstrosity after another'. Second-placed singer Amy Winehouse was described as 'exploding beehives above, tacky polka-dots below', and Blackwell dismissed actress Mary-Kate Olsen, who came third, as 'a tattered toothpick trapped in a hurricane'. The top 10 for 2007 were as follows:

1 .... Victoria Beckham	6 .... Eva Green
2 .... Amy Winehouse	7 .... Avril Lavigne
3 ....Mary-Kate Olsen	8 .... Jessica Simpson
4 ... Fergie (the singer, not the former Royal)	9 .... Lindsay Lohan
5 .... Kelly Clarkson	10..................... Alison Arngrim

TOP CELEBRITY TOTS

Brad Pitt and Angelina Jolie's children – Shiloh, Zahara, and Pax – took 3 of the top 5 places in *Forbes*'s December 2007 list of most influential celebrity infants (5 and under). The results, assessed by web presence and press clippings, were as follows:

1 .... Shiloh Jolie-Pitt	9 .... Romeo Beckham
2 .... Suri Holmes-Cruise	9 .... Cruz Beckham
3 .... Zahara Jolie-Pitt	
4 ....Sean Preston Federline	† Daughter of Tiger Woods and his wife, Elin.
5 .... Pax Jolie-Pitt	‡ Daughter of Anna Nicole Smith and Larry
6 .... Sam Alexis Woods†	Birkhead. During her short life, Dannielynn
7 .... David Banda Ritchie	has already been the subject of contested pater-
7 ....Dannielynn Hope‡	nity and suffered the tragic death of her mother.

CELEBRITY QUOTES

KATHERINE HEIGL (to *Eve*) · I satisfy my vices instead of fighting them. Mostly just the smoking. Well. There's the drinking and cursing ... ❦ EVA LONGORIA PARKER (to the *Daily Mail*) · I was very dark, scrawny and the only one in my family with black hair. I hated it. ❦ NICOLE KIDMAN (to *Vogue*) · You're either going to walk through life and experience it fully or you're going to be a voyeur. And I'm not a voyeur. ❦ JAMES McAVOY (to *Details*) · I think inside all actors there's a kid who secretly yearns to jump off buildings and say 'Yippeekayay, motherfucker!' ❦ ANGELINA JOLIE (to *Vanity Fair*) · It's very easy to get married, but it's not easy to build a family and be parents together. ❦ AMY WINEHOUSE (to *Rolling Stone*) · I'm young, and I'm in love, and I get my nuts off sometimes. ❦ MADONNA (to *Interview*) · We live very comfortable lives, and unfortunately, we have to have our noses rubbed in other people's pain and suffering to realize how much we have and how much we have to be grateful for. ❦ JENNIFER LOVE HEWITT (on her blog, after comments on bikini photos) · A size 2 is not fat! Nor will it ever be. And being a size 0 doesn't make you beautiful. ❦ RENÉE ZELLWEGER (to *Harper's Bazaar*) · It's weird to have fame precede you in any situation ... and I'm very proud of myself that I've not been to Betty Ford yet ... never say never! ❦ ROSIE O'DONNELL (to *Us Weekly*) · Frankly, most celebrities are annoying ... and I suppose I'm the most annoying [see p.122]. ❦ JANET JACKSON (to *Us Weekly*) · You don't know how many people come up to me and say, 'This child was conceived listening to you'. ❦

Paris Hilton

MADONNA (to Z100-FM) · I'm not sure I can sing 'Holiday' or 'Like a Virgin' ever again ... unless somebody paid me like $30m or something. [Like if] some Russian guy wants me to come to the wedding he's going to have to a 17-year-old. ❦ KATHERINE HEIGL (on her movie *Knocked Up*, to *Vanity Fair*) · [It's] a little sexist. It paints the women as shrews, as humorless and uptight, and it paints the men as lovable, goofy, fun-loving guys. ❦ LINDSAY LOHAN (on nude *New York* magazine photos, to AP) · I didn't have to put much thought into it. I mean, Bert Stern? Doing a Marilyn shoot? When is that ever going to come up? ❦ PARIS HILTON (in Johannesburg, in *People*) · I love Africa in general: South Africa and West Africa, they are both great countries. ❦ SCARLETT JOHANSSON (to AP) · I am engaged ... to Barack Obama. My heart belongs to Barack! ❦ ANG LEE (to AP) · Working with Heath [Ledger] was one of the purest joys of my life. ❦ MILEY CYRUS (on her controversial *Vanity Fair* photos, to *Good Morning America*) · Anyone who was 15 years old can't say they haven't made a mistake. ❦ GUY RITCHIE (to the *Daily Mirror*) · Think of the calories in sugar. Fat kills more people than anything else. Sugar is responsible for a lot of deaths, arguably more than crack cocaine. ❦ SHARON STONE (in the *Guardian*, on China's Tibet policies) · Then all this earthquake ... happened, and I thought, is that karma? When you're not nice, that the bad things happen to you? ❦ BLAKE LIVELY (to *Seventeen*) · I don't dance on tables and I don't like sex tapes. ❦ JESSICA SIMPSON (to *Elle*) · Tony [Romo] understands me. He appreciates my talent. He's the first person I've spiritually connected with.

THE 'BRITNEY INDUSTRIAL COMPLEX'

The bizarre soap opera that is Britney Spears's life continued to fascinate the media throughout 2008, and in its February 2008 issue, *Condé Nast Portfolio* estimated that the annual value of the entire 'Britney industry' could be as much as $120m. Below are some aspects of what *Portfolio* called the 'Britney Industrial Complex':

Sale of 83m records since her debut album in 1999 .... >$400m
Ticket sales on her tours.. $150m
Fee for a Britney appearance .... $250,000–$400,000
Sales of Britney's 3 perfumes: *Believe, Curious,* and *Fantasy* $100m
Paparazzi photos of Britney (average shot fetches $125–$700) ....$250,000–$100,000+
Celebrity magazine covers .... 33% addition to sales

CELEB MAGS

While other forms of print media have fallen into decline, the public appetite for celebrity news and gossip has shown little sign of diminishing. As of the end of 2007, the most prominent 'gossip rags' in the United States, based on circulation, were:

Magazine	circulation† 2007	2006	founded	editor
People	3·67m	3·78m	1974	Martha Nelson
Us Weekly	1·90m	1·77m	1977	Janice Min
Star	1·41m	1·52m	1974	Candace Trunzo
In Touch Weekly	1·29m	1·22m	2002	Richard Spencer
OK!	0·87m	0·64m	2005	Sarah Ivens
Life & Style	0·71m	0·72m	2004	Richard Spencer

† Average total paid circulation, Audit Bureau of Circulation figures. ❦ Over the past years, gossip mags have taken an increasing interest in celebrity pregnancies and have started paying ever-larger sums for exclusive shots of star babies. Recent reported fees include: $15m for Angelina Jolie and Brad Pitt's twins; $6m for Jennifer Lopez and Marc Anthony's twins; $3m for Camila Alves and Matthew McConaughey's son; $1m for Nicole Richie and Joel Madden's daughter; $1·5m for Christina Aguilera and Jordan Bratman's daughter; and $1m for rights to Jamie Lynn Spears's pregnancy story.

TOP-SELLING CELEBRITY COVER STARS

Jennifer Aniston is the star most likely to sell celebrity magazines, according to a *Forbes* analysis of covers stars and copy sales in the first 6 months of 2007. Below are the 10 circulation-boosting celebrity faces (excluding cover collages and special issues):

1 ....Jennifer Aniston	6 ....Katie Holmes	[*Forbes* also incorporated
2 ....Brad Pitt	7 ....Carrie Underwood	the E-Poll Market Research
3 .....Scarlett Johansson	8 ......Jennifer Hudson	'likability' score for each
4 .... Angelina Jolie	8 . Valerie Bertinelli [*tie*]	star, which may help explain
5 ....Reese Witherspoon	10........... Kelly Ripa	Britney Spears's absence.]

MOST-DESIRED CELEB FEATURES

Each year, plastic surgeons Toby G. Mayer and Richard W. Fleming poll their *c.*1,500 clients at the Beverly Hills Institute of Aesthetic & Reconstructive Surgery about the celebrity features they consider to be the most desirable. The 2008 list:

♀	*most desirable feature*	♂
Katherine Heigl, Amy Adams, Nicole Kidman	nose	*Leonardo DiCaprio, Heath Ledger, Jake Gyllenhaal*
Katie Holmes, Megan Fox, Ellen Pompeo	eyes	*Daniel Craig, Brad Pitt, Justin Timberlake*
Angelina Jolie, Jessica Alba, Scarlett Johansson	lips	*Matt Damon, Nick Lachey, John Mayer*
Carrie Underwood, Tyra Banks, Jennifer Love-Hewitt	jaw/chin	*Christian Bale, Will Smith, Ben Affleck*
Keira Knightley, Kate Bosworth, Halle Berry	cheeks	*George Clooney, Johnny Depp, Keanu Reeves*
Jessica Biel, Beyoncé Knowles, Charlize Theron	body	*David Beckham, Hugh Jackman, Matthew McConaughey*
Paris Hilton, Christina Applegate, Heidi Klum	skin	*Ashton Kutcher, Zac Efron, Orlando Bloom*

12m cosmetic operations were performed in the US in 2007, according to the American Society of Plastic Surgeons – 59% more than in 2000. Breast augmentation is the most common procedure.

INSURED BODY PARTS

In March 2008, Dutch wine producer Ilja Gort insured his nose and sense of smell for €5m ($7·7m) at Lloyd's of London, which designed a custom insurance policy especially for him. Other body parts that have been insured for large sums include:

Star	*body part*	*reported amount*
Michael Flatley (Riverdance &c.)	pair of legs	£25m (*c.*$50m)
America Ferrera	smile	$10m†
Keith Richards	hand	£1m (*c.*$2m)
Bruce Springsteen	voice	$1m
Betty Grable	legs	$1m
Marlene Dietrich	voice	$1m
Jamie Lee Curtis	legs	$1m
Dolly Parton	breasts	$600,000
Fred Astaire	legs	$75,000 (per leg)
Jimmy Durante	schnozzle	$50,000

1920s silent movie star Ben Turpin is generally cited as the first celebrity to take out an insurance policy against a body part; he took out a $20,000 insurance policy against his eyes uncrossing. † Aquafresh insured Ferrera's pearly whites in 2007 as part of a marketing campaign to raise money for Smiles for Success, a charity that provides free dental care for women. [Sources: *Times*; ABC News]

AMERICAN IDOL 7

25-year-old 'rock interpreter' and former bartender David Cook was crowned the seventh American Idol on May 21, 2008, in a landslide victory over 17-year-old crooner David Archuleta. Amid declining ratings, the 7th season of the recurring spectacle introduced several changes, including allowing contestants to play their own instruments. Some saw the move as a bonus for the guitar-playing Cook, who became the first male rocker to win the show. As usual, there was an assortment of mini-scandals, including a kerfuffle over Archuleta's father, as well as gaffes from judges (notably 'Castrogate' on 4/29, when Paula Abdul appeared to judge Jason Castro's performance before it began). The top 12 left in the following order:

March 12	David Hernandez	April 23	Carly Smithson
March 19	Amanda Overmyer	April 30	Brooke White
March 26	Chikezie	May 7	Jason Castro
April 2	Ramiele Malubay	May 14	Syesha Mercado
April 10	Michael Johns	Runner-up	David Archuleta
April 16	Kirsty Lee Cook	WINNER	David Cook

DANCING WITH THE STARS 6

Former figure skating champion Kristi Yamaguchi won the mirror-ball trophy in the sixth season of *Dancing With the Stars*, to become the show's first female winner since soap star Kelly Monaco won in the first season. Though earlier criticized for emotionally lackluster performances, Yamaguchi and partner Mark Ballas wowed judges in the finals, earning perfect scores during the final 3 dances (cha-cha, free-style, and jive). The celebrity contestants were eliminated in the following order:

March 25	Penn Jillette	April 29	Shannon Elizabeth
March 25	Monica Seles	May 6	Mario
April 1	Steve Guttenberg	May 13	Marissa Jaret Winokur
April 8	Adam Carolla	May 20	Cristián de la Fuente
April 15	Priscilla Presley	May 20	Jason Taylor
April 22	Marlee Matlin	WINNER	Kristi Yamaguchi

OTHER REALITY SHOW WINNERS

Network	show	winner (prize)
VH1	*Flavor of Love 3*	Thing 2 (Flavor Flav's 'lurve')
The CW	*Top Model 10*	Whitney Thompson (Elite & CoverGirl contracts; *Seventeen* shoot)
CBS	*Survivor: Micronesia*	Parvati Shallow ($1m)
BRAVO	*Top Chef 4*	Stephanie Izard (new kitchen; $100,000; &c.)
NBC	*The Celebrity Apprentice*	Piers Morgan ($250,000 for charity of choice)
BRAVO	*Project Runway 4*	Christian Siriano (*Elle* feature; $100,000; Saturn Astra; &c.)
ABC	*The Bachelor: London Calling*	Shayne Lamas (marriage to Matt Grant)
Fox	*So You Think You Can Dance 4*	Joshua Allen ($250,000, role in *Step Up 3D*)

MISS AMERICA · 2008

The 19-year-old former Miss Michigan, Kirsten Haglund, was crowned Miss America on January 26, 2008. A classic blonde whose grandmother was Miss Michigan in 1944, Haglund aspires to tread the boards on Broadway, and she plans to use the $50,000 prize scholarship to complete a bachelor's degree in musical theater at the University of Cincinnati. During the talent segment of the competition, Haglund sang *Over the Rainbow* clad in an ice-blue gown with a voluminous train; during the interview segment, she cited 'honesty' as an important personal characteristic when discussing sexually transmitted diseases. Haglund will travel *c*.20,000 miles a month during her reign, speaking in support of her platform issue,

'Raising Awareness of Eating Disorders' (as a teenager, Haglund battled with anorexia). ❦ The 2008 pageant served as the finale of a reality TV series, *Miss America: Reality Check*, which followed the contest's attempts to embrace an updated image. For the first time, the pageant featured a dance-music DJ on-stage, blue jeans during the opening parade of states, and donuts delivered to ousted contestants. Viewers were also able to vote via text-message for their favorite contestant – a title won by Miss Utah, Jill Stevens, an Army medic who served in Afghanistan. Miss Indiana, Nicole Elizabeth Rash, was the first runner-up to Miss America, while the second runner-up was Miss Washington, Elyse Umemoto.

FAVORITE TV PERSONALITY

Ellen DeGeneres is America's favorite TV personality, according to a 2008 poll by Harris Interactive. Below are the favorites overall, and those among various groups:

OVERALL FAVORITES	FAVORITE AMONG ...
1 . . . . Ellen DeGeneres	♂ . . . . Jay Leno
2 . . . . Oprah Winfrey	♀ . . . . Ellen DeGeneres
3 . . . . Jay Leno	*18–30 years*. . . . . Stephen Colbert
4 . . . . Hugh Laurie	31–42= . . . . Jay Leno & Jon Stewart
5 . . . . Jon Stewart	43–61 . . . . Oprah Winfrey
6= . . . . D. Letterman & S. Colbert	≥62= . . . . . . O. Winfrey & Bill O'Reilly
8 . . . . Bill O'Reilly	Republicans . . . . Bill O'Reilly
9= . . . Ray Romano & Homer Simpson	Dems= . . . E. DeGeneres & O. Winfrey

SESAME STREET CELEBRITY CAMEOS

Some of the celebrity stars on *Sesame Street*'s 39th season, beginning August 2008:

David Beckham (sharing his favorite word, 'persistence') · Feist (singing *1234*)
Neil Patrick Harris (as the *Fairy Shoe Person*) · LL Cool J (with Oscar, Elmo, and Abby)
Sandra Oh (as the *Cookie Fairy*) · Brian Williams (reporting on a 'selfishness epidemic')

DIGITAL TV

On February 17, 2009, all full-power TV stations in the United States will switch off their analog broadcast channels and transmit signals solely on digital channels. According to the Federal Communications Commission, the switch is being made to free segments of the broadcast spectrum for emergency communications, as well as for services like wireless broadband. In addition, digital TV offers enhanced picture and sound quality, although some have found digital signals more subject to interference. The first city in the US to make the switch to digital TV was Wilmington, North Carolina, which agreed to serve as an early test city for the transition by switching off its analog signals at noon on September 8, 2008. Below is a timeline of selected technological developments in television in the US:

1923	*Vladimir Zworkin patented a TV*	1948	*early tests of cable television*
	transmission tube, 'the iconscope'	1957	*first practical remote control, the*
1927	*Philo Farnsworth patented the*		*Zenith 'Space Commander'*
	first complete electronic TV,	1962	*first transatlantic TV satellite*
	the 'Image Dissector'	1970	*fiber-optic cable introduced*
1929	*first TV studio opened*	1972	*VCR introduced*
1930	*first commercial was broadcast*	1981	*HDTV first demonstrated*
1936	*coaxial cable was introduced*	1990	*first HDTV introduced*
1946	*first color TV system introduced*	1999	*TiVo launched*

THE HARDING TEST

In March 2008, a music video by the eccentric hip-hop duo Gnarls Barkley (best known for their 2006 hit *Crazy*) briefly attracted press attention after reportedly failing the Harding Test, which screens for images that can trigger epileptic attacks. Developed in 2001 by Cambridge Research Systems and English neuroscientist Graham Harding, the Harding Broadcast Flash and Pattern Analyser tests TV, film, and video game content frame-by-frame for images that flash, flicker, or appear intermittently, or that include certain formations of pattern[†]. Such images have been known to induce seizures in those with photosensitive epilepsy, which reportedly affects *c*.1 in 4,000 worldwide. The Gnarls Barkley video, which featured pop star Justin Timberlake as the host of a fictional 1990s public access TV show called 'City Vibin', was re-edited before it was released on MTV.

In June 2007, an animated logo for the London 2012 Olympics triggered a number of complaints from viewers with photosensitive epilepsy. The UK's Office of Communication (OfCom) reported that within the animation a sequence of '45 frames (*c*.2 seconds in length) contained an excessive number of "flashes" that were clearly in breach of the guidelines'. ❦ † According to OfCom, since television 'is by nature a flickering medium', it is 'impossible to eliminate the risk of television causing convulsions in viewers with photosensitive epilepsy'. However, OfCom warns of 3 dangers: *potentially harmful flashes* (an increase in luminance followed by a decrease, or a decrease followed by an increase); *rapidly changing image sequences* (e.g., fast cuts) where they result in areas of the screen that flash; and *potentially harmful regular patterns* (such as more than 5 light-dark pairs of clearly discernible stripes in any orientation).

DIVERSITY ON SCREEN

The Screen Actors Guild (SAG) annually assesses the diversity of actors cast in movies and television during the previous year. As in prior years, the 2007 report found that the majority of roles are given to actors <40, and that women >40 are particularly underrepresented. Although women ≥40 form 45·2% of the US population, they played 26% of 2006 movie and TV roles. The breakdown below compares the demographics of the actors on screen in 2006 to the US as a whole:

Group	% US	% roles	% lead roles	% supporting roles
Men <40	58·6	58·0	60·0	57·0
Men ≥40	41·4	40·0	39·0	40·0
Women <40	54·8	72·0	76·0	68·0
Women ≥40	45·2	26·0	23·0	29·0
Caucasian	73·4	72·3	75·4	70·9
African American	11·5	14·5	13·2	15·4
Latino/Hispanic	10·6	6·3	6·5	6·2
Asian/Pacific Islander	3·7	3·4	2·5	4·0
N American Indian	0·79	0·2	0·1	0·4
Unknown/other race	–	3·3	1·0	4·0

In 2007, a Gay and Lesbian Alliance Against Defamation (GLAAD) analysis found that during the 2007–08 season only 7 (1%)[†] of the regular characters on scripted, prime-time network TV were lesbian, gay, bisexual, or transgender (LGBT). Below is a breakdown of the LGBT characters on prime-time TV during that season:

LGBT characters	lead roles	supporting roles	recurring roles	gay men	lesbians	bisexual men	bisexual women	transgender
Broadcast networks	2	5	13	14	2	1	1	2
Mainstream cable networks	16	24	17	25	19	6	5	1

† The seven characters were: Kevin Walker and Saul Ashman on *Brothers and Sisters*; Caitlin on *Cashmere Mafia*; Andrew Van De Kamp on *Desperate Housewives*; Marc and Alexis on *Ugly Betty*; and Oscar on *The Office*. Six of the characters appeared on ABC programs, while *The Office* is broadcast on NBC.

GLAAD also found the following ethnicities among TV characters during the season:

499 whites · 81 African Americans · 40 Latino/as · 18 Asian Pacific Islanders
4 multiracial people · 1 person of Middle Eastern origin
1 Tlingit (Native Alaskan) · 6 nonhumans (aliens, &c.)
(Among lead & recurring characters on scripted, prime-time, network TV)

According to GLAAD, the network totals for 2007–08 season regular characters were:

	Whites	people of color	LGBT		Whites	people of color	LGBT
ABC	152	36	6	NBC	106	32	1
CBS	114	35	0	FOX	71	16	0
				The CW	56	26	0

——————— PRIME-TIME EMMYS · 2007 ———————

Award	winner
Drama series	*The Sopranos* · HBO
Drama, actor	James Spader · *Boston Legal*
Drama, actress	Sally Field · *Brothers & Sisters*
Drama, directing	Alan Taylor · *The Sopranos*, 'Kennedy and Heidi'
Drama, writing	David Chase · *The Sopranos*, 'Made in America'
Comedy series	*30 Rock* · NBC
Comedy, actor	Ricky Gervais · *Extras*
Comedy, actress	America Ferrera · *Ugly Betty*
Comedy, directing	Richard Shepard · *Ugly Betty*, 'Pilot'
Comedy, writing	Greg Daniels · *The Office*, 'Gay Witch Hunt'
Miniseries	*Broken Trail* · AMC
Made-for-TV movie	*Bury My Heart at Wounded Knee* · HBO
Miniseries or movie, actor	Robert Duvall · *Broken Trail*
Miniseries or movie, actress	Helen Mirren · *Prime Suspect: The Final Act*
Variety, music, or comedy series	*The Daily Show w. Jon Stewart* · Comedy Central
Reality-competition program	*The Amazing Race* · CBS

The actors and shows that have earned the most Emmys, through the 2007 awards:

Most Emmys won by a(n) ...		
Individual	James L. Brooks [19]	Series ... *Frasier* [37]
♂ performer	Carl Reiner [9]	Miniseries ... *Angels in America* [11]
♀ performer	Cloris Leachman [8]	Series, single season *West Wing* [2000; 9]
		Network, single year .... CBS [1974; 44]

——————— DAYTIME EMMYS · 2008 ———————

Award	winner
Drama series	*General Hospital* · ABC
Drama, lead actress	Jeanne Cooper · *The Young & the Restless*
Drama, lead actor	Anthony Geary · *General Hospital*
Drama, supporting actress	Gena Tognoni · *Guiding Light*
Drama, supporting actor	Kristoff St John · *The Young & the Restless*
Children's series	*Greatest Inventions with Bill Nye* · Discovery Channel; and *Jack Hanna's Into the Wild* · Syndicated
Preschool children's series	*Sesame Street* · PBS
Talk show, entertainment	*Rachael Ray* · Syndicated
Talk show, informative	*The Tyra Banks Show* · Syndicated
Talk show host	Ellen DeGeneres · *The Ellen DeGeneres Show*
Game show	*Cash Cab* · Discovery Channel
Game show host	Alex Trebek · *Jeopardy!*
Lifestyle show	*Everyday Italian* · Food Network
Lifestyle host	Giada De Laurentiis · *Everyday Italian*
Children's animated program	*Curious George* · PBS
Original song	*Chemistry* and *Little Starr* · *One Life to Live*

─────────── FREEDOM OF THE PRESS ───────────

A December 2007 poll released by the BBC World Service asked 11,344 people in 14 countries which of the following statements most closely matched their beliefs:

'Freedom of the press to report the news truthfully is very important to ensure we live in a fair society, even if it sometimes leads to unpleasant debates or social unrest.'	*'While freedom of the press to report news truthfully is important, social harmony and peace are more important, which sometimes means controlling what is reported for the greater good.'*

Respondents in N America and W Europe were most likely to value press freedom, whereas those in India, Singapore, and Russia were more likely to chose stability:

Country	press freedom	stability			
US	70%	28%	Egypt	55	45
Germany	67	26	Brazil	52	48
Great Britain	67	29	Mexico	51	46
Venezuela	64	36	UAE	51	48
South Africa	63	34	Singapore	43	48
Kenya	62	37	India	41	48
Nigeria	56	43	Russia	39	47
			(WORLD	56	40)

Respondents were also asked to assess the freedom of their national press and broadcasters to report the news 'truthfully and without bias'. Respondents were given a 5-point scale, where 5 was 'very free' and 1 was 'not at all free'. Below are the percentages of respondents in each country who rated their press 4 or 5 on this scale:

Kenya	81%	UK	56	South Africa	49
India	72	Germany	55	Russia	46
Egypt	64	US	53	Mexico	41
Venezuela	63	Brazil	52	(WORLD	56)

─────────── TOP NEWS SOURCES WORLDWIDE ───────────

The world overwhelmingly turns to television as its number-one news source, according to a Pew Global Attitudes survey released in October 2007. However, radio remains the dominant source in several African nations, while the internet has been gaining ground in N America and W Europe. Below are the percentages of those around the world who cite various media as their *first* or *second* news source:

(%)	TV	papers	radio	net		TV	papers	radio	net
Britain	83	58	29	21	Israel	80	45	38	26
Canada	82	51	30	25	Mexico	90	30	31	4
Ethiopia	65	25	81	5	Poland	92	45	33	15
France	81	53	34	25	Russia	95	51	27	6
Germany	84	62	26	19	S Africa	86	47	54	3
					US	83	47	22	35

───NEWS INTEREST INDEX───

Since 1986, the Pew Center for the People and the Press has regularly interviewed Americans about their level of interest in the major news stories of the day. A 2007 report from Pew tracked the trends in interest in news stories of various types between the years 1986–2006. Below are the percentages of Americans who said they were following stories on various topics 'very closely' during the years surveyed:

% following 'very closely'	'86–'89	'90–'99	'00–'06
War/terrorism (US-linked)	44	36	43
Bad weather	42	40	40
Money	23	29	40
Natural disasters	61	38	37
Man-made disasters	54	33	34
Health & safety	–	25	29
Crime & social violence	24	30	27
War/terrorism (non-US)	26	15	27
Domestic policy	30	23	26
Other politics	–	18	26
Campaigns & elections	25	20	24
Washington politics	17	19	24
US foreign policy	18	17	22
Political scandals	22	20	19
Sports	25	20	19
Personalities & ents	9	17	17
Celebrity scandals	22	13	17
Science & technology	33	15	16
Other nations	25	16	16
ALL STORIES	30	23	30

Below are the individual stories that drew the most and least interest 1986–2006:

MOST INTEREST		LEAST INTEREST	
Story　　*% following 'very closely'*		*Story*　　*% following 'very closely'*	
Challenger disaster [1986]	80	Reform Party convention [1999]	1
Terror attacks on US, gen. [2001]	78	Tom Cruise's split from wife [1990]	2
9/11 attacks [2001]	74	W. Allen–M. Farrow breakup [1992]	3
Hur. Katrina & Rita impact [2005]	73	Pinochet extradition case [1998]	3
San Francisco earthquake [1989]	73	Charles & Di marital probs [1996]	3

─WHITE HOUSE CORRESPONDENTS' ASSOC. DINNER─

The 2008 White House Correspondents' Association (WHCA) dinner was held on April 26 at the Washington Hilton. Although Craig Ferguson (host of the *Late Late Show*) was the featured entertainer[†], President George W. Bush provided the evening's most played sound-bite. In a nod to recent campaign controversies, Bush joked that 'Senator Clinton couldn't get into the building because of sniper fire, and Senator Obama's at church'.

❦ WHCA dinners fête members of the press covering the White House, and have been held since 1920. The WHCA was founded in 1914, after Woodrow Wilson announced he would be holding (then unprecedented) weekly press conferences, and amid rumors that a congressional committee would choose the journalists permitted to attend. While the rumor was unfounded, the WCHA still works to 'champion inclusiveness' in press access to the President.

[†] Ferguson was generally seen as a compromise between the brave, incendiary, and much-YouTubed 2006 speech made by Stephen Colbert and the milquetoast performance given by Rich Little in 2007.

——————————— NEWSPAPERS ———————————

Below are the top 10 newspapers in the US, based on average paid daily circulation:

Est.	title	editor	owned by	circulation†
1982	*USA Today*	Ken Paulson	Gannett Co.	2,284,219
1889	*Wall Street Journal*	Robert Thomson	News Corp.	2,069,463
1851	*New York Times*	Bill Keller	New York Times Co.	1,077,256
1881	*Los Angeles Times*	Russ Stanton	Tribune Co.	773,884
1919	*NY Daily News*	Martin Dunn	M.B. Zuckerman	703,137
1801	*New York Post*	Col Allan	News Corp.	702,488
1877	*Washington Post*	Leonard Downie Jr.	Washington Post Co.	673,180
1847	*Chicago Tribune*	Ann Marie Lipinski	Tribune Co.	541,663
1901	*Houston Chronicle*	Jeff Cohen	Hearst Corp.	494,131
1890	*Arizona Republic*	Randy Lovely	Gannett Co.	413,332

The percentage of Americans who read a newspaper at least once a week in 2007:

18–24 *years old*.... 33%	35–44 43	55–64 59
25–34 34	45–54 53	65+ 66

† Daily average for the 6 months ending 3/31/08. [Sources: *Editor & Publisher*; Scarborough Research]

——————————— '-30-' ———————————

Since the Civil War, and perhaps before, US journalists have used '-30-' (the number 30 flanked by dashes) as an in-house notation to mark the end of an article. The origins of this mark are hotly debated, but it seems plausible that the practice originated with telegraphers, who reportedly once ended their dispatches 'XXX' – the Roman numeral for 30. Another theory has it that the earliest (handwritten) stories employed a system wherein 'X' denoted the end of a line, 'XX' the end of a paragraph, and 'XXX' the end of a story. More baroque speculations concern a letter written to the East India Company, which apparently ended with the Bengali figure for 'farewell'. This figure was misread as '30', which was in turn adopted as a sign-off in subsequent communications. The *New York Times* has speculated that the mark developed as a form of protest by journalists demanding a 'living wage of $30 a week'. Although the notation has now fallen out of use, for a time in the C20th it was so widespread among journalists that within the trade '30' came also to mean 'the last', 'the end', and even 'death'. In a newspaper account from 1938, the funeral of a journalist killed in the Spanish Civil War is described as featuring a shield of white carnations, with the number '30' spelled out in red carnations.

[Sources: *American Journalism Review*; various] '–30–' was the title of the final episode of HBO series *The Wire*, which aired on March 9, 2008. Created, produced, and co-written by a former *Baltimore Sun* journalist, the show followed the intertwined fates of police, politicians, drug dealers, and reporters in Baltimore, earning critical acclaim (and a 2004 Peabody Award) for its depth and verisimilitude.

2008 NEWSROOM BAROMETER

The World Editors Forum conducted a survey of >700 newspaper editors and senior news executives from over 120 countries in March 2008, with the aim of gauging opinion on the future of newspapers. A selection of the results appears below:

In 10 years, what do you think will be the most common way of reading news?

%	2006	2008
Print	35	31
Online	41	44
Mobile phone	11	12
e-paper	7	7

In the next 10 years, do you think the quality of journalism will:

%	2006	2008
Worsen	27	28
Be about the same	16	22
Improve	50	45

Do you think in the future opinion and analysis pages will:

%	2006	2008
Increase	66	67
Be about the same	20	23
Decrease	12	9

What do you view as the greatest threat to the future of your newspaper?

	%
Declining youth readership	58
Internet & digital media	38
Lack of editorial innovation	36
Lack of investment	29
Free newspapers	13
Radio & TV	5
None of the above	6

What do you view as the principal threat to newspapers' editorial independence?

	%
Advertising pressure	23
Shareholder pressure	20†
Political pressure	19
PR firms	12

† Only 3% in N America saw political pressure as a primary threat, compared with 23% for shareholder pressure.

BLOGGING ARRESTS

35 people across the world were arrested for blogging about political issues in 2007, according to a 2008 World Information Access report. Since 2003, 64 have been arrested because of content on their blog. A summary of these arrests is below:

Blogging activity	Number of arrests · 2007	'03–'07
Using blog to organize/cover social protest	Burma (2), China (1) Egypt (4), Iran (1)	15
Violating cultural norms	China (1), Egypt (2), India (1) Hong Kong (1), Philippines (1)	14
Posting comments on public policy	Fiji (1), Malaysia (1) Pakistan (1), Saudi Arabia (1) Thailand (1), Syria (1)	12
Exposing corruption/human rights violations	China (3), Tunisia (1)	9
Posting comments about political figures	Egypt (1), Iran (1) Kuwait (1), Russia (1)	6
Other	China (1), Egypt (1), Fiji (1) Malaysia (1), Thailand (1), USA (2)	8

——————— PULITZER PRIZE · JOURNALISM · 2008 ———————

PUBLIC SERVICE AWARD
The *Washington Post* for '*the work of Dana Priest, Anne Hull, and Michel du Cille in exposing mistreatment of wounded veterans at Walter Reed Hospital, evoking a national outcry and producing reforms by federal officials*'

BREAKING NEWS REPORTING
The *Washington Post* staff for its '*exceptional, multi-faceted coverage of the deadly shooting rampage at Virginia Tech, telling the developing story in print and online*'

INTERNATIONAL REPORTING
Steve Fainaru of the *Washington Post* for his '*heavily reported series on private security contractors in Iraq that operate outside most of the laws governing American forces*'

BREAKING NEWS PHOTOGRAPHY
Andrees Latif of Reuters for his '*dramatic photograph of a Japanese videographer, sprawled on the pavement, fatally wounded during a street demonstration in Myanmar*'

EXPLANATORY REPORTING
Amy Harmon of the *New York Times* for her '*striking examination of the dilemmas and ethical issues that accompany DNA testing, using human stories to sharpen her reports*'

NATIONAL REPORTING
Jo Becker and Barton Gellman of the *Washington Post* for their '*lucid exploration of Vice President Dick Cheney and his powerful yet sometimes disguised influence on national policy*'
[See Pulitzer.org for other prizes]

——————— 67th PEABODY AWARDS ———————

Some of the programming chosen by the Peabody Awards, which honor the previous year's best in electronic media. (The awards do not recognize specific categories.)

CNN Presents: God's Warriors · CNN
To Die in Jerusalem · HBO
Art:21 · PBS
30 Rock · NBC
Speaking of Faith: The Ecstatic Faith of Rumi · American Public Media
Planet Earth · Discovery Channel
CBS News Sunday Morning: The Way Home · CBS
Fight for Open Records · WTAE-TV
Project Runway · BRAVO
Security Risks at Sky Harbor KNXV-TV
Dexter · Showtime
Nimrod Nation · Sundance Channel
Mad Men · AMC
The Colbert Report · Comedy Central
White Horse · BBC America

60 Minutes: The Killings in Haditha · CBS
Virginia Tech Shooting: The First 48 Hours · WSLS-TV
Independent Lens: Sisters in Law · PBS
Design Squad · PBS
Mental Anguish and the Military · NPR
A Journey Across Afghanistan: Opium and Roses · Balkan News Corporation
Taxi to the Dark Side · Jigsaw Pictures
The MTT Files American Public Media
Money for Nothing · WFAA-TV
The Buried and the Dead · WFAA-TV
Television Justice · WFAA-TV
Kinder Prison · WFAA-TV
Judgment Day: Intelligent Design on Trial · PBS

———————————— RADIO LISTENING ————————————

The average amount of time Americans spend listening to the radio each week:

Time spent listening	*hr:min per week*		
12–17 years old	♀ 13:15 ♂ 10:45	35–44	♀ 19:00 ♂ 21:00
18–24	♀ 16:45 ♂ 17:45	45–54	♀ 19:30 ♂ 21:30
25–34	♀ 18:00 ♂ 20:15	55–64	♀ 18:45 ♂ 20:30
		≥ 65	♀ 18:45 ♂ 18:45

The top radio genres in the United States, based on their average share of listeners:

Country
Listener share† .... 12·7%
No. stations nationwide 1,683
Listener gender...53·7% ♀ · 46·3% ♂
Top listening location............... car
Top region.........East South Central‡

Adult Contemporary
Listener share† .... 7·2%
No. stations nationwide 798
Listener gender...65·3% ♀ · 34·7% ♂
Top listening location............work
Top region............... New England

News/Talk/Info
Listener share† .... 10·7%
No. stations nationwide 1,553
Listener gender...43·9% ♀ · 56·1% ♂
Top listening location........... home
Top region....... West North Central§

Pop Contemporary
Listener share† .... 5·6%
No. stations nationwide 381
Listener gender...63·3% ♀ · 36·7% ♂
Top listening location............... car
Top region............... New England

† Share based on the number of people 12 years and older who are listening to a genre for 5 minutes or more within an average 15-minute period from 6am–midnight. ‡ Includes KY, TN, MS, and AL. § Includes ND, SD, NE, KS, MN, IA, and MO. Source: *Radio Today*, 2008 edition, Arbitron.

———————————— HOUSEHOLD TELEPHONES ————————————

16% of US households have only a cell phone (i.e., no landline), according to 2008 data from the National Health Interview Survey by the Centers for Disease Control and Prevention (CDC). Below is the percent of households with a cell phone only, a landline only, and with a cell phone as well as a landline, since 2004:

%	*landline only*	*cell only*	*both phones*		*landline only*	*cell only*	*both phones*
Jan–June 2004	39·6	5·0	43·2	July–Dec 2005	32·4	8·4	42·6
July–Dec 2004	38·7	6·1	43·1	Jan–June 2006	30·9	10·5	45·6
Jan–June 2005	34·4	7·3	42·4	July–Dec 2006	29·6	12·8	44·3
				Jan–June 2007	23·8	13·6	58·9
				July–Dec 2007	21·8	15·8	58·8

Not surprisingly, households with unrelated adult roommates were the most likely to use only cell phones (56·9% during the last 6 months of 2007). During the same time period, men (15·9%) were also somewhat more likely than women (13·2%) to live in households with only cell phones. In general, households whose inhabitants were younger and had lower incomes were more likely to use cell phones, while older inhabitants and those with a higher income were more likely to use landlines.

——————— MEDIA SLOGANS ———————

New York Times publisher Adolph Simon Ochs coined the famous slogan 'All the News That's Fit to Print' in 1896, as a way of distinguishing his brand from the sensationalist 'penny papers' then popular in New York. Since its first appearance on October 25, 1896, the phrase has become one of the most memorable mottos associated with any news organization. Other recent media slogans are listed below:

ABC News	*Start Here*	*O, the Oprah Magazine*	
CBS	*We are CBS*		*Live Your Best Life*
CNN	*The Most Trusted Name in News*	*BARk*	*Dog is my Co-Pilot*
Chicago Tribune	*What's in It for You?*	*Portfolio*	*Business Intelligence*
Esquire	*Man at His Best*	Wikipedia	*The free encyclopedia that*
Economist	*Sparks and Mensa*		*anyone can edit*
FOX News	*We Report. You Decide*	*Wall Street Journal*	*The Daily Diary of*
	Fair and Balanced		*the American Dream*
GQ	*Look Sharp + Live Smart*	*Weekly World News*	
MSNBC.com	*A fuller spectrum of news*		*The World's Only Reliable Newspaper*
NBC News	*America's News Leader*	*Onion*	*America's Finest News Source*

——————— ADVERTISING WALK OF FAME ———————

Since 2004, the public has been invited to vote for its favorite advertising characters and slogans as part of Advertising Week, an annual jamboree of industry events and conferences held in New York. The winners are commemorated with bronze plaques on the Madison Avenue Advertising Walk of Fame, between 49th and 50th in Manhattan. In September 2007, Orville Redenbacher and the Chick-fil-A Cows[†] were voted the favorite characters, while the winning slogans were '*The Few. The Proud. The Marines*' (US Marine Corps), and '*DING! You are now free to move about the country!*' (Southwest Airlines). Below are the winners from previous years:

2006	2004 (inaugural)
Colonel Sanders · Kool-Aid Man	M&Ms Characters · AFLAC Duck
Don't Mess with Texas	Mr Peanut · Pillsbury Doughboy
(State of TX Dept of Transportation)	Tony the Tiger
When it absolutely, positively has	*Melts in your mouth,*
to be there overnight (FedEx)	*not in your hands* (M&Ms)
	Sometimes you feel like a nut,
2005	*sometimes you don't* (Almond Joy/Mounds)
Juan Valdez · Geico Gecko	*Where's the beef?* (Wendy's)
Imagination at work (GE)	*A mind is a terrible thing to waste*
When you care enough to	(United Negro College Fund)
send the very best (Hallmark)	*Can you hear me now?* (Verizon)

† The Chick-fil-A Cows have served as mascots for the Atlanta-based chain since 1995. They usually appear with signs reading *Eat Mor Chikin* [sic], an attempt to save their own species from consumption. They have also been known to parachute into football stadiums and steal burgers from children.

Music & Movies

Listen, kid, take my advice, never hate a song that has sold half a million copies.
— IRVING BERLIN to Cole Porter [attributed]

FREE MUSIC & 360-DEGREE DEALS

The ease with which people can download music from the internet and share it for free has severely hit record company profits – in the US, the value of recorded music sold fell by 11·8% between 2006 and 2007, according to the Recording Industry Association of America (RIAA). By contrast, attendance at arena shows has grown, making touring an increasingly profitable endeavor. In light of this move away from record store sales, established bands like Radiohead have embraced the flexibility of downloads, giving away their music in return for larger crowds at their gigs. Meanwhile, record companies have introduced so-called 360-degree record deals, under which they take a slice of a musician's entire portfolio of earnings, including touring and sponsorship. Some recent developments in these areas:

360-degree deals

{10/07} Madonna signed a revolutionary recording, publishing, and touring contract with Live Nation reportedly worth $120m; she was the first major star to shun a traditional record deal in favor of an all-in-one contract. {03/08} Groove Armada signed an integrated marketing deal with Bacardi allowing the drinks company to release a 4-track EP by the band, with the option to use the music in its advertising. The group also agreed to play a series of Bacardi-sponsored live concerts. {03/08} U2 signed a 12-year deal with Live Nation. Although the band's physical recordings will still be distributed through Universal Music Group, Live Nation will handle digital distribution, branding rights, and merchandising. {05/08} Jay-Z became the third major artist to sign a 360-degree deal with Live Nation. Reportedly worth $150m, the deal includes albums, tours, and the creation of a new entertainment venture, Roc Nation, which may include Jay-Z's own label and talent management. {07/08} Shakira signed a 10-year deal, worth an estimated $70–$100m, covering touring, recording, merchandise, and sponsorship.

Free music

{07/07} Prince gave away free copies of his new album, *Planet Earth*, with the UK's *Mail on Sunday*, prompting criticism from some music retailers. {10/07} The Charlatans allowed their 10th studio album to be downloaded for free from UK radio station Xfm's website. {10/07} Radiohead announced that their album *In Rainbows* would be available to download for whatever fans decided to pay. {03/08} Nine Inch Nails gave away 9 songs from their instrumental album, *Ghosts I–IV*. {05/08} Coldplay allowed fans to download their new single *Violet Hill* for free from their website for one week only. {05/08} Nine Inch Nails released *The Slip* for free on their website after their deal with Universal ended.

———————————— US MUSIC SALES · 2007 ————————————

PHYSICAL SALES	2007	± 2006–07
CDs	511·1m	–17·5%
CD singles	2·6m	+51·5%
LP/EPs	1·3m	+36·6%
Music videos	27·5m	+18·6%
Total value	$7,985·8m	–19·1%

DOWNLOADS	2007	± 2006–07
Singles	809·9m	+38·1%
Albums	42·5	+54%
Music videos	14·2	+43·0%
Total value	$1,257·5m	+43·2%

[Source: RIAA]

———————————— US FAVORITE MUSIC GENRES · 2007 ————————————

A breakdown of 2007 music sales by genre, based on an RIAA survey of purchasers:

Genre†	*% of sales*
Rock	32·4
R&B/urban	11·8
Country	11·5
Rap/hip-hop	10·8
Pop	10·7
Religious	3·9
Children's	2·9
Jazz	2·6
Classical	2·3
Soundtracks	0·8
Oldies	0·4
New age	0·3
Other	7·1

† Respondents were asked to classify the music they purchased within the past month. 'Other' includes Big Band, Broadway shows, comedy, electronic, emo, ethnic, exercise, folk, goth, &c.

———————————— US RECORD LABEL MARKET SHARE ————————————

Four record labels (the 'Big 4') currently dominate the US music industry. Below are their market shares by % of albums sold, since 2003 (Sony and BMG merged in 2004):

%	Universal	Sony BMG		Warner	EMI	indies
2007	31·9	25·0		20·3	9·4	13·5
2006	31·6	27·4		18·1	10·2	12·6
2005	31·7	25·6		15·0	9·5	18·1
2004	29·5	13·2 Sony	15·2 BMG	14·6	9·9	17·3
2003	28·0	13·7 Sony	15·5 BMG	16·4	9·7	16·7

———————————— DIGITAL MUSIC WORLDWIDE ————————————

Below is the growth in global revenue from digital music between 2004 and 2007:

Digital music revenue		% of total music market
$2·9bn	2007	15%
$2·1bn	2006	11%
$1·1bn	2005	5%
$0·4bn	2004	2%

In the US, digital music accounts for 30% of the music market. South Korea is the only country where digital sales outstrip physical – 60% of all music sold in the country is digital. [Source: IFPI]

——————— GLOBAL BESTSELLING ALBUMS · 2007 ———————

Album	artist	publisher
High School Musical 2	Cast soundtrack	Disney Music Group
Back to Black	Amy Winehouse	Universal
Noel	Josh Groban	Warner
The Best Damn Thing	Avril Lavigne	Sony BMG
Long Road out of Eden	Eagles	Eagles Recording Co./Universal
Minutes to Midnight	Linkin Park	Warner
As I Am	Alicia Keys	Sony BMG
Call Me Irresponsible	Michael Bublé	Warner
Life in Cartoon Motion	Mika	Universal
Not Too Late	Norah Jones	EMI

[Source: International Federation of the Phonographic Industry. Includes physical and digital sales.]

——————— MUSIC SALES WORLDWIDE ———————

	2007 (US $)	Canada	650m	South Korea	334m
USA	10,394m	Australia	619m	Mexico	304m
Japan	4,897m	Italy	536m	Brazil	276m
UK	2,976m	Russia	426m	Switzerland	233m
Germany	2,277m	Spain	423m	India	213m

[Source: International Federation of the Phonographic Industry. Includes physical and digital sales.]

——————— ROCK & ROLL HALL OF FAME ———————

Madonna stole the spotlight at the 2008 *Rock & Roll Hall of Fame* ceremony. After being introduced by Justin Timberlake, the Material Girl thanked 'the ones that said I was talentless, that I was chubby, that I couldn't sing, that I was a one-hit wonder', adding she was 'grateful for their resistance'. The 2008 inductees were:

Leonard Cohen · The Dave Clark Five (Dave Clark, Lenny Davidson, Rick Huxley, Denis Payton, Mike Smith) · Kenny Gamble & Leon Huff
Madonna · John Mellencamp · The Ventures (Bob Bogle, Nokie Edwards, Gerry McGee, Mel Taylor, Don Wilson) · Little Walter

——————— MUSIC SALES AWARDS ———————

Below are the 2008 albums with the highest RIAA certifications, as of 7/24/08:

Multiplatinum (2,000,000+)	Lil Wayne, *Tha Carter III*
Platinum (1,000,000+)	Mariah Carey, *E=MC²* · Jack Johnson, *Sleep Through the Static* · Leona Lewis, *Spirit*

WORLDWIDE MUSIC MAP

The Gracenote Media Recognition Service is used by iTunes and other applications to recognize and display information from audio CDs. Since 2007, Gracenote has maintained a 'music map' which displays the artists and albums most often accessed in various parts of the world. The top artists as of January 2008 were:

Place	*top artist (genre)*
Afghanistan .... Queen (classic hard rock)	Kazakhstan ...... Linkin Park (rap metal)
Australia.... Ministry of Sound (trance)	Kenya............... Alkaline Trio (emo)
Canada .... The Beatles (rock)	Malaysia...... Avril Lavigne (teen rock)
California .... The Beatles (rock)	New York .... The Beatles (rock)
Cuba........ Joaquín Sabina (Latin rock)	Russian Fed...... Linkin Park (rap metal)
Egypt .... Elissa (Lebanese pop)	Pakistan .... Jal (rock/pop)
France .... The Beatles (rock)	Spain .... The Beatles (rock)
Germany .... Die Ärzte (punk)	South Korea.......... Bigbang (hip-hop)
India............ Linkin Park (rap metal)	United Kingdom..... The Beatles (rock)
Iran .... Pink Floyd (psychedelic rock)	Venezuela... Wisin & Yandel (reggaetón)
Ireland......... U2 (adult alternative rock)	[Genre according to Gracenote, MySpace, &c.]

'SUBSTANCES' IN MUSIC

Popular music is rife with references to substance use, according to a 2008 analysis led by Dr Brian Primack of the University of Pittsburgh Medical School. Based on an assessment of the 279 most popular songs of 2005 (according to *Billboard* charts), researchers concluded that Americans 15–18 years old hear *c.*84 references to drugs, alcohol, tobacco, &c., per day and >30,000 each year. However, some musical genres featured such substances significantly more often than did others:

References per song-hour:	*country*	*pop*	*R&B*	*rap*	*rock*	*all*
Tobacco	1	0	0	1	1	1
Alcohol	30	1	9	22	2	14
Marijuana	1	0	3	38	0	11
Any substance (incl. 'other')	34	2	14	105	7	35

WORST LYRICISTS

Sting's 'mountainous pomposity and cloying spirituality' earned him the number-one spot on *Blender* magazine's 2007 list of the Worst Lyricists in Rock. Sting was faulted for abandoning 'new-wave songs about hookers' for lyrics that 'rip off' Chaucer, St Augustine, and Shakespeare. The complete top ten list was as follows:

1 .... Sting	5 .... Dan Fogelberg	9 .... Donovan
2 ...... Neil Peart (Rush)	6 . Tom Marshall (Phish)	10 .... Jim Morrison
3 ... Scott Stapp (Creed)	7 .... Paul Stanley (Kiss)	† Songwriter responsible for
4 .. N. Gallagher (Oasis)	8 .... Diane Warren†	'Blame It on the Rain', &c.

———————— LOVED & HATED CHRISTMAS SONGS ————————

In December 2007, Edison Media Research played 10-second snippets of 579 Christmas songs to a sample of American women aged 30–49, and asked for their reactions. The panel rated the following seasonal tunes their most loved and loathed:

MOST LOVED	MOST HATED
Nat King Cole ..... *The Christmas Song*	Singing Dogs................*Jingle Bells*
Bing Crosby...........*White Christmas*	Cartman..................*O Holy Night*
Johnny Mathis ..... *Do You Hear What I Hear*	Elmo & Patsy ....*Grandma Got Run Over by a Reindeer*
Burl Ives........*A Holly Jolly Christmas*	Jackson 5 ...*S. Claus Is Coming to Town*
Harry S. Chorale.. *Little Drummer Boy*	Barbra Streisand............*Jingle Bells*

———————— WORLD'S GREENEST BAND ————————

Radiohead is the world's greenest band, according to a January 2008 list compiled by the British music magazine *NME*. The ranking was based on an analysis by carbonfootprint.com, which measured the amount of CO_2 produced by various recent tours. The Police scored exceptionally poorly, because their 2007–08 reunion tour favored large stadiums that often forced fans to travel long distances. Various bands were ranked on a scale that ranged from 0 ('as carbon neutral as Bob Geldof's bathwater') to 10 ('as good for the earth as an oil spill'). The results were:

Band	CO_2 *rank*			
Radiohead..............2	The Cribs...............4		Bands ranked by	
Babyshambles 4	Kasabian...............7		carbonfootprint.com on	
	The Police 7		the basis of their last tour.	

According to MusicMatters, a US marketing firm that helps bands reduce their environmental impact, a single stadium concert can produce 500–1,000 tons of CO_2. By comparison, the average medium-sized car produces about 6 tons of CO_2 per year (according to renewable energy firm NativeEnergy).

———————— TOP-EARNING WOMEN IN MUSIC ————————

Madonna is the richest woman in music according to *Forbes*, which in 2008 estimated she earned $72 from June 2006 to June 2007. Combining sales of concert tickets, albums, and merchandise, as well as earnings from clothing and fragrance lines and product endorsements, the top 10 richest women in music were:

Earnings June '06–June '07	$m		
Madonna...........................72	Christina Aguilera[†] 20		
Barbra Streisand.....................60	Faith Hill.............................19		
Celine Dion[†].........................45	Dixie Chicks 18		
Shakira 38	Mariah Carey[†] 13		
Beyoncé[†] 27			
Gwen Stefani[†].......................26	† Artists who have perfumes; Madonna, Beyoncé & Stefani have clothing lines.		

———————GRAMMY AWARDS · 2008———————

The 50th Grammy awards were held on February 10, 2008. The evening featured tributes to popular music past and present, including: a duet between (a live) Alicia Keys and (a still dead) Frank Sinatra; Beyoncé and Tina Turner in coordinated outfits; and a reunion of '80s pop-funk ensemble the Time, fronted by Rihanna. The evening's intrigue was supplied by soul sensation and tabloid bête noire Amy Winehouse, whose performance was beamed in from London after her visa application was declined. Herbie Hancock's Album of the Year win surprised some since it had sold just 55,000 copies, and was only the second jazz album to win in the category.

Record of the year..Amy Winehouse · *Rehab*
Album of the year.........................Herbie Hancock · *River: The Joni Letters*
Song of the year..Amy Winehouse · *Rehab*
New artist.. Amy Winehouse
Female pop vocal performance.............................Amy Winehouse · *Rehab*
Male pop vocal performance ..J. Timberlake · *What Goes Around ... Comes Around*
Pop vocal album ....Amy Winehouse · *Back to Black*
Dance recording ....Justin Timberlake, Nate (Danja) Hills & Timbaland
LoveStoned/I Think She Knows
Electronic/dance album......................Chemical Brothers · *We Are the Night*
Solo rock vocal performance ....Bruce Springsteen · *Radio Nowhere*
Rock song..................................Red Hot Chili Peppers · *Dani California*
Rock album ....Foo Fighters · *Echoes, Silence, Patience & Grace*
Alternative music album................................. White Stripes · *Icky Thump*
Female R&B vocal performance ....Alicia Keys · *No One*
Male R&B vocal performance...........................Prince · *Future Baby Mama*
R&B song..................... Dirty Harry, Jerry Brothers & Alicia Keys · *No One*
R&B album...Chaka Khan · *Funk This*
Contemporary R&B album................................. Ne-Yo · *Because of You*
Rap song ....A. Davis, Mike Dean, Faheem Najm & Kanye West · *Good Life*
Rap album .... Kanye West · *Graduation*
Country song ....Carrie Underwood · *Before He Cheats*
Country album ....Vince Gill · *These Days*
Bluegrass album.............................Jim Lauderdale · *The Bluegrass Diaries*
Traditional blues album . Henry James Townsend et al. *Last of the Great Mississippi Delta Bluesmen: Live in Dallas*
Contemporary jazz album.................Herbie Hancock · *River: The Joni Letters*
Latin pop album ....Alejandro Sanz · *El tren de los momentos*
Reggae album..Stephen Marley · *Mind Control*
Polka album.................Jimmy Sturr and His Orchestra · *Come Share the Wine*
Spoken word album ....Barack Obama
The Audacity of Hope: Thoughts on Reclaiming the American Dream
Compilation soundtrack album................................. The Beatles · *Love*
Score soundtrack album ....Michael Giacchino · *Ratatouille*
Classical album....................*cond.* Leonard Slatkin · *Tower: Made in America*
Producer of the year, non-classical ....Mark Ronson
Short-form music video ....Johnny Cash · *God's Gonna Cut You Down*

OTHER NOTABLE MUSIC AWARDS

Awards	prize	*winner*
American Music ['07]	*Pop/rock album*	Daughtry · *Daughtry*
	Pop/rock male artist	Justin Timberlake
	Pop/rock female artist	Fergie
	Country album	Carrie Underwood · *Some Hearts*
	Soul/R&B album	Justin Timberlake
		FutureSex/LoveSounds
	Rap/hip-hop album	T.I. · *T.I. vs T.I.P.*
	Favorite soundtrack	*High School Musical 2*
	Adult contemporary artist	Daughtry
	Latin artist	Jennifer Lopez
	Alternative artist	Linkin Park
Country Music ['07]	*Entertainer of the year*	Kenny Chesney
	Vocalist of the year, female	Carrie Underwood
	Vocalist of the year, male	Brad Paisley
	Single	Carrie Underwood · *Before He Cheats*
	Album	George Strait · *It Just Comes Natural*
	Vocal group	Rascal Flatts
	Horizon Award	Taylor Swift
Eurovision ['08]	*Winner*	Dima Bilan · *Believe* [Russia]
People's Choice ['08]	*Singer, female*	Gwen Stefani
	Singer, male	Justin Timberlake
	Song, rock	Daughtry · *Home*
	Song, hip-hop	Timbaland feat. Justin Timberlake & Nelly
		Furtado · *Give It to Me*
	Song, R&B	Rihanna · *Shut Up and Drive*
	Song, pop	Justin Timberlake
		What Goes Around ... Comes Around
	Song, country	Rascal Flatts · *Stand*
NAACP Image ['08]	*Album*	Alicia Keys · *As I Am*
	Artist, male	Chris Brown
	Artist, female	Alicia Keys
	Duo or group	Eddie & Gerald Levert
	Outstanding new artist	Jordin Sparks
	Jazz artist	Herbie Hancock
MTV VMAs ['07]	*Video of the year*	Rihanna feat. Jay-Z · *Umbrella*
	Video, male	Justin Timberlake
	Video, female	Fergie
	Best group	Fall Out Boy
	Monster Single of the Year	Rihanna feat. Jay-Z · *Umbrella*
	Best New Artist	Gym Class Heroes
	Quadruple Threat of the Year	Justin Timberlake
PLUG Independent	*Album of the Year*	Arcade Fire · *Neon Bible*
Music Awards ['08]	*New Artist of the Year*	Justice
	Female Artist of the Year	Annie Clark
	Male Artist of the Year	Andrew Bird

NORTH KOREA & THE 'GERSHWIN OFFENSIVE'

On February 25, 2008, the New York Philharmonic (with 165 guests and press) landed in Pyongyang, N Korea. At the center of this 48-hour visit was a 90-minute concert for 1,400 of the N Korean elite – a quasi-diplomatic event that *Time* called the 'Gershwin offensive' [see p.300]. While some accused the orchestra of pandering to a dictator, and US diplomats kept their distance, conductor Lorin Maazel called the event a way to 'bring people and their cultures together on common ground'.

Itinerary: {2/25/08, 4:10pm} Orchestra and entourage arrive via private 747. A heated truck is driven from S Korea to transport instruments in the freezing temperatures. {5:30pm} Check-in at Yanggakdo International Hotel, on an island in the Taedong River. Guides are assigned for every 4 people. {7pm} Orchestra and guests attend a show of traditional dance and drumming. {9pm} A lavish banquet features quail eggs, pheasant-ball soup, and crab au gratin. {2/26, 11am} Dress rehearsal at East Pyongyang Grand Theater, after which the Americans give musical supplies to local students. {3pm} Several philharmonic musicians teach master classes; the rest of the group goes sightseeing. {6pm} The concert begins at the East Pyongyang Grand Theater, broadcast live on N Korean television and radio. There are tears, and a 5-minute ovation. President Kim Jong-il does not attend. The program is:

North Korean national anthem
The 'Star-Spangled Banner'
Wagner, Prelude to Act III of *Lohengrin*
Dvořák, Symphony No. 9,
From the New World
Gershwin, *An American in Paris*
Encores:
Bizet, *L'Arlésienne*
Bernstein, Overture to *Candide*
Arirang [Korean folk song]

{9:15pm} At the celebratory post-concert banquet, philharmonic president Zarin Mehta says he is 'over the moon'. {2/27, 11am} The musicians attend a performance at an elite music school. {3pm} The group leaves N Korea.

The philharmonic's visit to N Korea was the first by a cultural group from the US. The event drew comparisons to the Boston Symphony Orchestra's trip to the Soviet Union in 1956, which was the first trip there by a major US orchestra. The BSO played 2 concerts each in Leningrad and Moscow, and earned a 10-minute standing ovation after the first Moscow performance. Some have termed such efforts 'symphonic diplomacy'; for other types of diplomacy, see p.300. ❦ On 2/26/08, the press reported that Eric Clapton (a purported favorite of Kim Jong-il's son Kim Jong Chol) had been invited to play Pyongyang; it was not certain he would attend. [Sources: NY Philharmonic, &c.]

KENNEDY CENTER HONORS

Each year, the John F. Kennedy Center for the Performing Arts in Washington, DC, honors several Americans for their 'lifetime of contributions to the performing arts'. In December 2007, the awards were presented to the following people:

Leon Fleisher (*pianist*) · Steve Martin (*actor & writer*) · Diana Ross (*singer*)
Martin Scorsese (*film director*) · Brian Wilson (*songwriter*)

SOME CLASSICAL ANNIVERSARIES · 2009

2009 marks a number of significant anniversaries for German(ic) composers. It is 200 years since the birth of FELIX MENDELSSOHN-BARTHOLDY (2/3/1809). G.F. HANDEL died 250 years ago (4/14/1759), and 200 years have passed since the death of FRANZ JOSEPH HAYDN (5/31/1809). Other classical anniversaries in 2009 are:

b.1659.................. Henry Purcell	*d*.1959.............Heitor Villa-Lobos†
b.1709................... Franz Benda	*d*.1959.................... Ernest Bloch
b.1859................. Basil Harwood	
b.1934..........Peter Maxwell Davies	† Brazilian by birth, he is considered to be the
b.1934.............Harrison Birtwistle	best-known classical composer from S America.

MOST-PERFORMED OPERAS

The operas most frequently staged by members of OPERA America and Opera.ca during the 2007–08 season, with the number of productions during the season:

Puccini · *La Bohème*..... 20 *productions*		Donizetti · *The Elixir of Love* 9
Puccini · *Tosca*........................15		Mozart · *The Magic Flute* 9
Verdi · *La Traviata* 13		Verdi · *Aïda*............................ 8
Mozart · *The Marriage of Figaro* 10		Puccini · *Madama Butterfly*.......... 8
Bizet · *Carmen* 9		Puccini · *Turandot*.................... 8
Mozart · *Don Giovanni*...............9		[Source: OPERA America]

While the classics above are clearly beloved, in 2008 two notable opera houses announced the production of modern, even populist, pieces. In May, Milan's La Scala announced that it would mount a production of Al Gore's *An Inconvenient Truth* for the 2011 season, and in June, the New York City Opera said it had commissioned an opera version of *Brokeback Mountain*, to premiere in 2013.

NEA OPERA HONORS

In May 2008, the National Endowment for the Arts (NEA) announced the winners of the annual Opera Honors awards, the first new national arts awards from the NEA in 25 years. According to the NEA, the awards are designed to honor 'luminaries who have made extraordinary contributions to opera in the US'. Ultimately, the NEA hopes the roster of winners will act as a kind of de facto 'hall of fame' for American opera. The $25,000 awards are given in four categories each year: composer, conductor, advocate, and singer. The inaugural class of winners is below:

Leontyne Price (singer)	*'known for her elegant musical style', 'great recording legacy'*
Carlisle Floyd (composer)	*'one of the most admired opera composers and librettists'*
Richard Gaddes (advocate)	*'trailblazing director' of the Santa Fe Opera and cofounder of the Opera Theater of St Louis*
James Levine (conductor)	*made the 'Metropolitan Opera Orchestra into one of the greatest orchestras in the world'*

──────────── 'BIG FIVE' PREMIERES ────────────

The following 'Big 5' US orchestras have long been considered the most prestigious, though the designation is not without controversy. Below are the works that were premiered by these orchestras in the 2007–08 season, from *Symphony* magazine:

BOSTON SYMPHONY ORCHESTRA
est. 1881

William Bolcom · *Symphony No. 8*
Elliott Carter · *Horn Concerto*
Brett Dean · *The Lost Art
of Letter Writing*†
Henri Dutilleux · *Le temps l'horloge*†
John Harbison · *Symphony No. 5*

CHICAGO SYMPHONY ORCHESTRA
est. 1891

Nico Muhly · *Step Team*
Matthias Pintscher · *Osiris*
Mark-Anthony Turnage
Chicago Remains

CLEVELAND ORCHESTRA
est. 1918

Thomas Adès · *Powder Her Face: Suite*†
Peter Eötvös · *CAP-KO*†
Matthias Pintscher
Five Orchestral Pieces†
Johannes Maria Staud · *Apeiron*†

NEW YORK PHILHARMONIC
est. 1842

Marc Neikrug · *Symphony No. 2,
'Quintessence'*
Tan Dun · *Piano Concerto*

PHILADELPHIA ORCHESTRA
est. 1900

Marc-André Dalbavie
La Source d'un regard†
Jennifer Higdon · *Concerto 4–3*†
Jennifer Higdon · *The Singing Rooms*†
Wolfgang Rihm · *Transformations 2*†
Herbert Willi · *Eirene*†

† US premiere. All other works are world premieres. ❧ According to data from the American Symphony Orchestra League, *c.*1,800 orchestras are based in the US: 350–400 professional; 800–900 volunteer; *c.*200 collegiate or conservatory; and 400–500 youth orchestras. Of the half million people involved in these orchestras, 75% volunteer their services.

──────────── 2008 MUSICIAN OF THE YEAR ────────────

Russian soprano Anna Netrebko was named 2008 Musician of the Year by Musical America, publishers of the *International Directory of the Performing Arts*. Netrebko was noted for possessing one of the 'finest female voices on the operatic stage', as well as for her 'natural beauty and fine acting skills'. Musical America has issued the award since 1960, when it was given to Leonard Bernstein. Some recent winners:

2007 . . . . Bernard Haitink (conductor)
2006 . . . . Esa-Pekka Salonen (conductor)
2005 . . . . .Karita Mattila (soprano)
2004 . . . . . . Wynton Marsalis (trumpeter)
2003 . . . . Kronos Quartet
2002 . . . . . . Sir Simon Rattle (conductor)
2001 . . . . Martha Argerich (pianist)
2000 . . . . Carnegie Hall
1999 . André Previn (conductor & pianist)

1998 . . . . Seiji Ozawa (conductor)
1997 . . . . .James Galway (flautist)
1996 . . . . Juilliard String Quartet
1995 . . . . Marilyn Horne (mezzo-soprano)
1994 . . . .Christa Ludwig (mezzo-soprano)
1993 . . . . Kurt Masur (conductor)
1992 . . . . .Robert Shaw (conductor)
1991 . . . .Gian Carlo Menotti (composer)
1990 . . Herbert von Karajan (conductor)

MUSIC & NOISE

In February 2008, the *EU Noise at Work Directive 2003/10/EC* came into effect for the European music and entertainment industries. The directive is intended to protect workers from damaging levels of noise, and establishes an average weekly workplace sound level of 85 decibels (dB). Once this level has been exceeded, the use of specially designed earplugs, noise-reducing screens, and other measures is required. While rock and pop music are more commonly associated with loud noise, the directive also caused some difficulty for classical musicians, since orchestras can also produce 'dangerous' decibel levels. (The German Federal Industrial Safety Commission noted that the noise produced by orchestra musicians is 'by all means comparable to the strain in main industrial work environments'.) After the directive came into effect, some musicians described the regulations as unworkable, and critics voiced concern that a number of pieces, such as those by Wagner[†] and Strauss, would be rendered virtually unplayable. Listed below are the average decibel levels of various musical instrument, with some other noises for comparison:

0 dB . . . . threshold of hearing	84 dB . . . . percussion
10 dB . . . . rustling leaves, whispering	86 dB . . . . flutes, double bass
30 dB . . . . ticking clock	87 dB . . . . trumpet
40 dB . . . . quiet living room	88 dB . . . . bassoon, horn, trombone
60 dB . . . . normal conversation	90 dB . . . . heavy truck, lawnmower
70 dB . . . . cars[‡], ringing telephone	100 dB . . . . dance club
80 dB . . . . . busy street, vacuum cleaner	110 dB . . . . jackhammer, rock band
82 dB . . . . harp	130 dB . . . . . absolute threshold of pain
83 dB . . . . violin	140 dB . . . . jet plane

† During Wagner's *Der Ring des Nibelungen*, trumpets and tubas can reach 110 dB, violins can hit 109 dB, and a deafening 118 dB (louder than a jackhammer) has been measured at the right ear of a flutist. ‡ In the extreme motor sport 'dB drag racing', enthusiasts compete to see who can produce the most noise inside a sealed car using only its motor and various amplifiers. At the time of writing, the loudest recorded car reportedly achieved 180·2 dB, in December 2007. [Sources: Arbeitsinspektion Austria; German health insurance firm Innungskrankenkasse; the German government; termpro.com]

GRAMOPHONE AWARDS · 2007

The Gramophone Awards, presented annually by *Gramophone* magazine, are chosen by a panel of critics, members of the industry, broadcasters, and 'celebrity' jurors.

Record of the year . . . . Nelson Freire, *cond.* Riccardo Chailly, Gewandhausorchester Leipzig · Brahms *Piano Concertos 1 & 2*
Artist of the year . . . . Julia Fischer
Young Artist of the Year . . . . Vasily Petrenko
Lifetime Achievement . . . . Montserrat Caballé
Label of the Year . . . . Deutsche Grammophon
Editor's Choice . . . . *cond.* Ivan Fischer, Budapest Festival Orchestra Mahler *Symphony No. 2*

WRITERS' STRIKE

On 11/5/2007, the Writers Guild of America (WGA) called 'pencils down' in a fight over new-media royalties, DVD residuals, and jurisdiction over reality and animation writers. Scarred by a 1985 deal which gave them only a small cut of home video revenues, WGA members boycotted work for 100 days while their representatives negotiated with the Alliance of Motion Picture & TV Producers (AMTP). The sticking point proved to be new-media revenues, but eventually a 'precedent-setting deal' was reached to give writers a piece of the action. The strike cost L.A.'s economy *c.*$2·5bn and very nearly canceled the Oscars. Below is a timeline of events:

{7/16/07} The WGA and AMPTP begin contract negotiations. {7/18} Talks end without progress. {9/19} Talks resume. '*The WGA made clear today that they … have a total disregard for the true state of the industry and its fundamental economics.*' – Nick Counter, AMPTP president. {10/5} Talks end; no progress. {10/19} 90% of the WGA votes to strike. {10/25} Talks resume. {10/31} Talks end; the WGA contract expires. {11/02} The WGA calls for a strike: '*The studios have not responded to a single one of our important proposals.*' – Patric Verrone, the WGA West President. {11/05} The strike begins; within days several shows suspend production. '*How greedy can you get, they won't even share the net!* ' – strike chant. {11/08} 4,000 striking writers picket LA's Avenue of the Stars. {11/26} Talks resume; *Last Call with Carson Daly* resumes production with nonunion writers. {12/07} Talks collapse. {12/11} The WGA approves a script waiver for the Screen Actors Guild Awards. {12/13} The WGA claims the AMPTP refused to bargain in good faith. {12/17} The WGA declines script waivers for Academy Award and Golden Globes telecasts. {1/2/08} Jay Leno, Conan O'Brien, and Jimmy Kimmel resume their shows without

NOTABLE STRIKE CHANTS

Hey, hey, ho, ho,
management can't
write the show!

No more scripts, no more
pages, soon we'll empty
all your stages!

They tried to make me
do a rewrite, but I said,
No! No! No!

writers. *The Late Show with David Letterman* resumes with writers after a one-off deal. {1/6} United Artists reaches a deal with the WGA. '*One-off deals do nothing to bring the WGA closer to a permanent solution for working writers.*' – AMPTP statement. {1/7} *The Daily Show with Jon Stewart* and *The Colbert Report* return without writers. {1/13} An ersatz, nominee-free Golden Globes ceremony airs: '*It's like an Irish wake where there's food and drink but somebody is missing.*' – Kevin Jacobsen, security guard. {1/18} The stalemate has ended, the WGA says. {1/23} Talks resume after the WGA agrees to withdraw its demands to organize reality and animation writers. '*Must be present to win.*' – mock Oscar-nomination certificate unveiled by Academy president Sid Ganis. {2/5} *Vanity Fair* cancels its annual Oscar party. {2/9} WGA board announces a tentative deal: '*Our strike has been a success.*' – P. Verrone. {2/10} The WGA East and West boards approve the contract. {2/12} WGA membership approves ending strike, by 92·5%. '*Can anyone remember what we were working on three months ago?*' – Shane Brennan, CBS producer, to writing staff. {2/24} Oscars air [see p.154]. {2/26} The WGA membership ratifies the new contract.

──────── US TOP-GROSSING MOVIES · 2007 ────────

Film	US box-office gross ($m)	director
Spider-Man 3	336·5	Sam Raimi
Shrek the Third	322·7	Chris Miller
Transformers	319·2	Michael Bay
Pirates of the Caribbean: At World's End	309·4	Gore Verbinski
Harry Potter & the Order of the Phoenix	292·0	David Yates
I Am Legend	251·7	Francis Lawrence
The Bourne Ultimatum	227·5	Paul Greengrass
300	210·6	Zack Snyder
Ratatouille	206·4	Brad Bird
National Treasure: Book of Secrets	205·7	Jon Turteltaub

[Source: MPAA. Includes box-office gross through February 2008.] Batman sequel *The Dark Knight* grossed more ($155·3m) during its opening weekend (July 18–20, 2008) than any other film in Hollywood history, not accounting for inflation. The film also broke a number of other records, including: highest single-day take ($67·9m on July 18); top-grossing midnight release ($18·5m on July 18); most screens at a time (4,366 on July 18); and top-grossing weekend on IMAX screens ($6·2m). The film drew additional attention as the last complete film of Australian actor Heath Ledger, who died on January 22, 2008, months after completing filming for his role as the Joker [see p.57].

──────── ALTERNATIVE MOVIE TITLES ────────

American title	Also known as …
Airplane (1980)	*Flying High!* (New Zealand, Philippines)
Annie Hall (1977)	*Io & Annie* (Italy);
	Der Stadtneurotiker ('The urban neurotic', Austria, West Germany)
Bend It Like Beckham (2002)	*Kick It Like Beckham* (Austria, Germany)
Cruel Intentions (1999)	*Sex Games* (Denmark); *Seduction Games* (Israel)
	The Temptation More Beautiful Than a Love (S Korea)
The Deer Hunter (1978)	*Die Durch die Hölle gehen*
	('Those who go through hell', Austria, West Germany)
East of Shanghai (1931)	*Rich and Strange* (UK)
The French Connection (1971)	*Focus Brooklyn* (Germany)
From the Mixed-Up Files of Mrs. Basil E. Frankweiler (1973)	*The Hideaways* (UK)
Gone with the Wind (1939)	*Lo que el viento se llevó* ('What the wind blew away',
	Spanish-speaking countries)
Never Been Kissed (1999)	*College Attitude* (France)
Out of Africa (1985)	*La mia Africa* ('My Africa', Italy)
Pulp Fiction (1994)	*Kriminale* (Bulgaria)
Snakes on a Plane (2006)	*Snake Flight* (Japan)
The Sound of Music (1965)	*Sonrisas y lágrimas* ('Smiles and Tears', Spain)
	Tutti insieme appassionatamente ('All together passionately', Italy)
The Magician (1959)	*The Face* (UK)
A View to a Kill (1985)	*The Beautiful Prey* (Japan)
Wild Things (1998)	*Sex Crimes* (France, Belgium)

—————————— BEST FILM COSTUME ——————————

The green dress worn by Keira Knightley in *Atonement* was voted best film costume in a January 2008 survey by Sky Movies and *InStyle*. The top five costumes were:

Keira Knightley's emerald green satin evening dress .... worn in *Atonement*
Marilyn Monroe's white halterneck dress....................... *The Seven Year Itch*
Audrey Hepburn's black Givenchy dress....................... *Breakfast at Tiffany's*
Olivia Newton-John's skin-tight pants... *Grease*
Kate Winslet's blue gown.. *Titanic*

—————————— FAVORITE MOVIE WEAPON ——————————

Luke Skywalker's gleaming light saber was the favorite movie weapon of 2,000 film-goers polled by 20th Century Fox in 2008. The top ten favorite movie weapons are:

Weapon	movie	
Light saber .... *Star Wars*	Golden gun ....
.44 Magnum ....*Dirty Harry*	*The Man with the Golden Gun*
Bullwhip................. *Indiana Jones*	Bow and arrow............*Robin Hood*
Samurai sword .... *Kill Bill*	Machine gun .... *Scarface*
Chainsaw.....*Texas Chainsaw Massacre*	The 'Death Star'............. *Star Wars*
	Bowler hat.................. *Goldfinger*

—————————— BEST FILMS BY GENRE ——————————

The American Film Institute (AFI) balloted a host of actors, critics, and filmmakers, in June 2008, to create a series of lists of the 10 greatest films across 10 different genres. According to AFI members, the top-ranking film of each genre is:

Animation	*Snow White & the Seven Dwarfs* (1937)
Fantasy	*The Wizard of Oz* (1939)
Gangster	*The Godfather* (1972)
Science fiction	*2001: A Space Odyssey* (1968)
Western	*The Searchers* (1956)
Sports	*Raging Bull* (1980)
Mystery	*Vertigo* (1958)
Romantic comedy	*City Lights* (1931)
Courtroom drama	*To Kill a Mockingbird* (1962)
Epic	*Lawrence of Arabia* (1962)

—————————— TOP-GROSSING MOVIES OF ALL TIME ——————————

Gone with the Wind ....$1·39bn	*Titanic*............................0·88bn
Star Wars........................1·22bn	*Jaws*...............................0·88bn
The Sound of Music.............0·98bn	*Doctor Zhivago* ....0·85bn
E.T.: The Extra-Terrestrial......0·98bn	*The Exorcist*.....................0·76bn
The Ten Commandments ....0·90bn	*Snow White & the 7 Dwarves* ...0·75bn

[North American box-office grosses adjusted for inflation. Source: *New York Times*]

—————————— HOLLYWOOD WALK OF FAME ——————————

Some of the celebrities awarded a star on the Hollywood Walk of Fame in 2008:

Charles Durning · Brian Keith · Susan Saint James · Holly Hunter
Sean 'Diddy' Combs · Michael Eisner · Kate Linder · Stephen Schwartz
Angela Bassett · Vince McMahon · Sherwood Schwartz
Suzanne Pleshette · Lucho Gatica · Elizabeth Montgomery

—————————— SOME 2008 MOVIE TAGLINES OF NOTE ——————————

Would you put your eggs … in this basket?	Baby Mama
Why so serious?	The Dark Knight
Summer 1994. The girls were fly. The music was dope.	
And Luke was just trying to deal.	The Wackness
Heroes never die … They just reload.	Rambo
One elephant, one world, one story	Horton Hears a Who!
Shoot first. Sightsee later.	In Bruges
A new age has begun.	The Chronicles of Narnia: Prince Caspian
The last man on earth is not alone.	I Am Legend
Get Carried Away	Sex and the City
Privilege. Ambition. Desire.	Brideshead Revisited
Put this in your pipe and smoke it	Pineapple Express
They grow up so fast.	Step Brothers
Choose your destiny	Wanted
His karma is huge.	The Love Guru

According to a 2008 survey released by branding agency Tagline Guru, the top tagline ever is, *In space no one can hear you scream* (from *Alien*), followed by *Houston, we have a problem* (*Apollo 13*), *They're back* (*Poltergeist II*), and *We are not alone* (*Close Encounters of the Third Kind*). The survey of 500 advertising pros rated taglines based on humor, attitude, expression, and influence on popular culture.

—————————— VIOLENT MOVIES & CRIME ——————————

Violent movies may actually deter violent crime, according to research presented at the 2008 annual meeting of the American Economic Association. Professors Gordon Dahl from the University of Rochester and Stefano DellaVigna from the University of California at Berkeley compared box-office attendance at violent and non-violent movies between 1995–2004 with daily crime reports from the US National Incident-Based Reporting System during the same period. Perhaps surprisingly, the researchers discovered that when audiences for violent films increased, reports of violent crime decreased. The effect was strongest from 6pm–12am, when for every additional million people attending a violent film, reports of violent crimes fell by 1·1–1·3%. The researchers surmised that the public is protected on nights when violent films are shown because would-be criminals choose to attend the films instead of roaming the streets, where they may engage in more volatile activities.

————80TH ACADEMY AWARD WINNERS · 2008————

The media breathed a sigh of relief when the Writers' Guild of America strike was settled in time for the 2008 Oscars [see p.150]. Yet for many the show failed to live up to the dazzle of previous years. A gang of bleak Best Picture nominees did nothing to lift a strike-bruised industry, and with little time to prepare the ceremony, host Jon Stewart's presentation was top-heavy with preprepared clips. Though no one film dominated, it was a good night for those outside the Hollywood elite – all 4 Best Actor awards went to people without a US passport. And the winners were ...

Leading actor	Daniel Day-Lewis · *There Will Be Blood*
Leading actress	Marion Cotillard · *La vie en rose*
Supporting actor	Javier Bardem · *No Country for Old Men*
Supporting actress	Tilda Swinton · *Michael Clayton*
Best picture	*No Country for Old Men*
Directing	Joel Coen & Ethan Coen · *No Country for Old Men*
Animated feature	Brad Bird · *Ratatouille*
Art direction	Dante Ferretti & Francesca Lo Schiavo · *Sweeney Todd*
Cinematography	Robert Elswit · *There Will Be Blood*
Costume design	Alexandra Byrne · *Elizabeth: The Golden Age*
Doc. feature	Alex Gibney & Eva Orner · *Taxi to the Dark Side*
Doc. short subject	Cynthia Wade & Vanessa Roth · *Freeheld*
Film editing	Christopher Rouse · *The Bourne Ultimatum*
Foreign language film	Stefan Ruzowitzky · *The Counterfeiters*
Makeup	Didier Lavergne & Jan Archibald · *La vie en rose*
Music (score)	Dario Marianelli · *Atonement*
Music (song)	Glen Hansard & Marketa Irglova, *Falling Slowly* · *Once*
Short film (animated)	Suzie Templeton & Hugh Welchman · *Peter & the Wolf*
Short film (live)	Philippe Pollet-Villard · *Le Mozart des pickpockets*
Sound mixing	Scott Millan, David Parker, & Kirk Francis *The Bourne Ultimatum*
Sound editing	Karen Baker Landers & Per Hallberg · *The Bourne Ultimatum*
Visual effects	Fink, Westenhofer, Morris, & Wood · *The Golden Compass*
Screenplay (adapted)	Joel Coen & Ethan Coen · *No Country for Old Men*
Screenplay (original)	Diablo Cody · *Juno*
Honorary award	Robert Boyle

QUOTES ❧ JON STEWART · Does this town need a hug? What happened? ❧ TILDA SWINTON · I have an American agent who is the spitting image of this. Really, truly the same shaped head and, it has to be said, the buttocks. ❧ MARION COTILLARD · Thank you, life. Thank you, love. It is true there are some angels in this city. ❧ JAVIER BARDEM · Thank you to the Coens ... [for putting] one of the most horrible haircuts in history over my head. ❧ DANIEL DAY-LEWIS (receiving his award from Dame Helen Mirren) · That's the closest I'll ever come to getting a knighthood. ❧ JOEL COEN · We're very thankful to all of you out there for letting us continue to play in our corner of the sandbox. ❧ HELEN MIRREN · Unfortunately, so often the roles are not good enough for the women, but the roles for the men are always wonderful. ❧ DIABLO CODY (*Juno* screenwriter) · This is for the writers.

OSCAR NIGHT FASHION · 2008

Star	dress	designer
Nicole Kidman	*simple black silk, empire line*	Balenciaga
Hilary Swank	*black, one-shoulder, netting fishtail skirt*	Versace
Tilda Swinton	*black silk, unstructured, asymmetric*	Lanvin
Ellen Page	*black, vintage flapper-style dress*	Jean Louis Scherrer
Cate Blanchett	*deep purple, empire line, flower details*	Dries Van Noten
Amy Adams	*dark green, corseted strapless, fishtail*	Proenza Schouler
Anne Hathaway	*bright red draped dress, garland shoulder detail*	Marchesa
Katherine Heigl	*bright red, sleek, one-shoulder*	Escada
Diablo Cody	*leopard print, chiffon*	Dior
Marion Cottilard	*pearl white, sequin-encrusted fish-scales*	Jean-Paul Gaultier

OSCAR SNUBS

Below is *Entertainment Weekly*'s 2008 list of the greatest performances in film history that never received an Academy Award nomination:

1 .... Jimmy Stewart · *Vertigo*
2 .... Anthony Perkins · *Psycho*
3 .. Cary Grant · *The Philadelphia Story*
4 .... Ingrid Bergman · *Casablanca*
5 ..... Samuel L. Jackson · *Jungle Fever*
6 .... Susan Sarandon · *Bull Durham*
7 .. John Cazale · *The Godfather, Part 2*
8 ..... Judy Garland · *The Wizard of Oz*
9 .. Marilyn Monroe · *Some Like It Hot*
10 .... Dennis Hopper · *Blue Velvet*

A 2008 poll by British film advertising company Pearl & Dean named prison drama *The Shawshank Redemption* the film that most deserved to win an Oscar but never did. *The Sixth Sense* was runner-up, followed by *Fight Club* and *Blade Runner*.

OSCAR ODDS

Oscar-watchers have long suspected that actors who perform in dramas are more likely to be nominated for an Academy Award. In January 2008, a team of Harvard and UCLA sociologists confirmed these suspicions by analyzing the Internet Movie Database records for every Oscar-eligible film released from 1927–2005. The researchers discovered that actors who appeared in dramas were 9× more likely to receive an Oscar nomination, when compared to actors who appeared in other genres. Women also had a higher chance of nomination, since there are fewer roles for the fairer sex but the same number of Oscar slots. An actor's chances of nomination were also increased by previous nominations and a higher placing in past movie credits, as well as by having a major distributor. Cast size and industry ties were found to have little effect.

THE OSCARS OF...

A variety of awards are touted as 'the Oscars of' various industries, including: the ERA Awards – the Oscars of electronic retailing; the Milken Family Foundation National Educator Award – the Oscars of teaching; the Codie Awards – the Oscars of software; the Stevie Awards – the Oscars of the business world; the W.C. Handy Award – the Oscars of the blues; the AVN Adult Movie Awards – the Oscars of porn.

———————— THE 65th GOLDEN GLOBES · 2008 ————————

The inane red carpet chitchat and star-studded shenanigans that usually accompany the Golden Globes were nowhere in sight in 2008, thanks to a strike by the Writers Guild of America [see p.150]. Since Guild members were not allowed to write for the ceremony, the traditional gala format was scrapped in favor of a 30-minute news conference. The awards themselves offered little by way of surprise – although Marion Cotillard's award for best actress in a musical or comedy was considered an upset, since Ellen Page (star of heartfelt teen-pregnancy comedy *Juno*) had been widely favored. And the winners – none of whom were actually present – were ...

Award	*winner*
Dramatic picture	*Atonement*
Dramatic actress	Julie Christie · *Away from Her*
Dramatic actor	Daniel Day-Lewis · *There Will Be Blood*
Picture, musical or comedy	*Sweeney Todd*
Actress, musical or comedy	Marion Cotillard · *La vie en rose*
Actor, musical or comedy	Johnny Depp · *Sweeney Todd*
Supporting actress	Cate Blanchett · *I'm Not There*
Supporting actor	Javier Bardem · *No Country for Old Men*
Director	Julian Schnabel · *The Diving Bell and the Butterfly*
Screenplay	Ethan and Joel Coen · *No Country for Old Men*
Original score	Dario Marianelli · *Atonement*
Original song	*Guaranteed* · *Into the Wild*
Animated feature film	*Ratatouille*
Foreign-language film	*The Diving Bell and the Butterfly*
Dramatic TV series	*Mad Men*
Actress, dramatic TV series	Glenn Close · *Damages*
Actor, dramatic TV series	Jon Hamm · *Mad Men*
TV series, musical or comedy	*Extras*
TV actress, musical or comedy	Tina Fey · *30 Rock*
TV actor, musical or comedy	David Duchovny · *Californication*
TV miniseries or movie	*Longford*
TV actress, miniseries or movie	Queen Latifah · *Life Support*
TV actor, miniseries or movie	Jim Broadbent · *Longford*
TV supporting actress, miniseries or movie	Samantha Morton · *Longford*
TV supporting actor, miniseries or movie	Jeremy Piven · *Entourage*

NBC's 1-hour telecast of the Golden Globes drew a paltry 5·8m viewers (a 71% decline on 2007), placing it 4th in ratings. At the same time, more people were watching the CBS miniseries *Comanche Moon*; ABC's *Extreme Makeover: Home Edition*; and *Family Guy* and *American Dad* (both on Fox).

NOTABLE QUOTES ❧ The Hollywood writers' strike took the glitz, the glamour, and roughly two thirds of the audience from this year's Golden Globes [David Germain, AP]. ❧ The preshow special looked hastily put together and awkward, an apt preview of the tensions that poisoned the no-frills announcement event [Alessandra Stanley, *New York Times*]. ❧ A half-hour before airtime, the photographers went wild: Mary Hart had arrived! It was the celebrity high point of the evening [Timothy M. Gray, *Variety*].

OTHER MOVIE AWARDS OF NOTE

ANNIE AWARDS 2008 · *annieawards.com*

Best animated feature.. *Ratatouille*
Best animated television production.................... *Creature Comforts America*
Best animated effects .... *Surf's Up*

DIRECTORS GUILD AWARDS 2008 · *dga.org*

Feature ....Joel Coen & Ethan Coen · *No Country for Old Men*
Documentary ....Asger Leth · *Ghosts of Cite Soleil*
Comedy series...................... Barry Sonnenfeld · *Pushing Daisies* ('Pie-lette')
Dramatic series...............Alan Taylor · *Mad Men* ('Smoke Gets in Your Eyes')
Commercials..........................Nicolai Fuglsig · *'Tipping Point'* (Guinness);
'It's Magic' (JC Penney)

GOLDEN RASPBERRIES 2008 · *razzies.com*

Worst picture .... *I Know Who Killed Me*
Worst director............................Chris Siverston · *I Know Who Killed Me*
Worst actor.. Eddie Murphy · *Norbit*
Worst actress............................ Lindsay Lohan · *I Know Who Killed Me*
Worst excuse for a horror movie .... *I Know Who Killed Me*

INDEPENDENT SPIRIT AWARDS 2008 · *filmindependent.org*

Best feature.. *Juno*
Best director.................... Julian Schnabel · *The Diving Bell and the Butterfly*
Best male lead............................. Philip Seymour Hoffman · *The Savages*
Best female lead.. Ellen Page · *Juno*

MTV MOVIE AWARDS 2008 · *mtv.com*

Best movie... *Transformers*
Best male performance ....Will Smith · *I Am Legend*
Best female performance ....Ellen Page · *Juno*
Best villain ....Johnny Depp · *Sweeney Todd*
Best fight.........................Sean Faris *vs* Cam Gigandet · *Never Back Down*
Best comedic performance ......J. Depp · *Pirates of the Caribbean: At World's End*
Best kiss .... Briana Evigan & Robert Hoffman · *Step Up 2 the Streets*

NATIONAL BOARD OF REVIEW 2007 · *nbrmp.org/awards*

Best film... *No Country for Old Men*
Best actor...................................... George Clooney · *Michael Clayton*
Best actress ....Julie Christie · *Away from Her*
Career achievement award....................................... Michael Douglas

SCREEN ACTORS GUILD AWARDS 2007 · *sagawards.org*

Cast performance .... *No Country for Old Men*
Best actor...................................Daniel Day-Lewis · *There Will Be Blood*
Best actress ....Julie Christie · *Away from Her*
Life achievement award... Charles Durning

SUNDANCE · 2008

Although some predicted that the Writers Guild of America strike [see p.150] would make 2008 a banner year for indie sales at the Sundance Film Festival, studios and distributors seemed relatively uninspired and big-money deals were few and far between. Critics noted that the festival, which is produced by Robert Redford's Sundance Institute to showcase the best in independent film, offered few crowd-pleasers in the vein of 2006's gem, *Little Miss Sunshine*. The celebrity vehicles on offer were poorly received and were outshone by bleak social realism pieces considering poverty (*Ballast*), Hurricane Katrina (*Trouble the Water*), and illegal immigration (*Frozen River*). Below are selected deals and quotes of note from Sundance 2008:

DEALS OF NOTE

Film	distributor (est. price)
Hamlet 2	Focus Features ($10m)
Choke	Fox Searchlight ($5m)
Henry Poole Is Here	Overture ($3·5m)
American Teen	Paramount Vantage ($1m)
Frozen River	Sony Pictures Classics (<$1m)

QUOTES OF NOTE

❦ ROBERT REDFORD · This year filmmakers are putting personal focus on issues relating to the world we live in rather than addressing them on a macro-political level. ❦ TIA LESSIN (codirector, *Trouble the Water*) · We couldn't have predicted that [out of] the despair and outrage that we felt in the aftermath of Katrina would emerge a story that is all about survival and hope. ❦ QUENTIN TARANTINO · Cinema, baby!

Grand jury prize, documentary	*Trouble the Water* · Tia Lessin & Carl Deal
Grand jury prize, dramatic	*Frozen River* · Courtney Hunt
World cinema jury prize, documentary	*Man on Wire* · James Marsh (UK)
World cinema jury prize, dramatic	*Ping Pongkingen* (King of Ping Pong) Jens Jonsson (Sweden)
Audience award, documentary	*Fields of Fuel* · Josh Tickell
Audience award, dramatic	*The Wackness* · Jonathan Levine
World cinema audience award, doc.	*Man on Wire* · James Marsh (UK)
World cin. audience award, dramatic	*Captain Abu Raed* · Amin Matalqa (Jordan)

FILM FESTIVAL PRIZES · 2008

Berlin · Golden Bear [FEB]	*Elite Squad* · José Padilha
Tribeca · Narrative Feature [APR/MAY]	*Let the Right One In* · Tomas Alfredson
Cannes · Palme d'Or [MAY]	*The Class* · Laurent Cantent
Moscow · Golden St George [JUN]	*As Simple as That* · Seyyed Reza Mir Karimi
Venice · Golden Lion [AUG/SEP '07]	*Lust, Caution* · Ang Lee
Toronto · People's Choice Award [SEP '07]	*Eastern Promises* · David Cronenberg
London · Sutherland Trophy [OCT '07]	*Persepolis* · Vincent Paronnaud and Marjane Satrapi

————— IMDb ON THE GLOBAL FILM INDUSTRY —————

Below are the countries with the most films listed in the Internet Movie Database (IMDb) as of June 2008 – along with the most common genres and keywords:

Country	films	common genres	common keywords
USA	209,802	short, comedy, drama	sex, independent film
France	35,645	short, drama, comedy	based on novel, character name in title
UK	33,443	drama, short, comedy	based on novel, independent film
Germany	22,777	short, documentary, drama	sex, based on novel
Italy	19,837	drama, comedy, short	based on novel, sex
India	19,754	drama, romance, action	based on novel, character name in title
Canada	19,273	short, documentary, drama	independent film, sex
Japan	16,303	drama, animation, action	based on novel, anime
Spain	15,291	short, comedy, documentary	based on novel, female nudity
Mexico	14,280	drama, short, documentary	melodrama, based on novel

————————————— METHOD ACTING —————————————

2008 Best Actor Oscar winner Daniel Day-Lewis is famous for his involved preparations before a role. He lived off the land for six months to prepare for *The Last of the Mohicans*, trained in the ring for nearly three years before his turn in *The Boxer*, and while shooting *My Left Foot*, in which he played a character with cerebral palsy, rarely left his wheelchair and was reportedly spoon-fed by crew members. Such measures are a more extreme form of method acting, which emphasizes emotional identification with the character one is to portray. The Russian theater director Konstantin Stanislavsky (1863–1938), usually cited as the father of method acting, urged a move away from the exaggerated, artificial style of theatrical performance towards a naturalistic approach emphasizing psychological depth. After founding the Moscow Art Theatre in 1897, he developed the Stanislavsky System, a set of techniques through which actors are trained to become their characters by drawing upon the experiences and emotions of their own life. These techniques were later refined at the Actors Studio in Manhattan, under the auspices of the formidable Lee Strasberg, an immigrant from the Ukraine. Strasberg drew upon Stanislavsky's theories to create a series of physical and psychological exercises that encouraged actors to plumb their own psyche as well as the motivations of their character. While a school of sorts, the Actors Studio (still extant) offers no final degree, and its membership is for life. Notable Actors Studio members include:

James Dean · Marlon Brando · Marilyn Monroe · Dustin Hoffman · Robert De Niro
Al Pacino · Sidney Poitier · Norman Mailer · Geraldine Page · Edward Albee
Montgomery Clift · Shelley Winters · Frank Corsaro · Julia Roberts

By most accounts, Stanislavsky and Lee Strasberg's ideas are now part of mainstream acting theory, although the 'method' also has its detractors. According to an oft-repeated anecdote, when Dustin Hoffman stayed awake for two days to 'get into' his character during the filming of *Marathon Man*, his costar Laurence Olivier is said to have quipped, 'Why don't you try acting? It's so much easier'.

THE HOLLYWOOD SIGN

The Hollywood sign was erected on the southern slope of Mt Lee in the Santa Monica Mountains in 1923, by property developer Harry Chandler, with the goal of publicizing a housing development below. The sign's prominent position soon made it a metonym both for the area and the burgeoning film industry. However, as the table below illustrates, the fluctuating fortunes of Hollywood have since been reflected in the changing typographical condition of the sign's 50'-tall letters:

The sign cost $21,000 but was only intended to last a year and a half.

Two decades of neglect resulted in the H toppling over in the late 1940s.

In 1949 the Hollywood Chamber of Commerce repaired the sign, removing the LAND.

During the 1970s the top of the D and the third O fell down,
and an arsonist set fire to the bottom of the second L.

In 1973 a practical joker altered the letters to encourage the loosening of laws on marijuana.

In 1978 Hugh Hefner hosted a gala fundraiser to restore the sign, with
celebrities sponsoring individual letters. Rocker Alice Cooper
bought an O, and crooner Andy Williams bought the W.

For three months in 1978, while the old sign was removed
and a new one constructed, Hollywood had no sign at all.

The sign was altered to mark Pope John Paul II's visit in 1987.

In March 2008, a Chicago-based investment group offered 138 acres above and left of the sign for $22m; inevitably, some groups have expressed fears that developing the land would overshadow the landmark. ❦ Hollywood has become so iconic that other entertainment-related locations have adopted names ending in '-wood', including: Bollywood (Bombay-based film industry), Lollywood (Lahore-based Pakistani film industry), Nollywood (Nigerian film industry), and Dollywood (Dolly Parton's Tennessee theme park). Hollywood, California, should not be confused with the Belfast suburb of Holywood, County Down, whose attractions include the Ulster Folk & Transport Museum.

Books & Arts

The more minimal the art, the more maximum the explanation.
— HILTON KRAMER (*b.*1928)

NOBEL PRIZE IN LITERATURE

The 2007 Nobel Prize in Literature was awarded to DORIS LESSING (1919–),

that epicist of the female experience, who with scepticism, fire,
and visionary power has subjected a divided civilisation to scrutiny

At 87, Doris Lessing is the oldest person to win the Nobel Prize in Literature – and the 11th woman. Upon learning of the award from a group of reporters on her doorstep, Lessing's response was characteristically sharp: 'Either they were going to give it to me sometime before I popped off, or not at all'. Indeed, many in the press saw the selection as somewhat tardy – coming as it did decades after the release of her most celebrated works. Yet few would deny that Lessing's fearlessness and insight had earned her the prize. ❦ Born in Iran in 1919, Lessing moved with her family to Rhodesia (now Zimbabwe), and her experiences there shaped her interest in racial, social, and sexual conflict. Her first book, *The Grass Is Singing* (1950), described a doomed love affair between a white woman and her African servant, and proved a near-instant bestseller. The *Children of Violence* series (1952–69) traced the intellectual development of heroine Martha Quest through turbulent mid-century Africa and England, furthering Lessing's themes and cementing her resonance with readers. Yet it was *The Golden Notebook* (1962) that earned Lessing her highest acclaim. The story of one woman as told through four journals, the book was embraced by the embryonic feminist movement for its intimate portrayal of a 'liberated' woman and her conflicted desires. Lessing never felt comfortable with her position as a feminist pioneer, sometimes calling *The Golden Notebook* her 'albatross', and preferring to see herself as a chronicler of the human condition. She followed *The Golden Notebook* with explorations of both inner and outer space, offering a vision of mental illness with *Briefing for a Descent into Hell* (1971), and turning towards science fiction with the *Canopus in Argos: Archives* series (1979–83). In 1984, she wrote two books under the pseudonym Jane Somers, to prove the difficulty of being published as an unknown writer (her British publisher rejected both). ❦ Lessing's Nobel acceptance speech extolled the value of literature and bemoaned the rise of the internet in today's 'fragmenting culture'. In May 2008, she called her Nobel win 'a bloody disaster', saying the relentless media attention made it near impossible to write a full novel.

WEEKLY US BESTSELLERS

USA Today tracks the bestselling books each week across all categories (fiction, nonfiction, paperback, and hardcover), based on reports from major bookstores, Amazon.com, Target, &c. The year's bestselling books through August 2008 were:

Week ending ...

1·06	*Eat, Pray, Love* ·	E. Gilbert
1·13	*Plum Lucky* ·	Janet Evanovich
1·20	*Eat, Pray, Love* ·	E. Gilbert
1·27	*Duma Key* ·	Stephen King
2·03	*The Appeal* ·	John Grisham
2·10	*A New Earth* ·	Eckhart Tolle†
2·17	*A New Earth* ·	Eckhart Tolle
2·24	*A New Earth* ·	Eckhart Tolle
3·02	*A New Earth* ·	Eckhart Tolle
3·09	*A New Earth* ·	Eckhart Tolle
3·16	*A New Earth* ·	Eckhart Tolle
3·23	*A New Earth* ·	Eckhart Tolle
3·30	*A New Earth* ·	Eckhart Tolle
4·06	*A New Earth* ·	Eckhart Tolle
4·13	*A New Earth* ·	Eckhart Tolle
4·20	*A New Earth* ·	Eckhart Tolle
4·27	*The Last Lecture* ·	Randy Pausch‡
5·04	*The Last Lecture* ·	Randy Pausch
5·11	*Audition* ·	Barbara Walters
5·18	*The Hollow* ·	Nora Roberts
5·25	*The Last Lecture* ·	Randy Pausch

6·01	*The Last Lecture* ·	Randy Pausch
6·08	*When You Are Engulfed in Flames*	
		David Sedaris
6·15	*Sail* ·	J. Patterson & H. Roughan
6·22	*Fearless Fourteen* ·	J. Evanovich
6·29	*Fearless Fourteen* ·	J. Evanovich
7·06	*Twilight* ·	Stephenie Meyer
7·13	*Tribute* ·	Nora Roberts
7·20	*Twilight* ·	Stephenie Meyer
8·03	*Breaking Dawn* ·	S. Meyer
8·10	*Breaking Dawn* ·	S. Meyer
8·17	*Breaking Dawn* ·	S. Meyer

In March 2008, Amazon bestseller charts in various countries showed that while Americans enjoyed pseudo-mystical books on self-improvement (*The Secret* was tops after *Harry Potter*), the British bought books by TV celebrity chefs, and the French chose more highbrow tomes. The top two books in Japan were *Face Massage* and *Inspiring Exercise*. † An Oprah's Book Club pick. ‡ Written with Jeffrey Zaslow.

FAVORITE BOOK OF ALL TIME & TOP GENRES

Below are the top answers to the question 'What is your favorite book of all time?', posed by a Harris Interactive online poll of 2,513 US adults during March 2008:

1	The Bible	6	Dan Brown · *The Da Vinci Code*
2	M. Mitchell · *Gone with the Wind*	7	Harper Lee · *To Kill a Mockingbird*
3	Tolkien · *Lord of the Rings* [series]	8	Dan Brown · *Angels and Demons*
4	J.K. Rowling · *Harry Potter* [series]	9	Ayn Rand · *Atlas Shrugged*
5	Stephen King · *The Stand*	10	J.D. Salinger · *Catcher in the Rye*

The poll also asked the genre of books read in the past year; the top answers were:

Read in past year	%				
Mystery/thriller &c.	48	Religion/spirituality	28	Self-help	20
History	35	Literature	27	Current affairs	16
Other fiction	34	Other nonfiction	27	Political	15
Biographies	31	Science fiction	25	True crime	14
		Romance	22	Business	13

ODDEST BOOK TITLE OF THE YEAR · 2007

The Diagram Group's prize for Oddest Title of the Year celebrated its 30th anniversary with its 2007 award. Administered by *The Bookseller*, and voted on by members of the book trade, the 'oddest' title of 2007, and the runners-up, were:

*If You Want Closure in Your
Relationship, Start with Your Legs*
Big Boom [winner]

*I Was Tortured by the
Pygmy Love Queen*
Jasper McCutcheon [2nd]

Cheese Problems Solved
P.L.H. McSweeney, editor [3rd]

How to Write a How to Write Book
Brian Piddock

Are Women Human?
Catharine A. MacKinnon

*People Who Mattered in Southend
and Beyond: From King Canute
to Dr Feelgood*
Dee Gordon

BULWER-LYTTON FICTION CONTEST

In 1982, the Department of English and Comparative Literature at San José State University created a literary contest in honor of E.G.E. Bulwer-Lytton (1803–73), who infamously opened his book *Paul Clifford* with 'It was a dark and stormy night'. The contest rewards the best 'bad' opening line to an imaginary novel. The 2008 winner was 41-year-old Garrison Spik from Washington, DC, whose entry was:

Theirs was a New York love, a checkered taxi ride burning rubber, and like the city their passion was open 24/7, steam rising from their bodies like slick streets exhaling warm, moist, white breath through manhole covers stamped 'Forged by DeLaney Bros., Piscataway, N.J.'

CELEBRITY AUTHORS

The wisdom and wit released by some notable celebrity (&c.) scribes during the year:

Title	celebrity author	publisher's description
American Son	Oscar De La Hoya	on achieving the American Dream
Audition	Barbara Walters	inspiring and riveting memoir
Born Standing Up	Steve Martin	illuminating guidebook to stand-up
Freckleface Strawberry	Julianne Moore	story of a little girl who's different
Just Who Will You Be?	Maria Shriver	for seekers of all ages
Losing It	Valerie Bertinelli	frank account of her life backstage
Out of Sync	Lance Bass	frankly discusses life as a gay man
sTORI Telling	Tori Spelling	the real life behind the rumors
Read All About It!	Laura & Jenna Bush	a classroom adventure
Thank You & You're Welcome!	Kanye West	entertaining volume of 'Kanye-isms'
What Happened?	Scott McClellan	candid look into who Bush is

—————— BAD SEX IN FICTION PRIZE · 2007 ——————

Each year the *Literary Review* awards its 'Bad Sex in Fiction' prize to a novel featuring the most 'inept, embarrassing, and unnecessary' sex scene. 2007's winner was the late Norman Mailer [see p.57] for this passage in *The Castle in the Forest*:

His mouth lathered with her sap, he turned around and embraced her face with all the passion of his own lips and face, ready at last to grind into her with the Hound, drive it into her piety.

—————— OTHER BOOK PRIZES OF NOTE · 2008 ——————

Caldecott Medal	Brian Selznick · *The Invention of Hugo Cabret*
Costa Book of the Year	A.L. Kennedy · *Day*
Children's prize	Ann Kelly · *The Bower Bird*
Biography	Simon Sebag Montefiore · *Young Stalin*
Poetry	Jean Sprackland · *Tilt*
First Novel	Catherine O'Flynn · *What Was Lost*
Edgar Allan Poe Awards: Novel	John Hart · *Down River*
Guardian first book award [2007]	Dinaw Mengestu · *Children of the Revolution*
Hugo Awards: Novel	Michael Chabon · *The Yiddish Policemen's Union*
Kingsley Tufts Poetry Prize	Tom Sleigh · *Space Walk*
Man Booker Prize [2007]	Anne Enright · *The Gathering*
National Book Awards: Fiction [2007]	Denis Johnson · *Tree of Smoke*
Nonfiction	Tim Weiner · *Legacy of Ashes: The History of the CIA*
Poetry	Robert Hass · *Time and Materials*
Young People's Literature	Sherman Alexie
	The Absolutely True Diary of a Part-Time Indian
National Book Critics Circle: Fiction	Junot Díaz
	The Brief Wondrous Life of Oscar Wao
Nonfiction	Harriet Washington · *Medical Apartheid*
Autobiography	Edwidge Danticat · *Brother, I'm Dying*
Nebula Awards: Novel	Michael Chabon · *The Yiddish Policemen's Union*
Newbery Medal	Laura Amy Schiltz
	Good Masters! Sweet Ladies! Voices from a Medieval Village
Orange Prize	Rose Tremain · *The Road Home*
PEN/Faulkner Award	Kate Christensen · *The Great Man*
PEN/Nabokov Award	Cynthia Ozick
Truman Capote Award for Literary Criticism	Helen Small · *The Long Life*

[Awards announced during 2008 unless otherwise noted]

Salman Rushdie's *Midnight's Children* won the 2008 'Best of the Booker' prize, given for the novel judged the finest in the 40-year history of the award. Rushdie's magical realist tale won 36% of an on-line vote, beating the 5 other finalists selected by a panel of 3 judges: *Oscar and Lucinda* by Australian Peter Carey; *Disgrace* by S African J.M. Coetzee; *The Conservationist* by S African Nadine Gordimer; *The Siege of Krishnapur* by J.G. Farrell; and *The Ghost Road* by Pat Barker (the latter are both British).

—————————AUTHORS' PAPERS—————————

In January 2008, the Pulitzer Prize-winning novelist Cormac McCarthy, author of *No Country for Old Men*, sold his papers to the Southwestern Writers Collection at Texas State University–San Marcos for $2m. McCarthy's 30 boxes of correspondence, notes, drafts, and proofs became available for scholars at the University's Alkek Library beginning in fall 2008, and the library has negotiated the right of first refusal for any future McCarthy papers (he is said to be at work on 3 novels). The papers of other notable authors may be found at the libraries below:

Alice Walker..Emory University Libraries
Jane Austen................. The Morgan Library, New York City · British Library
William S. Burroughs .... New York Public Library
George Eliot (Mary Ann Evans) .... Beinecke Library, Yale · British Library
William Faulkner .... University of Virginia Library
Graham Greene.. Lauinger Library, Georgetown Univ. · Boston College Libraries
Ernest Hemingway .... John F. Kennedy Presidential Library
Joyce Carol Oates..Syracuse University Library
George Orwell (Eric Blair) .... University College London Library
Upton Sinclair .... Lilly Library, Indiana University at Bloomington
Mark Twain .... Bancroft Library, University of California, Berkeley
Virginia Woolf...Sussex University Library

—————————DEAD PEOPLE'S LIBRARIES—————————

The website LibraryThing.com allows readers to list and catalogue their personal libraries in a format that can be viewed and discussed by other bibliophiles. The site also includes the discussion group *I See Dead People's Books*, in which users reconstruct the collections of the famous deceased by searching institutional catalogs, scholarly works, and other materials. A sampling from these libraries is below:

JAMES JOYCE
Tobias Smollett, *Humphry Clinker*
Bertrand Russell, *Principles of Social
Reconstruction* · William Francis
Collier, *History of Ireland for Schools*

TUPAC SHAKUR
The Diary of Anaïs Nin, 1931–34
Maya Angelou,
I Know Why the Caged Bird Sings
John Steinbeck, *The Grapes of Wrath*

SUSAN B. ANTHONY
Charles Dickens, *Bleak House*
Thomas Paine, *Common Sense*
Julia Smith, *Abby Smith & Her Cows*

ERNEST HEMINGWAY
William A. Robinson, *10,000 Leagues
over the Sea* · US Navy Department,
The 1931 International Code of Signals
Mary (Davis) Gillies, *All About
Modern Decorating*

F. SCOTT FITZGERALD
Sinclair Lewis, *Babbitt* · Karl Marx,
Manifesto of the Communist Party
L. Carroll, *Through the Looking Glass*

EZRA POUND
Aristotle, *The Metaphysics*
Wyndham Lewis, *Doom of Youth*
Hugh Kenner, *The Invention of China*

—————— NABOKOV & UNFINISHED MANUSCRIPTS ——————

When Vladimir Nabokov died in 1977, he left behind the unfinished manuscript of a novel tentatively titled *The Original of Laura*. Before his death, Nabokov ordered the remains of the manuscript to be destroyed, but his family chose to disobey this wish. For over 30 years, the manuscript (in the form of 50 index cards) has languished in a Swiss safe deposit box. In March 2008, Dmitri Nabokov, Vladimir's son, hinted that a decision on the fate of *Laura* could be near. A series of press articles followed, focusing on Dmitri's dilemma – whether to burn the manuscript, as his father had requested, or whether to publish it, satisfying the demands of Nabokov scholars and devotees. In April, Dmitri revealed plans to publish the book, telling Germany's *Der Spiegel* that his father had appeared to him and said, 'You're stuck in a right old mess. Just go ahead and publish'. ❦ *Other unfinished works by authors of note*: Charles Dickens completed only 6 of the 12 planned installments of *The Mystery of Edwin Drood* before he died in 1870. This meant that the work's central mystery, the disappearance of Mr Drood, was never solved. Notably,

Dickens is said to have offered to share the story's denouement with Queen Victoria only months before he died – an offer she declined. ❦ Franz Kafka published very little during the course of his life, and left his 3 major novels (*The Trial*, *The Castle*, and *Amerika*) unfinished at his death in 1924. Before he died, he asked his friend Max Brod to destroy all his work, a request that Brod ignored. ❦ The Latin epic poem the *Aeneid* was unfinished when its author, Virgil, died in 19 BC. However, Emperor Augustus (commissioner of the poem) ignored Virgil's request to burn the manuscript, and asked that it be published with as few changes as possible. ❦ When Mark Twain died in 1910, he left behind 3 unfinished manuscripts on similar themes: *The Chronicle of Young Satan*, *Schoolhouse Hill*, and *No. 44, the Mysterious Stranger*. Albert Bigelow Paine, Twain's biographer, combined the 3 into a single work, released in 1916 as *The Mysterious Stranger*. Today the compilation is seen as badly compromised, and a poor synthesis of Twain's attempt to write a dark social commentary on 'the damned human race'.

————————————— NEW BOOK SMELL —————————————

The fall 2007 launch of Amazon.com's 'reading device' Kindle stimulated discussion on the pleasures and perils of the book in paper form. A 2007 survey by e-book site CafeScribe revealed what people most love and loathe about the paper book:

Most loved characteristic	%	*Most hated characteristic*	%
Feel of turning a page	30	Weight	54
New book smell	30	'Carrying them around'	16
Old book smell	13	Wear & tear from previous readers	8
Wear & tear from previous readers	5	Storage space required	7
Weight	4	Waste (dead trees)	5

———————————— LARGEST US LIBRARIES ————————————

Below are the largest libraries in the US, in terms of the number of volumes held:

Library	volumes		
Library of Congress	32,124,001	Columbia University	9,455,312
Harvard University	15,826,570	Univ. of Texas at Austin	9,022,363
Boston Public Library	15,686,902	University of Michigan	8,273,050
Yale University	12,368,757	Stanford University	8,200,000
University of Illinois†	10,524,935		
University of California‡	10,094,417	† Urbana-Champaign ‡ Berkeley	
		[Source: American Library Association, 2008]	

———————————— PUBLIC LIBRARY USAGE ————————————

The percent of people who visited a library in the past year, by demographic group:

Generation Y† (18–30)	62%	College degree	68
Generation X† (31–42)	59	High school diploma	44
Income >$40,000	59	Parents with children at home	63
Income <$40,000	48	Adults without children at home	48

[† See p.91. Source: Pew Internet & American Life Project and Univ. of Illinois, December 2007]

——— MOST FREQUENTLY CHALLENGED BOOKS · 2007 ———

Gay penguins again proved the most controversial subject in US public schools and libraries, as Justin Richardson and Peter Parnell's *And Tango Makes Three* topped the 2007 list of most frequently challenged books. In library parlance, a 'challenge' is a formal complaint requesting the removal of a book from a library or school due to 'content or appropriateness'. The most-challenged books of 2007:

And Tango Makes Three† — Justin Richardson & Peter Parnell	*challenge:* anti-ethnic, sexism, homosexuality, anti-family, religious viewpoint, unsuited to age group
The Chocolate War · Robert Cormier	sexually explicit, offensive language, violence
Olive's Ocean · Kevin Henkes	sexually explicit, offensive language
The Golden Compass · Philip Pullman	religious viewpoint
The Adventures of Huckleberry Finn · Mark Twain	racism
The Color Purple · Alice Walker	homosexuality, sexually explicit, offensive language
TTYL · Lauren Myracle	sexually explicit, offensive language, unsuited to age group
I Know Why the Caged Bird Sings · Maya Angelou	sexually explicit
It's Perfectly Normal · Robie Harris	sex education, sexually explicit
The Perks of Being a Wallflower — Stephen Chbosky	homosexuality, sexually explicit, offensive language, unsuited to age group

† *And Tango Makes Three* is based on the true story of two male penguins in the Central Park Zoo, Roy and Silo, who formed a couple and successfully hatched and raised a penguin chick named Tango.

──────────── FUTURE OF BOOKS ────────────

A survey of over 1,300 publishing professionals from 86 countries at the October 2007 Frankfurt Book Fair revealed some of the challenges facing the book industry:

What is the greatest threat to the
publishing industry today?   %
Competition from other media 50
Overpublishing 31
Piracy...............................23
Literacy levels 17
Conglomeration 15
Censorship 7

Which of the following will be
obsolete in fifty years' time?   %
Main Street booksellers..............23
The printed book 11
The electronic reader...............10·5
The editor 6
The publisher 4
None of the above ....55·5

Which of the following do you see
as a major area of future growth?   %
E-books..............................44
Audiobooks 41
Books in translation 27
Educational publishing..............27
Graphic novels & comics............18
Children's literature..................17
Commercial fiction 15
Literary fiction 10

What is the most important challenge
currently facing the book industry?   %
Digitization 53
Globalization.........................24
User-generated content..............22
Rights issues.........................15

──────────── KIDS & READING ────────────

A 2008 survey by children's publisher Scholastic examined the reading habits and attitudes of American children aged 5–17. Some notable results from the survey:

Children who ...   %
Read every day......................24
– 4–6 times a week...................19
– 2–3 times a week...................21
– Once a week 14

Children who said ...   %
It is extremely important to
read books for fun 27
– Very important....................41
– A little important 24
– Not important 8

Top reasons given for not
reading more books for fun   %
I would rather do other things 31
Too much homework................27
Trouble finding books I like.........26
I read other things 19

Top places for ideas on what to read   %
Mom 65
Friends 61
Teachers 57
Library or librarian..................48
Dad..................................43
Bookstore/other store...............41

Books vs the net: which is better for ...
Using your imagination.... *books* (63%)
Reading for fun .... *books* (54%)
Inspiring characters ....*tie* (50/50%)
Long-lasting understanding .. *net* (51%)
[Among 9- to 17-year-olds]

Children who ...   %
Have read *Harry Potter*...............58
Say reading *HP* made them interested
in reading other books...............74

───────── THE PULITZER PRIZE · LETTERS & DRAMA ─────────

The 2008 Pulitzers awarded a Special Citation to Bob Dylan for his 'profound impact on popular music and American culture, marked by lyrical compositions of extraordinary poetic power'. Other 2008 Pulitzer Prizes in the arts were awarded to:

Fiction............................Junot Díaz · *The Brief Wondrous Life of Oscar Wao*
Drama...Tracy Letts · *August: Osage County*
History.............................Daniel Walker Howe · *What Hath God Wrought*
Biography .... John Matteson · *Eden's Outcasts*
Poetry....................................... Robert Hass · *Time and Materials*
General nonfiction....................Saul Friedländer · *The Years of Extermination*
Music................................. David Lang · *The Little Match Girl Passion*

───────────── STATE POETS LAUREATE ─────────────

In 1915, longtime librarian and Californian woman of letters Ina Coolbrith was named the first State Poet Laureate. Her crowning took place at the Panama Pacific International Exposition, where Sen. James D. Phelan lay a laurel wreath upon her head and named her the 'sole living representative of the golden age of Californian letters'. Today, 37 states have official Poets Laureate; a list as of January 2008 is below:

AL.......... Sue Walker	ME..........Betsy Sholl	SC...... Marjory Heath
AS......... Peggy Vining	MD .. Michael S. Glaser	Wentworth
CA ....Al Young	MS .. Winifred Hamrick	SD .. David Allan Evans
CO..........Mary Crow	Farrar	TN Margaret B. Vaughn
CT ..... Marilyn Nelson	MO ...... Walter Bargen	TX .... Steven Fromholz
DE.........Fleda Brown	MT............Greg Pape	UT..... Katharine Coles
FL....Edmund Skellings	NE .. William Kloefkorn	VT .... Ruth Stone
GA ......David Bottoms	NH.....Patricia Fargnoli	VA..............Carolyn
IL ....Kevin Stein	NY .... Billy Collins	Kreiter-Foronda
IN...... Joyce Brinkman	NC..... Kathryn S. Byer	WV.....Irene McKinney
IA .... Robert Dana	ND.....Larry Woiwode	WI .... Denise Sweet
KS..........Denise Low	OK..N. Scott Momaday	WY.... David Romtvedt
KY .. Jane Gentry Vance	OR.....Lawson F. Inada	
LA.... Brenda M. Osbey	RI .... Lisa Starr	[Source: Library of Congress]

AK has a 'State Writer Laureate' – Jerah Chadwick; ID has a 'Writer-in-Residence' – Kim Barnes.

───────────── US POET LAUREATE ─────────────

Kay Ryan was named the 16th US Poet Laureate on 7/24/2008. Born in California in 1945, Ryan is known for rigorously spare work that explores moments of every-day life. Interviewed by the *New York Times* after the award's announcement, Ryan revealed that she crafts her poems to function as almost-empty suitcases, contain-ing just a few items: 'the reader starts taking them out, but they keep multiplying'.

———————— ATTACKS ON WORKS OF ART ————————

In October 2007, intruders broke into the Musée d'Orsay in Paris and punched a 4" hole in Claude Monet's *Le Pont d'Argenteuil*. French police later arrested five people, whose motive for attacking the Impressionist masterpiece remains unknown. Some other notable examples of deliberate attacks on works of art are listed below:

The Portland Vase
British Museum, London
In 1845, an 'intemperate vandal' smashed the 1st-century Roman glass vase, causing significant damage.

The Nightwatch · Rembrandt
Rijksmuseum, Amsterdam
This painting has been attacked 3 times: in 1911 and 1975 with a knife, and in 1990, when a psychiatric patient sprayed it with sulphuric acid.

The Rokeby Venus · Velázquez
National Gallery, London
In 1914, suffragette Mary Richardson slashed the Venus in protest against the imprisonment of Emmeline Pankhurst.

Virgin & Child with St Anne & St John the Baptist · Leonardo da Vinci
National Gallery, London
In 1962, a schizophrenic German artist threw ink at the da Vinci; in 1987, it was shot by a former soldier.

The Thinker · Rodin
Cleveland Museum of Art, Ohio
In 1970, radical student group the Weathermen dynamited the sculpture.

Pietà · Michelangelo
St Peter's, Rome
An unhinged geologist smashed the Virgin's forearm and nose in 1972.

Guernica · Pablo Picasso
Museo Reina Sofia, Madrid
In 1974, an antiwar protester sprayed *Guernica* with 'Kill Lies All' while it was on loan to MOMA, New York.

Assorted statues
Villa Borghese Gardens, Rome
A biology professor broke the noses off 80 stone statues of historic figures, in 1985. By way of explanation, he reportedly said, 'the KGB are after me'.

Myra · Marcus Harvey
Royal Academy, London
Harvey's painting of Myra Hindley was attacked twice during the calculatedly controversial Saatchi-backed show *Sensation* in 1997.

Bamiyan Buddhas
Northern Afghanistan
In 2001, these giant statues (which were at least 1,300 years old) were blown up by the Taliban, who claimed they were un-Islamic idols.

Fountain · Marcel Duchamp
Centre Pompidou, Paris
Duchamp's Dadaist artwork (a porcelain urinal) was attacked twice by Pierre Pinoncelli. In 1993, he urinated in it, and 3 years later he cracked it with a hammer. Pinoncelli claimed his attacks were themselves a work of performance art.

In October 2007, the waters of Rome's Trevi fountain ran red after a man poured in a bucket of dye before fleeing. Leaflets found on the scene said the act was a protest against the expense of the Rome Film Festival, and a reference to the event's red carpet. ❦ In July 2008, a German man was arrested after ripping the head off a wax Adolf Hitler at the newly opened Berlin Madame Tussauds.

THE TURNER PRIZE · 2007

Founded in 1984, the Turner Prize is awarded each year to a British artist (defined, somewhat loosely, as an artist working in Britain or a British artist working abroad) under 50, for an outstanding exhibition or other presentation in the twelve months prior to each May. The winner receives £25,000 – and three runners-up £5,000.

Mark Wallinger won the 2007 Turner Prize for his installation *State Britain*, which replicated veteran campaigner Brian Haw's antiwar protest outside Parliament. The award was presented in Liverpool (the first time the ceremony has taken place outside London), to mark the city's status as 2008 European Capital of Culture. It took 15 people 6 months to make *State Britain*, which re-creates in exact detail the banners, flags, and tarpaulin shelter of Haw's iconic camp. Haw had initially rejected Wallinger's proposal (telling him politely to 'piss off'), but later discovered that the two 'shared the same heart'. Haw even attended the Turner prize ceremony. ❦ Wallinger presented a different work in Liverpool – the film *Sleeper*, in which he wanders around Berlin's National Gallery dressed in a bear costume. ❦ Born in 1959, Mark Wallinger studied at Goldsmiths College – the alma

Mark Wallinger

mater of many other members of the YBA (Young British Artist) movement, which emerged in the late 1980s. Wallinger switched from painting to sculpture to 'steel [himself] to work in other ways'. He is best known for *Ecce Homo* – a statue of Christ, which stood on the fourth plinth in Trafalgar Square in 1999. ❦ Wallinger, who lost out to Damian Hirst's pickled animals in the 1995 Turner, was the clear favorite to win the 2007 contest. The jury praised his work for its 'immediacy, visceral intensity, and historic importance', commenting that it combined 'a bold political statement with art's ability to articulate fundamental human truths'. ❦ The Stuckists, an anti-conceptual group of artists and self-publicists, failed to picket the ceremony as usual – although its cofounder Charles Thomson predictably described the entries as 'utter bilge'.

The following artists have been short-listed for the 2008 Turner Prize: *video artist* Runa Islam · *video artist* Mark Leckey · *installation artist* Goshka Macuga · *installation artist and sculptor* Cathy Wilkes.

ORDWAY PRIZE

The 2008 Ordway Prize was awarded to Brazilian artist Cildo Meireles and Los Angeles curator James Elaine. Bestowed biennially by Creative Link for the Arts and the New Museum of Contemporary Art, the $100,000 prize is intended to honor midcareer artists, critics, and curators who have made a 'significant impact on the field of contemporary art', but have yet to achieve public visibility. One of the most influential artists in Latin America, Meireles is known for producing formally innovative and politically engaged conceptual work. Elaine, currently at UCLA's Hammer Museum, has been commended for discovering talented young artists.

————————TOP TEN ARTISTS BY REVENUE · 2007————————

Artprice annually publishes a ranking of artists based on sales generated by their works at auction. 2007 marked the first time in a decade that Picasso was not No. 1:

Rank artist *('06 rank)*	2007 sales ($)
1 .... Andy Warhol (2) 420m	6 .... Henri Matisse (9) 114m
2 .... Pablo Picasso (1) 319m	7 ... Jean-Michel Basquiat (36) . 102m
3 .... Francis Bacon (19) 245m	8 .... Fernand Léger (26).......... 92m
4 .... Mark Rothko (78).......... 207m	9 .... Marc Chagall (6)............ 89m
5 .... Claude Monet (14)......... 165m	10... Paul Cézanne (17).......... 87m
	[Source: Artprice.com]

According to *Artprice*, the global art market saw an overall rise in prices in 2007, perhaps because a shaky stock market drove interest in 'alternative' forms of investment. Yet by the first quarter of 2008, the art market was showing its first signs of diminishing since the attacks of September 11, 2001.

————————THE MOST POWERFUL PEOPLE IN ART————————

The owner of Christie's was named the most powerful person in art in 2007, earning the distinction for the second year in a row. *ArtReview* magazine's top 10 were:

1 .. François Pinault.. *owner of Christie's*	6 .. Damien Hirst† .... *artist*
2 .. Larry Gagosian.......*dealer/gallerist*	7 .. Charles Saatchi.... *collector/gallerist*
3 .. Nicholas Serota ... *museum director*	8 .. Jay Jopling†...........*dealer/gallerist*
4 .. Glenn D. Lowry .. *museum director*	9 .. Steven A. Cohen .... *collector*
5 .. Eli Broad .... *collector*	10. David Zwirner ....*dealer/gallerist*

† Hirst is represented by Jopling's White Cube Gallery which, in 2007, sold for a reported $100m a diamond-encrusted human skull he had created – the most expensive single work by a living artist.

————————FBI's TOP TEN ART CRIMES————————

Since 2005, the FBI has maintained a list of the 'Top Ten Art Crimes' in order to raise public awareness of the stolen property. Below is the list as of July 29, 2008:

Item(s)	stolen from	in	est. $ value
7,000–10,000 Iraqi artifacts	Iraq	2003	'priceless'
12 Isabella Stewart Gardner Museum paintings	USA	1990	300m
Caravaggio · *Nativity with San Lorenzo and San Francesco*	Italy	1969	20m
Davidoff-Morini Stradivarius violin	USA	1995	3m
2 Van Goghs	Netherlands	2002	30m
Cézanne · *View of Auvers-sur-Oise*	England	1999	5.9m
2 Maxfield Parrish murals	USA	2002	4m
4 artworks from the Museu Chácara do Céu	Brazil	2006	unavailable
Frans Van Mieris · *A Cavalier*	Australia	2007	1m
1 Cézanne and 1 Degas	Switzerland	2008	unavailable

——————— TOP EXHIBITIONS · 2007 ———————

The *Art Newspaper*'s figures for the most popular art exhibitions in the world illustrate the continuing success of shows in Japan. Below are the most popular art exhibitions of 2007 around the world – and in NY – by the number of daily visitors:

GLOBAL TOP TEN

2007 exhibition	museum	daily attendance
The Mind of Leonardo	Tokyo National	10,071
Monet's Art and Its Posterity	National Art Center, Tokyo	9,273
Legacy of the Tokugawa	Tokyo National	9,067
Richard Serra Sculpture: 40 Years	Museum of Modern Art, NY	8,585
Masterpieces of French Painting	Museum of Fine Arts, Houston	7,268
Milkmaid by Vermeer	National Art Center, Tokyo	6,856
From Cézanne to Picasso	Musée d'Orsay, Paris	6,239
Masterpieces of French Painting	Neue Nationalgalerie, Berlin	6,115
Tutankhamun and the Pharaohs	Franklin Institute, Philadelphia	5,375
What Is Painting?	Museum of Modern Art, NY	5,269

NEW YORK TOP TEN

Richard Serra Sculpture: 40 Years	Museum of Modern Art	8,585
What Is Painting?	Museum of Modern Art	5,269
The Age of Rembrandt	Metropolitan Museum of Art	5,192
Cézanne to Picasso	Metropolitan Museum of Art	4,824
Ron Mueck	Brooklyn Museum	3,970
Annie Leibovitz: A Photographer's Life	Brooklyn Museum	3,970
Family Pictures	Guggenheim Museum	3,917
Brice Marden: A Retrospective	Museum of Modern Art	3,856
Manet & the Execution of Maximilian	Museum of Modern Art	3,812
Americans in Paris, 1860–1900	Metropolitan Museum of Art	3,788

——————— REPATRIATED ART ———————

In the past few years, museums around the world have expanded efforts to return art and artifacts to the countries and peoples from which they were taken. Such efforts reflect a growing awareness of the value of cultural property, and a renewed focus on repatriation by nations, such as Italy, which have lost many pieces. Below is a selection of pieces returned by American institutions during late 2007 and 2008:

Object	returned by	returned to
Eucharides calyx krater	Metropolitan Museum of Art	Italy
Remains of 55 people	Museum of Natural History	Canada
Thousands of Machu Picchu relics	Yale	Peru
The Danilov Bells	Harvard	Russia
4 ancient artifacts	Princeton	Italy
2 Greek goddess acroliths	University of Virginia	Italy
Limestone and marble Aphrodite statue	Getty Museum	Italy

THE END OF 'RENT'

The groundbreaking rock musical *Rent* closed on September 7, 2008, after a 12-year run at New York's Nederlander Theatre. Written during the early 1990s by the young composer Jonathan Larson, who died on the night of the show's final dress rehearsal, the musical is an adaptation of Puccini's *La Bohème* set among the struggling artists, addicts, and bohemians of New York's East Village. During its engagement, the show played 5,012 performances and 16 previews, grossing $280m (as of January 2008), winning multiple Tonys and one Pulitzer Prize. Below are the original cast members when the show opened on Broadway in April 1996:

Character	*actor*		
Mark Cohen	Anthony Rapp	Angel Schunard	
Roger Davis	Adam Pascal		Wilson Jermaine Heredia
Mimi Marquez	Daphne Rubin-Vega	Maureen Johnson	Idina Menzel
Tom Collins	Jesse L. Martin	Joanne Jefferson	Fredi Walker
		Benjamin Coffin III	Taye Diggs

THE 'VILLAGE VOICE' OBIE AWARDS · 2008

The Obie Awards are presented by a committee of critics and other theater professionals to 'publicly acknowledge and encourage' Off- and Off-Off-Broadway theater. Obies have been given each year since 1955, when they were established by the *Village Voice* theater editor Jerry Tallmer. The 2008 awards are listed below:

PERFORMANCE
Veanne Cox · 'sustained excellence'[†]
Sean McNall · 'sustained excellence'[†]
LisaGay Hamilton · *The Ohio State Murders*
Joel Hatch · *Adding Machine*
Francis Jue · *Yellow Face*
Kate Mulgrew · *Iphigenia 2·0*
Heidi Shreck
Drum of the Waves of Horikawa
Rebecca Wisocky
Amazons and Their Men
Ensemble · *Passing Strange*

DESIGN
Jane Greenwood · 'sustained excellence'[†]
David Zinn · 'sustained excellence'[†]
Takesha Kata, Keith Parham
Adding Machine
Peter Ksander · *Untitled Mars (This Title May Change)*
Katchor, Findlay, Sugg & Champa
The Slug Bearers of Kayrol Island

DIRECTION
David Cromer · *Adding Machine*
Krzysztof Warlikowski · *Krum*

PLAYWRITING
Horton Foote · *Dividing the Estate*
David Henry Hwang · *Yellow Face*

SPECIAL CITATION
David Greenspan · *The Argument*
Nature Theater of Oklahoma · *No Dice*

LIFETIME ACHIEVEMENT
Adrienne Kennedy

ROSS WETZSTEON MEMORIAL
AWARD · Cherry Lane Theater
Mentor Project

BEST NEW THEATER PIECE
Stew, Heidi Rodewald, Annie Dorsen
Passing Strange
† Awards overall achievement

———— TONY AWARDS · 2008 ————

Though the beloved Rodgers & Hammerstein musical *South Pacific* won 7 awards at the 2008 Tonys, the evening also honored several less established productions, including the salsa- and hip-hop-tinged musical *In the Heights*, and the rock musical *Passing Strange*, written by the single-monikered Stew. The major awards were:

Best play...*August: Osage County*
Best musical...*In the Heights*
Best original score..*In the Heights*
Best revival of a play..*Boeing-Boeing*
Best revival of a musical...*South Pacific*
Best leading actor in a play...........................Mark Rylance · *Boeing-Boeing*
Best leading actress in a play.............Deanna Dunagan · *August: Osage County*
Best leading actor in a musical...........................Paulo Szot · *South Pacific*
Best leading actress in a musical..............................Patti LuPone · *Gypsy*
Best featured actor in a play...............................Jim Norton · *The Seafarer*
Best featured actress in a play...................Rondi Reed · *August: Osage County*
Best featured actor in a musical...............................Boyd Gaines · *Gypsy*
Best featured actress in a musical............................Laura Benanti · *Gypsy*
Best direction of a play...................Anna D. Shapiro · *August: Osage County*
Best direction of a musical............................Bartlett Sher · *South Pacific*
Best choreography...........................Andy Blankenbuehler · *In the Heights*
Best orchestration...............Alex Lacamoire and Bill Sherman · *In the Heights*
Lifetime achievement in theater...................................Stephen Sondheim

———— NEW BROADWAY SHOWS · 2007–08 ————

Below are the 36 new productions that opened on Broadway in the 2007–08 season:

*The 39 Steps · August: Osage County · A Bronx Tale · Boeing-Boeing
A Catered Affair† · Cat on a Hot Tin Roof · Come Back, Little Sheba
The Country Girl · Cry-Baby† · Cymbeline · Cyrano de Bergerac
Dr Seuss' How the Grinch Stole Christmas!† · The Farnsworth Invention
Glory Days† · Grease · Gypsy† · The Homecoming · In the Heights† · Is He Dead?
Les Liaisons Dangereuses · The Little Mermaid† · Macbeth · Mauritius · November
Old Acquaintance · Passing Strange† · Pygmalion · The Ritz · Rock & Roll
South Pacific† · Sunday in the Park with George† · The Seafarer · Thurgood
Top Girls · Xanadu† · Young Frankenstein†* († musical)

———— GHOST LIGHTS ————

Many theaters around the world leave a light permanently lit onstage overnight between performances and for the duration between productions. These 'ghost lights', as they are known, perform two tasks: they act as working lights for the crew, and they mollify the superstitious who believe a theater should never be 'dark'.

————————— 'SATURDAY NIGHT LIVE' HOSTS —————————

Hosts and musical guests for season 33 of *Saturday Night Live* (episodes 625–636):

Date	host	musical guest			
9·29·07	LeBron James	Kanye West	3·15·08	Jonah Hill	Mariah Carey
10·6·07	Seth Rogen	Spoon	4·5·08	C. Walken	Panic at the Disco
10·13·07	Jon Bon Jovi	Foo Fighters	4·12·08	A. Kutcher	Gnarls Barkley
11·3·07	Brian Williams	Feist	5·10·08	Shia LaBeouf	My Morning Jacket
2·23·08	T. Fey	C. Underwood			
3·1·08	Ellen Page	Wilco	5·17·08	Steve Carell	Usher
3·8·08	A. Adams	Vampire Weekend	[George Carlin was *SNL*'s first host; see below]		

————— 2008 MARK TWAIN PRIZE & 'FILTHY WORDS' —————

The Kennedy Center Mark Twain Prize was created in 1998 to recognize comedians who 'elbow American culture to see if it's still alive'. On June 17, 2008, the Kennedy Center announced that George Carlin would be awarded the 2008 prize in a November ceremony; sadly, on June 22, Carlin died of heart failure. ❦ Like Mark Twain, Carlin was widely admired for using humor as a means of social commentary. And, though he released 22 albums and 3 books during his 50-year career, he is best remembered for his daring routine '7 Words You Can Never Say on Television', which became the centerpiece in a landmark free speech case, after it was broadcast on a NYC radio station in 1973. In 1978, the Supreme Court ruled that the routine was 'indecent', and that the FCC had the authority to regulate the broadcast of such material – including banning it during hours when children were likely to be listening. This ruling forms the basis for broadcast decency standards still in force. Carlin's 7 words were: [1] the Middle Low German word for dung; [2] a Latin onomatopoeic term for urination; [3] a (likely) Scandinavian term for sexual intercourse; [4] a pre-historic Germanic term for female genitalia; [5] slang that includes the French term for rooster and a verb for drawing liquid; [6] a derogatory term derived from an incestuous act; and [7] a term for female anatomy that also refers to any bird of the genus Parus.

————————————— 2007 THURBER PRIZE —————————————

The Thurber Prize annually celebrates the best American humor writing. It is given in memory of humorist James Thurber (1894–1961), known for his gently witty short stories and *New Yorker* cartoons. In 2007, former *Frasier* executive producer Joe Keenan won for his novel *My Lucky Star*, a Hollywood farce about two playwrights forced to pen the memoirs of a failed starlet. Keenan is the author of the novels *Blue Heaven* and *Putting on the Ritz*, and has written scripts for *Frasier* (for which he won an Emmy in 1996), as well as *Desperate Housewives*. 2007 runners-up included Bob Newhart for *I Shouldn't Even Be Doing This!: and Other Things That Strike Me as Funny*, and Merrill Markoe for *Walking in Circles Before Lying Down*.

ARTISTS IN AMERICA

Approximately 2m Americans are employed full time as artists, according to a 2008 National Endowment for the Arts report. *Artists in the Workforce, 1990–2005* analyzed occupational data from the US Census Bureau on actors, announcers, architects, visual artists, dancers, choreographers, designers, entertainers, performers, musicians, photographers, producers, directors, and writers, to create a profile of artistic employment nationwide. Below is a selection of notable results:

Artist type	No. in US	% ♀	% minority	median age	% <35	avg. income
Designers	779,359	54·9	20·3	40	37·0	$42,000
Fine artists	216,996	47·4	15·8	44	25·7	42,800
Architects	198,498	22·2	19·1	43	26·6	63,500
Writers & authors	185,276	54·9	10·8	44	26·8	50,800
Musicians	169,647	36·1	27·0	45	28·7	38,600
Photographers	147,389	42·8	20·5	39	42·0	37,600
Producers & directors	139,996	35·3	20·1	38	39·0	52,500
Announcers (radio &c.)	55,817	22·4	24·4	35	49·4	36,800
Entertainers &c.	41,128	45·1	25·1	35	49·8	39,900
Actors	39,717	45·1	23·4	35	49·9	31,500
Dancers &c.	25,651	75·9	40·1	26	80·8	34,600
All artists	1,999,474	45·9	19·9	40	35·0	45,200
Civilian labor force	144,898,471	46·4	30·4	40	36·9	38,700

Fine artists includes art directors and animators; dancers includes choreographers; entertainers includes performers. [Based on 2003–05 data collected through the American Community Survey.]

The metropolitan areas with the highest number of artists overall, in 2000:

Los Angeles–Long Beach 140,620
NYC.......................... 132,990
Chicago 64,800
Washington, DC...............47,360
Boston.......................38,885
Philadelphia...................35,670
San Francisco..................35,470
Atlanta.......................34,350
Detroit 33,215
Minneapolis–St Paul...........28,685

20% of all artists live in the top 5 areas.

The metro areas with the most artists of a specific type, in 2000:

Announcers ....Alexandria, LA
Fine artists.................... Santa Fe
Actors..................... Los Angeles
Architects.................... Santa Fe
Dancers......................Las Vegas
Designers............... San Francisco
Musicians.................... Nashville
Producers/directors .... Los Angeles
Entertainers ....Orlando
Photographers........... San Francisco
Writers....................... Santa Fe

[Ranked by the % of artists in the labor force]

In 2000, there were *c.*68 artists for every 10,000 people in the US, including:

27 designers · 8 fine artists · 7 architects · 6 musicians · 6 writers · 5 producers
4 photographers · 2 announcers · 1 actor · 1 dancer · 1 entertainer

─────── WORLD'S TALLEST BUILDING ───────

In 2008, a race to construct the world's tallest building developed among the oil-rich Arab states. In April, Riyadh-based company Kingdom Holding announced plans for the $10·7bn 'Mile High Tower' in the Saudi Arabian city of Jeddah, which will be taller than the Burj Dubai, currently under construction in Dubai and due for completion in 2009. (Although the Burj Dubai's owners have not revealed its final height, the tower is expected to exceed 2,600'.) Yet another 'super skyscraper' is planned for Kuwait. Currently, the world's five tallest buildings are:

Building	built	location	stories	feet
Taipei 101	2004	Taipei, Taiwan	101	1,667
Petronas Towers	1998	Kuala Lumpur, Malaysia	88	1,483
Sears Tower	1974	Chicago, USA	110	1,454
Jin Mao	1999	Shanghai, China	88	1,380
Two Intl Finance Center	2003	Hong Kong	88	1,362

The Council on Tall Buildings and Urban Habitat, which compiled this list, takes as its measurement the distance from the pavement level of the main entrance to the architectural top of the building, which includes spires, but does not include antennae, signage, or flag poles. A structure qualifies as a building (as opposed to a telecommunications tower) if at least 50% of its height is occupied by usable floor area. The council, founded in 1969, is based at the Illinois Institute of Technology in Chicago.

─────── LEANING TOWER OF SUURHUSEN ───────

The small village of Suurhusen in northern Germany caused a minor architectural sensation in November 2007, when Guinness World Records declared the community's church steeple the world's 'most tilted tower' – banishing the Leaning Tower of Pisa to an inglorious second. According to officials who measured both towers, the steeple in Suurhusen reportedly tilts at 5·19°, while the tower at Pisa leans at 3·97°. Though the 1,200 inhabitants of Suurhusen, and their famous medieval brick church, are becoming a worldwide tourist attraction, Pisan mayor Paolo Fontanelli took the news calmly, telling German newspaper *Die Welt*: 'They've got a tower with a tilt of more than 5 degrees? Well, then it will soon collapse.' The steeple in Suurhusen tilts at such an angle because of its wooden foundations, which have been caving in since the 19th century due to subsiding levels of ground water.

─────── SECOND LIFE ARCHITECTURE AWARDS ───────

A semitransparent ball of blue and white vapor won the Grand Prize at the first annual *Second Life* Architecture Awards, held in September 2007 at Austria's Ars Electronica festival. The awards are intended to spotlight 'spatially interesting and aesthetically independent' examples of private homes, corporate architecture, and other constructions inside *Second Life*, an online world that allows inhabitants to design their bodies, clothes, buildings, &c. The vapor ball, titled 'Living Cloud,' was designed by Berliner Tanja Meyle to act as a portable house for her online avatar.

—————— TOP CITIES NOTED FOR DESIGN ——————

In June 2008, the architectural firm RMJM Hillier compiled a ranking of the top 10 US cities noted for design. In creating the list, cities with >500,000 residents were assessed in 10 design-related categories, such as the number of LEED-certified[†] buildings, the quality of public transit, the number of buildings on the National Register of Historic Places, and the number of design and architectural awards won by each city. Chicago's history of architectural innovation and its dedication to the environment helped the city take first place. Below are the top 10 cities for design:

1 . . . . .Chicago	5 . . . . . Portland, Oregon	9 . . . . Philadelphia
2 . . . . New York	6 . . . . .San Francisco	10 . . . . Washington
3 . . . . Boston	7 . . . . .Seattle	
4 . . . . .Los Angeles	8 . . . . .Denver	[Source: *Business Week*]

† Developed by the nonprofit US Green Building Council, LEED (Leadership in Energy and Environmental Design) is a rating system that assesses building sustainability, by examining energy efficiency, use of water, material selection, &c. Chicago currently has 37 LEED-certified buildings.

—— AMERICAN INSTITUTE OF ARCHITECTS AWARDS ——

The AIA GOLD MEDAL is the highest honor given by the institute to an individual; it awards those whose work 'has had a lasting influence on the theory and practice of architecture'. In 2008 the medal was given to Italian architect Renzo Piano, perhaps best known for his work on the Centre Pompidou in Paris. Piano's projects in America include the Nasher Sculpture Center in Dallas, the renovation of the Morgan Library in New York, and the High Museum expansion in Atlanta. His work has been praised by the AIA as 'sculptural, beautiful, technically accomplished, and sustainable'.

The AIA ARCHITECTURE FIRM AWARD is the highest award given by the institute to a firm; it recognizes practices that have produced 'distinguished architecture' for at least a decade. In 2008 the award was won by Philadelphia group KieranTimberlake Associates, which has been lauded for its commitment to sustainable design and research. The group's projects have included SmartWrap (a plastic building material), the Pierson and Davenport Colleges at Yale, the Atwater Commons at Middlebury College, and the Melvin J. and Claire Levine Hall at the University of Pennsylvania.

—————— PRITZKER ARCHITECTURE PRIZE ——————

The Pritzker Prize honors living architects whose work 'has produced consistent and significant contributions to humanity and the built environment'. At a June 2 ceremony in Washington, DC, the 2008 Pritzker was awarded to Jean Nouvel, the bulk of whose work has been in his native France – including the Institut du Monde Arabe (1987) and the Cartier Foundation for Contemporary Art (1994), both in Paris. Nouvel received a $100,000 grant as well as a bronze medallion.

─────────HAUTE COUTURE & PRÊT-À-PORTER─────────

Haute couture ('high dress-making') is the exclusive design and creation of the finest made-to-measure garments. Englishman Charles Worth became known as the 'father of haute couture' after he established the first elite Parisian couture house in 1858, designing and showing finished couture outfits for the *beau monde*. In 1868, Worth established the *Chambre Syndicale de la Haute Couture Parisienne* to protect couture designs from being copied. Since 1945, the production of haute couture has been protected by law. Originally, fashion houses only qualified to use the title if they met the following rules: couturiers had to produce a minimum of 50 original designs for each collection, show their collections twice a year, and employ at least 20 artisans in their atelier. In 1992 the rules were relaxed to allow new designers to produce couture for a trial 2-year period, during which they need only employ 10 people in their workshop and produce 25 designs per collection (more established houses must still employ 15 technicians and show 35 designs per collection). Costs are so prohibitive (reportedly ≥$150,000 for an evening gown) that it is rumored that there are only *c*.300 couture clients worldwide. Recently many haute couture houses have closed, preferring to concentrate on their more profitable ready-to-wear (*prêt-à-porter*) lines. In 1946 there were 106 official couture houses, but by 2008 only a handful of these remained – they are:

Adeline André · Anne Valérie Hash · Chanel · Christian Dior
Christian Lacroix · Dominique Sirop · Elie Saab[†] · Emanuel Ungaro
Franck Sorbier · Givenchy · Maison Martin Margiela[†] · Giorgio Armani[†]
Jean Paul Gaultier · Maurizio Galante · Valentino[†]

[†] These non-French designers are allowed to show as 'correspondent' haute couture houses.

─────────CFDA AWARDS · 2008─────────

Some winners of the 2008 Council of Fashion Designers of America Awards:

Womenswear designer.....................	*Swarovski Award for Menswear*..........
Francisco Costa for Calvin Klein	Scott Sternberg for Band of Outsiders
Swarovski Award for Womenswear.......	*Accessory designer* ....Tory Burch
Kate & Laura Mulleavy for Rodarte	*Geoffrey Beene Lifetime Achievement*
Menswear designer............Tom Ford	*Award*................Carolina Herrera

─ACCESSORIES COUNCIL EXCELLENCE AWARDS · 2008─

Some winners of the 2008 Accessories Council Excellence Awards, which honor those who have had a 'positive impact on accessory consumption' in the past year:

Designer of the year.....................	*Retailer of the year*....Banana Republic
Nicolas Ghesquière for Balenciaga	*Fashion influencer* .... Cate Adair,
Brand of the year......... Jimmy Choo	costumer on *Desperate Housewives*

COLOR FORECAST · 2008–09

Clariant · *'bright, layered colors, contrasted with earthy, neutral tones'* · *'the dark green of chlorophyll'* · *'an independent violet symbolizing the power of self-expression'* · *'the strong, saturated yellow used in flags, taxis, and street paint'* [2009 forecast]

Pantone Fashion Color Report · *'cooler blues, greens and purples'* like Caribbean Blue, Blue Iris, & Royal Lilac · *'variations of warm red, orange and yellow'* like Burnt Orange & Ochre [Fall 2008 forecast]

Sherwin-Williams · *'complex hybrid shades'* such as Wood Violet and Cayenne · *'Whisper-soft, atmospheric colors'* like Mountain Air balancing *'grounded, earthy shades'* like Granite Peak · Energetic vibrant shades such as Gecko and Blackberry [2008 forecast]

Pantone View Home + Interiors · *rich gold, scarlet red, Dijon yellows* · *'grapevine greens and lusty wines'* · *anime-inspired colors* · *russet brown, iris blue, rosy mauve* [2009 forecast. Source · GDUSA]

MOST STYLISH KIDS

According to celebrity magazine *In Touch Weekly*, Gwen Stefani's young son, Kingston, is the 'most stylish kid' in Hollywood. When apprised of the news, Stefani was able to confirm that her son is indeed a 'chilled-out little guy'. Below are the top-five most stylish celebrity tots, according to the list released in February 2008:

#	child	born	parents
1	Kingston Rossdale	5/26/2006	Gwen Stefani & Gavin Rossdale
2	Suri Cruise	4/18/2006	Tom Cruise & Katie Holmes
3	Leni Klum	5/04/2004	Heidi Klum & Flavio Briatore
4	Brooklyn Beckham	3/04/1999	David & Victoria Beckham
5	Ava Phillippe	9/09/1999	Reese Witherspoon & Ryan Phillippe

KEFFIYEH CHIC

The *keffiyeh* – a woven, fringed, (often) checkered scarf traditionally worn by Arab men – was among 2008's more unusual fashion trends. The scarf first surfaced outside its original context as a fad in Tokyo in the early 2000s, began appearing on the shoulders of fashionable young urbanites in Europe and America *c.*2005, and became something of a fixture in those circles during 2008. Yet the keffiyeh's association with Arab nationalism – the scarf was first adopted by Palestinian insurgents in the 1930s and popularized by Yasser Arafat in the 1960s – proved problematic during the year. In January 2008, Urban Outfitters pulled the scarf from shelves after criticism from some Jewish and Arab groups. In May, Dunkin' Donuts pulled an online ad featuring chef Rachael Ray in a version of the scarf, after a conservative commentator accused Ray of indulging in 'jihadi chic'. Yet despite its association, during the year the *keffiyeh* was seen on celebrities such as Colin Farrell, Kirsten Dunst, and others, as well as on US troops, who use the scarves in the traditional manner – to shield their faces from sun and sand.

———————— MACARTHUR FELLOWS · 2007 ————————

The MacArthur Fellowships have been awarded each year since 1981 by the John D. and Catherine T. MacArthur Foundation. Known colloquially as the 'Genius Awards', the MacArthurs are designed to reward individuals of 'exceptional creativity' in any field. No applications are accepted, and nominations come from an anonymous pool of experts invited by the MacArthur committee. Fellows are unaware of their nomination until they receive a telephone call informing them of their windfall – $500,000 over a span of 5 years, to pursue any project of their interest. 24 fellowships were announced in September 2007. A selection appears below:

MERCEDES DORETTI · forensic anthropologist, *for* 'unearthing evidence of crimes against humanity and seeking justice on behalf of populations whose immense losses have been omitted from the historical record'

COREY HARRIS · blues musician, *for* 'leading a revival of Mississippi Delta blues by infusing traditional styles with influences from jazz, reggae, gospel, and African and Caribbean folk styles'

CHERYL HAYASHI · spider silk biologist, *for* 'integrating the understanding of spider phylogenetics & the development of such biomimetic materials as biodegradable fishing lines'

WHITFIELD LOVELL · artist, *for* 'paying tribute to the daily lives of anonymous African Americans through poetic and intricately constructed tableaux'

YOKY MATSUOKA · computer scientist and neuroroboticist, *for* 'devising complex prosthetic devices and rehabilitation strategies that hold life-changing potential for those suffering from brain injuries and manipulation disabilities'

JONATHAN SHAY · clinical psychiatrist/classicist, *for* 'drawing parallels between ancient texts and the experiences of Vietnam veterans that deepen our understanding of the effects of warfare on individuals'

———ARTS & HUMANITIES NATIONAL MEDALS · 2007———

NATIONAL MEDAL OF ARTS	NATIONAL HUMANITIES MEDAL
Morten Lauridsen (*composer*)	Stephen H. Balch (*founder, National Association of Scholars*)
N. Scott Momaday (*essayist, poet, professor, painter*)	Russell Freedman (*children's author*)
Roy R. Neuberger (*patron*)	Victor Davis Hanson (*historian*)
R. Craig Noel (*theater director*)	Roger Hertog (*benefactor*)
Les Paul (*guitarist, inventor*)	Cynthia Ozick (*novelist*)
Henry Steinway (*patron*)	Richard Pipes (*historian*)
George Tooker (*painter*)	Pauline L. Schultz (*curator*)
University of Idaho Lionel Hampton International Jazz Festival (*music competition & festival*)	Henry Snyder (*scholar-administrator*)
	Ruth Wisse (*Yiddish academic*)
Andrew Wyeth (*painter*)	Monuments Men (*345 WWII curators &c. who saved monuments from bombings & lootings*)

Sci, Tech, Net

Men have become tools of their tools.
— HENRY DAVID THOREAU, *Walden*, 1854

———————————— ETHANOL ————————————

Once heralded as the key to breaking American's 'addiction' to (foreign) oil, ethanol fell from grace in 2008, as a growing chorus questioned its environmental and economic impact. ❦ Ethanol (ethyl alcohol, C_2H_5OH – known also as grain alcohol or moonshine) is the alcoholic intoxicant in wine, beer, and liquor. It is widely used throughout science and industry as a preservative, solvent, and disinfectant. ❦ In 1925, Henry Ford told the *New York Times* that 'the fuel of the future is going to come from fruit like that sumac by the road, or from apples, weeds, sawdust – almost anything'. Indeed, Ford's Model T was designed to run on ethanol as well as gas. Yet ethanol's use as a fuel failed to attract mainstream attention until the 1970s, when the oil embargo of 1973 and the Iranian revolution of 1978 led to spikes in oil prices. Ethanol soon found favor as a gasoline extender, usually in a 10% ethanol to 90% gasoline blend known as 'gasohol' or E10. (Today, most cars in the US can run on E10, though only specially-equipped vehicles, known as Flexible Fuel Vehicles or FFVs, can run on higher blends.) Ethanol received another boost in the late-1980s amid concerns about air pollution; and after the 1990 Clean Air Act Amendments mandated certain oxygen levels in fuel, ethanol became a popular additive when another

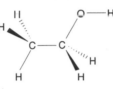

oxygenate (Methyl Tertiary Butyl Ether) was found to contaminate ground and surface water. After 9/11, energy security concerns again rose, and the Energy Policy Act of 2005 set ambitious targets for ethanol use, which were further raised by the Energy Independence & Security Act of 2007. Today, all US gasoline refiners and importers are required to incorporate a percentage of biofuel [7·7% in 2008] – and, thanks in part to significant subsidies and tariffs, the biofuel of choice is usually ethanol made in the US from corn. ❦ Although some argue that ethanol has raised corn prices to the benefit of farmers, scientists are divided as to whether ethanol produces a net energy gain, and many note the vast amounts of fossil fuel and water required for its production. Several studies in 2008 argued that ethanol has contributed to the eradication of rainforests and other lands, as pressures on grain supplies lead countries to convert forests to crops. The UN, IMF, and World Bank all have all expressed concern over the biofuel's contribution to the 2008 food crisis [see p.16]. Yet despite these concerns, ethanol remains politically popular – not least due to an influential lobby. Few commercially viable alternatives exist and US relationships to oil-producing countries don't appear to be getting warmer any time soon.

─────── NOBEL PRIZES IN SCIENCE · 2007 ───────

THE NOBEL PRIZE IN PHYSICS

Albert Fert
*Université Paris-Sud; Unité Mixte de
Physique CNRS/Thales, France*

Peter Grünberg
Forschungszentrum Jülich, Germany

'for the discovery of Giant
Magnetoresistance'

Fert and Grünberg independently discovered a method of layering magnetic material and nonmagnetic material, allowing tiny magnetic changes to produce large differences in electrical resistance – an effect called Giant Magnetoresistance (GMR). GMR has enabled extremely sensitive read-out heads to be made for devices that register data magnetically, such as hard drives and iPods, in turn allowing these devices to be produced on a minuscule scale. Because GMR depends on structures only a few atoms in size, it is considered one of the first real applications of nanotechnology.

THE NOBEL PRIZE IN CHEMISTRY

Gerhard Ertl
*Fritz-Haber-Institut der Max-Planck-
Gesellschaft, Germany*

'for his studies of chemical processes
on solid surfaces'

By demonstrating how chemical reactions take place on microscopic surfaces, Ertl pioneered a methodology now used in both academic and industrial surface chemistry. Ertl's methods have provided insights into everything from car exhaust emissions and the ozone layer to the Haber-Bosch process, which has been used since WWI to produce ammonia for artificial fertilizers, though its mechanism was previously little understood.

THE NOBEL PRIZE IN
PHYSIOLOGY OR MEDICINE

Mario R. Capecchi
University of Utah

Sir Martin J. Evans
Cardiff University

Oliver Smithies, *University of North
Carolina at Chapel Hill*

'for their discoveries of principles
for introducing specific gene
modifications in mice by the use of
embryonic stem cells'

The work of Capecchi, Evans, and Smithies led to a technology called 'gene targeting' that allows scientists to study the roles of individual genes in mice. Capecchi and Smithies created a method of pinpointing and manipulating individual genes at the cellular level, while Evans, using embryonic stem cells, discovered a way to transfer the genetic manipulations to the animal – creating so-called knockout mice. Because mice and humans share many genes, 'mouse models' provide insight into human growth, aging, and disease, and are now used to explore and test gene therapies.

——————ABEL PRIZE——————

The Abel Prize, awarded for outstanding scientific work in the field of mathematics, was presented in 2008 to John Griggs Thompson of the University of Florida and Jacques Tits of the Collège de France. Thompson and Tits won the *c.*$1·2m prize for their 'profound achievements in algebra and in particular for shaping modern group theory', which is also known as the 'science of symmetries'.

——————COPLEY MEDAL——————

The Copley Medal is presented by the British Royal Society; it is the world's oldest prize for scientific achievement. The 2007 award, worth *c.*$10,000, was given to Lord Robert May for his 'seminal studies of interactions within and among biological populations'. The prize has been awarded since 1731, and has previously been won by Charles Darwin, Albert Einstein, Louis Pasteur, and Stephen Hawking.

——————IG NOBEL PRIZES——————

Ig Nobel prizes are awarded for scientific 'achievements that cannot or should not be reproduced'. Below are some notable honors presented at the 2007 ceremony:

AVIATION · Patricia V. Agostino, Santiago A. Plano, and Diego A. Golombek (Universidad Nacional de Quilmes, Argentina) *for their discovery that Viagra assists jet lag recovery in hamsters.*

MEDICINE · Brian Witcombe (Gloucestershire Royal NHS Foundation Trust) and Dan Meyer (Sword Swallowers' Association International) *for their penetrating medical report 'Sword Swallowing and Its Side Effects'.*

PHYSICS · L. Mahadevan (Harvard University) and Enrique Cerda Villablanca (Universidad de Santiago de Chile) *for studying how sheets become wrinkled.*

CHEMISTRY · Mayu Yamamoto (Intl Medical Center of Japan) *for developing a way to extract vanillin (vanilla fragrance and flavoring) from cow dung.*

LINGUISTICS · Juan Manuel Toro, Josep B. Trobalon, and Núria Sebastián-Gallés (Universitat de Barcelona) *for showing that rats sometimes cannot tell the difference between a person speaking Japanese backwards and a person speaking Dutch backwards.*

PEACE · The US Air Force Wright Laboratory *for instigating research and development on a chemical weapon – the so-called gay bomb – that will make enemy soldiers become sexually irresistible to each other.*   [Source: improb.com]

——————DARWIN AWARDS——————

A 58-year-old Texan who died after consuming three liters of sherry via enema won the 2007 Darwin Award, which commemorates *'those who improve our gene pool by accidentally removing themselves from it'.* According to the wife of the deceased, enemas were a favorite mode of intoxication for her husband, named by the awards only as 'Michael'. Toxicology reports found he had a blood alcohol level of 0·47%.

───── UNIVERSAL ETHICAL CODE FOR SCIENTISTS ─────

In September 2007, the British government's chief scientific adviser, Sir David King, unveiled a Universal Ethical Code for Scientists. Developed by a government working group over a period of years, the code is in part a response to a series of scandals that have eroded public trust in scientists, such as the Woo Suk Hwang[†] cloning brouhaha. The code is intended to restore public confidence, remind scientists of their own responsibilities, and provide support for potential whistle-blowers. While the code is not mandatory, King has encouraged its adoption by scientists in the UK and across the world. The code's seven commandments are:

[1] *Act with skill and care in all scientific work. Maintain up-to-date skills and assist their development in others.*

[2] *Take steps to prevent corrupt practices and professional misconduct. Declare conflicts of interest.*

[3] *Be alert to the ways in which research derives from and affects the work of other people, and respect the rights and reputations of others.*

[4] *Ensure that your work is lawful and justified.*

[5] *Minimize and justify any adverse effect your work may have on people, animals, and the natural environment.*

[6] *Seek to discuss the issues that science raises for society. Listen to the aspirations and concerns of others.*

[7] *Do not knowingly mislead, or allow others to be misled, about scientific matters. Present and review scientific evidence, theory, or interpretation honestly and accurately.*

[Source: UK Government Office for Science]

† In 2004, Hwang reported that he had successfully created stem cells from cloned human embryos; he was later found to have falsified key data, among other violations. Yet in 2008 there were reports of a Hwang comeback. In July, the *New Scientist* confirmed that Hwang was to begin research on animal cloning at a private lab in Seoul. The California-based BioArts International also announced a partnership with Hwang on a project to clone pet dogs for the highest bidders in 5 online auctions.

───────── THE EDGE ANNUAL QUESTION · 2008 ─────────

Each year, the online science and culture magazine *Edge* invites notable scientists, philosophers, and others to answer an unusual open-ended question. In 2008, the question was, 'What have you changed your mind about? Why?' Some responses:

DAVID MYERS (social psychologist)
Newborns are not the blank slates I once presumed.

NICK BOSTROM (philosopher)
Everything.

SIMON BARON-COHEN (psychologist)
Whilst it is a wonderfully cosy, warm, feel-good idea, I have changed my mind about equality.

LEE M. SILVER (molecular biologist)
'If we could just get people to understand the science, they'd agree with us'. Not.

MARK HENDERSON (science editor)
Consulting the public about science isn't always a waste of time.

RANDOLPH M. NESSE (psychiatrist)
I used to believe that you could find out what is true by relying on experts.

——— GENES OF NOTE ———

*Some of the year's notable
discoveries in genetic research:*

A variant of the *KIF6* gene was found to raise the risk of heart attack and increase the chances of benefiting from intensive statin therapy. ❧ A *BDNF* gene variant was linked to a tendency towards obsessive worry, though with different effects in women and young girls. ❧ 5 different genetic variants, 3 located on chromosome 8, and 2 on chromosome 17, were found to significantly increase the odds of prostate cancer. ❧ 4 *FKBP5* gene variants were found to increase susceptibility to post-traumatic stress disorder in those who have suffered an abusive childhood. ❧ Mutations in the adenomatous polyposis coli (*APC*) gene are known to increase significantly the odds of developing colonic polyps and colorectal cancer. Researchers in Utah demonstrated that two such mutations, not found in the UK, could nonetheless be traced back to an American couple who sailed from England *c.*1630. ❧ Variants of the *GRIK2* and *GRIA3* genes were found to increase the likelihood of suicidal thoughts in patients with major depression treated with certain drugs. ❧ A mutation in the *ASIP* gene was found to increase the likelihood of red hair, freckles, and also skin cancer, even in populations rarely exposed to the sun. ❧ A variant of the *CHRNA5* gene has been linked to a higher chance of developing lung cancer. ❧ A variant of the *FTO* gene in children was linked to increased difficulty recognizing satiety. ❧ A variant of the Duffy antigen receptor for chemokines (*DARC*) gene which confers protection to Africans against some forms of malaria, was shown to increase susceptibility to HIV by *c.*40%, but also to be associated with slower disease progression.

——— ANIMAL GENOMES ———

In November 2007, US researchers announced they had for the first time successfully mapped the entire genetic code of a feline – a four-year-old Abyssinian named Cinnamon. Scientists hope that deciphering an animal's complete set of DNA will provide clues about its evolution and behavior as well as insights into disease. Other animals and insects whose genomes have been mapped include:

*chimpanzee · mouse · rat · dog · platypus
rhesus macaque · orangutan · cow
honey bee · fruit fly · horse · opossum*

In September 2007, French and Italian researchers said they were the first to genetically map a fruit: the pinot noir grape. In June 2008, the confectioners Mars announced the Chocolate Genome Project, to map the cacao tree's genome.

——— 'DOOMSDAY' VAULT ———

In January 2008, the first shipment of seeds arrived at the Svalbard Global Seed Vault on the remote Arctic island of Spitsbergen, Norway. Maintained by the UN-backed Global Crop Diversity Trust, the seed vault was designed as an 'insurance policy' for the world's food supply', in response to the threat of climate change, natural disasters, and global catastrophe. >4·5m seeds, eventually including samples of every major food crop, will be stored at a constant temperature of *c.*–15°C, 390ft deep inside an ice-cold mountain, protected internally by motion detectors and externally by prowling polar bears. Experimental data have shown that some seeds can survive *c.*10,000 years under optimum conditions, though, in practice, scientists plan to 'refresh' seeds in the vault every 20–100 years.

—————— ANTHROPOCENE & GEOLOGICAL TIME ——————

As most schoolchildren learn, the layers of rock on Earth can be divided into eons, eras, periods, and epochs – units of 'geological time' which correspond to various events in the environmental history of the planet. In January 2008, scientists at the Geological Society of London (GSL) proposed that, because of human impact on the environment, the earth had entered into a new geological epoch: the 'Anthropocene'. According to the GSL paper, the Anthropocene epoch [*anthro*: human + *cene*: new] is distinct because of environmental changes that began during the industrial revolution and are likely to leave distinct marks on the planet. As evidence, the paper cites increased erosion and denudation of the continents, higher CO_2 levels and accompanying temperature changes, animal and plant extinctions, rising sea levels, and increasing ocean acidity. Although a final decision on formal adoption of the Anthropocene rests with the International Union of Geological Sciences (IUGS), the term has been used informally by many since it was coined on the spur of the moment by the Nobel laureate Paul Crutzen at a 2000 conference.

————————————— HUMAN LIMITS —————————————

In 2008, the BBC magazine *Focus* compiled findings on the theoretical and actual limits of human endurance. According to the magazine, the following have been generally established as the 'absolute ceiling of human endeavour' [*do* NOT *attempt!*]:

Blood loss	a loss of ≥50% (3·4–4·9 pints)
Spiciness	5g capsaicin is theoretically the most one could survive; the impact is similar to a severe allergic reaction [see p.220]
Cold	a body temperature <32°F is likely fatal; <86°F produces unconsciousness
Noise	>200 decibels will rupture lungs and is generally fatal
Water consumption	17·5 pints per hour; more will dilute electrolytes to the point of seizure or death
Bee stings	the greatest number of stings survived is 2,243; >600 bee stings gives a 50% chance of death
Electrical shock	a sustained current of 200 milliamps can stop the human heart

————————————— VIAGRA'S OTHER USES —————————————

In recent years, scientists have discovered numerous alternative uses for Viagra, which is used by *c.*30m men around the world to treat erectile dysfunction. Some of Viagra's other benefits include: A protective effect on heart tissue deprived of oxygen before and after heart surgery [*Journal of Molecular and Cellular Cardiology*, 2007]. ❦ Lowering blood pressure in the lungs of patients with chronic bronchitis and emphysema [American College of Chest Physicians, 2006]. ❦ A reduction in attacks of Raynaud's phenomenon, which interrupts blood flow to extremities [*Circulation*, 2005]. ❦ An increase in blood flow to the uterus, which may help women become pregnant [*Human Reproduction*, 2000]. ❦ A freshener for cut flowers, which last *c.*1 week longer when 1mg Viagra is added to their water. [*Plant Physiology & Biochemistry*, 1998].

STN SIGNIFICA

Some (in)significa(nt) Sci, Tech, Net footnotes to the year. ❦ Google Trends showed that between 2004–07, internet users in Chile, Mexico, and Colombia were the most likely to search for the word 'gay'; users in Ireland, the UK, and the US for 'hangover'; and those in Philippines, Australia, and the US for 'love'. ❦ Britain's Royal Astronomical Society scrapped plans to report that 'minor planet 2007 VN84' looked set to miss Earth by just 3,500 miles, after scientists discovered that the 'planet' was in fact the European space probe Rosetta. ❦ Dutch police arrested a teenager for allegedly stealing €4,000 ($6,000) worth of virtual furniture in the virtual online game *Habbo Hotel*. ❦ Activists installed a virtual Guantánamo Bay inside *Second Life*, as a means of illustrating the predicament of detainees. ❦ A 26-year-old Moroccan engineer was arrested in Casablanca for 'villainous activities', after he created a fake Facebook profile for Prince Moulay Rachid, who is second in line to the Moroccan throne. ❦ A British survey by electronics retailer Comet found that 47% of UK men said they would forego sex for 6 months in return for a 50" plasma TV. ❦ S Korea developed a special 'space kimchi' for the country's first astronaut to take into space, using radiation to limit bacteria and reducing the smell by 'one-third or by half'. ❦ As part of a recruitment drive, the notoriously secretive Israeli spy agency Shin Bet launched a blog on which 4 agents described their work. ❦ Parents in Europe complained about the online game *Miss Bimbo*, in which girls 9–16 are encouraged to buy their virtual 'bimbos' diet pills and fake breasts. ❦ Scientists who created a synthe-sized genome of the bacterium *Mycoplasma genitalium* left a 'watermark' on their creation by including a series of amino acids with the same initials as lead researchers. The researchers added the mark to brand the bacteria as man-made. ❦ NASA celebrated the 40th anniversary of the Beatles' song *Across the Universe* (as well as NASA's own 50th birthday) by beaming the tune at the North Star Polaris, 431 light-years away. ❦ An E Carolina University biologist who discovered a new species of trapdoor spider honored his favorite rocker, Neil Young, by naming the arachnid *Myrmekiaphila neilyoungi*. ❦ Bhutan's national assembly banned lawmakers from bringing laptops into House chambers, for fear they would spend government sessions playing computer games. ❦ Bioengineers at MIT created a wintergreen-scented version of *E. coli*, after growing tired of hours in the lab with the 'poopy'-smelling organism. ❦ Two children were admitted to a mental health institution in Spain to be treated for cell phone addiction. ❦ Brazil banned sales of computer games *Counter-Strike* and *EverQuest*, saying they encouraged 'the subversion of public order'. ❦ The Internet Corporation for Assigned Names & Numbers relaxed rules on the net's address system, opening the way for URL endings beyond .com, .org, .net, and country-based addresses. ❦ Brazilian researchers photographed one of the world's last uncontacted tribes, in the Amazon rainforest; *c.*100 are said to still exist. ❦ Honda's Asimo robot led the Detroit Symphony in 'Impossible Dream' from *Man of La Mancha*. It was the first time a robot had conducted a live symphony performance.

——SOME NOTABLE SCIENTIFIC RESEARCH · 2007–08——

{OCT 2007} · Paleontologists in Argentina and Brazil discovered a 90m-year-old dinosaur skeleton that may represent a new species. During the Cretaceous period, the *Futalognkosaurus dukei* would have measured *c.*105' and weighed 60–70 tons, making it among the biggest dinosaurs. ❦ An analysis in *Evolution & Human Behavior* found that mothers with more fat around their hips tend to have children who achieve higher scores on cognition tests, leading scientists to theorize that the polyunsaturated fatty acids deposited around the hips may contribute to brain development in utero. ❦ Researchers at Yale and the University of California found that subjects given a set of nearly identical pictures were more likely to notice the difference between the pictures when they involved an animal. This finding led scientists to suggest that ancient predator-detection mechanisms are still at work in the brain. ❦ Researchers at Indiana University helped explain why people often respond with an eerie sensation to robots that are too lifelike. After monitoring the emotions of 140 subjects shown lifelike robots, the scientists found that the emotions subjects experienced (fear, nervousness, disgust) were similar to those provoked by images of diseased human bodies. {NOV} · A team at Yale found that 6-month-old babies who watched a 'puppet show' that depicted toys displaying social and antisocial behaviors were more likely to choose the 'social' toys to play with later, suggesting a time frame for social development . ❦ Astronomers discovered a 5th planet circling the star 55 Cancri, making it the largest known planetary system outside our own. ❦

Research presented to the American Society of Plastic Surgeons suggested no correlation between breast-feeding and mammary ptosis (sagging breasts). However, pregnancy in general, smoking, age, and the failure to wear proper bras were all found to contribute to a decline in breast elasticity. {DEC} · Research from Yale and University of California psychologists found that those whose first names began with a C or D earned lower grades than those whose names began with an A or B. Researchers attributed the finding to a psychological process called the 'name letter effect', whereby people favor things that remind them of their own name. {JAN 2008} · Researchers at New York's Rensselaer Polytechnic Institute created the darkest man-made material ever. Constructed from carbon nanotubes, the material reflects only very low levels of light, and has applications in electronics and solar energy. ❦ Scientists at the University of Minnesota created a beating rat's heart by injecting cells from a newborn rat into the hollowed-out structure of a dead one. Scientists suggested that human hearts might one day be created in a similar fashion. ❦ California Institute of Technology economists used brain scans to show that people enjoyed wine more when they were told it was expensive, regardless of its actual quality or price. ❦ A team of researchers at the J. Craig Venter Institute created the largest man-made DNA structure to date, by assembling the entire genome of the bacterium *Mycoplasma genitalium* from its synthesized components. {FEB} · University of Utah scientists proposed a method of tracking where people have lived by analyzing their

───── NOTABLE SCIENTIFIC RESEARCH · 2007–08 cont. ─────

hair for traces of drinking water. The model is based on the discovery that oxygen and hydrogen isotopes found in drinking water vary geographically, and that these isotopes remain in hair even after it has been cut. It is hoped that the discovery will assist forensic analysis. ❧ After analyzing data from mental health studies in 72 countries, researchers from the University of Warwick and Dartmouth College proposed that levels of happiness follow a 'U' shape throughout life, rising in the 20s and 70s but dipping significantly during middle age. ❧ Italian researchers refuted the theory that Napoleon died of arsenic poisoning, after analyzing 4 hairs taken from his head during various stages of his life. While the hairs showed levels of arsenic high by modern standards, the researchers found no marked rise during the course of Napoleon's life. {MAR} · A team from the University of Ulster and UAE University found that the skin of the S American paradoxical frog (*Pseudis paradoxa*) contains a substance that can stimulate the release of insulin. ❧ Astronomers at the California Institute of Technology's jet propulsion laboratory reported the first discovery of an organic molecule in the atmosphere of a planet outside Earth's solar system. A molecule of methane was found on the planet Vulpecula, where scientists also confirmed the presence of water. {APR} · University of Oregon and University of Copenhagen archaeologists found 14,000-year-old fossilized human feces in Oregon's Paisley Caves; it is the strongest evidence yet of the earliest humans in N America. ❧ Swedish researchers proposed a link between rhythm and intelligence, after men who

performed best on a drumming test were shown to have higher IQs. ❧ US scientists writing in *Science* described a new drug derived from salmonella that can protect cells exposed to radiation, without diminishing the effectiveness of cancer treatment. {MAY} · Scientists from the University of Pittsburgh and Carnegie Mellon reported in *Nature* that monkeys fitted with small brain sensors had learned to control a mechanical arm using only their thoughts. ❧ Archaeologists at the University of Sheffield performed carbon-dating tests on human remains at Stonehenge, and discovered that the site was used as a burial ground from the earliest days of its construction, *c.*3000 BC. {JUN} · Psychologists at the University of Plymouth found that students asked to estimate the steepness of a slope assessed it as 10–15% less steep if they had a friend helping them make the judgment. ❧ Researchers at Northwestern University found that the gap between boys and girls on math test scores narrowed or disappeared altogether in countries with higher measures of gender equality [see p.80]. ❧ Australian researchers who conducted high-resolution brain scans on 15 heavy marijuana users (>5 joints per day for >10 years) found that their hippocampi were 12% smaller, and amygdalae 7·1% smaller, when compared to nonusers. {JUL} · A trial of the drug Abiraterone on 21 patients with advanced prostate cancer found significant tumor shrinkage and other major improvements. ❧ German scientists discovered that seven types of small mammal living in western Malaysia regularly drink fermented palm nectar, which has an alcohol level similar to beer.

———————————— ASTEROID COLLISION THREAT ————————————

A team of US engineers won a $50,000 Planetary Society prize in February 2008 for designing a space probe capable of tracking an asteroid that threatens to collide with Earth. The asteroid – 99942 Apophis[†] – will pass close enough to Earth in 2029 to be seen by the naked eye, and there is a slim chance it might collide with us in 2036. (NASA estimates there is a <1 in 45,000 chance that Apophis will strike Earth on April 13, 2036). ❦ The contestants were asked to design a craft capable of planting a tracking device on Apophis which could collect sufficient data about the asteroid's trajectory to enable governments to decide by 2017 if action is required to drive it off course. At present the winning design, the spacecraft Foresight, is only a concept, but Bruce Betts of the Planetary Society said, 'We hope the winning entries will catalyze the world's space agencies to move ahead with designs and missions to protect Earth from potentially dangerous asteroids'.

† In Ancient Egyptian mythology, Apophis (also known as Apep) was the spirit of evil and darkness.

———————————— PLANETARY EVENTS 2009 ————————————

January 4 . . . . Perihelion: Earth is at orbital position closest to Sun
January 26 . . . . . Annual solar eclipse: visible across Indian Ocean and W Indonesia
February 9 . . . Penumbral lunar eclipse: visible in Alaska, Hawaii, Australia, E Asia
March 20 . . . . Equinox: Sun passes northward over Equator at 11:43 GMT
June 21 . . . . Solstice: Sun directly above Tropic of Cancer at 5:45 GMT
July 4 . . . . Aphelion: Earth is at orbital position farthest from Sun
July 7 . . . . Penumbral lunar eclipse: not visible to naked eye
July 22 . . . . . Total solar eclipse: visible in India, China, parts of Japan and S Pacific
August 6 . . . . Penumbral lunar eclipse: not visible to naked eye
September 22 . . . . Equinox: Sun passes southward over Equator at 21:18 GMT
December 21 . . . . . . Solstice: Sun directly above Tropic of Capricorn at 17:47 GMT
December 31 . . . . Partial lunar eclipse: visible in Eastern Hemisphere

———————————— NEW SUNSPOT CYCLE ————————————

On January 4, 2008, sunspot AR10981 appeared on the N hemisphere of the Sun. While this event may have gone unnoticed by the public, it was of crucial importance to astronomers, since AR10981 heralded a new solar cycle – Cycle 24. Sunspots are regions of lower temperature and heightened magnetic activity that appear as dark patches on the Sun's surface; they have been found to wax and wane in a 'solar cycle' of approximately 11 years. As the number of sunspots increases, so too does other solar activity, such as solar flares. Tracking the evolution of solar cycles is not simply of academic interest, since periods of intense solar activity can impede aeronautic and military communications, disable satellites, and threaten the stability of power grids. Periods of intense solar activity generally take place towards the middle of each solar cycle, which is next expected during 2011 or 2012. (The previous cycle peaked between 2000 and 2002, when there were major solar storms.)

KEY SPACE MISSIONS OF 2008

JULES VERNE · In April 2008, the European Space Agency's (ESA) automated transfer vehicle (ATV), known as Jules Verne, became the first unmanned, fully-automated space vehicle to dock successfully with the International Space Station. The huge ATV transported *c.*5 tons of vital supplies to the ISS, including air, food, and water. The ESA has agreed to build and launch 5 ATVs between 2008–15, in lieu of payment to become part of the ISS project.

JASON-2 · A joint venture between the French space agency CNES and NASA, the Jason-2 satellite was launched in June 2008. The mission aims to measure the effects of climate change by minutely mapping the oceans. It is hoped that images from Jason-2 will allow scientists to measure the extent of rising sea levels.

COLUMBUS · In February 2008, ESA's space lab Columbus docked with the ISS. Columbus will enable astronauts aboard the ISS to carry out hundreds of experiments, including research into the effects of gravity on plant growth.

PHOENIX · NASA's Phoenix lander arrived on Mars in May 2008 with a mission to use a robotic arm to gather samples of water ice. Despite initial problems caused by the surprisingly sticky soil on the Red Planet, Phoenix did eventually retrieve samples of water in July 2008. Although water ice had previously been identified by the Mars Odyssey orbiter, this was the first time samples of Martian water had been collected and analyzed. It is hoped that this breakthrough will allow researchers to explore if Mars might one day be habitable.

GLAST · In June 2008, the Glast space telescope was launched on a five-year mission to examine some of the most dramatic events in space. The NASA project will photograph gamma rays – the highest-energy form of light – that are created in explosive situations such as when neutron stars merge or where supermassive black holes exist. It is hoped that, through the study of these 'energetic objects', fundamental questions about the nature of the universe might be answered.

THE KAVLI PRIZES

The Kavli Prizes in astrophysics, nanoscience, and neuroscience were awarded for the first time in May 2008. The $1m awards, which are to be presented every other year, are a joint venture of the Norwegian Academy of Science and Letters, the Norwegian Ministry of Education and Research, and the California-based Kavli Foundation, which was established in 2000 by the Norwegian-born physicist, entrepreneur, and philanthropist Fred Kavli. The inaugural set of awards went to:

ASTROPHYSICS · Maarten Schmidt of the California Institute of Technology
and Donald Lynden-Bell of Cambridge University (UK)
NANOSCIENCE · Louis E. Brus of Columbia University
and Sumio Iijima of Meijo University (Japan)
NEUROSCIENCE · Pasko Rakic of the Yale School of Medicine, Thomas Jessell
of Columbia University, and Sten Grillner of the Karolinska Institute (Sweden)

——————SOME INVENTIONS OF NOTE · 2007–08——————

{OCT 2007} · Legend Technologies began marketing the PistolCam, a lightweight digital camera that attaches to a handgun's barrel and begins recording automatically whenever the gun is drawn. ❧ Japan's Kaneko Sangyo Co. developed a portable toilet for cars, equipped with a privacy curtain and bag for waste, for use in traffic jams and emergencies. ❧ A University of California team unveiled a device only a few atoms large that is able to receive radio waves and transmit them as sound – paving the way for nano-sized radios &c. ❧ Researchers at Queen's University Belfast won *c.*$1m for developing a 'bone cement' that can help repair fractures. {NOV} · A team from Hokkaido Industrial Research in Japan built 3 'melody roads' engraved with grooves that emit tones when cars drive over them. {DEC} · Research from the Air Force Institute of Technology demonstrated software that can be used to identify potential office saboteurs or industry spies, by scanning emails both for communication on sensitive topics and for lack of communication on 'normal' or social activities. According to researchers, people flagged as both socially alienated and communicating on sensitive topics are likely to pose a risk. {JAN 2008} · ❧ TN Games designed a USB-enabled 'gaming vest', using special air pockets to mimic the sensation of G-force, bullet wounds, &c. {FEB} · Scientists at Simon Fraser University in Canada unveiled a knee-mounted electrical generator that harvests the power produced by walking. The device, which engages at the end of each stride, can produce *c.*5 watts of power if worn on each knee – enough to run 10 cell phones. ❧

Scientists at the Marine Biological Laboratory in Massachusetts reported that they had trained black sea bass to associate a specific musical tone with being fed. The scientists hope the bass will eventually remember the tone long enough to be raised in the open ocean, then follow the tone to a cage. ❧ The finalists of Microsoft's NextGen PC Design competition included a neck-mounted camera called Momenta, which records everything in front of the viewer and logs the footage whenever it detects a spike in heart rate. {MAR} · A company called ThruVision developed a new kind of body-scanning technology for use in airports, arenas, &c. The technology is based on terahertz rays, which are normally used to study dying stars and are said to be less damaging than X-rays. ❧ A scientist at the USDA created a biodegradable packaging film containing the antimicrobial agent nisin, which kills bacteria that cause food poisoning. {MAY} · A Swiss pilot developed his own set of jet-powered wings, using 4 turbines strapped to his back. The wings allowed him to fly 186mph and perform tricks, after jumping out of a plane 7,500ft above the Alps. {JUN} · Israeli researchers developed a gesture-recognition system that allows surgeons to access images on a computer during surgery, simply by gesticulating. The system uses a video camera hooked up to a PC, which recognizes a basic vocabulary of gestures and translates them into computer commands [see p.15]. {JUL} · NASA announced plans to develop a GPS-like system for use on the moon, using beacons linked to space suits and other devices to help astronauts traverse the lunar surface.

——————————STANDBY ('VAMPIRE') POWER——————————

Many electronic appliances have a 'standby mode' in which the device is neither in use nor fully switched off. These 'lopomos' (LOw POwer MOdes) range from computer 'sleep' functions to the default mode of power adapters, cell phone chargers, and the like. While devices on standby may appear to be off, they continue to draw electricity as long as they remain plugged in and, since these drains are continuous and take place while devices are 'asleep', they have been nicknamed 'vampire loads'. Below are the average amounts of electricity consumed by appliances on standby:

Device	watts				
Cable box	10·8	DVD player	4·2	Computer	1·7
VCR	6·0	Answering machine	3·0	When in use, the average TV	
Inkjet printer	5·0	Microwave oven	2·9	consumes 210 watts.	
TV	5·0	Portable stereo	2·2	[Source: Lawrence Berkeley	
		Clock radio	1·7	National Laboratory]	

The proliferation of electronic devices with lopomos has made vampire loads an increasing cause of concern. The International Energy Agency (IEA) estimates that a typical European or North American home now contains 20 devices constantly on standby, which together account for 5–10% of residential electricity, and ultimately 1% of global CO_2 emissions. The table below illustrates the average use of standby power in the homes of various OECD countries, according to the IEA:

Av. residential standby power use (watts)		% annual resid. electricity			
87	Australia	12	37	Netherlands	10
27	France	7	100	New Zealand	11
44	Germany	10	19	Switzerland	3
46	Japan	9	32	UK	8
			50	US	5
			[Estimates based on a variety of studies]		

——————————X-PRIZES &c.——————————

In 1996 the X-Prize Foundation offered $10m to the first team able to build a privately funded passenger spaceship that could fly into space and back twice in two weeks. The success of the prize led to a new wave of scientific contests, including:

ARCHON X-PRIZE FOR GENOMICS *Goal*: Sequence 100 human genomes within 10 days · *Purse*: $10m

PETA IN VITRO MEAT PRIZE · *Goal*: Produce in vitro chicken meat & sell it to public by 6/30/2012 · *Purse*: $1m

VIRGIN EARTH CHALLENGE · *Goal*: Design a viable technology to remove anthropogenic greenhouse gases from the atmosphere · *Purse*: $25m

NETFLIX PRIZE · *Goal*: Develop a movie-recommendation algorithm that performs 10% better than Netflix's current system · *Purse*: $1m

In June 2008, John McCain said that, if elected President, he would offer a $300m prize ('$1 for every man, woman, and child in the US') to anyone who could build a more efficient car battery.

———————— SCI, TECH, NET WORDS OF NOTE ————————

GLOBALONEY · 'the ability to declaim for portentous minutes about the revolution in world affairs brought about by technological change/environmental degradation/the fundamental decline in moral values' – David Brooks.

SAVIOR SIBLINGS · children born (or bred) specifically to provide transplant material for extant children. *Also* SPARE PART BABIES.

EXABYTE · a billion gigabytes – previously an unthinkably large quantity of data, but now, thanks to data mining &c., increasingly common.

OFF-GRID · existing independently from the 'grid' of power, water, phones, &c. *Also* living below the radar of state or corporate surveillance.

G-PHONE · a mobile phone supposedly being developed by Google; superseded in November 2007 by ANDROID – a Google suite of open-source mobile phone software.

QWERTY TUMMY · illness caught from dirty computer keyboards [see p.202].

CYBRIDS · human-animal embryos used to grow stem cells; a controversial practice banned in some countries but allowed by UK authorities in September 2007.

METAVERSE · online 3-D social environments such as *Second Life* &c.; coined in Neal Stephenson's *Snow Crash*.

SHUFFLE SHAME · to be embarrassed by a poor song on a random playlist.

SEXTING · sending naked photos by text message, or flirting via SMS.

FACESLAMMING · to deny a Facebook friend request. *Also* FACEBOOK SUICIDE · to delete one's online profile.

RHYTHM GAMES · a genre of video games involving music (e.g., *Guitar Hero*) that are increasingly a feature of school physical education classes. *Also* WiiHABILITATION · the use of Wii consoles in physical therapy.

NETHOOD · Internet communities based on real-life proximity, in which users share services and information relevant to their location.

COPYFRAUD · false copyright claims, such as on public domain materials, that demand license fees when none are required.

KAVOSHGAR-1 · reportedly the first rocket successfully launched into space by Iran (in February 2008).

NANO-GENERATORS · tiny fibers, embedded in fabric &c., that convert mechanical energy (i.e., movement) into electricity.

NERDIC · the language of geeks.

GRIEFERS · online gamers who disrupt, harass, and annoy fellow players; the most famous are the Patriotic Nigras, whose misanthropic slogan is 'Ruining *Second Life* Since 2006'.

RICKROLLING · the practice of duping people into viewing Rick Astley's 1980's classic 'Never Gonna Give You Up', by sending them a supposedly vital URL.

GOOGLEGÄNGER · a namesake who shares the same Google search listings. *Also* GOOGLE TWINS.

──────── SCI, TECH, NET WORDS OF NOTE cont. ────────

GEEK DEFENSE · *Wired*'s term for the legal strategy of presenting highly intelligent (geeky) defendants as weird misfits who should not be judged by society's norms.

EVIL METER · term used by Google CEO Eric Schmidt, who said of the company's mission statement, '*"Don't be evil" is misunderstood. We don't have an evil meter ... the rule allows for conversation. I thought when I joined the company this was crap ... it must be a joke. I was sitting in a room in the first six months ... talking about some advertising ... and someone said that it is evil. It stopped the product. It's a cultural rule, a way of forcing the conversation, especially in areas that are ambiguous*'.

TWEETS · short status updates sent from cell phones or instant messaging services through the website Twitter.

FAIL-GREEN · fail-safe mechanisms that fail in an eco-friendly way.

CYBERCHONDRIACS · those people who (obsessively) search the internet for medical information.

ECO-FATIGUE · ennui or annoyance brought on by sanctimonious peddling of 'green' alternatives.

UNBOXING · the unlikely YouTube trend of uploading videos of people un-packing newly purchased technology products. An offshoot of TECHPORN.

E-VENGERS · those (exes) who wreak revenge online.

UPCYCLING · where recycling materials increases their value (e.g., when packing materials are reformed into insulation).

JAILBREAK · to escape from Apple's supposed iPhone iSLAVERY.

NSFW · website or email content that is Not Safe For Work; often used as a warning to others.

MULLET SITES · websites that (like the '70's haircut) have a professional front-end but user-generated content within. *Similarly* POOPULAR · popular on the outside, poopy on the inside.

FAT TV · a non-flat-screen television.

WEBLEBRITY · an internet-only celeb.

SNIPES · informational and advertising graphics overlayed across TV shows.

FANBOY · a fanatical fan, usually of one niche [splendidly, the term dates from 1919].

EARLY-NERD SPECIAL · midnight screenings of cult films (*Star Wars* &c.) designed especially for fanboys &c.

NOTOX · using radio waves, rather than chemicals, to reduce the signs of aging.

PLUTOID · International Astronomical Union's new designation for all 'dwarf planets lying beyond Neptune' [see p.77].

SPORN · porn created in the game *Spore*.

PASSWORD FATIGUE · the annoyance of having to remember a plethora of passwords. *Also* PASSZHEIMER'S · the inability to remember one's passwords.

TELEPUTING · using a TV to view computer content (games, photos, &c.).

JOURNOSAUR · a journalist who rails against online media.

——COMPUTER USAGE AROUND THE WORLD——

While computer usage is widespread in the US and Canada and across W Europe, the number of people who use a computer at least some of the time varies widely elsewhere in Europe, Latin America, and Africa. Below, according to 2007 data from the Pew Research Center, are the countries with the highest and lowest percent of residents who said they used a computer 'at least occasionally' at home or work:

Most computer use	%	*Least computer use*	%	*Biggest gainers*			%
					'02	'07	±
Sweden	82	Bangladesh	5				
South Korea	81	Tanzania	6	Brazil	22	44	+22
US	80	Pakistan	9	Slovakia	52	73	+21
Canada	76	Uganda	11	Bulgaria	19	38	+19
Britain	76	Indonesia	11	Britain	59	76	+17

——INTERNET ATTITUDES——

A sampling of American views on the internet, according to Zogby International:

Americans who say ...

The net has brought them closer to God	10% [6% 'more distant'; 80% 'no difference']
They would be 'very' or 'somewhat' likely to implant a device in their brain to access the net, if it was safe	11% [9% 'somewhat unlikely'; 76% 'not at all likely']
The internet can serve as a substitute for a significant other	24%
The net should be regulated like TV to protect kids from obscene content	29%
Internet video should have a rating system similar to the one used in film	24%
The internet has become an important part of who they are	14%

[Source: 463 Communications/Zogby International, October 2007]

——NET POPULATIONS——

Population of		*comparable to*
MySpace	230m†	Indonesia
Google	121m§	Japan
Yahoo!	116m§	Mexico
AOL	91m§	Philippines
eBay	83m§	Germany
Facebook	70m†	Turkey
Friendster	65m†	Iran
Wikipedia	56m§	Italy
Second Life	13m†	Guatemala
W. of Warcraft	10m‡	Hungary

† Users as of 5/08. ‡ Subscribers as of 1/08.
§ Unique visitors during 4/08.

——2008 WEBBY AWARDS——

Activism	*loveisrespect.org*
Best homepage	*lafilm.com*
Best writing	*wired.com*
Blog – political	*huffingtonpost.com*
Community	*flickr.com*
Education	*earth.columbia.edu*
Fashion	*journeys.louisvuitton.com*
Humor	*theonion.com*
Lifestyle	*cinchouse.com*
Magazine	*ngm.com*
Music	*bbc.co.uk/radio1/djs*
News	*nytimes.com*
Politics	*factcheck.org*
Sports	*sports.yahoo.com*

———————————VIDEO GAME RATING SYSTEM———————————

Video game ratings are assigned by the Entertainment Software Rating Board (ESRB), which was established in 1994 by the Entertainment Software Association (ESA). Participation is voluntary. To receive a rating, game publishers complete a questionnaire about potentially objectionable content, which they submit to the board alongside game footage. At least three 'specially trained raters', who must have experience with children, review each submission. The various ESRB ratings are:

EC *(Early childhood)* · Content may be suitable for ≥3s. Contains no inappropriate material.

E *(Everyone)* · Content may be suitable for ≥6s. Titles may contain minimal cartoon, fantasy, or mild violence; and/or infrequent mild language.

E10+ *(Everyone ≥10)* · Content may be suitable for ≥10s. Titles may contain more cartoon, fantasy, or mild violence, mild language, and/or minimal suggestive themes.

T *(Teen)* · Content may be suitable for ≥13s. Titles may contain violence, suggestive themes, crude humor, minimal blood, and/or infrequent use of strong language.

M *(Mature)* · Content may be suitable for ≥17s. Titles may contain intense violence, blood and gore, sexual content, and/or strong language.

AO *(Adults Only)* · Content only for ≥18s. Titles may include prolonged scenes of intense violence and/or graphic sexual content and nudity.

RP *(Rating Pending)* · Titles awaiting ESRB rating – used on prerelease advertising.

On April 29, 2008, Rockstar Games released *Grand Theft Auto IV*, and sold *c*.3·6m copies (worth $310m) worldwide. *GTA IV*, in which players can steal cars, visit prostitutes, and assault police officers, is rated 'M', for mature.

ESRB ratings also generally include 'content descriptors' based on subject matter that contributed to the rating and may be of concern. Some of the 24 possible descriptors include: *alcohol reference* – 'reference to and/or images of alcoholic beverages'; *animated blood* – 'discolored and/or unrealistic depictions of blood'; *fantasy violence* – 'violent actions of a fantasy nature, involving human or non-human characters'; and *cartoon violence* – 'involving cartoon-like situations and characters'.

———————————VIDEO GAME LANGUAGE———————————

Partly as a response to public concern over video game violence, Microsoft maintains a section of its Xbox website devoted to educational materials for parents. Included on the site is a guide to video gaming lingo; a selection appears below:

BUTTON MASHING – pressing all the buttons on a controller at once CAMPING – staying in one place EASTER EGG – hidden item in a game FRAG – to defeat an opponent

KICK – to remove a player from a server · OWNED – defeated soundly PATCH – addition developed after a game is released · POWER-UP – item that gives a player temporary powers

―――――――――――――――ONLINE SHOPPING―――――――――――――――

875m people (*c.*85% of the world's online population) have purchased something over the internet, according to 2008 data from Nielsen Online. S Korea had the highest percentage of internet shoppers (99% of the country's online population), followed by Germany, Japan, and the UK (all at 97% of those online). Below are the percentage of internet users who have shopped online, by region of the world:

Region	shopped online (%)	never shopped online (%)
Europe	93	7
N America	92	8
Asia Pacific	84	16
Latin America	79	21
Middle East	67	33

In all the countries surveyed, books were the items most commonly purchased:

Item	% who bought in past 3 months†
Books	41
Clothing/accessories/shoes	36
Videos/DVDs/games	24
Airline tickets	24
Electronic equipment	23

† % of global internet users

―――――――――――――――SOCIAL NETWORKING―――――――――――――――

Percent of internet users	Canada	53%	USA	34%
who belong to a social net-	China	42%	France	17%
working site, by country:	UK	39%	Germany	12%

57% of *all* internet users belonged to a social networking site in 2008, according to Universal McCann, allowing them to meet, poke, and spy on an ever increasing number of 'friends'. Below is a breakdown of popular sites around the world.

Canada	USA	Germany
Facebook . . 15·5m *users*†	MySpace . . . 60·4m *users*	Class Onl. . . . . . 3m *users*
Blogger . . . . 8·6m	Facebook 25m	Blogger . . . . 2·8m
Wind. LiveSp. . . . . . 6·3m	Class Onl. . . . . 13·6m	MySpace . . . . 2·4m

UK	France	China
Facebook . . . . 9·9m *users*	Skyrock . . . . 7m *users*	YeeYoo . . . . 6m *users*
Blogger . . . . 5·6m	Overblog 6m	9158.com . . . . 5·9m
MySpace . . . . 5·6m	Blogger . . . . 5·2m	Zhiji.com . . . . 3·1m

† Users for all sites are unique users per month, March 2008. Other social networking sites include: Bebo (popular in Ireland and NZ), Orkut (popular in Brazil), LinkedIn (business networking, popular in the US), hi5 (popular in Central America), Together We Served (US military), BlackPlanet. com (mainly US African Americans), Sagazone (mainly UK >50s), FaithBase (mainly US Christians), and MyHeritage (networking through genealogy). [Sources: OfCom; Datamonitor; Ipsos]

—————————FIRST COMPUTER SPAM—————————

Computer 'spam' turned 30 in 2008, though birthday celebrations were likely few and far between. The first piece of spam is said to have been sent on May 3, 1978, by an employee of the computer maker Digital Equipment Corporation (DEC). The message was sent via Arpanet, the US government-run antecedent of the internet, and invited 393 people to view 'the newest members of DECSYSTEM-20 family' at 2 product demonstrations in California. The reaction was almost universally negative, and DEC was chastised by the US Defense Communications Agency, the Arpanet overseer. Today, the security firm Sophos estimates that 95% of all email is spam, with the following dozen countries sending out the most such emails in 2007:

% of global spam			
United States .... 22·5	Russia .... 4·7	Spain .... 2·7
South Korea .... 6·5	Brazil .... 3·8	Italy .... 2·7
China .... 6·0	France .... 3·5	India .... 2·6
Poland .... 4·9	Germany .... 3·5	
	Turkey .... 3·1	[Source: Sophos, 2008]

Spam ('spiced' + 'ham') is a proprietary Hormel brand name. According to the BBC, the first person to use the term with regard to junk email (in 1993) was Joel Furr, an active early member of the Usenet online discussion system. Furr was reportedly inspired by the famous Monty Python sketch in which Eric Idle (as Mr. Bun) and Graham Chapman (as Mrs. Bun) are thwarted in their attempts to order a restaurant meal that does not include the processed meat product [see *Schott's Almanac 2007*].

————SPAM CATEGORIES————

The most common spam categories detected by Symantec (July–Dec 2007):

Commercial products	27%
Internet (spam toolkits &c.)	20
Finance	13
Scams	10
Health	10
Adult	7
Fraud	7
Leisure	6

————SPAM PER CAPITA————

The countries that relay the highest number of spam messages per capita, according to IT security firm Sophos:

1	Pitcairn Islands (in S Pacific)
2	Niue (island in S Pacific)
3	Tokelau Islands (3 atolls in S Pacific)
4	Anguilla (islands in Caribbean)
5	Faroe Islands (in N Europe)
6	Monaco
7	Bermuda

————————————SPOETRY————————————

Dubbed 'spoetry' in a 2006 *Guardian* article by Eva Wiseman, the seemingly random juxtaposition of words found in many spam messages (a device to foil anti-spam filters) can occasionally provide brief flashes of beauty. Over the past several years a variety of websites and contests devoted to 'spoems' have blossomed on the internet. An entry titled 'Almagest' on one such website, spampoetry.org, reads: *Machinery, and quiet vassily/ marvelous, his magician!/ have, cervix, dealt the blow.*

─────────── SOME INTERNET MALADIES ───────────

Condition   primary symptoms
Blog Streaking......................................*overexposing oneself via a blog*
MySpace Impersonation.......... *assuming false (often famous) identities on the net*
Photolurking...... *rummaging through online photo albums for private information*
Wikipediholism............... *excessive checking and correction of Wikipedia articles*
Egosurfing..*excessively Googling your own name*
Google Stalking............... *snooping on friends and enemies via the search engine*
Infornography................... *unhealthy addiction to new and current information*
Cyberchondria ....*fear of maladies diagnosed on the internet*
YouTube Narcissism ....*believing the whole world is waiting for your vacation video*

[Source: *New Scientist*, 2007] In the May 2008 issue of the *American Journal of Psychiatry*, Dr Jerald J. Block argued that internet addiction should be listed in the next edition of the *DSM*, the US classification of psychiatric conditions. According to Block, internet addiction has 3 subtypes (gaming, sexual preoccupations, and email/text messaging), and is characterized by: excessive use; anger or depression when the computer is inaccessible; and negative repercussions such as social isolation.

─────────── LOLCATS & LOLSPEAK ───────────

'Lolcats' are photographs of felines in various poses, adorned with weirdly spelled captions designed to appear as if they were spoken by the cats themselves (lol = 'laugh out loud'). This perplexing internet phenomenon became a nearly inescapable part of online culture in 2008. Lolcat captions tend to recycle jokes from the internet, gaming, and elsewhere. They are written in an imagined (and nauseating) feline baby talk – 'kitty pidgin' – which has come to be known as 'Lolspeak'. Like the hacker slang 'Leet speak' (of which it is a relative), Lolspeak is constantly evolving, yet it relies on several established formulas. One of the most popular is '*I'm in ur* [noun], [verb]-*ing your* [noun]', which apparently derives from a posting in an online game forum which read: 'I'm in ur base killing ur d00ds'. Another common formula depicts a cat licking some item and proclaiming: '[noun] *haz a flavor*'. Although the precise origins of lolcats are disputed, the website 'I Can Has Cheezburger?' (the most popular lolcat URL) posted its first lolcat picture in January 2007. Lolcats have given rise to numerous spin-offs, including lolgays, lolruses (walruses), loldogs, lolbees, lolpresidents, lolbrarians, lolgoths, lolmaps, and even lolchairs. Inevitably, in January 2008, a lolcat book project was announced.

Like lolcats, 'All Your Base Are Belongs to Us' (sometimes AYBABTU or AYB) spread rapidly and inexplicably across the internet. The phrase derives from the video game *Zero Wing*, released in Japanese in 1989, and in English in 1991. The English adaptation included some unfortunate subtitles, including 'All your base are belongs to us', uttered by the menacing villain 'CATS' during the game's opening sequence. In the late 1990s, the subtitle attracted attention on the 'Zany Video Game Quotes' forum, and in 1998, a Kansas City programmer created a flash animation in which the phrase takes over the world – appearing on planes, a *Time* cover, and at the UN. The animation was widely forwarded and posted on numerous sites, garnering mainstream news coverage in 2001. Some attribute its popularity to gamer nostalgia for all things '80s. Like lolcats, the phrase has yet to die a natural death.

REDEFINING THE BASE UNITS

Seven base units are used to measure the physical properties of the universe. These units form the fundamental building blocks of the *Système International d'Unités* (SI units), which are the legal standard of measurement for science and trade in most countries. However, in recent years a number of scientists have voiced concerns over one of the most widely used base units – the kilogram – which remains the only base unit defined by reference to a physical artifact. Since 1889, the mass of a kilogram has been fixed to a lump of platinum and iridium alloy held in a vault at the International Bureau of Weights and Measures in Sèvres, France. Unfortunately, the mass of this lump – which is too precious for routine measurement – changes slightly over time. Thus, in November 2007, the General Conference on Weights and Measures resolved to encourage experiments redefining the kilogram in terms of an invariable property of nature (such as the mass of a certain number of photons). The conference also encouraged experiments regarding the redefinition of other base units, since the demands of modern research call for increasingly precise measurements. Below are the SI base units with some of their proposed redefinitions:

METER · *Measures*: length. *Definition*: length of the path traveled by light in a vacuum during 1/299,792,458 of a second. *Proposed redefinition*: none.

KILOGRAM · *Measures*: mass. *Definition:* mass of the prototype in Sévres, France. *Proposed redefinition*: mass of a body whose energy is equal to that of a number of photons whose frequencies add up to a particular total (tied to the Planck constant).

SECOND · *Measures*: time. *Definition*: time taken for 9,192,631,770 periods of vibrations of the electromagnetic radiation emitted by a caesium-133 atom. *Proposed redefinition*: none.

AMPERE · *Measures*: electric current. *Definition*: the current in a pair of straight, parallel conductors of infinite length 1 meter apart in a vacuum that produces a force of 2×10^{-7} newtons per meter in their length. *Proposed redefinition*: the electric current in the direction of the flow of a certain number of elementary charges per second.

KELVIN · *Measures*: thermodynamic temperature. *Definition*: the fraction 1/273·16 of the thermodynamic temperature of the triple point of water (the temperature and pressure at which ice, liquid water, and water vapor exist). *Proposed redefinition*: the change of thermodynamic temperature that results in a change of thermal energy by a specific amount (tied to the Boltzmann constant).

CANDELA · *Measures*: luminous intensity. *Definition*: the luminous intensity of a source of frequency 540×10^{12} hertz whose radiant intensity is 1/683 watts per steradian. *Proposed redefinition*: none.

MOLE · *Measures*: substance (used in chemistry). *Definition*: amount of substance that contains as many elementary units as there are atoms in 0·012 kgs of carbon-12. *Proposed redefinition*: such that the Avogadro constant is $6·0221415 \times 10^{23}$ per mole.

[Sources: *New Scientist*; NIST]

Final decisions are expected at the 2011 meeting of the General Conference on Weights & Measures.

SI PREFIXES

Below are the SI prefixes and symbols for the decimal multiples and submultiples of SI units from 10^{24} to 10^{-24}.

10^{24}	yotta	Y	1 000 000 000 000 000 000 000 000
10^{21}	zetta	Z	1 000 000 000 000 000 000 000
10^{18}	exa	E	1 000 000 000 000 000 000
10^{15}	peta	P	1 000 000 000 000 000
10^{12}	tera	T	1 000 000 000 000
10^{9}	giga	G	1 000 000 000
10^{6}	mega	M	1 000 000
10^{3}	kilo	k	1 000
10^{2}	hecto	h	100
10	deca	da	10
1			1
10^{-1}	deci	d	0.1
10^{-2}	centi	c	0.01
10^{-3}	milli	m	0.001
10^{-6}	micro	µ	0.000 001
10^{-9}	nano	n	0.000 000 001
10^{-12}	pico	p	0.000 000 000 001
10^{-15}	femto	f	0.000 000 000 000 001
10^{-18}	atto	a	0.000 000 000 000 000 001
10^{-21}	zepto	z	0.000 000 000 000 000 000 001
10^{-24}	yocto	y	0.000 000 000 000 000 000 000 001

SOME USEFUL CONVERSIONS

A	A *to* B *multiply by*	B *to* A *multiply by*	B
inches	25·4	0·0397	millimeters
inches	2·54	0·3937	centimeters
feet	0·3048	3·2808	meters
yards	0·9144	1·0936	meters
miles	1·6093	0·6214	kilometers
acres	0·4047	2·471	hectares
square feet	0·0929	10·76	square meters
square miles	2·5899	0·3861	square kilometers
UK pints	0·5682	1·7598	liters
UK gallons	4·546	0·2199	liters
cubic inches	16·39	0·0610	cubic centimeters
ounces	28·35	0·0353	grams
pounds	0·4536	2·2046	kilograms
stones	6·35	0·157	kilograms
miles/gallon	0·3539	2·825	kilometers/liter
miles/US gallon	0·4250	2·353	kilometers/liter
miles/hour	1·609	0·6117	kilometers/hour

°C – °F

°C	°F	°C	°F
100	212	49	120·2
99	210·2	48	118·4
98	208·4	47	116·6
97	206·6	46	114·8
96	204·8	45	113
95	203	44	111·2
94	201·2	43	109·4
93	199·4	42	107·6
92	197·6	41	105·8
91	195·8	40	104
90	194	39	102·2
89	192·2	38	100·4
88	190·4	37	98·6
87	188·6	36	96·8
86	186·8	35	95
85	185	34	93·2
84	183·2	33	91·4
83	181·4	32	89·6
82	179·6	31	87·8
81	177·8	30	86
80	176	29	84·2
79	174·2	28	82·4
78	172·4	27	80·6
77	170·6	26	78·8
76	168·8	25	77
75	167	24	75·2
74	165·2	23	73·4
73	163·4	22	71·6
72	161·6	21	69·8
71	159·8	20	68
70	158	19	66·2
69	156·2	18	64·4
68	154·4	17	62·6
67	152·6	16	60·8
66	150·8	15	59
65	149	14	57·2
64	147·2	13	55·4
63	145·4	12	53·6
62	143·6	11	51·8
61	141·8	10	50
60	140	9	48·2
59	138·2	8	46·4
58	136·4	7	44·6
57	134·6	6	42·8
56	132·8	5	41
55	131	4	39·2
54	129·2	3	37·4
53	127·4	2	35·6
52	125·6	1	33·8
51	123·8	0	32
50	122	-1	30·2
		-2	28·4

Normal body temp.
= 98·6°F (37°C)
range 97·7–98·9°F
(36·1–37·2°C)

Travel & Leisure

Men travel faster now, but I do not know if they go to better things.
— WILLA CATHER, *Death Comes for the Archbishop*, 1927

―――――――――― VACATIONS & THE ECONOMY ――――――――――

Despite rising gas prices and other economic woes [see p.19], Americans have yet to abandon their annual summer vacation, according to a 4/2008 poll by AOL Travel/ Zogby. Respondents revealed the following about their 2008 summer travel plans:

Gas prices will have no impact	%	Planning trips >1 week long	%
Northeast *residents*	70	Northeast	47
South	70	South	60
Midwest	67	Midwest	49
West	69	West	51

Vacationing >6 hours from home	%	Less money for vacation than last year	%
Northeast	51	Northeast	59
South	65	South	60
Midwest	56	Midwest	52
West	65	West	57

A 2008 TripAdvisor poll showed how travelers planned to cut costs while away:

Said they would ...	%	Travel to a destination with	
Take fewer car trips to save fuel	37	a favorable exchange rate	32
Take shorter car trips to save fuel	18	Stay at cheaper accommodations	19

Many businesses sought to ameliorate 2008's economic woes by offering 'recession specials' of various kinds – below is a selection from around the US and abroad:

Padre's Modern Mexican in Phoenix, AZ, offered a free drink to anyone with a foreclosure notice. ❦ Harry's Bar in Venice, Italy, beloved by US tourists, offered a 20% discount on its menu to 'American victims of subprime loans'. ❦ Bars across the US featured 'recession relief' happy hours and drink deals, such as the $2 'Late-on-Your-Rent Lager' at Denver's Below Bar, or the 'Inflation Libation' special at LA's Table 8. ❦ Several fast-food chains expanded their 'dollar menus', including $1 Burger King cheeseburgers in some areas and $1 coffee in selected Starbucks. ❦ A restaurant in Covent Garden, London, offered a cut-price 'credit crunch brunch'. ❦ A boutique opened in Nolita, Manhattan, allowing customers to rent rather than buy designer dresses. ❦ Lamborghini began offering 'certified pre-owned vehicles' for the first time in the US. ❦ The 'recession special' has long been a fixture at NYC hot dog chain Gray's Papaya: 2 dogs and a drink for $3.50. [Sources: CNN Money; MSN Money; *Foreign Policy*]

———————————CARS & DRIVING———————————

State	license plate slogan
Alabama	*Stars Fell On*
Alaska	*Celebrating Statehood 1959–2009*
Arizona	*Grand Canyon State*
Arkansas	*The Natural State*
Connecticut	*Constitution State*
Delaware	*The First State*
DC	*Taxation Without Representation*
Florida	*Sunshine State*
Hawaii	*Aloha State*
Idaho	*Famous Potatoes*
Illinois	*Land of Lincoln*
Indiana	*Lincoln's Boyhood Home*
Kentucky	*Unbridled Spirit*
Louisiana	*Sportsman's Paradise*
Maine	*Vacationland*
Massachusetts	*The Spirit of America*
Minnesota	*10,000 Lakes*
Missouri	*Show Me State*
Montana	*Big Sky Country*
Nevada	*The Silver State*
New Hampshire	*Live Free or Die*
New Jersey	*Garden State*
New Mexico	*Land of Enchantment*
New York	*The Empire State*
North Carolina	*First in Flight*
North Dakota	*Discover the Spirit*
Ohio	*Birthplace of Aviation*
Oklahoma	*Native America*
Rhode Island	*Ocean State*
South Dakota	*Great Faces, Great Places*
Tennessee	*The Volunteer State*
Texas	*The Lone Star State*
Utah	*Life Elevated*
Vermont	*Green Mountain State*
Washington	*Evergreen State*
West Virginia	*Wild, Wonderful*
Wisconsin	*America's Dairyland*

[Slogans on standard plates issued in 2008;
not all states have a slogan]

MOST CARS PER CAPITA

Iowa	0·58
Connecticut	0·57
Ohio	0·56
California	0·54
North Dakota	0·54

FEWEST CARS PER CAPITA

Colorado	0·18
Nevada	0·27
DC	0·28
Kansas	0·31
Arkansas	0·34

[Includes private and commercial vehicles]

MOST DRIVERS PER 1,000 POP.

Connecticut	800
Alabama	797
New Hampshire	781
Florida	773
Montana	766

FEWEST DRIVERS PER 1,000 POP.

New York	577
Minnesota	597
DC	615
Illinois	629
California & Georgia	631

MOST MILES OF ROAD

Texas	305,272
California	170,290
Kansas	140,380
Illinois	138,996
Minnesota	132,309

FEWEST MILES OF ROAD

DC	1,500
Hawaii	4,330
Delaware	6,179
Rhode Island	6,528
Vermont	14,406

[Source: Federal Highway Administration,
Highway Statistics, 2006]

---------------- CAR COLOR CONFIDENCE INDEX ----------------

In 2008, CNW Marketing Research developed a 'color-confidence index' by asking 1,900 Americans how they felt about their life, and what color their car was. Clearly, more robust measures of mental health exist, yet the results are intriguing:

Car color	confidence (%± average)		
Emerald green	+5·5	Silver .... +1·2	Bright blue .... −5·5
Dark blue	+3·2	White .... *average*	Bright yellow .... −8·3
		Sunny yellow .... −3·7	Red .... −8·8
		Orange .... −4·1	Black .... −14·6

---------------- DRIVER AGES ----------------

More and more American teenagers are giving up the hallowed national ritual of applying for a drivers license as soon as they turn 16, according to Federal Highway Administration statistics released in 2008. According to the *New York Times*, a tightening of state laws, as well as higher insurance premiums, may be to blame.

% of 16-year-olds with a driver's license		% of each age group with a driver's license, 2006			
2006	29·8	<16 years old	4·9	30–34	89·9
2005	29·0	16	29·8	35–39	91·3
2004	30·2	17	51·1	40–44	93·3
2003	30·8	18	66·6	45–49	92·3
2002	32·1	19	74·2	50–54	92·1
2001	34·3	20	78·0	55–59	94·0
2000	37·0	21	79·0	60–64	88·8
1999	37·2	22	79·3	65–69	89·0
1998	43·8	23	83·3	70–74	86·9
1997	43·3	24	83·8	75–79	83·3
1996	40·6	25–29	84·2	80–84	74·6
				≥85	51·0
				[Source · FHA]	

---------------- BUMPER STICKERS & ROAD RAGE ----------------

While bumper stickers may be a source of fleeting amusement during traffic jams, in 2008 Colorado State University scientists uncovered a darker side to the garish plastic rectangles. In three separate studies on car adornment and driving behavior, the researchers discovered that the more bumper stickers, window decals, and mirror hangings students displayed on their vehicle, the more likely they were to report aggressive road behavior or 'road rage'. Interestingly, drivers with more car adornments also reported greater feelings of attachment to their vehicles, and the researchers posited that drivers who decorate their cars may be more prone to confusing the social norms of private property protection with the norms for sharing a public space. i.e., a road. Intriguingly, the researchers found no relationship between the content of the bumper stickers (whether religious, sporting, political, patriotic, punning, or other) and reports of a tendency towards aggressive driving.

—————— US TRANSPORTATION FATALITIES · 2006 ——————

Selected type	fatalities	%
Car occupants	17,800	39·6
Light-truck occupants	12,721	28·3
Motorcycle riders	4,810	10·7
Pedestrians†	4,784	10·7
Large-truck occupants	805	1·8
Pedal cyclists†	773	1·7
Other vehicle occupants	739	1·7
Recreational boating	710	1·6
General aviation	698	1·6

Railroad trespassers	520	1·2
Air carriers	50	0·11
Water transport (vessel-related)	48	0·11
Water transport (non-vessel)	39	0·09
Heavy-rail transit (subway &c.)	32	0·07
Bus occupants	27	0·06
Rail employees	19	0·04

Other fatalities occurred during the year.
† Struck by car or truck. [Source: DOT; 2006]

—————— DRIVING WITH CELL PHONES &c. ——————

At any given moment during daylight, *c.*11% of vehicles driven in America are being operated by someone using a cell phone, according to the National Highway Traffic Safety Administration (NHTSA). The NHTSA collects these data using the National Occupant Protection Use Survey, in which observers are sent to a randomly selected sample of 1,500 road sites to log driver behavior. Below is the percentage of drivers observed using cell phones, cell phones with headsets, and other devices, in 2007:

%	holding phone to ear	using a headset	handling a device†
All drivers	6	0·6	0·7
♂	5	0·6	0·5
♀	8	0·5	0·9

White	6	0·6	0·7
Black	8	0·9	0·6
Other race	6	0·3	0·4

† Visibly manipulating a PDA, phone, &c.

In July, California became the fifth state to require that drivers talking on cell phones use a headset. Yet chatting is just one distracting activity in which drivers engage; a 2006 Pew study found that 16% of Americans admit to grooming in their cars (or as the *LA Times* called it, 'driving while primping').

—————————— DRUNK DRIVING ——————————

17,602 people died in alcohol-related crashes† in the US in 2006, according to the National Highway Traffic Safety Administration, which also reported the following:

Highest drunk-driving rates, 2006 (per 100m vehicle miles traveled)	
Montana	0·91
South Carolina	0·84
Louisiana	0·80
Mississippi	0·77
South Dakota	0·75

2006 drunk-driving fatalities†	No.
Car occupants	14,861
Pedestrians	2,367
Pedal cyclists	302
Others/unknown	72

† Crashes in which one driver or nonoccupant has a BAC of ≥0·01 grams per deciliter.

Between 2001–05, more fatal alcohol-related crashes occurred on January 1 (54) than any other day.

SUBWAYS OF THE WORLD

System	est. annual ridership	no. stations	single fare	single fare US$
Tokyo Subway	2·9bn	282	160–300¥	$1·55–$2·9
Moscow Metro	2·6bn	172	19 rubles	77¢
NYC Subway	1·5bn	468	$2	$2
Seoul Metropolitan Subway	1·5bn	263	900 won	95¢
Mexico City Metro	1·4bn	175	2 pesos	20¢
Paris Metro	1·4bn	380	€1·60	$2·3
London Underground	976m	275	£4	$8
Osaka Municipal Subway	880m	123	≥200¥	≥$1·9
Hong Kong MTR	867m	53	$4–26	51¢–$3.33
St Petersburg Metro	810m	58	14 rubles	58¢

Below are the transit fares for some other cities of note, in US$ as of March 2008:

City	single fare ($)		
Athens	1·52	Montreal	2·79
Boston	2	Philadelphia	2
Helsinki, Finland	3·04	Rome	1·52
Lisbon, Portugal	1·14–1·59	São Paolo	1·41
Los Angeles	1·25	Stockholm	6·32
		Washington, DC	1·65–4·50

[Sources: NYC MTA, Hong Kong MTR, Transport for London, City of St Petersburg, Virgin Atlantic, Metro International. Currency conversions are approximate guides and current at time of writing.]

WORLD'S BEST PUBLIC TRANSPORTATION

London's public transportation system is the best in the world, according to 2,000 travelers polled by TripAdvisor in October 2007. Below are the top five winners for the best, the cleanest, and the safest public transportation system in the world:

Best	Cleanest	Safest
1 .... London	1 ...... Washington, DC	1 .... London
2 .... New York	2 .... Tokyo	2 ...... Washington, DC
3 .... Paris	3 .... Paris	3 .... Paris
4 ...... Washington, DC	4 .... London	4 .... New York
5 .... Hong Kong	5 .... Montreal	4 .... Tokyo [*tie*]

TRAIN TRESPASSER FATALITIES

486 people died after trespassing on the rails in 2007 – the top cause of rail-related deaths, according to the Dept of Transportation. The states with the most fatalities:

California	82	Florida	36	Pennsylvania	23
Texas	49	Illinois	27	North Carolina	23

————————BUSIEST INTERNATIONAL AIRLINES————————

Rank	country	airline	passengers (m)	passenger km (bn)
1	USA	American	98·1	224·3
2	USA	Delta	73·5	158·9
3	USA	United	69·3	188·7
4	USA	Northwest	54·8	116·8
5	Germany	Lufthansa	51·2	114·7
6	France	Air France	49·4	128·7
7	Japan	All Nippon Airways	49·2	58·0
8	Japan	JAL	48·9	89·3
9	USA	Continental	46·7	122·7
10	China	China Southern Airline	40·8	59·6
11	Ireland	Ryanair	40·5	39·8

[Source: International Civil Aviation Organization, 2006]

————————BUSIEST INTERNATIONAL AIRPORTS————————

Rank	airport	airport code	passengers	% change 2006–07
1	Atlanta	ATL	89,379,287	+5·3
2	Chicago	ORD	76,159,324	−0·2
3	London	LHR	68,068,554	+0·8
4	Tokyo	HND	66,671,435	+1·3
5	Los Angeles	LAX	61,895,548	+1·4
6	Paris	CDG	59,919,383	+5·4
7	Dallas/Ft Worth	DFW	59,784,876	−0·7
8	Frankfurt	FRA	54,161,856	+2·6
9	Beijing	PEK	53,736,923	+9·4
10	Madrid	MAD	52,122,214	+14·0

[Source: Airports Council International, 2007]

————————WORLDWIDE AIR TRAFFIC DATA · 2007————————

Region	2007 passengers	'06–'07 ±%
Africa	129,614,596	+13·7
Asia-Pac	1,055,287,061	+7·7
Europe	1,450,522,474	+7·3
Latin Am.	304,586,180	+8·4
Mideast	126,249,405	+16·5
N Am.	1,579,595,445	+3·3

SYSTEM-WIDE TRAFFIC	
Passengers†	4·5bn
Intl passengers‡	1·8 bn
All passenger traffic, ±'06–'07	+6·4%
Cargo (incl. mail)	80·3m tons
International freight	48·3m tons
Landings & takeoffs	68·6m

Between Jan–May 2008, international passenger traffic rose by 6·1%; however, domestic passenger traffic rose by only 0·9%. † All passengers enplaning and deplaning; those in transit are only counted once. ‡ Passengers traveling between airports in different countries. [Source: Airports Council Intl]

US FLYING TIMES

The estimated average flying times between some American cities (hrs:mins)

to	to Boston	to Chicago	to Dallas	to Detroit	to LA	to Miami	to NYC	to Phoenix	to SF
to Chicago	2:10								
to Dallas	3:30	2:15							
to Detroit	1:45	1:10	3:00						
to LA	5:20	3:50	2:50	4:15					
to Miami	3:05	3:20	3:10	3:00	5:45				
to NYC	1:15	2:50	3:45	2:15	6:30	3:20			
to Phoenix	4:45	3:20	2:20	3:45	1:30	4:00	4:45		
to SF	5:30	4:10	3:25	4:30	1:25	5:15	5:20	1:55	
Seattle	5:00	3:50	3:45	4:00	2:30	5:30	5:15	2:45	2:10

MOST LATE FLIGHTS

Airline	% of on-time flights
Atlantic Southeast Airlines	66·4
American Airlines	66·9
American Eagle	68·8
United Airlines	69·1
Comair	69·5

For the 12 months ending May 2008.
[Source: Bureau of Transportation]

MOST LOST LUGGAGE

Airline	reports per 1,000 passengers[†]
American Eagle	13·6
Comair	11·4
Atlantic Southeast Airlines	11·2
Skywest Airlines	10·9
Mesa Airlines	10·5

† Of lost, damaged, or delayed bags in 2007, per 1,000 passengers. [Source: BOT]

WORST 2007 AIR ACCIDENTS

Deaths	date	location	airline (plane)
187	7/17	São Paulo, Brazil	TAM (Airbus A320-233)
114	5/05	Douala, Cameroon	Kenya Airways (Boeing 737-8AL)
102	1/01	off Ujung Pandang, Indonesia	Adam Air (Boeing 737-4Q8)
90	9/16	Phuket, Thailand	One-Two-Go (McDonnell Douglas MD-82)
57	11/30	Isparta, Turkey	Atlasjet (McDonnell Douglas MD-83)

[Source: Aircraft Crashes Record Office]

WORLD'S WORST AIRPORTS

Foreign Policy's list of the world's 5 worst airports in 2007, and why they're so bad:

Léopold Sédar Senghor, Dakar, Senegal .... *3-hour immigration lines, no seats*
Indira Gandhi, New Delhi, India .... *filthy toilets, used syringes on terminal floor*
Mineralnye Vody, SW Russia .... *snow, ice, and feral cats inside terminal*
Baghdad, Iraq .... *pilots employ terrifying landing techniques to avoid missiles*
Charles de Gaulle, Paris, France .... *rude staff, dirty terminals, overpriced food*

TOURISM TRENDS OF NOTE

STAYCATIONS
Stay-at-home vacations, inspired by high (gas) prices and recession woes.

CLIMATE SIGHTSEEING
Visiting areas threatened by climate-change (e.g., glaciers and rainforests). *Also* ECO-TOURISM: low-impact travel that fosters environmental awareness. *Also* GREEN TRAVEL: choosing sustainable alternatives, buying carbon offsets, &c.

DEBAUCHERISM
'Spring Break'-esque excess in the Caribbean, Las Vegas, &c. The trend for British stag and hen parties to cause mayhem in cities like Prague, Dublin, Amsterdam, and Bratislava has been called ALCOHOL TOURISM.

DARK TOURISM
Travel to sites of horror, death, or destruction (e.g., the 'killing fields' of Cambodia, Auschwitz, &c.) whether for educational motives or from mor-bid fascination[†]. (*Also* HOLOCAUST, SLAVERY, PRISON, BATTLEFIELD, or CEMETERY TOURISM.)

DIASPORA TOURISM
Migrants returning to see relatives, use local services, or explore their heritage, reportedly popular among Eastern Europeans.

VOLUNTOURISM
Do-gooder vacations, such as trips to New Orleans to build homes for those displaced by Hurricane Katrina.

GASTRO-TOURISM
Expeditions to outstanding restaurants (e.g., El Bulli), or areas with culinary fame (e.g., the Napa Valley). The 'Michelin effect', where food awards prompt an increase in tourism, has recently hit Tokyo in the wake of Japan's recent triumph [see p.224].

MEDICAL TOURISM
Trips for medical procedures, either to visit a specific center of excellence or to avoid high costs and/or long waits. *Also* REPRODUCTIVE TOURISM: travel for fertility treatments. *Also* PLASTIC SURGERY TOURISM.

PROCREATION VACATIONS
Holidays in conducive environments taken by couples hoping to conceive – sometimes featuring 'fertility-boosting' food, massages, treatments, &c.

BABYMOONS
Romantic getaways taken by parents before the birth of their child, or to celebrate its arrival.

SLOW TRAVEL
Trips that eschew hectic schedules to 'savor the journey' (e.g., traveling by train, staying in rural areas, &c).

SUICIDE TOURISM
When the terminally ill travel to places where euthanasia is legal (e.g., Switzerland) to end their lives; or when people travel to landmarks (e.g., Golden Gate Bridge, Eiffel Tower, &c.) to kill themselves 'in style'[‡].

[†] Madeleine McCann's 2007 disappearance has inspired hundreds of tourists on DISAPPEARANCE TOURS, to visit Praia da Luz, Portugal, from where she vanished. [‡] According to a 2007 report from the New York Academy of Medicine, more than 1 in 10 people who killed themselves in Manhattan (1990–2004) were 'suicide tourists'. [Sources: *USA Today*; World Travel Market; *New Scientist*; SlowPlanet.com; JWT; *Time Out New York*; *Forbes*; *Washington Post*; The Dark Tourism Forum; &c.]

—————————— FOREIGN VISITORS ——————————

More people visited the US from foreign countries in 2007 than in any prior year, according to the US Commerce Department. The nation had 56·7m foreign visitors, 11% more than in 2006. Below are top 10 countries of origin for visitors:

Country	2007 visitors				
Canada	17,735,000	Japan	3,531,489	Australia	669,536
Mexico	15,089,000	Germany	1,524,151	Brazil	639,431
UK	4,497,858	France	997,506	Italy	634,152
		South Korea	806,175	TOTAL	56,716,277

—————————— FOREIGN VISITING ——————————

64m United States residents traveled abroad in 2007, a 1% rise compared to 2006, according to the Commerce Department. The growth came almost entirely from overseas travel, which grew by 4%, while travel to Mexico and Canada declined:

Country	US visitors	±'06–'07			
Mexico (ground)	19,453,000	–1%	France	2,217,000	–1%
Canada (ground)	13,371,000	–3%	Germany	1,936,000	+15%
UK	3,123,000	–5%	Japan	1,718,000	+12%
Italy	2,373,000	+8%	Jamaica	1,530,000	–9%
			China	1,374,000	+4%

————— SALUTATIONS OF DIFFERENT NATIONS —————

The 1881 etiquette manual *Our Deportment* by John H. Young offers an amusing (if somewhat credulous) guide to the methods of greeting used in some foreign lands:

In SOUTHERN AFRICA, it is the custom to rub toes.

In LAPLAND, your friend rubs his nose against yours.

The TURK folds his arms upon his breast and bends his head very low.

The MOORS OF MOROCCO have a somewhat startling mode of salutation: they ride at a gallop toward a stranger, as though they would unhorse him, and when close at hand suddenly check their horse and fire a pistol over the person's head.

The EGYPTIAN solicitously asks you, 'How do you perspire?' and lets his hand fall to the knee.

The CHINESE bows low and inquires, 'Have you eaten?'

The SPANIARD says, 'God be with you, sir,' or, 'How do you stand?'

And the NEAPOLITAN piously remarks, 'Grow in holiness.'

The GERMAN asks, 'How goes it with you?'

The FRENCHMAN bows profoundly and inquires, 'How do you carry yourself?'

Our Deportment adds a cautionary note to untraveled Americans on the subject of kissing, tactfully noting, 'Foreigners are given to embracing. In France and Germany the parent kisses his grown-up son on the forehead, men throw their arms around the necks of their friends, and brothers embrace like lovers. It is a curious sight to Americans, with their natural prejudices against publicity in kissing.'

MOST VISITED US CITIES

Below are the American cities international travelers visited most often in 2007:

Rank	city	intl visitors in 2007	tourism slogan
1	New York City	7,646,000	*I ♡ New York*†
2	Los Angeles	2,652,000	*Discover Los Angeles*
3	Miami	2,341,000	*Express Yourself*
4	San Francisco	2,270,000	*Only in San Francisco*
5	Orlando	2,055,000	*Say Yes to Orlando*
6	Las Vegas	1,720,000	*What Happens Here, Stays Here*
7	Honolulu	1,553,000	*Oahu, the Heart of Hawaii*‡
8	Washington, DC	1,195,000	*Create Your Own Power Trip*
9	Chicago	1,147,000	*A Great Urban Adventure*§
10	Boston	1,075,000	*America's Walking City*
11	San Diego	645,000	*San Diego – The Road to Happiness*§
12	Philadelphia	550,000	*Philly's More Fun*
13	Atlanta	478,000	*City Lights, Southern Nights*
14	Houston	478,000	*My Houston*
15	Anaheim	430,000	*It's So California!*

† Though frequently associated with NYC, the famous slogan is also used throughout the state.
‡ Island-wide slogan. § Summer 2008 slogan. [Sources: Intl Trade Admi.; Dept of Commerce]

ATTRACTIVE RESIDENTS

Miami is home to the most attractive people in the US, while Philadelphia has the least attractive residents, according to a *Travel & Leisure*/CNN Headline News poll of 60,000 people. The cities said to have the most and least attractive people were:

Most attractive	Least attractive
Miami · San Diego · Charleston	Philadelphia · Wash., DC · Dallas/Ft
Austin · Honolulu	Worth · San Antonio · Orlando

The poll also asked respondents which city had the most intelligent residents (Seattle), the most stylish people (New York), and the most diversity overall (New York). Charleston was said to be the most friendly, while New Orleans denizens were said to be the most 'fun'. [Source: *Travel & Leisure*, 2007]

FAVORITE LEISURE ACTIVITIES

Below are America's favorite pastimes (based on the percentage who participated in the last year):

Dining out 40%	Going to the beach ..23	Cooking for fun......18
Entertaining..........40	Playing cards 22	Bars/clubs 18
Reading books 39	Computer games.....20	[Source: Mediamark
Barbecuing 34	Baking................19	Research, 2006 data]

───────────MEAL & HOTEL COSTS IN THE US───────────

Two adults traveling together in the US in 2008 could expect to spend an average of $244 per day on meals and lodging, according to the American Automobile Association. The AAA's 2008 *Annual Vacation Costs Survey*, based on prices at 60,000 businesses in AAA travel guides, found an average cost of $164 per night for accommodations (double occupancy) and $80 for meals (excluding tips and beverages). Of course, costs varied across the country. The most and least expensive cities were:

MOST EXPENSIVE				LEAST EXPENSIVE			
$	*room*	*meals*	*combined*	$	*room*	*meals*	*combined*
Honolulu†	546	127	673	Tulsa	116	62	179
New York	477	129	606	Albuquerque	121	58	179
Miami	281	90	371	Wichita	119	75	194
San Diego	244	117	361	Okl. City	133	62	195
Las Vegas	224	134	358	Fresno	126	81	207

In 1950, the first year the AAA began tracking vacation costs, the average price for a day's meals and lodgings in the United States was $13. † Hawaii state officials disputed this ranking, claiming the average daily expenditure for tourists in Hawaii was about $358 per couple per day as of May 2008.

───────────THE COST OF CULTURE───────────

London is one of the world's most expensive cities for cultural experiences, according to a 2008 survey by the UK Post Office, which compared the price of a range of cultural activities (museums, classical music concerts, visits to the opera and ballet, and heritage sites) in 10 major tourist destinations. A look at costs in 3 major cities:

BERLIN	NEW YORK	LONDON
Total: $419	Total: $510	Total: $613
Pergamonmuseum · $13	*Guggenheim* · $18	*Tate Modern* · free
Checkpoint Charlie · $21	MoMA · $20	*Natural History Museum* free
Museum of Natural History · $10	*Museum of Natural History* · $15	*Victoria and Albert Museum* · free
Berlin Phil. · $116	*New York Philharmonic* $82	*London Philharmonic* $64
Berlin State Opera $112	*Met Opera* · $238	*Royal Opera* · $272
Berlin State Ballet $112	*NYC Ballet* · $93	*Royal Ballet* · $161
Berlin Cathedral · $8	*Empire State Building* $19	*Buckingham Palace* $57
Reichstag · *free*	*Statue of Liberty* · free	*Hampton Court* · $27
Charlottenburg Palace $26	*Harlem Renaissance Tour* $25	*Tower of London* · $33

The costs for a day of culture in the other 7 cities: Warsaw ($150); Prague ($206); Lisbon ($215); Amsterdam ($329); Rome ($415); Paris ($490); Barcelona ($515). All conversions are approximate.

SPOILED & UNSPOILED ISLANDS

Due to their delicate ecosystems, islands are particularly vulnerable to climate change, invasive species, and the consequences of tourism. In November 2007, *National Geographic Traveler* asked 522 experts in sustainable tourism to rank 111 selected islands using a number of criteria, including: environmental and ecological quality; the condition of historic buildings; social and cultural integrity; and the quality of tourism management. The highest- and lowest-ranking islands are below:

Least-spoiled	*Most-spoiled*
Faroe Islands, Denmark	St Thomas, US Virgin Islands
Azores, Portugal	Ibiza, Spain
Lofoten, Norway	Providenciales, Turks & Caicos
Shetland Islands, Scotland	Jamaica
Chiloé, Chile	Hilton Head, USA

GREAT BACKYARD BIRD COUNT

Record numbers of Pine Grosbeak and Common Redpolls were recorded during the 2008 Great Backyard Bird Count, in which volunteers around the country are asked to record bird sightings in their area for 15 minutes over a period of 4 days. During the 2008 event (held February 15–18), 85,725 checklists were submitted and 635 species identified. The most commonly seen birds in the US and Canada:

Rank	species				
1	*Northern Cardinal*	4	*Downy Woodpecker*	8	*Tufted Titmouse*
2	*Mourning Dove*	5	*American Goldfinch*	9	*Black-capped*
3	*Dark-eyed Junco*	6	*Blue Jay*		*Chickadee*
		7	*House Finch*	10	*American Crow*

BEST BEACHES

Each year, Dr Stephen Leatherman, director of Florida International University's Laboratory for Coastal Research, produces a ranking of America's best beaches. The list is based on 50 criteria, including water and sand quality, safety, and environmental management. In 2008 the following ten beaches were at the top of his list:

Rank	beach & location		
1	Caladesi Island State Park, FL	6	Main Beach, East Hampton, NY
2	Hanalei Beach, Kauai, HI	7	Hamoa Beach, Maui, HI
3	Siesta Beach, Sarasota, FL	8	Cape Hatteras, NC
4	Coopers Beach, Southampton, NY	9	Cape Florida State Park, FL
5	Coronado Beach, San Diego, CA	10	Beachwalker Park,
			Kiawah Island, SC

The beach named the best each year is excluded from future rankings. Some recent winners: *Ocracoke Lifeguard Beach* in Outer Banks, NC [2007]; *Fleming Beach Park* in Maui, HI [2006]; *Fort DeSoto Park's North Beach* in St Petersburg, FL [2005]; *Hanauma Bay*, Oahu, HI [2004]; Kaanapali, HI [2003].

————————HEALTH ADVICE FOR TRAVELERS————————

Tips for traveling from the Centers for Disease Control and Prevention: ❦ JET LAG · During the flight, stay away from large meals, caffeine, and alcohol. To address symptoms, 'persons traveling eastward should seek bright light in the morning, while those traveling westward should seek bright light in the afternoon'. ❦ MOTION SICKNESS · To reduce symptoms, 'choose seats with the smoothest ride', which are usually at the front of a car, boat, or train, and over the wings on an airplane. 'Focus on distant objects or keep eyes closed', 'minimize head movement'. Symptoms usually improve about 15 minutes after motion has stopped. ❦ EXTREME COLD · Warning signs of hypothermia include 'shivering, confusion, memory loss, drowsiness, exhaustion, fumbling hands, and slurred speech'. Skin that is frostbitten appears white, grayish-yellow, and firm, waxy, or numb. To prevent hypothermia and frostbite, travelers should dress warmly (but remove layers that cause excessive perspiration) and drink warm beverages. Treatment includes 'getting the person warm'. ❦ SUNBURN · Symptoms usually begin '*c.*4 hours after sun exposure, worsen within 24–36 hours, and resolve in 3–5 days'. Skin peeling begins 3-8 days later. Eyes can also become sunburned, which will make them feel red, dry, gritty, and painful. ❦ EXTREME HEAT · The symptoms of heatstroke include a body temperature >103°F, red, hot, and dry skin, a rapid pulse, headache, dizziness, and nausea. People with these symptoms should 'rest, drink cool nonalcoholic beverages', and take a cool shower or swim. If symptoms progress, seek emergency treatment, as heatstroke can be fatal. ❦

ALTITUDE SICKNESS · results from traveling to a high-altitude area (>6,000–8,000ft) faster than the body can adapt. Symptoms may resemble those of a hangover, and include headache, fatigue, and nausea. 'There is no reason for someone to die from altitude illness unless trapped by weather or geography' and unable to descend. If on a group trek, 'acknowledge and verbalize' altitude sickness symptoms should they develop. ❦ SWIMMING · 'Murky water, hidden underwater objects, unexpected drop-offs, and aquatic plant life are hazardous'. Always wear a personal flotation device when boating or water skiing; '"water wings" and "noodles" are toys and should not be used in place of life jackets'. If scuba diving, avoid shiny watches. Do not swim with diarrhea. ❦ ANIMALS · Free-ranging macaque monkeys may pose a herpes B risk, so avoid scratches, splashes, and bites. While 'deaths from snakebite are relatively rare', leave all snakes alone, as 'most snakebites are the direct result of startling, handling, or harassing snakes'. Therapy for snakebites is controversial. ❦ AIR TRAVEL · Those with ear, nose, or sinus infections or severe congestion may experience pain while flying. Stomach gases also expand during flight, and so passengers sensitive to bloating should avoid carbonated beverages and gas-producing foods. ❦ FOOD & DRINK · Never bring home perishable seafood. Avoid salads, uncooked vegetables, and unpasteurized milk products. Food from street vendors should be cause for suspicion. Beware of assuming food and drink onboard aircraft are safe.

[Source: *Health Information for Intl Travel,* 2008]

———— NEWLY INSCRIBED WORLD HERITAGE SITES ————

Below are the sites inscribed on the World Heritage List by UNESCO during 2008:

CULTURAL SITES: *Archaeological site of al-Hijr (Madâin Sâlih)*, Saudi Arabia
Armenian monastic ensembles, Iran · *Baha'i holy places in Haifa & W Galilee*, Israel
Berlin modernism housing estates, Germany · *Carpathian mountain area*, Slovakia
Chief Roi Mata's domain, Vanuatu · *Fortifications of Vauban*, France
Frontiers of the Roman Empire†, Germany and UK
Historic center of Berat and Gjirokastra†, Albania
Historic center of Camagüey, Cuba · *Kuk early agricultural site*, Papua N Guinea
Le Morne cultural landscape, Mauritius · *Mantua and Sabbioneta*, Italy
Mountain Railways of India†
Melaka and George Town, historic cities of the Straits of Malacca, Malaysia
Mijikenda Kaya forests, Kenya · *Palaeolithic cave art of northern Spain†*
San Marino historic center and Mount Titano, San Marino
Stari Grad Plain, Croatia
The wooden churches of the Slovak part of Preah Vihear Temple, Cambodia
Rhaetian railway in the Albula/Bernina landscapes, Switzerland/Italy
San Miguel and the Sanctuary of Jesús de Nazareno de Atotonilco, Mexico

NATURAL PROPERTIES:
Joggins fossil cliffs, Canada · *Lagoons of New Caledonia*, France
Monarch butterfly biosphere reserve, Mexico · *Mt Sanqingshan Ntnl Park*, China
Saryarka – steppe and lakes of northern Kazakhstan · *Socotra Archipelago*, Yemen
Surtsey, Iceland · *Swiss tectonic arena Sardona*, Switzerland
† Extensions of sites inscribed in previous years

———— MUSEUMS & GALLERIES IN MAJOR CITIES ————

City	population	national museums	other museums	public art galleries
London	7·6m	22	162	92
New York	8·3m	16	85	N/A
Paris	2·2m	19	138	59
Shanghai	9·8m	6	100	6
Tokyo	8·5m	8	71	40

[Source: *Museums Journal*, April 2008]

———— DISTINCTIVE DESTINATIONS ————

Each year the National Trust for Historic Preservation selects a dozen American vacation spots with a 'strong commitment to historic preservation and revitalization'. In 2008, the following were selected: *Aiken*, SC; *Apalachicola*, FL; *Columbus*, MS; *Crested Butte*, CO; *Fort Davis*, TX; *Friday Harbor*, WA; *Portland*, OR; *Portsmouth*, NH; *Red Wing*, MN; *Ste Genevieve*, MO; *San Juan Bautista*, CA; *Wilmington*, NC.

———————— UNUSUAL MUSEUMS OF NOTE ————————

A selection from the many unusual and offbeat museums found around the world:

American International Rattlesnake Museum............Albuquerque, New Mexico
Atomic Testing Museum...Las Vegas, Nevada
Bakelite Museum .... Williton, Somerset, England
Barometer World & Museum ....Okehampton, Devon, England
Big Daddy Don Garlits Museum of Drag Racing......................Ocala, Florida
Big Mac Museum...................................North Huntingdon, Pennsylvania
Bramah Museum of Tea and Coffee.............................. London, England
British Lawnmower Museum ....Southport, Lancashire, England
Bunny Museum.. Pasadena, California
Burlingame Museum of Pez Memorabilia .... Burlingame, California
Carrot Museum.. Berlotte, Belgium
Cockroach Hall of Fame Museum .... Plano, Texas
Conspiracy Museum (JFK & other assassinations) ....Dallas, Texas
Cumberland Pencil Museum...........................Keswick, Cumbria, England
Dutch Cheese Museum.....................Alkmaar, North Holland, Netherlands
Ice Museum...Fairbanks, Alaska
Icelandic Phallological Museum (phallic specimens)................... Húsavík, Iceland
Jesse James Museum... Stanton, Missouri
Kool-Aid: Discover the Dream (dedicated to Kool-Aid; see p.289) .....Hastings, Nebraska
Leila's Hair Museum....................................... Independence, Missouri
Le Musée de la Banane (Banana Museum)...................Sainte-Marie, Martinique
Matchbox Museum .... Tomar, Portugal
Mount Horeb Mustard Museum.......................... Mount Horeb, Wisconsin
Museo del Jamón-Centro de Interpretación del Cerdo Ibérico
(Cured Ham Museum and Ibérico Pig Interpretation Center) .... Aracena, Spain
Museum of Brands, Packaging, and Advertising................... London, England
Museum of Broken Relationships...........................traveling (brokenships.com)
Museum of Drinking Water....................................Taipei, Taiwan
Museum of Questionable Medical Devices........................St Paul, Minnesota
Museum of Roller Skating.......................................Lincoln, Nebraska
Museum of Temporary Art .... Tübingen, Germany
Muzium Padi (National Rice Museum)................................Kedah, Malaysia
National Great Blacks in Wax Museum ....Baltimore, Maryland
Norwegian Canning Museum ....Stavanger, Norway
Owl Art and Craft Museum ....Seoul, South Korea
Phosphate Museum .... Mulberry, Florida
Salt Museum.......................................Northwich, Cheshire, England
Shin-Yokohama Ramen Museum ....Yokohama, Japan
Spam Museum (the food, not the email) .... Austin, Minnesota
Sulabh International Museum of Toilets ....New Delhi, India
Telephone Historical Centre (call before visiting) ....Edmonton, Alberta, Canada
US Border Patrol Museum...El Paso, Texas
Williams Hall Museum of Kitsch Art...........................Burlington, Vermont
World Brick Museum ....Maizuru City, Japan

———————————— THE GHOST CHILI ————————————

The Bhut Jolokia – or 'Ghost Chili', as it is known in its native land of India – was pronounced the world's hottest chili pepper by Guinness World Records in October 2007. The Ghost Chili yields 1m Scoville Heat Units (SHU), almost twice the amount contained in former chili champion the Red Savina. Scientists at New Mexico State University discovered the pepper after being alerted to its existence by the Indian Defense Research Laboratory. Researchers are said to be excited about its commercial possibilities, since a minute amount of the dehydrated pepper can provide extremely potent spice. ❦ In 1912 American chemist Wilbur Scoville created a method of measuring the amount of spice in a chili pepper, by progressively mixing its extract with sugar water until a panel of tasters could no longer discern any heat. The more sugar water necessary, the higher the number of Scoville Heat Units assigned. Although the method used to arrive at SHUs has since evolved, the rating system remains in use. Below are the SHUs for some chilis (and chili products) of note:

Pure capsaicin......SHU = 16,000,000
Pepper spray (commercial) . 2,000,000
Bhut Jolokia................. 1,000,000
Red Savina 577,000
Habanero...................... 200,000
Thai........................... 100,000
Cayenne........................ 50,000
Jalapeño 5,000

———————————— GENDER & FOOD PREFERENCES ————————————

Women are more likely to eat vegetables, whereas men prefer meat – according to not very surprising research released by the Foodborne Disease Active Surveillance Network in 2008. The goal of the research was to discover whether men and women have different preferences for unsafe foods, or those likely to cause illnesses like *E. coli*. After monitoring the habits of 14,000 US adults from May 2006–April 2007, men were found to prefer undercooked hamburgers and runny eggs, while women displayed an inexplicable love of alfalfa sprouts. The researchers also noted that:

Men ate more ...	*Women ate more ...*
veal · duck · ham · shrimp	carrots · tomatoes · blueberries
oysters · brussels sprouts · asparagus	yogurt · almonds · walnuts

———————————— MOST-FATTENING ICE CREAM ————————————

Below are the most-fattening ice creams available in 2008, according to *Newsweek*:

Brand & flavor	*calories*	*fat (per ½-cup serving)*
Häagen-Dazs Chocolate Peanut Butter	360	24g
Ben and Jerry's Chubby Hubby	330	20g
Häagen-Dazs Butter Pecan	310	23g
Sheer Bliss Pomegranate with chocolate chips	320	20g
Ben and Jerry's Vermonty Python [see p.121]	300	19g

──────── TOP TAP WATER & WATER SOMMELIERS ────────

While Los Angelenos may complain about local air quality, their drinking water is among the best in the world, according to the judges at the 2008 Berkeley Springs International Water Tasting. After evaluating 120 waters from around the world on taste, texture, odor, and clarity, the panel of food critics and judges at the annual event in Berkeley Springs, West Virginia, awarded the gold medal for Best Municipal Water to the Metropolitan Water District of Southern California, as well as the town of Clearbook, British Columbia. Below are the other gold medalists:

Non-carbonated bottled water .... Tumai Water, Martinsburg, WV
Purified drinking water .... Great Blue, Federalsburg, MD
Carbonated bottled water ..... Salvus Mineralwasser Medium, Emsdetten, Germany
People's choice for package design .... Mist Premium Spring Water, Atlanta, GA

'Water sommeliers' have infested certain fine dining establishments since *c.*2002, tasked with understanding the characteristics of various waters and recommending harmonious water pairings for food and wine. In 2007, two Nestlé waters, San Pellegrino and Acqua Panna, and L'Association de la Sommellerie Internationale, released the Water Codex II – a guide to water tasting and service for sommeliers and others. According to this Codex, waters can be divided into 2 categories: HEAVY-BODIED (sparkling, mildly acidic, stimulates salivation) and LIGHT-BODIED (still, low acid, velvety). The Codex suggests that heavy-bodied waters should be paired with red wines, rich food, and meats, whereas light-bodied waters are best with white wine, salads, and light dishes of chicken or fish. Those who wish to perform their own water tasting are advised by the Codex to adopt the following five steps:

[1] *Pour* water into the appropriate glass; [2] *Taste* a sip of *c.*15ml, allow it to linger on the tongue, then distribute throughout the mouth; [3] *Observe* the water at eye level, then lower the glass and view from above; [4] *Smell* the water, breathing deeply at regular intervals; and [5] *Taste* again, allowing the water to rest on the tongue.

──────────── MOST CAFFEINATED CITY ────────────

Chicago is the most caffeinated city in America, according to a 2007 survey conducted by Prince Market Research. The survey asked 2,000 people in 20 major cities to describe their total caffeine consumption, including coffee, tea, chocolate, and energy drinks. The cities with the most and least caffeine consumption were:

Most caffeinated	*Least caffeinated*
[1] Chicago [2] Tampa	[1] San Francisco/Oakland
[3] Miami [4] Phoenix	[2] Philadelphia [3] NYC
[5] Atlanta	[4] Detroit [5] Baltimore

Not surprisingly, Seattle ranked first in coffee consumption, and Seattleites were the most likely to say caffeine is good for you. Chicagoans drank the most cola and ate the most chocolate, while Miamians consumed the most tea, and those in Riverside/San Bernardino, CA, slurped the most energy drinks.

MUSIC & WINE

Listening to certain styles of music can enhance the taste of wine, according to psychologists at Heriot Watt University. The researchers first identified four songs which exemplified certain styles of music: *Carmina Burana* by Orff (which was classified as 'powerful and heavy'), Tchaikovsky's *Waltz of the Flowers* from *The Nutcracker* ('subtle and refined'), *Slow Breakdown* by Michael Brook ('mellow and soft'), and *Just Can't Get Enough* by Nouvelle Vague ('zingy and refreshing'). Then, subjects were given wine to quaff while listening to these tracks and were asked if the music influenced its flavor. White wine was rated as 40% more 'zingy' when drunk while listening to Nouvelle Vague, but only 26% more 'mellow and soft' while listening to Michael Brook. Red wine was most enhanced (by 60%) when imbibed during *Carmina Burana*. The Chilean winemaker Aurelio Montes (who admitted he is wont to play hypnotically soothing monastic chants to his wines as they mature) commissioned the research in May 2008, and subsequently recommended the following complimentary wine and music combinations:

SYRAH *best drunk with ...*	CABERNET SAUVIGNON
Nessun Dorma · Puccini	*Honky Tonk Woman* · Rolling Stones
Chariots of Fire · Vangelis	*Won't Get Fooled Again* · The Who
Orinoco Flow · Enya	*Live & Let Die* · Paul McCartney
MERLOT	CHARDONNAY
Easy · Lionel Ritchie	*Atomic* · Blondie
Heartbeats · Jose Gonzalez	*Spinning Around* · Kylie Minogue
Over the Rainbow · Eva Cassidy	*Rock DJ* · Robbie Williams

'WINE SPECTATOR' TOP 100

The 4 'most exciting' wines of 2007, from *Wine Spectator* magazine's 'Top 100' list:

[1] Clos des Papes *Châteauneuf-du-Pape* 2005
[2] Ridge *Chardonnay Santa Cruz Mountains Santa Cruz Mt Estate* 2005
[3] Le Vieux Donjon *Châteauneuf-du-Pape* 2005
[4] Antinori *Toscana Tignanello* 2004

WINE IMPORT & EXPORT

The top exporting and importing wine countries in 2007, according to the USDA:

Wine IMPORTS	*hectoliters*	*% total*	*Wine* EXPORTS	*hectoliters*	*% total*
European Union	12·9m	31	European Union	18·4m	39
USA	8·4m	20	Australia	7·8m	17
Russia	6·5m	16	Chile	6·1m	13
Canada	3·1m	8	South Africa	5·0m	11
Switzerland	1·9m	5	USA	4·1m	9

'FOOD & WINE' BEST NEW CHEFS · 2008

Jim Burke .... *James*........................... Philadelphia
Gerard Craft .... *Niche* .... St Louis, Missouri
Tim Cushman........................ *O Ya* .... Boston
Jeremy Fox .... *Ubuntu* .... Napa, California
Koren Grieveson................. *Avec*................................Chicago
Michael Psilakis..................... *Anthos* ....NYC
Ethan Stowell .... *Union*..................................Seattle
Giuseppe Tentori..................... *Boka* ....Chicago
Eric Warnstedt .... *Hen of the Wood* .... Waterbury, Vermont
Sue Zemanick....................... *Gautreau's*....................... New Orleans

JAMES BEARD AWARDS · 2008

Below is a selection of the honors bestowed at the James Beard Awards in 2008:

Outstanding restaurateur .... Joe Bastianich & Mario Batali,
Babbo Ristorante e Enoteca, NYC
Outstanding chef......................................Grant Achatz, *Alinea* · Chicago
Outstanding restaurant .... *Gramercy Tavern* · NYC
Best new restaurant .... *Central Michel Richard* · Washington, DC
Rising star chef..................................... Gavin Kaysen, *Café Boulud* · NYC
Outstanding pastry chef...Elisabeth Prueitt & Chad Robertson, *Tartine Bakery* · SF
Outstanding wine service ....*Eleven Madison Park* · NYC
Outstanding wine and spirits professional................................ Terry Theise
Terry Theise Estate Selections, Silver Spring, MD
Outstanding service award...................................... *Terra* · St Helena, CA
Cookbook of the year... Hugh Fearnley-Whittingstall · *The River Cottage Meat Book*
Cookbook Hall of Fame...Paula Wolfert
Couscous and Other Good Food from Morocco
TV show, national or local............................... *Gourmet's Diary of a Foodie*
Restaurant reviews .... Brad A. Johnson, *Angeleno*
'Hampton's', 'Sona', 'The Penthouse'
Website..Epicurious.com
Radio Food Show ....*The Splendid Table*

'RESTAURANT MAGAZINE' TOP TABLES · 2008

Restaurant Magazine's top 10 of the world's best restaurants in 2008:

El Bulli .... Spain	*Per Se*............................... USA
The Fat Duck........................UK	*Bras*.............................. France
Pierre Gagnaire.................. France	*Arzak* .... Spain
Mugaritz........................... Spain	*Tetsuya's*.......................Australia
The French Laundry............... USA	*Noma* ....Denmark

AMERICAN MICHELIN STARS

The *Michelin Guide* was first published in 1900 by the Michelin Tire Company. Its editors employ a 3-star rating system using a deceptively simple set of criteria: [*] 'A very good restaurant in its category'; [**] 'Excellent cooking, worth a detour'; [***] 'Exceptional cuisine, worth a special trip'. In reality, the award of one Michelin star confers instant recognition; two stars confer fame; and three stars are the culinary equivalent of a Nobel prize. New York City was the first N American city to receive a guide, for 2006; a guide to San Francisco, the Bay Area, and the surrounding Wine Country followed for 2007; and guides to Los Angeles and Las Vegas were released for 2008. As of the 2008 editions, the following US restaurants had earned 3 stars:

Restaurant	location	cuisine
Jean-Georges	Manhattan	French
Le Bernardin	Manhattan	French, seafood
Per Se	Manhattan	American Nouveau, French
The French Laundry	Yountville, CA	American with French influences
Joel Robuchon	Las Vegas	French

(No LA restaurants earned 3 stars.) Tokyo now boasts more Michelin-starred restaurants than any other city, with 150 in total. In 2008, an anonymous Michelin inspector revealed the grueling job he undertakes: each inspector is paid to eat out five times a week and sleep in 150 hotels annually, writing more than 1,000 reports and driving on average 18,640 miles per year. Recognizing the health impact of all that rich food, the company provides health checks and cholesterol tests every 6 months.

SOME UNUSUAL DELICACIES

A few of the many delicacies around the world that a brave traveler might enjoy:

Delicacy	eaten in ...	Delicacy	eaten in ...
Bull penis	China	Kangaroo	Australia
Camel	North Africa	Live octopus	Korea, Japan
Cat	China, Peru	Ortolan†	France
Cricket	Cambodia	Puffer fish‡	Japan
Crocodile	Australia	Putrefied shark	Iceland
Dog	China, Korea, Congo	Rat	Ghana, Thailand, Vietnam, Togo
Flying fox bat	Guam	Reindeer	Finland
Frog	France, Asia, Peru	Sea slug	China, Japan
Grasshoppers	Thailand	Snails	France, China
Guinea Pig	Peru, Ecuador	Snake blood	Vietnam, Indonesia
Horse	France, Italy, Germany	Tarantula	Cambodia
		Whale	Japan

† In French cuisine, these songbirds are traditionally force-fed and then drowned alive in Armagnac, although the practice has been banned since 1999. Former French President François Mitterrand was said to have consumed two during his last meal before dying of cancer. ‡ Puffer fish, known as fugu in Japan, is lethal if prepared incorrectly; only master fugu chefs are allowed to prepare the dish. [Sources include: *Science Lunch*, *National Geographic*, the London *Times*, BBC, & MSNBC]

—————————— POLITICAL PLAYING CARDS ——————————

In 2003, US forces in Iraq were given 'Most Wanted' playing cards to assist in their hunt for Saddam Hussein and his cronies. Playing cards are now being used for purposes beyond games of snap or identifying possible war criminals, for example:

Archaeology cards	*Criminal cases cards*	*Foxhunting cards*
In July 2007, the US Dept of Defense issued cards depicting Iraqi & Afghan archaeological sites and artifacts in an attempt to educate troops about the environment of the areas in which they were deployed.	Since July 2007, inmates of Florida state jails have been given cards depicting details of 'cold cases', in an attempt to crack unsolved crimes. A resulting tip has led to two being charged with a 2004 murder.	In 2004, the UK's Countryside Alliance produced playing cards featuring Members of Parliament believed to be opposed to foxhunting and other blood sports, before a vote on an anti-hunting bill.

In July 2008, a German publishing house released a card game featuring famous world dictators, called the 'Das Führer-Quartett'. Based on a popular German children's game called 'Quartett' (which usually depicts flowers), the cards give biographical information on various despots (Hitler, Stalin, Mao, &c.), written with an ironic touch. Key facts include the revelation that Romanian dictator Nicolae Ceauşescu had a fondness for Vlad the Impaler. ❦ The 'Starz Behind Barz' playing cards, launched in 2004, are patterned on the miliary's 'Most Wanted' cards but feature police mug shots of various celebrities, such as Ozzy Osbourne and O.J. Simpson; Michael Jackson is the Joker.

—— WORLD SCRABBLE CHAMPIONSHIP & SCRABULOUS ——

40-year-old Nigel Richards from New Zealand won the 2007 World Scrabble Championship, held in Mumbai, India, on November 9–12. Richards defeated Ganesh Asirvatham of Malaysia in the final game by earning 4 bonus scores for *dirtiest, overapt, recopies,* and *equinias,* each of which used all of Richards's 7 letters. Though burdened with an unhelpful number of vowels, Asirvatham did manage to score 122 points in the final game with the word *tailleur.* ❦ The biannual competition has been held each year since 1991, and the winner currently receives $15,000. The 2007 competition was the first to be played under the rules of the World English-language Scrabble Players Association; the tournament's official dictionary was the *Collins Scrabble Tournament & Club Word List.*

In January 2008, Facebook was asked to remove the popular application Scrabulous after Scrabble's owners, Hasbro and Mattel, claimed the game infringed their copyright. On July 24, Hasbro, owners of the rights to Scrabble in N America, sued the developers of Scrabulous, Calcutta-based brothers Rajat Agarwalla and Jayant Agarwalla. On July 29, Scrabulous was pulled from Facebook for North American users, despite the protestations of thousands who had joined a 'Save Scrabulous' group. Addicted players were forced to migrate to Scrabulous. com, though many choose to take up a similar Agarwalla application called Wordscraper. Fewer chose to play the Hasbro-sanctioned Scrabble introduced to the site in July – whether out of spite, or due to a number of bugs.

──────────── NATIONAL TOY HALL OF FAME ────────────

Each year, the Strong National Museum of Play in Rochester, NY, inducts several toys into the National Toy Hall of Fame. To be so honored, toys must have 'achieved longevity and national significance in the world of play and imagination'. The public may submit nominations, although final decisions are made by a panel of judges based on the toy's 'icon status'; its longevity throughout generations; its ability to foster learning or creativity; and evidence that the toy has 'profoundly changed play or toy design'. In November 2007, the following toys were inducted into the Hall:

Atari 2600 Game System.....*'made video games a part of everyday play in the home'*
Raggedy Andy............................*'Raggedy Andy yearned to join his big sister'*
The kite.......*'people ... of all ages have learned the many and varied uses of the kite'*

Since opening in 1998, the NTHOF has enshrined the following toys: alphabet blocks; Barbie; the bicycle; Candy Land; the cardboard box; checkers; Crayola crayons; Duncan yo-yo; Easy-Bake Oven; Erector Set; Etch A Sketch; Frisbee; G.I. Joe; hula hoop; Jack-in-the-box; jacks; the jigsaw puzzle; the jump rope; Lego; Lincoln logs; Lionel trains; marbles; Monopoly; Mr Potato Head; Play-Doh; Radio Flyer Wagon; Raggedy Ann; the rocking horse; roller skates; Scrabble; Silly Putty; Slinky; the teddy bear; Tinkertoy; Tonka trucks; and View-Master. Nominate toys at: strongmuseum.org.

──────────── TOY OF THE YEAR AWARDS ────────────

The Toy Industry Association's Toy of the Year Awards (the 'TOTYs') honor the best toys developed for the North American market. Below are some of the winners at the 8th annual TOTYs, which were held on February 16, 2008, in New York City:

Toy of the year ....Air Hogs Havoc Heli Laser Battle
Infant/preschool toy of the year......................Moon Sand Adventure Island
Girl toy of the year.. Littlest Pet Shop: Display & Play Round & Round Pet Town
Playset *and* Troop Groovy Girls [TIE]
Boy toy of the year [*sic*].........................Transformers Movie Deluxe Figures
Game of the year...Rubik's Revolution
Most innovative toy of the year ....Smart Cycle Physical Learning
Property of the year...Hannah Montana

──────────── BARBIES OF THE YEAR ────────────

Some of the special-edition Barbie dolls produced by Mattel in 2007 and 2008:

Barbie Mariposa	*purple and pink wings, butterfly tiara, removable skirt*
E! Live from the red carpet	*midnight blue crepe &*
by Badgley Mischka Barbie	*chiffon gown, gold & blue accessories*
Dallas Cowboys cheerleader Barbie	*star-spangled vest & belt, white shorts*
Speed racer Barbie	*dressed as Trixie, Speed Racer's girlfriend, in shift dress, leggings, and pink heels*

———————— WESTMINSTER DOG SHOW · 2008 ————————

A beagle took Best in Show at the 2008 Westminster Kennel Club Dog Show, for the first time in the contest's history. Uno, a caramel-colored 2-year-old, drew roaring applause as he was paraded around the carpet at Madison Square Garden, and received a standing ovation when his win was announced. Asked why no representative from the beloved breed had ever won before, one judge replied, 'Maybe the others just didn't have it'. Uno bested *c.*2,600 dogs in 169 breeds and varieties.

Group	*winner*	*breed*
Working	Ch.† Redwitch Reason to Believe	akita
Terrier	Ch. Efbe's Hidalgo at Goodspice	Sealyham terrier
Toy	Ch. Smash JP Win a Victory	poodle (toy)
Nonsporting	Ch. Brighton Minimoto	poodle (standard)
Sporting	Ch. Colsidex Seabreeze Perfect Fit	Weimaraner
Hound	Ch. K-Run's Park Me in First [won Best in Show]	beagle
Herding	Ch. Vinelake Collinswood Yablon OA OAJ	Australian shepherd

† 'Champion' denotes a dog who has earned fifteen points at other American Kennel Club shows.

———————————— DOG WALK OF FAME ————————————

The first ever canine 'walk of fame' was established in London's Battersea Park in November 2007, to record the legacy of the legendary dogs of film and television. The first six dogs to be immortalized with a permanent plaque on the walk were:

Dog	film or TV series	*breed*
Bullseye	*Oliver!* (1968)	bull terrier
Lassie	*Lassie* (TV 1958–74); *Lassie Come Home* (1943)	collie
Toto	*The Wizard of Oz* (1939)	cairn terrier
Bobby	*Greyfriars Bobby* (1961)	Skye terrier
Gromit	*Wallace & Gromit* (1989–)	cartoon beagle
Chance & Shadow	*Homeward Bound* (1963)	bulldog, golden retriever
Fang	The *Harry Potter* films (2001–)	Neapolitan mastiff†

Dogs were chosen by an online vote at Skymovies.com, which sponsored the walk along with the Kennel Club. † In *Harry Potter* books, Fang is a boarhound; in the films, he is portrayed by a mastiff.

———————————— MOST POPULAR DOG NAMES ————————————

Below are the most popular names for dogs as of 2008, according to Veterinary Pet Insurance (based on the most popular names in their database of insured pets):

♂ dogs	♀ dogs
Max · Buddy · Rocky · Bailey · Jake	Bella · Molly · Lucy · Maggie · Daisy
Charlie · Jack · Toby · Cody · Buster	Sophie · Sadie · Chloe · Bailey · Lola

——————ANIMALS IN THE NEWS · 2007——————

Some of the year's more unusual animal stories. ❦ Philippines customs officials at a mail processing center were unsettled to discover in a package marked 'personal clothing' 300 live scorpions and tarantulas. ❦ According to the London *Times*, there were only two sightings of the Loch Ness monster in 2007 (as of the end of September) – a marked decline from previous years that could spell doom for regional tourism. ❦ New York and Houston are the cities most at risk from rat infestation, according to poison maker d-CON. ❦ An Indian man married a dog in the hope it would lift the curse he claims he has been under since stoning to death two other dogs. ❦ A man was questioned by police at LaGuardia airport in New York after smuggling a monkey under his hat on a flight from Peru, with a stopover in Florida. ❦ A jellyfish invasion wiped out the only salmon farm in Northern Ireland, killing more than 100,000 fish. ❦ In New Zealand, the Christmas song 'A Very Silent Night' was recorded at a frequency only audible to dogs, and released to raise money for an animal charity. ❦ Newquay Zoo in Cornwall, England, was condemned by conservation groups for euthanizing two Sulawesi crested black macaques because the monkeys would not stop fighting. ❦ The long-eared jerboa, a tiny, nocturnal desert creature with one of the biggest ear-to-body ratios of any mammal, was caught on camera for the first time in the Gobi Desert. ❦ Male monkeys 'pay' for sex by grooming female monkeys, according to a study of macaques in Kalimantan Tengah, Indonesia, reported in the *New Scientist*. In areas where there are fewer females, males are forced to

groom their partners for up to twice as long before they are able to have sex with them. ❦ A female orangutan called Nonja, thought to be the oldest in captivity, died at the Miami Metro Zoo at the age of 55, a decade past the age to which most orangutans survive. ❦ Scientists from a university in Hungary developed a computer program that 'translates' dog barks, and can classify them with 'reasonable' accuracy. ❦ Hamster prices tripled in China after the Year of the Rat began on February 7, 2008; wary parents deemed the cuddly creatures an acceptable rodent substitute. ❦ An octopus at an aquarium in Newquay, England, became so possessive of his new Mr Potato Head toy that he began to attack anyone who tried to take it from him. ❦ A man who was seized by a crocodile in N Australia was accidentally shot by a colleague who came to his rescue; the croc dropped his victim, who was then flown to the hospital to be treated for bite and bullet wounds. ❦ A team at the University of Melbourne in Australia concluded that chameleons first evolved the ability to change color to make themselves more noticeable to other chameleons, rather than to blend in to their background. ❦ Animal rights campaigners welcomed the announcement by the British Ministry of Defence that it will no longer use live goats in experiments to measure the risks of 'the bends' for crews trapped in submarines. ❦ A New Zealand man was charged with assault after using a hedgehog as a weapon; the animal left a large welt and several puncture wounds. ❦ A British study found that human yawns are contagious for dogs; 72% of 29 dogs tested yawned after watching humans do so.

Sports

*I just wanted to make sure I took every single moment in and every single swim in,
every single moment with my teammates, so I would remember them.*
— MICHAEL PHELPS [see p.230]

———— 'SPORTS ILLUSTRATED' COVERS OF NOTE ————

Date	cover star(s)
01·14·08	Glenn Dorsey, LSU Tigers
01·21·08	Brett Favre, Green Bay Packers
01·28·08	Eli Manning, New York Giants
02·04·08	Michael Strahan, NY Giants & Tom Brady, New England Patriots
02·11·08	David Tyree, NY Giants & Rodney Harrison, New England Patriots
02·18·08	Dale Earnhardt Jr., Hendrick Motorsports
02·25·08	Johan Santana, New York Mets
03·03·08	Jason Kidd, Dallas Mavericks
03·10·08	Tyler Hansbrough, North Carolina Tar Heels
03·17·08	Brett Favre, Green Bay Packers
03·24·08	DaJuan Summers, Georgetown
03·31·08	Ryan Braun, Milwaukee Brewers; Justin Upton, AZ Diamondbacks; and Troy Tulowitzki, Colorado Rockies
04·07·08	Tyler Hansbrough, North Carolina Tar Heels
04·14·08	Mario Chalmers, Kansas Jayhawks
04·21·08	Kobe Bryant, Los Angeles Lakers & Kevin Garnett, Boston Celtics
04·28·08	Johnny Unitas, Baltimore Colts
05·05·08	Kosuke Fukudome, Chicago Cubs
05·12·08	Chris Paul, New Orleans Hornets & Tony Parker, San Antonio Spurs
05·19·08	Danica Patrick, Andretti Green Racing
05·26·08	Derek Jeter, New York Yankees
06·02·08	Josh Hamilton, Texas Rangers
06·09·08	Magic Johnson, Los Angeles Lakers
06·16·08	Kobe Bryant, Los Angeles Lakers
06·23·08	Tiger Woods
06·30·08	Kevin Garnett, Boston Celtics
07·07·08	Tim Lincecum, San Francisco Giants
07·14·08	Rafael Nadal
07·28·08	Michael Phelps
08·04·08	David Tyree, New York Giants
08·11·08	Brandon Spikes, Florida Gators
08·18·08	Michael Phelps
08·25·08	Michael Phelps

[Various special issues were also published in the months above. For the swimsuit issue, see p.233]

————— THE US AT THE OLYMPICS · BEIJING 2008 —————

The US sent 596 athletes (310 men and 286 women) to compete in Beijing, and brought home more medals (110) than any other country – though China won the most golds [see p.23]. Below are some zeniths (and nadirs) from the XXIX Olympics:

The 2008 games transformed Michael Phelps into a household name, and made swimming a must-see spectator sport. Phelps won 8 golds, the most ever in a single Olympics, taking his career total to 14 and making him the most successful Olympian of all time. Phelps's triumphs included a spectacular finish in the 100m butterfly, when he beat Serbian Milorad Cavic by one-hundredth of a second and won his 7th gold – tying with Mark Spitz's 1972 tally. Earlier in the games, Phelps nearly lost his chance to beat Spitz's record when the French team looked set to win the 4×100m freestyle relay – but US teammate Jason Lezak marshaled spectacular strength to push past Alain Bernard, taking the gold by eight-hundredths of a second and keeping Phelps's dream alive. In women's swimming, American Natalie Coughlin won 6 medals, the most ever by a female US athlete in a single Olympics. ❧ After a mediocre performance in 2004, the 2008 US men's basketball 'Redeem Team' roared back to dominance, beating Spain 118–107 to take the team's first gold since 2000. The women's basketball team also earned a place at the top of the podium, pummeling Australia 92–65 for their fourth consecutive gold. ❧ The men's volleyball team won its first gold medal in 20 years, with a 3–1 win against top-ranked Brazil. This victory was especially poignant in light of the tragedy that befell coach Hugh

PHELPS'S EIGHT GOLDS	
400m individual mly	4:03·84†
4×100m freestyle rly	3:08·24†
200m freestyle	1:42·96†
200m butterfly	1:52·03†
4×200m freestyle rly	6:58·56†
200m individual mly	1:54·23†
100m butterfly	0:50·58
4×100m medley relay	3:29·34†

† World record

McCutcheon, whose father-in-law was murdered and mother-in-law seriously wounded in an unprovoked attack in Beijing a day after the opening ceremony. ❧ The track and field team had a disappointing Games, with several disqualifications and some lukewarm performances. They dropped the baton during both the men's and women's 4×100m relay prelims, which resulted in America missing the finals of these events for the first time in many years. Overall, the US won 7 track and field golds (one more than America's all-time Olympic low of 6). ❧ Gymnasts Nastia Liukin and Shawn Johnson beat China to win the gold and silver in the women's gymnastics all-around – the first time America had taken both medals in the event. The men's chances looked poor after 2004 all-around champion Paul Hamm and his twin, Morgan, missed the games due to injury; but the US unexpectedly took bronze in the team finals and silver in the horizontal bar. ❧ The baseball and softball teams played amid controversy over the IOC's decision to drop the sports from the 2012 program. (IOC president Jacques Rogge said that MLB officials needed to release star players for the games and adhere to stricter doping standards.) Neither team managed to take gold: the softball team won silver, and the baseball team bronze. ❧ Women's volleyball stars Kerri Walsh and Misty May-Treanor beat China to win their second straight gold – and their 108th consecutive match.

———————— BEIJING 2008 · MISCELLANY ————————

CONSTRUCTION AND COST · China spent *c.*$43bn on the 2008 games and constructed 12 spectacular new venues, notably the National Stadium (called the 'Bird's Nest' after its latticework structure), and the National Aquatics Center (aptly called the 'Water Cube'). The Bird's Nest, which hosted the opening and closing ceremonies, has 91,000 seats, uses 2·8m square feet of space, and cost *c.*$500m. (In 2004, Athens reportedly spent just $15bn on its Olympics; London 2012 has an estimated budget of $17·5bn.)

MASCOTS · The 2008 Olympic mascots were five fanciful creatures inspired by the colors of the Olympic rings: *Beibei* [a fish], *Jingjing* [a panda], *Huanhuan* [the Olympic flame], *Yingying* [a Tibetan antelope], and *Nini* [a swallow]. Together, they were known as the *Fuwa*, which equates to 'the friendlies'. When combined, their names spell out *Bei Jing Huan Ying Ni* – 'Welcome to Beijing'.

TORCH RELAY · The Olympic torch relay was disrupted by pro-Tibet protests in a number of countries [see *Chronicle*]. It was noted that the idea of lighting the Olympic torch in Greece and running it through different countries was first conceived by the Nazis as a propaganda stunt before the 1936 Berlin games.

NBC & VIEWERSHIP · 211m Americans watched the Olympics, according to NBC, making it the most-viewed single event in US TV history. *c.*39·9m saw Michael Phelps win his 8th gold. NBC reportedly spent $894m in acquiring the rights to the Beijing games.

PROTESTS · In response to criticism of China's human rights record, Beijing designated 3 'protest zones' for demonstrations during the games (Purple Bamboo Park, Ritan Park, and World Park). However, the city said that only 77 applications to protest had been received, all of which were 'withdrawn' or rejected. The press reported that Chinese citizens applying for permission to demonstrate were detained, and some were sentenced to 'reeducation through labor'. Additionally, a number of foreign demonstrators were arrested, including 8 Americans who were detained and sentenced to 10 days in prison following peaceful pro-Tibet protests. After spending 4 days in jail, they were deported.

———————— US MEDAL TABLE · BY SPORT ————————

Sport	Gd	Sv	Bz	All	Sport	Gd	Sv	Bz	All
Swimming	12	9	10	31	Beach volleyball	2	0	0	2
Track & field	7	9	7	23	Sailing	1	1	0	2
Gymnastics	2	6	2	10	Volleyball	1	1	0	2
Shooting	2	2	2	6	Tennis	1	0	1	2
Fencing	1	3	2	6	Water polo	0	2	0	2
Cycling	1	1	3	5	Soccer	1	0	0	1
Equestrian	1	1	1	3	Softball	0	1	0	1
Rowing	1	1	1	3	Baseball	0	0	1	1
Wrestling	1	0	2	3	Boxing	0	0	1	1
Tae kwon do	0	1	2	3	Judo	0	0	1	1
Basketball	2	0	0	2	TOTAL	36	38	36	110

———— 2007 SPORTSMAN OF THE YEAR ————

New York Jets quarterback Brett Favre, long a beloved icon of the Green Bay Packers, was named *Sports Illustrated*'s Sportsman of the Year for 2007. Awarded since 1954, the magazine's honor is annually bestowed upon a team or athlete that most 'embodies the spirit of sportsmanship and achievement'. Favre was commended for a spectacular 2007 season with the Packers as well as for his 'perseverance and his passion' – qualities that helped him to win three MVPs and one Super Bowl (XXXI) during his 16 years in the NFL. Below are a few of Favre's many records:

Most AP NFL MVP awards (1995, 1996, and 1997) · *Most consecutive starts by an NFL quarterback* (253) · *Most wins by a starting NFL quarterback, regular season* (160) · *Most career passing touchdowns* (442) · *Most career passing yards* (61,655) *Most career pass completions* (5,377) · *Most career pass attempts* (8,758)

[Source: *Sports Illustrated*; officialbrettfavre.com. Records as of 8/08.] Favre announced his retirement from the NFL at a teary press conference in March 2008. However, after a period of contentious negotiations, he was reinstated effective 8/3/08, and traded to the New York Jets shortly thereafter.

——————— THE ESPY AWARDS · 2008 ———————

The ESPYs were created by ESPN in 1993 to commemorate the sports achievements of the previous year. Tiger Woods and the New York Giants earned the most honors at the 2008 awards, held on July 16 in LA – Woods won 3 trophies and his 5th Best Male Athlete award, for a record 21 career ESPYs. Justin Timberlake hosted the event, winning praise both for his original rock opera and a segment in which he pretended to chastise Oklahoma State football coach Mike Gundy for owning a Jonas Brothers poster. A selection of 2008 ESPY awards appears below:

♂ *athlete*.................. Tiger Woods
♀ *athlete*............... Candace Parker
Team.....................Boston Celtics
Coach..........Pat Summitt, Tennessee
    Women's Basketball
Game.................2008 Super Bowl
Moment......... 'Great Sportsmanship'
    (S. Tucholsky, M. Holtman, L. Wallace)†
Breakthrough athlete... Adrian Peterson
Champ. performance......Tiger Woods,
    2008 US Open
Play.............. Eli Manning's pass to
    David Tyree at the 2008 Super Bowl

Upset.................2008 Super Bowl
Arthur Ashe Courage Award.............
    John Carlos & Tommie Smith
Jimmy V Award for Perseverance.........
    Kevin Everett
Record-breaking performance.. B. Favre
Best comeback...........Josh Hamilton
♀ *college athlete*.............Tim Tebow
♂ *college athlete*............ Candace Parker
♂ *athlete w/a disability*.... Ryan Kocer
♀ *athlete w/a disability*.... Shay Oberg
International ♂ *athlete*... Rafael Nadal
International ♀ *athlete* ..Lorena Ochoa

† The 'Best Moment' award honored Division II softball players Sara Tucholsky, of W Oregon, and Central Washington's Mallory Holtman and Liz Wallace. During a game on April 26, Tucholsky collapsed with a knee injury after hitting the first home run of her college career; her Washington opponents astonished spectators by carrying Tucholsky around the bases so the home run would count.

—BEST-PAID ATHLETES—

The top 10 on *Sports Illustrated*'s list of the highest-earning US athletes, based on pay, endorsements, winnings, and appearances in the most recent season:

#	athlete (sport)	2007–08 earnings
1	Tiger Woods (golf)	$128m
2	Phil Mickelson (golf)	$62m
3	LeBron James (basketball)	$40m
4	Floyd Mayweather (boxing)	$40m
5	Kobe Bryant (basketball)	$35m
6	Shaquille O'Neal (basketball)	$35m
7	Alex Rodriguez (baseball)	$35m
8	Kevin Garnett (basketball)	$31m
9	Peyton Manning (football)	$31m
10	Derek Jeter (baseball)	$30m

—FAVORITE ATHLETES—

Below are the winners of a June 2008 Harris Interactive poll that asked 2,454 American adults to name their favorite sports celebrity:

#	athlete	sport
1	Tiger Woods	golf
2	Michael Jordan	basketball
3	Brett Favre	football
4	Kobe Bryant	basketball
5	Jeff Gordon	NASCAR
6	Dale Earnhardt Jr.	NASCAR
7	Derek Jeter	baseball
8	Peyton Manning	football
9	Tom Brady	football
10	Kevin Garnett	basketball

THE LAUREUS AWARDS · 2008

The Laureus World Sporting Academy encourages the 'positive and worthwhile in sport' and presents awards to athletes in all disciplines. Some 2008 winners were:

World sportsman of the year .... Roger Federer (tennis)
World sportswoman of the year .... Justine Henin (tennis)
World team of the year .... South African Rugby Team
World breakthrough of the year .... Lewis Hamilton (F1)
Comeback of the year .... Paula Radcliffe (running)
World sportsperson of the year with a disability .... Esther Vergeer (tennis)
World action sportsperson of the year ..... Shaun White (snow- & skateboarding)
Spirit of sport award .... Dick Pound (World Anti-Doping Agency)
Sport for good award ...... Brendan and Sean Tuohey (PeacePlayers International)
Lifetime achievement award .... Sergey Bubka (pole vault)

THE S.I. SWIMSUIT ISSUE

The 2008 *Sports Illustrated* swimsuit issue cover featured model Marisa Miller draped in blue jewels and little else, pictured at sunset on the beach in the US Virgin Islands. The issue also featured galleries of NFL cheerleaders, 'bodypainting masterpieces', and 2008 Indy Japan 300 champion Danica Patrick in a white bikini and half of her racing jumpsuit. Will Ferrell appeared in character as Jackie Moon (owner of fictional 1970s basketball team the Flint Tropics), draped by Heidi Klum in an aqua suit and white go-go boots. Recent *S.I.* cover girls include: Beyoncé Knowles [2007]; Veronica Varekova, Elle Macpherson, Rebecca Romijn, Rachel Hunter, Daniela Pestova, Elsa Benitez, Carolyn Murphy, Yamila Diaz [2006]; and Carolyn Murphy [2005].

——————— BASEBALL · THE 2007 WORLD SERIES ———————

BOSTON RED SOX *bt* COLORADO ROCKIES 4–0

The Red Sox proved the 'Curse of the Bambino' [see below] was gone for good when they beat the Colorado Rockies in their second sweep of the World Series since 2000. Although the Rockies came in on a scorching season, earning their first Fall Classic appearance, they proved no match for BoSox dynamism and confidence. If some found the games themselves less than thrilling, few Boston fans complained.

> *[This] is even more enjoyable, because you can enjoy it rather than be so exhausted after the relief of 86 years.*
> — JASON VARITEK, catcher, Boston Red Sox

No.	date	result	city	sang *God Bless America*
1	10·24·07	Red Sox 13, Rockies 1	Boston	Ashanti
2	10·25·07	Red Sox 2, Rockies 1	Boston	Boyz II Men
3	10·27·07	Red Sox 10, Rockies 5	Denver	Philip Bailey
4	10·28·07	Red Sox 4, Rockies 3	Denver	Lonestar

Third baseman Mike Lowell earned Series MVP after hitting ·400 with 4 RBI and 6 runs scored.

——————— SOME BASEBALL CURSES OF NOTE ———————

The failure of the Red Sox to win a World Series from 1918–2004 was often blamed on the 'Curse of the Bambino'. Believers say the curse was caused by the 1919 sale of Babe 'the Bambino' Ruth to the Yankees, and for years fans attempted numerous exorcisms, including: placing a Red Sox cap blessed by a Lama at the summit of Mount Everest; dredging up a piano that Babe had pushed into a Sudbury, Massachusetts, pond; and conducting a Fenway Park 'exorcism' with the help of Father Guido Sarducci from *Saturday Night Live*. Thankfully, the 2004 sweep put such ceremonies to rest. ❦ According to some, the Chicago Cubs haven't reached the World Series since 1945 because of a billy goat. Legend has it that über-fan Billy Sianis, owner of the Billy Goat Tavern, attempted to bring his goat to a 1945 World Series game but was ejected because of the animal's odor. It is said an incensed Sianis then proclaimed there would never be another World Series at Wrigley Field, a curse that seems to have lasted until today. ❦ Anaheim Stadium is said by some to be cursed because it was built on a Native American burial ground. Former owner Gene 'the Singing Cowboy' Autry reportedly hired a tribal shaman to exorcise the curse and, after his death, Autry's widow was said to have considered appeasing the spirits by burying his ashes under home plate. Yet the existence of the burial ground was never confirmed, and fears eased after the Angels' 2002 title. [Sources include *Rounding the Bases*, by Joseph L. Price.]

A surprising number of athletes featured on the cover of *Sports Illustrated* have begun losing streaks (or even perished) soon after their appearance – a phenomenon sometimes called the 'cover curse'.

2007 MLB PLAYOFFS

American League Division Series

Indians *bt* Yankees[†] 3–1
10·04·07....... Indians 12–3
10·05·07 ...... Indians 2–1
10·07·07....... Yankees........... 8–4
10·08·07....... Indians 6–4

Red Sox *bt* Angels 3–0
10·03·07.......Red Sox............ 4–0
10·05·07.......Red Sox............ 6–3
10·07·07.......Red Sox............ 9–1

American League Championship Series

Red Sox *bt* Indians 4–3
10·12·07.......Red Sox............ 10–3
10·13·07....... Indians 13–6
10·15·07....... Indians 4–2
10·16·07....... Indians 7–3
10·18·07.......Red Sox............ 7–1
10·20·07.......Red Sox.......... 12–2
10·21·07.......Red Sox.......... 11–2

National League Division Series

Diamondbacks *bt* Cubs 3–0
10·03·07... Diamondbacks 3–1
10·04·07... Diamondbacks 8–4
10·06·07... Diamondbacks 5–1

Rockies[†] *bt* Phillies 3–0
10·03·07...... Rockies............ 4–2
10·04·07...... Rockies........... 10–5
10·06·07...... Rockies............ 2–1

National League Championship Series

Rockies *bt* Diamondbacks 4–0
10·11·07...... Rockies............ 5–1
10·12·07...... Rockies............ 3–2
10·14·07...... Rockies............ 4–1
10·15·07...... Rockies............ 6–4

† Wild card team

2007 BATTING LEADERS

American League		National League
Magglio Ordonez, Tigers [.363]	*batting average*	Matt Holliday, Rockies [.340]
Alex Rodriguez, Yankees [54]	*home runs*	Prince Fielder, Brewers [50]
Alex Rodriguez, Yankees [156]	*runs batted in*	Matt Holliday, Rockies [137]

2007 BASEBALL AWARDS OF NOTE

American League	*award*	National League
Alex Rodriguez (Yankees)	MVP	Jimmy Rollins (Phillies)
Carsten C. Sabathia (Indians)	Cy Young	Jake Peavy (Padres)

2007 TOP BASEBALL ATTENDANCE

Team	*avg. home game attendance*
New York Yankees	52,739
Los Angeles Dodgers	47,614
New York Mets	47,579
St. Louis Cardinals	43,853
Los Angeles Angels	41,551

[Source: ESPN]

──────────── SUPER BOWL XLII · 2008 ────────────

NEW YORK GIANTS *bt* NEW ENGLAND PATRIOTS 17–14

February 3, 2008 · University of Phoenix Stadium, Glendale, Arizona
National Anthem: Jordin Sparks · Viewers: 97·5m (most-watched Super Bowl ever)

The Giants achieved the improbable at Super Bowl XLII, vanquishing the unbeaten Patriots in one of the most remarkable upsets in football history. The Patriots played with their eyes on immortality: a Super Bowl win would have given them the first perfect season since the 1972 Miami Dolphins. But the Giants dashed these hopes with a mix of rugged defense and stunning fourth-quarter plays. The Giants opened the game with the longest opening drive in Super Bowl history, leaving them 3 points ahead by the end of the first quarter. But while the Patriots bounced back with a touchdown from Laurence Maroney, they failed to put the game away. Notably, the Giants sacked Patriots quarterback Tom Brady twice during the second quarter (5 times during the game overall, more than any other opponent during the season). The halftime show offered an aging, and bearded, Tom Petty, aptly singing 'I Won't Back Down', among other favorites, but the real excitement was left to the fourth quarter. With less than 3 minutes left, and the Giants trailing 14–10, Eli Manning escaped from an attempted sack and threw the ball 32 yards to David Tyree, who leapt to catch the ball and then kept it safe by clutching it to his helmet. Manning's 13-yard pass to Plaxico Burress sealed the deal, ending a career-defining 83-yard drive from Manning as well as the Patriots' hope for a perfect season.

A 'Rocky'-themed Budweiser spot (featuring a Clydesdale training to pull the Bud wagon) topped several postgame polls of Super Bowl ads; a Coke battle between gigantic balloons at the Macy's Thanksgiving Day Parade came a close second. The most TiVo'ed ad was for E*Trade Financial, in which a baby day-trader used the service to buy stocks before vomiting. Two animated ads for Salesgenie.com generated mild controversy – one, in which a family of pandas speak with Chinese accents, was later pulled. Advertisers paid up to \$2·7m for 30 seconds, a Super Bowl record.

──────────── 2008 NFL PLAYOFFS ────────────

The Patriots became the first NFL team to enter the Super Bowl 18–0, while the Giants beat the Packers and Brett Favre to become the season's top underdogs:

NFC Wild Card Playoffs	*AFC Wild Card Playoffs*
01·05·08.... Seahawks 35–Redksins 14	01·05·08........ Jaguars 31–Steelers 29
01·06·08..... Giants 24–Buccaneers 14	01·06·08........ Chargers 17–Titans 6
NFC Divisional Playoffs	*AFC Divisional Playoffs*
01·12·08..... Packers 42–Seahawks 20	01·12·08........ Patriots 31–Jaguars 20
01·13·08...... Giants 21–Cowboys 17	01·13·08........ Chargers 28–Colts 24
NFC Championships	*AFC Championships*
01·20·08........ Giants 23–Packers 20	01·21·08..... Patriots 21–Chargers 12

———————2008 BOWL CHAMPIONSHIP SERIES———————

BCS CHAMPIONSHIP: LSU TIGERS *bt* OHIO STATE BUCKEYES 38–24

After a college football season full of twists and turns, the Louisiana State U. Tigers beat the Ohio State Buckeyes in front of a roaring Superdome crowd to become the first team with two BCS national championship titles. Despite a first-quarter lead by the Buckeyes, and an early 65-yard touchdown from Ohio's Chris Wells, the Tigers offense rallied in the second quarter thanks to quarterback Matt Flynn, who threw 4 touchdown passes and earned offensive MVP. The Buckeyes crumbled and earned 5 personal fouls, forcing them to face their 2nd championship loss in a row.

ROSE BOWL
1·1·08 · Pasadena
USC Trojans (6) *bt*
Illinois Fighting Illini (13) 49–17

FIESTA BOWL
1·2·08 · Glendale
West Virginia Mountaineers (11) *bt*
Oklahoma Sooners (3) 48–28

SUGAR BOWL
1·1·08 · New Orleans
Georgia Bulldogs (4) *bt*
Hawaii Warriors (10) 41–10

ORANGE BOWL
1·3·08 · Miami
Kansas Jayhawks (8) *bt*
Virginia Tech Hokies (5) 24–21

———————2007 HEISMAN TROPHY———————

In 2008, Florida Gators quarterback Tim Tebow became the first sophomore to win the Heisman Trophy – awarded annually since 1953 to the most outstanding college football player. (All other winners have been juniors or seniors.) Despite his relative youth, Tebow managed the first '20-20 season' (more than 20 touchdown passes and 20 touchdown rushes) by a Division I-A player. Tebow finished his regular season with 3,132 passing yards and 29 touchdowns against 6 interceptions, and ran for 838 yards with 22 touchdowns. He is the third Gators quarterback to win the trophy, after Steve Spurrier did so in 1966, and Danny Wuerffel in 1996.

——2008 NCAA WOMEN'S BASKETBALL CHAMPIONSHIP——

TENNESSEE LADY VOLUNTEERS *bt* STANFORD CARDINAL 64–48

The Tennessee Lady Volunteers captured a stunning eighth national title on April 8, 2008, becoming the first repeat champions since the Connecticut Huskies won a trophy each year from 2002 to 2004. Candace Parker was named the Most Outstanding Player of the Final Four (for the second year in a row), after she scored 17 points for the unstoppable Lady Vols despite playing with an injured shoulder.

Championship	*1*	*2*	*T*	*National semifinal*
Cardinal	29	19	48	4·6·08 .. Lady Vols 47–Lady Tigers 46
Lady Volunteers	37	27	64	4·6·08 ....Cardinal 82–Huskies 73

2008 NBA FINALS

BOSTON CELTICS *bt* LOS ANGELES LAKERS 4–2

The Boston Celtics took home their 17th NBA Championship on June 17, 2008, destroying the LA Lakers in the series finale of a stunning comeback season. The Celtics had their new 'Big 3' to thank: Kevin Garnett, Ray Allen, and Paul Pierce – though it was Pierce who was honored as MVP, the first NBA title of his career, after supplying 26 points in game 6. The Lakers fell from lofty heights as the pre-Finals favorites, but they couldn't manage to slip out from under the 3–1 series lead the Celtics established in Game 4. Game 6 saw the highest score ever in the history of the Finals, and the Celtics won their title with the second-highest-ever margin of victory.

No.	date	result	city
1	06·05·08	Celtics 98, Lakers 88	Boston
2	06·08·08	Celtics 108, Lakers 102	Boston
3	06·10·08	Lakers 87, Celtics 81	Los Angeles
4	06·12·08	Celtics 97, Lakers 91	Los Angeles
5	06·15·08	Lakers 103, Celtics 98	Los Angeles
6	06·17·08	Celtics 131, Lakers 92	Boston

2008 NBA PLAYOFFS

Eastern Conference Quarterfinals
Celtics *bt* Hawks, 4–3 [games]
Pistons *bt* 76ers, 4–2
Magic *bt* Raptors, 4–1
Cavaliers *bt* Wizards, 4–2

Western Conference Quarterfinals
Lakers *bt* Nuggets, 4–0 [games]
Hornets *bt* Mavericks, 4–1
Spurs *bt* Suns, 4–1
Jazz *bt* Rockets, 4–2

Eastern Conference Semifinals
Pistons *bt* Magic, 4–1
Celtics *bt* Cavaliers, 4–3

Western Conference Semifinals
Spurs *bt* Hornets, 4–3
Lakers *bt* Jazz, 4–2

Eastern Conference Finals
Celtics *bt* Pistons, 4–2

05·20·08	Celtics	88–79
05·22·08	Pistons	103–97
05·24·08	Celtics	94–80
05·26·08	Pistons	94–75
05·28·08	Celtics	106–102
06·30·08	Celtics	89–81

Western Conference Finals
Lakers *bt* Spurs, 4–1

05·21·08	Lakers	89–85
05·23·08	Lakers	101–71
05·25·08	Spurs	103–84
05·27·08	Lakers	93–91
05·29·08	Lakers	100–92

2008 NBA ANNUAL AWARDS

MVP	Kobe Bryant, Lakers	Rookie	K. Durant, SuperSonics
Coach	Byron Scott, Hornets	Sportsmanship	Grant Hill, Suns

NCAA 'MARCH MADNESS' · 2008

2008 NCAA Division I Men's Basketball Championship
San Antonio

National Championship · April 7

* * *
KANSAS (1)
beat
MEMPHIS (1)
75–68
* * *

Column stages (left to right)
1st Round March 20–21 · 2nd Round March 22–23 · Sweet Sixteen March 27–28 · Elite Eight March 29–30 · Final Four April 5 · National Championship April 7

South region

1st Round
- 87 Memphis (1 / 63 Texas Arl. (16
- 76 Miss St (8 / 69 Oregon (9
- 72 Mich St (5 / 61 Temple (12
- 82 Pittsburgh (4 / 63 Oral Rob (13
- 74 Marquette (6 / 66 Kentucky (11
- 77 Stanford (3 / 53 Cornell (14
- 78 Miami (7 / 64 St Mary's (10
- 74 Texas (2 / 54 Austin P (15

2nd Round: 77 Memphis / 74 Mississippi S / 65 Michigan St / 54 Pittsburgh / 81 Marquette / 82 Stanford / 72 Miami / 75 Texas

Sweet Sixteen: 92 Memphis / 74 Michigan St / 62 Stanford / 82 Texas

Elite Eight: 85 Memphis / 67 Texas

Final Four: 78 Memphis

West region

1st Round
- 70 UCLA (1 / 29 MVSU (16
- 62 BYU (8 / 67 Tex A&M (9
- 99 Drake (5 / 101 W Kent (12
- 69 Conn (4 / 70 S Diego (13
- 90 Purdue (6 / 79 Baylor (11
- 73 Xavier (3 / 61 Georgia (14
- 75 W Virginia (7 / 65 Arizona (10
- 71 Duke (2 / 70 Belmont (15

2nd Round: 51 UCLA / 49 Texas A&M / 72 W Kentucky / 63 San Diego / 78 Purdue / 85 Xavier / 73 W Virginia / 67 Duke

Sweet Sixteen: 88 UCLA / 78 W Kentucky / 79 Xavier / 75 W Virginia

Elite Eight: 76 UCLA / 57 Xavier

Final Four: 63 UCLA

East region

1st Round
- 113 UNC (1 / 74 MSM (16
- 72 Indiana (8 / 86 Arkansas (9
- 68 N. Dame (5 / 50 G. Mason (12
- 71 Wash St (4 / 40 Winthrop (13
- 72 Oklahoma (6 / 64 St Joseph (11
- 79 Louisville (3 / 61 Boise St. (14
- 81 Butler (7 / 61 S Alabam (10
- 72 Tennessee (2 / 57 Amer U (15

2nd Round: 108 UNC / 77 Arkansas / 41 N. Dame / 61 Wash State / 48 Oklahoma / 78 Louisville / 71 Butler / 76 Tennessee

Sweet Sixteen: 68 UNC / 47 Wash St / 79 Louisville / 60 Tennessee

Elite Eight: 83 UNC / 73 Louisville

Final Four: 66 UNC

Midwest region

1st Round
- 85 Kansas (1 / 75 Port St (16
- 71 UNLV (8 / 58 Kent St (9
- 69 Clemson (5 / 75 Villanova (12
- 62 Vanderbilt (4 / 83 Siena (13
- 67 USC (6 / 80 Kansas St (11
- 71 Wisconsin (3 / 56 Cal S Ful (14
- 76 Gonzaga (7 / 82 Davidson (10
- 66 C'town (2 / 47 UMBC (15

2nd Round: 75 Kansas / 56 UNLV / 84 Villanova / 72 Siena / 55 Kansas State / 72 Wisconsin / 74 Davidson / 70 Georgetown

Sweet Sixteen: 72 Kansas / 57 Villanova / 56 Wisconsin / 73 Davidson

Elite Eight: 59 Kansas / 57 Davidson

Final Four: 84 Kansas

{ 2008 NCAA Women's Championship }
Tennessee *beat* Stanford 64–48

Play-in game, 3/18/08; Mt. St Mary's vs Coppin State : Mt. St Mary's played N Carolina in 1st Round

TOUR DE FRANCE · 2008

As Spain's Carlos Sastre crossed the Paris finish line to win the 2008 Tour de France, there were hopes that the tour was emerging from years darkened by doping scandals. 33-year-old Sastre, nicknamed Don Limpio (Mr Clean), became the third successive Spaniard to win the tour in what was arguably Spain's greatest sporting year (victory in soccer's Euro 2008 [see p.247], and Nadal's triumph at Wimbledon [see p.245]). The specter of doping still haunted the event (3 competitors were expelled early in the tour), but race commentators praised the return of more fallible riders – a fact that seemed to indicate an absence of drug abuse. Sastre laid the foundations for his win with a daring sprint away from the pack at the bottom of the Alpe-d'Huez, creating a 1min & 34s lead over Cadel Evans. Pre-race favorite Evans had the chance to reclaim the yellow jersey in a decisive time-trial, but despite his much-vaunted speed he failed to trim enough seconds off Sastre's lead. Australian Evans was runner-up in the 2007 tour, but was not able to translate that promise into victory in 2008, again coming in second. The final standings were:

1	Carlos Sastre [ESP]	Team CSC	87 hours, 52 mins, 52 secs
2	Cadel Evans [AUS]	Silence – Lotto	+58s
3	Bernhard Kohl [AUT]	Gerolsteiner	+1 min 13s

THE MASTERS · 2008

South African Trevor Immelman beat Tiger Woods by 3 shots to win the 2008 Masters, with the highest final round score (3-over 75) for a champion since 1962.

Trevor Immelman...	$1,350,000.. 280		Brandt Snedeker	$435,000.. 284
Tiger Woods	$810,000.. 283		Phil Mickelson........	$273,750.. 286
Stewart Cink	$435,000.. 284		[The total purse for the event was $7,500,000.]	

GOLF MAJORS · 2008

♂	course	winner	
US OPEN	Torrey Pines, California	Tiger Woods[†] [USA]	−1
BRITISH OPEN	Royal Birkdale, England	Padraig Harrington [IRE]	+3
USPGA	Oakland Hills, Michigan	Padraig Harrington [IRE]	−3
♀			
KRAFT NABISCO	Mission Hills, California	Lorena Ochoa [MEX]	−11
LPGA	Havre de Grace, Maryland	Yani Tseng [TAI]	−12
US OPEN	Interlachen, Minnesota	Inbee Park [KOR]	−9
BRITISH OPEN	Sunningdale, England	Ji-Yai Shin [KOR]	−18

† Woods won the 2008 US Open on the first hole of sudden-death playoff against Rocco Mediate, despite playing the entire weekend with a torn ligament in his left knee. Shortly thereafter, Woods said he would miss the rest of the 2008 season to undergo reconstructive surgery. In other golf news, in May, Anika Sorenstam announced that she would retire from golf at the end of the 2008 season.

——————— TRACK & FIELD RECORDS ———————

Event		set by	when	record
♂	100m	Usain Bolt [JAM] [see p.22]	2008	9·69s†
♀	100m	Florence Griffith-Joyner [USA]	1988	10·49s
♂	110m hurdles	Dayron Robles [CUB]	2008	12·87s
♀	100m hurdles	Yordanka Donkova [BUL]	1988	12·21s
♂	200m	Usain Bolt [JAM] [see p.22]	2008	19·30s†
♀	200m	Florence Griffith-Joyner [USA]	1988	21·34s
♂	400m	Michael Johnson [USA]	1999	43·18s
♀	400m	Marita Koch [GDR]	1985	47·60s
♂	400m hurdles	Kevin Young [USA]	1992	46·78s
♀	400m hurdles	Yuliya Pechonkina [RUS]	2003	52·34s
♂	800m	Wilson Kipketer [DEN]	1997	1:41·11
♀	800m	Jarmila Kratochvílová [TCH]	1983	1:53·28
♂	1,500m	Hicham El Guerrouj [MAR]	1998	3:26·00
♀	1,500m	Yunxia Qu [CHN]	1993	3:50·46
♂	Mile	Hicham El Guerrouj [MAR]	1999	3:43·13
♀	Mile	Svetlana Masterkova [RUS]	1996	4:12·56
♂	5,000m	Kenenisa Bekele [ETH]	2004	12:37·35
♀	5,000m	Tirunesh Dibaba [ETH]	2008	14:11·15†
♂	10,000m	Kenenisa Bekele [ETH]	2005	26:17·53
♀	10,000m	Junxia Wang [CHN]	1993	29:31·78
♂	Marathon	Haile Gebrselassie [ETH]	2007	2:04:26
♀	Marathon	Paula Radcliffe [GBR]	2003	2:15:25
♂	High jump	Javier Sotomayor [CUB]	1993	2·45m
♀	High jump	Stefka Kostadinova [BUL]	1987	2·09m
♂	Long jump	Mike Powell [USA]	1991	8·95m
♀	Long jump	Galina Chistyakova [URS]	1988	7·52m
♂	Triple jump	Jonathan Edwards [GBR]	1995	18·29m
♀	Triple jump	Inessa Kravets [UKR]	1995	15·50m
♂	Pole vault	Sergey Bubka [UKR]	1994	6·14m
♀	Pole vault	Yelena Isinbaeva [RUS]	2008	5·05m†
♂	Shot put	Randy Barnes [USA]	1990	23·12m
♀	Shot put	Natalya Lisovskaya [URS]	1987	22·63m
♂	Discus	Jürgen Schult [GER]	1986	74·08m
♀	Discus	Gabriele Reinsch [GDR]	1988	76·80m
♂	Hammer	Yuriy Sedykh [URS]	1986	86·74m
♀	Hammer	Tatyana Lysenko [RUS]	2007	78·61m
♂	Javelin	Jan Zelezný [CZE]	1996	98·48m
♀	Javelin	Osleidys Menéndez [CUB]	2005	71·70m
♂	Decathlon	Roman Šebrle [CZE]	2001	9,026pts
♀	Heptathlon	Jackie Joyner-Kersee [USA]	1988	7,291pts
♂	4×100m relay	Jamaica	2008	37·10s†
♀	4×100m relay	German Democratic Republic	1985	41·37s
♂	4×400m relay	USA	1993	2:54·29
♀	4×400m relay	USSR	1988	3:15·17

[Records correct as of 8·16·08 · † Awaiting ratification]

────────── MIXED MARTIAL ARTS ──────────

A combat sport based on a variety of martial arts, Mixed Martial Arts (MMA) has grown in popularity over in years. Once labeled 'human cockfighting' – by John McCain – the sport has since adopted safety precautions and become increasingly standardized. The primary American MMA organization is the Ultimate Fighting Championship (UFC), whose weight classes and reigning champs are listed below:

Category	lb			
Lightweight	145–155	Welterweight..... >155–170	Lt Heavyweight .. >185–205	
		Middleweight.... >170–185	Heavyweight..... >205–265	

Weight	champion	since	fighting styles
Lightweight	BJ 'the Prodigy' Penn [USA]	1/19/08	Brazilian jujitsu
Welterweight	Georges 'Rush' St. Pierre [CAN]	4/19/08	boxing, Muay Thai, Brazilian jujitsu, wrestling, freestyle
Middleweight	Anderson 'the Spider' Silva [BRA]	10/14/06	boxing, Muay Thai, Brazilian jujitsu
Light Heavyweight	Forrest Griffin [USA]	7/5/08	boxing, Brazilian jujitsu, freestyle
Heavyweight	Randy 'the Natural' Couture† [USA]	3/3/07	wrestling

† The UFC has labeled Brazilian Antonio Rodrigo 'Minotauro' Nogueira its interim heavyweight champion, due to a contract dispute with Randy Couture, who says he has resigned from the sport.

────── WORLD BOXING CHAMPIONS · AS OF 8·24·2008 ──────

Weight	WBC	WBA	IBF	WBO
Heavy	Peter [NGR]	Chagaev [UZB]	Klitschko [UKR]	Klitschko [UKR]
Cruiser	vacant	Arslan [GER]	Cunnningham [USA]	vacant
Light heavy	Diaconu [ROM]	Garay [ARG]	Tarver [USA]	Erdei [HUN]
Super middle	vacant	Kessler [DEN]	Bute [CAN]	Calzaghe [GBR]
Middle	Pavlik [USA]	Sturm [GER]	Abraham [GER]	Pavlik [USA]
Junior middle	Mora [USA]	Santos [PUR]	Phillips [USA]	Dzinziruk [UKR]
Welter	Berto [USA]	Margarito [MEX]	vacant	Williams [USA]
Junior welter	Bradley [USA]	Kotelnik [UKR]	Malignaggi [USA]	Holt [USA]
Light	Pacquiao [PHI]	Kobori [JPN]	Campbell [USA]	Campbell [USA]
Junior light	vacant	Valero [VEN]	Baloyi [RSA]	Arthur [GBR]
Feather	Larios [MEX]	John [INA]	vacant	Luevano [USA]
Junior feather	Vázquez [MEX]	Caballero [PAN]	Molitor [CAN]	López [PUR]
Bantam	Hasegawa [JAP]	Moreno [PAN]	Agbeko [GHA]	Peñalosa [PHI]
Junior bantam	Mijares [MEX]	Concepción [PAN]	Darchinyan [ARM]	Montiel [MEX]
Fly	Naito [JAP]	Sakata [JAP]	Donaire [PHI]	Narváez [ARG]
Junior fly	Sosa [MEX]	Canchila [COL]	Solis [MEX]	Calderón [PUR]
Straw	Palacios [NCA]	Niida [JAP]	García [MEX]	Nietes [PHI]

Category	lb					
Straw	105	Jr bantam....115	Jr light.......130	Jr middle 154	Cruiser.......200
		Bantam......118	Light.........135	Middle.......160	Heavy......>200
Jr fly 108		Jr feather.....122	Jr welter 140	Spr middle...168	[The UK uses
Fly 112		Feather.......126	Welter 147	Light heavy ..175	different names.]

WIMBLEDON · 2008

All England Lawn Tennis & Croquet Club, London, UK · June 23–July 6, 2008

It is a dream to play on this court, my favorite tournament,
but to win I never imagined. — RAFAEL NADAL
One of the greatest tennis matches ever played. — *New York Times*

MEN'S SINGLES
Rafael Nadal [ESP]
bt Roger Federer [SUI]
6–4, 6–4, 6–7 (5–7), 6–7 (8–10), 9–7

LADIES' SINGLES
Venus Williams [USA]
bt Serena Williams [USA]
7–5, 6–4

It's monumental. — VENUS WILLIAMS

MEN'S DOUBLES
Daniel Nestor [CAN]
& Nenad Zimonjic [SRB]
bt Jonas Bjorkman [SWE]
& Kevin Ullyett [ZIM]
7–6 (14–12), 6–7 (3–7), 6–3, 6–3

LADIES' DOUBLES
Venus Williams [USA]
& Serena Williams [USA]
bt Lisa Raymond [USA]
& Samantha Stosur [AUS]
6–2, 6–2

MIXED DOUBLES
Bob Bryan [USA]
& Samantha Stosur [AUS]
bt Mike Bryan [USA]
& Katarina Srebotnik [SLO]
7–5, 6–4

Round (singles†)	*prize money*
Winner	£750,000
Runner-up	£375,000

† Winnings for doubles differ.

2007 · US OPEN

Flushing Meadows Corona Park, Queens, NY · August 27–September 9, 2007

MEN'S SINGLES
Roger Federer [SUI]
bt Novak Djokovic [SRB]
7–6 (4), 7–6 (2), 6–4

WOMEN'S SINGLES
Justine Henin [BEL]
bt Svetlana Kuznetsova [RUS]
6–1, 6–3

MEN'S DOUBLES
Simon Aspelin [SWE]
& Julian Knowle [AUT]
bt Lukas Dlouhy [CZE]
& Pavel Vizner [CZE]
7–5, 6–4

WOMEN'S DOUBLES
Nathalie Dechy [FRA]
& Dinara Safina [RUS]
bt Yung-Jan Chan [TPE]
& Chia-Jung Chuang [TPE]
6–4, 6–2

MIXED DOUBLES
Victoria Azarenka [BLR]
& Max Mirnyi [BLR]
bt Meghann Shaughnessy [USA]
& Leander Paes [IND] · 6–4, 7–6 (6)

Round (singles)	*prize money*
Winner	$1·4m
Runner-up	$700,000

───────TENNIS GRAND SLAM TOURNAMENTS───────

Event	month	surface	♂ winner	♀
Australian Open	Jan	Plexicushion	Novak Djokovic	Maria Sharapova
French Open	May/Jun	clay	Rafael Nadal	Ana Ivanovic
Wimbledon	Jun/Jul	grass	Rafael Nadal	Venus Williams
US Open [2007]	Aug/Sep	cement	Roger Federer	Justine Henin

───────────────THE DAVIS CUP───────────────

The Davis Cup is an international men's tennis tournament that includes 131 countries, of which 16 qualify to play in the World Group. (The rest fight it out in continental leagues, in an effort to gain promotion into the elite World Group.) The US has belonged to the World Group since 1989, and has won 32 times, including in 2007. The 2008 World Group results at the time of writing are listed below:

February 8–10 · 2008 WORLD GROUP 1ST ROUND
Russia *bt* Serbia 3–2
Czech Republic *bt* Belgium 3–2
Argentina *bt* Great Britain 4–1
Sweden *bt* Israel 3–2
Germany *bt* South Korea 3–2
Spain *bt* Peru 5–0
France *bt* Romania 5–0
United States *bt* Austria 4–1

April 11–13 · 2008 WORLD GROUP QUARTERFINALS
Russia *bt* Czech Republic 3–2
Argentina *bt* Sweden 4–1
Spain *bt* Germany 4–1
United States *bt* France 4–1

[World Group semifinals are Sep 19–21, 2008, and finals Nov 21–23, 2008. See daviscup.com]

───────ATP & WTA RANKINGS · AS OF 8·29·2008───────

♂	race	ATP	rank	♀	race	WTA
Rafael Nadal [ESP]	1175	6700	1	Ana Ivanovic [SRB]	2821	3612
Roger Federer [SUI]	721	5930	2	Jelena Jankovic [SRB]	2970	3515
Novak Djokovic [SRB]	785	5105	3	Serena Williams [USA]	2680	3341
David Ferrer [ESP]	322	2865	4	S. Kuznetsova [RUS]	1932	3181
N. Davydenko [RUS]	387	2700	5	E. Dementieva [RUS]	2405	3070
Andy Murray [GBR]	380	2415	6	Maria Sharapova [RUS]	2515	3131
David Nalbandian [ARG]	180	1975	7	Dinara Safina [RUS]	2673	3047
Andy Roddick [USA]	279	1845	8	Venus Williams [USA]	1856	2586
James Blake [USA]	294	1725	9	Vera Zvonareva [RUS]	1735	2117
Stanislas Wawrinka [SUI]	256	1725	10	A. Radwanska [POL]	1805	2076

MLS CUP · 2007

HOUSTON DYNAMO *bt* NEW ENGLAND REVOLUTION 2–1
November 18, 2007 · Field: RFK Stadium, Washington, DC · Attendance: 39,859
MLS Cup MVP · Dwayne De Rosario

	total shots	shots on goal	fouls	offsides	corner kicks	saves
Houston Dynamo	14	7	15	1	3	7
New England Revolution	14	8	15	1	4	5

EUROPEAN SOCCER CHAMPIONSHIPS 2008

On June 29, 2008, Spain beat Germany in a thrilling final, fulfilling years of promise to take their first international soccer title since 1964. Hosted by Switzerland
and Austria, the tournament got off to a lively start as the new guard – Croatia,
Turkey, Holland, Russia, and Spain – left old-guard teams such as France and
world champions Italy looking staid. In the end, Luis Aragonés's young squad was
widely considered the team of the tournament and worthy championship winners.

THE QUARTERFINALS

Germany *bt* Portugal 3–2
Turkey *bt* Croatia 1–1 (*pens* 3–1)

Russia *bt* Holland 3–1
Spain *bt* Italy 0–0 (*pens* 4–2)

THE SEMIFINALS

Germany *bt* Turkey 3–2

Spain *bt* Russia 3–0

– THE FINAL –

SPAIN *bt* GERMANY 1–0
June 29, 2008 · Ernst Happel Stadion, Vienna
Player of the tournament: Xavi [ESP] · Golden Boot: David Villa [ESP]

SUMMER X GAMES · 2008

July 31–August 3, 2008 · Los Angeles

SKATE

Big Air	Bob Burnquist
Street ♀ Elissa Steamer; ♂ R. Shekler
Vert	♀ Karen Jones; ♂ Pierre-Luc Gagnon
SuperPark	Rune Gilfberg

MOTO X

Best Trick	Kyle Loza
Racing	♀ Tara Gieger; ♂ Josh Hansen

Freestyle	Jeremy Lusk
SuperMoto	Jeff Ward
Speed & Style	Kevin Johnson
Step Up	Ricky Carmichael

BMX

Freestyle Vert	Jamie Bestwick
Freestyle SuperPark	Daniel Dhers
Big Air	Chad Kagy
Street	Garrett Reynolds

RALLY

Rally Car	Travis Pastrana

50th DAYTONA 500

February 18, 2008 · Estimated crowd: 180,000
National Anthem: Trisha Yearwood · Prize purse: $18,689,238

Ryan Newman triumphed in the 50th running of the Daytona 500, foiling Tony Stewart in his 10th attempt to win the 'Great American Race'. For the second year in a row, the race was decided in the last lap, when teammate Kurt Busch gave Newman a 'push from heaven' while coming off Turn 2. The win was significant for owner Roger Penske, winner of 14 Indy 500s, but never before a Daytona victor.

Driver (start)	Sponsor	total points	earnings
Ryan Newman (12)	Alltel	190	$1,506,045
Kurt Busch (2)	Miller Lite	175	$1,063,870
Tony Stewart (20)	Home Depot	170	$871,049
Kyle Busch (18)	M&M's	170	$652,938

The Harley J. Earl trophy was plated in gold in 2008 to commemorate the 50th running of the Daytona 500. 7-time Daytona winner Richard Petty waved the green flag as the Honorary Starter, while 1960 winner and former owner Junior Johnson drove a 2008 Corvette Z06 as the pace car.

2007 NEXTEL CUP CHAMPION

Jimmie Johnson of Hendrick Motorsports won the Nextel Cup Championship in 2007, his second championship win in a row. Jeff Gordon placed second, trailing Johnson by 77 points. Below are Johnson's final numbers, according to NASCAR:

Starts	poles	wins	top-5	top-10	laps	winnings
36	4	10	20	24	10,318	$7,646,421

92nd INDIANAPOLIS 500

May 25, 2008 · Estimated crowd: 400,000
Distance: 500 miles · Average speed: 143.567mph · Cautions: 8

Driver (start)	team	total points	earnings $
Scott Dixon (1)	Target Chip Ganassi Racing	191	2,988,065
Vitor Meira (8)	Delphi National Guard	98	1,273,215
Marco Andretti (7)	Team Indiana Jones (Blockbuster)	130	782,065
Helio Castroneves (4)	Team Penske	176	482,815
Ed Carpenter (10)	Menards/Vision Racing	120	399,665
Ryan Hunter-Reay (20)	Rahal Letterman Racing Team Ethanol	105	328,065
Hideki Mutoh (9)	Formula Dream	113	307,115
Buddy Rice (17)	Dreyer & Reinbold Racing	88	311,415
Darren Manning (14)	ABC Supply Co./AJ Foyt Racing	92	301,815
Townsend Bell (12)	Dreyer & Reinbold William Rast Racing	52	275,315

———————————— SPORTS PARTICIPATION ————————————

The National Sporting Goods Association regularly polls the number of Americans (aged 7 or over) who participate in a range of sports more than once during the year. Charted below are the levels of participation during the period 1997–2007:

Sport · Millions of participants	2007	2005	2003	2001	1999	1997
Aerobic exercising	30·3	33·7	28·0	26·3	26·2	26·3
Archery (target)	6·6	6·8	3·9	4·7	4·9	4·8
Backpack/wilderness camp	13·0	13·3	15·1	14·5	15·3	12·0
Baseball	14·0	14·6	15·4	14·9	16·3	14·1
Basketball	24·1	29·9	27·9	28·1	29·6	30·7
Bicycle riding	37·4	43·1	38·3	39·0	42·4	45·1
Billiards/pool	29·5	37·3	33·0	32·7	32·1	36·0
Boating, motor/power	31·9	27·5	24·2	23·9	24·4	27·2
Bowling	43·5	45·4	41·9	41·9	41·6	44·8
Camping (vacation/overnight)	47·5	46·0	53·4	48·7	50·1	46·6
Cheerleading	–	3·3	–	3·7	–	–
Exercise walking	89·8	86·0	81·6	78·3	80·8	76·3
Exercising with equipment	52·8	54·2	50·2	43·9	45·2	47·9
Fishing	35·3	43·3	42·7	44·4	46·7	44·7
Football (tackle)	9·2	9·9	8·7	8·2	8·4	8·2
Golf	22·7	24·7	25·7	26·6	27·0	26·2
Hiking	28·6	29·8	26·7	26·1	28·1	28·4
Hockey (ice)	2·1	2·4	1·9	2·2	1·9	1·9
Hunting w/bow & arrow	5·7	6·6	5·0	4·7	5·8	5·3
Hunting with firearms	19·5	19·4	17·9	19·2	17·1	17·0
In-line roller skating	10·7	13·1	16·0	19·2	24·1	26·6
Kayaking/rafting	5·9	7·6	–	3·5	3·0	2·9
Mountain biking (off road)	7·4	9·2	8·2	6·9	6·8	8·1
Muzzleloading	3·6	4·1	3·4	3·2	3·3	2·9
Paintball games	7·4	8·0	7·4	5·6	5·1	–
Running/jogging	30·4	29·2	23·9	24·5	22·4	21·7
Scooter riding	10·6	10·4	11·9	12·7	–	–
Skateboarding	10·1	12·0	9·0	9·6	7·0	6·3
Skiing (alpine)	5·5	6·9	6·8	7·7	7·4	8·9
Skiing (cross-country)	1·7	1·9	1·9	2·3	2·2	2·5
Snowboarding	5·1	6·0	6·3	5·3	3·3	2·8
Soccer	13·8	14·1	13·0	13·9	13·2	13·7
Softball	10·0	14·1	12·4	13·2	14·7	16·3
Swimming	52·3	58·0	52·3	54·8	57·9	59·5
Target shooting	20·9	21·9	17·9	17·3	17·7	18·5
Target shooting – airgun	6·6	6·7	3·8	2·9	3·5	3·4
Tennis	12·3	11·1	9·6	10·9	10·9	11·1
Volleyball	12·0	13·2	10·4	12·0	11·7	17·8
Waterskiing	5·3	6·7	5·5	5·8	6·6	6·5
Weight lifting	33·2	35·5	25·9	23·9	–	–
Workout at club	33·8	34·7	29·5	26·5	24·1	21·1

──── READY RECKONER OF OTHER RESULTS · 2007–08 ────

AMATEUR ATHLETICS · AAU James E. Sullivan Memorial Award	Tim Tebow
AUTO RACING · F1 UK Grand Prix	Lewis Hamilton [GBR]
F1 World Drivers Championship [2007]	Kimi Räikkönen [FIN] · Ferrari
F1 World Constructors Championship [2007]	Ferrari [ITA]
BADMINTON · World Championship [2007]	
Singles	♂ Lin Dan [CHI] · ♀ Zhu Lin [CHI]
Doubles ♂ M. Kidho/H. Setiawan [INA] ·	♀ Yang Wei/Zhang Jiewen [CHI]
Mixed doubles	Nova Widianto/Lilyana Natsir [INA]
BASEBALL · MLB All-Star Game	American League *bt* National League 4–3
BASKETBALL · NBA All-Star Game	Eastern Conf. *bt* Western Conf. 134–128
BOWLING · USBC Masters [2007]	Sean Rash *bt* Steve Jaros 269–245
Denny's US Open	Norm Duke *bt* Mika Koivuniemi 224–216
Denny's World Championship	Norm Duke *bt* Ryan Shafer 202–165
PBA Tournament of Champions	Michael Haugen Jr *bt* Chris Barnes 215–214
USBC Queens Tournament	Lynda Barnes *bt* Amy Stolz 215–195
BOXING · *Ring Magazine* Fight of the Year [2007]	I. Vazquez *bt* R. Marquez
Ring Magazine Fighter of the Year [2007]	Floyd Mayweather
CHESS · FIDE World Championship [2007]	Vishwanathan Anand
US Chess Championship	Yury Shulman
US Women's Chess Championship	Anna Zatonskih
ELEPHANT POLO · World Championships [2007]	Chopard *bt* Chivas Regal Scotland
DIRECTORS' CUP · NCAA Division I	Stanford
Division II	Grand Valley State
Division III	Williams
NAIA	Azusa Pacific
DIVING · FINA Diving World Cup	China [11 medals]
DRAGON BOAT RACING · IDBF CCWC Premier Mixed 2000m	
	Mayfair Predators [CAN]
FISHING · Bassmaster Classic Championship	Alton Jones
IGFA Inshore World Championship	Robert Collins
IGFA Offshore World Championship	Outdoor Channel Offshore Classic [USA]
GYMNASTICS · Acrobatic Gymnastics World Cup Series	
Mixed pairs	Stanislav Barbarykin & Olga Sviridova [RUS] 28·960
Women's pairs	Katsiaryna Murashko & Alina Yushko [BLR] 28·853
Men's pairs	Alexei Dudchenko & Konstantin Pilipchuk [RUS] 28·859
ICE HOCKEY · World Championship	Russia *bt* Canada 5–4
LACROSSE · Division I NCAA Men's Champ.	Syracuse *bt* Johns Hopkins 13–10
Division I NCAA Women's Champ.	Northwestern *bt* Pennsylvania 10–6
LITTLE LEAGUE BASEBALL · World Series [2007]	Warner Robins, GA, Little League
LITTLE LEAGUE SOFTBALL · World Series	South, Simpsonville, SC, Little League
MOBILE PHONE THROWING · World Champ. [2007]	Tommi Huotari [FIN] 294'
MONSTER TRUCK RALLY · Monster Jam World Finals	
Racing	*Batman*, driven by John Seasock
Freestyle	*Taz*, driven by Adam Anderson
MOTORCYCLE RACING · US Grand Prix	Valentino Rossi [ITA]
PARAGLIDING · World Cup [2007]	Switzerland

— READY RECKONER OF OTHER RESULTS · 2007–08 cont. —

PARACHUTING · FAI World Champions Formation Skydiving 8-way	France, 151pts
FAI World Champions Formation Skydiving 4-way	United States, 195pts
POKER · World Series of Poker [2007]	Jerry Yang
PUZZLES · US Puzzle Championship	Thomas Snyder, 365pts
ROCK PAPER SCISSORS · USARPS Championship	Sean Sears
RODEO · World Championships [2007]	Shawn Minor
Bareback Riding Champion	Billy Griffin
Steer Wrestling Champion	Jordan Wiseman
Saddle Bronc Riding Champion	Shawn Minor
Tie-down Roping Champion	Steve Brickey
Bull Riding Champion	Nathan Tull
Barrel Racing Champion	Mesa Leavitt
SNOWSHOEING · USSSA Nat. Snowshoe Champ.	♂ J. Middaugh; ♀ K. Nelson
SOCCER · European Championship	Spain *bt* Germany 1–0
SOFTBALL · ASA Men's major fast pitch	Patsy's
ASA Women's major fast pitch	Southern California Hurricanes
USSSA Men's major slow pitch [2007]	Resmondo
SQUASH · Super Series Finals	Gregory Gaultier [FRA] *bt* Amr Shabana [EGY]
Women's World Open [2007]	Rachael Grinham [AUS] *bt* Natalie Grinham [AUS]
SUDOKU · World Sudoku Championship	Thomas Snyder [USA]
SWIMMING · FINA World Swimming Championships (25m)	
200m backstroke	♂ Markus Rogan [AUT]; ♀ Kirsty Coventry [ZIM]
200m breaststroke	♂ Kristopher Gilchrist [GBR]; ♀ Suzaan van Biljon [RSA]
50m freestyle	♂ Duje Draganja [CRO]; ♀ Marleen Veldhuis [NED]
100m freestyle	♂ Nathan Adrian [USA]; ♀ Marleen Veldhuis [NED]
400m freestyle	♂ Yuriy Prilukov [RUS]; ♀ Kylie Palmer [AUS]
TENNIS · Fed Cup [2007]	Russia *bt* Italy 4–0
WTA Champ. [2007]	Justine Henin *bt* Maria Sharapova 5–7, 7–5, 6–3
TEXT MESSAGING · National Texting Champion	Morgan Pozgar
TRIATHLONS · Kelowna ITU Triathlon Premium Pan American Cup	
Elite Women	Paula Findlay [CAN] 02:08·35
Elite Men	Brent McMahon [CAN] 01:54·44
Aquathalon World Championship [2007]	Sergio Sarmiento [MEX] 0:29·54
Ironman World Championship [2007]	Chris McCormack [USA] 8:15·34
WOMEN'S HOCKEY · NCAA Championship	
	Minnesota Duluth *bt* Wisconsin Badgers 4–0
WRESTLING · NCAA Division I	Iowa Hawkeyes
X GAMES 14 · Snowboard SuperPipe	♂ Shaun White; ♀ Gretchen Bleiler
Snowboard Slopestyle	♂ Andreas Wiig; ♀ Jamie Anderson
Snowboard Big Air	Torstein Horgmo
Snowboarder X	♂ Nate Holland; ♀ Lindsey Jacobellis
SuperPipe Ski	♂ Tanner Hall; ♀ Sarah Burke
Ski Big Air	Jon Olsson
Ski Slopestyle	Andreas Hatveit
Skier X	♂ Daron Rahlves; ♀ Ophelie David

All events took place in 2008, unless otherwise stated.

The Nation

*If [America] forgets where she came from, if the people lose sight of
what brought them along, if she listens to the deniers and mockers,
then will begin the rot and dissolution.* — CARL SANDBURG (1878–1967)

——— US GEOGRAPHIC SPECIFICATIONS & EXTREMES ———

Highest point . . . . Mount McKinley, Alaska (20,320ft above sea level)
Lowest point . . . . Death Valley, California (282ft below sea level)
Mean elevation . . . . ≈2,500ft
Northernmost point . . . . Point Barrow, Alaska
Southernmost point . . . . Ka Lae (South Cape), Hawaii
Easternmost point . . . . West Quoddy Head, Maine
Westernmost point . . . . Cape Wrangell, Alaska

GEOGRAPHIC AREA
Total . . . . .3,794,083 sq mi
Land . . . . .3,537,438 sq mi
Water . . . . .256,645 sq mi
[includes only the 50 States and DC]
LAND BOUNDARIES
Total . . . . .7,478 mi
Canada . . . . .5,526 mi
[including 1,539 mi with Alaska]
Mexico . . . . .1,952 mi
Guantánamo Bay† . . . . 17 mi
Coastline . . . . 12,380 mi
MARITIME CLAIMS
Territorial sea . . . . 12 nautical miles
Contiguous zone . . . . 24 nm
Exclusive economic zone . . . . . .200 nm
Continental shelf . . . . .not specified
LAND USE (2005)
Arable land .18·01%
Permanent crops . . . . 0·21%
Other . . . . .81·78%
Different calculations exist.
[Sources: USGS; CIA; Dept of the Interior]

US Commonwealth & Territories
American Samoa · Guam
Northern Mariana Islands
Puerto Rico · Virgin Islands

Freely Associated States
Republic of the Marshall Islands
Federated States of Micronesia
Republic of Palau (status review in 2009)

Other areas under US jurisdiction
Midway Atoll · Palmyra Atoll
Wake Atoll · Baker Island
Howland Island · Jarvis Island
Johnston Atoll · Kingman Reef
Navassa Island (claimed by Haiti)

Extremes calculated based on the geographic center of the US, including Alaska and Hawaii. † Since 1903, the US has leased Guantánamo Bay from Cuba for *c*.$4,000 per year – although as an act of protest, the Cuban government refuses to cash the checks.

There are 663 WILDERNESS AREAS in the US covering 105,764,330 acres (an area greater than California). The 1864 Wilderness Act gave Congress the authority to designate and protect these unique areas 'where the earth and its community of life are untrammeled by man, where man himself is a visitor who does not remain...'

LARGEST US CITIES

City	state	2005 pop.	± since 2000 (%)	nickname(s)
New York	NY	8,143,197	134,919 (1·7)	*The Big Apple; Gotham City*
Los Angeles	CA	3,844,829	150,009 (4·1)	*City of Angels; La La Land*
Chicago	IL	2,842,518	−53,498 (−1·8)	*The Windy City; Big Town*
Houston	TX	2,016,582	62,951 (3·2)	*Magnolia City; Clutch City*
Philadelphia	PA	1,463,281	−54,269 (−3·6)	*City of Brotherly Love*
Phoenix	AZ	1,461,575	140,530 (10·6)	*Valley of the Sun*
San Antonio	TX	1,256,509	111,863 (9·8)	*Alamo City; Mission City*
San Diego	CA	1,255,540	32,140 (2·6)	*Plymouth of the West*
Dallas	TX	1,213,825	25,245 (2·1)	*The Big D*
San Jose	CA	912,332	17,389 (1·9)	*Capital of Silicon Valley*

[As of July 1, 2005 · Source: US Census · Some cities have additional or alternative nicknames]

AMERICAN SUPERLATIVES OF NOTE

Biggest waterfall (volume)	Niagara Falls, New York	168,000m³ per minute
Deepest depression	Death Valley, California	282ft below sea level
Deepest canyon	Grand Canyon, Arizona	1·1mi
Highest active volcano	Wrangell, Alaska	14,163ft
Highest dam	Oroville Dam, California	770ft
Highest sea cliffs	Moloka'i, Hawaii	3,300ft
Highest waterfall	Yosemite Falls, California	2,425ft
Largest delta	Mississippi River Delta	11,000mi²
Largest desert	Great Basin, Nevada, Utah, &c.	190,000mi²
Largest geyser	Steamboat, Yellowstone National Park	>300ft
Largest glacier	Bering, near Cordova, Alaska	126mi
Largest lake	Michigan-Huron, USA/Canada	45,410mi²
Largest national forest	Tongass, Alaska	17m acres
Largest state	Alaska	571,951mi²
Longest cave	Mammoth Cave, Kentucky	365mi
Longest mountain range	Rocky Mountains	*c*.3,000mi
Longest rail tunnel	New Cascade, Washington	7·8mi
Longest road tunnel	Ted Williams/I-90 Extension, MA	1·6mi
Longest river system	Mississippi-Missouri river system	3,890mi
Longest suspension bridge	Verrazano Narrows, New York	4,260ft
Smallest city (area)	West New York Town, New Jersey	1mi²
Smallest state	Rhode Island	1,045mi²
Tallest dunes	Great Sand Dunes, Colorado	>750ft
Tallest inhabited building	Sears Tower, Chicago	110 stories, 1,450ft
Tallest monument	Gateway Arch, St Louis, Missouri	630ft
Tallest structure	KVLY TV mast, North Dakota	2,063 ft
Tallest tree	Hyperion, Redwood National Park, CA	379·1ft

Unsurprisingly, a degree of uncertainty and debate surrounds some of these entries and their specifications.

—ALLEGIANCE PLEDGE—

According to the US Code, the PLEDGE OF ALLEGIANCE should be made facing the flag, standing to attention, with the right hand over the heart. Men not in uniform should remove their headdress with their right hand and hold it at the left shoulder. Those in uniform should remain silent, face the flag, and salute. The Pledge of Allegiance is:

I pledge allegiance to the flag of the United States of America and to the Republic for which it stands, one Nation, under God, indivisible, with Liberty and Justice for all.

The Youth's Companion, a magazine in Boston, first published the Pledge of Allegiance in 1892 to celebrate the 400th anniversary of America's discovery. However, the publication of the Pledge was not without controversy, since two writers at the *Companion*, James B. Upham and Francis Bellamy, both claimed authorship. A number of tribunals ruled in favor of Bellamy, and in 1957 the Library of Congress confirmed his claim. The original text pledged allegiance to 'my flag', and in 1923 the National Flag Conference added a specification of the US flag (presumably a bid to avoid confusion and prevent any possible ambiguity amongst those who were born in other countries). In 1942, the Pledge was given official recognition by Congress; and, on June 14, 1954, the phrase 'under God' was added by Congressional decree. President Eisenhower stated, 'In this way we are reaffirming the transcendence of religious faith in America's heritage and future; in this way we shall constantly strengthen those spiritual weapons which forever will be our country's most powerful resource in peace and war'.

—AMERICAN'S CREED—

The AMERICAN'S CREED is as follows:

I believe in the United States of America as a government of the people, by the people, for the people; whose just powers are derived from the consent of the governed; a democracy in a republic; a sovereign Nation of many sovereign States; a perfect union, one and inseparable; established upon those principles of Freedom, Equality, Justice, and Humanity for which American patriots sacrificed their lives and fortunes. I therefore believe it is my duty to my country to love it, to support its Constitution, to obey its laws, to respect its flag, and to defend it against all enemies.

It was written by William Tyler Page (a descendent of President Tyler) in 1917, as an entry for a national competition for a composition that embodied the principles of America. The competition, conceived by Henry Sterling Chapin, the Commissioner of Education in NY, prompted over 3,000 entries. Page's text was formally adopted by the House of Representatives in April 1918.

—NATIONAL MOTTO—

The NATIONAL MOTTO, 'In God We Trust', was established by the 84th Congress, and approved by Eisenhower in 1956. It seems the motto dates from a popular movement during the Civil War to recognize God on US coinage. Secretary of the Treasury Salmon P. Chase declared in 1861, 'No nation can be strong except in the strength of God, or safe except in His defense. The trust of our people in God should be declared on our national coins'. 'In God We Trust', which first appeared on US notes in 1957, may be based on 'In God is our trust' from the fourth verse of *The Star-Spangled Banner*.

———————COLUMBIA———————

A feminized form of 'Columbus', 'Columbia' was used as a label for the New World as early as 1697, when it appeared in Samuel Sewall's *Phaenomena Quaedam Apocalyptica.* During the American Revolution, an idealized Columbia figure began to appear as an allegory of the national spirit in American songs and poems. (One early and famous example is Boston poet Phillis Wheatley's 1775 *To His Excellency, General Washington*.) As a personification of the nation, 'Columbia' proved a useful counter-symbol to 'Britannia', and there was even some debate about changing America's name to the 'United States of Columbia'. (When the Spanish colony New Granada declared independence from Spain in 1819 and became Columbia Grande, this idea was dropped.) After a long tradition of depicting the New World as a bare-breasted 'Indian Queen', images of Columbia began to appear in political cartoons and engravings, where she was shown draped in a modest white gown and wearing a liberty cap[†]. According to scholars, this image of Columbia represented liberty, progress, and American unity, although it was a somewhat fluid image that lent itself to a variety of associations, including the arts and the sciences. Columbia had fallen out of favor by the early C20th, ceding her place in the national pantheon to masculine images like Uncle Sam. Yet the name Columbia survives across the States in Columbia University (renamed from Kings College in 1784); Columbia, SC (named in 1786); 'Hail Columbia' (an early national anthem now used as an entry song for the Vice President); and, of course, the District.

† Originally a small cap, often of red felt, which Romans would place on the head of freed slaves.

———————YANKEE———————

While the origin of the word *Yankee* is much debated, many scholars believe the term derives from Dutch settlers in America. *Yankee* is said to come from either *Janke*, a diminutive form of the name *Jan* (John), or *Jan Kees*, a disparaging nickname which translates as *John Cheese*. For reasons that are unclear, the Dutch colonists called the neighboring English settlers in northern Connecticut *Yankees*, and the term somehow became a nickname for any New Englander. By the War of Independence, the British had begun using *Yankee* as a term of contempt for the colonists. *Yankee Doodle* was originally a popular (and mocking) marching song in the British Army (*doodle* originally meant someone silly or foolish), which was only later claimed by the American troops. During the Civil War, Southerners used the term as an insult for Northerners. By WWI, American soldiers were often called *Yankees* (or *Yanks*) elsewhere in the world. Today, *Yankee* is still used outside the US as a mildly disparaging term for an American, although within the States, it is generally a neutral term for a New Englander.

———————FEDERAL HOLIDAYS———————

Federal law [5 U.S.C. 6103] establishes these public holidays for federal employees:

New Year's Day · Birthday of Martin Luther King Jr · Washington's Birthday · Memorial Day Independence Day · Labor Day Columbus Day · Veterans Day Thanksgiving · Christmas Day

[See also the Ephemerides, p.342]

THE WHITE HOUSE

The White House is composed of 3 major parts: the East Wing, the West Wing, and the Residence. The Residence is the oldest part of the building, and originally included the President's living and working quarters. Some notable rooms:

GROUND FLOOR

Map Room · Roosevelt's 'situation room' during WWII[†]; now used for private meetings. Decorated in the Chippendale style of the C18th.

Diplomatic Reception Room · Used to present ambassadors to the President (first by Theodore Roosevelt, in 1903). Also the site of FDR's 'fireside chats'.

China Room · Displays the White House china. Decorated with a red color scheme, inspired by the room's portrait of Grace Coolidge.

Vermeil Room · Also called the Gold Room; used as a display room and sitting room for formal occasions. Contains the White House collection of vermeil (gold-dipped silver).

Library · A 'Gentlemen's Ante-Room' until 1935, when it was remodeled as a library. Includes a collection of books begun by Abigail Fillmore in the 1850s. Often used for teas and meetings, and decorated in late-Federal-period style.

FIRST FLOOR

State Dining Room · Used for formal dinners; can seat 140 guests. Modeled after neoclassical English houses of the late-C18th.

Red Room · Formerly the President's antichamber, then the Yellow Drawing Room, when it hosted Dolley Madison's parties. Now used as a parlor and for small dinner parties.

Blue Room · A reception room decorated in French Empire style. Van Buren introduced the blue scheme in 1837.

Green Room · Formerly a dining and card room; now a drawing room. Federal-period furniture, with eagle motifs throughout the room.

East Room · Used mainly for large ceremonies and other gatherings. Decorated in late-C18th-classical style. Apart from a grand piano and portrait of George Washington, the room is sparsely furnished – Theodore Roosevelt's children sometimes used it for roller-skating.

The second floor of the Residence holds the First Family and guest bedrooms. The third floor is used for leisure, and includes a sun room, workout room, billiards room, and music room (the latter added by the Clintons). ❦ The East and West Wing were originally built as extensions of the Residence to connect to nearby offices. The President worked on the second floor of the Residence (often in what is now the Lincoln bedroom) until 1902, when overcrowding forced a move to the West Wing:

The WEST WING includes the Oval Office, Cabinet Room, Roosevelt Room, Press Briefing Room, and executive staff offices. Taft built the first OVAL OFFICE in 1909; it was moved to its present location in 1934. Each President redecorates the office; George W. Bush has chosen several paintings of Texas scenes. ❦ The EAST WING was built in 1942, in part to cover an air-raid bunker. It now houses office space for the First Lady and her staff, as well as the President's theater.

[Sources include the White House Museum]

† The SITUATION ROOM is a 5,000-square-foot intelligence briefing area on the ground floor of the West Wing, and nicknamed 'The Woodshed'. It was created by JFK after the Bay of Pigs invasion.

21-GUN SALUTES

Dispute surrounds the history and significance of the 21-gun salute. It seems that all such salutes derive from the universal tradition of abasing one's weapons as a sign of respect and peaceful intent. Some African tribes would trail their spears in the ground to signify passivity, and it is not unlikely that the handshake developed, like the open-handed salute, as a way of proving one was unarmed. According to the estimable *Oxford Companion to Ships and the Sea*, there were originally two forms of naval salute. When in narrow seas or foreign territorial waters, ships would vail [lower] their topsails. In other circumstances, they would fire guns. Significantly, ships would fire their salutes with their bows pointing towards the vessel being saluted to demonstrate (and ensure) no hostile intent. Originally, the firing of salutes had no formal regulation and was governed by each captain's predilection for loud noise and his supply of gunpowder. Anxious to preserve valuable ammunition, the Secretary to the British Navy (and diarist) Samuel Pepys devised a scale for naval gun salutes (always in odd numbers†) ranging from 3 (the minimum) to 19 (for the Admiral of the Fleet). The Royal or Presidential salute was the maximum: 21‡. A number of sources suggest that ships were obliged to fire salutes to exhaust their ammunition or render themselves defenseless while they rearmed. In the years that Britain ruled the waves, the Royal Navy would expect weaker nations to salute first, and would even recognize the ships of monarchies with more gunfire than those from parvenu republics. ❦ According to the US Army's Center of Military History, in 1810 the National salute was established by the War Dept as the number of states in the Union (then 17), and was required to be made by all military installations on Independence Day, at 1pm. In 1818, US Navy regulations designated a 21-gun salute for any Presidential visit to a ship (at the time the number of states numbered 21). In 1842, the Presidential salute was established at 21 guns, and in 1875, the US formally adopted the international convention of saluting foreign vessels with 21 guns. In 1890, the National salute was designated as 21 guns, and the Independence Day salute was renamed the Salute to the Union and designated as equal to the number of states in the Union. ❦ Nowadays, military protocol surrounding military salutes is carefully gradated. For example, Presidents, former Presidents, Presidents-elect, and foreign royalty or heads of state all receive 21 guns; the Vice President receives 19 guns, as do Cabinet members, Prime Ministers, and Premiers. Chairmen of Congressional Committees receive 17, and Consuls accredited to the US receive 11.

---

† The *Oxford Companion* states, 'odd numbers were chosen for salutes because even numbers were always fired at naval funerals as a sign of mourning for the dead officer'. Virgil declared that 'odd numbers please the gods', and in *The Merry Wives of Windsor*, Shakespeare wrote, 'they say there is divinity in odde Numbers, either in nativity, chance, or death'. ‡ The significance of the 21 is much debated. It has been mooted that it was the product of multiplying the Sacraments (7) by the Trinity (3), and in America there is some discussion of a link to the Declaration of Independence (1+7+7+6=21).

PRESIDENTIAL ESTATES

Some of the notable homes and estates inhabited by various American presidents:

President	estate name	state	notable features
Washington	Mt Vernon	VA	*c.8,000 acres, whiskey distillery*
Adams	Peacefield	MA	*orchards, 14,000-volume library*
Jefferson	Monticello	VA	*5,000 acres, plantation, octagonal dome*
Madison	Montpelier	VA	*forests, cemeteries, 'Madison Temple'*
Monroe	Highland	VA	*plantation, boxwood garden*
Jackson	The Hermitage	TN	*c.1,120 acres, cotton plantation, springs*
Van Buren	Lindenwald	NY	*linden groves, intricate woodwork*
Harrison	Grouseland	IN	*walnut grove, 13 fireplaces*
Tyler	Sherwood Forest	VA	*1,600 acres, longest frame house in US*
Buchanan	Wheatland	PA	*wheat fields, smokehouse, icehouse*
Hayes	Spiegel Grove	OH	*31 rooms, 12,000-volume library*
Garfield	Lawnfield	OH	*windmill, granary, chicken coop*
Cleveland	Westland Mansion	NJ	*billiard room, marble mantelpieces*
Roosevelt	Sagamore Hill	NY	*23 rooms, tennis court*
FDR	Springwood	NY	*forestry experiments, stuffed bird collection*
Eisenhower	Eisenhower Farm	PA	*putting green, skeet range, barbecue*
JFK	Hyannisport	MA	*waterfront, theater, swimming pool*
LBJ	Johnson Ranch	TX	*2,700 acres, 'showcase ranch'*
Nixon	La Casa Pacifica	CA	*swimming pool, security wall*
Ford	Rancho Mirage	CA	*bordered Thunderbird Country Club*
Reagan	Rancho del Cielo	CA	*adobe house, overlooking Pacific*
Bush Sr.	Walker's Point	ME	*oceanfront, stone cottages, tennis courts*
Bush Jr.	Prairie Chapel Ranch	TX	*native limestone, solar panels, 7 canyons*

PRESIDENTIAL & CONGRESSIONAL AWARDS

Some of the Presidential and Congressional awards bestowed in 2007 and 2008:

CONGRESSIONAL GOLD MEDAL
to Dr Michael Ellis DeBakey
to Aung San Suu Kyi

MEDAL OF HONOR
to Lt Michael P. Murphy
to MSG Woodrow W. Keeble
to Navy Seal MA Michael A. Monsoor
to Spc. Ross McGinnis

PRESIDENTIAL MEDAL OF FREEDOM
to Gary S. Becker, Dr Oscar Elias
Biscet, Dr Francis S. Collins,
Benjamin L. Hooks,

Rep. Henry J. Hyde, Brian P. Lamb,
Harper Lee, and Ellen Johnson Sirleaf

and to Benjamin S. Carson Sr, Anthony S. Fauci, Tom Lantos, General
Peter Pace, Donna Edna Shalala, and
Laurence H. Silberman

The President also awards the Enrico Fermi
Award, Presidential Citizens Medal, President's
Award for Distinguished Federal Civilian
Service, Presidential Award for Excellence in
Mathematics and Science Teaching, Preserve
America Presidential Awards, &c.

―――――――――――CITIZENSHIP OATH―――――――――――

The Oath of Allegiance is taken by those who wish to become naturalized citizens of the United States of America. According to USCIS, 'it is not until an applicant takes the Oath of Allegiance that he or she actually becomes a citizen'. The oath must be taken at a public ceremony and a signed copy must be submitted to the government. Taking the oath acknowledges a willingness to 'support and defend the Constitution and the laws of the US', and a willingness to serve in the army, vote, pay taxes, serve on a jury, and 'abide by the will of the majority and support the US government'.

I hereby declare, on oath, that I absolutely and entirely renounce and abjure all allegiance and fidelity to any foreign prince, potentate, state, or sovereignty of whom or which I have heretofore been a subject or citizen; that I will support and defend the Constitution and laws of the United States of America against all enemies, foreign and domestic; that I will bear true faith and allegiance to the same; that I will bear arms on behalf of the United States when required by the law; that I will perform noncombatant service in the Armed Forces of the United States when required by the law; that I will perform work of national importance under civilian direction when required by the law; and that I take this obligation freely without any mental reservation or purpose of evasion; so help me God.

Applicants who can demonstrate that their religious beliefs prohibit army service may omit the relevant clauses. Additionally, those whose religious beliefs or conscience interfere with the words 'on oath' or 'so help me God' may use the words 'solemnly affirm' or omit the passage concerning God. Those with foreign orders or titles of nobility must renounce them during the oath-taking ceremony.

―――――――――SECESSION MOVEMENTS OF NOTE―――――――――

When Norman Mailer died in November 2007 [see p.57], many obituaries recalled that in 1969 he ran for New York City mayor on a platform that called for the city to secede from the state. Currently, several states have secessionist groups driven by assorted concerns. Below are some of the movements to break away from the US:

Second Vermont Republic	*(mostly) leftist group that seeks to reclaim Vermont's 1777–91 status as an independent republic*
League of the South	*secessionist group that views the South as its own nation*
Cascadia	*term for a proposed country formed from (usually) British Columbia, Washington, Oregon, and based on ecological and cultural similarities*
Atlantica	*hypothetical Atlantic US and Canada zone of economic integration*
Alaskan Independence Party	*libertarians calling for Alaskan secession*
Hawaiian Sovereignty movement	*diverse collection of groups calling for Hawaiian self-determination; some see US as occupying force*
Californians for Independence	*calls for 'Californian solutions to Californian problems'; one of many groups calling for California to secede*
Republic of New Hampshire	*leftist group calling for the state to leave the US*
Republic of Texas	*disputes 1845 annexation of Texas; one of several groups calling for Texan nationhood*

─────────────── LIBRARY OF CONGRESS ───────────────

The Library of Congress, on Capitol Hill in Washington, DC, was established in 1800 as a reference library for members of Congress. The original bill creating the library, signed by President John Adams, merely called for 'such books as may be necessary for the use of Congress – and for putting up a suitable apartment for containing them therein'. Today the Library of Congress is the largest library in the world (according to *Guinness World Records* [and see p.167]), and it currently holds:

> 32m books & other printed materials, 2·8m recordings, 12·5m photographs
> 5·3m maps, 5·5m music items, 59·5m manuscripts, 530 miles of bookshelves
> >700,000 rare books, the papers of 23 presidents ... 134m items total

The Library, which is open to the public for research, receives 22,000 items each workday and adds 10,000 a day to its own collection (the rest are distributed to other libraries). According to a rule known as 'Mandatory Deposit' [section 407 of title 17 of the United States Code], all publishers must submit to the library within three months of publication two copies of any work under copyright protection that is published or distributed within the US. Since 1962, the Library has maintained overseas offices in New Delhi, Cairo, Rio de Janeiro, Jakarta, Nairobi, and Islamabad, to acquire, catalog, and preserve materials not otherwise available.

A 2007 review of the Library of Congress general collection found that 17% of materials requested could not be found. Officials said they did not believe the materials were lost, but simply misplaced. Subsequent review reduced the total to 13%, but lawmakers still called the news 'deeply troubling'.

─────────────── METONYMIC PLACES ───────────────

A metonym is a figure of speech in which a word or phrase is substituted for another concept with which it is associated. Metonyms often take the form of nouns used as symbols for broader concepts, such as 'crown' for 'monarchy'. In the United States, a variety of places have come to serve as metonyms for various aspects of the nation:

What	*where*	*stands for ...*
K Street	Washington, DC	lobbying
Wall Street	New York City	finance
Madison Avenue	New York City	advertising
Hollywood [see p.160]	California	film industry
Nashville	Tennessee	country music
Capitol Hill	Washington, DC	Congress
Broadway	New York City	theater
The White House	Washington, DC	the President
The Pentagon	Washington, DC	the Department of Defense
Washington	Washington, DC	federal politics
Detroit	Michigan	auto industry
Silicon Valley	California	computer industry
Houston	Texas	NASA ('Houston, we have a problem')

——————————— US TIME ZONES ———————————

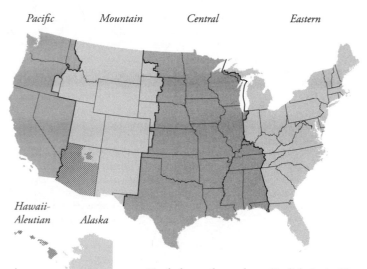

| *Pacific* | *Mountain* | *Central* | *Eastern* |

*Hawaii-
Aleutian*   *Alaska*

Hatched areas do not observe Daylight Saving Time
[Adapted from *The National Atlas*]

± hours from UTC	DST	Standard
Atlantic	–3	–4
Eastern	–4	–5
Central	–5	–6
Mountain	–6	–7
Pacific	–7	–8
Alaska	–8	–9
Hawaii-Aleutian	–9	–10
Samoa†	NA	–11
Chamorro‡	NA	+10

Coordinated Universal Time (UTC or just UT) is an international time standard essentially identical to good old-fashioned Greenwich Mean Time (GMT). † Samoa Standard Time Zone includes that part of the US that is between 169°30W – 172°30W, but does not include any part of Hawaii or Alaska. ‡ The 9th US Time Zone was established by Congress in December 2000, for Guam and the Northern Marianas west of the International Date Line. The Chamorro Time Zone, named after the region's indigenous people, is 14 hours ahead of Eastern Standard Time.

Daylight Saving Time (DST) is not observed in Hawaii, American Samoa, Guam, Puerto Rico, the Virgin Islands, or the state of Arizona, with the exception of the Navajo Indian Reservation, which does observe DST. (Indiana adopted DST in 2006; 18 counties use Central Daylight Time, and 74 Eastern Daylight Time.) The Energy Policy Act of 2005 extended DST for one month so that, where it is observed in the United States, it will start and end on the following days:

DST *begins* *at 2am*	year [Spring forward, Fall back]	DST *ends* *at 2am*
Mar 8	2009	Nov 1
Mar 14	2010	Nov 7
Mar 13	2011	Nov 6
Mar 11	2012	Nov 4
Mar 10	2013	Nov 3
Mar 9	2014	Nov 2
Mar 8	2015	Nov 1
Mar 13	2016	Nov 6

─────── AVERAGE US MONTHLY TEMPERATURES ───────

	avg. temp	± avg. C20 temp			
Sept 2007	...67·5°F	...........+2·1°F	Feb.	..............34·9	.... +0·2
Oct	.............56·9	.... +2·1	March	..........42·0	.... −0·4
Nov	.............44·1	.... +1·6	April	.............51·0	.... −1·0
Dec	.............33·6	.... +0·2	May	.............60·3	.... −0·7
Jan 2008	.......30·5	.... −0·3	June	.............70·4	.... +1·1
			July	.............74·9	.... +0·7

─────── 2009 HURRICANE NAMES ───────

The National Hurricane Center began naming storms in 1953, after identification by latitude and longitude proved clumsy. (Female names were used until 1979, when male names were added following charges of sexism.) Six lists of names, maintained by the World Meteorological Organization (WMO), are used in rotation (i.e., the 2009 list will be reused in 2015), although storm names are sometimes retired†. Below are the names to be used in the 2009 Atlantic hurricane season:

Ana	Grace	Mindy	Teresa
Bill	Henri	Nicholas	Victor
Claudette	Ida	Odette	Wanda
Danny	Joaquin	Peter	
Erika	Kate	Rose	[Source: National
Fred	Larry	Sam	Weather Service]

† The names given to particularly damaging storms are thereafter permanently retired and replaced with a new name beginning with the same letter. Since 2000, the WMO has retired: Keith [2000]; Allison, Iris, Michelle [2001]; Isidore, Lili [2002]; Fabian, Isabel, Juan [2003]; Charley, Frances, Ivan, Jeanne [2004]; Dennis, Katrina, Rita, Stan, Wilma [2005]; and Dean, Felix, Noel [2007].

─────── SOME WINDS OF NOTE ───────

Blue Norther or Blue Whistler .. Texas cold front (*Blue Darter, Blue Blizzard* in Oklahoma)
Chinook...................................dry, warm, westerly wind from the Rockies
Diablo ....hot, dry, northeasterly wind from the San Francisco Bay Area
Kona....................................stormy, rainy, southwesterly wind in Hawaii
Matanuska.................. strong, northeasterly winter wind near Palmer, Alaska
Mauka............................. cool, light wind from the mountains in Hawaii
Nor'easter...........storm with heavy, northeasterly winds along the Atlantic coast
Santa Ana ..strong, dry wind blowing from canyons to the coast in SW California
Sou'easter......................................any strong, southeasterly wind or gale
Sundowner.......... warming, late-afternoon downslope winds near Santa Barbara
Taku ....strong, north-northeasterly wind near Juneau, Alaska

Iran is home to a northwesterly wind called the *Sansar*, which reportedly translates as 'the icy wind of death'. The *Bad-I-Sad-O-Bist-Roz* also affects the region from June onwards, and can last 120 days.

─────────────── DISASTER DECLARATIONS ───────────────

When a disaster occurs, the US President may declare either a federal 'Emergency' or 'Major Disaster'. Such declarations are made only after an appeal has been received from a governor, who has determined that the disaster has outstripped the state's resources. The process leading to a federal disaster declaration is outlined below:

1. Local governments respond to the disaster with volunteer agencies &c.

2. If necessary, the local government turns to the state, which may mobilize the National Guard and state agencies.

3. A preliminary damage assessment (PDA) is conducted by state and federal officials. Based on the damage assessment, the governor may request a declaration of Emergency or Major Disaster from the President. (In severe

cases, the damage assessment may occur after the request.)

4. The Federal Emergency Management Agency (FEMA) evaluates the request and the type of assistance necessary.

5. Based on FEMA's recommendation, the President declares an Emergency or Major Disaster. While both activate federal funds and assistance, a 'Major Disaster' declaration also initiates long-term federal recovery programs.

Notable disasters of the year included the tornadoes across the Southern US on February 5–6, 2008, which killed 55; the floods that stretched from TX to PA March 17–19, which killed 13; the tornadoes that hit MS, OK, and GA on May 11, which killed *c*.20; and the major June flooding in MS.

─────────────── US HOMELAND SECURITY STATUS ───────────────

In response to the terrorist outrages of September 11, 2001, President George W. Bush created the Department of Homeland Security to 'anticipate, pre-empt and deter' terrorist and other threats. The Department employs a five-point, color-coded Security Advisory System to indicate the perceived level of risk – the higher the 'threat condition', the greater the risk of an attack in probability and severity:

Threat	*color*	GUARDED..........Blue	HIGH............Orange
LOW..............Green		ELEVATED.......Yellow	SEVERE............Red

The threat condition was established at YELLOW; since then its changes have been:

Period	*shift*	*cause*
09·10·02–09·24·02	yellow–orange	*1st anniversary of the September 11 attacks*
02·07·03–02·27·03	yellow–orange	*the time of the Muslim Hajj*
03·17·03–04·16·03	yellow–orange	*start of allied military attacks on Iraq*
05·20·03–05·30·03	yellow–orange	*intelligence reports of potential attacks*
12·21·03–01·09·04	yellow–orange	*intelligence reports of holiday season attacks*
08·01·04–11·10·04	yellow–orange	*specific warning for East Coast financial areas*
07·07·05–08·12·05	yellow–orange	*specific mass-transit warning after London bombs*
08·10·06–	yellow–orange (& briefly red)	*specific shift for the airline industry*

—— DEPARTMENT OF DEFENSE UNIFIED COMMANDS ——

The US Department of Defense maintains five regional Unified Combatant Commands (COCOMs), which are together responsible for 'military-to-military and security relationships' across the globe. Each COCOM is led by a Combatant Commander, who exercises authority over all US military forces in the region and reports directly to the Secretary of Defense. The most recently established Command is the US Africa Command (AFRICOM), which was projected to become fully operational in October 2008. The regional Unified Commands as of 2007:

PACOM · *established* 1947
Area of responsibility · The Asia-Pacific region, including Hawaii and Alaska, also China, Russia, India, &c.
Mission · 'Promotes security and peaceful development in the Asia-Pacific region by deterring aggression, advancing regional security cooperation, responding to crises, and fighting to win'
Commander · Adm. Timothy Keating
Location · Camp H.M. Smith, HI

CENTCOM · *established* 1983
Area of responsibility · Egypt and most of the Middle East
Mission · 'Conducts operations to attack, disrupt and defeat terrorism, deter and defeat adversaries, deny access to WMD, assure regional access, strengthen regional stability', &c.
Commander
General David H. Petraeus
Location · MacDill Air Force Base, FL

SOUTHCOM · *established* 1947
Area of responsibility · Central and S America, the Caribbean (except US commonwealths, territories, and possessions), Cuba and the Bahamas, Panama Canal
Mission · 'Conduct military operations and promote security cooperation to achieve US strategic objectives'
Commander
Admiral James G. Stavridis
Location · Miami, FL

NORTHCOM · *established* 2002
Area of responsibility · Continental US, Canada, Mexico, and waters to *c.*500 nautical miles; air/land/sea approaches
Mission · 'Anticipates and conducts Homeland Defense and Civil Support operations within the assigned area of responsibility to defend, protect, and secure the US and its interests'
Commander · General Gene Renuart
Location · Peterson Air Force Base, Colorado Springs, CO

EUCOM · *established* 1952
Area of responsibility · All of Europe, parts of the Middle East
Mission · 'Maintain ready forces to conduct the full range of operations unilaterally or in concert with coalition partners; enhance transatlantic security through support of NATO; promote regional stability; counter terrorism; and advance US interests in the area of responsibility'
Commander · Gen. Bantz J. Craddock
Location · Stuttgart, Germany

AFRICOM · *announced* 2007
Area of responsibility · The African continent, minus Egypt
Mission · AFRICOM will work closely with the AU and African nations on security cooperation, and 'continue developing capabilities of African nations to help solidify our relations'
Commander
Gen. William E. 'Kip' Ward
Temp. location · Stuttgart, Germany

[Source: Dept of Defense]

───── AMERICAN WAR STATISTICS (1775–1991) ─────

AMERICAN REVOLUTION (1775–83)
Total US service members 217,000
Battle deaths 4,435
Non-mortal woundings.......... 6,188

WAR OF 1812 (1812–15)
Total US service members 286,730
Battle deaths 2,260
Non-mortal woundings.......... 4,505

INDIAN WARS (c.1817–98)
Total US service members 106,000
Battle deaths 1,000

MEXICAN WAR (1846–48)
Total US service members 78,718
Battle deaths 1,733
Other deaths in service 11,550
Non-mortal woundings.......... 4,152

CIVIL WAR (1861–65)
Union
Total US service members .. 2,213,363
Battle deaths 140,414
Other deaths in service 224,097
Non-mortal woundings....... 281,881
Confederate
Total service members 1,500,000
Battle deaths 74,524
Other deaths in service† 59,297
Non-mortal woundings...... unknown

[† *Does not include 26,000–31,000*
who died in Union prisons]

SPANISH-AMERICAN WAR (1898–1902)
Total US service members ,,,, 306,760
Battle deaths 385
Non-theater deaths in service.... 2,061
Non-mortal woundings.......... 1,662

WORLD WAR I (1917–18)
Total US service members .. 4,734,991
Battle deaths 53,402
Non-theater deaths in service...63,114
Non-mortal woundings....... 204,002
Living veterans 1

WORLD WAR II (1941–45)
Total US service members .16,112,566
Battle deaths 291,557
Non-theater deaths in service. 113,842
Non-mortal woundings....... 671,846
Living veterans 2,498,000

KOREAN WAR (1950–53)
Total US service members .. 5,720,000
Battle deaths 33,741
Other deaths (in theater) 2,833
Non-theater deaths in service...17,672
Non-mortal woundings....... 103,284
Living veterans 2,400,000

VIETNAM WAR (1964–75)
Total US service members .. 8,744,000
Deployed to SE Asia........ 3,403,000
Battle deaths 47,424
Other deaths (in theater) 10,785
Non-theater deaths in service...32,000
Non-mortal woundings....... 153,303
Living veterans 7,203,600

DESERT SHIELD/STORM (1990–91)
Total US service members .. 2,322,000
Deployed to Gulf 694,550
Battle deaths 147
Other deaths (in theater) 235
Non-theater deaths in service.... 1,590
Non-mortal woundings........... 467
Living veterans 2,269,000

AMERICA'S WARS TOTAL (1775–1991)
Wartime military service...41,891,368
Battle deaths 651,022
Other deaths (in theater) 308,797
Non-theater deaths in service. 230,279
Non-mortal woundings..... 1,431,290
Living war veterans 17,484,000
Living veterans (periods of war & peace) ...
23,532,000

As of May 2008. For casualty statistics from the
Global War on Terror see pp.20–21.
[Sources: Depts of Defense & Veterans Affairs]

——— NATO MILITARY SPENDING & FORCES ———

[Source: NATO]

(Iceland has no forces)

	Defense spending (% of GDP)		Effective annual strength of armed forces (No., % of labor force)				
	1985–89 (average)	2007	1985	1990	1995	2000	2007
Belgium	2·7	1·1	107k (2·8%)	106k (2·7%)	47k (1·2%)	42k (1·0%)	39k (0·9%)
Bulgaria	NA	2·3	NA	NA	NA	NA	41k (1·6%)
Canada	2·1	1·3	83k (0·9%)	87k (0·9%)	70k (0·7%)	59k (0·5%)	65k (0·5%)
Czech Republic	NA	1·6	NA	NA	NA	52k (1·4%)	25k (0·7%)
Denmark	2·0	1·3	29k (1·4%)	31k (1·4%)	27k (1·3%)	24k (1·1%)	18k (0·8%)
Estonia	NA	1·6	NA	NA	NA	NA	5k (1·0%)
France	3·7	2·4	560k (2·7%)	548k (2·6%)	502k (2·3%)	394k (1·8%)	354k (1·6%)
Germany	3·0	1·3	495k (2·3%)	545k (2·5%)	352k (1·3%)	319k (1·0%)	247k (0·7%)
Greece	5·1	2·8	201k (6·1%)	201k (5·7%)	213k (5·7%)	205k (5·1%)	142k (3·4%)
Hungary	NA	1·1	NA	NA	NA	50k (1·5%)	20k (0·6%)
Italy	2·2	1·8	504k (2·5%)	493k (2·4%)	435k (2·2%)	381k (1·8%)	298k (1·3%)
Latvia	NA	1·7	NA	NA	NA	NA	6k (0·5%)
Lithuania	NA	1·2	NA	NA	NA	NA	10k (0·8%)
Luxembourg	0·8	0·7	1·2k (0·9%)	1·3k (0·9%)	1·3k (0·9%)	1·4k (0·8%)	1·6k (0·8%)
Netherlands	2·7	1·5	103k (2·0%)	104k (1·8%)	67k (1·2%)	52k (0·9%)	51k (0·7%)
Norway	2·9	1·4	36k (2·3%)	51k (2·9%)	38k (2·3%)	32k (1·8%)	20k (1·0%)
Poland	NA	1·9	NA	NA	NA	191k (1·5%)	150k (1·2%)
Portugal	2·5	1·5	102k (2·6%)	87k (2·1%)	78k (1·8%)	68k (1·5%)	41k (0·9%)
Romania	NA	1·9	NA	NA	NA	NA	76k (1·0%)
Russian Federation	NA	?	NA	NA	?	?	?
Slovak Republic	NA	1·7	NA	NA	NA	NA	18k (0·9%)
Slovenia	NA	1·6	NA	NA	NA	NA	7k (0·8%)
Spain	2·1	1·2	314k (2·7%)	263k (2·1%)	210k (1·6%)	144k (1·1%)	132k (0·8%)
Turkey	3·3	2·7	814k (4·7%)	769k (4·0%)	805k (3·8%)	793k (3·6%)	496k (2·2%)
United Kingdom	4·5	2·3	334k (1·9%)	308k (1·7%)	233k (1·3%)	218k (1·1%)	190k (0·9%)
United States	6·0	4·0	2,244k (2·9%)	2,181k (2·6%)	1,620k (1·9%)	1,483 (1·5%)	1,346k (1·4%)

US MILITARY RANKS

PAY	ARMY	NAVY & COAST GUARD†	MARINES	AIR FORCE	Number
O-11‡	General of the Army	Fleet Admiral	—	General of the Air Force	—
O-10	General	Admiral	General	General	40
O-9	Lieutenant General	Vice Admiral	Lieutenant General	Lieutenant General	130
O-8	Major General	Rear Admiral (Upper Half)	Major General	Major General	284
O-7	Brigadier General	Rear Admiral (Lower Half)	Brigadier General	Brigadier General	446
O-6	Colonel	Captain	Colonel	Colonel	11,447
O-5	Lieutenant Colonel	Commander	Lieutenant Colonel	Lieutenant Colonel	28,404
O-4	Major	Lieutenant Commander	Major	Major	45,086
O-3	Captain	Lieutenant	Captain	Captain	69,032
O-2	First Lieutenant	Lieutenant Junior Grade	First Lieutenant	First Lieutenant	26,328
O-1	Second Lieutenant	Ensign	Second Lieutenant	Second Lieutenant	22,928
W-5	Chief Warrant Officer	Chief Warrant Officer	Chief Warrant Officer	—	599
W-4	Chief Warrant Officer	Chief Warrant Officer	Chief Warrant Officer	—	2,815
W-3	Chief Warrant Officer	Chief Warrant Officer	Chief Warrant Officer	—	4,683
W-2	Chief Warrant Officer	Chief Warrant Officer	Chief Warrant Officer	—	5,572
W-1	Warrant Officer	Chief Warrant Officer	Warrant Officer	—	3,461
E-9	Sgt Major of the Army	MCPO of the Navy	Sgt Major of the Marine Corps	Ch. Master Sgt of the Air Force	10,669
E-9	Command Sgt Major/Sgt Major	Fleet/Command MCPO	Sgt Major/Master Gunnery Sgt	Command Chief Master Sgt	↑
E-9		Master Chief Petty Officer		Chief Master Sgt/First Sgt	↑
E-8	First Sgt/Master Sgt	Senior Chief Petty Officer	First Sgt/Master Sgt	Senior Master Sgt/First Sgt	27,042
E-7	Sgt First Class/Platoon Sgt	Chief Petty Officer	Gunnery Sergeant	Master Sgt/First Sgt	97,788
E-6	Staff Sergeant	Petty Officer First Class	Staff Sergeant	Technical Sergeant	168,619
E-5	Sergeant	Petty Officer Second Class	Sergeant	Staff Sergeant	245,116
E-4	Corporal/Specialist	Petty Officer Third Class	Corporal	Senior Airman	255,821
E-3	Private First Class	Seaman	Lance Corporal	Airman First Class	196,803
E-2	Private	Seaman Apprentice	Private First Class	Airman	82,347
E-1	Private	Seaman Recruit	Private	Airman Basic	49,064

† The US Coast Guard is a part of the Dept of Transportation in peacetime and the Navy in times of war. Coast Guard ranks are essentially the same as Navy ranks. ‡ Reserved for wartime only. · Numbers are Active Duty Military Personnel as of 04-30-2007. [Source: Department of Defense] Within the O-10 rank, each service has a Chief of Staff or Commandant.

———FOREIGN TERRORIST ORGANIZATIONS———

In accordance with section 219 of the US Immigration and Nationality Act, the Secretary of State may designate certain groups Foreign Terrorist Organizations (FTOs). FTOs are defined as foreign organizations that engage in terrorism or terrorist activity (or that have the 'capability and intent' to engage in such activities), and whose terrorist activities threaten national security. For FTO designation purposes:

Terrorism is defined as 'premeditated, politically motivated violence perpetrated against noncombatant targets by subnational groups or clandestine agents'. *Terrorist activity* is defined as unlawful activity involving 'highjacking or sabotage of any conveyance'; hostage-taking; 'a violent attack upon an internationally protected person'; an assassination; use of biological, chemical, or nuclear weapons; use of other weapons 'other than for mere personal monetary gain'; the 'threat, attempt, or conspiracy to do any of the foregoing'. (Activities such as fund-raising for a terrorist group may also be problematic; see state.gov.)

Once an organization has been defined as an FTO by the State Department, it is illegal for anyone subject to US jurisdiction to knowingly provide the group with 'material support or resources'. FTO members who are aliens may not enter the US, and in some cases may be removed. In addition, US financial institutions must retain control over any FTO funds they may possess, and report the funds to the Treasury Dept. The active FTOs listed in the 2007 *Country Reports on Terrorism* are:

Abu Sayyaf Group [ASG] · Formed in 1990s; seeks an Islamic state in parts of the Southern Philippines.

Ansar al-Islam [AS] · Sunni jihadist group in Iraq. Wants to expel Coalition forces and establish Islamic state.

Al-Aqsa Martyrs Brigade · Cells of Palestinian militants loyal to Fatah.

Armed Islamic Group [GIA] · Aims to overthrow Algerian regime and replace it with a fundamentalist Islamic state.

Asbat al-Ansar · Lebanon-based Sunni group with ties to al-Qaeda.

Aum Shinrikyo [Aum/Aleph] · Japanese doomsday cult, responsible for 1995 Tokyo sarin gas attack.

Basque Fatherland & Liberty [ETA] · Aims to establish independent Basque homeland based on Marxist principles.

Communist Party of Philippines/New People's Army [CPP/NPA] · Maoist group formed in 1969; aims to overthrow government using guerrilla warfare.

Continuity Irish Republican Army [CIRA] · Splinter group formed 1994 as armed wing of Republican Sinn Fein.

Gama'a al-Islamiyya [IG] · Egypt's largest militant group, active since 1970s.

Islamic Resistance Movement [HAMAS] · Formed at onset of the first Palestinian Intifada in 1987.

Harakat ul-Mujahedin [HUM] · Islamic militant group operating in Kashmir.

Hezbollah · Lebanon-based radical Shia group formed after Israeli invasion of Lebanon in 1982; allied with Iran.

———FOREIGN TERRORIST ORGANIZATIONS cont.———

Islamic Jihad Group [IJG] · Calls for an Islamic government in Uzbekistan.

Islamic Movement of Uzbekistan [IMU] · Islamic militants from Central Asian states allied with al-Qaeda.

Jaish-e-Mohammed [JEM] · Group aims to unite Kashmir with Pakistan, and has declared war against the US.

Jemaah Islamiya Organization [JI] · Seeks the establishment of an Islamic caliphate across Southeast Asia.

Kahane Chai [Kach] · Israeli group that seeks to restore biblical state of Israel.

Kongra-Gel [KGK/PKK] · Turkish Kurds, originally Marxist-Leninist separatists.

Lashkar e-Tayyiba [LT] · Fights in Kashmir against India.

Lashkar i Jhangvi [LJ] · Focuses on anti-Shia attacks in Pakistan; linked to the murder of journalist Daniel Pearl.

Liberation Tigers of Tamil Eelam [LTTE] · Tamil secessionist group in Sri Lanka.

Libyan Islamic Fighting Group [LIFG] · Targets Libyan interests; has tried to assassinate President Gadhafi four times.

Moroccan Islamic Combatant Group [GICM] · Calls for Moroccan Islamic state; operates in W Europe diasporas.

Mujahedin-e Khalq Organization [MEK] · 'Cult-like' group blend of Marxism, Islam, and feminism; seeks overthrow of Iranian regime.

National Liberation Army [ELN] · Colombian Marxist insurgent group

formed in 1965, inspired by Fidel Castro and Che Guevara.

Palestinian Islamic Jihad [PIJ] · Formed In Gaza Strip in 1970s; seeks destruction of Israel.

Popular Front for the Liberation of Palestine [PFLP] · Marxist-Leninists focused on struggle against Western imperialism. (Splinter groups include *PFLP–GC* and *Palestine Liberation Front*).

Al-Qaeda · Established by Osama bin Ladin in 1988. Goal is to overthrow all 'non-Islamic' regimes.

Al-Qaeda in Iraq [AQI] · Largest terrorist group in Iraq. Targets Coalition forces and Shia civilians.

Al-Qaeda in the Islamic Maghreb [AQIM] · Mission is to overthrow Algerian government and install Islamic regime.

Real IRA [RIRA] · Dedicated to removing British forces from N Ireland.

Revolutionary Armed Forces of Colombia [FARC] · Latin America's oldest and largest insurgency; nominally Marxist.

Revolutionary Organization 17 November · Radical leftists that seek to sever Greek ties to the EU and NATO. *Revolutionary Nuclei* is a similar group.

Revolutionary People's Liberation Party/ Front [DHKP/C] · Anti-US and NATO; wants to a create socialist Turkish state.

Shining Path [SL] · Militant Peruvian Maoists; calls for a peasant revolutionary regime; has ties to drug trafficking.

List does not include currently inactive groups.

The States

The metaphor of the melting pot is unfortunate and misleading. A more accurate analogy would be a salad bowl, for, though the salad is an entity, the lettuce can still be distinguished from the chicory, the tomatoes from the cabbage.
— CARL N. DEGLER, *Out of Our Past*, 1970

─────────── INDUSTRIES OF THE STATES ───────────

Many states have illustrious agricultural and industrial histories now forgotten. In 1896, the almanac A Perpetual Calendar, *by L.S.F Pinaud, named each state's top products:*

ALABAMA ranks fourth in *cotton*. ❦ ARIZONA ranks second in *silver*. ❦ CALIFORNIA ranks first in *barley, grape culture, sheep, gold,* and *quicksilver*. ❦ COLORADO ranks first in *silver*. ❦ CONNECTICUT ranks first in *clocks*. ❦ DELAWARE is way up in *peaches*. ❦ DAKOTA is the finest *wheat-growing* state. ❦ FLORIDA ranks third in *sugar* and *molasses*. ❦ GEORGIA ranks second in *rice* and *sweet potatoes*. ❦ INDIANA ranks second in *wheat*. ❦ ILLINOIS ranks first in *oats, meat packing, lumber traffic, malt* and *distilled liquors,* and *miles of railway*. ❦ IOWA ranks first in average *intelligence* of population, first in production of *cord,* and first in number of *swine*. ❦ IDAHO ranks sixth in *gold* and *silver*. ❦ KANSAS ranks fifth in *cattle, corn,* and *rye*. ❦ KENTUCKY ranks first in *tobacco* and has a worldwide reputation for *thoroughbred horses* and *cattle*. ❦ LOUISIANA ranks first in *sugar* and *molasses*. ❦ MAINE ranks first in *ship building, slate* and *granite* quarries, *lumbering,* and *fishing*. ❦ MARYLAND ranks fourth in *coal*. ❦ MASSACHUSETTS ranks first in *cotton, woolen,* and *worsted* goods, and in *cod* and *mackerel* fisheries. ❦ MICHIGAN ranks first in *copper, lumber,* and *salt*. ❦ MINNESOTA ranks fourth in *wheat* and *barley*. ❦ MISSISSIPPI ranks second in *cotton*. ❦ MISSOURI ranks first in *mules*. ❦ MONTANA ranks fifth in *silver* and *gold*. ❦ NEW MEXICO's *grazing facilities* can't be beat. ❦ NEBRASKA has abundant crops of *rye, buckwheat, barley, flax,* and *hemp*. ❦ NEVADA ranks second in *gold*. ❦ NEW HAMPSHIRE ranks third in the manufacture of *cotton goods*. ❦ NEW JERSEY ranks first in *fertilizing marl*†, *zinc,* and *silk* goods. ❦ NEW YORK ranks first in the *value of manufactures, soap, printing* and *publishing, hops, hay, potatoes, buckwheat,* and *milch cows*‡. ❦ NORTH CAROLINA ranks first in *tar* and *turpentine*. ❦ OHIO ranks first in *agricultural implements* and *wool*. ❦ OREGON takes the palm for *cattle raising*. ❦ PENNSYLVANIA ranks first in *rye, iron, steel, petroleum,* and *coal*. ❦ RHODE ISLAND, in proportion to its size, outranks all other states in *value of manufactures*. ❦ SOUTH CAROLINA ranks first in *phosphates*. ❦ TENNESSEE ranks second in *peanuts*. ❦ TEXAS ranks second in *cattle* and *cotton*. ❦ UTAH ranks third in *silver*. ❦ VERMONT ranks fourth in *copper*. ❦ VIRGINIA ranks first in *peanuts*. ❦ WEST VIRGINIA ranks fifth in *salt* and *coal*. ❦ WISCONSIN ranks second in *hops*.

† A mixture of clay and calcium carbonate that was once prized for its ability to correct soil acidity. ‡ A milk cow. 'Milch' now refers to a dairy animal, though the term once denoted any domestic animal.

THE UNITED STATES

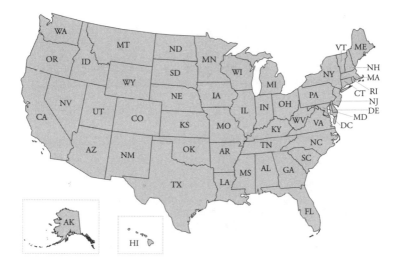

KEY TO TABLES OVERLEAF

Overleaf are a range of tables designed to allow comparisons to be made between the various states and, where relevant, Washington, DC, and the USA as a whole. A degree of debate and dispute surrounds a number of entries, and data sources are the most recent at the time of writing. Below is a key to some entries:

Land area	US Census Bureau
Racial & ethnic breakdown	2000 · US Census Bureau
Resident population	July 2007 · US Census Bureau
Unemployment rate	% of civilian labor force · 2005 · US Bureau of Labor Statistics
Home ownership rate	% of owner households · 2005 · US Census Bureau
Persons below poverty line	2005 · US Census Bureau
Average annual pay	2005 · US Bureau of Labor Statistics
Violent crime	per 100,000 population · 2005 · FBI
Infant mortality rate	deaths of infants <1/1,000 live births · 2005 · US NCHS
Doctors	per 100,000 resident population · 2004 · American Medical Association
Traffic fatalities	per 100 million vehicle miles · 2004 · US NHSTA
Energy consumption	million BTUs per person · 2003 · US Energy Information Admin
Mobile homes	% of total housing units · 2005 · US Census Bureau
Degree	persons ≥25 with a bachelor's degree or higher · 2005 · US Census Bureau
Highway miles	miles of functional roads (interstate–local) · 2003 · US Fed. Highway Admin
Geographic center & highest & lowest points	US Geographic Survey
Morgan Quitno state rankings	2008 · morganquitno.com (with thanks)
Temperatures	December 2003 · National Oceanic and Atmospheric Administration (NOAA)

———— STATES · MAPS, CAPITALS, ADMISSION, &c. ————

California · CA
155,959 sq mi
Sacramento
31st State on
9·9·1850

Georgia · GA
57,906 sq mi
Atlanta
4th State on
1·2·1788

Iowa · IA
55,869 sq mi
Des Moines
29th State on
12·28·1846

Maryland · MD
9,774 sq mi
Annapolis
7th State
on 4·28·1788

Missouri · MO
68,886 sq mi
Jefferson City
24th State on
8·10·1821

Arkansas · AR
52,068 sq mi
Little Rock
25th State on
6·15·1836

Florida · FL
53,927 sq mi
Tallahassee
27th State on
3·3·1845

Indiana · IN
35,867 sq mi
Indianapolis
19th State on
12·11·1816

Maine · ME
30,862 sq mi
Augusta
23rd State on
3·15·1820

Mississippi · MS
46,907 sq mi
Jackson
20th State on
12·10·1817

Arizona · AZ
113,635 sq mi
Phoenix
48th State on
2·14·1912

Delaware · DE
1,954 sq mi
Dover
1st State on
12·7·1787

Illinois · IL
55,584 sq mi
Springfield
21st State on
12·3·1818

Louisiana · LA
43,562 sq mi
Baton Rouge
18th State on
4·30·1812

Minnesota · MN
79,610 sq mi
St Paul
32nd State on
5·11·1858

Alaska · AK
571,951 sq mi
Juneau
49th State on
1·3·1959

Connecticut · CT
4,844 sq mi
Hartford
5th State on
1·9·1788

Idaho · ID
82,747 sq mi
Boise
43rd State on
7·3·1890

Kentucky · KY
39,728 sq mi
Frankfort
15th State
on 6·1·1792

Michigan · MI
56,804 sq mi
Lansing
26th State on
1·26·1837

Alabama · AL
50,744 sq mi
Montgomery
22nd State on
12·14·1819

Colorado · CO
103,717 sq mi
Denver
38th State on
8·1·1876

Hawaii · HI
6,423 sq mi
Honolulu
50th State on
8·21·1959

Kansas · KS
81,815 sq mi
Topeka
34th State on
1·29·1861

Massachusetts · MA
7,840 sq mi
Boston
6th State
on 2·6·1788

——— STATES · MAPS, CAPITALS, ADMISSION, &c. ———

Montana · MT 145,552 sq mi *Helena* 41st State on 11-8-1889	Nebraska · NE 76,872 sq mi *Lincoln* 37th State on 3-1-1867	Nevada · NV 109,826 sq mi *Carson City* 36th State on 10-31-1864	New Hampshire NH · 8,968 sq mi *Concord* 9th State on 6-21-1788	New Jersey · NJ 7,417 sq mi *Trenton* 3rd State on 12-18-1787
New Mexico · NM 121,356 sq mi *Santa Fe* 47th State on 1-6-1912	New York · NY 47,214 sq mi *Albany* 11th State on 7-26-1788	North Carolina · NC 48,711 sq mi *Raleigh* 12th State on 11-21-1789	North Dakota · ND 68,976 sq mi *Bismarck* 39th State on 11-2-1889	Ohio · OH 40,948 sq mi *Columbus* 17th State on 3-1-1803
Oklahoma · OK 68,667 sq mi *Oklahoma City* 46th State on 11-16-1907	Oregon · OR 95,997 sq mi *Salem* 33rd State on 2-14-1859	Pennsylvania · PA 44,817 sq mi *Harrisburg* 2nd State on 12-12-1787	Rhode Island · RI 1,045 sq mi *Providence* 13th State on 5-29-1790	South Carolina · SC 30,109 sq mi *Columbia* 8th State on 5-23-1788
South Dakota · SD 75,885 sq mi *Pierre* 40th State on 11-2-1889	Tennessee · TN 41,217 sq mi *Nashville* 16th State on 6-1-1796	Texas · TX 261,797 sq mi *Austin* 28th State on 12-29-1845	Utah · UT 82,144 sq mi *Salt Lake City* 45th State on 1-4-1896	Vermont · VT 9,250 sq mi *Montpelier* 14th State on 3-4-1791
Virginia · VA 39,594 sq mi *Richmond* 10th State on 6-25-1788	Washington · WA 66,544 sq mi *Olympia* 42nd State on 11-11-1889	West Virginia · WV 24,077 sq mi *Charleston* 35th State on 6-20-1863	Wisconsin · WI 54,310 sq mi *Madison* 30th State on 5-29-1848	Wyoming · WY 97,100 sq mi *Cheyenne* 44th State on 7-10-1890

——— STATES · RESIDENTS, SYMBOLS, &c. ———

State	Residents called	State tree	State flower	State bird	Abbreviation
Alabama	Alabamian, Alabama	Southern Longleaf Pine	Camellia	Yellowhammer	Ala.
Alaska	Alaskan	Sitka Spruce	Forget-me-not	Willow Ptarmigan	Alaska
Arizona	Arizonan, Arizonian	Palo Verde	Blossom of the Saguaro Cactus	Cactus Wren	Ariz.
Arkansas	Arkansan	Loblolly Pine	Apple Blossom	Mockingbird	Ark.
California	Californian	California Redwood	Golden Poppy	California Valley Quail	Calif.
Colorado	Coloradan, Coloradoan	Colorado Blue Spruce	Rocky Mountain Columbine	Lark Bunting	Colo.
Connecticut	Connecticuter, Nutmegger	White Oak	Mountain Laurel	American Robin	Conn.
Delaware	Delawarean	American Holly	Peach Blossom	Blue Hen Chicken	Del.
DC	Washingtonian	Scarlet Oak	American Beauty Rose	Wood Thrush	D.C.
Florida	Floridian, Floridan	Sabal Palm	Orange Blossom	Mockingbird	Fla.
Georgia	Georgian	Live Oak	Cherokee Rose	Brown Thrasher	Ga.
Hawaii	Hawaiian	Kukui or Candlenut	Native Yellow Hibiscus	Nene or Hawaiian Goose	Hawaii
Idaho	Idahoan	Western White Pine	Syringa	Mountain Bluebird	Idaho
Illinois	Illinoisan	White Oak	Purple Violet	Cardinal	Ill.
Indiana	Indianan, Indianian, Hoosier	Tulip Tree	Peony	Cardinal	Ind.
Iowa	Iowan	Oak	Wild Rose	Eastern Goldfinch	Iowa
Kansas	Kansan	Cottonwood	Native Sunflower	Western Meadowlark	Kans.
Kentucky	Kentuckian	Tulip Poplar	Goldenrod	Cardinal	Ky.
Louisiana	Louisianan, Louisianian	Bald Cypress	Magnolia	Eastern Brown Pelican	La.
Maine	Mainer	Eastern White Pine	White Pinecone and Tassel	Chickadee	Maine
Maryland	Marylander	White Oak	Black-eyed Susan	Baltimore Oriole	Md.
Massachusetts	Bay Stater	American Elm	Mayflower	Chickadee	Mass.
Michigan	Michigander(-ian), Michiganite	Eastern White Pine	Apple Blossom	Robin	Mich.
Minnesota	Minnesotan	Red or Norway Pine	Pink & White Lady's Slipper	Common Loon	Minn.
Mississippi	Mississippian	Magnolia	Magnolia	Mockingbird	Miss.
Missouri	Missourian	Flowering Dogwood	Hawthorn	Eastern Bluebird	Mo.

———STATES · RESIDENTS, SYMBOLS, &c.———

State	Residents called	State tree	State flower	State bird	Abbreviation
Montana	Montanan	Ponderosa Pine	Bitterroot	Western Meadowlark	Mont.
Nebraska	Nebraskan	Cottonwood	Goldenrod	Western Meadowlark	Nebr.
Nevada	Nevadan, Nevadian	Singleleaf Pinyon & Pine	Sagebrush	Mountain Bluebird	Nev.
New Hampshire	New Hampshirite	White Birch	Purple Lilac	Purple Finch	N.H.
New Jersey	New Jerseyite, New Jerseyan	Northern Red Oak	Purple Violet	Eastern Goldfinch	N.J.
New Mexico	New Mexican	Pinyon Pine / Piñon	Yucca	Roadrunner	N.Mex.
New York	New Yorker	Sugar Maple	Rose	Eastern Bluebird	N.Y.
North Carolina	North Carolinian	Longleaf Pine	Dogwood	Cardinal	N.C.
North Dakota	North Dakotan	American Elm	Wild Prarie Rose	Western Meadowlark	N.Dak.
Ohio	Ohioan	Buckeye	Scarlet Carnation	Cardinal	Ohio
Oklahoma	Oklahoman	Redbud	Mistletoe	Scissor-tailed Flycatcher	Okla.
Oregon	Oregonian	Douglas Fir	Oregon Grape	Western Meadowlark	Oreg.
Pennsylvania	Pennsylvanian	Eastern Hemlock	Mountain Laurel	Ruffed Grouse	Pa.
Rhode Island	Rhode Islander	Red Maple	Blue Violet	Rhode Island Red Hen	R.I.
South Carolina	South Carolinian	Sabel Palm / Palmetto Tree	Yellow Jessamine	Great Carolina Wren	S.C.
South Dakota	South Dakotan	Black Hills Spruce	Pasqueflower	Ring-necked Pheasant	S.Dak.
Tennessee	Tennessean, Tennesseean	Tulip Poplar	Iris	Mockingbird	Tenn.
Texas	Texan	Pecan	Bluebonnet	Mockingbird	Tex.
Utah	Utahan, Utahn	Blue Spruce	Sego Lily	California Seagull	Utah
Vermont	Vermonter	Sugar Maple	Red Clover	Hermit Thrush	Vt.
Virginia	Virginian	Flowering Dogwood	American Dogwood	Northern Cardinal	Va.
Washington	Washingtonian	Western Hemlock	Western Rhododendron	Willow Goldfinch	Wash.
West Virginia	West Virginian	Sugar Maple	Big Rhododendron	Cardinal	W.Va.
Wisconsin	Wisconsinite	Sugar Maple	Wood Violet	Robin	Wis.
Wyoming	Wyomingite	Plains Cottonwood	Indian Paintbrush	Western Meadowlark	Wyo.

STATES · NAME ORIGINS

Some of the (many) theories surrounding the names of each state:

Alabama · From a Choctaw word that can be translated to mean 'thicket cleaners', or 'plant reapers'. ❧ **Alaska** · Derived from the Aleut word *Alyeska*, often thought to mean 'great land'. Some linguists argue the term actually means 'mainland', or more precisely, 'the object toward which the action of the sea is directed'. ❧ **Arizona** · Possibly from the Papago for 'little spring', although some argue it is instead derived from the Spanish *arida* for dry and *zona* for area. ❧ **Arkansas** · Likely the French version of the Illinois tribe's name for the Quapaw Indians. ❧ **California** · Often linked to the 1510 novel *Las Sergas de Esplandián* by Garci Ordóñez de Montalvo. The book describes a mythical island called California, which was populated by black Amazons and ruled by the beautiful Queen Calafia. Some believe that explorers (who initially thought they had discovered an island) were inspired by the popular novel. ❧ **Colorado** · Said to come from the Spanish for 'red-colored', after the ruddy waters of the Colorado river.

❧ **Connecticut** · From the Mohican word *Quinnehukqut*, for 'long river' or 'beside the long tidal river'. ❧ **Delaware** · Named after Sir Thomas West, Lord de la Warr, first British Governor of the Colony of Virginia. ❧ **District of Columbia** · Named in honor of Christopher Columbus. ❧ **Florida** · After the Spanish Feast of the Flowers at Easter (*Pascua de Florida*), and named by Spanish explorer Ponce de León after he found the region on Easter Sunday. ❧ **Georgia** · For George II of England. ❧ **Hawaii** · The origin is unknown, although it may come from the islands' traditional discoverer Chief Hawaii Loa. ❧ **Idaho** · Some historians believe the name was invented by (unsuccessful) congressional hopeful George M. Willing, who (falsely) claimed the term was of Native American origin. ❧ **Illinois** · After the Native American tribe the Inini, which means 'perfect and accomplished men'. ❧ **Indiana** · Meaning 'land of the Indians'. ❧ **Iowa** · The French version of the Dakota name for a tribe in the region; believed by some to mean 'sleepy heads', 'snakes', 'dusty noses', or 'this is the place'. ❧ **Kansas** · From a Sioux word for

'people of the south wind'. ❧ **Kentucky** · From the Wyandot for 'land of tomorrow'. ❧ **Louisiana** · After 'La Louisianne', the name given by explorer Sieur de La Salle to the area, after Louis XIV. ❧ **Maine** · Named either to distinguish the mainland from the nearby islands, or in tribute to Charles I's wife, Queen Henrietta Maria, feudal proprietor of the French province of Mayne. ❧ **Maryland** · In honor of Queen Henrietta Maria (Queen Mary). Some argue the colony's Catholic founders also approved of the association with the Virgin Mary. ❧ **Massachusetts** · After the Massachusetts tribe; the word allegedly means 'large hill place'. ❧ **Michigan** · Some attribute the name's origin to the Chippewa word for 'clearing', others to a local word meaning 'great lake' or 'swimming turtle'. ❧ **Minnesota** · Named for the Minnesota River, after the Dakota words for 'milky water' or 'cloudy'; some translate the term as 'water reflecting cloudy skies'. ❧ **Mississippi** · From local Native American words that mean 'Father of Waters'. ❧ **Missouri** · Named for the Missouri River, which was named after the Missouri Indians; the term is said to mean

STATES · NAME ORIGINS

'those who have large canoes'. ✿ Montana · Possibly from the Latin word for 'mountainous'. ✿ Nebraska · From local words for 'flat or spreading water', in reference to the Platte and Nebraska rivers. ✿ Nevada · From *Sierra Nevada*, or 'snowy range' in Spanish. ✿ New Hampshire · Named after the English county of Hampshire. ✿ New Jersey · Named after the island of Jersey in the English Channel. ✿ New Mexico · New Mexico means 'place of Mexitli', an Aztec war god. The area was named *Nuevo Mexico* by early explorers who hoped to discover the same bounty they'd found in Mexico. ✿ New York · Named in honor of the brother of Charles II, the Duke of York and Albany. ✿ North Carolina · First named in honor of France's Charles IX and then England's Charles I and II; 'Carolina' is the feminized form of the Latin *Carolinus*, an adjective derived from Charles. North and South Carolina were one colony until 1729. ✿ North Dakota · Named for the Dakota tribal grouping, also called the Sioux. In the group's own language, 'dakota' means 'allies' or 'friends'. 'Sioux' is the French version of an Ojibway term meaning 'enemy'. ✿ Ohio · Named for the Ohio River; *oheo* is Iroquois for 'beautiful river' or 'great river'. ✿ Oklahoma · Allegedly suggested by Native American missionary Rev. Allen Wright, from Choctaw words meaning 'red person'. ✿ Oregon · Of greatly disputed origin. One theory attributes the name to the Spanish *orejon*, or 'big ear', used to describe several tribes in the region. Possibly also from the French word for 'hurricane' – Canadian fur traders may have once called Oregon's Columbia River the 'river of storms'. ✿ Pennsylvania · In honor of Adm. Sir William Penn, father of William Penn. *Sylvania* is Latin for 'woods', and therefore the name is thought to literally mean 'Penn's woods'. However, 'Penn' is also Welsh for 'head' or 'headland', and the name can also be translated as 'high woodlands'. ✿ Rhode Island · Possibly from the Dutch for 'red island', after the state's red clay shores. Also possibly for the Greek island of Rhodes. ✿ South Carolina · See North Carolina. ✿ South Dakota · See North Dakota. ✿ Tennessee · From the Cherokee name *Tanasi*, for a town on the Tennessee River; the meaning is unknown. ✿ Texas · Said by some to be the Caddo term for 'hello friend', which the Spanish used to describe friendly tribes throughout the region. Also said to be the Native Americanization of the Spanish *tejas*, or 'allies'. ✿ Utah · According to one theory, the name derives from the White Mountain Apache word for the Navaho, meaning 'one that is higher up'. Others say the name comes from the Ute tribe. ✿ Vermont · From the French for 'green mountain'. ✿ Virginia · In honor of Queen Elizabeth I, popularly known as the 'Virgin Queen'. ✿ Washington · Named in honor of George Washington. ✿ West Virginia · See Virginia. ✿ Wisconsin · Possibly from either the Chippewa word for 'grassy place' or the Ojibway word for 'gathering of the waters'. ✿ Wyoming · From Delaware words which may mean 'at the big flats' or 'large meadows'. ✿ *A great deal of dispute surrounds many of these entries.*

[Selected sources: State government websites (various); *Illustrated Dictionary of Place Names: US and Canada*, Keslie B. Harder, Ed.]

STATES · RACE & ETHNICITY

Race and Ethnicity 2000	State Population 2000	White alone, not Hispanic or Latino %	Hispanic or Latino (Any Race) %	2 or more races %	Other %	Hawaiian & Pacific Islands %	Asian %	American Indian & Alaskan Native %	Black & African American %	White %
Alabama	4,447,100	70.3	1.7	1.0	0.7	0.0	0.7	0.5	26.0	71.1
Alaska	626,932	67.6	4.1	5.4	1.6	0.5	4.0	15.6	3.5	69.3
Arizona	5,130,632	63.8	25.3	2.9	11.6	0.1	1.8	5.0	3.1	75.5
Arkansas	2,673,400	78.6	3.2	1.3	1.5	0.1	0.8	0.7	15.7	80.0
California	33,871,648	46.7	32.4	4.7	16.8	0.3	10.9	1.0	6.7	59.5
Colorado	4,301,261	74.5	17.1	2.8	7.2	0.1	2.2	1.0	3.8	82.8
Connecticut	3,405,565	77.5	9.4	2.2	4.3	0.0	2.4	0.3	9.1	81.6
Delaware	783,600	72.5	4.8	1.7	2.0	0.0	2.1	0.3	19.2	74.6
DC	572,059	27.8	7.9	2.4	3.8	0.1	2.7	0.3	60.0	30.8
Florida	15,982,378	65.4	16.8	2.4	3.0	0.1	1.7	0.3	14.6	78.0
Georgia	8,186,453	62.6	5.3	1.4	2.4	0.1	2.1	0.3	28.7	65.1
Hawaii	1,211,537	22.9	7.2	21.4	1.3	9.4	41.6	0.3	1.8	24.3
Idaho	1,293,953	88.0	7.9	2.0	4.2	0.1	0.9	1.4	0.4	91.0
Illinois	12,419,293	67.8	12.3	1.9	5.8	0.0	3.4	0.2	15.1	73.5
Indiana	6,080,485	85.8	3.5	1.2	1.6	0.0	1.0	0.3	8.4	87.5
Iowa	2,926,324	92.6	2.8	1.1	1.3	0.0	1.3	0.3	2.1	93.9
Kansas	2,688,418	83.1	7.0	2.1	3.4	0.0	1.7	0.9	5.7	86.1
Kentucky	4,041,769	89.3	1.5	1.1	0.6	0.0	0.7	0.2	7.3	90.1
Louisiana	4,468,976	62.5	2.4	1.1	0.7	0.0	1.2	0.6	32.5	63.9
Maine	1,274,923	96.5	0.7	1.0	0.2	0.0	0.7	0.6	0.5	96.9
Maryland	5,296,486	62.1	4.3	2.0	1.8	0.0	4.0	0.3	27.9	64.0
Massachusetts	6,349,097	81.9	6.8	2.3	3.7	0.0	3.8	0.2	5.4	84.5
Michigan	9,938,444	78.6	3.3	1.9	1.3	0.0	1.8	0.6	14.2	80.2
Minnesota	4,919,479	88.2	2.9	1.7	1.3	0.0	2.9	1.1	3.5	89.4
Mississippi	2,844,658	60.7	1.4	0.7	0.5	0.0	0.7	0.4	36.3	61.4
Missouri	5,595,211	83.8	2.1	1.5	0.8	0.1	1.1	0.4	11.2	84.9

STATES · RACE & ETHNICITY

Race and Ethnicity 2000	White %	Black & African American %	American Indian & Alaskan Native %	Asian %	Hawaiian & Pacific Islands %	Other %	2 or more races %	Hispanic or Latino (Any Race) %	White alone, not Hispanic or Latino %	State Population 2000
Montana	90.6	0.3	6.2	0.5	0.1	0.6	1.7	2.0	89.5	902,195
Nebraska	89.6	4.0	0.9	1.3	0.0	2.8	1.4	5.5	87.3	1,711,263
Nevada	75.2	6.8	1.3	4.5	0.4	8.0	3.8	19.7	65.2	1,998,257
New Hampshire	96.0	0.7	0.2	1.3	0.0	0.6	1.1	1.7	95.1	1,235,786
New Jersey	72.6	13.6	0.2	5.7	0.0	5.4	2.5	13.3	66.0	8,414,350
New Mexico	66.8	1.9	9.5	1.1	0.1	17.0	3.6	42.1	44.7	1,819,046
New York	67.9	15.9	0.4	5.5	0.0	7.1	3.1	15.1	62.0	18,976,457
North Carolina	72.1	21.6	1.2	1.4	0.0	2.3	1.3	4.7	70.2	8,049,313
North Dakota	92.4	0.6	4.9	0.6	0.0	0.4	1.2	1.2	91.7	642,200
Ohio	85.0	11.5	0.2	1.2	0.0	0.8	1.4	1.9	84.0	11,353,140
Oklahoma	76.2	7.6	7.9	1.4	0.1	2.4	4.5	5.2	74.1	3,450,654
Oregon	86.6	1.6	1.3	3.0	0.2	4.2	3.1	8.0	83.5	3,421,399
Pennsylvania	85.4	10.0	0.1	1.8	0.0	1.5	1.2	3.2	84.1	12,281,054
Rhode Island	85.0	4.5	0.5	2.3	0.1	5.0	2.7	8.7	81.9	1,048,319
South Carolina	67.2	29.5	0.3	0.9	0.0	1.0	1.0	2.4	66.1	4,012,012
South Dakota	88.7	0.6	8.3	0.6	0.0	0.5	1.3	1.4	88.0	754,844
Tennessee	80.2	16.4	0.3	1.0	0.0	1.0	1.1	2.2	79.2	5,689,283
Texas	71.0	11.5	0.6	2.7	0.1	11.7	2.5	32.0	52.4	20,851,820
Utah	89.2	0.8	1.3	1.7	0.7	4.2	2.1	9.0	85.3	2,233,169
Vermont	96.8	0.5	0.4	0.9	0.0	0.2	1.2	0.9	96.2	608,827
Virginia	72.3	19.6	0.3	3.7	0.1	2.0	2.0	4.7	70.2	7,078,515
Washington	81.8	3.2	1.6	5.5	0.4	3.9	3.6	7.5	78.9	5,894,121
West Virginia	95.0	3.2	0.2	0.5	0.0	0.2	0.9	0.7	94.6	1,808,344
Wisconsin	88.9	5.7	0.9	1.7	0.0	1.6	1.2	3.6	87.3	5,363,675
Wyoming	92.1	0.8	2.3	0.6	0.1	2.5	1.8	6.4	88.9	493,782
USA	75.1	12.3	0.9	3.6	0.1	5.5	2.4	12.5	69.1	281,421,906

——— STATES · SOCIAL INDICATORS ———

State (& rank)	Resident population		Unemployment %		Home ownership %		% of people below the poverty line		Av. annual pay ($)		Violent crime rate per 100,000 pop.	
Alabama	4,627,851	23rd	4·0	38th	76·6	3rd	17·0	7th	34,598	31st	432	22nd
Alaska	683,478	47th	6·8	3rd	66·0	43rd	11·2	33rd	40,216	15th	632	7th
Arizona	6,338,755	16th	4·7	29th	71·1	27th	14·2	15th	38,154	21st	513	16th
Arkansas	2,834,797	32nd	4·9	25th	69·2	37th	17·2	6th	31,266	45th	528	13th
California	36,553,215	1st	5·4	12th	59·7	49th	13·3	20th	46,211	5th	526	14th
Colorado	4,861,515	22nd	5·0	20th	71·0	29th	11·1	35th	41,601	10th	397	24th
Connecticut	3,502,309	29th	4·9	25th	70·5	32nd	8·3	48th	52,954	1st	275	37th
Delaware	864,764	45th	4·2	35th	75·8	6th	10·4	39th	44,622	6th	632	6th
DC	588,292	–	6·5	–	45·8	–	19·0	–	66,696	–	1,459	–
Florida	18,251,243	4th	3·8	42nd	72·4	20th	12·8	24th	36,800	23rd	708	3rd
Georgia	9,544,750	9th	5·3	15th	67·9	41st	14·4	13th	39,096	18th	449	20th
Hawaii	1,283,388	42nd	2·8	50th	59·8	48th	9·8	44th	36,353	25th	255	41st
Idaho	1,499,402	39th	3·8	42nd	74·2	8th	13·9	17th	30,777	46th	257	40th
Illinois	12,852,548	5th	5·7	9th	70·9	30th	12·0	28th	43,744	8th	552	11th
Indiana	6,345,289	15th	5·4	12th	75·0	7th	12·2	27th	35,431	30th	324	29th
Iowa	2,988,046	30th	4·6	31st	73·9	11th	10·9	37th	33,070	38th	291	31st
Kansas	2,775,997	33rd	5·1	19th	69·5	36th	11·7	31st	33,864	34th	387	25th
Kentucky	4,241,474	26th	6·1	6th	71·6	23rd	16·8	8th	33,965	33rd	267	39th
Louisiana	4,293,204	25th	7·1	2nd	72·5	19th	19·8	2nd	33,566	35th	594	9th
Maine	1,317,207	40th	4·8	27th	73·9	11th	12·6	25th	32,701	40th	112	49th
Maryland	5,618,344	19th	4·1	36th	71·2	25th	8·2	49th	44,368	7th	703	4th
Massachusetts	6,449,755	14th	4·8	27th	63·4	45th	10·3	40th	50,095	3rd	457	19th
Michigan	10,071,822	8th	6·7	5th	76·4	5th	13·2	22nd	41,214	11th	552	10th
Minnesota	5,197,621	21st	4·0	38th	76·5	4th	9·2	46th	40,800	12th	297	30th
Mississippi	2,918,785	31st	7·9	1st	78·8	2nd	21·3	1st	29,763	48th	278	36th
Missouri	5,878,415	18th	5·4	12th	72·3	22nd	13·3	20th	35,951	26th	525	15th

STATES · SOCIAL INDICATORS

State (& rank)	Resident population		Unemployment %		Home ownership %		% of people below the poverty line		Av. annual pay ($)		Violent crime rate per 100,000 pop.	
Montana	957,861	44th	4.0	38th	70.4	33rd	14.4	13th	29,150	49th	282	35th
Nebraska	1,774,571	38th	3.8	42nd	70.2	34th	10.9	37th	32,422	42nd	287	32nd
Nevada	2,565,382	35th	4.1	36th	63.4	45th	11.1	35th	38,763	19th	607	8th
New Hampshire	1,315,828	41st	3.6	45th	74.0	10th	7.5	50th	40,551	14th	132	47th
New Jersey	8,685,920	11th	4.4	32nd	70.1	35th	8.7	47th	49,471	4th	355	26th
New Mexico	1,969,915	36th	5.3	15th	71.4	24th	18.5	3rd	32,605	41st	702	5th
New York	19,297,729	3rd	5.0	20th	55.9	50th	13.8	18th	51,937	2nd	446	21st
North Carolina	9,061,032	10th	5.2	18th	70.9	30th	15.1	12th	35,912	27th	468	18th
North Dakota	639,715	48th	3.4	49th	68.5	38th	11.2	33rd	29,956	47th	98	50th
Ohio	11,466,917	7th	5.9	8th	73.3	15th	13.0	23rd	37,333	22nd	351	27th
Oklahoma	3,617,316	23rd	4.4	32nd	72.9	17th	16.5	9th	31,721	43rd	509	17th
Oregon	3,747,455	27th	6.1	6th	68.2	40th	14.1	16th	36,588	24th	287	33rd
Pennsylvania	12,432,792	6th	5.0	20th	73.3	15th	11.9	29th	39,661	17th	425	23rd
Rhode Island	1,057,832	43rd	5.0	20th	63.1	47th	12.3	26th	38,751	20th	251	42nd
South Carolina	4,407,709	24th	6.8	3rd	73.9	11th	15.6	10th	32,927	39th	761	1st
South Dakota	796,214	46th	3.9	41st	68.4	39th	13.6	19th	29,149	50th	176	46th
Tennessee	6,156,719	17th	5.6	10th	72.4	20th	15.5	11th	35,879	28th	753	2nd
Texas	23,904,380	2nd	5.3	15th	65.9	44th	17.6	5th	40,150	16th	530	12th
Utah	2,645,330	34th	4.3	34th	73.9	11th	10.2	41st	33,328	36th	227	45th
Vermont	621,254	49th	3.5	47th	74.2	8th	11.5	32nd	34,197	32nd	120	48th
Virginia	7,712,091	12th	3.5	47th	71.2	25th	10.0	43rd	42,287	9th	283	34th
Washington	6,468,424	13th	5.5	11th	67.6	42nd	11.9	29th	40,721	13th	346	28th
West Virginia	1,812,035	37th	5.0	20th	81.3	1st	18.0	4th	31,347	44th	273	38th
Wisconsin	5,601,640	20th	4.7	29th	71.1	27th	10.2	41st	35,471	29th	242	43rd
Wyoming	522,830	50th	3.6	45th	72.8	18th	9.5	45th	33,251	37th	230	44th
USA	301,621,157	–	5.1	–	68.9	–	13.3	–	40,677	–	469	–

──────── STATES · SOCIAL INDICATORS ────────

State (& rank)	Infant mortality rate		Doctors per 100,000 resident population		Traffic fatalities per 100m vehicle miles		Energy consumption million BTU/person		Mobile homes as % of all housing units		% of >25s with a BA or higher	
Alabama	9.4	4th	213	40th	1·95	13th	447	8th	14·6	7th	19·8	46th
Alaska	5.9	37th	222	34th	2·02	10th	1,175	1st	5·6	33rd	28·7	19th
Arizona	6.9	24th	208	43rd	2·01	12th	246	47th	12·1	12th	27·9	20th
Arkansas	7.9	14th	203	44th	2·22	3rd	416	11th	13·3	8th	17·5	49th
California	5.3	43rd	259	20th	1·25	35th	229	48th	4·1	40th	30·4	12th
Colorado	6.4	33rd	258	21st	1·45	24th	297	36th	4·8	34th	35·4	5th
Connecticut	5.8	39th	363	4th	0·92	49th	255	41st	0·9	48th	36·9	1st
Delaware	9.0	5th	248	24th	1·44	26th	383	18th	11·2	13th	25·6	26th
DC	14·1	–	798	–	1·15	–	329	–	0·0	–	46·7	–
Florida	7.2	22nd	245	25th	1·65	18th	252	43rd	10·5	16th	25·5	27th
Georgia	8.2	9th	220	37th	1·45	24th	343	25th	10·5	16th	26·9	23rd
Hawaii	6.5	31st	310	7th	1·46	23rd	248	45th	0·2	50th	30·6	11th
Idaho	6.1	35th	169	50th	1·77	15th	341	26th	10·8	14th	25·9	24th
Illinois	7.4	17th	272	11th	1·24	37th	310	34th	3·1	43rd	29·5	16th
Indiana	8.0	12th	213	39th	1·30	31st	470	6th	5·9	30th	22·5	42nd
Iowa	5.3	44th	187	46th	1·24	37th	400	15th	4·4	37th	24·5	36th
Kansas	7.4	18th	220	36th	1·58	21st	410	13th	5·7	32nd	30·4	12th
Kentucky	6.6	27th	230	31st	2·04	6th	456	7th	12·7	10th	19·0	48th
Louisiana	10·1	2nd	264	15th	2·03	9th	822	3rd	12·5	11th	19·7	47th
Maine	6.9	25th	267	13th	1·30	31st	366	20th	9·6	20th	24·2	37th
Maryland	7.3	19th	411	2nd	1·16	41st	281	40th	1·8	45th	36·3	3rd
Massachusetts	5.2	47th	450	1st	0·87	50th	248	46th	0·9	48th	36·8	2nd
Michigan	7.9	13th	240	27th	1·12	43rd	313	33rd	6·2	29th	24·6	35th
Minnesota	5.1	48th	281	10th	1·00	46th	355	21st	4·0	42nd	34·3	7th
Mississippi	11·4	1st	181	48th	2·28	1st	411	12th	15·7	3rd	21·9	44th
Missouri	7.5	15th	239	29th	1·64	19th	322	29th	7·5	26th	24·9	34th

STATES · SOCIAL INDICATORS

State (& rank)	Infant mortality rate		Doctors per 100,000 resident population		Traffic fatalities per 100m vehicle miles		Energy consumption million BTU/person		Mobile homes as % of all housing units		% of >25s with a BA or higher	
Montana	7.0	23rd	221	35th	2.04	6th	410	14th	12.9	9th	25.4	28th
Nebraska	5.6	42nd	239	30th	1.32	28th	372	19th	4.5	35th	25.1	31st
Nevada	5.8	41st	186	47th	2.04	6th	292	39th	7.4	27th	23.5	40th
New Hampshire	5.3	45th	260	19th	1.29	33rd	254	42nd	6.5	28th	32.8	8th
New Jersey	5.2	46th	306	8th	1.00	46th	298	35th	1.0	47th	36.3	3rd
New Mexico	6.1	34th	240	28th	2.18	4th	353	22nd	17.8	2nd	27.2	21st
New York	5.8	40th	389	3rd	1.08	44th	220	49th	2.6	44th	30.3	14th
North Carolina	8.8	7th	253	23rd	1.62	20th	314	32nd	15.5	4th	25.4	28th
North Dakota	6.0	36th	242	26th	1.32	28th	624	4th	9.0	22nd	27.2	21st
Ohio	8.3	8th	261	18th	1.15	42nd	349	23rd	4.3	38th	22.9	41st
Oklahoma	8.1	11th	171	49th	1.67	17th	425	10th	9.7	19th	24.0	39th
Oregon	5.9	38th	263	16th	1.28	34th	295	38th	9.6	20th	25.1	18th
Pennsylvania	7.3	20th	294	9th	1.38	27th	321	30th	4.5	35th	25.8	25th
Rhode Island	6.5	32nd	351	6th	0.98	48th	212	50th	1.4	46th	29.2	17th
South Carolina	9.4	3rd	230	32nd	2.11	5th	389	16th	18.5	1st	24.2	37th
South Dakota	7.2	21st	219	38th	2.24	2nd	345	24th	10.6	15th	25.1	31st
Tennessee	8.9	6th	261	17th	1.82	14th	388	17th	10.5	16th	21.6	45th
Texas	6.6	29th	212	41st	1.55	22nd	560	5th	7.9	23rd	25.4	28th
Utah	4.5	50th	209	42nd	1.20	39th	296	37th	4.3	38th	29.8	15th
Vermont	6.5	30th	352	5th	1.25	35th	252	44th	7.6	25th	34.4	6th
Virginia	7.5	16th	270	12th	1.17	40th	329	28th	5.9	30th	30.7	10th
Washington	5.1	49th	265	14th	1.01	45th	316	31st	7.8	24th	30.9	9th
West Virginia	8.1	0th	229	33rd	2.02	10th	433	9th	15.4	5th	15.1	50th
Wisconsin	6.6	28th	254	22nd	1.31	30th	335	27th	4.1	40th	25.1	31st
Wyoming	6.8	26th	188	45th	1.77	15th	919	2nd	14.8	6th	22.0	43rd
USA	6.9	–	266	–	1.44	–	339	–	7.0	–	27.5	–

——————————STATES · CENTER & ELEVATIONS——————————

State	Geographic center	Highest elevation	feet (')	Lowest elevation	feet (')	difference (')
Alabama	12 mi SW of Clanton	Cheaha Mountain	2,407	Gulf of Mexico	0	2,407
Alaska	60 mi NW of Mount McKinley	Mount McKinley (Denali)	20,320	Pacific Ocean	0	20,320
Arizona	55 mi ESE of Prescott	Humphreys Peak	12,633	Colorado River	70	12,563
Arkansas	12 mi NW of Little Rock	Magazine Mountain	2,753	Ouachita River	55	2,698
California	38 mi E of Madera	Mount Whitney	14,494	Death Valley	-282	14,776
Colorado	30 mi NW of Pikes Peak	Mount Elbert	14,433	Arikaree River	3,315	11,118
Connecticut	East Berlin in Hartford County	Mount Frissell	2,380	Long Island Sound	0	2,380
Delaware	11 mi S of Dover	Ebright Road	448	Atlantic Ocean	0	448
Florida	12 mi NNW of Brooksville	Britton Hill	345	Atlantic Ocean	0	345
Georgia	18 mi SE of Macon	Brasstown Bald	4,784	Atlantic Ocean	0	4,784
Hawaii	20°15' N 156°20' W, off Maui Island	Pu'u Wekiu	13,796	Pacific Ocean	0	13,796
Idaho	At Custer, SW of Challis	Borah Peak	12,662	Snake River	710	11,952
Illinois	28 mi NE of Springfield	Charles Mound	1,235	Mississippi River	279	956
Indiana	14 mi NNW of Indianapolis	Hoosier Hill	1,257	Ohio River	320	937
Iowa	5 mi NE of Ames	Hawkeye Point	1,670	Mississippi River	480	1,190
Kansas	15 mi NE of Great Bend	Mount Sunflower	4,039	Verdigris River	679	3,360
Kentucky	3 mi NNW of Lebanon	Black Mountain	4,145	Mississippi River	257	3,888
Louisiana	3 mi SE of Marksville	Driskill Mountain	535	New Orleans	-8	543
Maine	18 mi N of Dover	Mount Katahdin	5,268	Atlantic Ocean	0	5,268
Maryland	4½ mi NW of Davidsonville	Hoye Crest	3,360	Atlantic Ocean	0	3,360
Massachusetts	North part of City of Worcester	Mount Greylock	3,491	Atlantic Ocean	0	3,491
Michigan	5 mi NNW of Cadillac	Mount Arvon	1,979	Lake Erie	571	1,408
Minnesota	10 mi SW of Brainerd	Eagle Mountain	2,301	Lake Superior	601	1,700
Mississippi	9 mi WNW of Carthage	Woodall Mountain	806	Gulf of Mexico	0	806
Missouri	20 mi SW of Jefferson City	Taum Sauk Mountain	1,772	Saint Francis River	230	1,542

STATES · CENTER & ELEVATIONS

State	Geographic center	Highest elevation	feet (')	Lowest elevation	feet (')	difference (')
Montana	11 mi W of Lewistown	Granite Peak	12,799	Kootenai River	1,800	10,999
Nebraska	10 mi NW of Broken Bow	Panorama Point	5,424	Missouri River	840	4,584
Nevada	26 mi SE of Austin	Boundary Peak	13,140	Colorado River	479	12,661
New Hampshire	3 mi E of Ashland	Mount Washington	6,288	Atlantic Ocean	0	6,288
New Jersey	5 mi SE of Trenton	High Point	1,803	Atlantic Ocean	0	1,803
New Mexico	12 mi SSW of Willard	Wheeler Peak	13,161	Red Bluff Reservoir	2,842	10,319
New York	12 mi S of Oneida; 26 mi SW of Utica	Mount Marcy	5,344	Atlantic Ocean	0	5,344
North Carolina	10 mi NW of Sanford	Mount Mitchell	6,684	Atlantic Ocean	0	6,684
North Dakota	5 mi SW of McClusky	White Butte	3,506	Red River	750	2,756
Ohio	25 mi NNE of Columbus	Campbell Hill	1,550	Ohio River	455	1,095
Oklahoma	8 mi N of Oklahoma City	Black Mesa	4,973	Little River	289	4,684
Oregon	25 mi SSE of Prineville	Mount Hood	11,239	Pacific Ocean	0	11,239
Pennsylvania	2½ mi SW of Bellefonte	Mount Davis	3,213	Delaware River	0	3,213
Rhode Island	1 mile SSW of Crompton	Jerimoth Hill	812	Atlantic Ocean	0	812
South Carolina	13 mi SE of Columbia	Sassafras Mountain	3,560	Atlantic Ocean	0	3,560
South Dakota	8 mi NE of Pierre	Harney Peak	7,242	Big Stone Lake	966	6,276
Tennessee	5 mi NE of Murfreesboro	Clingmans Dome	6,643	Mississippi River	178	6,465
Texas	15 mi NE of Brady	Guadalupe Peak	8,749	Gulf of Mexico	0	8,749
Utah	3 mi N of Manti	Kings Peak	13,528	Beaver Dam Wash	2,000	11,528
Vermont	3 mi E of Roxbury	Mount Mansfield	4,393	Lake Champlain	95	4,298
Virginia	5 mi SW of Buckingham	Mount Rogers	5,729	Atlantic Ocean	0	5,729
Washington	10 mi WSW of Wenatchee	Mount Rainier	14,411	Pacific Ocean	0	14,411
West Virginia	4 mi E of Sutton	Spruce Knob	4,863	Potomac River	240	4,623
Wisconsin	9 mi SE of Marshfield	Timms Hill	1,951	Lake Michigan	579	1,372
Wyoming	58 mi ENE of Lander	Gannett Peak	13,804	Belle Fourche River	3,099	10,705

—— STATES · RANKINGS & TEMPERATURES ——

State	2008 Morgan Quitno State Rankings (morganquitno.com)				Record State Temperatures				
	Safest	Healthiest	Dangerous	Livable	Highest	recorded at	Lowest	recorded at	difference
Alabama	36th	42nd	15th	44th	112°F	Centerville	-27°F	New Market	139°F
Alaska	43rd	38th	8th	29th	100°F	Fort Yukon	-80°F	Prospect Creek Camp	180°F
Arizona	46th	40th	5th	36th	128°F	Lake Havasu City	-40°F	Hawley Lake	168°F
Arkansas	40th	37th	11th	46th	120°F	Ozark	-29°F	Pond	149°F
California	38th	17th	13th	30th	134°F	Greenland Ranch	-45°F	Boca	179°F
Colorado	26th	29th	25th	14th	118°F	Bennett	-61°F	Maybell	179°F
Connecticut	11th	11th	40th	11th	106°F	Danbury	-32°F	Coventry	138°F
Delaware	39th	41st	12th	27th	110°F	Millsboro	-17°F	Millsboro	127°F
Florida	42nd	46th	9th	28th	109°F	Monticello	-2°F	Tallahassee	111°F
Georgia	32nd	45th	19th	40th	112°F	Greenville	-17°F	CCC Camp F-16	129°F
Hawaii	23rd	8th	28th	21st	100°F	Pahala	12°F	Mauna Kea Obs 111.2	88°F
Idaho	9th	23rd	42nd	9th	118°F	Orofino	-60°F	Island Park Dam	178°F
Illinois	30th	33rd	21st	26th	117°F	East St Louis	-36°F	Congerville	153°F
Indiana	25th	27th	26th	30th	116°F	Collegeville	-36°F	New Whiteland	152°F
Iowa	8th	6th	43rd	5th	118°F	Keokuk	-47°F	Elkader	165°F
Kansas	27th	15th	24th	17th	121°F	Alton (near)	-40°F	Lebanon	161°F
Kentucky	18th	32nd	33rd	48th	114°F	Greensburg	-37°F	Shelbyville	151°F
Louisiana	49th	49th	2nd	45th	114°F	Plain Dealing	-16°F	Minden	130°F
Maine	2nd	4th	49th	20th	105°F	North Bridgton	-48°F	Van Buren	153°F
Maryland	44th	35th	7th	16th	109°F	Cumberland & Frederick	-40°F	Oakland	149°F
Massachusetts	22nd	5th	29th	13th	107°F	New Bedford & Chester	-35°F	Chester	142°F
Michigan	41st	22nd	10th	38th	112°F	Mio	-51°F	Vanderbilt	163°F
Minnesota	17th	1st	34th	4th	114°F	Moorhead	-60°F	Tower	174°F
Mississippi	28th	50th	23rd	50th	115°F	Holly Springs	-19°F	Corinth	134°F
Missouri	33rd	34th	18th	39th	118°F	Warsaw & Union	-40°F	Warsaw	158°F

STATES · RANKINGS & TEMPERATURES

State	2008 Morgan Quitno State Rankings (morganquitno.com)				Record State Temperatures				
	Safest	Healthiest	Dangerous	Livable	Highest	recorded at	Lowest	recorded at	difference
Montana	7th	25th	44th	19th	117°F	Medicine Lake	-70°F	Rogers Pass	187°F
Nebraska	16th	7th	35th	6th	118°F	Minden	-47°F	Oshkosh	165°F
Nevada	50th	47th	1st	35th	125°F	Laughlin	-50°F	San Jacinto	175°F
New Hampshire	1st	2nd	50th	1st	106°F	Nashua	-47°F	Mt Washington	153°F
New Jersey	20th	16th	31st	7th	110°F	Runyon	-34°F	River Vale	144°F
New Mexico	48th	48th	3rd	33rd	122°F	Waste Isolation Pilot Plant	-50°F	Gavilan	172°F
New York	19th	30th	32nd	24th	108°F	Troy	-52°F	Old Forge	160°F
North Carolina	35th	31st	16th	42nd	110°F	Fayetteville	-34°F	Mt Mitchell	144°F
North Dakota	3rd	9th	48th	10th	121°F	Steele	-60°F	Parshall	181°F
Ohio	29th	21st	22nd	40th	113°F	Gallipolis (near)	-39°F	Milligan	152°F
Oklahoma	34th	43rd	17th	32nd	120°F	Tipton	-27°F	Watts	147°F
Oregon	21st	19th	30th	22nd	119°F	Pendleton	-54°F	Seneca	173°F
Pennsylvania	24th	18th	27th	34th	111°F	Phoenixville	-42°F	Smethport	153°F
Rhode Island	12th	10th	39th	25th	104°F	Providence	-25°F	Greene	129°F
South Carolina	47th	44th	4th	49th	111°F	Camden	-19°F	Caesars Head	130°F
South Dakota	5th	24th	46th	15th	120°F	Gannvalley	-58°F	McIntosh	178°F
Tennessee	45th	36th	6th	47th	113°F	Perryville	-32°F	Mountain City	145°F
Texas	37th	39th	14th	37th	120°F	Monahans	-23°F	Seminole	143°F
Utah	13th	12th	38th	2nd	117°F	Saint George	-69°F	Peter's Sink	186°F
Vermont	4th	3rd	47th	8th	105°F	Vernon	-50°F	Bloomfield	155°F
Virginia	15th	20th	36th	12th	110°F	Balcony Falls	-30°F	Mtn. Lake Bio. Stn	140°F
Washington	31st	13th	20th	18th	118°F	Ice Harbor Dam	-48°F	Mazama & Winthrop	166°F
West Virginia	14th	26th	37th	43rd	112°F	Martinsburg	-37°F	Lewisburg	149°F
Wisconsin	10th	14th	41st	23rd	114°F	Wisconsin Dells	-55°F	Couderay	169°F
Wyoming	6th	28th	45th	3rd	115°F	Basin	-66°F	Riverside R.S.	181°F

Government

*Too bad all the people who know how to run the country
are busy driving cabs and cutting hair.*
— GEORGE BURNS (1896–1996)

————GEORGE WALKER BUSH · 43rd PRESIDENT————

Sworn into office: January 20, 2001 & January 20, 2005 · *Party*: Republican
Born: July 6, 1946, New Haven, Connecticut · *Professed religion*: Methodist
Yale University (graduated 1968) & Harvard University Business School (graduated 1975)
Served as 46th Governor of Texas 1994–2000
Marriage: November 5, 1977, to Laura Welch (born November 4, 1946, in Midland, Texas)
Children: twins Barbara (1981–), Jenna (1981–)
Pets: Barney & Miss Beazley (dogs); India 'Willie' Bush (cat); Ofelia (cow)

Medical exam	2001	2002	2003	2004	2005	2006	2007
Weight (lbs)	189.75	189.0	194.0	199.6	191.6	196.0	192.0
Blood pressure	118/74	106/70	110/62	110/60	110/64	108/68	117/71

————THE CABINET & CABINET RANKING MEMBERS————

Vice President	Richard B. Cheney
Secretary of State	Condoleezza Rice
Secretary of the Treasury	Henry M. Paulson Jr
Secretary of Defense	Robert M. Gates
Attorney General	Michael B. Mukasey
Secretary of the Interior	Dirk Kempthorne
Secretary of Agriculture	Edward Schafer
Secretary of Commerce	Carlos M. Gutierrez
Secretary of Labor	Elaine Chao
Secretary of Health & Human Services	Michael O. Leavitt
Secretary of Housing & Urban Development	Steven Preston
Secretary of Transportation	Mary E. Peters
Secretary of Energy	Samuel W. Bodman
Secretary of Education	Margaret L. Spellings
Secretary of Veterans Affairs	Dr James Peake
Secretary of Homeland Security	Michael Chertoff
Administrator, Environmental Protection Agency	Stephen Johnson
Director, Office of Management and Budget	Rob Portman
Director, Office of National Drug Control Policy	John Walters
US Trade Representative	Ambassador Susan Schwab
White House Chief of Staff	Joshua B. Bolten

————— RANKING OF PRESIDENTIAL GREATNESS —————

Presidents ranked by 'greatness' %	Great & near great	Below av. Average & failure	[Zogby, Feb 2008]	Great & near great	Below av. Average & failure
Franklin D. Roosevelt	69	15	3	George H.W. Bush	27	50	23
John F. Kennedy	67	23	4	Jimmy Carter	25	36	35
Ronald Reagan	62	23	14	George W. Bush	22	25	52
Harry Truman	45	33	4	Lyndon B. Johnson	19	45	27
Dwight D. Eisenhower	43	40	3	Gerald R. Ford	18	58	18
Bill Clinton	42	29	28	Richard M. Nixon	15	30	50

————————— DRINKING THE KOOL-AID —————————

To 'drink the Kool-Aid' is to give unthinking, quasi-brainwashed support to a cause or individual. The construction has long been a media cliché; during the interminable 2007–08 primaries, supporters of almost every contender were accused at one time or another of drinking their candidate's Kool-Aid. The popular use of the phrase seems to date to two events. In 1968, Tom Wolfe published *The Electric Kool-Aid Acid Test*, a pioneering work of 'new journalism' that described the trans-American travels of Ken Kesey, the 'Pied Piper of the psychedelic era' (according to the *New York Times*) and author of *One Flew Over the Cuckoo's Nest*. Of all Kesey's hedonistic excesses, the act that captured the public's attention (and gave Wolfe his title) was the 'Acid Test', where Kesey and his followers challenged members of the public to drink Kool-Aid laced with LSD to see if they 'freaked out'. Ten years later, on November 18, 1978, in Jonestown, Guyana, the maverick preacher Jim Jones induced 913 members of his People's Temple cult (including 276 children) to commit suicide by drinking fruit juice spiked with cyanide. Although there is some debate about what type of juice this was (a 1979 FBI report refers variously to 'a flavored water drink', 'flavor aid', and 'Kool-Aid'), the tragically submissive Jonestown murder-suicides have ever since been associated with 'drinking the Kool-Aid'.

Kool-Aid was first marketed in *c.*1915 as a soft drink syrup called Fruit Smack by Perkins Products Co. of Nebraska. In 1927, the syrup was concentrated into a powder (in cherry, grape, lemon-lime, orange, strawberry, and raspberry flavors) and renamed Kool-Aid. Kool-Aid is now made by Kraft.

———————— PRESIDENTIAL TAX RETURNS ————————

According to the White House, President and Laura Bush earned an adjusted gross income of $923,807 in 2007, on which they paid $221,635 in federal tax. The income included a $150,000 advance to Laura Bush for *Read All About It!*, a children's book written with her daughter Jenna about a boy named Tyrone who is reluctant to read. The Bushes donated $165,660 to charity, including to the fire department in Crawford, TX. The Cheneys declared an adjusted gross income of $3.04m, on which they paid $602,651 in federal tax, and from which they donated $166,547.

president	born	star sign	birth state	age at inaug.	term of office	political party	religion	handedness	owned slaves	facial hair	red-headed	Mt Rushmore	assassinated	served as VP	at Harvard	on a banknote	Nobel Prize	children	6ft or taller	salary	died in office	date of death	age
George Washington	02-22-1732	♓	VA‡	57	1789–1797	F	E	r	■			■				■			■	$25k		12-14-1799	67
John Adams	10-30-1735	♏	MA‡	61	1797–1801	F	U	r						■	■			5		$25k		07-04-1826	90
Thomas Jefferson	04-13-1743	♈	VA‡	57	1801–1809	DR	D	r	■		■	■		■		■		6	■	$25k		07-04-1826	83
James Madison	03-16-1751	♓	VA‡	57	1809–1817	DR	E	r	■											$25k		06-28-1836	85
James Monroe	04-28-1758	♉	VA‡	58	1817–1825	DR	E	r	■									2	■	$25k		07-04-1831	73
John Q. Adams	07-11-1767	♋	MA‡	57	1825–1829	DR	U	r							■			4		$25k		02-23-1848	80
Andrew Jackson	03-15-1767	♓	SC‡	61	1829–1837	D	P	r	■		□								■	$25k		06-08-1845	78
Martin Van Buren	12-05-1782	♐	NY	54	1837–1841	D	Re	r		■				■				4		$25k		07-24-1862	79
William Harrison	02-09-1773	♒	VA‡	68	1841	W	E	r	■									10		$25k	■	04-04-1841	68
John Tyler	03-29-1790	♈	VA	51	1841–1845	W	E	r	■					■				14	■	$25k		01-18-1862	71
James Knox Polk	11-02-1795	♏	NC	49	1845–1849	D	M	r	■											$25k		06-15-1849	53
Zachary Taylor	11-24-1784	♐	VA	64	1849–1850	W	E	r	■								6		$25k	■	07-09-1850	65
Millard Fillmore	01-07-1800	♑	NY	50	1850–1853	W	U	r			□			■			2			$25k		03-08-1874	74
Franklin Pierce	11-23-1804	♐	NH	48	1853–1857	D	E	r									3			$25k		10-08-1869	64
James Buchanan	04-23-1791	♉	PA	65	1857–1861	D	P	r										■	$25k		06-01-1868	77
Abraham Lincoln	02-12-1809	♒	KY	52	1861–1865	R	L	r		■		■	■			■	4	■	$25k	■	04-15-1865	56
Andrew Johnson	12-29-1808	♑	NC	56	1865–1869	D/U/R	?	r	■					■			5		$25k		07-31-1875	66
Ulysses S. Grant	04-27-1822	♉	OH	46	1869–1877	R	M	r	■	■						■	4		*$50k		07-23-1885	63
Rutherford Hayes	10-04-1822	♎	OH	54	1877–1881	R	M	r		■					■		8		$50k		01-17-1893	70
James Garfield	11-19-1831	♏	OH	49	1881	R	Di	l		■			■				7	■	$50k	■	09-19-1881	49
Chester Arthur	10-05-1829	♎	VT	50	1881–1885	R	E	r		■				■			3	■	$50k		11-18-1886	56
Grover Cleveland	03-18-1837	♓	NJ	47	1885–1889	D	P	r								■	5		$50k		06-24-1908	71
Benjamin Harrison	08-20-1833	♌	OH	55	1889–1893	R	P	r		■	□						3		$50k		03-13-1901	67
Grover Cleveland	03-18-1837	♓	NJ	55	1893–1897	D	P	r								■	5		$50k		06-24-1908	71

US PRESIDENTS cont.

president	born	star sign	birth state	age at inaug.	dates of term	political party	religion	handedness	owned slaves	facial hair	red-headed	Mt Rushmore	assassinated	served as VP	at Harvard	on a banknote	Nobel Prize	children	salary	died in office	date of death	age of death
William McKinley	01-29-1843	♒	OH	54	1897–1901	R	M	r					■			■		2	$50k	■	09-14-1901	58
Theodore Roosevelt	10-27-1858	♏	NY	42	1901–1909	R	Re	r		■		■	□	■	■		■	6	$50k		01-06-1919	60
William Taft	09-15-1857	♍	OH	51	1909–1913	R	U	r		■								3	$75k		03-08-1930	72
Woodrow Wilson	12-28-1856	♑	VA	56	1913–1921	D	P	r								□	■	3	$75k		02-03-1924	67
Warren Harding	11-02-1865	♏	OH	55	1921–1923	R	B	r										.	$75k	■	08-02-1923	57
Calvin Coolidge	07-04-1872	♋	VT	51	1923–1929	R	C	r						■				2	$75k		01-05-1933	60
Herbert Hoover	08-10-1874	♌	IA	54	1929–1933	R	Q	?			□							2	$75k		10-20-1964	90
Franklin D. Roosevelt	01-30-1882	♒	NY	51	1933–1945	D	E	r					□					6	$75k	■	04-12-1945	63
Harry S. Truman	05-08-1884	♉	MO	60	1945–1953	D	B	l					□	■				1	*$100k		12-26-1972	88
Dwight D. Eisenhower	10-14-1890	♎	TX	62	1953–1961	R	P	r										2	$100k		03-28-1969	78
John F. Kennedy	05-29-1917	♊	MA	43	1961–1963	D	Ro	r					■		■			3	$100k	■	11-22-1963	46
Lyndon B. Johnson	08-27-1908	♍	TX	55	1963–1969	D	Di	r						■				2	$100k		01-22-1973	64
Richard Nixon	01-09-1913	♑	CA	56	1969–1974	R	Q	r						■				2	$200k		04-22-1994	81
Gerald Ford	07-14-1913	♋	NE	61	1974–1977	R	E	l					□	■				4	$200k		12-26-2006	93
James 'Jimmy' Carter	10-01-1924	♎	GA	52	1977–1981	D	So	r										4	$200k			
Ronald Reagan	02-06-1911	♒	IL	69	1981–1989	R	Di	?					□					4	$200k		06-05-2004	93
George H.W. Bush	06-12-1924	♊	MA	64	1989–1993	R	E	l						■				6	$200k			
William 'Bill' Clinton	08-19-1946	♌	AR	46	1993–2001	D	B	l										.	$200k			
George W. Bush	07-06-1946	♋	CT	54	2001–	R	M	r							■			2	$400k			

NOTES: Considerable debate and dispute surround a number of these entries. ‡ = Born British. *Party:* [F]ederalist; [C]onfederationalist; [U]nitarian; [D]eist; [P]resbyterian; [R]eformed Dutch; [M]ethodist; [L]iberal; [Di]sciples of Christ; [B]aptist; [Q]uaker; [Ro]man Catholic; [So]uthern Baptist. A number of Presidents changed their religion. *Handedness* data are equivocal. *Slave ownership* is disputed and not necessarily while in office. *Heights* are problematic. *Red-headedness* is often subjective (e.g., 'FK). *Children* includes those who died as infants; Jefferson's activity with the slave Sally Hemings is disputed; one of Reagan's sons was adopted. *Salary:* * indicates the President also received the preceding salary. Hollow boxes indicate an assassination attempt, an obsolete banknote design, or uncertain hair color.

───── 2008 STATE OF THE UNION ADDRESS ─────

Delivered by President George W. Bush · January 28, 2008
Start: 9·09pm EST · *Finish*: 10·02pm EST · *Duration*: 53 mins
Words: 5,723 · *Interruptions*: applause, 72; laughter, 1 [White House analysis]

Some thematic extracts

ELECTIONS · In this election year, let us show our fellow Americans that we recognize our responsibilities and are determined to meet them. Let us show them that Republicans and Democrats can compete for votes and cooperate for results at the same time.

ECONOMY · As we meet tonight, our economy is undergoing a period of uncertainty. America has added jobs for a record 52 straight months, but jobs are now growing at a slower pace. Wages are up, but so are prices for food and gas. Exports are rising, but the housing market has declined. At kitchen tables across our country, there is a concern about our economic future.

EARMARKS · The people's trust in their government is undermined by congressional earmarks – special interest projects that are often snuck in at the last minute, without discussion or debate.

SUBPRIME · These are difficult times for many American families, and by taking these steps, we can help more of them keep their homes.

ENERGY · To build a future of energy security, we must trust in the creative genius of American researchers and entrepreneurs and empower them to pioneer a new generation of clean energy technology. Our security, our prosperity, and our environment all require reducing our dependence on oil.

IMMIGRATION · We must also find a sensible and humane way to deal with people here illegally. Illegal immigration is complicated, but it can be resolved. And it must be resolved in a way that upholds both our laws and our highest ideals.

IRAQ · The American and Iraqi surges have achieved results few of us could have imagined just one year ago. When we met last year, many said that containing the violence was impossible. A year later, high-profile terrorist attacks are down, civilian deaths are down, sectarian killings are down.

IRAN · Iran's rulers oppress a good and talented people. And wherever freedom advances in the Middle East, it seems the Iranian regime is there to oppose it. Iran is funding and training militia groups in Iraq, supporting Hezbollah terrorists in Lebanon, and backing Hamas's efforts to undermine peace in the Holy Land. Tehran is also developing ballistic missiles of increasing range, and continues to develop its capability to enrich uranium, which could be used to create a nuclear weapon.

PALESTINE · The time has come for a Holy Land where a democratic Israel and a democratic Palestine live side by side in peace.

ON AMERICA · The miracle of America is that our greatness lies not in our government, but in the spirit and determination of our people ... And so long as we continue to trust the people, our nation will prosper, our liberty will be secure, and the state of our Union will remain strong.

2008 SOTU · REACTION & ANALYSIS

Washington Post · While aides insist he is not dwelling on his legacy, the 'unfinished business' agenda he outlined seemed geared toward consolidating past achievements and focusing strategically on where he can win a few more.

LA Times · ... a short-term scramble for a long-term legacy.

Chicago Tribune · A lame duck skirting the edges of relevance in his last year in office, Bush angled to get the country's attention via the pocketbook. He called for quick passage of a bipartisan economic stimulus package to address a credit crunch that has aroused deep anxiety on Wall St and Main St.

Wall Street Journal · Perhaps the best service Mr. Bush can do in his final months is push back against a public pessimism that could escalate into retreat from world leadership.

New York Times · Mr. Bush still has a year left – and many serious problems to address. It is time, finally, for him to put aside the partisanship, the bluster and the empty rhetoric. The state of the union is troubled. The nation yearns for leadership.

Seattle Times · He spoke of trust in people – taxpayers, homeowners, medical researchers, doctors and patients, students, workers, energy entrepreneurs and others – to drive their own success and that of the country. The unspoken message: Government isn't the answer.

Jay Leno · [last year] President Bush said, 'The economy is on the move.' This year he said, 'Where'd it go?'

Jon Stewart · By my count, Dick Cheney smiled twelve times during that speech, meaning he only has four smiles left for the entire year.

WORD FREQUENCY & MICROSOFT'S AUTO SUMMARY

America	65	World	13	Freedom	9	Business	5
Iraq	39	Country	12	School	9	Care	5
People	29	Enemy	12	Afghanistan	8	Iran	5
Congress	27	Al-Qaeda	11	Free	8	Democracy	4
Nation	24	Child	11	Liberty	8	Education	4
Terror	23	Empower	11	Peace	8	Energy	4
Trust	17	Government	11	Power	8	Nuclear	4
Tax	16	Hope	11	Extremist	7	Palestinian	4
Agreement	14	Citizen	10	Health	7	Immigration	3
Fight	14	Leader	10	Law	7	Oil	3
Future	13	Economy	9	Families	6	War	3
Security	13	Federal	9	Progress	6	Washington	3

When the text of George W. Bush's speech is entered into Microsoft Word's Auto-Summarize feature, and distilled down to *c.*1% of its original length, the result is:

In Afghanistan, America, our 25 NATO allies, and 15 partner nations are helping the Afghan people defend their freedom and rebuild their country. We launched a surge of American forces into Iraq. A free Iraq will deny al-Qaeda a safe haven. America opposes genocide in Sudan. America is leading the fight against disease. God bless America.

————————— PRESIDENTIAL MISCELLANY —————————

PRESIDENTS' DAY · For many in America, the holiday on the third Monday in February is known as 'Presidents' Day'. However, the day was not originally designed as an opportunity to celebrate the service of all Presidents, and in fact, the official title for the federal holiday is Washington's Birthday. ❦ Long before his death, Washington's February 22 birthday was a cause for popular celebration. The proposal (by Arkansas senator Steven Wallace Dorsey) to mark the day as an official federal holiday passed in 1879, after meeting little dissent. However, in 1968 a bill was proposed to create a single 'Presidents' Day' in honor of both Washington and Abraham Lincoln – whose February 12 birthday was also a holiday in some states. While that version of the bill was never passed, the 1968 *Uniform Holidays Act* fixed Washington's official birthday on the third Monday of February, in order to create a long weekend. Today a confusing patchwork of regulations has meant that the state holiday is called 'Presidents' Day' in some areas, while the federal holiday is still known as 'Washington's Birthday'. A push from retail advertisers has helped cement the idea of a single day to honor all presidents, though many note that the patriotic significance of the day has long since dimmed.

THE PRESIDENT'S DESK · In the Oval Office the President of the United States sits behind the *Resolute* desk. The desk is named after the HMS *Resolute* ship, from which it was fashioned. In 1854, a British crew abandoned the HMS *Resolute* when it became embedded in Arctic ice. An American crew found the ship a year later, rescued and repaired it, and presented it to Queen Victoria as a goodwill gesture. In return, once the ship was retired, the Queen ordered a desk fashioned from its timbers, which she presented to President Hayes in 1880. Since then, most Presidents have used the desk in either private studies or the Oval Office. Notably, it was modified by FDR, who ordered a carved panel fitted to the kneehole to conceal his wheelchair.

TECUMSEH'S CURSE · The 'Curse of Tecumseh' is sometimes offered as an explanation for the curious fact that between 1840 and 1960, every US President elected in a year ending with zero died in office. Thus, William Henry Harrison†, elected in 1840, died of pneumonia; Lincoln, elected in 1860, was assassinated; both Garfield (1880) and McKinley (1900) were shot; Harding (1920) perished after a stroke; Roosevelt (1940) died of a cerebral hemorrhage; and Kennedy (1960) was, of course, assassinated. Reagan is thought to have 'broken' the curse by winning the 1980 election and surviving a 1981 assassination attempt. (The next president in line would have been George W. Bush.) The curse is named after the famous Shawnee tribe leader Tecumseh (*c.*1768–1813), whose forces were defeated by William Henry Harrison's men at the 1811 Battle of Tippecanoe. Legend has it that Tecumseh (or perhaps his brother Tenskwatawa) pronounced the curse at some point after his ignominious defeat. It is unclear how Tecumseh knew Harrison would become president, or why the curse only afflicted presidents elected in years ending in zero.

† Harrison caught pneumonia on his inaugural day and died after one month in office, serving the shortest term of any US President.

———————— PRESIDENTIAL CAMPAIGN SONGS ————————

While the musical interludes of the 2008 campaigns frequently focused on Obama Girl's unofficial tribute *I Got a Crush on Obama* [see p.24], campaign theme songs have been a part of presidential elections since Washington used the rousing *Follow Washington* in 1789 *('And follow, follow Washington/He will lead the way, my lads')*. Early campaign songs were often written especially for a candidate, and based on popular tunes such as *Yankee Doodle*. More recently, candidates have appropriated preexisting songs to serve as their anthem. Below are selected campaign songs of note:

Candidate	*year*	*song*
Hillary Clinton	2008	Céline Dion · *You and I*
Al Gore	2000	The Call · *Let the Day Begin*
George W. Bush	2000	Billy Ray Cyrus · *We the People*
Bill Clinton	1992 & 1996	Fleetwood Mac · *Don't Stop*
Bob Dole	1996	*I'm a Dole Man*
Ross Perot	1992	Patsy Cline · *Crazy*
Michael Dukakis	1988	Neil Diamond · *Coming to America*
Jimmy Carter	1976	*Ode to the Georgia Farmer*
Gerald Ford	1976	*I'm Feeling Good About America*
George McGovern	1972	Paul Simon · *Bridge Over Troubled Water*
Lyndon B. Johnson	1964	*Hello, Lyndon*
John F. Kennedy	1960	Frank Sinatra · *High Hopes*
Harry Truman	1948	*I'm Just Wild About Harry*
Franklin D. Roosevelt	1932	*Happy Days Are Here Again*
Herbert Hoover	1928	*If He's Good Enough for Lindy*
Calvin Coolidge	1924	*Keep Cool and Keep Coolidge*
Woodrow Wilson	1912	*Wilson – That's All!*
Theodore Roosevelt	1912	*We're Ready for Teddy Again*
William H. Taft	1908	*Get on a Raft With Taft*
James A. Garfield	1880	*If the Johnnies Get Into Power Again*
Rutherford B. Hayes	1876	*The Boys in Blue*
Abraham Lincoln	1860	*Lincoln and Liberty*
James Buchanan	1856	*The White House Chair*
Henry Clay	1844	*Old Dan Tucker*
James Polk	1844	*Jimmy Polk of Tennessee*
William Henry Harrison	1840	*Tippecanoe and Tyler Too*
Martin Van Buren	1840	*Rockabye, Baby*
John Quincy Adams	1828	*Little Wat Ye Wha's a-Comin*
Thomas Jefferson	1800	*For Jefferson and Liberty*

John McCain's campaign favored Darryl Worley's *I Will Hold my Ground*, Chuck Berry's *Johnny B. Goode*, and ABBA's *Take a Chance on Me*, among others. Barack Obama frequently played Motown favorites and favored U2's *City of Blinding Lights*. However, his campaign was also honored with an independent music video from the hip-hop artist will.i.am featuring a motley crew of celebrity cameos. The *Yes We Can* song, based on Obama's New Hampshire primary speech, became an internet sensation during the year and won an Emmy for Best New Approaches in Daytime Entertainment. [Sources include Oscar Brand's CD *Presidential Campaign Songs*. Not all song choices were official.]

110th CONGRESS

HOUSE

Democrat	232 (53·3%)
Republican	201 (46·2%)
Independent	0 (0·0%)
Vacancy	2 (0·5%)

Members	435
Delegates	4
Resident Commissioner	1
Female members	74 (17·0%)
Black members	42 (9·7%)
Hispanic members	26 (6·0%)
Asian Pacific members	7 (1·6%)
American Indian members	1 (0·2%)
Foreign-born members	11 (2·5%)
Average age	55·93 years
Prior military service	102 (23·4%)

SENATE

Democrat	49 (%)
Republican	48 (%)
Independent	2 (%)
Vacancy	1 (%)

Members	100
(Vice President votes in event of a tie)	
Vice President	Richard B. Cheney
Female members	16 (%)
Black members	1 (%)
Hispanic members	3 (%)
Asian Pacific members	2 (%)
American Indian members	0 (%)
Foreign-born members	1 (%)
Average age	61·7 years
Prior military service	29 (%)

CONSTITUTIONAL QUALIFICATION
Article I, Section 2
No person shall be a Representative who shall not have attained to the Age of twenty five Years, and been seven Years a Citizen of the United States, and who shall not, when elected, be an Inhabitant of that State in which he shall be chosen.

CONSTITUTIONAL QUALIFICATION
Article I, Section 3
No Person shall be a Senator who shall not have attained to the Age of thirty Years, and been nine Years a Citizen of the United States, and who shall not, when elected, be an Inhabitant of that State for which he shall be chosen.

Speaker
Nancy Pelosi [CA-D]
Majority Leader
Steny H. Hoyer [MD-D]
Minority Leader
John A. Boehner [OH-R]

President Pro Tempore
Robert C. Byrd [WV-D]
Majority Leader
Harry M. Reid [NV-D]
Minority Leader
Mitch McConnell [KY-R]

Speaker's salary	$217,400
Maj. & Min. Leaders' slry	$188,100
Members' salary	$169,300

President Pro Tempore's slry	$188,100
Maj. & Min. Leaders' slry	$188,100
Senators' salary	$169,300

Chaplain
Rev. Daniel P. Coughlin
Clerk of the House
Lorraine C. Miller
Sergeant at Arms
Wilson (Bill) Livingood

Chaplain
Barry C. Black
Secretary
Nancy Erickson
Sergeant at Arms
Terrance Gainer

[Congressional membership data as at election · Sources: Congressional Research Service, & others]

80th–110th CONGRESSES

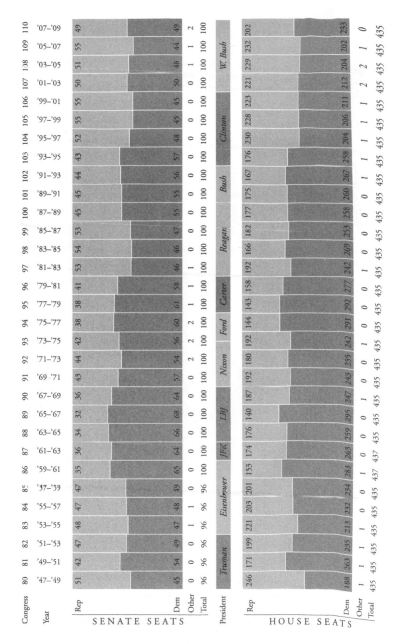

Congress	Year	Rep	Dem	Other	Total	President	Rep	Dem	Other	Total
110	'07–'09	49	49	2	100	*W. Bush*	202	233	0	435
109	'05–'07	55	44	1	100		232	202	1	435
108	'03–'05	51	48	1	100		229	204	2	435
107	'01–'03	50	50	0	100		221	212	2	435
106	'99–'01	55	45	0	100	*Clinton*	223	211	1	435
105	'97–'99	55	45	0	100		228	206	1	435
104	'95–'97	52	48	0	100		230	204	1	435
103	'93–'95	43	57	0	100		176	258	1	435
102	'91–'93	44	56	0	100	*Bush*	167	267	1	435
101	'89–'91	45	55	0	100		175	260	0	435
100	'87–'89	45	55	0	100		177	258	0	435
99	'85–'87	53	47	0	100	*Reagan*	182	253	0	435
98	'83–'85	54	46	0	100		166	269	0	435
97	'81–'83	53	46	1	100		192	242	1	435
96	'79–'81	41	58	1	100	*Carter*	158	277	0	435
95	'77–'79	38	61	1	100		143	292	0	435
94	'75–'77	38	60	2	100	*Ford*	144	291	0	435
93	'73–'75	42	56	2	100	*Nixon*	192	242	1	435
92	'71–'73	44	54	2	100		180	255	0	435
91	'69–'71	43	57	0	100		192	243	0	435
90	'67–'69	36	64	0	100	*LBJ*	187	247	1	435
89	'65–'67	32	68	0	100		140	295	0	435
88	'63–'65	34	66	0	100		176	259	0	435
87	'61–'63	36	64	0	100	*JFK*	174	263	0	437
86	'59–'61	35	65	0	100		153	283	1	437
85	'57–'59	47	49	0	96	*Eisenhower*	201	234	0	435
84	'55–'57	47	48	1	96		203	232	0	435
83	'53–'55	48	47	1	96		221	213	1	435
82	'51–'53	47	49	0	96	*Truman*	199	235	1	435
81	'49–'51	42	54	0	96		171	263	1	435
80	'47–'49	51	45	0	96		246	188	1	435
		Rep	Dem	Other	Total	President	Rep	Dem	Other	Total
		SENATE SEATS					HOUSE SEATS			

——110th CONGRESS · COMMITTEES——

HOUSE	SENATE
Committee on Agriculture	Cmte on Agri., Nutrition, & Forestry
Chair · *Collin C. Peterson* [MN-D]	Chair · *Tom Harkin* [IA-D]
Committee on Appropriations	Committee on Appropriations
Chair · *David R. Obey* [WI-D]	Chair · *Robert C. Byrd* [WV-D]
Committee on Armed Services	Committee on Armed Services
Chair · *Ike Skelton* [MO-D]	Chair · *Carl Levin* [MI-D]
Budget Committee	Banking, Housing, Urban Aff. Cmte
Chair · *John Spratt* [SC-D]	Chair · *Christopher J. Dodd* [CT-D]
Cmte on Education and Labor	Committee on the Budget
Chair · *George Miller* [CA-D]	Chair · *Kent Conrad* [ND-D]
Cmte on Energy and Commerce	Cmte on Comm., Science, & Transp.
Chair · *John D. Dingell* [MI-D]	Chair · *Daniel Inouye* [HI-D]
Committee on Financial Services	Cmte on Energy & Natural Resources
Chair · *Barney Frank* [MA-D]	Chair · *Jeff Bingaman* [NM-D]
Committee on Foreign Affairs	Cmte on Environ. and Public Works
Chair · *Howard L. Berman* [CA-D]	Chair · *Barbara Boxer* [CA-D]
Committee on Homeland Security	Committee on Finance
Chair · *Bennie G. Thompson* [MS-D]	Chair · *Max Baucus* [MT-D]
Committee on House Administration	Committee on Foreign Relations
Chair · *Robert A. Brady* [PA-D]	Chair · *Joseph R. Biden Jr* [DE-D]
Committee on the Judiciary	Health, Edu., Labor, & Pensions Cmte
Chair · *John Conyers, Jr.* [MI-D]	Chair · *Ted Kennedy* [MA-D]
Committee on Natural Resources	Homeland Sec. & Gov. Affairs Cmte
Chair · *Nick J. Rahall, II* [WV-D]	Chair · *Joe Lieberman* [CT-ID]
Cmte on Oversight & Gov. Reform	Committee on the Judiciary
Chair · *Henry A. Waxman* [CA-D]	Chair · *Patrick. J Leahy* [VT-D]
Committee on Rules	Cmte on Rules and Administration
Chair · *Louise M. Slaughter* [NY-D]	Chair · *Dianne Feinstein* [CA-D]
Cmte on Science and Technology	Small Bus. & Entrepreneurship Cmte
Chair · *Bart Gordon* [TN-D]	Chair · *John Kerry* [MA-D]
Committee on Small Business	Committee on Veterans' Affairs
Chair · *Nydia M. Velázquez* [NY-D]	Chair · *Daniel Kahikina Akaka* [HI-D]
Standards of Official Conduct	Committee on Indian Affairs
Chair · *Stephanie Tubbs Jones* [OH-D]	Chair · *Byron L. Dorgan* [ND-D]
Cmte on Transport & Infrastructure	Select Committee on Ethics
Chair · *James Oberstar* [MN-D]	Chair · *Barbara Boxer* [CA-D]
Committee on Veterans' Affairs	Select Committee on Intelligence
Chair · *Bob Filner* [CA-D]	Chair · *Jay Rockefeller* [WV-D]
Committee on Ways and Means	Special Committee on Aging
Chair · *Charles B. Rangel* [NY-D]	Chair · *Herb Kohl* [WI-D]
Permanent Select Cmte on Intelligence	
Chair · *Silvestre Reyes* [TX-D]	Joint Committee on Printing
Select Cmte on Energy Independence	Joint Committee on Taxation
and Global Warming	Joint Committee on the Library
Chair · *Edward Markey* [MA-D]	Joint Economic Committee

THE LIFE CYCLE OF A BILL

A refresher course on the perilous journey of a bill through the House and Senate:

Any member of Congress may INTRO-DUCE a bill. In the House, a Representative introduces a bill by placing it in the hopper on the House Clerk's desk. Senators introduce legislation to the floor after gaining approval from the presiding officer.

The bill is referred to a COMMITTEE by the Speaker of the House or by the Senate presiding officer. Bills may be sent to more than one committee, or parts sent to multiple committees.

The committee chairman may refer the bill to a SUBCOMMITTEE, where the bill is studied in further detail and hearings may be held. The subcommittee then reports its findings to the full committee.

The full committee holds a MARK-UP SESSION to debate and vote upon revisions. If substantial revisions are made, the committee may order a clean bill marked with a new number. The committee then holds a final vote.

If the bill passes the committee, staff prepare a report on the bill and send it to the full House or Senate. The bill is then placed on the House or Senate CALENDAR.

Once a bill reaches the floor, it is again debated. DEBATE in the full House is guided by the sponsoring committee, and limited by the terms set in the Rules committee. All amendments must be germane to the bill. In the Senate, debate is unlimited (unless cloture is invoked), amendments do not need to be germane, and riders are frequently included.

The House or Senate VOTE on the bill. If the bill passes in the House, it is sent to the Senate. If it passes in the Senate, it is sent to the House. Both chambers must approve the bill before it can be signed by the President.

If necessary, a CONFERENCE COMMITTEE (with members of both the House and Senate) is created to iron out any differences between the bill passed in each chamber. Once a compromise is reached, the conference committee sends a 'conference report' back to both the House and Senate. Once both houses approve the report, the bill is sent to the President.

THE PRESIDENT may: (a) sign the bill, in which case it becomes law; (b) ignore the bill, in which case it becomes law in 10 days if Congress is in session or does not become law if Congress adjourns within 10 days; or (c) veto the bill.

If the President vetoes the bill, the chamber originating the bill can override the VETO by a vote of two-thirds of those present. If the other chamber also votes to override the veto, the bill becomes law.

Some of the bills considered in the House and Senate during the 110th Congress: a resolution designating May 2008 as 'National Be Bear Aware and Wildlife Stewardship Month' · the Genetic Information Nondiscrimination Act of 2007 · the Professional Boxing Amendments Act of 2007 · the Great Cats and Rare Canids Act of 2007 · the Positive Aging Act of 2007 · 'A resolution reaffirming the constitutional and statutory protections accorded sealed domestic mail' · the Safe Babies Act of 2007.

─────────── ON FORMS OF DIPLOMACY ───────────

MADMAN DIPLOMACY involves deliberately presenting oneself as irrational, unstable, and dangerous in order to intimidate one's opponents and/or conceal a weak position. It was famously used by Richard Nixon, who attempted to persuade the N Vietnamese and Russians that he would 'do anything', including going nuclear, to halt the war. Since then, Nikita Khrushchev, Saddam Hussein, Fidel Castro, Vladimir Putin, Mahmoud Ahmadinejad, Kim Jong-il, and even George W. Bush have been accused of madman diplomacy.

BLADDER DIPLOMACY was a tactic of President Assad of Syria, who would speak to foreign politicians and diplomats at inordinate length while relentlessly plying them with drinks.

DOLLAR DIPLOMACY (or ECONOMIC IMPERIALISM) involves the imposition of economic influence over other countries and the use of political influence (and ultimately force) to protect overseas investments. Although a host of powers through history have exercised such influence (and still do), the phrase is usually associated with William Taft's presidency (1909–13), when America sought control over Latin America and E Asia by guaranteeing loans.

MEGAPHONE DIPLOMACY involves the public statement of demands in place of actual negotiation. Usually these demands are not backed by a credible threat of force – either because no capability for force exists, or because there is insufficient desire to exercise it.

MORAL DIPLOMACY is premised on either a (self-defined) moral code, or the moral authority of an individual. The former was somewhat unsuccessfully advocated by Woodrow Wilson, who declared, 'no nation is fit to sit in judgment upon any other nation'. Examples of *personal* moral diplomacy include a host of intercessions by various popes, and the Elders – a group of freelance moral diplomats whose members include Desmond Tutu, Kofi Annan, Nelson Mandela, Mary Robinson, and Aung San Suu Kyi.

CULINARY DIPLOMACY is the use of food and drink to lubricate negotiations and to disseminate information about a culture through its cuisine. It is no mistake that state banquets are opulent and lavish, nor that they invariably showcase national dishes and indigenous produce. (When George W. Bush hosted dinner for Queen Elizabeth II in May 2007, much was made of the President foregoing his Tex-Mex favorites for a banquet featuring American caviar and Napa Valley wines.) ☜ At its most brutal, culinary diplomacy involves halting food exports, blockading food imports, or supplying food by force (e.g., the Berlin airlift or the Iraqi oil-for-food program). Recent agflation suggests that states with food to spare may see their diplomatic stock rise. And, as Cyclone Nargis has shown, the importance of food in the wake of disasters cannot be overestimated [see p.26].

The essence of PANDA DIPLOMACY is twofold: (a) giant pandas are adored universally; and (b) China has a giant panda monopoly. Since the Tang dynasty (618–907), when Japan was presented with 2 of the species, China has been using *Ailuropoda melanoleuca* to spread goodwill. The zenith of modern panda diplomacy was 1972, when the Sino-American summit was sealed by China's gift of 2 pandas to the US; similar gifts followed to Japan,

─────────── ON FORMS OF DIPLOMACY cont. ───────────

France, Britain, Mexico, Spain, and Germany. However, in 2006, Taiwan rejected China's offer of 2 pandas, citing 'ecological concerns' – but it seems that Taiwan was fearful that accepting a *transfer* of these 'Trojan pandas' would strengthen China's claim to the island.

In 2003, George W. Bush identified the BUSH DOCTRINE as one 'defined by action, as opposed to by words'. In 2006, *Time* concluded that Bush's post-9/11 stance on geopolitics ('Either you are with us, or you are with the terrorists') was dead and declared 'the end of COWBOY DIPLOMACY'.

PING-PONG DIPLOMACY dates to 1971, when the US table tennis team became the first Americans to enter China since 1949. Nixon capitalized on this sporting encounter to facilitate his historic visit to the country in 1972. Examples of SPORTING DIPLOMACY have been seen throughout history, from the jousting and archery on the Field of the Cloth of Gold in 1520 to the part a sports boycott of South Africa played in the collapse of apartheid. The diplomacy currently surrounding Beijing's hosting of the Olympics could hardly be more fraught – with some calling for a boycott, comparing the Chinese games to 'Hitler's Olympics' in 1936.

MEDICAL DIPLOMACY seeks to exploit a superiority in medical resources for political gain. The US Surgeon General boasted, 'America's compassion and generosity to use our medical expertise and financial resources can be a powerful instrument in spreading hope, health, dignity, *and democracy* to many nations around the world' [emphasis added]. Yet, medical diplomacy is not a tool exclusive to major powers. Since the 1959

revolution, Cuba has punched above its weight with a program of DOCTOR DIPLOMACY. By exporting medical personnel to at least 68 countries, Castro has ameliorated relations with foreign governments and drawn political and economic assistance into Cuba. Recently, Hugo Chávez has emulated Castro's policy by offering free eye surgery to Latin America's poor.

The NY Philharmonic Orchestra's 2008 performance in Pyongyang was hailed as a landmark in relations with N Korea, and decried as a 'disgrace'. Either way, it was a fine illustration of CULTURAL DIPLOMACY, which, through the years, has also been described variously as CONCERT, ART, MUSICAL, VIOLIN, or ORCHESTRA DIPLOMACY. ❦ Like its culinary counterpart, CULTURAL DIPLOMACY seeks to soften the hard edges of geopolitics, using the creative arts as a way of spanning international divides – from reciprocal gift-giving between sovereigns to state-sponsored cultural programs. (Bona fide cultural diplomacy is often not helped by the tendency of governments to use it as cover for espionage; often the diplomatic title 'Cultural Attaché' is so transparent a cover for intelligence gathering as to be risible.) ❦ Cultural diplomacy can easily slip into cultural imperialism – or worse. After the 2003 invasion of Iraq, many questioned why Allied troops literally stood by while the country's treasures were looted. Donald Rumsfeld famously dismissed the episode with two words: 'Stuff happens'. But not everyone was convinced that the failure to protect Iraq's antiquities was an oversight. If a country is defined by its cultural identity, then allowing that identity to be sacked may be useful. As the journalist Simon Jenkins observed, 'Even the Nazis protected the Louvre'.

CRIME & PUNISHMENT

Some of the year's most notable crime and legal stories. {SEP 2007} The 'Jena 6' case began in 8/06, when a black student at a Jena, LA, high school asked a principal if he could sit beneath the 'white tree', so named because it was favored by white students. The student was told he could sit where he liked. In an apparent response, the next morning 3 white students hung nooses from the tree. The students were suspended, but the incident inflamed local racial tensions. On 12/4, 6 black students allegedly attacked a white student, beating him unconscious. The 6 were arrested and charged with attempted 2nd-degree murder; 5 were charged as adults, including one who was 16. Parents and activists complained of a racist double standard, arguing that the black students faced punishments that outstripped their crimes, while white students had been shown leniency after perpetrating a 'hate crime'. National media attention increased, and on 9/20/07, *c.*10,000 demonstrated in Jena, led by Al Sharpton; the march was described as one of the largest civil rights demonstrations in years. Eventually, charges for all of the 'Jena 6' were reduced. As of 8/08, one of the 6 had been convicted, of 2nd-degree battery; trials of the remaining 5 were ongoing. {OCT} 21-year-old Genarlow Wilson was freed from prison after the GA Supreme Court ruled that his 10-year sentence for consensual oral sex with a 15-year old when he was 17 constituted cruel and unusual punishment. Because of his case, consensual sex between minors in GA was changed from a felony to a misdemeanor. {NOV} The US Sentencing Cmsn lowered the recommended sentences for crack co-

The 'white tree'

caine offenses, from 10 years and 1 month to an average of 8 years and 10 months. The change came after years of complaints from civil rights advocates, who said that tougher sentences for crack contributed to the rise in the black prison population [see p.116]. {DEC} A Youngstown, OH, couple described as the 'goth Bonnie and Clyde' were arrested for stealing $8·4m from an armored car company the Monday after Thanksgiving. Some initially praised the bloodless heist ('one for the common man'), but the pair were caught after leaving a trail of clues during their escape to WV. {APR '08} 3 NYC police detectives were found not guilty in the 2006 death of Sean Bell, an unarmed black man who died in a hail of bullets outside a strip club hours before his wedding. The case led to outrage and charges of police brutality, especially after it was revealed that Bell had been shot with 50 bullets; *c.*1,000 staged protests against the acquittal. ❦ 2 retired NYC detectives said they believed that a gang of serial killers was responsible for the drowning deaths of *c.*40 college-age men, mostly in the Midwest, since 1997. The detectives dubbed the group the 'Smiley Face Killers' after the symbols painted near 22 of the crime scenes. {MAY} The Supreme Court upheld the 2003 Protect Act, which makes it illegal to offer or solicit child pornography, even if the pornography does not exist. {JUL} A former hedge fund manager faked his suicide the day he was to begin a 20-year prison term for defrauding investors of >$400m. He surrendered to police 23 days after leaving his car near a NY bridge, with the words 'suicide is painless' scrawled on the hood.

─────────── SUPREME COURT JUSTICES ───────────

Justice	*date of birth*	*state*	*law school*	*appointed by*	*term began*
John G. Roberts Jr†	01·27·1955	NY	Harvard	Bush Jr [R]	09·29·2005
John Paul Stevens	04·20·1920	IL	Northwestern	Ford [R]	12·19·1975
Antonin Scalia	03·11·1936	NJ	Harvard	Reagan [R]	09·26·1986
Anthony M. Kennedy	07·23·1936	CA	Harvard	Reagan [R]	02·18·1988
David H. Souter	09·17·1939	MA	Harvard	Bush Sr [R]	10·09·1990
Clarence Thomas	06·23·1948	GA	Yale	Bush Sr [R]	10·23·1991
Ruth Bader Ginsburg	03·15·1933	NY	Columbia	Clinton [D]	08·10·1993
Stephen G. Breyer	08·15·1938	CA	Harvard	Clinton [D]	08·03·1994
Samuel A. Alito Jr	04·01·1950	NJ	Yale	Bush Jr [R]	01·31·2006

† Chief Justice · [Sources: Supreme Court; Cornell Law School] · Antonin Scalia was the funniest Supreme Court Justice of the 2006–07 term, according to a study in the *Yale Law Journal*'s online magazine that analyzed the number of times the notation 'laughter' was inscribed in the court transcript. According to the study, Scalia earned 54 laughs during the term, trailed by Justice Breyer's 30 and Chief Justice Roberts's 19. Clarence Thomas earned no laughter notations, to come in dead last.

─────────────── JURY DUTY ───────────────

65% of United States adults have been called to jury duty, according to a December 2007 Harris Interactive poll. Yet, only 44% bothered to attend†, and only 24% actually served as part of a jury deliberating a case. Below are some opinions on juries:

Adults who ...
Would trust a jury over a judge to give a fair verdict ...... 50% (23% said a judge)
Would trust a jury over a judge to give a fair sentence .... 31% (48% said a judge)
Said people on trial have a fair and impartial jury all or most of the time..... 58%
(63% of whites, 55% of Hispanics, and 37% of blacks)

† The penalties for ignoring a jury summons vary from state to state. In general, since a summons is an official court order, failure to appear can result in a fine or imprisonment for contempt of court.

─────────── WACKIEST WARNING LABELS ───────────

The Michigan-based group Lawsuit Abuse Watch runs an annual 'wacky warning label contest' to highlight 'how lawsuits and fear of lawsuits have driven the proliferation of common-sense warnings on US products'. Below are the 2007 winners:

Grand prize ....*Danger: Avoid death* (on a tractor)
Second place .... *Do not iron while wearing shirt* (on an iron-on T-shirt transfer)
Third place .... *Do not put child in bag* (on a baby stroller with storage pouch)
Honorable mention....... *Caution: Safety goggles recommended* (on a letter opener)
Honorable mention.... *The Vanishing Fabric Marker should not be used as a writing instrument for signing checks or any legal documents* (on fabric marker)

—————————WORLD ORGANIZATIONS—————————

United Nations [UN]
(est. 1945 · 192 member states)
Initially created in a bid to maintain
peace and security after WWII, the
UN now works across a broad range
of areas, spanning international law
and economic development. To
manage its ever-growing remit, the
UN administers a number of agencies
with more specific focuses, such as
the Security Council, whose prime
responsibility is international peace.
Nearly every recognized state in the
world is a UN member (save the
Vatican, Palestine, Taiwan,
Niue, and the Cook Islands).

North Atlantic Treaty Organization
[NATO] · (est. 1949 · 26 members)
A military alliance of Western
countries, originally established to
counter a perceived threat from the
Soviet Union. NATO now promotes
mutual defense and cooperation.
In 1995, NATO undertook its first
aggressive action – bombing Serbian
positions around Sarajevo. NATO has
held a peacekeeping role in
Afghanistan since 2003.

World Bank (or *International Bank for
Reconstruction & Development*)
(est. 1944 · 185 members)
An agency of the UN providing
low-interest loans, policy advice,
and technical assistance to low- and
middle-income countries to cut
poverty and aid development.

World Trade Organization [WTO]
(est. 1995 · 151 members)
International organization that
aims to facilitate business links.
The WTO negotiates rules of trade
between nation states and arbitrates
international trade disputes.

The Paris Club
(est. 1956 · 19 members)
Informal group of creditor countries
that works to ease the burden of
debtor countries by renegotiating
and rescheduling their debts.

*Organization for Economic
Cooperation and Development* [OECD]
(est. 1961 · 30 members)
Group of industrialized countries
cooperating on social and economic
policy and development.

International Monetary Fund
[IMF] · (est. 1945 · 185 members)
Works to promote world monetary
stability, economic development, and
high levels of employment.

*Organization of Petroleum
Exporting Countries* [OPEC]
(est. 1960 · 11 members)
Encourages cooperation amongst
petroleum-producing countries and
works to achieve 'stable and fair' prices
for oil producers, and a consistent
supply of fuel.

Group of Eight [G8] · (est. 1975)
A group of the most powerful (and
wealthy) nations – USA, Japan,
Germany, Britain, France, Canada,
Italy, and Russia – that meets annually
to discuss economic and
political cooperation.

*United Nations Education, Scientific
and Cultural Organization* [UNESCO]
(est. 1945 · 191 member states,
and 6 associate members)
Fosters collaboration between
member states in areas of science, arts,
heritage, and culture. Most notably,
UNESCO works to preserve
the World Heritage sites [see p.218].

WORLD ORGANIZATIONS cont.

World Health Organization [WHO]
(est. 1948 · 193 members)
UN agency that aims to attain the
highest possible levels of health across
the globe, and raise awareness of
important health-related issues.

International Atomic Energy Agency
[IAEA] · (est. 1957 · 144 members)
An intergovernmental organization
that reports to the UN, the IAEA aims
to promote positive uses for nuclear
energy, and ensure that it is not used
for military purposes.

*International Committee of
the Red Cross* [ICRC]
(est. 1863 · 18 individual members,
all Swiss nationals)
Formed to provide humanitarian
aid during wartime, the ICRC now also
lends help to refugees and responds
to natural disasters.

Association of Southeast Asian Nations
[ASEAN] · (est. 1967 · 10 members)
Aims to further economic growth,
assist social and cultural development,
and create regional stability amongst
Southeast Asian countries.

The Commonwealth
(est. 1926 · 53 member states)
A voluntary group of states that
were formerly part of (or associated
with) the British Empire. The
Commonwealth fosters cooperation,
development, and trade between
member states.

Commonwealth of Independent States
[CIS] · (est. 1991 · 12 states)
Established to provide coordination
of defense, foreign, and economic
policies for states that were formerly
part of the USSR.

Council of Europe
(est. 1949 · 47 member countries)
Works to encourage unity between
member states, to safeguard European
heritage, and to promote human
rights and European laws.

*European Bank for Reconstruction
& Development* [EBRD]
(est. 1991 · 63 members)
The EBRD aims to foster market
economies and democracies in 27
countries in central and eastern
Europe, and central Asia.

League of Arab States (or *Arab League*)
(est. 1945 · 22 members)
Supports economic, social, political,
and military unity amongst Arab states.

Organization of the Islamic Conference
[OIC] · (est. 1969 · 57 states)
Promotes unity and cooperation
between Muslim countries, works to
safeguard holy places, and aims to
eliminate racial discrimination.

*Unrepresented Nations & Peoples
Organization* [UNPO]
(est. 1991 · 70 members)
Works to empower occupied nations,
indigenous people, and national
minorities who lack representation
elsewhere.

African Union [AU]
(est. 1999 · 53 nations)
Aims to encourage solidarity amongst
African nations, and to foster peace,
socioeconomic cooperation,
and integration.

The Quartet · (est. 2002)
Informal grouping of the parties (EU,
UN, Russia, and the US) concerned
with securing Middle East peace.

NEW COUNTRY GROUPINGS

In recent years, a range of informal terms have been popularized to describe groups of countries that are linked by economic, political, or military influence:

BRIC
Brazil, Russia, India, and China
*From this group, a number
of terms have developed:*
BRIMC = BRIC + Mexico
BRICS = BRIC + South Africa
BRICA = BRIC + the Arab Gulf
Cooperation Council (GCC) states:
Saudi Arabia, Kuwait, UAE,
Oman, Bahrain, and Qatar
BRICET = BRIC + Eastern Europe
and Turkey

CHINDIA
China and India

FOUR ASIAN TIGERS
Hong Kong, Singapore,
South Korea, and Taiwan

NEXT ELEVEN (N-11)
Bangladesh, Egypt, Indonesia,
Iran, Mexico, Nigeria, Pakistan,
Philippines, Turkey,
Vietnam, and South Korea

'FREE & FAIR' ELECTIONS

According to the US State Dept 'free and fair elections increase the likelihood of a peaceful transfer of power. They help to ensure that losing candidates will accept the validity of the election's results and cede power to the new government'. However, in a warning that chimes with Russia's controversial 2008 presidential election, the State Dept cautions that 'elections alone do not assure democracy since dictators can use the resources of the state to tamper with the election process'. Listed below are the State Dept's prerequisites for elections to be considered free and fair:

Universal suffrage for all eligible men and women to vote. ❦ Freedom to register as a voter or run for public office. ❦ Freedom of speech for candidates and political parties. ❦ Numerous opportunities for the electorate to receive objective information from a free press. ❦ Freedom to assemble for political rallies and campaigns. ❦ Rules that require party representatives to maintain a distance from polling places on election day; election officials, volunteer poll workers, and international monitors may assist voters with the voting process but not the voting choice. ❦ An impartial or balanced system of conducting elections and verifying election results; either trained election officials must be politically independent or those overseeing elections should be representative of the parties in the election. ❦ Accessible polling places, private voting space, secure ballot boxes, and transparent ballot counting. ❦ Secret ballots. ❦ Legal prohibitions against election fraud, and enforceable laws to prevent vote tampering (e.g., double counting, ghost voting). ❦ Recount and contestation procedures. ❦ Voting methods should include: paper ballots; ballots with pictures of candidates or party symbols so that illiterate citizens may cast the correct vote; electronic systems with touch-screen or push-button machines; and absentee ballots, allowing those who will not be able to vote on election day to cast their ballots prior to the election.

COLOR REVOLUTIONS

In recent years, popular protest movements have led to bloodless coups in several former Soviet nations. These revolutions have come to be called the 'Color Revolutions'. They are said to be inspired by the 1989 Velvet Revolution, when massive protests and a general strike led to the renouncement of power by the Communist regime in the former Czechoslovakia. The Color Revolutions include:

Rose Revolution · A 2003 coup in the former Soviet state of Georgia. Eduard Shevardnadze sparked mass protests after he claimed to have won a parliamentary election which many denounced as fraudulent. Protesters stormed Parliament, with leader Mikhail Saakashvili holding a long-stemmed rose. The crowd forced Shevardnadze to flee, and Saakashvili was elected president [see p.31].

Orange Revolution · After offical reports showed that Moscow-backed Viktor Yanukovych had won Ukraine's 2004 presidential election, thousands of protesters took to the streets wearing orange, the color of opposition leader Viktor Yushchenko's party. The protesters claimed massive election fraud and

other abuses; Yushchenko claimed he'd been poisoned. The protests were successful, and a new presidential election was ordered by the Supreme Court. Yushchenko won.

Tulip Revolution · In 2005, after weeks of protests in Kyrgyzstan following a disputed parliamentary election, protesters stormed the presidential palace. President Askar Akayev was forced to flee, and later signed a resignation letter from Moscow. The revolution was reportedly named for the country's rich assortment of tulips.

Some in the press saw fit to label the September 2007 Burmese protests the *Saffron Revolution*, after the saffron sashes worn by the Buddhist monks leading the movement.

Other revolutions that have come to be associated with specific colors or symbols:

Carnation Revolution	largely peaceful spring 1974 military coup in Portugal
Cedar Revolution	2005 revolt in Lebanon after the assassination of former PM Rafik Hariri; protesters called for Syrian withdrawal
Denim Revolution	unsuccessful revolt in Belarus after the 2006 presidential election; jeans were reportedly waved as a symbol of freedom
Green Revolution	controversial change in Third World agriculture methods beginning in the 1940s; credited with increasing cereal yields
Purple Revolution	term used by George W. Bush to praise the 2005 Iraq elections; named for the ink used to stain voters' fingers [see p.15]
White Revolution	program of reforms enacted by the Shah of Iran in 1963

The Carnation Revolution was named because the flowers were then in bloom; the cedar is a Lebanese emblem. ❦ The Cedar and Denim revolutions are also sometimes called Color Revolutions by those who wish to emphasis their peaceful tactics and popular base. Bush's use of the term 'Purple Revolution' also sought to associate Iraq with such peaceful transitions to democracy. ❦ The Tulip Revolution has also been called the Lemon Revolution, since yellow was the color of the opposition. One Kyrgi leader said that yellow was seen as the color of change because of its use on a traffic light.

Money

Money can't buy friends, but you can get a better class of enemy.
— SPIKE MILLIGAN (1918–2002)

———— MONEY · MANUFACTURE & LIFE SPAN ————

Currency	no. produced in 2007	average life span	animal equivalent
$1 bill	3,827,200,000	21 months	woolly opossum
$2 bill	0	9 years	fox
$5 bill	1,132,800,000	16 months	worker bee
$10 bill	403,200,000	18 months	deer mouse
$20 bill	2,099,200,000	2 years	field mouse
$50 bill	224,000,000	4½ years	alpine marmot
$100 bill	1,113,600,000	7½ years	African giant rat
Coins	14,445,870,000	25–30 years	hippopotamus

On 5/20/2008, a Washington, DC, federal appeals court ruled that the Treasury discriminates against the blind by failing to issue paper currency that is readily distinguishable to those without sight. The ruling could force the US to begin issuing bills that vary in size or shape based on denomination. [Sources: US Mint; Treasury Dept · Note production for fiscal year; coin production, calendar year]

———— PRESIDENTS &c. ON BANK NOTES ————

Portrait	bill
George Washington	$1
Thomas Jefferson	$2
Abraham Lincoln	$5
Alexander Hamilton	$10
Andrew Jackson	$20
Ulysses S. Grant	$50
Benjamin Franklin	$100
†William McKinley	$500
†Grover Cleveland	$1,000
†James Madison	$5,000
†Salmon P. Chase	$10,000
†Woodrow Wilson	$100,000

† These notes are no longer in production.

———— CRUDE OIL PRICES ————

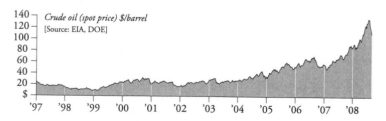

Crude oil (spot price) $/barrel
[Source: EIA, DOE]

POVERTY IN THE USA

According to the US Census, the official poverty rate in 2006 was 12·3% – down from 12·6% in 2005. 36·5m people were living in poverty (not statistically different from 2005) – and 2006 rates were statistically unchanged from 2005 for non-Hispanic whites (8·2%), blacks (24·3%), and Asians (10·3%). Charted on the right are the poverty levels by race from 1959, the first year for which estimates are available. Below are the Office of Management and Budget's 2006 money income thresholds used to determine who is in poverty: 'If a family's total income [pre-tax, excluding benefits] is less than that family's threshold, then that family and every individual in it is considered in poverty.'

% of the US population in poverty

Blacks · Hispanics · All races · Whites

For example: if a family of six, including 2 children <18, had a total income <$28,360, they would all be considered to be living in poverty.

| Family unit | related children <18 | | | | | | | | |
	NONE	1	2	3	4	5	6	7	≥8
	family income $								
One person									
<65 years	10,488								
≥65 years	9,669								
Two people									
householder <65 years	13,500	13,896							
householder ≥65 years	12,186	13,843							
Three people	15,769	16,227	16,242						
Four people	20,794	21,134	20,444	20,516					
Five people	25,076	25,441	24,662	24,059	23,691				
Six people	28,842	28,957	28,360	27,788	26,938	26,434			
Seven people	33,187	33,394	32,680	32,182	31,254	30,172	28,985		
Eight people	37,117	37,444	36,770	36,180	35,342	34,278	33,171	32,890	
Nine people or more	44,649	44,865	44,269	43,768	42,945	41,813	40,790	40,536	38,975

OIL PRICES & TRADING SIGNALS

On 1/2/2008, the price of oil hit a (psychologically) significant milestone when a trader on the New York Mercantile Exchange (NYMEX) bid $100 for a single barrel of crude oil futures. Although some dismissed this as a headline-grabbing 'vanity trade', in the months that followed, the price of oil has yo-yoed upwards [see p.308], influenced by a host of complex dynamics including: the anemic US dollar, post-subprime credit illiquidity, booming demand from China and India, and supply-side tensions in Iran, Iraq, Nigeria, &c. The effect of such turbulence on public confidence (as well as on prices at the pump) has sparked increased interest in oil brokerage. And, perhaps because they are more photogenic than numbers on a screen, the bizarre gesticulations of the remaining 'open outcry' oil traders have, for the media, become a metonym for the market. Demonstrated below are the signals used on floor of the NYMEX.

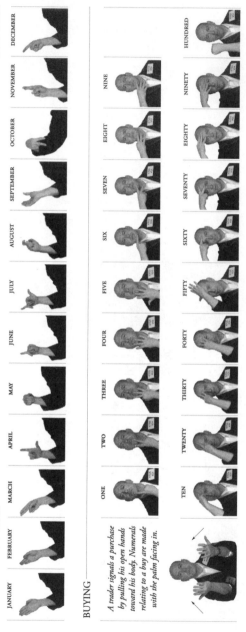

MONTHS OF THE YEAR

BUYING

A trader signals a purchase by pulling his open hands toward his body. Numerals relating to a buy are made with the palm facing in.

OIL PRICES & TRADING SIGNALS cont.

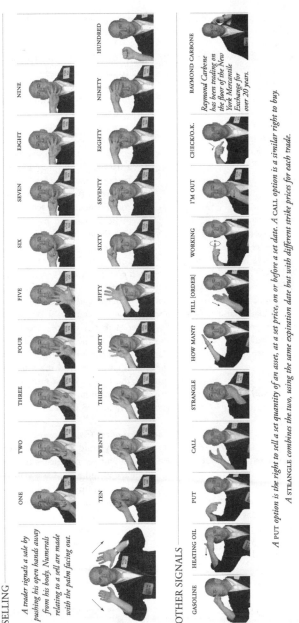

SELLING

A trader signals a sale by pushing his open hands away from his body. Numerals relating to a sell are made with the palm facing out.

ONE · TWO · THREE · FOUR · FIVE · SIX · SEVEN · EIGHT · NINE · HUNDRED

TEN · TWENTY · THIRTY · FORTY · FIFTY · SIXTY · SEVENTY · EIGHTY · NINETY

OTHER SIGNALS

GASOLINE · HEATING OIL · PUT · CALL · STRANGLE · HOW MANY? · FILL [ORDER] · WORKING · I'M OUT · CHECK/O.K.

RAYMOND CARBONE

Raymond Carbone has been trading on the floor of the New York Mercantile Exchange for over 20 years.

A PUT option is the right to sell a set quantity of an asset, at a set price, on or before a set date. A CALL option is a similar right to buy.
A STRANGLE combines the two, using the same expiration date but with different strike prices for each trade.

Some suggest that these open outcry signals are an arcane and dying art, threatened by electronic systems and supported by a dwindling number of exchanges around the world. However Raymond Carbone [pictured above] who trades energy options on the floor of the NYMEX for his company, Paramount Options, is upbeat about open outcry: 'People have been saying that these signals will only be around for another couple of years. But they've been saying that for a decade.' And, he notes, 'I can signal a trade faster than you can type it'.

THE $1 BILL

Below is a guide to the symbols and signs decorating the American one-dollar bill:

FACE

The image of George Washington is based on the 'Athenaeum' portrait by Gilbert Stuart [1755–1828]. Stuart, one of the leading portraitists of his day, was commissioned to paint this likeness of Washington by Martha Washington *c.*1796. The painting is known as the 'Athenaeum' because it was acquired by the Boston Athenaeum museum after Stuart's death.

The serial number is found in the top right and bottom left corners. The prefix letter indicates the issuing Reserve Bank: A is for Boston, B New York, C Philadelphia, D Cleveland, E Richmond, F Atlanta, G Chicago, H St Louis, I Minneapolis, J Kansas City, K Dallas, and L San Francisco. The suffix letter shows the number of times the serial number has been used: A is for once, B twice, and so on.

The small numbers and letters found on the lower right and top left of the bill indicate the position of the note on the plate from which it was printed. The *plate serial number*, identifying the plate itself, appears next to the letter in the lower-right corner.

The series year found on the bottom right of the portrait changes not with the calendar but after a new design has been introduced. When a minor change is made, a suffix letter is added.

The medallion to the left of the portrait is the *Federal Reserve Seal*, and includes the letter of the issuing bank. The *Treasury Seal* appears to the right.

BACK

The motto *In God We Trust* has been used on paper money produced since 1957, though it appeared on coins far earlier – first on two-cent coins, in 1864.

The *obverse of the Great Seal* appears on the right, showing a bald eagle gripping an olive branch (peace) and a bundle of arrows (war). The nation's commitment to peace is said to be symbolized by the fact that the eagle is facing the olive branches rather than the arrows. The motto held in the eagle's beak is *E pluribus unum* ('out of many, one'). The stripes on the shield symbolize the states, and the crest of stars above the eagle's head is said to symbolize 'America in the world'. According to some scholars, the head of the eagle also represents the President; the top of the shield, Congress; and the nine tail feathers, the Judiciary. The number 13 reappears throughout the seal, symbolizing the original 13 states.

The *reverse of the Great Seal* appears on the left. The pyramid is said to symbolize strength and permanence, although it is depicted as unfinished as a symbol of the nation's future perfection. The Roman numerals at its base represent 1776, and the motto etched below – *Novus Ordo Seclorum* – means 'a new order of the ages'. The glowing Eye of Providence represents the all-seeing eye of God. *Annuit Coeptis* is Latin for 'He [God] favors our undertakings'.

The plate serial number for the back of the bill appears on the lower right.

US COINAGE

	Cent	Nickel	Dime	Quarter	Half Dollar	Presidential Dollar	Golden Dollar*
2007 Production	4,401,200,000	1,198,840,000	2,098,500,000	2,796,640,000	8,200,000	943,110,000	9,380,000
Composition	copper-plated Zn	cupro-nickel	cupro-nickel	cupro-nickel	cupro-nickel	manganese-brass	manganese-brass
Weight	2·5g	5g	2·268g	5·670g	11·340g	8·1g	8·1g
Diameter	19·05mm	21·21mm	17·91mm	24·26mm	30·61mm	26·50mm	26·50mm
Thickness	1·55mm	1·95mm	1·35mm	1·75mm	2·15mm	2·00mm	2·00mm
Edge	plain	plain	reeded	reeded	reeded	edge lettering	plain
No. of Reeds‡	none	none	118	119	150	none	none
Obverse	Lincoln	Jefferson	Roosevelt	Washington	Kennedy	Statue of Liberty	Sacagawea & son
Designed by	V.D. Brenner	Felix Schlag	John R. Sinnock	John Flannagan	Gilroy Roberts	Don Everhart	Glenna Goodacre
Date of Issue	1909	1938	1946	1932	1964	from 2007	2000
Reverse	Lincoln Memorial	Monticello	Torch, oak, &c.	Eagle	Presidential Arms	various	Eagle in Flight
Designed by	Frank Gasparro	Felix Schlag	John R. Sinnock	John Flannagan	Frank Gasparro	various	Thomas D. Rogers
Date of Issue	1959	1938	1946	1932‡	1964‡	various	2000

[Source: US Mint] The above specifications are for US Mint legal tender coins currently in circulation. * The 'Golden' Dollar is actually 88·5% Cu; 6·0% Zn; 3·5% Mn; 2·0% Ni. † Traditionally, when coins were minted from precious metals (silver, gold, &c.), they were milled with 'reeding', or grooves, in order to foil counterfeiters and protect their edges (reeded edges show when coins have been clipped or filed for their precious metals). Although no gold coins have circulated in the US since 1934, and by the 1980s silver had also been abandoned, reeded edges remain to help the visually impaired distinguish similar size coins by touch. ‡ 1975–76 Bicentennial reverses were minted. These coins are dated 1776–1976; none was individually dated 1975 or 1976. ● According to the US Mint's website, in FY2005, a penny cost $0·0097 to make, factoring in metal, fabrication, labor and overhead, and transportation. However, increases in metal prices raised costs, and 'producing pennies and nickels using metal purchased on April 28, 2006 (e.g., $1·49/lb for zinc, $3·23/lb for copper, and $8·69/lb for nickel) would result in a unit cost for the penny of approximately 1·4 cents'. The Mint projected that 'the annualized cost for the penny in FY 2006 would be approximately 1·23 cents'. Consequently, the Mint states that 'although the metal compositions of most US coins are established by law, the US Mint, as part of its ongoing research and development efforts, will continue to examine the feasibility of alternative metal alloys for coinage. The US Mint will continue to produce all denominations of US coins in accordance with its statutory composition and fabrication requirements'.

———————— US MEDIAN INCOMES BY GENDER ————————

Below is the difference in median male and female earnings between 1960–2006.

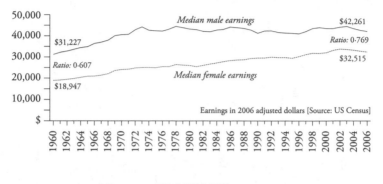

———————————————— US SAVINGS ————————————————

Personal saving as a percentage of disposable personal income was 0·3% in the 1st quarter of 2008, according to the BEA. Below this indicator is charted since 1970:

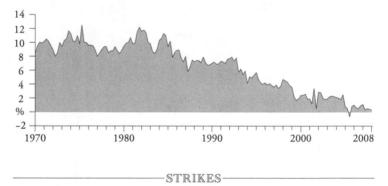

———————————————————— STRIKES ————————————————————

Major strikes idled 189,000 workers for 1·3m workdays in 2007, according to the BLS. Below are the days lost from strikes involving ≥1,000 workers, 1947–2007:

──────────── INTERNAL REVENUE SERVICE DATA ────────────

Below is a brief snapshot of the Internal Revenue Service's activities during 2007:

Tax collected by type	*gross collection*	*refunds*	*net collection*
USA TOTAL	2,691,537,557	295,246,560	2,396,290,997
· corporation income tax	395,535,825	27,054,347	368,481,478
· individual income tax	1,366,241,437	248,641,454	1,117,599,983
· employment taxes	849,732,729	11,690,664	838,042,065
· estate and gift taxes	26,977,953	969,331	26,008,622
· excise taxes	53,049,612	6,890,764	46,158,848

Tax files returned, by type	*number*	
USA TOTAL	235,348,000	· employment taxes........30,740,000
· income tax	183,091,000	· tax-exempt orgs.............. 901,000
· estate tax	50,000	· excise taxes 907,000
· gift tax	253,000	· supplemental docs........19,496,000

Activity · fiscal year	1987	1997	2007
Gross collection ($)	886,290,590	1,623,272,071	2,691,537,557
Operating costs ($)	4,365,816	7,163,541	10,764,736
Cost of collecting $100 ($)	0·49	0·44	0·40
Average tax per capita ($)	3,627	5,928	[preliminary] 8,871

[Source: Internal Revenue Service Data Book, 2007; see this for detailed notes to these charts.]

──────────── STATE QUARTERS ────────────

The State Quarters program of the United States Mint, honoring each State in the order of its admittance into the Union, concluded in 2008 with the following coins:

State	*statehood*	*coin design (reverse)*	*additional inscription*
OK	11·16·1907	Scissortail flycatcher (bird), Indian blanket (flower)	N/A
NM	01·06·1912	Zia sun symbol, state outline	*Land of Enchantment*
AZ	02·14·1912	Saguaro cactus, Grand Canyon	*Grand Canyon State*
AK	01·03·1959	Grizzly bear with salmon in mouth	*The Great Land*
HI	08·21·1959	King Kamehameha I†; 8 islands in outline	
			Ua Mau Ke Ea O Ka Aina I Ka Pono‡

All State Quarters also include the name of the State and the year of its admittance to the Union. ❦ In 2009, the Mint will issue 6 quarters in honor of US nonstates: first, the District of Columbia, then 5 United States Territories, in the following order: the Commonwealth of Puerto Rico, Guam, American Samoa, the United States Virgin Islands, and the Commonwealth of the Northern Mariana Islands. At the time of writings, designs were still under evaluation. † King Kamehameha I, also known as Kamehameha the Great (*c.*1738–1819), was the first ruler to unite the Hawaiian islands; he is remembered for preserving traditional customs while encouraging trade and ushering in a period of prosperity. ‡ Hawaiian state motto meaning, 'The life of the land is perpetuated in righteousness'.

———— UNEMPLOYMENT · DATA & EXPLANATION ————

8·8 million people were unemployed in the US in July 2008 – a rate of 5·7% [BLS].

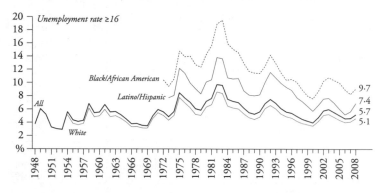

The reasons why the nonworking population of America was not working were explored in a September 2007 report from the US Census (analyzing first quarter 2004 data). Of the 227m people (≥15) in the US at that time, 35% had not worked at a paid job in the preceding 4 months. As can be seen below, 38% of nonworkers were retired, and 19% were attending school; 15% had a chronic illness or disability. Below, the reasons given for not working are tabulated by age:

Reason for not working	All	15–19	20–24	25–44	45–54	55–64	≥65
Unable to find work	4·3	3·1	12·3	10·0	7·9	3·0	0·3
On layoff	1·7	0·2	2·8	4·2	4·8	1·8	0·1
Temporary injury or illness	1·7	0·2	1·2	3·9	5·0	2·1	0·5
Chronic illness/disability	14·7	1·2	5·4	19·3	38·3	32·4	7·4
Pregnancy/childbirth	0·8	0·6	3·5	2·7	0·2	–	–
Retired	37·9	–	–	0·4	7·3	42·8	85·9
Going to school	19·1	89·7	46·6	7·6	1·9	0·3	0·1
Caring for children/others	3·2	1·9	19·5	43·6	22·2	8·1	1·7
Not interested in working	3·6	1·3	3·6	3·3	8·2	6·8	2·4
Other	2·9	1·8	5·2	5·0	4·3	2·8	1·6

———————— TAX RATES WORLDWIDE ————————

According to the OECD, 55·4% of an average Belgian's salary goes to taxes (counting both income tax and social security contributions), giving the country the highest tax rate in the OECD. The US has the 7th lowest rate (29·1%). The countries with the highest and lowest rates are shown below, from the OECD's 2005 data:

Highest rates	%			*Lowest rates*	%		
Belgium	55·4	Hungary	50·5	Korea	17·3	N Zealand	20·5
Germany	51·8	France	50·1	Mexico	18·2	Japan	27·7
		Sweden	47·9			Iceland	29·0

——————— FEDERAL & STATE INCOME TAX RATES ———————

Below are the basic rates of federal income tax and an indication of each State's income tax rate. For further information, seek expert advice.

2008 Federal Rate	Single Filers	Married Filing Jointly or Qualifying Widow(er)	Married Filing Separately	Head of Household	
10%	$0–$8,025	$0–$16,050	$0–$8,025	$0–$11,450	10%
15%	$8,026–$32,550	$16,051–$65,100	$8,026–$32,550	$11,451–$43,650	15%
25%	$32,551–$78,850	$65,101–$131,450	$32,551–$65,725	$43,651–$112,650	25%
28%	$78,851–$164,550	$131,451–$200,300	$65,726–$100,150	$112,651–$182,400	28%
33%	$164,551–$357,700	$200,301–$357,700	$100,151–$178,850	$182,401–$357,700	33%
35%	$357,701+	$357,701+	$178,851+	$357,701+	35%
	[Schedule X]	[Schedule Y-1]	[Schedule Y-2]	[Schedule Z]	

State	income tax rate (%)
Alabama	2.0–5.0
Alaska	none
Arizona	2.59–4.54
Arkansas	1.0–7.0
California	1.0–9.3
Colorado	4.63
Connecticut	3.0–5.0
Delaware	2.2–5.95
Florida	none
Georgia	1.0–6.0
Hawaii	1.4–8.25
Idaho	1.6–7.8
Illinois	3.0
Indiana	3.4
Iowa	0.36–8.98
Kansas	3.5–6.45
Kentucky	2.0–6.0
Louisiana	2.0–6.0
Maine	2.0–8.5
Maryland	2.0–5.5
Massachusetts	5.3
Michigan	4.35
Minnesota	5.35–7.85
Mississippi	3.0–5.0
Missouri	1.5–6.0
Montana	1.0–6.9
Nebraska	2.56–6.84
Nevada	none
New Hampshire	(intrst & dvend)
New Jersey	1.4–8.97
New Mexico	1.7–5.3
New York	4.0–6.85
North Carolina	6.0–7.75
North Dakota	2.1–5.54
Ohio	0.618–6.24
Oklahoma	0.5–5.5
Oregon	5.0–9.0
Pennsylvania	3.07
Rhode Island	25% of Fed taxes
South Carolina	0–7.0
South Dakota	none
Tennessee	(intrst & dvend)
Texas	none
Utah	5.0
Vermont	3.6–9.5
Virginia	2.0–5.75
Washington	none
West Virginia	3.0–6.5
Wisconsin	4.6–6.75
Wyoming	none
Washington, DC	4.0–8.5

─────────── THE EURO ───────────

The euro, introduced in 1999, is currently legal currency in the following territories:

OFFICIAL CURRENCY
Austria, Belgium, Cyprus, Finland,
France, Germany, Greece, Ireland,
Italy, Luxembourg, Malta,
the Netherlands, Portugal,
Spain, Slovenia

DE FACTO CURRENCY
Andorra, Kosovo, Montenegro

SPECIAL ARRANGEMENTS
Monaco, Vatican City,
San Marino

OVERSEAS TERRITORIES
Guadeloupe, French Guiana,
Martinique, Mayotte, Réunion,
Saint Pierre and Miquelon, French
Southern & Antarctic Territories

Charted below is the value of the € against the $; July 2008 saw a peak of >1·58:

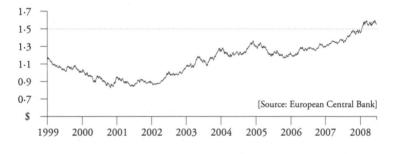

[Source: European Central Bank]

─────── UNITED STATES POSTAL SERVICE REWARDS ───────

The United States Postal Service offers rewards for 'information and services leading to the arrest and conviction of any person for the following offenses' which include:

Murder or manslaughter of an on-duty USPS employee $100,000
Mailing bombs or explosives $100,000
Mailing threats or dangerous chemicals, weapons, or biological materials.... $100,000
Forcibly assaulting any on-duty USPS employee $50,000
Mailing illegal drugs, or the proceeds from the sale of illegal drugs............. $50,000
Mailing money that has been obtained illegally; or money laundering......... $50,000
The unlawful use, reuse, or forgery of postage stamps &c. $50,000
Robbery or attempted robbery of any property under USPS control............. $50,000
Using the mail to traffic in child pornography, or aid any child sexual abuse .. $50,000
Breaking into any USPS post office or building................................ $10,000
Possession, theft, or counterfeiting of postal money orders &c................... $10,000
Theft, destruction, obstruction, or retardation of mail &c....................... $10,000

The USPS also publishes a 'most wanted' list, at the top of which (at the time of writing) was the person responsible for the Sept. 2001 anthrax mailings, despite the Aug. 2008 death of suspect Bruce Ivins.

—INTEREST RATES · FEDERAL RESERVE PRIME RATE—

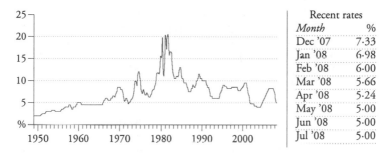

Recent rates	
Month	%
Dec '07	7·33
Jan '08	6·98
Feb '08	6·00
Mar '08	5·66
Apr '08	5·24
May '08	5·00
Jun '08	5·00
Jul '08	5·00

——NATIONAL HOUSING CHARACTERISTICS & PRICE——

Number of rooms	%	Value ($) [occupied]	%	Year structure built	%
1	0·5	<10,000	2·4	2005–09	0·8
2	1·1	10–20k	1·7	2000–04	7·4
3	8·8	20–30k	1·7	1995–99	7·1
4	18·3	30–40k	1·9	1990–94	5·6
5	23·0	40–50k	2·3	1985–89	7·1
6	20·4	50–60k	2·6	1980–84	6·0
7	12·3	60–70k	3·8	1975–79	10·2
8	7·1	70–80k	4·5	1970–74	8·6
9	3·4	80–100k	8·5	1960–69	12·2
≥10	5·0	100–120k	6·8	1950–59	10·5
Number of bedrooms	%	120–150k	9·8	1940–49	6·4
0	1·0	150–200k	13·0	1930–39	4·8
1	11·8	200–250k	8·9	1920–29	4·3
2	27·6	250–300k	6·6	1919 or earlier	7·5
3	40·9	>300,000	25·5	*Median year*	1973
≥4	18·7	*Median value*	$165,344	[American Housing Survey, 2005]	

Below are the percentage changes in house prices, ranked by Census division, for the year ending March 31, 2008. [Source: Office of Federal Housing Enterprise Oversight]

	Census division (% change)	*1 year*	*quarter*	*5 year*	*since 1980*
1	West South Central	3·86	0·41	28·43	134·29
2	East South Central	3·61	0·65	29·32	198·58
3	West North Central	1·26	0·40	25·38	205·56
4	Mountain	0·88	−0·29	51·79	285·87
5	Middle Atlantic	0·48	0·11	49·09	439·10
6	East North Central	0·47	0·51	19·21	220·16
7	New England	−0·93	0·01	33·27	515·46
8	South Atlantic	−1·03	−0·41	52·11	317·32
9	Pacific	−5·60	−2·61	60·20	462·44
	USA	−0·03	−0·23	38·88	287·54

FORBES MAGAZINE RICH LIST · 2008

No.	Billionaire	nationality	$ billion	business	marital status (kids)
1	Warren Buffett	American	62·0	investing	married (3)
2	Carlos Slim Helu	Mexican	60·0	telecoms	widowed (6)
3	William Gates III	American	58·0	software	married (3)
4	Lakshmi Mittal	Indian	45·0	manufacturing	married (2)
5	Mukesh Ambani	Indian	43·0	manufacturing	married (3)
6	Anil Ambani	Indian	42.0	various	married (2)
7	Ingvar Kamprad & family	Swedish	31·0	retail (Ikea)	married (4)
8	K.P. Singh	Indian	30·0	real estate	married (3)
9	Oleg Deripaska	Russian	28·0	various	married (2)
10	Karl Albrecht	German	27·0	retail (Aldi)	married (2)

MINIMUM WAGE

Covered nonexempt workers are entitled to a minimum wage of not less than $6·55/hour effective July 24, 2008, and $7·25/hour effective July 24, 2009. ❦ The minimum wage generally applies to employees of firms with an annual turnover >$500,000, as well as smaller enterprises engaged in interstate business. All federal, state, and local government employees are covered, as are domestic workers. That said, a host of exceptions apply, for example, to workers with disabilities, full-time students, those <20 early in their employment, tipped employees, &c. ❦ Some states have their own minimum wage; where state and federal wages differ, employees are entitled to the higher rate. Below are DoL data from July 2008:

AL.......no law	HI....... $7·25	MA..... $8·00	NM..... $6·50	SD....... $6·55
AK...... $7·15	ID....... $5·55	MI....... $7·40	NY ...... $7·15	TN......no law
AZ....... $6·90	IL .... $7·75	MN..... $5·25	NC...... $6·55	TX . federal rate†
AR...... $6·25	IN....... $6·55	MS......no law	ND...... $6·55	UT . federal rate†
CA ...... $8·00	IA .... $7·25	MO..... $6·65	OH...... $7·00	VT ...... $7·68
CO ..... $7·02	KS....... $2·65	MT..... $6·55	OK . federal rate†	VA.. federal rate†
CT ...... $7·65	KY....... $6·55	NE ...... $6·55	OR ..... $7·95	WA...... $8·07
DE ...... $7·15	LA.......no law	NV...... $6·85	PA....... $7·15	WV...... $7·25
FL....... $6·79	ME...... $7·00	NH..... $6·55	RI .... $7·40	WI....... $6·50
GA ..... $5·15	MD...... $6·55	NJ....... $7·15	SC.......no law	WY...... $5·15

This is a basic guide only. † States whose legislation specifies a minimum wage set at the federal level.

TOP HEDGE FUND MANAGERS

The highest-earning hedge fund managers of 2007, according to *Alpha* magazine:

John Paulson† ....*earned* $3·7bn	Phil Falcone.....................$1·7bn
George Soros....................$2·9bn	Ken Griffin......................$1·5bn
James Simons ....$2·8bn	† Reportedly Wall Street's largest ever paycheck.

─────── CHARITABLE GIVING ───────

Despite economic fears, charitable giving in the US was estimated at $306·39bn in 2007 (2·2% of the GDP): a rise of 3·9% from 2006 and the first time the total has ever exceeded $300bn, according to the Giving USA Foundation. (Notwithstanding the early primary season, FEC data show that presidential campaigns raised $580·4m in 2007 – less than 0·25% of the total.) Below is a breakdown of 2007 recipients and donors, by type:

RECIPIENT *type*	%		DONOR *type*	%
Religion	33·4	Arts, culture, &c. ....4·5	Individuals	74·8
Education	14·1	Intl affairs ....4·3	Foundations	12·6
Human services	9·7	Envrnmt/animals ....2·3	Bequests	7·6
Health	7·6	Gifts to foundations .9·1	Corporations	5·1
Public society	7·4	Other & deductions carried over..........7·7	[All figures are rounded]	

65% of Americans gave money to charity in 2007, according to the first American Express Charitable Gift Survey. Yet, in this age of high-profile 'billanthropy', it is notable that 66% of these donations were for less than $100, and 45% were for less than $50. The average charitable donation was $172, though donors proved more generous to religious causes. The report noted that 6% of Americans had donated online, yet the medium of donating (online *vs* offline) did not significantly affect the sums given. (64% of those who gave online said that the internet was fast, convenient, and allowed them to respond to an urgent need; 20% were prompted to give by an email or a website.) At right are the average sums donated by method and recipient type. Parsing gifts to *secular* organization, AmEx found that while 20%

Average charitable donation ($)

Method	All	religious	secular
Online	165	334	144
Offline	174	280	137
Both	172	284	138

gave to health charities, and 2% gave to arts or cultural charities, average donations to the latter outstripped donations to the former $313 to $102. (Donors were most generous to educational institutions, to whom the average gift was $375.)
❦ A December 2007 Bank of America report proposed 12 'archetypes' of high-net-worth households (i.e., those with a net worth of >$1m, or an annual income of >$200k). Of course, individuals or households can fit more than one archetype.

The Very Wealthy..*with a net worth of* ≥$50m
The Bequeather ....*with a will that leaves* ≥25% *to charity*
The Devout Donor *. regularly attends religious services and donates to religious causes*
The Secular Donor......*seldom attends religious services or donates to religious causes*
The Entrepreneur............*with* ≥50% *of their net worth in entrepreneurial assets*
The Dynast...........................*gives their children money to donate to charity*
The Metropolitan........*primary residence is in a city with a population* ≥500,000
The High-Frequency Volunteer.................*who volunteers* >200 *hours per year*
The Strategic Donor...................*with foundations &c. who give to a few groups*
The Transactional Donor.........*with no foundations &c. who give to many groups*
The Altruistic Donor ....*motivated more by a sense of altruism than by wealth*
The Financially Pragmatic Donor............*who would give more if they felt richer*

──────────── GAMBLING ────────────

Because most gambling legislation is enacted at a state level, there is a paucity of national data and state-by-state comparisons. The American Gaming Association (AGA) reports that 11 states have commercial casinos, 28 have Indian casinos, 41 (+DC) have lotteries, 43 have pari-mutuel wagering†, and 47 (+DC) have charitable gaming [see table at right]. Below is a selection of the latest data available on gambling:

65% of Americans gamble, according to a December 2007 poll by Gallup (♂67%:♀63%). Below are the most popular forms of gambling in the US:

Bought state lottery ticket 46%
Visited a casino 24
Participated in an office pool 14
Played a video poker machine 12
Other gambling not mentioned 9
Bet on professional sports 7
Played bingo for money 7
Bet on a horse race 5
Bet on a college sports event 4
Bet on a boxing match 3
Gambled for money online 2

Gallup found only modest differences in rates of gambling by age: older Americans (59%) are marginally less likely to gamble than younger adults (66%), or the middle aged (69%). There are no significant differences in gambling between college graduates and nongraduates, but gambling is much more common among higher-income (72%) and middle-income (66%) Americans, than lower-income (55%) Americans. A Gallup poll on US morality in May 2007 found that 32% thought gambling to be 'morally wrong' (by comparison, 27% thought the death penalty was morally wrong).

US lottery sales totaled $52·6bn in 2005, according to the North American Association of State and Provincial Lotteries. New York topped the state table with sales of $6·3bn, followed by Massachusetts with sales of $4·5bn.

A 2006 Harrah Casinos report showed that >25% of US adults (age ≥21) gambled at a casino at least once in 2005 – a rate stable since 2002. On average, Americans visit casinos 6·1 times a year. Interestingly, the gender ratio of casino visitors exactly matches the gender ratio in US society (♀52%:♂49%). Below are the most popular casino games:

VIDEO POKER 71%
· ¢1–¢2 7
· ¢5–¢10 19
· ¢25–¢50 38
· $1–$4 7
· $5+ 1
TABLE GAMES 14%
· blackjack/21 9
· roulette 2
· craps 2
· live poker 2
OTHER/DON'T KNOW 14%

The 2006 top-10 US casino markets, according to the 2007 AGA report are:

Location	revenue $
Las Vegas Strip, Nev.	6·689bn
Atlantic City, N.J.	5·208bn
Chicagoland, Ind./Ill.	2·595bn
Connecticut	1·734bn
Detroit, Mich.	1·303bn
Tunica/Lula, Miss.	1·252bn
St Louis Mo./Ill.	990·98m
Reno/Sparks, Nev.	939·50m
Boulder Strip, Nev.	929·70m
Shreveport, La.	847·18m

Consumers spent $32·4bn in casinos in 2006, up from $17·1bn in 1996. [AGA]

———— GAMBLING cont. ————

Poker's popularity has been stoked in recent years by celebrity endorsement and televised competitions. The AGA estimates that 14% of all Americans played poker in 2006 (18% in 2004 and 2005; 12% in 2003) – of whom:

Location of poker game	%
Played with friends or family	87
On the internet for money‡	32
In a casino or tournament	30
On the internet just for fun	13

Thought poker was	%
A game of skill	45
A game of chance	41
Don't know/refused	14

Reason for playing	%
Spending time with friends &c.	58
Skill and strategy involved	21
Chance to win money	9
It's a popular game	8
Don't know/refused	4

‡ The FBI states that it is illegal to place 'cyber bets' on sporting events or virtual card games; transfer money electronically for gambling; or bet in online offshore casinos if you live in the US.

As of March 4, 2008, casinos and other sponsors of poker tournaments have been required to report all winnings of >$5,000 to the Internal Revenue Service, usually on the form W-2G. In so doing, sponsors are freed from any obligation to withhold federal income tax from winners, who themselves have long been required to declare income from tournaments on their tax return.

† Pari-mutuel [see right] is a system of race betting where the winners divide the total sum bet (after the deduction of any expenses) in proportion to the sums wagered individually.

Forms of legal gaming by state	Commercial casinos	Tribal casinos	Pari-mutuel wagering	Lotteries	Racetrack casinos	Charitable gaming
Alabama	·	$	·	$	·	$
Alaska	·	$	·	·	·	$
Arizona	·	$	$	$	·	$
Arkansas	·	·	·	$	·	$
California	·	$	$	$	·	$
Colorado	$	$	$	$	·	$
Connecticut	·	$	$	$	·	$
Delaware	·	·	$	$	$	$
DC	·	·	$	·	·	$
Florida	·	$	$	$	·	$
Georgia	·	·	·	$	·	$
Hawaii	·	·	·	·	·	·
Idaho	·	$	$	$	·	$
Illinois	$	·	$	$	·	$
Indiana	·	$	$	$	$	$
Iowa	$	$	$	$	$	$
Kansas	·	$	$	$	·	$
Kentucky	·	·	$	$	·	$
Louisiana	$	$	$	$	$	$
Maine	·	·	$	$	$	$
Maryland	·	·	$	$	·	$
Massachusetts	·	·	$	$	·	$
Michigan	$	$	$	$	·	$
Minnesota	·	$	$	$	·	$
Mississippi	$	$	·	·	·	$
Missouri	$	·	$	$	·	$
Montana	·	$	$	$	·	$
Nebraska	·	$	$	$	·	$
Nevada	$	·	·	·	·	$
New Hampshire	·	·	$	$	·	$
New Jersey	$	·	$	$	·	$
New Mexico	·	$	$	$	$	$
New York	·	$	$	$	$	$
North Carolina	·	$	$	·	·	$
North Dakota	·	$	·	$	·	$
Ohio	·	·	$	$	·	$
Oklahoma	·	$	$	$	$	$
Oregon	·	$	$	$	·	$
Pennsylvania	†	·	$	$	$	$
Rhode Island	·	·	$	$	$	$
South Carolina	·	·	$	$	·	$
South Dakota	$	$	$	$	·	$
Tennessee	·	·	$	$	·	·
Texas	·	$	$	$	·	$
Utah	·	·	·	·	·	·
Vermont	·	·	$	$	·	$
Virginia	·	·	$	$	·	$
Washington	·	$	$	$	·	$
West Virginia	·	·	$	$	$	$
Wisconsin	·	$	$	$	·	$
Wyoming	·	$	·	$	·	$

† Legal but not operational.
[Source: American Gaming Association]

─────────────────── IDENTITY THEFT ───────────────────

A relatively novel avenue of crime, identity theft was only included in the National Crime Victimization Survey in 2004. The latest data from that survey (2005 figures reported in Nov. 2007) indicate that 6·4m US households (5·5% of all households) experienced at least one type of identity theft. Statistical and anecdotal data suggest that without action by consumers and banks this figure is likely to rise. Below is a breakdown of ID theft from the 2007 Bureau of Justice Statistics special report:

	number of households	%		number of households	%
Identity theft	6,426,200	5·5	existing credit card	2,966,500	2·5
No identity theft	109,206,700	93·3	other existing accounts	1,586,500	1·4
Unknown	1,477,800	1·3	personal information	1,083,100	0·9
Total	117,110,800	—	multiple types	790,200	0·7

A similar survey by the Federal Trade Commission showed that 3·7% of US adults (*c.*8·3m people) discovered they were victims of ID theft in 2005. 10% of victims reported a loss of ≥$6,000 in goods and services; 5% reported a loss of >$13,000. The latest 'Aftermath Survey' by the Identity Theft Resource Center (ITRC) shows that victims of ID theft in 2006 typically spent $1,342–$1,884 in out-of-pocket expenses and 97–231 hours rectifying their credit. Tabulated below is the ITRC's 2006 analysis of the many and various uses that are made of stolen identities:

Victim's identity used to/for...	%		
New credit account in victim's name	60	Get apartment or home as victim.	11
Get new cell phone	30	Access victim's online banking account	9
New home phone	29	Take over existing checking	9
Get new cable/utility.	29	Obtain auto loan/car purchase as victim.	8
Charges over internet	28	Take over/modify existing cellular account	8
Charges on victim's card.	27	Lease car using victim's info.	8
Change details of an existing credit a/c.	18	Open internet account	7
Other loans	17	Take over/modify to existing cable/utility	7
Make charges on stolen card	16	Take over/modify to existing home phone	7
Open new checking or savings account	12	Mortgage or 2nd mortgage as victim.	3
Create checks with false account info	12	File bankruptcy under victim's info	2
		[Respondents could report more than 1 use]	

ITRC data also shed light upon the various sources of stolen ID data, and the time which elapsed between the first incident of fraud and its discovery by victims:

Source of stolen information	%	*Time passed prior to discovery*	%
Friend or family member	41	0–3 months	33
Work	12	4–6 months	16
Wallet/handheld/planner	8	7–12 months	13
Home/car by a thief.	8	13–18 months	5
Mail	7	19–23 months	8
Internet.	7	2–3 years	8
Scam.	5	≥3 years	17
Fraudulent address change.	4		
Trash.	1	[Respondents could report more than 1 source]	

——HISTORICAL ECONOMIC INDICATORS OF NOTE——

Indicator · Year		2007	2006	2005	2004	2003	2002	2001	2000	1999
President		Bush	Bush	Bush	Bush	Bush	Bush	Bush	Clinton	Clinton
Gross Domestic Product (GDP)	current $bn	13,841.3	13,194.7	12,433.9	11,685.9	10,960.8	10,469.6	10,128.0	9,817.0	9,268.4
Gross Domestic Product (GDP)	% change	4.9	6.1	6.4	6.6	4.7	3.4	3.2	5.9	6.0
Change in consumer prices (all urban consumers)	%	4.1	2.5	3.4	3.3	1.9	2.4	1.6	3.4	2.7
Unemployment rate (civilian labor force)	%	4.6	4.6	5.1	5.5	6.0	5.8	4.7	4.0	4.2
Average weekly hours worked (non-agricultural)	hours	33.8	33.9	33.8	33.7	33.7	33.9	34.0	34.3	34.3
Average gross weekly earnings (non-agricultural)	current $	589.72	567.87	544.33	529.09	518.06	506.75	493.79	481.01	463.15
Industrial output as a percentage of total capacity	%	81.0	80.9	80.2	78.0	76.0	74.8	76.3	81.8	81.9
Disposable income, per capita	current $	33,705	32,183	30,677	29,563	28,053	27,167	26,235	25,472	23,968
Personal expenditure, per capita	current $	32,223	30,831	29,381	27,911	26,476	25,504	24,722	23,862	22,491
Change in real, per capita, personal disp. income	%	2.1	2.1	0.8	2.7	1.2	2.1	0.9	3.7	1.8
Savings as % of disposable income	%	0.5	0.4	0.5	2.1	2.1	2.4	1.8	2.3	2.4
Consumer credit – total outstanding	$bn	2,523.6	2,387.5	2,284.9	2,191.3	2,078.0	1,974.1	1,867.2	1,717.5	1,532.1
Prime rate charged by banks	%	8.05	7.96	6.19	4.34	4.12	4.67	6.91	9.23	8.00
NYSE Composite index (Dec 2002=5,000)		9,649	8,358	7,349	6,613	5,447	5,579	6,398	6,806	6,547
Dow Jones Industrial Average		13,170	11,409	10,548	10,317	8,994	9,226	10,189	10,735	10,465
NASDAQ Composite (Feb 1971=100)		2,579	2,263	2,099	1,987	1,647	1,540	2,035	3,784	2,728
Net farm income	$bn	88.7	59.0	77.1	85.9	59.7	40.1	55.0	50.7	47.7
Total corporate profits after tax	$bn	1,140.1	1,351.9	1,186.7	897.3	664.8	575.8	503.8	508.2	517.2
Federal finance surplus/deficit		-162.0	-248.2	-318.3	-412.7	-377.6	-157.8	128.2	236.2	125.6
US Trade, balance on current account	$m	-731,214	-788,116	-728,993	-624,993	-523,400	-461,275	-384,699	-417,426	-301,630
US Dollar/GB Pound ($/£)		2.00	1.84	1.82	1.83	1.63	1.50	1.44	1.51	1.62
US Dollar/euro ($/€)		1.37	1.26	1.24	1.24	1.13	0.94	0.90	0.92	1.06
GB Pound/euro (£/€)		1.46	1.47	1.46	1.47	1.45	1.59	1.61	1.64	1.52
Gold price per troy ounce	$	696	604	443	409	364	310	271	279	279

[Sources: Economic Indicators, Government Printing Office; US Annual Statistical Abstract; HM Treasury; Bank of England]

Form & Faith

It is impossible, in our condition of society, not to be sometimes a Snob.
— WILLIAM MAKEPEACE THACKERAY (1811–63)

HAVES & HAVE-NOTS

The percentage of Americans who believe that their society is divided into haves and have-nots has risen dramatically, from 26% in 1988 to 48% in 2007 – according to a Pew Research Center poll from November 2007. And, given the recent economic upheaval caused by the subprime credit crunch, it seems likely that this figure may have risen further over the last 12 months. Below is a tabulation of recent Pew data:

Is America divided into haves and have-nots?

%	yes	no	d/k
1988	26	71	
2001	44	53	
2007	48	48	

If you had to choose, are you in the haves or have-nots?

%	haves	have-nots	d/k
1988	59	17	24
2001	52	32	16
2007	45	34	21

Below are those who, in 2007, said that America *is* split into haves and have-nots:

Group	%				
All Americans	48	Men	56	30–49s	51
Republicans	33	Women	51	50–64s	49
Democrats	63	Whites	45	≥65s	45
Independents	46	Blacks	67		
		18–29s	49	[Source: Pew Research Cntr]	

AMERICANS & CLASS

Since 1972, the General Social Survey has asked Americans whether they thought they belonged to the lower, working, middle, or upper class. The results are below:

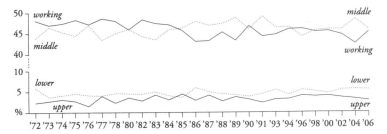

FORMS OF ADDRESS

Personage	envelope	letter opening	verbal address
President	The President, The White House	Dear Mr President	Mr President
Vice President	The Vice President, Old Executive Office Building	Dear Mr Vice President	Mr Vice President
Former US President	The Honorable {A} {B}	Dear Mr {B}	Mr {B}; President {A} {B}
Attorney General	The Honorable {A} {B}	Dear Mr Attorney General	Mr Attorney General
Cabinet Members	The Honorable {A} {B}, Secretary of {department}	Dear Mr Secretary	Mr Secretary
Postmaster General	The Honorable {A} {B}, Postmaster General	Dear Mr Postmaster General	Mr Postmaster General
President of the Senate	The Honorable {A} {B}, President of the Senate	Dear Mr President	Mr President
Speaker of the House of Rep.	The Honorable {A} {B}, Speaker of the House of Rep.	Dear Mr Speaker	Mr Speaker; Speaker
US Senator	The Honorable {A} {B}, US Senate	Dear Senator {B}	Senator {B}
Congressman/woman	The Honorable {A} {B}, House of Representatives	Dear Mr/Madam {B}	Congressman/woman ({A} {B})
Secretary General of the UN	His/Her Excellency {A} {B}, Secretary General of the UN	Dear Mr Secretary General	Mr Sec. Gen./Excellency
Ambassador of the US	The Honorable {A} {B}, American Ambassador	Dear Mr Ambassador	Mr Ambassador
Foreign Ambassador	His/Her Excellency {A} {B}, Ambassador of {X}	Dear Mr Ambassador	Mr Ambassador
Chief Justice of the Supreme Ct	The Chief Justice, The Supreme Court of the US	Dear (Mr) Chief Justice	Mr Chief Justice ({B})
Assoc. Justice of the Supreme Ct	Mr/Mrs Justice {B}, The Supreme Court of the US	Dear (Mr) Justice	Mr Justice ({B})
State Governor	The Honorable {A} {B}, The Governor of {X}	Dear Governor {B}	Governor {B}
Lieutenant Governor	The Honorable {A} {B}, Lieutenant Gov. of {X}	Dear Mr {B}	Mr {B}
Mayor	The Honorable {A} {B}, Mayor of {X}	Dear Mayor {B}	Mr Mayor
King/Queen	His/Her Majesty {name}, King/Queen of {X}	Your Majesty	Your Majesty
President of a Republic	His/Her Excellency {A} {B}, President of the Rep. of {X}	Dear Mr President	Mr President
Prime Minister	His/Her Excellency {A} {B}, The Prime Minister of {X}	Dear (Mr) Prime Minister	(Mr) Prime Minister
US Armed Forces	{Rank} {A} {B} {USA, USN, USAF, USMC, USCG}	Dear {Rank} {B}	{Rank} {B}

{A} = first name; {B} = last name ❦ Throughout, where appropriate, 'Madam' should be substituted for 'Mr'. ❦ For reasons of space, some titles have been abbreviated; they should not be so truncated in practice. ❦ Considerable debate and dispute surround 'correct' forms of address. The above tabulation has been compiled from a number of, often contradictory, sources. Readers in need of detailed advice, such as on the styling of US military ranks, are advised to consult the relevant organization. (The British Peerage is so complex that its custom are the subject of a series of specialist texts that detail, for example, the correct way to address the wives of younger sons of Earls.)

JENNA BUSH'S WEDDING

George Walker Bush's younger (by one minute) daughter, Jenna Welch Bush, married Henry Chase Hager of Richmond, Virginia, on May 10, 2008. Despite speculation that the wedding might take place within the White House, the couple spliced their troth outdoors at the Bushes' Prairie Chapel Ranch in Crawford, Texas. The ceremony was conducted at sunset, in front of a bespoke limestone altar and before 200 family members and friends. Below are some of the wedding day details:

Bride's dress · embroidered white silk organza by Oscar de la Renta
Groom's suit · dark blue with powder blue tie
Aisle music · 'Trumpet Voluntary' (played by a mariachi band)
Pastor · Kirbyjon Caldwell, Houston's Windsor Village United Methodist Church
Ceremony readings · from Corinthians, read by George H.W. & Barbara Bush
Wedding singer · Tyrone 'Super T' Smith
First dance · Taj Mahal's *Lovin' in My Baby's Eyes*
Father-daughter dance · Joe Cocker's *You Are So Beautiful*
Menu · fried oysters on tostadas, lump Gulf crab parfait, grilled Rio Grande ranch flatiron steak, spinach with pine nuts, churros with chocolate
Cake · tres leches (bride's), chocolate (groom's)

In March 2008, Bush told the Hispanic Chamber of Congress, 'I had to face some very difficult spending decisions, and I've had to conduct sensitive diplomacy. That's called planning for a wedding'.

THREE TYPES OF MARRIAGE

If a man marries for	LOVE	CONVENIENCE & COMFORT	A DOWRY
He gets	a wife	a mistress	a madam
Who will	love him	honor him	suffer him
He has her for	himself	his house & friends	society
She will	agree with him	oblige him	dictate to him
When he is ill she will	nurse him	visit him	inquire after him
When he dies she will	shed tears	sigh	wear mourning

– Adapted from an observation attributed to JACOB COHEN, *c.*1899

LUCKY DAYS ON WHICH TO MARRY

January .... 2 ~ 4 ~ 11 ~ 19 ~ 21
February .... 1 ~ 3 ~ 10 ~ 19 ~ 21
March .... 3 ~ 5 ~ 12 ~ 20 ~ 23
April .... 2 ~ 4 ~ 12 ~ 20 ~ 22
May .... 2 ~ 4 ~ 12 ~ 20 ~ 23
June .... 1 ~ 3 ~ 11 ~ 19 ~ 21
July .... 1 ~ 3 ~ 12 ~ 19 ~ 21 ~ 31

August .... 2 ~ 11 ~ 18 ~ 20 ~ 30
September .... 1 ~ 9 ~ 16 ~ 18 ~ 28
October .... 1 ~ 8 ~ 15 ~ 17 ~ 27 ~ 29
November .... 5 ~ 11 ~ 13 ~ 22 ~ 25
December .. 1 ~ 8 ~ 10 ~ 19 ~ 23 ~ 29

[A. Cielo, *Signs, Omens, & Superstitions*, 1918]

ON DEMEANOR

WALK *groundly* · TALK *profoundly* · DRINK *roundly* · SLEEP *soundly*

PATRIOTIC TOASTS

The Perfect Gentleman; or, Etiquette and Elegance, published in 1860, provides a variety of toasts suitable for patriotic occasions. A selection of these appear below:

America – The birthplace of liberty, and the asylum for the oppressed of every land.

May all Americans share equally the blessings of liberty, and ever stand ready to contend for the rights and liberties of mankind.

The American eagle – May she build her nest on every forest on this continent.

The progress of our country – May it never be fettered by faction.

Uncle Sam – May the venerable old gentleman soon sweep our legislative halls clean of pugilists, duellists, and thieves.

May civil and religious liberty ever go hand-in-hand.

May the weight of our taxes never break the back of our credit.

Where liberty dawned, may it rise to its meridian splendor.

The Press – Free without licentiousness, and bold without intolerance.

Wealth, security, & resistance to oppression.

The spot where we were born – 'where the women can all love, and the men can all fight – the latter all day, the former all night'.

TRADITIONAL WASHINGTON RECEPTION DAYS

'Usage has set apart certain days when the ladies of the households of receiving officials are "at home." The designation of certain days for certain classes of officials was adopted as a matter of convenience to the public, and to give the lady of the house time to attend to her own social duties on other days, without interruption or disappointment to her friends. The Rule for days "at home" now in vogue is:'

Mondays.......... *ladies of the families of Justices of the Supreme Court and 'Capitol Hill'*
Tuesdays ....*ladies of the families of the Speaker, Representatives, and Generals of the Army*
Wednesdays............................. *ladies of the families of Members of the Cabinet*
Thursdays........................ *ladies of the families of the Vice President and Senators*
Fridays .. *ladies of the 'West End' or fashionable quarter of the city in and out of official life*
Saturdays.............. *the Drawing Rooms of the Presiding Lady of the Executive Mansion*

– Randolph Keim De Benneville, *Hand-book of Official and Social Etiquette and Public Ceremonials at Washington*, 1889

─ON CONVERSATION─

Pearls of wisdom on the conversational arts, harvested from a variety of sources.

Look at the person to whom you speak, but do not stare at him. Endeavor both by your expression and manner to show confidence without boldness, and ease without familiarity. ⁓ Be sparing of puns and proverbs. Too many of them render conversation trite and stiff. ⁓ A short, pithy quotation adds a sparkle to discourse; a very long one is wearisome. ⁓ In conversation, as in music, attend to time. In your words, do not hurry and become a gabbler; neither speak so slowly as to be sententious. A harsh, loud voice is vulgar, but it is an unpleasant piece of affectation to speak so low that you are only heard with difficulty. ⁓ Never attempt to engross all of the conversation. You might as well try to help yourself to all the dinner. ⁓ The very essence of conversation is reciprocity; and those who pay no attention to the sentiments of others lose all the benefit of interchange of thought. ⁓ When parents enter into details about the wonderful quickness, beauty, talents, &c., of their children, listen patiently. If you are yourself a parent, you will excuse parental partiality. If you are not, perhaps you may be one at some future time. But papas and mammas should beware of putting the patience of the general hearer to the test by very lengthy accounts of the clever speeches or wonderful achievements of their hopeful progeny. ⁓ Be particularly careful in all that relates to the letter 'h'. Do not drop it where it should be sounded, nor introduce it where it has no right to be.

A tale should be judicious, clear, succinct.
The language plain,
and incidents well linked.
Tell not as new what everybody knows,
And new or old, still hasten to a close;
There, centring in a focus round and neat,
Let all your rays of information meet.

– WILLIAM COWPER (1731–1800)

⁓ Conversation should bring into play all the amiable qualities of kindness, politeness, patience, and forbearance. [Anon, *Cassell's Handbook of Etiquette*, 1860] ❦ There is no such thing as conversation. It is an illusion. There are intersecting monologues, that is all. – REBECCA WEST ❦ In refined society conversation may be classed as the highest order of entertainment. Music may be ranked next, and dancing last. ⁓ Persons engaged in conversation should maintain a respectful distance. It is not always agreeable to maintain too close proximity, no matter how important or interesting the subjects under consideration. ⁓ High sounding expressions in conversation are not an evidence of learning, or even ordinary intelligence. Let every one speak naturally. ⁓ Vulgarity of expression is to be condemned in all. Double entendres, intentionally made, are an evidence of a vulgar mind, and should be rebuked. [Randolph Keim, *Hand-book of Official & Social Etiquette & Public Ceremonials at Washington*, 1869] ❦ Conversation has a kind of charm about it, an insinuating and insidious something that elicits secrets from us just like love or liquor. – SENECA ❦ He who takes a side which he at length finds not to be tenable, should frankly confess his inability to maintain it. Let him not think it an exposure of his own weakness; it will be received as the indication both of his candor and of his discrimination … He who can cheerfully and unreservedly own himself confuted, has won a more glorious victory than his confuter. [G.W. Hervey, *Rhetoric of Conversation; or, Bridles & Spurs for the Management of the Tongue*, 1853] ❦

ON CONVERSATION cont.

A good listener is not someone who has nothing to say. A good listener is a good talker with a sore throat. – KATHERINE WHITEHORN ❧ Never make yourself the hero or heroine of your own story. – Speak to entertain rather than to distinguish yourself. – It is exceedingly unpleasant to hear the English language butchered by bad grammar and the misapplication of words. – No one has a right to go into society unless he can be sympathetic, unselfish, and animating as well as animated. Society demands cheerfulness and unselfishness, and it is the duty of every one to help make and sustain it in these features. The manner of conversation is quite as important as the matter. – Do not lose your temper in society; avoid all coarseness and undue familiarity in addressing others; never attack the character of others in their absence; avoid all cant; do not ask the price of articles you observe, except from intimate friends, and then very quietly; never give officious advice; and especially avoid contradictions and interruptions. [W.R. Houghton &c., *Rules of Etiquette & Home Culture*, 1889] ❧ Put power into the lower notes of the voice, and sweetness into the higher ones. There is magnetism in a melodious voice to which no one can be insensible. The dullest talker can hold his hearers if he utters his platitudes agreeably. – Every one, man and woman, has a repertoire of persuasive notes, of caressing tones. It was said of Gibbon, the historian, when in love with the mother of Mme. de Stael, that his only idea of reaching the heart was by piercing the ears! – Flippancy grates upon one's nerves if long continued. – Disputatious persons ought to be muzzled. [George Rippey Stewart, *Correct Social Usage*, 1906] ❧ Beware of the conversationalist who adds 'in other words'. He is merely starting afresh. – ROBERT MORLEY ❧ Gesticulations are in excessively bad taste. If you do not wish to attract censorious remark, converse quietly and without gesture. – Do not whistle, loll about, scratch your head, or fidget with any portion of your dress while speaking. 'Tis excessively awkward, and indicative of low-breeding. – Unless you are actually afflicted with deafness, never ask to have a sentence repeated. It implies a wandering attention. – Business men do not go into the world of polite society to carry their shop, and they will not thank you for reminding them of work in their hours of relaxation. [S.A. Frost, *Frost's Laws & By-laws of American Society*, 1869] ❧ Silence is the virtue of fools. – FRANCIS BACON ❧ Tones, gestures, glances, attitudes, and smiles supply a color, so to speak, remaining indelibly impressed upon the memory, and which no book can ever impart. – Nearly all eccentricity whatever is in fact only shallow vanity. Avoid oddity of every kind whatever in your external appearance or manners or conversation. – It is wrong to be always in the right. – Rely upon it, if you converse well enough to excite interest, the world will soon know everything about you. [Charles Godfrey Leland, *The Art of Conversation*, 1865]

There must, in the first place, be knowledge, there must be materials; in the second place, there must be a command of words; in the third place, there must be imagination, to place things in such views as they are not commonly seen in; and in the fourth place, there must be presence of mind, and a resolution that is not to be overcome by failures: this last is an essential requisite; for want of it many people do not excel in conversation.

– SAMUEL JOHNSON (1709–84)

TYPES OF LAUGHTER

A taxonomy of laughter from *The Perfect Gentleman; or, Etiquette & Eloquence* (1860):

The DIMPLERS
The *dimple* is practiced to give a grace
to the features, and is frequently made
a bait to entangle a gazing lover.

The SMILERS
The *smile* expresses our satisfaction
in a sort of liberal approbation.

The LAUGHERS
The *laugh* is the common risus of the
ancients, and is simply an expansion
of the smile, accompanied by a slight
cachinnation.

The GRINNERS
The *grin*, by writers of antiquity, is
called the Syncrusian, and was then,
as it is now, made use of to display
a beautiful set of teeth.

The HORSE-LAUGHERS
The *horse-laugh* is an undue
expansion of the laugh, accompanied
by a boisterous noise, and is not
allowable in polite society.

The Perfect Gentleman notes that 'immoderate
laughter is exceedingly unbecoming in a lady'.

DISCIPLES OF THE WISE

According to Hebraic tradition, *Six things are a disgrace to the disciple of the wise:*

To walk abroad perfumed;
To walk alone by night;
To wear old, clouted shoes;
To talk with a woman in the street;
To sit at table with illiterate men;
To be late at the synagogue.

TUSSER'S 'PRINCIPLE POINTS OF RELIGION'

1 .... To pray to God continually,
2 ..... To learn to know Him rightfully
3 .... To honor God in Trinity,
The Trinity in Unity,
The Father in his Majesty,
The Son in his Humanity,
The Holy Ghost's Benignity,
Three persons, one in Deity
4 .... To serve Him always, Holily,
5 ..... To ask Him all things, needfully,
6 .... To praise Him in all company,
7 ...... To love Him always, steadfastly,
8 ...... To dread Him always, fearfully,
9 ....To ask Him mercy, penitently,

10 ..... To trust Him always, faithfully,
11 ...... To obey Him always, willingly,
12 ..... To abide Him always, patiently,
13 ... To thank Him always, thankfully,
14 ...... To live here always, virtuously,
15 ..... To use thy neighbour, honestly,
16 .... To look for death still, presently,
17 .... To help the poor, in misery,
18 .... To hope for Heaven's felicity,
19 .... To have faith, hope, and charity,
20 ....To count this life but vanity.

– THOMAS TUSSER, *Five Hundred
Points of Good Husbandry*, 1663

ON HANDSHAKES

There are many theories regarding the history of the handshake. While some speculate that the gesture may have evolved in pre-history as a display of trust designed to show the absence of a weapon, such theories are difficult to confirm. As a greeting, the handshake was known in Assyria, Babylonia, Greece, and Rome, then spread throughout the Roman Empire. In Rome, the right-hand clasp was included during the signing of contracts and used in the marriage ceremony (some scholars have noted that the right hand was considered sacred to the Roman godess of fidelity, Fides). Yet the extent to which these gestures were similar to the handshake of today is a matter of debate, and there are those who attribute its modern usage to, variously, the Quakers, English, Italians, Germans, or French. All that seems certain is the vital importance of the handshake in both business and political dealings, and that scores of books have been written regarding its proper deployment:

An 'anonymous authority' cited by the 1881 etiquette manual *Our Deportment* offers the following advice: A man has no right to take a lady's hand until it is offered · It is the privilege of a superior to offer his or her hand first, so that an inferior should never put his forward first. · The right hand should always be offered, unless it be so engaged as to make it impossible, and then an excuse should be offered. · The French give the left hand, as nearest the heart.

❦ In her 2005 *Guide to Excruciatingly Correct Behavior*, Miss Manners notes that the 'lady/older/ranking person should initiate' the handshake, though she does not provide any advice to help determine which category applies. ❦ Today business-etiquette experts frequently implore one to avoid the limp 'dead fish' handshake, although there are also those who feel Americans have gone too far in favor of the firm handshake, which can seem aggressive.

The ubiquity of the handshake has made it a convenient form of identification for secret societies. The internet teems with guides to Masonic handshakes, including:

The Boaz .... *thumb pressed against the other Mason's first knuckle*
The Shibboleth.................... *thumb pressed between the first and second knuckle*
The Jachin............................ *thumb pressed hard against the second knuckle*
The Tubalcain .... *thumb pressed between second and third knuckle*
The Ma-Ha-Bone........... *thumbs interlaced, fingers spread and pressed to the wrist*

Secret handshakes are also a feature of many street gangs, and gang-prevention organizations have encouraged school districts to compile a list of their ever-changing attributes. ❦ While not quite a secret society, the Scout movement has its own special handshake: all Scouts shake with their left hand, a curious tradition that has been attributed to the practices of various African tribes. ❦ For unknown reasons, Mussolini is reported to have banned normal handshakes in favor of the raised fist.

The hand gesture that drew the most attention in 2008 was likely the fist bump [see p.15], made famous by Barack and Michelle Obama on the night the former claimed the Democratic nomination. Though some have noticed that young men (and germaphobes) are increasingly taking to the gesture, many in the business world caution that it is not an appropriate replacement for the handshake.

─────── GREETINGS FROM THE PRESIDENT &c. ───────

United States citizens may request official greetings from the President and First Lady on the following occasions, by writing to the White House Greetings Office:

BIRTHDAYS · Available for individuals turning 80 years or older.

BIRTH · Requests must be made within a year of the child's birth, and may not be made until the child is born.

WEDDINGS · Requests should be made after the wedding.

ANNIVERSARY · Available to couples celebrating their 50th or greater wedding anniversary.

Requests may be made by visiting the White House website at whitehouse.gov.

The Queen of England will send a congratulatory card via the Royal Mail to citizens of Her Realms or UK Overseas Territories on their 60th, 65th, and 70th wedding anniversaries, and every anniversary thereafter; as well as on 100th and 105th birthdays, and every birthday thereafter.

The German President will send a letter of congratulation to citizens on 65th, 70th, and 75th wedding anniversaries, as well as 100th and 105th birthdays, and every birthday thereafter. The President will also become honorary godparent to the 7th child of any family; this includes a gift of €500 (*c.*$780).

─────────── FIRST WORLD WAR VETERANS ───────────

The last known German, French, Austrian, and Turkish WWI veterans died in 2008:

Erich Kästner†
3·10·1900–1·1·2008 (aged 107)
In 1918, Kästner served in the German army for 4 months and was sent to the Western Front. During WWII he was in the Luftwaffe, stationed mainly in France.

Franz Künstler
7·24·1900–5·27·2008 (aged 107)
Künstler was born to the German minority in the (then) Hungarian town of Soos, and was drafted into the Austrian army in Feb. 1918, where he served as a gunner in Italy.

Lazare Ponticelli
12·7·1897–3·12·2008 (aged 110)
Born in Italy, Ponticelli moved to France as a boy. In 1914, he joined the French Foreign Legion and the next year, when Italy joined the Allies, the Italian army.

Yakup Satar
3·11·1898–4·2·2008 (aged 110)
Satar joined the Ottoman army in 1915 and fought in the 1917 Mesopotamian campaign against the British. Captured by them at Kut, he was a POW for over a year.

On March 6, 2008, Frank Buckles of Charlestown, WV, was honored at a White House ceremony as the last living WWI veteran to have served in the American forces. (The occasion of the celebration was a Pentagon photography exhibit depicting nine WWI veterans). Buckles (*b.*1901) joined the Army at 16, after lying about his age, and served as an ambulance driver in both England and France.

† Verification of Kästner's status is problematic since Germany keeps no records of its war veterans.

RELIGIOUS AFFILIATION IN THE US

Religious affiliation amongst US adults is 'very diverse and extremely fluid' according to a landmark 2008 poll by the Pew Forum on Religion and Public Life. The survey of 35,000 Americans found:

28% have left the faith in which they were raised in favor of another religion – or no religion at all. And, if change in faith includes changes within various types of Protestantism, this rate is 44%.

America is 'on the verge of becoming a minority Protestant country', as just 51·3% report an affiliation with Protestantism, which itself is 'characterized by significant internal diversity and fragmentation, encompassing hundreds of different denominations'.

Catholicism has seen the greatest losses in affiliation: while 31% were raised as Catholics, only 24% describe themselves so as adults. Yet, the overall decline in Catholicism has been checked by immigration (which has also buoyed Buddhism, Islam, and Hinduism). Amongst all foreign-born Americans, Catholics outnumber Protestants by 46% to 24%.

16·1% report that they are unaffiliated with any specific faith, which makes 'unaffiliated' the fourth largest religious group in the country. That said, there is considerable diversity within this group, and 'it is simply not accurate to describe this entire group as nonreligious or "secular"'.

The religions that best retain childhood members into adulthood are Hinduism (with an 84% 'retention rate'), Judaism (76%), Orthodox Christian (73%), and Mormon (70%). Jehovah's Witnesses have the lowest rate of retention (37%).

US religious affiliation	%	%	%
CHRISTIAN	78·4		
Protestant	51·3		
Evangelical		26·3	
Mainline		18·1	
Historic Black		6·9	
Catholic	23·9		
Mormon	1·7		
Jehovah's Witness	0·7		
Orthodox	0·6		
Greek			<0·3
Russian			<0·3
Other			<0·3
Other Christian	0·3		
OTHER RELIGIONS	4·7		
Jewish	1·7		
Reform		0·7	
Conservative		0·5	
Orthodox		<0·3	
Other		0·3	
Buddhist	0·7		
Zen		<0·3	
Theravada		<0·3	
Tibetan		<0·3	
Other		0·3	
Muslim†	0·6		
Sunni		0·3	
Shia		<0·3	
Other		<0·3	
Hindu	0·4		
Other world religions	<0·3		
Other faiths	1·2		
Unitarians & other liberal		0·7	
New Age		0·4	
Native American religions		<0·3	
UNAFFILIATED	16·1		
Atheist	1·6		
Agnostic	2·4		
Nothing in particular	12·1		
Secular unaffiliated		6·3	
Religious unaffiliated		5·8	
D/K or REFUSED	0·8		

† 2007 Pew Data; some figures are rounded.
[Source: Pew Forum on Religion & Public Life, 2008 US Religious Landscape Survey, Adults.]

——————— WORLD RELIGIONS & LANGUAGES ———————

Religion	%	Language	%
Christian	33·3	Mandarin Chinese	13·2
Roman Catholic	17·0	Spanish	4·9
Protestant	5·8	English	4·7
Orthodox	3·5	Arabic	3·1
Anglican	1·3	Hindi	2·7
Muslim	21·0	Portuguese	2·7
Hindu	13·3	Bengali	2·6
Buddhist	5·8	Russian	2·2
Sikh	0·4	Japanese	1·9
Jewish	0·2	Standard German	1·4
Other religions	12·0	Wu Chinese	1·2

[In % of world population · Only first-language speakers · Source: CIA World Factbook, 2008]

——————————— BELIEF IN GOD ———————————

While 100% of Mormons believe in God, according to a 2008 survey by the Pew Forum on Religion and Public Life, the same is not the case with other religions:

Believe in God	%				
Mormon	100	Catholic	97	Jewish	83
Jehovah's Witness	98	Orthodox	95	Buddhist	75
Protestant	98	Muslim	92	Unaffiliated	70
		Hindu	92	ALL AMERICANS	92

Below is the percentage of believers in each religious group who say they view God as a 'person with whom people can have a relationship', or as an impersonal force:

% personal		% impersonal			
91	Mormon	6	41	Muslim	42
82	Jehovah's Witness	11	31	Hindu	53
72	Protestant	19	25	Jewish	50
60	Catholic	29	20	Buddhist	45
49	Orthodox	34	28	Unaffiliated	35
			60	ALL AMERICANS	25

The remaining portion of believers did not know whether they believed in a personal God, or in God as an impersonal force. The unaffiliated includes atheists, agnostics, and those classified as 'secular' unaffiliated or 'religious' unaffiliated. Strangely, 22% of atheists said they believed in God [see p.340].

——————————— THE BIBLE ———————————

Americans who say the Bible is ...	%		
The word of God	30	An ancient book of fables	22
Inspired by God	46	No opinion	3
		[Source: Gallup, May 2008]	

──────── EINSTEIN ON RELIGION ────────

In May 2008, a letter in which Albert Einstein discussed his views on religion was bought at a London auction for £170,000 (*c.*$334,000). The recipient of the letter (sent 3·1·1954) was philosopher Eric Gutkind, who had sent Einstein his book *Choose Life: The Biblical Call to Revolt*. This extract gives a flavor of Einstein's belief:

> *The word God is for me nothing more than the expression and product of human weaknesses, the Bible a collection of honorable, but still primitive legends which are nevertheless pretty childish. No interpretation no matter how subtle can (for me) change this. These subtilized interpretations are highly manifold according to their nature and have almost nothing to do with the original text. For me the Jewish religion like all other religions is an incarnation of the most childish superstitions.*

──────── TEMPLETON PRIZE ────────

The *Templeton Prize for Progress Toward Research or Discoveries About Spiritual Realities* was awarded in 2008 to Michael Heller, a Polish theologian and cosmologist. Heller's work has sought to answer some of the most fundamental and abstract questions of the universe (e.g., 'why is there something rather than nothing?') by drawing on knowledge from both science and religion. Interviewed by the *New York Times* soon after his win, Heller noted the necessity of reconciling the two fields, saying that 'science gives us knowledge, and religion gives us meaning. Both are prerequisites of the decent existence'. ❦ Sir John Templeton, who died on July 8, 2008, founded his prize in 1972, 'to encourage and honor the advancement of knowledge in spiritual matters'. The £820,000 prize (>$1·6m), is said to be the richest annual prize given to an individual. Templeton stipulated its value always be greater than the Nobel Prize, to 'underscore that research and advances in spiritual discoveries can be quantifiably more significant than disciplines recognized' by the Nobels.

──────── RELIGION AS AN INSURANCE FOR HAPPINESS ────────

Religious believers enjoy higher levels of 'life satisfaction', according to research among Europeans by Andrew Clark and Orsolya Lelkes presented to the Royal Economic Society in March 2008. In their paper 'Deliver Us from Evil: Religion as Insurance', Clark and Lelkes also asserted that religion 'insure[s] against some of life's adverse events' (e.g., unemployment and divorce), and that people seem to become happier the more often they attend church or pray. The authors also claimed that religious people tend to conservatism, in that they are 'both anti-divorce and anti-job creation programs for the unemployed'. And, while both Catholics and Protestants are less hurt by marital separation than the nonreligious, Protestants suffer less than Catholics do. The authors conclude: 'Over and above denomination, churchgoing and prayer are also associated with greater satisfaction. Religion tempers the impact of adverse life events: it has current as opposed to after-life rewards.'

—————— POPE BENEDICT XVI's VISIT TO THE US ——————

Pope Benedict XVI made his first Papal visit to the US in 2008. While he raised the issues of immigration, human rights, and abortion in a series of speeches, for many the defining theme of Benedict's tour was his determination to address the priest abuse scandal, in part by meeting with victims. Below is a timeline of his US visit:

{4/15, 4pm} Arrived on 'Shepherd One' in Washington, DC. {4/16, 10:30am} White House welcoming ceremony and speech on South Lawn, followed by private meeting with George W. Bush. {5:30} Prayer service and meeting with 350 bishops at Basilica of the National Shrine of the Immaculate Conception. {4/17, 10am} Said Mass before 46,000 at Nationals Park baseball stadium. (Unscheduled) private meeting with victims of the priest abuse scandal, the first such meeting by a Pope since the scandal broke in 2002. {5pm} Speech to Catholic educators at the John Paul II Cultural Center, followed by a meeting with Buddhist, Muslim, Hindu, Jewish, and other faith representatives. {4/18, 10:45am} Speech at the UN, emphasizing human rights as a means of halting violence, war, and poverty. {6pm} Visit to the Park East Synagogue, the first Papal visit to an American synagogue, followed by prayer service at St Joseph's Church. {4/19, 9:15am} Mass at St Patrick's Cathedral. {4:30} Meeting with young Catholics at St Joseph's Seminary. Rally and prayer service afterwards; Kelly Clarkson performed. {4/20, 9:30am} Visit to and consecration of Ground Zero. {2:30pm} Mass at Yankee Stadium. {8pm} Farewell ceremony at JFK airport; the Pope departed for Rome.

The Pope celebrated his 81st birthday on 4/16 with a lemon cake and a chorus of 'Happy Birthday' sung by 9,000 on the White House lawn. [Sources: *USA Today, Washington Post, New York Times*, &c.]

————————— THE VATICAN & ALIENS —————————

In an interview with the Vatican's newspaper, *L'Osservatore Romano*, in May 2008, the director of the Vatican Observatory, Father José Gabriel Funes, said that belief in aliens does not contradict a belief in God. In the article, titled 'Aliens Are My Brother', Funes went on to say that the existence of aliens cannot be ruled out: 'Just as there is a multiplicity of creatures over the Earth, so there could be other beings, even intelligent [beings], created by God. This is not in contradiction with our faith, because we cannot establish limits to God's creative freedom.'

————————— PAPAL GUIDANCE BY TEXT MESSAGE —————————

Words of wisdom from Pope Benedict XVI (and his papal predecessor, John Paul II) are now available in Italy via text message. In February 2008, JPII's former spokesman Joaquin Navarro Valls joined with Vodafone to offer the daily SMS service. Each text message costs the equivalent of US 35¢, although for 52¢ the message is accompanied by an image of the late pontiff. Rival firm Telecom Italia already sends out a weekly message with selections from the Pope's Sunday address.

NEW SAINTS

In the Roman Catholic Church, a saint is one who has been canonized by the Pope and is thus declared worthy of 'public veneration' throughout the church. (Canonization is distinct from beatification, in which the church grants permission to venerate an individual with the titular suffix 'Blessed', but only within a particular diocese or other specified area.) Canonization is a lengthy and complex procedure, often spanning centuries, which depends on evidence of a candidate's exceptional sanctity as well as proof of several miracles†. At the time of writing, Pope Benedict XVI was scheduled to canonize the following saints during 2008:

Fr. Gaetano Errico
(1791–1860 · § 10·12·2008)
Devoted teacher who founded the Congregation of the Missionaries of the Sacred Hearts of Jesus and Mary at Secondigliano, Italy, after St Alphonsus Liguori commanded him so to do in a vision in 1818.

Maria Bernarda Butler
(1848–1924 · § 10·12·2008)
Founded the Franciscan Missionaries of Mary Help of Christians in Ecuador, and later performed healing miracles in Colombia. First modern Swiss woman to be canonized.

Alphonsa Muttathupandathu
(1910–1946 · § 10·12·2008)
A sister of the Congregation of Poor Clares of the Third Order of St Francis, she was revered for her devotion to the church despite frequent health problems. India's first saint.

Narcisa de Jesus Martillo Moran
(1832–69 · § 10·12·2008)
An Ecuadorian laywoman renowned for her religious instruction of children and young people. She reportedly spent four hours a night in religious mortification, including sometimes wearing a crown of thorns.

† In February 2008 the *Vatican's Congregation for the Causes of Saints* issued a directive demanding care in the beatification and canonization process. The 45-page statement called for 'greater sobriety and rigor' from officials, including those assessing the required miracles, as well as 'rigorous historical research'. Pope John Paul II beatified 1,340 and canonized 482, significantly more than his predecessors; his own sainthood case is pending, with reports of an expected beatification in spring 2009.

SEVEN NEW DEADLY SINS

In March 2008, the Vatican added to the traditional enumeration of deadly sins 7 further sins for the modern era. Bishop Gianfranco Girotti, head of the Apostolic Penitentiary (which rules on matters of conscience and grants absolutions), said 'while sin used to concern mostly the individual, today it has mainly a social resonance, due to the phenomenon of globalization.' The new 'social sins' are:

Taking or dealing in drugs
Genetic manipulation
'Morally debatable' scientific experiments
Environmental pollution
Social inequalities & injustice

Causing poverty
Accumulating excessive wealth

The original 7, laid down in the C6th, are anger, envy, gluttony, greed, lust, pride, and sloth.

--- ATHEISM ---

In the past few years, the debate over atheism has been animated by a number of bestselling books, not least *The God Delusion* by biologist Richard Dawkins and *God Is Not Great* by journalist Christopher Hitchens. According to a 2007 study by the Barna Group, *c.*20m Americans (*c.*9%) are atheist, agnostic, or identify themselves as having 'no faith', though rates of disbelief seem to vary with age [see right].

Age	% atheist
18–22	19
23–41	14
42–60	9
61+	6
[Includes agnostics &c.]	

A 2006 University of Minnesota study found Americans were less accepting of atheists than of other minorities. Nearly 40% said atheists did not share their 'vision of society', and *c.*48% said they would disapprove if their child married an atheist. Shown below is how atheists compare with other minority groups on these questions:

% who agree the group below 'does not at all fit' their vision of society		*% who would disapprove if their child wanted to marry a(n) …*	
Atheists	39·6	Atheist	47·6
Muslims	26·3	Muslim	33·5
Homosexuals	22·6	African American	27·2
Conservative Christians	13·5	Asian American	18·5
Recent immigrants	12·5	Hispanic	18·5
Hispanics	7·6	Jew	11·8
Jews	7·4	Conservative Christian	6·9

Data from the 2007 Pew Global Attitudes Project show also that in many parts of the world, a majority of people feel one must believe in God in order to be moral:

'It is necessary to believe in God to be moral and to have good values'			
	South Africa	74	Germany	39
	India	66	Canada	30
	Lebanon	66	Russia	26
	Unites States	57	Britain	22
Egypt … 99% *agreed*	Mexico	53	China	17

--- EVOLUTION & BIOLOGY TEACHERS ---

Below, according to a 2008 survey carried out by Pennsylvania State University, is the percentage of US high school biology teachers who 'agree' or 'strongly agree' with the following statements on teaching CREATIONISM and INTELLIGENT DESIGN:

I emphasize that these are valid alternatives to Darwinian explanations	48%
I emphasize that many reputable scientists view these as valid alternatives	49%
I acknowledge these as valid religious perspectives, but which are not appropriate for a science class	40%
I emphasize that almost all scientists reject these as valid accounts of the origin of species	32%

———————— FEDERAL HOLIDAYS ————————

According to the US Office of Personnel Management, federal law (5 USC 6103) establishes the following public holidays for federal employees. Most federal employees work on a Monday-through-Friday schedule. For these employees, when a holiday falls on a nonworkday, Saturday or Sunday, the holiday is usually observed on Monday (if the holiday falls on a Sunday) or Friday (if on a Saturday).

Holiday	2009	2010	2011	2012
New Year's Day	Jan 1	Jan 1	Jan 1	Jan 2
BD Martin Luther King Jr	Jan 19	Jan 18	Jan 17	Jan 16
Washington's Birthday	Feb 16	Feb 15	Feb 21	Feb 20
Memorial Day	May 25	May 31	May 30	May 28
Independence Day	Jul 3	Jul 5	Jul 4	Jul 4
Labor Day	Sep 7	Sep 6	Sep 5	Sep 3
Columbus Day	Oct 12	Oct 11	Oct 10	Oct 8
Veterans Day	Nov 11	Nov 11	Nov 11	Nov 12
Thanksgiving Day	Nov 26	Nov 25	Nov 24	Nov 22
Christmas Day	Dec 25	Dec 24	Dec 26	Dec 25

— TRADITIONAL WEDDING ANNIVERSARY SYMBOLS —

1st ....Paper	10th ....Tin	35th ....Coral, Jade
2nd ....Cotton	11th ....Steel	40th ....Ruby
3rd...............Leather	12th ....Silk	45th .... Sapphire
4th..........Linen, Silk	13th ....Lace	50th .... Gold
5th................ Wood	14th ....Ivory	55th ....Emerald
6th..................Iron	15th ....Crystal	60th .... Diamond
7th....... Wool, Copper	20th ....China	70th ....Platinum
8th.............. Bronze	25th ....Silver	75th .... Diamond
9th..............Pottery	30th .... Pearl	*British symbols differ.*

[Debate rages about the order of paper and cotton, and other symbols exist for certain anniversaries.]

—————— KEY TO SYMBOLS USED OVERLEAF ——————

[★ FH] ....US Federal holiday	[§ *patronage*]...................Saint's day
[●] ....Clocks change (USA)	[WA *year*].......... Wedding anniversary
[UK] .... UK Bank holiday	[Admis *year*].... Admission day [US States]
[ND]...................... National day	◑/◯......... Full/New moon [GMT]
[NH]................... National holiday	[✦].............Annual meteor shower
[ID *year*]..............Independence day	[UN]................United Nations day
[BD *year*].......................Birthday	[●] ....Eclipse [see p.192]
[† *year*] ....Anniversary of death	[£] .... Union Flag to be flown (UK)

Certain dates are subject to change, or tentative at the time of printing. Zodiac dates are approximate.

───────── JANUARY ─────────

Capricorn [♑]　　　*Birthstone* · GARNET　　　*Aquarius* [♒]
(Dec 22–Jan 20)　　　*Flower* · CARNATION　　　(Jan 21–Feb 19)

1★........ New Year's Day [★FH] · L(afayette) Ron(ald) Hubbard [†1986] ....Th
2 ....David Bailey [BD1938] · Georgia [Admis1788] ....F
3 ....Mel Gibson [BD1956] · Alaska [Admis1959]....................Sa
4 .... Quadrantids [𝄞] · Utah [Admis1896] ....Su
5 ....Twelfth night · St Edward the Confessor [†1066] ....M
6 ....Epiphany · New Mexico [Admis1912] ....Tu
7 ....Gerald Durrell [BD1925] · Hirohito [†1989] ....W
8 ..... Dame Shirley Bassey [BD1937] · Professor Stephen Hawking [BD1942] ....Th
9 ....Joan Baez [BD1941] · Connecticut [Admis1788]..................F
10........Grigori Rasputin [BD1872] · Dame Barbara Hepworth [BD1903] ....Sa
11...... ◗ · National Unity Day, Nepal [NH] · Francis Scott Key [†1843]......Su
12........................ Dame Agatha Christie [†1976] ....M
13..............St Hilary of Poitiers [§ *snake-bites*] · James Joyce [†1941] ....Tu
14.............. Humphrey Bogart [†1957] · Anthony Eden [†1977] ....W
15............Ivor Novello [BD1893] · Martin Luther King Jr [BD1929]............Th
16.................Carole Lombard [†1942] · Kate Moss [BD1974]..................F
17.......St Anthony of Egypt [§ *basket-makers*] · Al Capone [BD1899] ....Sa
18.........................Rudyard Kipling [†1936] ....Su
19★ ....Martin Luther King Jr Day [★FH] · Dolly Parton [BD1946] ....M
20...... Presidential Inauguration Day · St Sebastian [§ *archers, soldiers, & athletes*].......Tu
21.............. Christian Dior [BD1905] · George Orwell [†1950] ....W
22.........................Lord Byron [BD1788] ....Th
23.............. St John the Almsgiver · Edouard Manet [BD1832] ....F
24......................... St Francis de Sales [§ *journalists*] ....Sa
25......Burns' Night, Scotland · Conversion of St Paul · St Dwyn [§ *lovers*] ......Su
26........ ☺ · [●] · Australia Day, Australia [NH] · Michigan [Admis1837].........M
27......Holocaust Memorial Day · Wolfgang Amadeus Mozart [BD1756].......Tu
28.................Charlemagne [†814] · King Henry VIII [†1547] ....W
29...... St Julian the Hospitaller [§ *innkeepers and boatmen*] · Kansas [Admis1861].......Th
30...................... Mahatma Gandhi [†1948 *assassinated*] ....F
31............. Guy Fawkes [†1606 *executed*] · Franz Schubert [BD1797] ....Sa

French Rev. calendar......*Nivôse* (snow)	Dutch month ......*Lauwmaand* (frosty)
Angelic governor................*Gabriel*	Saxon month.......*Wulf-monath* (wolf)
Epicurean calendar.....*Marronglaçaire*	Talismanic stone ....*Onyx*

❧ The Latin month *Ianuarius* derives from *ianua* ('door'), since it was the opening of the year. It was also associated with *Janus* – the two-faced Roman god of doors and openings who guarded the gates of heaven. Janus could simultaneously face the year just past and the year to come. ❧ *If January Calends be summerly gay, 'Twill be winterly weather till the calends of May.* ❧ *Janiveer – Freeze the pot upon the fier.* ❧ *He that will live another year, Must eat a hen in Januvere.* ❧ On the stock market, the *January effect* is the trend of stocks performing especially well that month. ❧

FEBRUARY

Aquarius [♒] (Jan 21–Feb 19)   **Birthstone · AMETHYST**   **Pisces [♓]**
    Flower · PRIMROSE   (Feb 20–Mar 20)

1 .... National Freedom Day · Buster Keaton [† 1966] .... Su
2 ....Candlemas · Groundhog Day .... M
3 ....St Blaise [§ *sore throats*] · Val Doonican [BD1927] .... Tu
4 .... Norman Wisdom [BD1915] · Liberace [† 1987] .... W
5 .... St Agatha [§ *bell founders*] .... Th
6 ....Waitangi Day – New Zealand · Massachusetts [Admis 1788] .... F
7 .... Charles Dickens [BD1812] · Eddie Izzard [BD1962] .... Sa
8 ....St Jerome Emiliani [§ *abandoned children and orphans*] .... Su
9 .... ☽ · [●] · St Apollonia [§ *dentists*] · Mia Farrow [BD1945]........... M
10 ....St Scholastica [§ *convulsive children*] · Bertolt Brecht [BD1898]........... Tu
11 .... Burt Reynolds [BD1936] · Sylvia Plath [† 1963 *suicide*]............... W
12 .... Abraham Lincoln [BD1809] .... Th
13 .... St Modomnoc [§ *bee-keepers*] · Catherine Howard [† 1542 *beheaded*].......... F
14 .... St Valentine [§ *lovers*] · Arizona [Admis1912] · Oregon [Admis1859]........ Sa
15 ....Susan B. Anthony Day · Sir Ernest Shackleton [BD1874] .... Su
16★ ..... Washington's Birthday [★ FH]· St Benedict Joseph Labre [§ *tramps*] .... M
17 .... Molière [† 1673] · Ruth Rendell [BD1930].................. Tu
18 ....Count Alessandro Volta [BD1745] · John Travolta [BD1954] .... W
19 .... Prince Andrew [BD1960] [£] · Saparmurat Niyazov [BD1940]..........Th
20 .... Sidney Poitier [BD1927] .... F
21 ....Int. Mother Language Day [UN] · Sir Douglas Bader [BD1910] .... Sa
22 .... George Washington [BD1732] · Andy Warhol [† 1987] .... Su
23 .... Samuel Pepys [BD1633] · John Keats [† 1821] .... M
24 ....George Harrison [BD1943] · Alain Prost [BD1955]................ Tu
25 .... ☺· Ash Wednesday · Tennessee Williams [† 1983].............. W
26 ....Levi Strauss [BD1829] · Johnny Cash [BD1932] .... Th
27 .... Dominican Republic [ID 1844] · Spike Milligan [† 2002] .... F
28 ....Henry James [† 1916] .... Sa

French Rev. calendar..... *Pluviôse* (rain)	Dutch month *Sprokelmaand* (vegetation)
Angelic governor...............*Barchiel*	Saxon month..........*Solmonath* (Sun)
Epicurean calendar.... *Harrengsauridor*	Talismanic stone .... *Jasper*

❦ Much mythology and folklore consider February to have the most bitter weather: *February is seldom warm.* ❦ *February, if ye be fair, The sheep will mend, and nothing mair; February, if ye be foul, The sheep will die in every pool.* ❦ *As the day lengthens, the cold strengthens.* ❦ That said, a foul February is thought to predict a fine year: *All the months in the year, Curse a fair Februeer.* ❦ The word *February* derives from the Latin *februum* – which means cleansing, and reflects the rituals undertaken by the Romans before Spring. ❦ Having only 28 days in non-leap years, February was known in Welsh as *y mis bach* – the little month. ❦ February is traditionally personified in pictures either by an old man warming himself by the fireside, or as 'a sturdy maiden, with a tinge of the red hard winter apple on her hardy cheek'. ❦

——————————— MARCH ———————————

Pisces [♓]   **Birthstone** · BLOODSTONE   **Aries** [♈]
(Feb 20–Mar 20)   **Flower** · JONQUIL   (Mar 21–Apr 20)

1 .... St David [§ *Wales*] · Nebraska [Admis1867] · Ohio [Admis1803] .... Su
2 .... Mikhail Gorbachev [BD1931] · John Irving [BD1942] .... M
3 .... Doll's Festival, Japan · Florida [Admis1845] .... Tu
4 .... Ronald Reagan & Nancy Davis [WA 1952] · Vermont [Admis1791] .... W
5 .... St Piran [§ *tin-miners*] · Patsy Cline [†1963] .... Th
6 .... Ghana [ID 1957] · Davy Crockett [†1836] .... F
7 .... St Felicity & St Perpetua of Carthage [§ *mothers separated from their children*] ...... Sa
8 .... [☉] · Women's Rights & Int. Peace Day [UN] .... Su
9 .... Napoleon Bonaparte & Joséphine de Beauharnais [WA 1796] .... M
10 .... ☽ · Prince Edward [BD1964] [£] · Sharon Stone [BD1958] .... Tu
11 .... Sir Alexander Fleming [†1955] .... W
12 .... Thomas Augustine Arne [BD1710] · Liza Minnelli [BD1946] .... Th
13 .... Earl Grey [BD1764] · Czar Alexander II [†1881 *assassinated*] .... F
14 .... St Matilda [§ *parents with many children*] .... Sa
15 .... Eduard Strauss [BD1835] · Maine [Admis1820] .... Su
16 .... St Urho [§ *Finnish immigrants in America*] · Aubrey Beardsley [†1898] .... M
17 .... St Patrick's Day [§ *Ireland*] · World Maritime Day [UN] .... Tu
18 .... Fra Angelico [†1455] · Ivan the Terrible [†1584] .... W
19 .... St Joseph [§ *fathers and carpenters*] · Bruce Willis [BD1955] .... Th
20 .... First Day of Spring · Sir Isaac Newton [†1727] .... F
21 .... Gary Oldman [BD1958] · Ayrton Senna [BD1960] .... Sa
22 .... World Day for Water [UN] · William Shatner [BD1931] .... Su
23 .... World Meteorological Day [UN] · Roger Bannister [BD1929] .... M
24 .... St Dunchad [§ *Irish sailors*] · Queen Elizabeth I [†1603] .... Tu
25 .... Annunciation Day · Elton John [BD1947] .... W
26 .... ☺ · Ludwig van Beethoven [†1827] · Cecil Rhodes [†1902] .... Th
27 .... Quentin Tarantino [BD1963] .... F
28 .... Sergei Rachmaninov [†1943] · Virginia Woolf [†1941 *suicide*] .... Sa
29 .... Robert Falcon Scott [†1912] · Elle Macpherson [BD1964] .... Su
30 .... Vincent van Gogh [BD1853] · Piers Morgan [BD1965] .... M
31 .... John Constable [†1837] · Charlotte Brontë [†1855] .... Tu

French Rev. cal. .... *Ventôse* (wind)	Dutch month .. *Lentmaand* (lengthening)
Angelic governor .... *Machidiel*	Saxon month ..... *Hrèth-monath* (rough)
Epicurean calendar .... *Oeufalacoquidor*	Talismanic stone .... *Ruby*

❦ The first month of the Roman year, March is named for Mars, the god of war but also an agricultural deity. ❦ The unpredictability of March weather leads to some confusion (*March has many weathers*), though it is generally agreed that March *comes in like a lion, and goes out like a lamb*. Yet, because March is often too wet for crops to flourish, many considered *a bushel of Marche dust* [a dry March] *is worth a ransom of gold*. ❦ March hares are 'mad' with nothing more than lust, since it is their mating season. ❦ The *Mars* bar is named after its creator, Frank Mars. ❦

─────── APRIL ───────

Aries [♈]   *Birthstone* · DIAMOND   *Taurus* [♉]
(Mar 21–Apr 20)   *Flower* · SWEET PEA   (Apr 21–May 21)

1 ....April Fool's Day [except in Canada] · Marvin Gaye [† 1984 *shot by father*].......W
2 ....St Urban of Langres [§ *vine dressers*] · Georges Pompidou [† 1974].........Th
3 ....Jesse James [† 1882] · Graham Greene [† 1991] ....F
4 ....Senegal [ID 1960] · Martin Luther King Jr [† 1968 *assassinated*]...........Sa
5 ......Palm Sunday · St Vincent Ferrer [§ *builders*] · Howard Hughes [† 1976].....Su
6 ....Harry Houdini [BD1874] · Sir John Betjeman [BD1906] ....M
7 ....World Health Day [UN] · W.K. Kellogg [BD1860] ....Tu
8 ....Flower Festival – Japan · Pablo Picasso [† 1973]..............W
9 .... ◗ · Passover · Isambard Kingdom Brunel [BD1806] ....Th
10 ....Good Friday · Omar Sharif [BD1932].....................F
11 ....St Stanislaw of Krakow [§ *Poland*] · Queen Margaret of Navarre [BD1492]....Sa
12 ....Easter Day · St Zeno [§ *Verona*] · Franklin D. Roosevelt [† 1945].........Su
13 ....Easter Monday · Chad [ND] · Garry Kasparov [BD1963] ....M
14 ....Abraham Lincoln [† 1865 *assassinated*] ....Tu
15 ....Leonardo da Vinci [BD1452] · Jean-Paul Sartre [† 1980].............W
16 ....St Drogo [§ *shepherds*] · Charlie Chaplin [BD1889]................Th
17 .... Benjamin Franklin [† 1790] ....F
18 ....Zimbabwe [ID 1980] · Albert Einstein [† 1955] ....Sa
19 ....Benjamin Disraeli [† 1881] · Dudley Moore [BD1935].............Su
20 .... Bram Stoker [† 1912] · Leslie Phillips [BD1924] ....M
21 .... Queen Elizabeth II [BD1926] [£] · Lyrids [☄] ....Tu
22 ....Jack Nicholson [BD1937] ....W
23 ....St George [§ *England*] · World Book & Copyright Day [UN]...........Th
24 .... William I of Orange [BD1533] · Daniel Defoe [† 1731].............F
25 .... ☺· Anzac Day – Australia & New Zealand · St Mark [§ *notaries*].........Sa
26 ....Lucille Ball [† 1989] ....Su
27 .... Sierra Leone [ID 1961] · St Zita [§ *bakers*] ....M
28 ....Francis Bacon [† 1992] · Maryland [Admis1788] ....Tu
29 ....Japan [ND] · Andre Agassi [BD1970].......................W
30 ....Édouard Manet [† 1883] · Louisiana [Admis1812]...............Th

French Rev. cal. .....*Germinal* (budding)	Dutch month ....*Grasmaand* (grass)
Angelic governor..............*Asmodel*	Saxon month...........*Eastre-monath*
Epicurean calendar........*Petitpoisidor*	Talismanic stone ....*Topaz*

❦ April, T.S. Eliot's 'cruellest month', heralds the start of Spring and is associated with new growth and sudden bursts of rain. ❦ Its etymology might derive from the Latin *aperire* ('to open') – although in Old English it was known simply as the *Eastre-monath*. ❦ *April with his hack and his bill, Plants a flower on every hill.* ❦ The custom of performing pranks and hoaxes on April Fool's Day (or *poisson d'avril*, as it is known in France) is long established, although its origins are much disputed. ❦ *If it thunders on All Fools' day, it brings good crops of corn and hay.* ❦ Cuckoos used to appear in letters to the London *Times* c.April 8; the last was on April 25, 1940. ❦

———————————— MAY ————————————

🐂 *Taurus* [♉]   *Birthstone* · EMERALD   *Gemini* [Ⅱ] 🚶🚶
  (Apr 21–May 21)   *Flower* · LILY OF THE VALLEY   (May 22–Jun 21)

1 .... May Day · Antonin Dvořák [†1904] .... F
2 ....Engelbert Humperdinck [BD1936] · David Beckham [BD1975] .... Sa
3 .... World Press Freedom Day [UN] · Bing Crosby [BD1904]............ Su
4 .... St Florian [§ *invoked against fire & water*] · Audrey Hepburn [BD1929] .... M
5 .... Eta Aquarids [☄] · Napoleon Bonaparte [†1821]................Tu
6 .... Robert Edwin Peary [BD1856] · Sigmund Freud [BD1856] .... W
7 .... Robert Browning [BD1812] .... Th
8 .... VE Day · Sir David Attenborough [BD1926].................. F
9 .... ◗ · Europe Day – European Union · Tenzing Norgay [†1986]........ Sa
10 .... Mother's Day · Bono [BD1960] .... Su
11 .... Bob Marley [†1981] · Minnesota [Admis 1858] .... M
12 ....Florence Nightingale [BD1820] · Katharine Hepburn [BD1907] ....Tu
13 ....Dame Daphne Du Maurier [BD1907]..................... W
14 ....Paraguay [ND] · George Lucas [BD1944].................... Th
15 ....International Day of Families [UN] · St Isidore [§ *rural life*]............. F
16 ....Sammy Davis Jr [†1990]........................... Sa
17 .... Sandro Botticelli [†1510] · Edward Jenner [BD1749] .... Su
18 ....Canada – Victoria Day · Gustav Mahler [†1911]................ M
19 ....St Yves [§ *lawyers & Brittany*] · Anne Boleyn [†1536 *executed*] ....Tu
20 ....St Bernardino of Siena [§ *advertising*]....................... W
21 ..... St Eugene de Mazenod [§ *dysfunctional families*] · Sir John Gielgud [†2000].....Th
22 .... International Day for Biological Diversity [UN]................. F
23 ....Joan Collins [BD1933] · South Carolina [Admis 1788]............... Sa
24 ....☺· Nicolaus Copernicus [†1543] · Queen Victoria [BD1819] .... Su
25★ .... Memorial Day Observed [★ FH] · Venerable Bede [†AD735].......... M
26 ....Samuel Pepys [†1703] · John Wayne [BD1907] ....Tu
27 ....Isadora Duncan [BD1878]........................... W
28 ....Azerbaijan [ND] · Anne Brontë [†1849]................... Th
29 ....Rhode Island [Admis 1790] · Wisconsin [Admis 1848]................. F
30 .... Traditional Memorial Day · Peter Fabergé [BD1846].............. Sa
31 ...The Visitation of the Blessed Virgin Mary · Franz Joseph Haydn [†1809] .. Su

French Rev. cal. .... *Floréal* (blossom)	Dutch month ...... *Blowmaand* (flower)
Angelic governor...............*Ambriel*	Saxon month....... *Trimilchi* [see below]
Epicurean calendar...........*Aspergial*	Talismanic stone .... *Garnet*

❧ Named after *Maia*, the goddess of growth, May is considered a joyous month, as Milton wrote: 'Hail bounteous May that dost inspire Mirth and youth, and warm desire'. ❧ However, May has long been thought a bad month in which to marry: *who weds in May throws it all away.* ❧ Anglo-Saxons called May *Trimilchi*, since in May cows could be milked three times a day. ❧ May was thought a time of danger for the sick; so to have *climbed May hill* was to have survived the month. ❧ Kittens born in May were thought weak, and were often drowned. ❧

JUNE

Gemini [♊︎]   *Birthstone* · PEARL   *Cancer* [♋︎]
(May 22–Jun 21)   *Flower* · ROSE   (Jun 22–Jul 22)

1 .... Kentucky [Admis1792] · Tennessee [Admis1796] .... M
2 .... Coronation of Elizabeth II [1953] [£] · Franz Kafka [†1924] .... Tu
3 .... St Kevin [§ *blackbirds*] · Tony Curtis [BD1925] .... W
4 .... Socrates [BD 470BC] · Sir Christopher Cockerell [BD1910] .... Th
5 .... World Environment Day [UN] · Denmark [ND] .... F
6 .... D Day · Björn Borg [BD1956] .... Sa
7 .... ◑ · Malta [ND] · Charles Rennie Mackintosh [BD1868] .... Su
8 .... St Medard [§ *good weather, prisoners, & toothache*] · Francis Crick [BD1916] .... M
9 .... Peter the Great [BD1672] · Cole Porter [BD1893] .... Tu
10 .... HRH Prince Philip [BD1921] [£] · Spencer Tracy [†1967] .... W
11 .... John Constable [BD1776] · Jacques Cousteau [BD1910].. .... Th
12 .... Russia [ID 1990] · The Philippines [ND] .... F
13 .. St Anthony of Padua [§ *horses, mules, & donkeys*] · William Butler Yeats [BD1865] .. Sa
14 .... Flag Day · Che Guevara [BD1928] · Steffi Graf [BD1969] .... Su
15 .... Ella Fitzgerald [†1996] · Arkansas [Admis1836] .... M
16 .... Stan Laurel [BD1890] .... Tu
17 .... St Botulph [§ *agricultural workers*] · Venus Williams [BD1980] .... W
18 .... Seychelles [ND] · Paul McCartney [BD1942] .... Th
19 .... J.M. Barrie [†1937] .... F
20 .... First Day of Summer · West Virginia [Admis1863] .... Sa
21 ... Father's Day · Niccolò Machiavelli [†1527] · New Hampshire [Admis1788]... Su
22 .... ☉ · St Thomas More [§ *lawyers*] · Fred Astaire [†1987] .... M
23 .... Midsummer Eve · Alan Turing [BD1912] .... Tu
24 .... St Jean Baptiste Day – Canada · Midsummer Day .... W
25 .... George Custer [†1876] · Virginia [Admis1788] .... Th
26 .... United Nations Charter Day [UN] .... F
27 .... Helen Keller [BD1880] · Jack Lemmon [†2001] .... Sa
28 .... King Henry VIII [BD1491] · Peter Paul Rubens [BD1577] .... Su
29 .... St Paul [§ *authors*] · Elizabeth Barrett Browning [†1861] .... M
30 .... St Theobald [§ *bachelors*] · Mike Tyson [BD1966] .... Tu

French Rev. cal. .... *Prairial* (meadow)	Dutch month ... *Zomermaand* (Summer)
Angelic governor .... *Muriel*	Saxon month .... *Sere-monath* (dry)
Epicurean calendar .... *Concombrial*	Talismanic stone .... *Emerald*

❦ *June* is probably derived from *iuvenis* ('young'), but it is also linked to the goddess *Juno*, who personifies young women. In Scots Gaelic, the month is known as *Ian t-òg-mbios*, the 'young month'; and in Welsh, as *Mehefin*, the 'middle'. ❦ According to weather lore, *Calm weather in June, Sets corn in tune*. ❦ To 'june' a herd of animals is to drive them in a brisk or lively manner. ❦ Wilfred Gowers-Round asserts that 'June is the reality of the Poetic's claims for May'. ❦ In parts of South Africa the verb 'to june-july' is slang for shaking or shivering with fear – because these months, while Summer in the north, are mid-Winter in the south. ❦

—————————————— JULY ——————————————

🦀 *Cancer* [♋]   *Birthstone* · RUBY   *Leo* [♌]   🦁
   (Jun 22–Jul 22)   *Flower* · LARKSPUR   (Jul 23–Aug 23)

1 ...... Canada Day – Canada [NH] · Somalia [ND] · Debbie Harry [BD1945] ..... W
2 .... Ernest Hemingway [† 1961 *suicide*] .... Th
3 .... St Thomas [§ *architects*] · Idaho [Admis1890] .... F
4★ .... Independence Day [★FH] · Marie Curie [† 1934] .... Sa
5 .... Cape Verde [ID 1975] · Cecil Rhodes [BD1853] .... Su
6 .... Dalai Lama [BD1935] · George W. Bush [BD1946] .... M
7 .... ◐ · [◉] · Sir Thomas More [† 1535 *executed*] .... Tu
8 .... Percy Bysshe Shelley [† 1822] · Kevin Bacon [BD1958] .... W
9 .... Dame Barbara Cartland [BD1901] · Tom Hanks [BD1956] .... Th
10 .... John Calvin [BD1509] · Wyoming [Admis1890] .... F
11 .... World Population Day [UN] · St Benedict [§ *inflammatory diseases*] .... Sa
12 .... Kiribati [ID 1979] · Erasmus Desiderius [† 1536] .... Su
13 .... St Margaret [§ *expectant mothers*] · Harrison Ford [BD1942] .... M
14 .... Bastille Day – France · Ingmar Bergman [BD1918] .... Tu
15 .... St Swithin's Day · Gianni Versace [† 1997 *murdered*] .... W
16 .... Feast of Our Lady of Mount Carmel · Ginger Rogers [BD1911] .... Th
17 .... Duchess of Cornwall [BD1947] [£] · Adam Smith [† 1790] .... F
18 .... Jane Austen [† 1817] · Nelson Mandela [BD1918] .... Sa
19 .... Matthew Flinders [† 1814] .... Su
20 .... St Wilgefortis [§ *difficult marriages*] · Bruce Lee [† 1973] .... M
21 .... Belgium [ND] · Robert Burns [† 1796] .... Tu
22 .... ☺· [◉] · St Mary Magdalene [§ *hairdressers & repentant women*] .... W
23 .... Prince Andrew & Sarah Ferguson [WA 1986] .... Th
24 ...... Simon Bolivar Day – Venezuela & Ecuador · Peter Sellers [† 1980] .... F
25 .... St James [§ *laborers*] · Samuel Taylor Coleridge [† 1834] .... Sa
26 .... Stanley Kubrick [BD1928] · New York [Admis1788] .... Su
27 .... St Aurelius [§ *orphans*] · Hilaire Belloc [BD1870] .... M
28 .... Delta Aquarids (South) [✦] · Johann S. Bach [† 1750] .... Tu
29 .... St Martha [§ *cooks*] · Vincent van Gogh [† 1890 *suicide*] .... W
30 .... Henry Ford [BD1863] · Arnold Schwarzenegger [BD1947] .... Th
31 ...... St Ignatius of Loyola [§ *those on spiritual exercises*] · J.K. Rowling [BD1965] .... F

French Rev. calendar.. *Messidor* (harvest)	Dutch month .... *Hooymaand* (hay)
Angelic governor .... *Verchiel*	Saxon month .... *Mæd-month* (meadow)
Epicurean calendar .... *Melonial*	Talismanic stone .... *Sapphire*

❦ July was originally called *Quintilis* (from *Quintus* – meaning 'fifth'), but it was renamed by Mark Antony to honor the murdered Julius Caesar, who was born on July 12. ❦ *A swarm of bees in May is worth a load of Hay; A swarm of bees in June is worth a silver spoon; But a swarm of bees in July is not worth a fly.* ❦ *If the first of July be rainy weather, 'Twill rain mair or less for forty days together.* ❦ *Bow-wow, dandy fly – Brew no beer in July.* ❦ July used to be known as the thunder month, and some churches rang their bells in the hope of driving away thunder and lightning. ❦

——————————— AUGUST ———————————

🦁 **Leo** [♌]   **Birthstone** · PERIDOT   **Virgo** [♍] 🙍
(Jul 23–Aug 23)   **Flower** · GLADIOLUS   (Aug 24–Sep 23)

1 ....St Alphonsus [§ *confessors & theologians*] · Colorado [Admis1876] .... Sa
2 .... Alexander Graham Bell [†1922] · Wes Craven [BD1939] .... Su
3 .... Civic Holiday, Canada · Joseph Conrad [†1924]............... M
4 ....Queen Mother [BD1900] · Hans Christian Andersen [†1875] ....Tu
5 ....Oyster Day, UK · Marilyn Monroe [†1962]................. W
6 .... ☾ · Delta Aquarids (North) [⚹] · [◉] · Sir Alexander Fleming [BD1881]...Th
7 ....Labor Day – Western Samoa · St Cajetan [§ *the unemployed*]............ F
8 ....,.... St Dominic [§ *astronomers*] · Dustin Hoffman [BD1937].............. Sa
9 .... International Day of the World's Indigenous People [UN]........... Su
10 ....St Lawrence [§ *cooks*] · Missouri [Admis1821].................... M
11 ....St Clare [§ *television & sore eyes*] · Enid Blyton [BD1897] ....Tu
12 ....Ian Fleming [†1964] · Perseids [⚹] .... W
13 ....John Logie Baird [BD1888] · Florence Nightingale [†1910]...........Th
14 .... Pakistan [ID 1947] · William Randolph Hearst [†1951].............. F
15 .... VJ Day · Assumption Day · Princess Anne [BD1950] [£]........... Sa
16 ....St Stephen the Great [§ *bricklayers*] · Elvis Presley [†1977]............. Su
17 .... Gabon [ND] · Mae West [BD1892]....................... M
18 ....Genghis Khan [†1227] · Patrick Swayze [BD1952]...............Tu
19 .... Afghanistan [ID 1919] · Blaise Pascal [†1662] .... W
20 .... ☽ · St Oswin [§ *the betrayed*] · Leon Trotsky [†1940 *assassinated*] ....Th
21 .... Princess Margaret [BD1930] · Hawaii [Admis1959]................. F
22 ....Ramadan · Claude Debussy [BD1862] · Dorothy Parker [BD1893]....... Sa
23 .... Gene Kelly [BD1912] · Rudolph Valentino [†1926]............... Su
24 .... Ukraine [ID 1991] · St Bartholomew [§ *tanners*].................. M
25 ....Michael Faraday [†1867] · Friedrich Nietzsche [†1900].............Tu
26 ....St Adrian of Nicomedia [§ *arms dealers, soldiers, & plague*] .... W
27 ....Titian [†1576] · Mother Teresa [BD1910] ....Th
28 ....Donald O'Connor [BD1925] .... F
29 .... St John the Baptist [§ *convulsive children*] · Ingrid Bergman [BD1915] [†1982].... Sa
30 ....Cleopatra [†30BC *suicide*] · Mary Wollstonecraft Shelley [BD1797] .... Su
31 ....Malaysia [ND] · Diana, Princess of Wales [†1997]................ M

French Rev. calendar... *Thermidor* (heat)	Dutch month ...... *Oostmaand* (harvest)
Angelic governor..............*Hamaliel*	Saxon month...... *Weod-monath* (weed)
Epicurean calendar...........*Raisinose*	Talismanic stone .... *Diamond*

❦ Previously called *Sextilis* (as the sixth month of the old calendar), August was renamed in 8BC, in honor of the first Roman Emperor, Augustus, who claimed this month to be lucky, as it was the month in which he began his consulship, conquered Egypt, and had many other triumphs. ❦ *Greengrocers rise at dawn of sun, August the fifth – come haste away, To Billingsgate the thousands run, Tis Oyster Day! Tis Oyster Day!* ❦ *Dry August and warme, Dothe harvest no harme.* ❦ *Take heed of sudden cold after heat.* ❦ *Gather not garden seeds near the full moon.* ❦ *Sow herbs.* ❦

———————— SEPTEMBER ————————

Virgo [♍]　　　*Birthstone* · SAPPHIRE　　　*Libra* [♎]　⚖
(Aug 24–Sep 23)　　　*Flower* · ASTER　　　(Sep 24–Oct 22)

1 .... St Giles [§ *cripples, lepers, & nursing mothers*] .... Tu
2 .... Keanu Reeves [BD1964] · J.R.R. Tolkien [† 1973] .... W
3 .... Oliver Cromwell [† 1658] .... Th
4 .... ◑ · St Ida of Herzfeld [§ *widows*] · Edvard Grieg [† 1907] .... F
5 ....Jesse James [BD1847] · Mother Teresa [† 1997].................. Sa
6 .... Swaziland [ND] · King James II [† 1701].................. Su
7★....................Labor Day [★ FH] · Keith Moon [† 1978] .... M
8 .... International Literacy Day [UN] · Nativity of Blessed Virgin Mary ...... Tu
9 ....Chrysanthemum Day, Japan · California [Admis1850]............. W
10 .... St Nicholas of Tolentino [§ *sick animals*] · Mungo Park [BD1771] ....Th
11 .... New Year – Ethiopia · D.H. Lawrence [BD1885]................ F
12 ....Jesse Owens [BD1913] · Johnny Cash [† 2003].................. Sa
13 ....Grandparents' Day · Milton Hershey [BD1857] .... Su
14 ...... Exaltation of the Holy Cross · William McKinley [† 1901 *assassinated*] ...... M
15 ....Battle of Britain Day · Guatemala [ND]..................... Tu
16 ....International Day for the Preservation of the Ozone Layer [UN] .... W
17 ....Baz Luhrmann [BD1962]............................ Th
18 ....☺· Chile [ND] · Lance Armstrong [BD1971] .... F
19 .... Rosh Hashanah · St Januarius [§ *blood banks*] · William Golding [BD1911].... Sa
20 ....Jakob Grimm [† 1863] · Sophia Loren [BD1934]................ Su
21 .... International Day of Peace [UN] · Stephen King [BD1947]........... M
22 .... First Day of Autumn · Mali [ND]........................ Tu
23 ....Wilkie Collins [† 1889] · Ray Charles [BD1930]................ W
24 .... Guinea-Bissau [ID 1973] · F. Scott Fitzgerald [BD1896] ....Th
25 .... St Cadoc of Llancarvan [§ *cramps*] · Mark Rothko [BD1903]........... F
26 .... St Cosmas & St Damian [§ *pharmacists & doctors*] · T.S. Eliot [BD1888] .... Sa
27 ....St Vincent de Paul [§ *charitable societies*] · Edgar Degas [† 1917]........... Su
28 ......Yom Kippur · Louis Pasteur [† 1895] · Arthur 'Harpo' Marx [† 1964] ..... M
29 .... Michaelmas Day · Miguel de Cervantes [BD1547] ....Tu
30 .... Botswana [ND] · Truman Capote [BD1924] .... W

French Rev. cal. ....*Fructidor* (fruit)	Dutch month .... *Herstmaand* (Autumn)
Angelic governor................. *Uriel*	Saxon month......*Gerst-monath* (barley)
Epicurean calendar............*Huîtrose*	Talismanic stone ....*Zircon*

❦ September is so named as it was the seventh month in the Roman calendar. ❦ *September blows soft, Till the fruit's in the loft. Forgotten, month past, Doe now at the last.* ❦ *Eat and drink less, And buy a knife at Michaelmas.* ❦ To be 'Septembered' is to be multihued in autumnal colors, as Blackmore wrote: 'His honest face was Septembered with many a vintage'. ❦ *Poor Robin's Almanack* (1666) states: 'now *Libra* weighs the days and night in an equal balance, so that there is not an hairs breadth difference betwixt them in length; this moneth having an R in it, Oysters come again in season'. ❦ The Irish name *Meán Fómhair* means 'mid-Autumn'. ❦

─────────── OCTOBER ───────────

♎ *Libra* [♎]   *Birthstone* · OPAL   *Scorpio* [♏]   🦂
(Sep 24–Oct 22)   *Flower* · CALENDULA   (Oct 23–Nov 22)

1 .... International Day of Older Persons [UN].................... Th
2 .... Mahatma Gandhi [BD1869] · Graham Greene [BD1904] .... F
3 .... Germany [ND] · William Morris [† 1896] .... Sa
4 .... ☽ · St Francis of Assisi [§ *animals & birds*] · Jackie Collins [BD1937]........ Su
5 ....International Teachers' Day [UN] · Bob Geldof [BD1954]........... M
6 .... Children's Day [UN] · Britt Ekland [BD1942].................. Tu
7 .... St Sergius [§ *Syria*] · Edgar Allen Poe [† 1849].................. W
8 ....Chevy Chase [BD1943]............................ Th
9 ....Jacques Tati [BD1908] · Che Guevara [† 1967]................ F
10............Fiji [ND] · Orson Welles [† 1985]......................... Sa
11............ St Gummarus [§ *glove-makers*] · Ulrich Zwingli [† 1531] .... Su
12 ★ .... Columbus Day [★ FH] · Thanksgiving – Canada............... M
13............Rudolf Virchow [BD1821] · Margaret Thatcher [BD1925]...........Tu
14..........Dwight D. Eisenhower [BD1890] · Ralph Lauren [BD1939] .... W
15.......St Teresa of Avila [§ *headache sufferers*] · Friedrich Nietzsche [BD1844] ....Th
16.................. World Food Day [UN] · St Hedwig [§ *brides*].................... F
17..... Int. Day for the Eradication of Poverty [UN] · Evel Knievel [BD1938]..... Sa
18...........☺· Alaska Day, USA · Jean-Claude Van Damme [BD1960] .... Su
19................ Jonathan Swift [† 1745] · John le Carré [BD1931] .... M
20............... St Acca [§ *learning*] · Sir Christopher Wren [BD1632]...............Tu
21........................ St Hilarion [§ *hermits*] · Orionids [✦]........................ W
22.................... Vatican [ND] · Kingsley Amis [† 1995]....................Th
23.............St John of Capistrano [§ *jurors*] · Al Jolson [† 1950]................. F
24................United Nations Day [UN] · Zambia [ND].................... Sa
25.............Kazakhstan [ND] · Geoffrey Chaucer [† 1400]................. Su
26......................... Domenico Scarlatti [BD1685]......................... M
27.............. Turkmenistan [ND] · Captain James Cook [BD1728] .... Tu
28............... St Simon the Zealot [§ *sawyers*] · Bill Gates [BD1955]............... W
29.............Turkey [ND] · Sir Walter Raleigh [† 1618 *executed*]................Th
30.....St Marcellus the Centurion [§ *conscientious objectors*] · Ezra Pound [BD1885]...... F
31........... Halloween · Nevada [Admis1864] · Harry Houdini [† 1926] .... Sa

French Rev. cal. ... *Vendémiaire* (vintage)	Dutch month .... *Wynmaand* (wine)
Angelic governor................*Barbiel*	Saxon month....... *Win-monath* (wine)
Epicurean calendar......... *Bécassinose*	Talismanic stone ....*Agate*

❧ October was originally the eighth month of the calendar. ❧ *Dry your barley land in October, Or you'll always be sober.* ❧ October was a time for brewing, and the month gave its name to a 'heady and ripe' ale: 'five Quarters of Malt to three Hogsheads, and twenty-four Pounds of Hops'. Consequently, *often drunk and seldom sober falls like the leaves in October.* ❧ In American politics, an *October surprise* is an event thought to have been engineered to garner political support just before an election. ❧ Roman Catholics traditionally dedicated October to the devotion of the rosary. ❧

—— NOVEMBER ——

Scorpio [♏]   *Birthstone* · TOPAZ   *Sagittarius* [♐]
(Oct 23–Nov 22)   *Flower* · CHRYSANTHEMUM   (Nov 23–Dec 21)

1 ....All Saints' Day ....Su
2 .....[●] · ❶ · All Souls' Day · N. Dakota [Admis1889] · S. Dakota [Admis1889] ... M
3 ....Election Day · Henri Matisse [†1954] ....Tu
4 ......St Charles Borromeo [§ *learning and the arts*] · Felix Mendelssohn [†1847] ..... W
5 ....Taurids [♌] · Art Garfunkel [BD1942]....................Th
6 .... St Leonard of Noblac [§ *against burglars*] ....F
7 .... Albert Camus [BD1913] · Steve McQueen [†1980] ....Sa
8 .... Montana [Admis1889] · Edmond Halley [BD1656] ....Su
9 .... Neville Chamberlain [†1940] · Charles de Gaulle [†1970] ....M
10 ....St Tryphon [§ *gardeners*] · Martin Luther [BD1483]................Tu
11★ ...Veterans Day [★FH] · Remem. Day, Canada · Washington [Admis1889] .... W
12 .... Roland Barthes [BD1915] · Grace Kelly [BD1929] ....Th
13 ....Camille Pissarro [†1903] · Whoopi Goldberg [BD1955].............. F
14 .... Prince Charles [BD1948] [£] · Claude Monet [BD1840] ....Sa
15 .... St Albert the Great [§ *scientists*] · J.G. Ballard [BD1930]..............Su
16 ....☺· International Day for Tolerance [UN] · Oklahoma [Admis1907].......M
17 ....Leonids [♌] · Auguste Rodin [†1917].....................Tu
18 ....St Odo of Cluny [§ *rain*] · Man Ray [†1976].................. W
19 ....Monaco [ND] · Indira Gandhi [BD1917]....................Th
20 ....Queen Elizabeth II & Prince Philip [WA 1947] [£] .... F
21 ....North Carolina [Admis1789] ....Sa
22 ....Aldous Huxley [†1963] · Boris Becker [BD1967] ....Su
23 ....St Felicity [§ *martyrs*] · Boris Karloff [BD1887].................M
24 ....Henri de Toulouse-Lautrec [BD1864] · Freddie Mercury [†1991]........Tu
25 .... St Catherine of Alexandria [§ *philosophers*].................... W
26★ ....Thanksgiving [★FH] · St John Berchmans [§ *altar boys & girls*] ....Th
27 ....Anders Celsius [BD1701] · Jimi Hendrix [BD1942] .... F
28 .... East Timor [ND] · William Blake [BD1757] ....Sa
29 ...................C.S. Lewis [BD1898] · Cary Grant [†1986] ....Su
30 ....St Andrew [§ *Scotland & Russia*] · Winston Churchill [BD1874] ....M

French Rev. calendar.....*Brumaire* (fog)	Dutch month ....*Slagtmaand* [see below]
Angelic governor.............*Advachiel*	Saxon month......*Wind-monath* (wind)
Epicurean calendar.......*Pommedetaire*	Talismanic stone ....*Amethyst*

❦ Originally, the ninth (*novem*) month, November has long been associated with slaughter, hence the Dutch *Slaghtmaand* ('slaughter month'). The Anglo Saxon was *Blotmonath* ('blood' or 'sacrifice month'). ❦ A dismal month, November has been the subject of many writers' ire, as J.B. Burges wrote: 'November leads her wintry train, And stretches o'er the firmament her veil Charg'd with foul vapours, fogs and drizzly rain'. ❦ Famously, Thomas Hood's poem *No!* contains the lines 'No warmth, no cheerfulness, no healthful ease ... No shade, no shine, no butterflies, no bees, No fruits, no flowers, no leaves, no birds —— November!' ❦

DECEMBER

Sagittarius [♐]   *Birthstone* · TURQUOISE   *Capricorn* [♑]
(Nov 23–Dec 21)   *Flower* · NARCISSUS   (Dec 22–Jan 20)

1 .... World AIDS Day [UN] · Woody Allen [BD1935]................. Tu
2 .... ❶ · Kyrgyzstan [ND] · Britney Spears [BD1981]................. W
3 .... International Day of Disabled Persons [UN] · Illinois [Admis1818] .... Th
4 .... St Ada [§ *nuns*] · Wassily Kandinsky [BD1866] .... F
5 .... Thailand [ND] · Walt Disney [BD1901] .... Sa
6 .... St Nicholas [§ *bakers & pawnbrokers*] · Roy Orbison [† 1988] .... Su
7 .... Pearl Harbor Day · Delaware [Admis1787].................... M
8 .... The Immaculate Conception · Sammy Davis Jr [BD1925] .... Tu
9 .... Clarence Birdseye [BD1886] · Dame Judi Dench [BD1934].......... W
10 ...Nobel Prizes awarded · Human Rights Day [UN] · Mississippi [Admis1817] .. Th
11 .... St Damasus [§ *archaeologists*] · Indiana [Admis1816] .... F
12 .... Hanukkah · Pennsylvania [Admis1787]...................... Sa
13 .... Soot Sweeping Day – Japan · Dick Van Dyke [BD1925] .... Su
14 .... Geminids [☄] · St Agnellus [§ *invoked against invaders*] · Alabama [Admis1819] .... M
15 .... National Bill of Rights Day · Walt Disney [† 1966]............. Tu
16 .... ☽ · Kazakhstan [ID 1991] · Sir Noël Coward [BD1899] .... W
17 .... Sow Day – Orkney Islands, Scotland · Simón Bolivar [† 1830] .... Th
18 .... Antonio Stradivari [† 1737] · New Jersey [Admis1787] .... F
19 .... Emily Brontë [† 1848] · Edith Piaf [BD1915].................... Sa
20 .... St Ursucinus of Saint-Ursanne [§ *against stiff neck*] · John Steinbeck [† 1968].... Su
21 .... Shortest Day · First Day of Winter · Jane Fonda [BD1937]........... M
22 .... George Eliot [† 1880] · Beatrix Potter [† 1943].................. Tu
23 .... Ursids [☄] · Japan [ND] .... W
24 .... Christmas Eve · Vasco da Gama [† 1524] .... Th
25★ .... Christmas Day [★ FH]· Dean Martin [† 1995].................. F
26 .... Boxing Day · Kwanzaa · St Stephen [§ *stonemasons & horses*] .... Sa
27 .... St John [§ *Asia Minor*] · Johannes Kepler [BD1571].................. Su
28 .... Denzel Washington [BD1954] · Iowa [Admis1846].............. M
29 .... Madame de Pompadour [BD1721] · Texas [Admis1845].............. Tu
30 .... Our Lady of Bethlehem · Tiger Woods [BD1975]................ W
31 .... [●] · New Year's Eve · Hogmanay – Scotland .... Th

French Rev. calendar.... *Frimaire* (frost)	Dutch month ... *Wiutermaand* (Winter)
Angelic governor................ Hanael	Saxon month...... *Mid-Winter-monath*
Epicurean calendar......... *Boudinaire*	Talismanic stone .... *Beryl*

❧ *If the ice will bear a goose before Christmas, it will not bear a duck afterwards.* ❧
Originally the tenth month, December now closes the year. ❧ *If Christmas Day be bright and clear there'll be two winters in the year.* ❧ The writer Saunders warned in 1679, 'In December, Melancholy and Phlegm much increase, which are heavy, dull, and close, and therefore it behoves all that will consider their healths, to keep their heads and bodies very well from cold'. ❧ Robert Burns splendidly wrote in 1795 – 'As I am in a complete Decemberish humor, gloomy, sullen, stupid'. ❧

ON FRIENDSHIP

In time of PROSPERITY friends will be *plenty*;
In time of ADVERSITY *one* out of *twenty*.

ANNIVERSARIES OF 2009

25th Anniversary (1984)
Torvill & Dean won gold at the
Winter Olympics with their Bolero
❦ The Bank of England replaced £1
notes with coins

50th Anniversary (1959)
Fidel Castro was sworn in as Cuban
Prime Minister ❦ Lunik III took the
first photos of the far side of the Moon

75th Anniversary (1934)
Driving tests were introduced in
Britain ❦ Bonnie Parker and Clyde
Barrow were killed in an ambush ❦
Donald Duck made his screen debut
in *The Wise Little Hen*

100th Anniversary (1909)
Louis Blériot became the first person
to fly across the Channel ❦ Selfridges
in London first opened its doors ❦
The Crystal Palace hosted the world's
first Boy Scout rally ❦
Robert Peary became the first
man to reach the North Pole

150th Anniversary (1859)
Charles Blondin became the first
person to cross Niagara Falls on a
tightrope ❦ Charles Darwin's
Origin of Species was published ❦
The clock known as Big Ben was
wound up for the first time
and it started ticking

200th Anniversary (1809)
Ecuador declared independence from
Spain ❦ The first Two Thousand
Guineas Stakes was run at Newmarket

250th Anniversary (1759)
The British Museum opened ❦
England's first board game, *A Journey
Through Europe*, went on sale

500th Anniversary (1509)
Henry VIII married the first of
his six wives, Catherine of Aragon

800th Anniversary (1209)
The Albigensian Crusade was
launched against the Cathars

TABULATION OF OCCULT CORRESPONDENCES

Archangel	Angel	Planet	Body part	Animal	Bird	Stone
Raphael	Michael	Sun	*heart*	lion	swan	carbuncle
Gabriel	Gabriel	Moon	*left foot*	cat	owl	crystal
Camael	Zamael	Mars	*right hand*	wolf	vulture	diamond
Michael	Raphael	Mercury	*left hand*	ape	stork	agate
Zadikel	Sachiel	Jupiter	*head*	hart	eagle	sapphire
Haniel	Anael	Venus	*generative organs*	goat	dove	emerald
Zaphhiel	Cassiel	Saturn	*right foot*	mole	hoopoe	onyx

— H. STANLEY REDGROVE, *Bygone Beliefs*, 1919

PHASES OF THE MOON · MMIX

	1	2	3	4	5	6	7	8	9	10	11	12	13	14	15	16	17	18	19	20	21	22	23	24	25	26	27	28	29	30	31
January																															
February																															
March																															
April																															
May																															
June																															
July																															
August																															
September																															
October																															
November																															
December																															

Key: ● New Moon · ◑ First Quarter · ○ Full Moon · ◐ Last Quarter · Dates are based on Universal Time (Greenwich Mean Time)

─────BENJAMIN FRANKLIN'S VIRTUOUS WEEK─────

In his autobiography, Benjamin Franklin (1706–90) tells how, aged 27, he 'conceived the bold and arduous project of arriving at moral perfection' by attempting 'to live without committing any fault at any time'. Surprised that this proved harder than he had imagined, Franklin decided to 'acquire the habitude' of the following virtues:

TEMPERANCE	*Eat not to dullness; drink not to elevation*
SILENCE	*Speak not but what may benefit others or yourself; avoid trifling conversation*
ORDER	*Let all your things have their places; let each part of your business have its time* [see p.359]
RESOLUTION	*Resolve to perform what you ought; perform without fail what you resolve*
FRUGALITY	*Make no expense but to do good to others or yourself; i.e., waste nothing*
INDUSTRY	*Lose no time; be always employed in something useful; cut off all unnecessary action*
SINCERITY	*Use no hurtful deceit; think innocently and justly; and, if you speak, speak accordingly*
JUSTICE	*Wrong none by doing injuries or omitting the benefits that are your duty*
MODERATION	*Avoid extremes; forbear resenting injuries so much as you think they deserve*
CLEANLINESS	*Tolerate no uncleanliness in body, clothes, or habitation*
TRANQUILLITY	*Be not disturbed at trifles, or at accidents common or unavoidable*
CHASTITY	[Franklin presumably thought this was self-explanatory]
HUMILITY	*Imitate Jesus and Socrates*

Imitating Pythagoras, Franklin decided that daily examination was required. So, on July 1, 1733, he began a 'little book' in which each virtue was allocated a page, thus:

	S.	M.	T.	W.	T.	F.	S.
TEMPERANCE *Eat not to dullness; drink not to elevation.*							
T[emperance]							
S[ilence]	O	O		O		O	
O[rder]	O O	O	O			O	O
R[esolution]			O		O		
F[rugality]		O		O			
I[ndustry]		O					
S[incerity]							
J[ustice]							
M[oderation]							
C[leanliness]							
T[ranquility]							
C[hastity]							
H[umility]							

Comparing himself to a gardener who does not attempt to eradicate all his weeds in one fell swoop, Franklin attended to one virtue each week, leaving the others 'to their ordinary chance'. He marked each day's transgressions, hoping to keep that week's virtue unsullied and to wean himself from his other faults. One 'course' of virtues would take thirteen weeks; four courses would cover a year. Franklin's initial dedication was such that he acquired a more durable notebook, but later, as his travels became more extensive, his enthusiasm flagged and he abandoned the project – though he always carried an annotated notebook with him. At the age of 79, Franklin wrote that he owed to 'this little artifice' the 'constant felicity' of his life.

─── BENJAMIN FRANKLIN'S ORDERED DAY ───

Benjamin Franklin was a sworn enemy of idling and the idle. 'Trouble springs from idleness, and grievous toil from needless ease', he wrote, asserting that 'sloth, like rust, consumes faster than labor wears, while the used key is always bright'. In an attempt to employ his time fruitfully and attain the virtue of Order, he devised this 'scheme of employment for the twenty-four hours of a natural day', which he copied into the diary of virtues that he carried with him everywhere [see p.358].

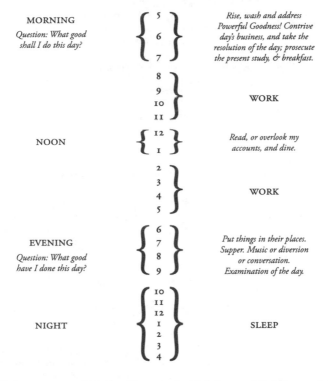

MORNING *Question: What good shall I do this day?*	5 6 7	*Rise, wash and address Powerful Goodness! Contrive day's business, and take the resolution of the day; prosecute the present study, & breakfast.*
	8 9 10 11	**WORK**
NOON	12 1	*Read, or overlook my accounts, and dine.*
	2 3 4 5	**WORK**
EVENING *Question: What good have I done this day?*	6 7 8 9	*Put things in their places. Supper. Music or diversion or conversation. Examination of the day.*
NIGHT	10 11 12 1 2 3 4	**SLEEP**

Of all the virtues to which Franklin aspired, this 'scheme of Order' proved the most problematic, since 'those who must mix with the world' cannot always be masters of their own time. Franklin was so troubled by his failure to adhere to his timetable that he admitted to being 'almost ready to give up the attempt, and content [himself] with a faulty character in that respect'. Citing the parable of the man who prides himself on a 'speckled' ax having failed to sharpen it completely, Franklin confessed to pretending that perfection would have made him 'envied and hated', and that 'a benevolent man should allow a few faults in himself, to keep his friends in countenance'. In reality, however, he found himself 'incorrigible with respect to order'. That said, though he 'never arrived at the perfection [he] had been so ambitious of obtaining', he was 'by the endeavor, a better and a happier man'.

──ANON'S ALPHABET OF WRITERLY ADVICE (c.1911)──

A *word out of place spoils the most beautiful thought.*   – VOLTAIRE

B *egin humbly. Labor faithfully. Be patient.*   – ELIZABETH STUART PHELPS

C *ultivate accuracy in words and things; amass sound knowledge; avoid affectation; write all topics which interest you.*   – F.W. NEWMAN

D *on't be afraid. Fight right along. Hope right along.*   – S.L. CLEMENS

E *very good writer has much idiom; it is the life and spirit of language.*   – W.S. LANDOR

F *ollow this: If you write from the heart, you will write to the heart.*   – BEACONSFIELD

G *enius may begin great works, but only continued labor completes them.*   – JOUBERT

H *alf the writer's art consists in learning what to leave in the ink-pot.*   – STEVENSON

I *t is by suggestion, not cumulation, that profound impressions form on the imagination.*   – LOWELL

J *oy in one's work is an asset beyond the valuing in mere dollars.*   – C.D. WARNER

K *eep writing, and profit by criticism. Use for a motto Michelangelo's wise words: 'Genius is infinite patience'.*   – L.M. ALCOTT

L *ord, let me never tag a moral to a story, nor tell a story without a meaning.*   – VAN DYKE

M *ore failures come from vanity than carelessness.*   – JOSEPH JEFFERSON

N *ever do a 'pot-boiler'. Let one of your best things go to boil the pot.*   – O. HENRY

O *riginality does not mean oddity, but freshness. It means vitality, not novelty.*   – NORMAN HAPGOOD

P *luck feathers from the wings of your imagination, and stick them in the tail of your judgment.*   – HORACE GREELEY

Q *uintessence approximates genius. Gather much thought into few words.*   – SCHOPENHAUER

R *evise. Revise. Revise.*   – E.E. HALE

S *implicity has been held a mark of truth: it is also a mark of genius.*   – CARLYLE

T *he first principle of composition of whatever sort is that it should be natural and appear to have happened so.*   – FREDERICK MACMONNIES

U *tilize your enthusiasms. Get the habit of happiness in work.*   – BEVERIDGE

V *ery few voices but sound repellent under violent exertion.*   – G.E. LESSING

W *hatever in this world one has to say, there is a word, and just one word, to express it. Seek that out and use it.*   – DE MAUPASSANT

Y *es, yes; believe me, you must draw your pen not once, nor twice, but o'er and o'er again through what you've written, if you would entice the man who reads you once to read you twice.*   – HORACE

Z *eal with scanty capacity often accomplishes more than capacity with no zeal at all.*   – GEORGE ELIOT

Index

'Make a long arm, Watson, and see what V has to say'. I leaned back and took down the great index volume to which he referred. Holmes balanced it on his knee, and his eyes moved slowly and lovingly over the record of old cases, mixed with the accumulated information of a lifetime. 'Voyage of the *Gloria Scott*', he read ... 'Victor Lynch, the forger. Venomous lizard or gila ... Vittoria, the circus belle. Vanderbilt and the Yeggman ... Vipers. Vigor, the Hammersmith wonder. Hullo! Hullo! Good old index. You can't beat it. Listen to this, Watson, Vampirism in Hungary. And again, Vampires in Transylvania'.

— ARTHUR CONAN DOYLE, *The Adventure of the Sussex Vampire*, 1924

$1 BILL – BHUT JOLOKIA

——— BHUTTO, BENAZIR – DAYLIGHT SAVING TIME ———

——————— 'GREENEST' BAND – MARRIAGE AGES ———————

—— MARRIAGE, ANNIVERSARIES – POLICE OFFICERS ——

─── STATES, DEPRESSED – ZIMBABWE ───

———————— ERRATA, CORRIGENDA, &c. ————————

In keeping with many newspapers and journals, *Schott's Miscellany* will publish in this section any significant corrections from the previous year. Below are some errata from *Schott's Miscellany 2008* – many of which were kindly noted by readers.

[p.72 *of the 2008 edition*] The 75,000 species of 'marine mammal' should have read 'marine animal or fauna', and the hairy crab *Kiwa hirsuta* deserved a capital 'k'. [p.204] The SI symbol for the prefix micro (10⁻⁶) – i.e., 'μ' – was missing; it has been added. [p.228] The story of Japanese people being gulled into buying lambs disguised as poodles seemed too unlikely to be true; it was. [p.243] The time and date of the men's 4×400m relay world record were incorrect; they have been corrected. [p.247] Edwin Valero, the WBA junior lightweight champion, is from Venezuela, not Panama. [p.273] Some of the notes to the States section had not been fully updated – although the actual data within the section had. [p.359] The symbols of the moon phases have been switched this year (now on p.357), so that New Moons are dark and Full Moons are light; this seemed more logical. [pp.344–55] Some of the monthly calendrical markers (e.g., the French Revolutionary months) have been shifted, though their position remains the subject of some debate.

———————— ACKNOWLEDGMENTS ————————

The author would like to thank:

Pavia Rosati · Jonathan, Judith, Geoffrey, & Oscar Schott, Anette Schrag
Benjamin Adams, Richard Album, Joanna Begent, Michael Binyon,
Martin Birchall, Ray Carbone, Andrew Cock-Starkey, James Coleman,
Aster Crawshaw, Jody & Liz Davies, Peter DeGiglio, Colin Dickerman,
Miles Doyle, Stephanie Duncan, Jennifer Epworth, Sabrina Farber,
Kathleen Farrar, Alona Fryman, George Gibson, Yelena Gitlin, Catherine Gough,
Mark & Sharon Hubbard, Max Jones, Amy King, Robert Klaber, Maureen Klier,
Alison Lang, James Ledbetter, Annik LeFarge, John Lloyd, Ruth Logan,
Josh Lovejoy, Chris Lyon, Sam MacAuslan, Jess Manson, Michael Manson,
Sarah Marcus, Susannah McFarlane, Sara Mercurio, Alice L. Miller, David Miller,
Peter Miller, Polly Napper, Nigel Newton, Sarah Norton, Elizabeth Peters,
Cally Poplak, Dave Powell, Alexandra Pringle, Todd Pruzan, Brian Rea,
Karen Rinaldi, David Shipley, Bill Swainson, Caroline Turner, & Greg Villepique.